R. G. M. NISBET

Collected Papers on Latin Literature

Edited by S. J. Harrison

CLARENDON PRESS · OXFORD

1995

Oxford University Press, Walton Street, Oxford OX2 6DP

Oxford New York
Athens Auckland Bangkok Bombay
Calcutta Cape Town Dar es Salaam Delhi
Florence Hong Kong Istanbul Karachi
Kuala Lumpur Madras Madrid Melbourne
Mexico City Nairobi Paris Singapore
Taipei Tokyo Toronto
and associated companies in
Berlin Ibadan

Oxford is a trade mark of Oxford University Press

Published in the United States
by Oxford University Press Inc., New York

British Library Cataloguing in Publication Data
Data available

Library of Congress Cataloging in Publication Data
Nisbet, R. G. M. (Robin George Murdoch)
Collected papers on Latin literature / R. G. M. Nisbet ;
edited by S. J. Harrison.
Includes bibliographical references.
1. Latin literature—History and criticism. I. Harrison, S. J.
II. Title.
PA6004.N57 1995 870.9′001—dc20 94-29830
ISBN 0-19-814948-4

1 3 5 7 9 10 8 6 4 2

Typeset by Joshua Associates Limited, Oxford
Printed in Great Britain on acid-free paper by
Biddles Ltd., Guildford and King's Lynn

FOREWORD

ROBIN NISBET's predecessor in the Corpus Christi Chair of Latin Language and Literature at Oxford, Sir Roger Mynors, was once asked why he had produced so few articles. 'It doesn't come out that way,' was the reply. That could have been said by his successor till fifteen or so years ago. He had been a Fellow and Tutor at Corpus Christi College since 1952, and became Corpus Professor in 1970. For twenty-five years his output consisted, almost exclusively, of three major books, the edition with commentary of Cicero's *In Pisonem* (1961), and in 1970 and 1978, the two remarkable commentaries on the first two books of Horace's *Odes*, fruit of collaboration with Margaret Hubbard. It is only since 1978, and indeed especially within the last six or seven years, that there has been a regular and rich flow of substantial articles.

Scholarly papers often spin off from larger undertakings, but for most of those collected in this volume that is not the case. The occasions repay examination. There is the occasional review; but Nisbet has been sparing in that genre. One (2) is of particular interest; to criticize Eduard Fraenkel's treatment of the text of Petronius in Konrad Müller's edition was a matter requiring tact when the great man was still very present in the Corpus common room. Other occasions were supplied by lectures, to the Virgil Society (7, 20) and elsewhere (26), or by invitations to address seminars (21, 25), or to contribute to volumes in honour of friends and colleagues (13, 15, 16, 19, 23). Several papers grew from Nisbet's own graduate classes (4, 9, 11, 13). One is the brilliant taking of a grand opportunity, the chance to give the first account of the new papyrus preserving lines of Cornelius Gallus (6), written in partnership with Peter Parsons next door in Christ Church; it is difficult to feel that much of permanent importance has accrued on that topic since. These impulses to write, and the variety of subject, are the marks of a scholar producing not for the sake of production, but as the outflow or overflow of a scholarly life, lived not in isolation but among colleagues and pupils who valued his opinion and welcomed his contributions.

These are the papers of one who is a leading textual critic. Nisbet practises on the major Latin poets, not afraid to apply the same rigour to the text of Horace that is used more freely on less grand authors. As for the lesser, 'I could not myself emend the *Aetna* or the *Anthologia Latina* because I have no instinct about what the authors might have written, nor do I care' (21). The most sustained effort, perhaps, has been put into the text of Juvenal. The early review of Clausen's Oxford Classical Text (2) already shows a willingness to heal by excision of lines; but it is only one of a series of important pronouncements, culminating in the masterly paper in the Skutsch Festschrift (15) and in the just and balanced assessment of Housman's edition (17). But there is also stimulating work on Catullus (5), and of course a continuing concern for the *Odes* of Horace (8, 12, 16). The thought processes involved in emendation are revealingly discussed in an attractively personal paper (21). It is, for Nisbet, not a self-promoting activity, but part of a great debate; and when another side of the argument is taken by a Shackleton Bailey, 'it is a privilege and delight to debate . . . about these interesting problems' (12). No less important, Nisbet's conjectures are only a part of his constant effort to make sense of a text. Texts are there to be understood, and a late paper (26) argues cogently, but against the modern trend, for the limiting of the ambiguities properly to be sought in them. Particularly illuminating then are the papers where Nisbet goes through a poem, revealing its structure and the progress of thought: a commentary more running than a formal volume would encourage, but showing in detail how one of the *Silvae* of Statius (3) or one of the *Tristia* of Ovid (9), or an *Epode* of Horace (10) works, and what light it can throw on, or receive from, the circumstances of its writing, the history of the times, and (a favourite concern) the person to whom it is addressed. In particular, the exposition of the Fourth *Eclogue* (4) uses a wide and profound learning to throw light on 'this supremely beautiful poem'; Norden himself would have admired the way in which this difficult territory is trodden. The same sort of technique is applied to a page of the Verrines (22). Nisbet sometimes uses 'working on prose' (with a good Scots 'r') as a high compliment to others; and the indications in the later papers of a return to Cicero are welcome indeed. The contribution to the Dover Festschrift (19) throws wide open the whole matter of sentence structure and rhythm in Cicero, and will have repercussions for other authors too.

'The style of a poet . . . is . . . the hardest part to characterize, which is why we all prefer to talk about other matters.' Hence the particular interest of the paper from which that remark is taken, a sensitive account of the manner of the *Eclogues* (20). In a sense, though, Nisbet is almost always talking about style. When he emends, it is to produce something that will be worthy of the author, and fit his style as well as the context. For 'textual critics are not simply concerned with grammatical absurdities, and in the great classical authors they look for something more felicitous than what satisfied a fourth-century schoolmaster' (17).

As for Nisbet's own manner, he talks (17) of 'a particularly English mode of scholarship, impatient of theory, sparing of words, displaying no more learning than necessary, going for the vital spot, empirical, commonsensical, concrete, sardonic'. The Scots mode, on this showing, is very much the same. Every sentence tells, and each deserves to be read with the care with which it was written. The lucidity is as unfailing as the politeness of the discourse, and the strokes of wit are not designed to hurt. These papers, like the distinguished commentaries, show how scholarship should be conducted.

This collection, to which Robin Nisbet himself and his pupil and colleague Stephen Harrison have devoted much labour, has been put together following his retirement in 1992, and will appear to mark his seventieth birthday in 1995. It is a reminder to us of the pleasure he has given us over so many years, and (I hope) will be an encouragement to him to continue writing. Eminent Latinists have recently devoted their retirement to *adversaria* on most of the Latin writers there are. This is not Robin's way. We should all welcome another Horace commentary, or more than one. But then there is all that prose waiting. We look forward to going on learning from one who could (though he would not) have written, with Cicero: 'facile sentio quam multorum non modo discendi sed etiam scribendi studia commoverim'.

Michael Winterbottom

Corpus Christi College, Oxford
September 1993

ACKNOWLEDGEMENTS

Oxford University Press is grateful for permission to reprint papers from the following (numbers in brackets refer to chapters):

Liverpool Classical Monthly and *Liverpool Classical Papers* (8, 23)

Bulletin of the Institute of Classical Studies and its Supplement 51 (4, 15)

Illinois Classical Studies (17)

Proceedings of the Virgil Society (7, 20)

Materiali e discussioni per l'analisi dei testi classici (21)

Papers of the Leeds International Latin Seminar (18)

Journal of Roman Studies (London: Society for the Promotion of Roman Studies (2, 3, 6, 9, 14)

Author and Audience in Latin Literature, ed. T. Woodman and J. Powell (Cambridge University Press) (22)

Poetry and Politics in the Age of Augustus, ed. T. Woodman and D. West (Cambridge University Press) (10)

Homo Viator. Classical Essays for John Bramble, ed. M. Whitby et al. (Bristol Classical Press, Gerald Duckworth & Co.)

Proceedings of the Cambridge Philological Society (5, 16)

Acta Antiqua Academiae Scientarum Hungaricae (11)

CONTENTS

1

Notes on Horace, *Epistles* 1

HORACE addresses *Epist.* 1. 5 and *Od.* 4. 7 (*diffugere nives*) to his friend
Torquatus. The superscription to the ode and ps.-Acro on the epistle
identify the recipient as Manlius Torquatus; the reference to Torquatus's lineage (line 23 of the ode) suits a member of this old patrician
family. Some editors have supposed that Horace's friend was C. Nonius
Asprenas, who was given the name 'Torquatus' after he had been
injured in the *lusus Troiae* (Suet. *Aug.* 43. 2). But Suetonius implies that
this accident happened shortly before the games were abandoned,
towards the end of the century;[1] and Asprenas must have been a boy at
the time.

In the epistle Horace invites Torquatus to supper, and gives particulars of the wine that will be drunk:

> vina bibes iterum Tauro diffusa palustris
> inter Minturnas Sinuessanumque Petrinum:[2]
> si melius quid habes arcesse, vel imperium fer.   (1. 5. 4–6)

Editors say that *imperium* is the authority of the *dominus convivii*, but
Münzer, *RE* 14. 1. 1193, sees an additional point: he suggests that
there is a joking allusion to the proverbial *imperia Manliana*, which are
often associated with the Manlii Torquati. The first person to bear the
name Torquatus, T. Manlius Imperiosus Torquatus, cos. 347, etc., was
famous for his stern discipline; everybody knew how he had executed
his son for disobedience on the battlefield. In Livy's account of this
episode the word *imperium* is used five times, culminating in an explicit
reference to *imperia Manliana* (8. 7. 8–22). In Livy 26. 22. 9 another
T. Manlius Torquatus, in refusing the consulship, says to the people,
'neque ego vestros mores consul ferre potero neque vos imperium
meum'. In *Fin.* 2. 105 Cicero is talking to his Epicurean friend

I wish to thank Mr Gordon Williams for his help.

[1] For the date cf. K. Schneider, *RE* 13. 2065.
[2] The three lines form a unity, and a colon should be printed after *Petrinum*.

Classical Quarterly, NS 9 (1959), 73–6.

L. Manlius Torquatus, and criticizing the Epicurean view that the wise man forgets his misfortunes; he says, 'sed res se tamen sic habet ut nimis imperiosi philosophi sit vetare meminisse. vide ne ista sint Manliana vestra aut maiora etiam, si imperes quod facere non possim.' For other references to *imperia Manliana* see Liv. 4. 29. 6, Gell. 1. 13. 7; even Augustine, in telling the story of Imperiosus Torquatus, says, 'quia contra imperium suum, id est contra quod imperaverat pater imperator . . . pugnaverat' (*Civ. Dei* 5. 18). So if Münzer is right, Horace is saying that Torquatus, though he came of a family which was used to giving orders, would have to receive them for once.[3] The case for this interpretation is by no means proved, but cannot be dismissed out of hand on grounds of obscurity; this is exactly the sort of point which, though obscure to us, would be clear to Horace's readers.

It seems to have been forgotten that another historical allusion has | previously been found in the same context.[4] The first of the Torquati, old Imperiosus himself, defeated the Latins in 340 between Sinuessa and Minturnae; see Livy 8. 11. 11, 'huic agmini Torquatus consul ad Trifanum—inter Sinuessam Minturnasque is locus est—occurrit'.[5] It looks as if Horace is deliberately offering his friend wine from his ancestor's battlefield; for wine with sentimental value cf. *Epod.* 13. 6, *Od.* 3. 21. 1 and especially 1. 20. 2, though wine from a battlefield is unique. Torquatus, a Roman patrician, must have known where his greatest ancestor (Cic. *Sull.* 32) was supposed to have fought his most decisive battle. It then becomes difficult to believe that Horace wrote the words in ignorance or with indifference. Sinuessa and Minturnae were only nine Roman miles apart, so the coincidence would be unusual. The district (and hence, one might guess, its associations) would be known to everybody who had travelled down the Appian Way to Campania. Horace does not say 'Trifanum' because it was an obscure place, ignored by Diodorus; in any case wine from a single village or estate would have been hard to obtain.

[3] Münzer also finds significance in line 21 where Horace says 'haec ego procurare et idoneus imperor et non invitus'; and indeed *imperor* is so strange that it needs some explanation.

[4] See I. G. F. Estré, *Horatiana Prosopographeia* (1846), 497. I owe this reference to Mr T. F. Higham; I originally thought that the point had been completely overlooked. As Estré does not argue his case, and his book is little known, it seems worth while reviving his idea and combining it with Münzer's.

[5] Diodorus 16. 90 says περὶ Σούεσσαν (Σινούεσσαν Sigonius). For difficulties about this campaign see Beloch, *Römische Geschichte*, 373, De Sanctis, *Storia dei Romani*, ii. 275 ff. One thing is clear: it was believed in Horace's time that a major battle had taken place in the triangle Minturnae-Sinuessa-Suessa.

This interpretation gains support from line 6 'si melius quid habes arcesse'. Horace's wine is of medium quality, six years old at the very most;[6] a man of Torquatus's position would be expected to keep a better cellar than Horace. In fact, on the conventional interpretation it is hard to understand the point of 'si melius quid habes arcesse'. But if the wine had a sentimental value Horace can challenge Torquatus to produce something better, without fear that his challenge will be accepted.

If we admit that Horace's wine has associations with Imperiosus Torquatus then Münzer's explanation of *imperium fer* becomes much easier.

> laetus sorte tua vives sapienter, Aristi,
> nec me dimittes incastigatum, ubi plura
> cogere quam satis est ac non cessare videbor.   (1. 10. 44–6)

The surface meaning of these lines is perfectly satisfactory, yet a special point may be seen if we consider the recipient of the epistle, Aristius Fuscus. Ps.-Acro says at the beginning of the epistle that he was a *grammaticus*; Porphyrio on *Sat.* 1. 9. 60 calls him 'praestantissimus grammaticus illo tempore'. A *grammaticus*, even when a professional grammarian and man of learning, was primarily a schoolmaster. *dimittere* is naturally used of dismissing pupils (e.g. Mart. 90. 68. 11); *castigatio*, both with *verba* and *verbera*, was an everyday activity of ancient schoolmasters. Horace seems to be gently mocking both his friend and himself.

Aristius Fuscus was the recipient of *Odes* 1. 22 (*integer vitae*), and in *Satires* 1. 9 he refuses to rescue Horace from the bore. There is another possible fact about him which is worth recalling, as it is omitted in the notices in *RE* and | *PIR*². In a grammatical fragment, *GL* 7. 35 (Keil), the manuscript reads 'abnesti fusti grammatici liber est ad assinum pollionum'. Usener's emendation *Aufusti* is accepted by Keil and Funaioli, but Haupt's *Aristi Fusci* (cf. *Opuscula* 2. 69) explains the corruption more simply. In *Satires* 1. 10. 83 ff. Aristius Fuscus and Asinius Pollio are mentioned in the same context as people who approved of Horace's poems. Admittedly, as Funaioli points out (*Gramm. Rom. Frag.* 507), writings by Aristius are not mentioned elsewhere.

---

[6] Taurus was consul for the second time in 26 BC; the book was published in 20.

> ut proficiscentem docui te saepe diuque
> Augusto reddes signata volumina, Vinni,
> si validus, si laetus erit, si denique poscet.   (1. 13. 1-3)

Horace is sending his collection of poems to Augustus; the bearer is one Vinnius (the manuscripts give no authority for the spelling *Vinius*). Ps.-Acro and the superscription in the manuscripts call him Vinnius Asellus (cf. 8 f. 'Asinaeque paternum cognomen vertas in risum'). Ps.-Acro on line 8 calls him C. Vinnius Fronto, but this may be a mistaken identification with some other person.

The elder Pliny mentions a centurion called Vinnius, a man of spectacular strength, who served in Augustus's praetorian guard: 'at Vinnius Valens meruit in praetorio divi Augusti centurio, vehicula culleis onusta donec exinanirentur sustinere solitus, carpenta adprehensa una manu retinere, obnixus contra nitentibus iumentis, et alia mirifica facere, quae insculpta monumento eius spectantur' (*NH* 7. 82). Horace emphasizes the weight of his parcel of poetry (line 6); he says to his Vinnius, 'viribus uteris per clivos flumina lamas' (line 10). Sufficient point is provided by the man's nickname Asina or Asellus, but it would add to the joke if the famous strong man were meant. Such an identification is obviously speculative; this note simply points to the possibility.

It is usually thought that Horace's correspondent is a humble friend of his own, and not somebody in Augustus's retinue. But this is by no means certain. Horace is asking Vinnius to make sure that Augustus is well and in the right mood, and this would not be easy for an unimportant messenger who had travelled a long journey and was far from his base. (Indeed, if Vinnius was a friend of Horace's, one might prefer to say that line 3 does not exactly represent Horace's verbal instructions, but is put into the written epistle out of courtesy to Augustus.) But if Vinnius is a subordinate of Augustus's, with regular access to him, the line suits perfectly; such a subordinate could proffer the poems immediately or withhold them as circumstances suggested. One may compare Martial's verses to Domitian's doorkeeper, in spite of the differences between the two societies: 'nosti tempora tu Iovis sereni cum fulget placido suoque vultu, quo nil supplicibus solet negare' (5. 6. 9 ff.).

It may be objected that the praetorian guard was a large body of nine cohorts, each consisting of six centuries; there may not have been close contact between every centurion and Augustus. Yet one of the duties of the force was to provide a personal bodyguard for the Princeps, which travelled about with him. Augustus, who shared some of his countrymen's tastes, was amused by *minuti pueri* (Suet. *Aug.* 83); he was presumably aware of this remarkable strong man in his own praetorian guard. Vinnius is the sort of person who might even have been singled out for special duty. |

Pliny's Vinnius belongs to the right place socially for Horace's slightly condescending jocularity; he looks like the type of centurion who had risen from below and reached his peak. Seeing that he is known to Pliny so long after, he must have been a familiar personality in the Rome of Augustus; his epitaph shows that he was a real 'character' of the type so much savoured by the Romans. The difficulty is that we cannot be sure that he flourished so early under Augustus as 23 BC; but supposing he did, then any Vinnius who is mentioned in line 2 in connection with Augustus, and not more explicitly defined till line 8 (*Asinae*), might most naturally remind people of the astonishing centurion of the guard.

2

Review and Discussion of K. Müller (ed.), *Petronii Arbitri Satyricon* and W. V. Clausen (ed.), *A. Persi Flacci et D. Iuni Iuvenalis Saturae*

THE elegant novel of Petronius Arbiter has been scandalously neglected by textual critics. Bücheler's *editio maior* has held the field since
1862, but though it marked an important advance its apparatus is
cumbrous, and its readings are often unintelligible. Friedländer collected useful information on the language of the *Cena*; Heraeus illu-
minated Trimalchio's table-talk from the Corpus of Glossaries;
M. Ernout translated the whole work in felicitous French, though his
text contains little that is new. It is a pity that scholars have spent so
much of their time on the monologues of the *Cena*. The narrative parts
of the book, written in terse and rhythmical Silver Age prose, show
equal artistry and wit. They also present problems of their own.

Dr Konrad Müller, who is already known for his edition of Curtius
Rufus, has now produced the standard text of Petronius. He has
collated the significant manuscripts with great care, and set out the
results clearly and systematically. It is possible at last to assess the
weight behind each reading, and many variants which clutter the
pages of Bücheler have been decisively eliminated. Of course when
contamination has been at work it is difficult to trace all the cross-
currents, and one suspects that Müller's stemma aims at too great
precision in the lower reaches. But there can be no doubt that his work
on the manuscripts represents a great step forward, which alone would
have made his book an important one.

In fact Müller offers very much more, chiefly through the excisions
that have been made in the text. It had previously been recognized
that there were a few interpolated phrases in Petronius, but Müller's
edition makes more than a hundred new deletions (besides further

Journal of Roman Studies, 52 (1962), 227–38, on Müller (ed.), *Petronii Arbitri Satyricon*
(Munich: Ernst Heimeran Verlag, 1961), and Clausen (ed.), *A. Persi Flacci . . . Saturae*
(Scriptorum Classicorum Bibliotheca Oxoniensis; Oxford: Clarendon Press, 1959).

suggestions in the apparatus). Of these Professor Fraenkel (to whom the book is dedicated) is responsible for more than half. In such matters it is always difficult to know where to draw the line, and there is plenty of room for debate about the details. It is therefore necessary to state firmly at the beginning that there are many more interpolations in the text of Petronius than have hitherto been recognized. Müller and Fraenkel have made an important breakthrough, and the new text of Petronius deserves the closest attention of all Latinists.

One category of interpolation consists of explanatory relative clauses. 16. 3 'mulier autem erat operto capite, illa scilicet quae paulo ante cum rustico steterat.' There is no reason why Quartilla's maid should be the same person as the rustic's companion, and Jacobs deleted *illa. . . steterat.* 25. 2 'continuoque producta est puella satis bella et quae non plus quam septem annos | habere videbatur et ea ipsa quae primum cum Quartilla in cellam venerat nostram.' It is astonishing to find that the girl who appeared in 17. 1 was only 7 years old, and Fraenkel deletes *et ea. . . nostram.* 72. 7 'nec non ego quoque ebrius qui etiam pictum timueram canem . . . in eundem gurgitem tractus sum.' Müller deletes the relative clause; Encolpius fell in because he was drunk, and the painted dog (29. 1) has nothing to do with the case. 102. 4 'nunc per puppim, per ipsa gubernacula delabendum est a quorum regione funis descendit qui scaphae custodiam tenet.' Müller deletes *a quorum. . . tenet*; the information is clumsily superfluous, but the deletion is given valuable support by the oddity of *custodiam tenet.*

I give a selection from other phrases which have been convincingly deleted. 22. 2 'iam ego etiam tot malis fatigatus.' Müller deletes *tot malis*, which occurs in the previous section (such repetitions are typical of the interpolator). 25. 5 'et subinde prodeuntibus annis maioribus me pueris applicui, donec ad hanc aetatem perveni.' Fraenkel deletes *hanc*. 30. 5 'cum conaremur in triclinium intrare.' Müller deletes *in triclinium*, which is superfluous in the context; he observes that elsewhere in Petronius *intrare* takes a direct object. 47. 8 'nec adhuc sciebamus nos in medio lautitiarum, quod aiunt, clivo laborare.' Fraenkel deletes *lautitiarum*; the addition of such genitives is characteristic of the interpolator. 67. 5 'applicat se illi toro in quo Scintilla Habinnae discumbebat uxor.' Fraenkel deletes *Scintilla* as a gloss. 71. 9 'te rogo ut naves etiam monumenti mei facias.' Something is wrong, and Müller's deletion of *monumenti mei* (only in the apparatus) seems the simplest solution. 85. 1 'excogitavi rationem qua non essem patri familiae suspectus amator.' Fraenkel's deletion of *amator* improves both the rhythm and the Latin. 94. 6 'cede insaniae, id est ocius foras exi.' Fraenkel deletes *id est* here and at 101. 2; 114. 5; 117. 2; 130. 7; Müller at 87. 1. 111. 13 'nemo invitus audit cum cogitur aut cibum sumere aut vivere.' Fraenkel restores sense by deleting *aut cibum sumere aut*. 117. 5 'in verba Eumolpi sacramentum iuravimus.' Fraenkel deletes *sacramentum*, which has been interpolated from the next section. 137. 5 'visoque ansere occiso sciscitata causam tristitiae . . .'. Müller deletes *tristitiae*; Proselenos is not asking why everybody is so glum (the reason is obvious), but why the goose is dead.

But though Petronius's text has been restored so expertly, some flakes of genuine paint seem to have come away in the cleaning. I list a few of the deletions which have not convinced me; others, though possibly right, are not absolutely necessary. 41. 8 'tum Trimalchio rursus adiecit "non negabitis me" inquit "habere Liberum patrem".' Fraenkel deletes *rursus adiecit*, in spite of the clausula (similarly at 68. 6, he deletes *adiecit*); yet for pleonastic *inquit* cf. Hofmann, *Syntax*, 615. 49. 2 'mirari nos celeritatem coepimus.' Fraenkel wishes to delete *coepimus*, and similarly at 49. 6; 62. 11; 86. 6; 126. 11. But the idiomatic use of *coepi* is common in Petronius, and the historic infinitive rare. 49. 3 'longe maior nobis porcus videbatur esse quam paulo ante aper fuerat.' Müller's deletion of *quam . . . fuerat* makes the meaning very obscure. 53. 2 'in praedio Cumano quod est Trimalchionis nati sunt pueri XXX, puellae XL.' Müller deletes *quod est Trimalchionis*, but the legal periphrasis surely did not spring from an interpolator. (Cicero, *Mur.* 26, makes fun of the circumlocution 'fundus qui est in agro qui Sabinus vocatur'.) 97. 5 'non est moratus Giton imperium.' Müller deletes *imperium*; yet cf. Apul. *Met.* 10. 3. 1 'nec adulescens aegrae parentis moratus imperium.' 105. 2 'simul ut notae quoque litterarum non adumbratae comarum praesidio totae ad oculos legentium acciderent.' Fraenkel deletes *adumbratae* and Müller emends *totae* to *tectae*; but Bücheler's *obumbratae* is a more economical solution. 111. 10 'donec ancilla vini certum ab eo odore corrupta . . .'. Müller omits *certum ab eo* with Fuchs and some manuscripts, but *certum habeo*, the reading of John of Salisbury, is plausible. For the use of this phrase in parenthesis cf. Sen. *Cont.* 10. 3. 2 'hoc, certum habeo, unusquisque vestrum suadebat.'

It is not immediately obvious when the interpolations were made; Müller assigns them to the ninth century, and promises a detailed discussion of the problem. He convincingly argues that the excerpts of Petronius were made in the Carolingian age, but this does not by itself

prove that the interpolations belong to the same period. Müller
suggests that the interpolation in 16. 3 ('illa scilicet quae paulo ante
cum rustico steterat') was an attempt to tie together a lacunose narrative. This argument is less than decisive: at 57. 1, for instance,
Fraenkel deletes 'is ipse qui supra me discumbebat' as another false
identification; yet here there is no lacuna to be tidied up. At 139. 4
'nondum querellam finieram' Fraenkel deletes *querellam*, which he
regards as interpolated from 139. 3, *querella* (before a lacuna). This is
an interesting idea, but it is not conclusive. Petronius says elsewhere
(70. 1) 'necdum finieram sermonem'; there Müller considers the
deletion of *sermonem*, but cf. Apul. *Met.* 5. 27. 1 'necdum sermonem
Psyche finierat.'

One plausible case of Carolingian interpolation is 14. 3 'sed praeter
unum dipondium sicel . . .'. Some editors accept the old emendation
cicer, which goes well with the following *lupinos*; but as a *sicel* was in
point of fact equivalent to a *dipondium*, Gaselee deleted the word as a
gloss. At 78. 7 'vigiles qui custodiebant vicinam regionem', Müller's
deletion of the relative clause makes the narrative neater. But perhaps
he goes too far when he implies that such an interpolation cannot | be
ancient; it might have been made not to explain who *vigiles* were, but
to smooth over their abrupt introduction in this context. 116. 8 'ad
summos honores perveniunt, id est soli militares soli fortissimi atque
etiam innocentes habentur.' Fraenkel rightly deletes *id. . . militares*, but
the interpolation need not be Carolingian: for the use of *militares* see
Amm. Marc. 14. 5. 3; 15. 5. 12; 15. 6. 1.

One feature that must be investigated is the prose-rhythm of the
interpolations. Some good clausulae have been removed or impaired
by deletions. See 4. 3, *atroci stilo effoderent*; 12. 4, *rustici emptoris*; 14. 5,
tenere clamavit; 15. 2, *pallium lucri facere*; 16. 3, *cum rustico steterat*; 25. 2,
venerat nostram; 26. 7, *liberae cenae*; 40. 8, *pendebant e dentibus*; 41. 8,
rursus adiecit; 49. 3, *ante aper fuerat*; 65. 6, *optime facere*; 88. 8, *Capitolii
tangant*; 102. 15, *ferrumine infigitur*; 105. 10, *lineamentis*; 105. 11, *decepta
supplicio*. One would like to know the likelihood of such interpolations
being made in the ninth century, or for that matter in late antiquity.
One feels some inclination to reduce the list; some of these deletions
are unconvincing (41. 8; 49. 3; 105. 10), and others are open to doubt.
Even so, some strange cases remain: for instance, the deletion in 25. 2
is very plausible ('et ea ipsa quae . . . in cellam venerat nostram'), yet
the word-order is artistic and the clausula excellent.

Besides deletions Müller's edition mentions some new emendations, of which the following seem most noteworthy. 23. 3, *huc huc* ⟨*cito*⟩ *convenite* (*convertite* Fraenkel: an ionic a maiore is expected). 62. 10, *in larvam intravi* (*larva intravi* Fraenkel). 88. 7, *ubi est dialectica? ubi astronomia? ubi sapientiae consultissima via?* (*occultissima via* Müller). 90. 1, *timui ego ne me poetam vocaret* (*pro poeta mulcarent* Müller). 91. 7, *nihil iam memini si bona fide paenitentiam* (*praeterita* Müller) *emendas*. 99. 2, *tantum omnem scabitudinem animo . . . deleret* (*delevet* Fraenkel) *sine cicatrice*. 99. 6, *ego cum Gitone quicquid erat in alt'* [i.e. *alter*] *compono* (*manticae impono* Fraenkel; yet *componere* is the Latin for 'to pack', and Bücheler's *in iter compono* may be right). 126. 8, *quid factum est quod tu proiectis, Iuppiter, armis inter caelicolas fabula muta taces?* (*iaces* Fraenkel, plausible in spite of Housman, *Luc.* 1. 260). 128. 4, *postquam omnes vultus temptavit quos solet inter amantes risus* (*lusus* Müller) *fingere*. Not all the new emendations are as interesting as these, and too many are received into the text.

Müller does not quote nearly enough old emendations; for this reason Bücheler's edition is still useful. I give a selection of conjectures which should have been recorded. 9. 8, *de ruina* (*de ruma* Housman, *CR* 18 (1904), 398). 14. 7, *nostram . . . ridebant invidiam* (*inscitiam* margo edit. Torn.). 26. 1, *thalamumque incesta* (*intexta* Auratus) *exornaverant veste*. 71. 6, *valde te rogo ut secundum pedes statuae meae catellam pingas* (*fingas* Scheffer). 91. 11, *ego ne mea quidem vestimenta ab officioso* (*officio* Erhard) *recepissem*. 93. 1, *animus errore lentus* (*laetus* Graevius) *iniurias diligit*. 93. 2, *et pictis anas renovata pennis* (*involuta pennis* Busche, *RhM* 66 (1911), 455. Busche should have quoted Mart. Cap. 9. 918 'nam candidus nivosis I olor involutus alis'). 94. 8, *cervicesque nodo condebam* (*indebam* Burman, cf. Tac. *Ann.* 15. 57. 2, *vinclo . . . indidit cervicem*). 97. 8, *insertans commissuris secure* (*securem* Bücheler). 101. 7, *nisi naufragium ponimus* (*patimur* Fuchs, cf. Sen. *Herc. Oet.* 118, *naufragium pati*). 105. 10, *prudentissimus* (*imprudentissimus* Scioppius). 109. 9, *nunc umbra nudata sua iam tempora maerent,I areaque attritis ridet* (*sordet* Junius) *adusta pilis*. 117. 1, *prudentior Eumolpus convertit ad novitatem rei mentem genusque divinationis* (*id invitationis* Haase, better *invitationis*) *sibi non displicere confessus est*. 117. 2, *non mehercules penam* (*peram* Pithoeus, i.e. πεῖραν) *istam differrem*. 128. 2, *totoque corpore velut laxato* (*luxato* Jungermann). 131. 9, *myrtoque florenti quietum* (*quietum aera* Ernout) *verberabat*. 135. 8, *hinc molli stillae latus* (*mollis tiliae lacus* Pithoeus) *et de caudice lento I vimineae lances* (cf. Ov. *Met.* 10. 92, *tiliae molles*, Pliny, *NH* 16. 207, *mollissima tilia*).

Sometimes an emendation, or variant, or the reading of the manuscripts might have been promoted from the apparatus to the text. In the following selection of passages I give my own preference in parentheses. 3. 4, *sine praedae spe* (*sine spe praedae* var. lect.). 23. 5, *perfluebant* (*profluebant* Ribbeck) *per frontem sudantis acaciae rivi*. 34. 8, *ut articuli eius vertebraeque laxatae* (*luxatae* Heinsius) *in omnem partem flecterentur*. 62. 4, *homo meus coepit ad stelas facere, sed⟨eo⟩ ego* (*sed ego pergo* Heraeus) *cantabundus et stelas numero*. 64. 7, *quo ⟨adspectu⟩ admonitus officii* (*quo admonitus officio* cod.). 77. 4, *susum cellationem* (*cenationem* Scheffer). 89, l. 13, *ad fata* (*furta* Bücheler) *compositus Sinon*. 118. 5, *praeterea curandum est ne sententiae emineant extra corpus orationis expressae, sed intexto vestibus* (*versibus* var. lect.) *colore niteant*. 130. 8, *levissima* (*lenissima* var. lect.) *ambulatione compositus* (cf. Cels. 3. 27. 4, *ambulationibus lenibus*, though at 1. 6. 2, Celsus's manuscripts read *ambulatione quamvis levi*). 141. 9, *Saguntini oppressi* (*obsessi* Rittershusius) *ab Hannibale*. It is more serious that the obelus is not used more freely. Often one is pulled up by nonsense; sometimes Müller himself comments on the obscurity in the apparatus, but the difficulty ought to be signalled in the text.

Müller's edition has shown how corrupt Petronius's text is and how much it needs discussion. I append some comments and suggestions. |

6. 1 'et dum in hoc dictorum aestu motus incedo, ingens scholasticorum turba in porticum venit.' Müller rightly rejects *in hortis*, a variant for *motus*; it gives an inferior clausula, and as he points out the conversation took place not in the garden but the colonnade. Yet *motus* can hardly be used absolutely for 'in a state of excitement'; and even if *in* is deleted (as Müller suggests in his apparatus) the word still seems too weak. Perhaps *mutus*: while Agamemnon produces a spate of words Encolpius stays dumb.

12. 6 'sed cum Ascyltos timeret fidem oculorum, ne quid temere faceret prius tamquam emptor propius accessit detraxitque umeris laciniam et diligentius temptavit.' *umeris* is a little odd, as it is not stated explicitly that the rustic's shoulders are meant. Perhaps the word is an interpolation derived from 12. 4 'iniecit contemplationem super umeros rustici.'

15. 2 'advocati tamen iam pene nocturni qui volebant pallium lucri facere flagitabant uti apud se utraque deponerentur.' Müller rightly deletes *qui . . . flagitabant* and obelizes *iam pene*; he suggests something on the lines of *in rem praesentem*. I have considered *importune* ('unseasonably').

16. 2 'cum et ipsi ergo pallidi rogaremus quis esset, "aperi" inquit

"iam scies". dumque loquimur, sera sua sponte delapsa cecidit re-
clusaeque subito fores admiserunt intrantem. mulier autem erat ...'.
intrantem is strangely tautologous; I suggest *instantem*.

17. 1 'tacentibus adhuc nobis et ad neutram partem assentationem
flectentibus intravit ipsa.' Müller, like many editors, accepts the early
emendation *assensionem*. Yet one of the two possibilities alluded to was
a *refusal* to enter discussions with Quartilla, and *assensionem* seems an
odd way of expressing this idea. Perhaps the word should be deleted as
an interpolation; in that case *flectentibus* would be intransitive.

17. 9 'neve traducere velitis tot annorum secreta quae vix mille
homines noverunt.' A joke does not seem suitable here, so Müller is
probably right to doubt *mille*. Perhaps *tres* (*iii* for *m*).

18. 6 'nam sane et sapiens contemptus iurgia nectit | et qui non
iugulat, victor abire solet.' The last line is odd. Quartilla does not seem
to be urging the virtues of forgiveness; and a reference to throat-
cutting is irrelevant. I have considered *iurgat* and *victus*.

22. 3 '... duo Syri expilaturi [lagoenam] triclinium intraverunt,
dumque inter argentum avidius rixantur, diductam fregerunt lagoenam. cecidit etiam mensa cum argento ...'. Jahn rightly deleted
lagoenam. I think it possible that *inter argentum* should also be deleted.
The *lagoena* which was pulled apart was made of earthenware; the
passage runs more smoothly if the mention of silver is postponed till
the next sentence. (Barth saw the difficulty, though his conjecture *inter
trahendum* has no merit.)

26. 9 '"quid vos?" inquit "nescitis hodie apud quem fiat?"' The
question-mark should come after *quid*, not *vos*; cf. 20. 5; 74. 6; 117. 12;
127. 4; D. R. Shackleton Bailey, *Towards a Text of Cicero ad Atticum*, 3.

44. 18 'antea stolatae ibant nudis pedibus in clivum, passis capillis,
mentibus puris, et Iovem aquam exorabant.' For *mentibus* Müller prints
Leo's conjecture *vestibus*. But *mente pura* is a common phrase in
religious contexts (*TLL* 8. 729. 34); Dr S. Weinstock calls my attention
to Aus. 369 P 'lautis manibus, mente pura.'

55. 6 'tuo palato clausus pavo pascitur | plumato amictus aureo
Babylonico.' Müller accepts Fraenkel's *Babylonicus*, but though Diodorus praises Babylonian peacocks it is awkward to take *aureo* as a
noun. Other editors interpret *Babylonico* as an eastern tapestry (cf. Jer.
Epist. 107. 12 'pellis Babyloniae vermiculata pictura'); this sustains the
metaphor of *plumato*, which means 'embroidered' as well as 'feathered'.

60. 5 'repente nova ludorum remissio hilaritatem [hic] refecit.'
Müller accepts Bücheler's *missio*; this word is used in late Latin of the

letting loose of beasts in the arena (cf. *Hist. Aug. Aur.* 17. 7, 'ut centum leones una missione simul exhiberet'). The metaphor is strange here, and the genitive *ludorum* inappropriate. I propose *commissio*, which is often used of the beginning of the public games. For a similar metaphor applied to private amusements cf. Plaut. *Pers.* 771 'age puere, ab summo septenis cyathis committe hos ludos.'

62. 10 'sudor mihi per bifurcum volabat.' For *volabat* Heinsius compared Sen. *Oed.* 992 'gelidus volat (*sic A*: fluit *E*) sudor per artus'; but it would take more than this to convince one that *sudor volat* is Latin. I have previously proposed *undabat*; *ūdabat* and *uolabat* are very similar.

73. 3 'invitatus balnei sono diduxit usque ad cameram os ebrium et coepit Menecratis cantica lacerare.' For *os diducere* ('to open one's mouth') cf. Gell. 5. 9. 2 'diduxit adulescens os clamare nitens.' For *usque ad cameram* cf. 40. 1 'sublatis manibus ad cameram', yet here it is hard to justify the expression even as a joke. If the phrase is deleted, sense and rhythm are improved. The interpolator may have thought that *diduxit os* meant 'he raised his voice'.

74. 13 'contra Trimalchio "quid enim?" inquit "ambubaia non me misit se de machillam illam sustuli".' Müller prints Fraenkel's proposal 'ambubaia non meminit se de machina? inde illam sustuli' (*meminit* Heinsius, *machina* Reiske). *inde* seems to make the passage a word too long; *de machina illam sustuli* gives a very convincing run. Bücheler proposed *ambubaia non meminit | sed . . .*; but one would prefer a question. I have considered *ambubaiam non meminisse!*, but feel that an indicative is more natural.

74. 13 'inflat se tamquam rana et in sinum suum conspuit.' Müller, like other modern editors, accepts Reiske's *non spuit*; but the Greek paroemiographers give the proverb in both a positive and a negative form. See Gregorius Cyprius, Mosq. 3. 27 εἰς κόλπον πτύεις· ἀντὶ τοῦ μεγαλορρημονεῖς, Juv. 7. 111 f. 'tunc immensa cavi spirant mendacia folles conspuiturque sinus.'

74. 15 'Agatho unguentarius here proxime seduxit me et "suadeo" inquit "non patiaris genus tuum interire".' *here proxime* is unparalleled, and Müller quotes with approval Leo's *tabernae proximae*; but 'just yesterday' suits the context admirably. Burman deleted *proxime*, but it would be better to delete *here*; *proxime* is used of time at 38. 10, and the ambiguity of the word might have encouraged a gloss.

79. 4 'prudens enim prudens, cum luce etiam clara timeret errorem, omnes pilas columnasque notaverat creta.' Müller accepts the deletion of the second *prudens*, an early emendation; but this leaves the first

prudens isolated in too short a phrase. *prudens enim pridie* is found in some manuscripts, though Müller regards it as an emendation. I have considered *prudens enim puer* (Giton is meant).

80. 9 'mox ubi ridendas inclusit pagina partes, I vera redit facies, assimulata perit.' Petronius is talking about actors on the stage, not characters in a book; so *pagina* should be obelized. Bücheler suggested *machina*, but a reference to the pegma is too specialized; one really expects a word meaning 'curtain'. I have considered *pergula* ('hut' or 'annexe'), which might conceivably have been used of the actors' dressing-room.

84. 2–3 'deinde qui solas extruere divitias curant, nihil volunt inter homines melius credi quam quod ipsi tenent. iactantur itaque, quacumque ratione possunt, litterarum amatores, ut videantur illi quoque infra pecuniam positi.' Müller obelizes *iactantur*, and proposes *inescant*; but if poets are courted by the rich, why are they so poor? Bücheler's *insectantur* makes better sense. *infra pecuniam positi* means 'of less importance than money' (cf. Cic. *Tusc.* 3. 15 'res humanas despicere atque infra se positas arbitrari'); one might have expected *illae* and *positae*.

85. 4 'forte cum in triclinio iaceremus, quia dies sollemnis ludum artaverat pigritiamque recedendi imposuerat hilaritas longior, fere circa mediam noctem intellexi puerum vigilare.' I feel doubt about *ludum artaverat*. Editors say that it means 'had shortened the class', but in this context one expects *ludus* to mean 'fun'. For *artaverat* one might expect *ampliaverat* or *prolataverat* or something of the kind.

89, ll. 27 f. 'ibat iuventus capta, dum Troiam capit, I bellumque totum fraude ducebat nova.' Bücheler explains *bellum totum* as *omnes Graecorum copias*; but one looks for an epigram which will make a contrast between *totum* and *nova*. For *ducebat* I have considered *cludebat* ('was ending'); cf. Stat. *Theb.* 11. 58, *claudere... bella*.

94. 11 'ego si te non invenissem, periturus ⟨per⟩ praecipitia fui.' *per* is found in the *editio Tornaesiana*, but Müller regards it as lacking authority. *per praecipitia* suggests a leap over a precipice, but Giton means that he nearly stabbed himself. I suggest *praecipiti via*; cf. below 'ad mortem viam quaero', Quint. 6, *prooem.* 6 'maximos cruciatus praecipiti via effugit' (though not there of suicide).

96. 3 'ego durante adhuc iracundia non continui manum, sed caput miserantis stricto acutoque articulo percussi.' *stricto articulo* should be compared with *stricta manu* (cf. Ov. *Am.* 1. 6. 14; *Trist.* 5. 2. 30), which in turn should be connected with *stricto gladio*. The adjective *acuto* does

not cohere with the participle *stricto*; I suggest that *acutoque* should be deleted.

101. 8 'poteris hanc simulationem et vultus confusione et lacrimis obumbrare, ut misericordia permotus gubernator indulgeat tibi.' One might have expected *tibi* to come second word in its phrase, after *gubernator*. Possibly *gubernator* should be deleted; the word occurs in the previous sentence and would be a typical interpolation here.

104. 4 'ceterum Lichas ut Tryphaenae somnium expiavit, "quis" inquit "prohibet navigium scrutari, ne videamur divinae mentis opera damnare?"' It is strange that Lichas should first 'expiate' Tryphaena's dream, and only then take steps to see if it was true. I propose *expiaret*; cf. 105. 4 'itaque ut tutela navis expiaretur, placuit quadragenas utrique plagas imponi.'

106. 1 '"o te" inquit "feminam simplicem, tamquam vulnera ferro praeparata litteras biberint".' This sentence is very difficult to understand and no simple emendation presents itself. Perhaps one might delete *tamquam... biberint.*

108. 9 'multi ergo utrimque sine morte labuntur, plures cruenti vulneribus referunt veluti ex proelio pedem.' Fraenkel plausibly deletes *veluti ex proelio. sine morte* is odd linguistically and makes a bad anticlimax. Burman's *sine more* (= ἀκόσμως) deserves consideration, but this expression is normally used with verbs like *ruere* and *furere*. Perhaps one might delete the offending words.

111. 9 'at illa ignota consolatione percussa laceravit vehementius pectus.' *ignota* is nonsense and I propose *ingrata* (*īgrata*); I have also considered *praeclusa* (ablative), but feel that *percussa* could stand. |

115. 9 '"hunc forsitan" proclamo "in aliqua parte terrarum secura expectat uxor, forsitan ignarus tempestatis filius, aut patrem utique reliquit aliquem cui proficiscens osculum dedit".' Müller accepts Fraenkel's insertion of *aut* after *patrem*, presumably because *patrem... aliquem* is an unusual phrase; but the tricolon is better balanced if only three people are mentioned.

115. 14 'ite cauti, et opes fraudibus captas per mille annos disponite.' *disponite* means 'set out for display', but *per* seems the wrong preposition. I suggest *in*.

117. 6 'serviliter ficti dominum consalutamus.' Fraenkel rightly doubts *ficti*; perhaps *vestiti.*

117. 11 'his ita ordinatis, "quod bene feliciterque eveniret" precati deos viam ingredimur.' The colon that runs from *quod bene* to *deos* seems too long for the rest of the sentence. Possibly *quod... eveniret*

should be deleted; the unadorned insolence of *precati deos* would suit Petronius.

118. 3 'ceterum neque generosior spiritus sanitatem amat neque . . .'. Müller accepts Fraenkel's deletion of the first *neque*. But Eumolpus dislikes *carminis tranquillitatem* and recommends *furentis animi vaticinatio*.

119, ll. 36 ff. 'iam Phasidos unda | orbata est avibus, mutoque in litore tantum | solae desertis adspirant frondibus aurae.' For *solae* editors quote Sen. *Phaedr.* 474 'solis et aer pervius ventis erit', yet here after *tantum* the word seems strange. I have considered *surdae* = 'voiceless'; abbreviation to *s'dae* could explain the corruption.

119, ll. 51 f., 'praeterea gemino deprensam gurgite plebem | faenoris illuvies ususque exederat aeris.' Palmerius's *ingluvies* is surely right; it belongs naturally in the same context as *gurgite* and *exederat*. Müller quotes the *Thesaurus* for *inluvies*, but the passage on which they rely is not a fair parallel: see Fulg. *Myth.* 79. 17, 'at vero quod eius prandia stercoribus foedant, ostendit fenerantium vitam rapinae inluvie esse sordidam.'

120, ll. 67 ff., 'est locus exciso penitus demersus hiatu | . . . Cocyti perfusus aqua; nam spiritus, extra | qui furit effusus, funesto spargitur aestu.' *effusus* is clumsy after *perfusus*; I propose *expulsus*.

122, ll. 163 f., 'sanguine Germano sexagintaque triumphis | esse nocens coepi.' Caesar had not yet achieved one triumph, let alone sixty. I suggest *tropaeis*; *tropheis* and *triüphis* might be confused. *triumphis* also occurs a few lines above (156 f. 'Saturnia tellus armis laeta meis olimque onerata triumphis'). There the word might be defended as an equivalent for *spoliis*, though cf. Luc. 2. 583 f. 'sed tota tenetur terra meis quocumque iacet sub sole tropaeis.' *tropaeis* is used by Petronius a few lines below (172).

124, ll. 264 ff., 'sentit terra deos mutataque sidera pondus | quaesivere suum; namque omnis regia caeli | in partes diducta ruit.' Perhaps *iamque*.

124, ll. 269 f., 'Magnum cum Phoebo soror et Cyllenia proles | excipit ac totis similis Tirynthius actis.' *totis* is weak, and untrue; Hercules was not similar to Pompey in respect of all his acts. I propose *tantis* (dative): Hercules resembled the great acts of Pompey (compendious comparison).

125. 3 'quid, si etiam mercennarius praesenti felicitate lassus indicium ad amicos detulerit totamque fallaciam invidiosa proditione detexerit?' I propose *insidiosa*.

126. 1 'quia nosti venerem tuam, superbiam captas vendisque

amplexus, non commodas.' Heinsius proposed *superbia me captas*,
Fraenkel *superbia lucrum captas*; but one feels that only the verb is
wrong. I suggest *superbiam iactas*, though I have no parallel; *ia* might
have been lost after *iā*. Müller considers the deletion of *non commodas*
(cf. 126. 4), but the words seem necessary.

126. 12 'itaque collegit altius tunicam flexitque se in eum daphnona
qui ambulationi haerebat.' No exact parallel presents itself for the use
of *haerere*; perhaps *adhaerebat*, which would also give a better clausula.

126. 15 'supercilia usque ad malarum scripturam currentia et rursus
confinio luminum paene permixta.' Fraenkel rightly deletes *luminum*.
For *scripturam* I propose *suturam*; cf. Cels. 8. 1. 4 'malae transversas
suturas habent.'

126. 16 'oculi clariores stellis extra lunam fulgentibus.' *extra lunam*
must mean 'outside the moonlight'; but this is an odd way of saying
'when there is no moon'. I propose *citra lunam*. For this use of *citra*,
almost equal to *sine*, cf. Quint. 12. 10. 76 'lucent igitur haec citra
solem.'

128. 1 '"quid est?" inquit "numquid te osculum meum offendit?
numquid spiritus ieiunio marcens? numquid alarum neglegens sudor?
puto si haec non sunt, numquid Gitona times?"' Müller follows
Fraenkel, who deletes *sudor puto* and inserts *sum* after *alarum*; yet one
would prefer a third noun to balance *osculum* and *spiritus*. I suggest
neglegens odor, which is a more plausible expression than *neglegens sudor*;
sudor puto might possibly be regarded as a scribe's emendation of *odor*.

132. 2 'manifestis matrona contumeliis verberata.' Müller quotes
Cic. *Pis.* 63, *convicio verberari*; but that passage refers to abusive words,
this to insulting actions. Bücheler tried *exacerbata*; I suggest *vexata*.

fr. xxv, 'cui voltur iecur intimum pererrat | et querit pectus in-
timasque fibras.' Müller quotes the early emendation *et pectus trahit*. I
suggest *pectusque eruit*.

I have discussed some of the above passages with Miss Margaret
Hubbard, Mr G. J. Toomer, and Mr A. F. Wells; I am greatly indebted
to them for their help. |

Professor Clausen prints virtually the same text of Persius as in his
admirable edition of 1956. The only significant changes are *prol* 9
'nostra verba'; 5. 59 'fregerit articulos' (both improvements). The 1956
apparatus gave an exemplary demonstration of the pattern formed by a
diffused tradition, where the truth may be preserved in unlikely places,
but it was rather long for most purposes; all variants of interest can be

found in the new Oxford text (except perhaps 1. 34, *vanum* P). The readings of Vat. Pal. lat. 1710, a manuscript of exceptional merit, are given in detail for the first time, and the lemmata of the scholia are clearly distinguished from the interpretations which they contain. 1. 60, Barth's *tentae* might have been recorded. 2. 2, *apponit* is better than *apponet*. 3. 107-9, the distribution of the parts seems to be mis-understood. 4. 5, *tacendaque* is better than *tacendave*. 5. 66 'cras hoc fiet idem' makes one sentence, as K. F. Hermann pointed out.

The text of Juvenal is new. Clausen cites a few more manuscripts than Housman (notably Parisinus 8072 and the Ambrosian, Orleans, and Antinoe fragments) and his reports are more accurate; yet the practical gain is slight. He rightly does not imitate Knoche's com-plicated apparatus; he points out that the relations of the 'vulgar' manuscripts (Housman's Ψ, Clausen's Φ) cannot be represented by any stemma. He mentions three emendations of his own in the ap-paratus (2. 168, *indulget*; 5. 104, *glaucis sparsus*; 10. 313, *ex ira*). His book will be convenient to use, and completely supersedes Owen's old Oxford text (which sensible people ignored); but it does not, and could not, replace Housman, whose edition is the best introduction to textual criticism in existence.

Some readers will regret that Clausen has not recorded one or two more emendations. Oxford texts aim at a *brevis adnotatio critica*, but conjectures take up little room, and it is better to give too many than too few; even when they fail to convince they can pinpoint a difficulty, add life to a text, or even lead to a solution. Some at least of the follow-ing are worth thinking about. 1. 104, *molli* Marshall (cf. Catull. 25. 1f. 'mollior ... imula oricilla'). 3. 23, *itidem cras* Damsté. 3. 205, *sub eodem e marmore* Housman. 6. 29, *exagitate* Hadr. Valesius. 6. 96, *corpore* var. lect. ap. Ruperti. 7. 102, *operis lex* var. lect. ap. Ruperti (cf. Hor. *Ars P.* 135 'operis lex'). 7. 205, after *Athenae* Heinrich marked a lacuna. 8. 49, *togatus* (Scriver and independently R. L. Dunbabin; right, I think). 8. 105, *atque audax Antonius* Knoche. 8. 161, *salutans* Leo. 8. 201, I have considered *et* for *aut*; cf. Cic. *Pis.* 73 'nec ... scutum et gladium', where *aut* is a variant. 9. 76, *migrabat* Highet. 10. 54, *aut vel perniciosa* Doederlein. 10. 184, *nollet* Housman. 10. 313, *lex irae debet* Housman. 10. 326, *erubuit coepto* Housman. 10. 351, *caeca vanaque* (or *pravaque*) Housman. 12. 31, after *undis* Weidner marked a lacuna. 13. 179, *dabit nimium* or *solum* Housman. 13. 226, *vindicet ignis* codd. dett.

Clausen's judgement commands respect, but in a work of this diffi-culty disagreement is occasionally to be expected. 1. 69f. 'occurrit matrona potens, quae molle Calenum porrectura viro miscet sitiente rubetam.' *rubeta* (PRV) seems necessary. *viro* must surely be a dative after *porrectura*, and *sitiente* gives a good contrast with *molle*; the construction of *miscet* is also made easier. 4. 116 and 5. 32, Housman's punctuation is adopted by Clausen, but fails to convince. 6. 157 f. 'hunc dedit olim barbarus incestae, dedit hunc Agrippa sorori.' Housman's *gestare* for *dedit hunc* is the best emendation that has ever been made in Juvenal, and it should have been adopted. 13. 43 f. 'nec puer Iliacus formonsa nec Herculis uxor ad cyathos et iam siccato nectare tergens bracchia Volcanus.' Schurtzfleisch's *saccato* must lie behind the scholiast, and it keeps up the humour of *ad cyathos* admirably. 13. 213 ff. 'sed vina misellus expuit, Albani veteris pretiosa senectus displicet.' For *sed vina* Herel and Withof proposed *Setina*; their conjecture has not been accepted by Housman, Knoche, or Clausen, but it is surely right.

Clausen deletes some thirty-six lines as interpolations, compared with Housman's fifteen; this is a notable improvement, but perhaps a few more excisions might have been made. See especially 1. 85–6 'quidquid agunt homines ... farrago libelli est' (E. Harrison, *CR* 51 (1937), 55 f., who proposed *ecquando* in 87); 3. 95 f. 'mulier nempe ipsa videtur, non persona loqui' (Jachmann); 3. 104 'non sumus ergo pares: melior, qui semper et omni' (Jahn); 3. 242 'namque facit somnum clausa lectica fenestra' (Pinzger); 7. 135 'et tamen est illis hoc utile. purpura vendit' (Knoche with U). Other proposed excisions might have been recorded in the apparatus: for instance 4. 73 (Jachmann); 5. 63 (Ribbeck); 6. 530 (Paldamus); 8. 140–1 (Knoche *dubitanter*); 8. 202 (Ruperti); 10. 146 (Pinzger). At 8. 111–12, Clausen accepts Manso's deletion; but the following sentence with its two adverbs is unconvincing ('forsitan imbellis Rhodios unctamque Corinthon despicias merito').

Perhaps the interpolations in Juvenal have not all been detected; some further suggestions for excisions are offered below. The method has been out of favour in some quarters recently, so apologies and excuses must first be offered. Interpolations in some quantity are known to have been made in Juvenal; it is therefore much more reasonable to make excisions in this author than in most other Latin poets. One cannot assume that the interpolator, fool though he was, always | wrote gibberish; it is sensible to keep a look-out for minor infelicities even if interpolation cannot be decisively proved. Wherever a passage is improved by a deletion it is worth examination; if the offending line gives a clumsy explanation of a point that has been made epigrammatically in the immediate context, then there is good reason for suspecting interpolation. The interpolated line is not always single and self-contained. Citation by the scholiast does not guarantee the authenticity of a line. It is an unfortunate complication that the interpolator was capable of changing words as well as adding lines (cf. 7. 50).

The interpolations may have come mainly from a single source, and they show some features in common. They are distinguished by what Housman calls an 'inanis strepitus verborum', and they reveal none of Juvenal's own vividness and point. Conjunctions and other particles are used freely, and sometimes imprecisely: note *ergo* (3. 104; 3. 281; 11. 99; 14. 119); *namque* (3. 242; 11. 161); *tamen* (7. 135); *sed* (8. 202; 14. 117); *nempe* (3. 95; 13. 166). Sometimes plurals are introduced in a context which contains vivid singulars. See 3. 112f. 'horum si nihil est aviam resupinat amici. [scire volunt secreta domus atque inde timeri].' 3. 280ff. 'cubat in faciem, mox deinde supinus: [ergo non aliter poterit dormire; quibusdam] somnum rixa facit' (for intrusive *quidam* see also 12. 50; 15. 107). 7. 50ff. 'nam si discedas laqueo tenet ambitios *um* [consuetudo mali, tenet insanabile multos] scribendi cacoethes, et aegro in corde senescit' (*multos* is a worse offence than *consuetudo mali*). 7. 134ff. 'spondet enim Tyrio stlattaria purpura filo [et tamen est illis hoc utile. purpura vendit] causidicum, vendunt amethystina; convenit illi et strepitu et facie maioris vivere census.' It must be admitted that there are also intrusive plurals at 11. 42, *dominis* (where, however, Heinrich proposed *damnis*), and at 3. 298f., *feriunt* and *faciunt* (I feel doubts about the genuineness of this sentence; elsewhere *vadimonium facere* is used of the defendant, as is pointed out in the Budé edition). I turn now to some suggestions on individual passages.

1. 142-6   poena tamen praesens cum tu deponis amictus
              turgidus et crudum pavonem in balnea portas.
              hinc subitae mortes atque intestata senectus.
              it nova nec tristis per cunctas fabula cenas;
              ducitur iratis plaudendum funus amicis.

          145 it *AL*²: et *PRVΦ*.

The difficulty of *intestata senectus* was pointed out by Madvig (*Adv. Crit.* 3. 249) and Housman (*CR* 13 (1899), 432ff.). It is true that they may have put their case too strongly: if the text is sound *senectus* must mean not 'old age' but 'old men', and *intestata*, coming after *subitae mortes*, must be interpreted 'die intestate'. Yet the line remains difficult;

intestatus, unlike English 'intestate', does not necessarily imply death (cf. 3. 273 f. 'ad cenam si intestatus eas'), and one cannot see why the rich patrons are described particularly as 'old men'. Madvig's own *infestata* is unintelligible; Housman's interpretation of *intestata* ('un-attested') is unparalleled, and would be confusing in a context which refers to death.

Knoche deletes 144–5 (*hinc . . . cenas*), but nobody has paid much attention: 145 is too convincing a line. I suggest that only 144 (*hinc . . . senectus*) should be deleted. Juvenal allows us to infer that the man is dead; the interpolator tries to make the connection of thought clear, but has difficulty (as elsewhere) in filling out the line. For the abrupt transition from the dinner to the funeral (without explicit mention of the death) cf. Persius 3. 100 ff. 'sed tremor inter vina subit calidumque trientem excutit e manibus, dentes crepuere retecti, uncta cadunt laxis tunc pulmentaria labris. hinc tuba, candelae.' It might be argued that *hinc* in Persius supports the authenticity of *hinc* in Juvenal; but one could equally suppose that Persius influenced the interpolator of Juvenal.

Two further observations may be added. I attach weight to the fact that plural *mortes* disrupts the series of singulars; see the cases quoted above of similar plurals in interpolations. Secondly, I assume that the reason for the friends' anger at the funeral is the scurvy treatment they have so recently received (thus Housman). But if 144 is retained they seem to be angry because the rich man has not had time to make a will. This involves a new train of thought which is unrelated to Juvenal's main theme, the punishment that awaits those who banquet alone.

2. 104–7   nimirum summi ducis est occidere Galbam
                  et curare cutem, summi constantia civis
                  Bebriaci(s) campis solium adfectare Palati
                  et pressum in faciem digitis extendere panem.

Housman points out some serious difficulties: the repetition of *summi* is awkward, seeing that *civis* does not repeat *ducis*; *ducis est* does not balance *constantia civis* (*est*); *constantia* when combined with *summi civis* naturally means 'firmness', whereas the context requires it to mean 'consistency'. I suggest that the simplest solution would be to delete *summi constantia . . . campis*, though the last | two words are in themselves unobjectionable. The motive for the interpolation might have been a wish to make it clear that *curare* and *adfectare* are not co-ordinate. Alternatively one might delete *et curare . . . civis*, but the pair of antitheses is attractive, *et curare cutem* is a convincing phrase, and there is no obvious motive for such an interpolation.

6. 63–6　　　chironomon Ledam molli saltante Bathyllo
　　　　　　　Tuccia vesicae non imperat, Apula gannit
　　　　　　　sicut in amplexu subito et miserabile longum.
　　　　　　　attendit Thymele: Thymele tunc rustica discit.

Housman pointed out that 65 *et* ought to join *miserabile* and *longum*, not *subito* and *miserabile*; he therefore transposed *gannit* and *longum*, in which he has been followed by Clausen. But though grammar is thus restored, *subito* is weak, and *miserabile* is even more unconvincing. Presumably this is why Knoche deleted *subito . . . attendit Thymele*. I suggest that it would be better to delete all of 65 (*sicut . . . longum*). *sicut in amplexu* can readily be spared, as it only weakens *gannit*; yet an interpolator might have thought that this word needed explanation (whereas on Knoche's theory no reason for the interpolation can be suggested). The repetition of *Thymele* is attractive, and should not be destroyed. Finally it may be noted that *tunc* suits the theory offered here a little better than Knoche's.

6. 107–10　　praeterea multa in facie deformia, sicut
　　　　　　　attritus galea mediisque in naribus ingens
　　　　　　　gibbus et acre malum semper stillantis ocelli.
　　　　　　　sed gladiator erat.

Thus Clausen with the manuscripts; but as Housman observed, it is strange that a swelling inside the nose should be produced by the chafing of a helmet. He also remarked on the superfluity of *que*. He therefore adopted Hadrianus Valesius's emendation *galeae* (thus taking *attritus* as a noun). Bücheler emended *sicut* to *ficus*, unconvincingly. I propose *sulcus*. See Ov. *Met.* 3. 276 'sulcavitque cutem rugis'; Stat. *Theb.* 7. 761 f. 'omnisque per artus sulcus et incisis altum rubet orbita membris'; Claud. *Eutrop.* 1. 110 'sulcisque genarum corruerat passa facies rugosior uva.' Professor Fraenkel points out to me Aesch. *Cho.* 25, ὄνυχος ἄλοκι νεοτόμῳ.

6. 159–60　　observant ubi festa mero pede sabbata reges
　　　　　　　et vetus indulget senibus clementia porcis.

　　　　　　　mero *Φ*: nudo *PRO, Arov.*

mero pede is an unusual expression for 'with bare feet'. It is explained by *Corp. Gloss. Lat.* 5. 652. 54 'me[t]ro pede id est nudo pede'; this gloss is found in a collection of notes on Juvenal, and has no independent authority. More valuable evidence is given by Prudentius, *Peristeph.* 6. 91 'stabat calce mera'; yet this passage is a little easier than ours, as the previous lines have dealt with the removal of the shoes (cf. 90 'vestigia pura'). I have considered, though with very little confidence, *udo pede*; a facetious reference to ritual foot-washing would be in Juvenal's manner. One could then assume that the comic *udo pede* was corrupted to the more normal *nudo pede*, and that metre was restored by *mero*. *P*'s blunders are normally sincere; it is the *Φ* group as a rule which deliberately tampers with the text. However, it must be admitted that at 11. 91, *P* interpolates *postremo* for *rigidique* (cf. Housman, p. xvii).

6. 565–8   consulit ictericae lento de funere matris,
            ante tamen de te Tanaquil tua, quando sororem
            efferat et patruos, an sit victurus adulter
            post ipsam; quid enim maius dare numina possunt?

quid ... possunt? seems to rub in unnecessarily a point that the reader should have taken for himself; after the series of epigrams it makes an anticlimax. I suggest that 568 (*post ... possunt*) should be deleted. The wicked woman asks whether her lover is going to live, i.e. recover from a serious illness; a person of this kind would not worry about the distant future. If *post ipsam* is right one would have to argue that Juvenal is humorously applying to an adulterous relationship the attitudes of marriage; yet one feels that after *matris, te, sororem, patruos,* the most effective climax comes at *adulter*. If the interpolator missed the point of *victurus* he would be tempted to supply *post ipsam* and fill out the line.

8. 167–72   indulge veniam pueris: Lateranus ad illos
            thermarum calices inscriptaque lintea vadit
            maturus bello Armeniae Syriaeque tuendis
            amnibus et Rheno atque Histro. praestare Neronem
            securum valet haec aetas. mitte Ostia, Caesar,
            mitte, sed in magna legatum quaere popina. |

There are two theories about Lateranus. Some suppose that he is Plautius Lateranus, consul-designate in 65, and executed in that year because of his part in the Pisonian conspiracy. But Juvenal's Lateranus actually reached the consulship: see 148 *mulio consul,* 150 *finitum tempus honoris cum fuerit,* 155 *interea* (i.e. while he is consul). If Juvenal means the consul-designate of 65 he has made a bad blunder. Others suppose that he is referring to T. Sextius Lateranus, consul 94, but this is contradicted by 170 *Neronem* (quoted above). Juvenal calls Domitian *calvo Neroni* (4. 38), but *Nero* without an adjective is a very different matter. In Martial 11. 33 'Nero' seems to be used as a cover-name for Domitian, but in a matter-of-fact statement, such as we have here, such ambiguity would be impossible. I suggest that *praestare... aetas* should be deleted: now the passage could refer to the consul of 94. In any case the line is a little strange: it would more naturally refer to the prefect of the praetorian guard than to an army commander on the frontier. If the deletion is made, *mitte Ostia* ('send him to the embarkation-port') follows naturally on the distant place-names.

9. 125-9   nunc mihi quid suades post damnum temporis et spes
            deceptas? festinat enim decurrere velox
            flosculus angustae miseraeque brevissima vitae
            portio; dum bibimus, dum serta unguenta puellas
            poscimus, obrepit non intellecta senectus.

flosculus involves a strange mixture of metaphors after *festinat...
decurrere velox*. 127 gives an extraordinary word-order, and makes a remarkable contrast with the two vigorous lines that follow. The obvious solution is to delete *velox ... brevissima*; this was in fact suggested tentatively by Ruperti, but nobody seems to have taken any notice. *vitae portio* by itself is sufficient, but an interpolator might have thought that *brevissima* was desirable.

10. 148-52   hic est quem non capit Africa Mauro
              percussa Oceano Niloque admota tepenti
              rursus ad Aethiopum populos aliosque elephantos.
              additur imperiis Hispania, Pyrenaeum
              transilit.

In 150 *altosque*, the reading of *PA* is obviously intolerable; *aliosque* (*Φ*, Prisc.) is also notoriously difficult, and people write articles on it from time to time. There is another oddity about the line which has not attracted attention: there is no connective to join the Nile and the Aethiopians (one expects *rursusque* not *rursus*). I suggest that 150 should perhaps be deleted. Juvenal may only have considered the north coast of Africa where Carthaginian power extended; the interpolator felt it necessary to point out that Africa extended far to the south as well. *altosque* may have been the handiwork of the interpolator; it would be worthy of him.

10. 159–62   exitus ergo quis est? o gloria! vincitur idem
              nempe et in exilium praeceps fugit atque ibi magnus
              mirandusque cliens sedet ad praetoria regis
              donec Bithyno libeat vigilare tyranno.

I suggest that 160 (*nempe* ... *magnus*) ought to be suspected. Hannibal did not in fact flee immediately after his defeat, but of course Juvenal might have made a careless mistake. It is more serious that the line says very little in a long-winded way; *nempe* is found elsewhere in interpolations. The literal-minded interpolator might have wished to avoid the abrupt transition from Hannibal's defeat to his attendance on the king of Bithynia.

11. 46–9   hi plerumque gradus: conducta pecunia Romae
             et coram dominis consumitur; inde, ubi paulum
             nescio quid superest et pallet faenoris auctor,
             qui vertere solum, Baias et ad ostrea currunt.

qui vertere solum is odd; this is the first we have heard of people who go into exile, yet *qui* implies that we have met them before. Line 48 also reveals a difficulty. *paulum nescio quid superest* means that the spendthrift has *still* a little left (which makes his defection all the worse), not that he has *only* a little left; therefore the creditor's pallor should not be mentioned at this point. I suggest that these difficulties could both be removed by the deletion of *et pallet* ... *solum* (though *et pallet faenoris auctor* is a good phrase). The subject of *currunt* can be supplied from the context, but the pedantic interpolator might have wished to see it explicitly named. |

11. 111–14   templorum quoque maiestas praesentior, et vox
              nocte fere media mediamque audita per urbem
              litore ab Oceani Gallis venientibus et dis
              officium vatis peragentibus.

The play on *media* and *mediam* is inept. Perhaps Juvenal wrote *tacitamque* (or something similar) and a scribe's eye jumped.

13. 23–5   quae tam festa dies ut cesset prodere furem,
             perfidiam, fraudes atque omni ex crimine lucrum
             quaesitum et partos gladio vel puxide nummos?

furem refers to a criminal, whereas the other accusatives in the sentence all refer to crimes. Perhaps one might emend to *furtum*. Such a corruption could have originated from the natural phrase *prodere furem*, 'to give away a thief' (cf. Ulp. *Dig.* 12. 5. 4. 1 'si dederit fur ne proderetur').

13. 107–8   tunc te sacra ad delubra vocantem
              praecedit, trahere immo ultro ac vexare paratus.

vexare, if right, must mean something like 'to jostle'; Duff quotes Suet. *Aug.* 53 'in turba . . . vexatus'. One could not say simply *vexare ad delubra*; so *trahere ac vexare* must be taken together as 'to pull and shove'. I propose *vectare*. The trickster walks in front of you to the temple; he actually pulls you along; best of all, he is ready to provide transport in his litter.

14. 4–13   si damnosa senem iuvat alea, ludit et heres
            bullatus parvoque eadem movet arma fritillo.
            nec melius de se cuiquam sperare propinquo
            concedet iuvenis, qui radere tubera terrae,
            boletum condire et eodem iure natantis
            mergere ficedulas didicit nebulone parente
            et cana monstrante gula. cum septimus annus
            transierit puerum, nondum omni dente renato,
            barbatos licet admoveas mille inde magistros,
            hinc totidem, cupiet lauto cenare paratu . . .

It is a little awkward that Juvenal first mentions the glutton as a *iuvenis* (7), and only later considers how you might educate him as a *puer* (11). I suggest that editors' punctuation may give the wrong meaning; perhaps one should have a comma after *fritillo* (5) and *gula* (10), and a full stop after *iuvenis* (7). When a father plays dice his small son will do the same, and he will be no better as a young man; *senem*, *bullatus*, and *iuvenis* balance each other. Then follows the example of the glutton.

14. 70–2   gratum est quod patriae civem populoque dedisti
            si facis ut patriae sit idoneus, utilis agris,
            utilis et bellorum et pacis rebus agendis.

Housman pointed out the awkwardness of repeating *patriae* without repeating *populo*; he therefore proposed *ut civis sit idoneus*. But difficulties remain: this rich man's son is not going to be an agricultural labourer, and *agris* is not co-ordinate with *bellorum et pacis rebus*. For *agris* one expects *armis*; this emendation in turn suggests *paci* for *patriae*, and the deletion of 72. Cf. Prop. 1. 6. 29 'non ego sum laudi, non natus idoneus armis'; 3. 9. 19 'hic satus ad pacem, hic castrensibus utilis armis'. One cannot propose changes on this scale with much confidence, but one can insist that something is wrong.

14. 265–9   an magis oblectant animum iactata petauro
                   corpora quique solet rectum descendere funem
                   quam tu, Corycia semper qui puppe moraris
                   atque habitas, coro semper tollendus et austro,
                   perditus ac vilis sacci mercator olentis.

ac vilis (PU, Ambr.) does not make sense; neither does *a siculis* (*Φ*); Clausen rightly obelizes. Housman proposed *ac similis* (i.e. the sea-sick merchant turns as yellow as his saffron); but the merchant would only turn yellow for short periods, and one expects a more permanent characteristic to be mentioned. I suggest *articulis*: the merchant was crippled by arthritis, as might well happen in damp ancient ships. *articulis . . . perditus* is an emendation by Madvig at Persius 1. 23 (approved by Housman and Clausen). The comment of the scholiast *tu foetide* may rest simply on a misunderstanding of *sacci olentis*. |

15. 140–7   quis enim bonus et face dignus
                        arcana, qualem Cereris volt esse sacerdos,
                        ulla aliena sibi credit mala? separat hoc nos
                        a grege mutorum, atque ideo venerabile soli
                        sortiti ingenium divinorumque capaces
                        atque exercendis pariendisque artibus apti
                        sensum a caelesti demissum traximus arce
                        cuius egent prona et terram spectantia.

'The fact that we can feel sympathy separates us from the brutes, and it is because we can feel sympathy that we have acquired from heaven a capacity for sympathy.' There is something wrong with the logic, as Duff points out. For *ideo* I suggest *adeo*. Juvenal now argues: 'A capacity for sympathy separates us from the brutes; *what is more* it is from heaven that we have acquired a feeling that the brutes lack.' I further suggest that 145 (*atque exercendis . . . apti*) may possibly be an interpolation; though it would suit remarks elsewhere about man's kinship with the divine, it has nothing to do with the matter in hand.

16. 13–20   Bardaicus iudex datur haec punire volenti
                   calceus et grandes magna ad subsellia surae
                   legibus antiquis castrorum et more Camilli
                   servato, miles ne vallum litiget extra
                   et procul a signis. 'iustissima centurionum

> cognitio est igitur de milite, nec mihi derit
> ultio, si iustae defertur causa querellae.'
> tota cohors tamen est inimica . . .

Housman pointed out that *igitur* (18) gives the wrong meaning; he proposed *inquis* or *inquit* or *sed enim*. Knoche retains the reading of the manuscripts, Clausen obelizes *igitur*. I suggest that 18 (*cognitio . . . derit*) should be deleted. The words within the quotation marks will now be spoken not by the aggrieved civilian (in which case they would be naïve) but by the military man. The point of the repetition *iustissima . . . iustae* is made sharper by the deletion. For *iusta* applied to *ultio* cf. Petr. 106. 4; Tac. *Hist.* 4. 6.

Some other lines arouse faint suspicions even though it is impossible to put forward a compelling case for deletion. 1. 29 could conceivably have been interpolated by a reader who shared the scholiast's views about 'summer rings'. (Crispinus should be guilty of vulgar excess, not of over-refinement; for the idiomatic use of *aestivum* cf. *matutino* in 4. 108 and 6. 523.) 6. 138, if removed, might make *inde* in the next line a little easier. In 6. 359, *tamen*, though defensible (see Housman), is at first sight misleading; if the line were removed and *illam* read in 358 the passage would gain in vigour. 6. 395 and 6. 588 are both expendable. 10. 243–5 are feeble compared with what has preceded. 10. 342 is perfectly good in itself, but might have been interpolated to rub in the point of the previous line. 10. 349 is weak compared with the following sentence, though Juvenal could have written it. 13. 101 is tolerable without being brilliant; yet if it had not been there in the original text it contains precisely the sort of explanation that the interpolator would have provided. 15. 167 is a poor line; if it were removed the Latin would be perfectly good (cf. Kühner–Stegmann, 2. 563 f.), though the interpolator would not have thought so. Of course one's doubts in these passages may be quite unjustified; Juvenal, though so often pointed and compressed, was capable of being garrulous and diffuse. Yet in a text known to contain interpolations one ought never to take anything for granted.

I have discussed some parts of this review with Dr R. Kassel, Mr G. J. Toomer, and Mr A. F. Wells; I am very grateful to them for their help.

3

Felicitas at Surrentum (Statius, *Silvae* 2. 2)

THE Surrentinum[1] of Pollius Felix encouraged Statius to play on the meaning of felicity. The villa's prospect extended to Naples and Limon[2] (near Pausilypum), where an inscription of AD 65 already attests the name of the family.[3] Nereids climbed the rocks to steal the fortunate proprietor's grapes, and Satyrs tumbled in the sea in the eagerness of their pursuit. A local Siren flew up to hear songs better than her own (112f.),

> hic ubi Pierias exercet Pollius artes,
> seu volvit monitus quos dat Gargettius auctor,
> seu nostram quatit ille chelyn, seu dissona nectit
> carmina, sive minax ultorem stringit iambon.

In other words Pollius was a poet (cf. 39f.; 3. 1. 66f.) who wrote hexameters,[4] elegiacs, and iambi; that is why Statius refers to his *eloquentia* and *facundia*,[5] for Schanz–Hosius[6] are wrong to include so private a person among the orators. In particular he seems to have composed didactic verse on Epicurean subjects.[7] In a context referring to the Siren and immediately after a mention of Pierian arts, *volvit monitus* (co-ordinate with *quatit, nectit, stringit*) surely refers to something more

An earlier version of this paper was read in London on 22 Mar. 1977 to the Society for the Promotion of Roman Studies. It originated from discussions of Statian prosopography with Mrs E. Darch. I owe much to comments and corrections from Mrs M. T. Griffin, Mr C. W. Macleod, Professor F. G. B. Millar, and Sir Ronald Syme.

[1] See P. Mingazzini and F. Pfister, *Forma Italiae, Regio I*, vol. 2. *Surrentum* (1946), 54f., 132f. with tav. i and xviii; the scale of the villa was probably less than supposed by J. Beloch, *Campanien*[2] (1890), 269f. (with pl. x).

[2] *Silv.* 2. 2. 81f.; 3. 1. 149.

[3] *ILS* 5798: 'Macrinus . . . hic ambulavit a villa Polli Felicis, quae est Epilimones, usque ad emissarium Paconianum, Nerva et Vestino cos.'; Mommsen, *Hermes*, 18 (1883), 158f.; J. H. D'Arms, *Romans on the Bay of Naples* (1970), 221f.

[4] For this use of *chelys* cf. 1. 3. 102; 5. 5. 33; *Theb.* 1. 33.

[5] 2. *praef.*; 3. *praef.*; 3. 1. 65; so 1. 3. 1 of the equally versatile Vopiscus (1. 3. 99f.).

[6] *Geschichte der röm. Lit.* 2[4], 839 n. 5.

[7] For the Epicurean traditions of the area cf. D'Arms, op. cit. (n. 3), 56f.

than an interest in philosophy (thus Vollmer's commentary) or an avoidance of public life (J. H. Mozley's Loeb edition).

From this point an Epicurean attitude begins to dominate the poem, just as Horace's odes are sometimes coloured by the philosophical position of his addressees. Already in the opening section Statius had used a series of double-edged words to relate the tranquil scene to the ἀταραξία of Pollius himself (26f.):[8]

> mira quies pelagi:[9] ponunt hic lassa furorem
> aequora, et insani spirant clementius austri,
> hic praeceps minus audet hiems, nulloque tumultu
> stagna modesta iacent dominique imitantia mores.

Now in the final paragraph *felix* takes on a more ethical and less materialistic connotation:[10] Pollius has made himself immune to fate by conquering hope and fear, and death will find him, in a phrase reminiscent of Lucretius,[11] 'abire paratum ac plenum vita' (128f.). The lush τοποθεσία gives place to more explicit Epicurean symbols: the Marina di Puolo, which seems still to preserve the name of Pollius, is transmuted into the haven of the wise,[12] the | sea becomes the tumult of the world[13] (as in the proem to Lucretius 2), the panoramic vista the *spectaculum* of human folly,[14] the secluded villa the citadel[15] of the mind (129f.):

> nos, vilis turba, caducis
> deservire bonis semperque optare parati,
> spargimur in casus: celsa tu mentis ab arce
> despicis errantis humanaque gaudia rides.

This subtle pastiche allusively combines several other Epicurean motifs: lack of αὐταρκεία (*Sent. Vat.* 67, 77), transitory 'goods' (contrast the immortal ἀγαθά of *Ep. Men.* 135, *Sent. Vat.* 78), infinite desires

---

[8] For γαληνισμός cf. Epicur. *Ep. Her.* 37, 83, frr. 413, 425, 429 (Usener); W. Schmid, *RAC* 5. 722. For similar correspondences between external and internal storms cf. D. Vessey, *Statius and the Thebaid* (1973), 93 f.

[9] For the *quies* of Pollius cf. 3. *praef.*

[10] 122 'Troica et Euphratae supra diademata felix'.

[11] 3. 938 'cur non ut plenus vitae conviva recedis . . .?'; Epicur. fr. 499 (= Cic. *Tusc.* 5. 118); *Sent. Vat.* 47.

[12] 140 'securos portus'; Epicur. fr. 544: Ἐπίκουρος τἀγαθὸν ἐν τῷ βαθυτάτῳ τῆς ἡσυχίας ὥσπερ ἐν ἀκλύστῳ λιμένι καὶ κωφῷ τιθέμενος; Virg. *Catal.* 5. 8f. 'nos ad beatos vela mittimus portus, magni petentes docta dicta Sironis'.

[13] 139 'illo alii rursus iactantur in alto'.

[14] Lucr. 2. 2 'e terra magnum alterius spectare laborem'; 2. 9f.

[15] Lucr. 2. 7f. 'sed nil dulcius est bene quam munita tenere edita doctrina sapientum templa serena'; Hor. *Serm.* 2. 6. 16; *Carm.* 2. 6. 21f.; *Ciris* 14.

(*Κύριαι Δόξαι* 15, frr. 454f.), vulnerability to fortune (cf. frr. 489, 584), a failure to give coherence to life (*spargimur*).[16] Yet though the passage is as eloquent as anything in Statius, it may seem too smug for modern taste: Pollius had perhaps been disappointed in minor ambitions at Puteoli,[17] but his serenity was based on immense wealth. What could such people know of storms?

One speaks advisedly of 'people', for Pollius had a wife who matched him in temperament as well as in name (9f.):

> trans gentile fretum placidi facundia Polli
> detulit et nitidae iuvenilis gratia Pollae.

Polla seems to have been an interesting person in her own right, as she receives similar compliments in the other poems addressed to the family;[18] by contrast, the wives of Statius's other addressees are generally ignored,[19] as is Pollius's own daughter, whose baby's birth is the occasion of 4. 8. In 2. 2 Polla is treated as an equal partner in her husband's felicity (107: 'sis felix, tellus, dominis ambobus'), and the poem ends with an Epicurean *envoi* to the tranquil pair (143: 'discite securi'), whose catastematic bliss preserves the laws of friendship (144f.: 'sanctusque pudicae servat amicitiae leges amor').[20] Most important of all is the preceding address to the wife alone (151f.):[21]

> non tibi sepositas infelix strangulat arca
> divitias avidique animum dispendia torquent
> faenoris: expositi census et docta fruendi
> temperies.

This eulogy of munificence strongly suggests that Polla herself was a patron of letters; for the drift one may compare the *Charites* of

[16] Epicurus spoke of the dissipation of life by wrong attitudes to time (cf. below, n. 100); see *Sent. Vat.* 14: ὁ δὲ βίος μελλησμῷ παραπόλλυται (contrast Hor. *Carm.* 3. 29. 41f.); Cic. *Fin.* 1. 62–3 (with J. S. Reid's parallels).

[17] 2. 2. 133f. Pollius had abandoned not poetry but politics: for text and interpretation cf. L. Håkanson, *Statius' Silvae* (1969), 64f. (*pulchrique*); better E. Courtney, *BICS* 18 (1971), 95 (*rectique*).

[18] 3. 1. 87, 159, 179; 4. 8. 13f.

[19] The exceptions are Priscilla, whose death is the actual subject of 5. 1, and Statius's mother, who is mentioned without being named in the *epicedium* on his father (5. 3. 240f.).

[20] Something of the same attitude to marriage may be observed behind the satire at Lucr. 4. 1278f. Bailey comments ad loc.: 'perhaps, too, there is the thought that long custom of living together approaches to the Epicurean conceptions of friendship'.

[21] In spite of the dislocation in the MS, there can be no doubt that these lines precede 143f., i.e. they refer to Polla; cf. Housman, *CR* 20 (1906), 42f. = *Classical Papers* 2. 646f.

Theocritus, where generosity to poets is encouraged more explicitly than was acceptable to Roman taste (16. 22 f.):

> δαιμόνιοι, τί δὲ κέρδος ὁ μυρίος ἔνδοθι χρυσὸς
> κείμενος; οὐχ ἅδε πλούτου φρονέουσιν ὄνασις,
> ἀλλὰ τὸ μὲν ψυχᾷ, τὸ δέ πού τινι δοῦναι ἀοιδῶν.

It is particularly significant that *docta fruendi temperies* is an imitation of Horace, *Carm.* 2. 2. 3 f., where Sallustius Crispus is described as hostile to silver *nisi temperato splendeat usu.* | Though Horace is too discreet to underline it, the point there must be that Sallustius, like Proculeius in the following stanza, was a patron of poets.[22]

Statius was fortunate in his friendship with ladies called Polla: the last poem in the same book, the *Genethliacon Lucani* (2. 7), was dedicated to Argentaria Polla, the widow of Lucan. The wife of Pollius was lovely, charming, serene, kind, virtuous and rich,[23] but Calliope ascribes no less attractive qualities to Lucan's widow (2. 7. 81 f.):

> nec solum dabo carminum nitorem,
> sed taedis genialibus dicabo
> doctam atque ingenio tuo decoram,
> qualem blanda Venus daretque Iuno
> forma simplicitate[24] comitate
> censu sanguine gratia decore.[25]

Such compliments were no doubt common enough in panegyrics on women, but it is a more interesting coincidence that Lucan's widow also gave encouragement to poets:[26] compare 2. *praef.* 'cludit volumen Genethliacon Lucani, quod Polla Argentaria, rarissima uxorum, cum hunc diem forte coleremus,[27] imputari sibi voluit', Mart. 7. 21-3 (a cycle of three epigrams clearly commissioned for the same occasion),[28] and 10. 64. 1 (where he significantly calls Polla his *regina*).[29] At this point one is tempted to ask whether the wife of Pollius and the widow

---

[22] Crinagoras is more candid (*A. Pl.* 40). For Proculeius cf. Juv. 7. 94, where he is linked with Maecenas.

[23] 2. 2. 10 and 3. 1. 87, *nitidae*; 2. 2. 10, *gratia*; 3. 1. 179, *placidae* (cf. 2. 2. 148 f.); 4. 8. 13 f., *benigno . . . sinu*; 2. 2. 144, *pudicae*; 2. 2. 152, *divitias*.

[24] So 3. 1. 32 (of Pollius) 'sed felix simplexque domus'.

[25] Cf. also 2. 7. 62, *castae*.

[26] As is made clear by P. White, *HSCPh*, 79 (1975), 280f.

[27] *consuleremus* of the MS is meaningless; F. Skutsch's *coleremus* is excellent in sense (cf. White, op. cit.) and rhythm.

[28] V. Buchheit, *Philologus*, 105 (1961), 90 ff.

[29] Cf. the use of *rex* at *Silv.* 3. 2. 92 f.; Hor. *Epist.* 1. 7. 37 (to Maecenas); White, op. cit. 285.

of Lucan might not be the same person. This possibility was suggested very tentatively by Markland in 1728 (below, n. 43), and was still thought worth summarily rejecting at *RE* 2. 706 (published in 1896), but is not even mentioned in the articles on Polla and Pollius Felix,[30] or in Vollmer's commentary, or in Schanz–Hosius, or in *PIR*, or in more recent studies of Flavian literary society. It may be worth while to ask why the identification is now thought so implausible, and then to consider the positive arguments in support.

First of all, there may be doubts about chronology. Lucan was born in 39 (*Vita Vaccae*) and died in 65; let us assume that Argentaria Polla was born between 40 and 45. It is usually taken for granted that Polla Pollii was twice a grandmother in 91[31] (3. 1. 175f.) and a third time in 95 (4. 8); that is compatible with an age similar to that of the other Polla. However, it seems more likely (as Mrs Griffin points out) that the grandchildren in question were those of Pollius by an earlier marriage: at 4. 8. 13 f. ('quaeque sibi genitos putat attollitque benigno Polla sinu'), Statius is probably saying that Polla treats her husband's grandchildren as if they were her own. Even so, Polla Pollii seems to have been middle-aged by 91, as is suggested by the 'impossible' protasis at 3. 1. 161, 'quod si dulce decus viridisque resumeret annos'. In that case the *iuvenilis gratia* of which the poet speaks (above, p. 31) must mean not that she was still young but that she had retained her youthful charm; even if she was not herself a grandmother, she could still have been old enough to be Lucan's widow.

There are questions about social status as well as chronology: it has recently been suggested that Pollius Felix was a freedman's son,[32] whose *cognomen* perhaps hints at servile origin, and the sources of his money have even been compared with those of Trimalchio.[33] But he was not only a man of great wealth, but of wide-ranging literary, artistic, and philosophical interests; the serene dilettante of Statius does not sound like a self-made parvenu. | He is more likely to have been a member of the local aristocracy. It is a basic fact of Roman social history that such families could be connected with the highest in the land, and the Annaei themselves had been no different in origin.

[30] *RE* 21. 1407f., 1419f.

[31] For the dating of the poems cf. Vollmer, op. cit. 6f.; H. Frère and H. J. Izaac (Budé edn.), vol. 1, xxiif.

[32] J. H. D'Arms, *JRS* 64 (1974), 111, mentioning as a possible father Cn. Pollius Cn. l. Victor, an *Augustalis* at Puteoli in 56 (*CIL* 10. 1574).

[33] D'Arms, op. cit. (n. 3), 125f.

Lucan's father, the unambitious Mela,[34] was not just equestrian but provincial,[35] as were both his grandfathers, the elder Seneca and Acilius Lucanus. After Lucan's suicide Polla might have felt no desire to marry again into a great political family.

But the main objection that is felt to our hypothesis is not chronological or social but sentimental. Scholars are reluctant to identify the happy wife of Pollius with the devoted widow of the *Genethliacon*, who kept Lucan's likeness over her bed and called him like Protesilaus from the underworld (2. 7. 120 f.):

> adsis lucidus et vocante Polla
> unum, quaeso, diem deos silentum
> exores: solet hoc patere limen
> ad nuptas redeuntibus maritis.[36]

But though the *univira*[37] enjoyed traditional esteem in Latin literature, second husbands[38] were common and unobjectionable, as was to be expected in a society where marriage was secular,[39] divorce easy, early death frequent, and the after-life meagre. Roman women of the highest character could be commended for *pietas* to two different husbands:[40] cf. *Carm. Epig.* 1578. 1 'semperque pudica maritis'; *CIL* 6. 19253, 'D. M. Anniae Helvidiae coiugi sanctissimae et incomparabili fecit P. Arrenius Gemellinus . . . con qua (*sic*) vixit annis XI et P. Aelio Filarguro marito virginio eius co[n quo] vixit annis XXI'; or, if that is too low a grade of society, *ILS* 8394 (*laudatio Murdiae*), 'gratum fidumque animum in viros'. In Epicurean circles the more liberal view would have prevailed, and Pollius might have repeated Anna's question to Dido: 'id cinerem aut manis credis curare sepultos?' (Virg. *Aen.* 4. 34). Or, to take a more auspicious instance of Virgil's illumination of conduct, Hector's widow Andromache has an obsessive devotion to the memory of her dead husband, but that does not keep her from marrying the less heroic but highly deserving Helenus (*Aen.* 3. 294 f.); Aeneas comments (495) 'vobis parta quies' (words that refer not to death but most emphatically to life), and if our theory is correct the

---

[34] Sen., *Contr.* 2. *praef.* 3 'hoc unum concupiscentem, nihil concupiscere'; Tac. *Ann.* 16. 17. 3 'petitione honorum abstinuerat per ambitionem praeposteram'.

[35] Tac. *Ann.* 14. 53. 5 'equestri et provinciali loco ortus' (the great Seneca).

[36] Cf. Mart. 7. 23. 3 f. 'tu, Polla, maritum saepe colas et se sentiat ille coli'.

[37] *RAC* 3. 1017 f.; M. Humbert, *Le Remariage à Rome* (1972), 59 f.

[38] Humbert, op. cit.; T. P. Wiseman, *Catullan Questions* (1969), 58 f.

[39] For the 'humanistic idea' of Roman marriage cf. F. Schulz, *Classical Roman Law* (1951), 103 f.

[40] Humbert, op. cit. 102 f., 108 f., 122.

same could be said to Polla. But to prove the point there is no need to look beyond Statius himself: he mentions the previous marriage of Priscilla, the dead wife of the mourning Abascantus (5. 1. 45 f.), and in comparing his own wife Claudia to Penelope and Laodamia, he does not hesitate to praise her *fides* to her former husband (3. 5. 50 f.):

> nec minor his tu nosse fidem vitamque maritis
> dedere. sic certe cineres umbramque priorem
> quaeris adhuc, sic exsequias amplexa canori
> coniugis ingentis iterasti pectore planctus
> iam mea.

That is to say, she was a Laodamia to her dead husband and a Penelope to her living one.

At this point there may be hope of introducing a more positive piece of evidence: our hypothesis seems to be treated as a fact by one ancient writer. Sidonius gives a long list of authors whom he professes to regard as inferior to the father of Consentius; after a mention of the Senecas and Martial, the climax comes with the following lines (*Carm.* 23. 165 f.):

> quid quos duplicibus iugata taedis
> Argentaria pallidat poetas? |

The poets are Lucan and Statius, not Pollius, of whose writings Sidonius was as ignorant as we are; and it is generally assumed[41] that to make the sentence balance, they are also the two husbands. But it is difficult to see how even Sidonius could have supposed that Polla was married to Statius: he knew well the *Silvae* in general[42] and the *Genethliacon* in particular, and he ought to have seen that Statius is addressing his wife in 3. 5 and not in 2. 7. It seems more likely that Sidonius regards the two husbands as Lucan and Pollius[43] (the circumstance is worth mentioning because the marriages marked the two stages of Polla's literary importance); in that case, *pallidat* refers not to the *pallor amantium* but to the pale cast of thought, as is naturally suggested by the collocation with *poetas*.[44] Unfortunately this conclusion

---

[41] Cf. *RE* 1. 2228; W. B. Anderson's Loeb edn. ad loc.

[42] *Carm.* 9. 226 f., 22 §6; R. Bitschofsky, *De L. Sollii Apollinaris Sidonii studiis Statianis* (1881).

[43] Cf. Markland on Stat., *Silv.* 2. *praef.* 'quod si verum sit ... Lucanum et Pollium eandem uxorem habuisse, omnis erroris liberatur Sidonius'. For the importance of Markland's *Silvae* see now C. Collard, *PCPS* 22 (1976), 1 f.

[44] Pers. *prol.* 4 'pallidamque Pirenen'; Juv. 7. 97 with Mayor's note. In Lucan's case Sidonius would be thinking of the *Adlocutio ad Pollam* (see next paragraph).

is of little practical importance: there was no ancient biography of
Statius, and Sidonius can have known nothing about his circle except
what he could glean from the poems. He is unsound elsewhere on
literary history: he thought[45] that Ovid's Corinna was Julia, scrupu-
lously distinguished the philosopher Seneca from the tragedian, and
assumed too confidently that Juvenal was exiled by an actor. He tells us
nothing that we could not have derived for ourselves; all we can say is
that he saw nothing unreasonable in the assumption that Lucan's
widow should have remarried.

Argentaria Polla deserves further investigation. Statius would
respect her not just for her graciousness and her money but for her
antecedents and poetical interests (2. 7. 83 'doctam atque ingenio tuo
decoram'); and when Martial reminds her of an improper epigram by
her late husband,[46] that implies an emancipated lady who knew the
rules of the genre. Sidonius pictures her as helping Lucan with his
poetry, though his other *exempla* suggest that he has no evidence
except a general feeling of appropriateness: 'saepe versum Corinna
cum suo Nasone complevit, Lesbia cum Catullo, Caesennia cum
Gaetulico, Argentaria cum Lucano, Cynthia cum Propertio, Delia cum
Tibullo' (*Epist.* 2. 10. 5). Lucan addressed her in the *Adlocutio ad
Pollam*[47] (perhaps part of his *Silvae*, since it is not mentioned as an
independent poem in Vacca's *Life*); this may have been the model for
Statius's address to his wife Claudia, in which he urges on her the
attractions of Campania as opposed to Rome (3. 5. 81 f.). It may also be
relevant that Lucan wrote *Epistulae ex Campania*, which were probably
in prose[48] rather than verse; the title suggests something more than a
temporary holiday, and such a link with Campania[49] would fit our
theory even though it does nothing to prove it. After Lucan's death his
widow might have retired to her husband's property on the Bay of
Naples, and in due course have married a kind Epicurean gentleman of
quieter literary and political tastes. Lucan had been a rich man;[50] when
his father was put to death in 66 for his own and his son's money, he
left a large sum to Tigellinus 'quo cetera manerent' (Tac. *Ann.*

---

[45] *Carm.* 23. 160 f.; 9. 232 f.; 9. 271 f.

[46] Lucan fr. 10 (Morel) = Mart. 10. 64. 6 'si nec pedicor, Cotta, quid hic facio?'

[47] Stat., *Silv.* 2. 7. 62 f. 'hinc castae titulum decusque Pollae iucunda dabis adlocutione'.

[48] *Vita Vaccae* (cf. *Silv.* 2. 7. 22); M. J. McGann, *RFIC* 99 (1971), 63 f. and *TAPA* 105
(1975), 213 f. against F. M. Ahl, *Lucan* (1976), 335 f.

[49] The Pisonian conspiracy that brought Lucan to his death centred round Piso's villa
at Baiae; cf. Tac. *Ann.* 15.52.1; F. M. Ahl, *TAPA* 102 (1971), 22 f.

[50] Juv. 7. 79 f. 'iaceat Lucanus in hortis marmoreis'; Tac. *Ann.* 16. 17. 4.

16. 17. 5). Perhaps some of the family fortunes (the childless Seneca's as well) found their way to Polla; perhaps she even diverted her second husband from Puteoli and Pausilypum, where he had his roots, by bringing him a splendid Surrentinum.

Where did she herself come from? The name 'Argentarius' was rare and in general undistinguished, but it was borne by one person of literary talent: this was the well-known declaimer, who plays a considerable part in the writings of Lucan's grandfather.[51] The elder Seneca not only wrote about declaimers but welcomed them into his family circle. | Porcius Latro was an associate from childhood till the day of his death (*Cont.* 1. *praef.* 13), Seneca's sons regarded the son of Clodius Turrinus with brotherly affection (10. *praef.* 14), one of them was ultimately adopted by Junius Gallio (*PIR*² I. 757), the great Seneca was a friend of Passienus Crispus, the grandson of the 'Passienus noster' of the *Controversiae.*[52] The declaimers cited by the elder Seneca belong in general to the Augustan period, when his sons were too young to listen (1 *praef.* 1 and 4), and Argentarius was the pupil of Cestius Pius (10. 3. 12), whose floruit is given by Jerome as 13 BC. Therefore he was presumably too senior to be the father of a woman born about AD 40-5, but he might have been the grandfather; a relationship was already suggested by F. Marx (*RE* 1. 2228). It has been observed that of the dozen inscriptions recording Argentarii three come from Spain (perhaps because of the silver mines), including one from Seneca's own *conventus Cordubensis.*[53] A number of the declaimers associated with the elder Seneca were Spaniards,[54] notably Porcius Latro, Gavius Silo, Clodius Turrinus, Cornelius Hispanus, Statorius Victor (the case of Junius Gallio rests only on conjecture).[55] On the other hand Seneca explicitly says that Argentarius was a Greek (*Cont.* 9. 3. 13), and this may suggest that his family or their patrons derived their name not from Spanish mines but from Greek banks.[56]

Though a connection with Argentarius cannot be definitely proved,

[51] See esp. Sen., *Cont.* 9. 3. 12-13; H. Bornecque, *Les Déclamations et les déclamateurs d'après Sénèque le père* (1902), 152f.; S. G. P. Small, *YCS* 12 (1951), 75f.

[52] 3. *praef.* 10; Bornecque, op. cit. 186f.; M. T. Griffin, *Seneca* (1976), 45.

[53] Small, op. cit. 73, citing *CIL* 2. 1562, 3283, 5493.

[54] H. de la Ville de Mirmont, *Annales de la faculté des lettres de Bordeaux, Bulletin Hispanique,* 12 (1910), 1f.; 14 (1912), 11f.; 15 (1913), 154f., 237f., 384f.; M. Griffin, *JRS* 62 (1972), 12.

[55] The 'sweet Gallio' born at Corduba (Stat. *Silv.* 2. 7. 30) is the elder Seneca's son; cf. A. Vassileiou, *RPh.* 46 (1972), 40f. (citing Sen. *NQ* 4. *praef.* 11).

[56] His teacher Cestius Pius came from Smyrna (Hier. *Chron.* ad ol. 191. 4), in spite of his Latin name.

it must be underlined that in spite of her unimportant name Argentaria was a person of culture and distinction in a society where literary
ladies were still rare enough to be noticed; when Statius speaks of her
lineage (2. 7. 86, *sanguine*), he may not be thinking in purely social
terms. Lucan shared his family's fondness for declamation, and the *Life*
of Vacca records speeches for and against Octavius Sagitta; as for his
epic, it is enough to mention[57] the morbid sensationalism, the fervid
denunciations of tyranny, the hyperbolical paradoxes, the epigrams
that reiterate rather than develop,[58] the heavy-handed use of point.
Though the elder Seneca speaks with no particular warmth of
Argentarius, it would have been quite appropriate that the young poet,
whose original ambitions were purely literary, should marry a member
of such a family; his own maternal grandfather, Acilius Lucanus,
though he is nowhere described as a declaimer, had been a well-known
orator from Corduba (*Vita Vaccae*). And if our central hypothesis turns
out to be correct, it would also be appropriate that the granddaughter
of a Romanized Greek should marry the Hellenizing Pollius,[59] whose
daughter in turn married the Neapolitan Julius Menecrates (4. 8).

The possibility of a link between Argentaria and Argentarius is
made more intriguing, and perhaps also more likely, by a further circumstance: the declaimer was probably the same person as M. Argentarius the epigrammatist.[60] Both have the same rare Latin name,
though the former was of Greek origin and the latter wrote in Greek;
the former worked under Augustus (as has been seen), the latter is
included in the *Garland of Philip*, which contains epigrams from the
time of Philodemus till the principate of Gaius.[61] Several epigrammatists of the *Garland of Philip* have been identified with declaimers
(Adaeus, Aemilianus, and Diocles), though unlike Argentarius they
declaimed in Greek; and several others mention declaimers.[62] In particular the pointed and sardonic style of M. Argentarius well suits the

---

[57] S. F. Bonner, *AJP* 87 (1966), 257f.; for the tragedies of Seneca see his *Roman
Declamation* (1949), 160f.

[58] Fronto, p. 151 (van den Hout) 'Annaee, quis finis erit?'

[59] Stat. *Silv.* 2. 2. 95f. 'macte animo quod Graia probas, quod Graia frequentas arva'.
He had a villa at the Greek city of Tarentum (110f.).

[60] Reitzenstein, *RE* 2. 712; Small, op. cit. (n. 51), 77f.; R. Del Re, *Maia* 7 (1955), 184f.;
Gow-Page, *Garland of Philip*, 2. 166. It is no objection that Argentaria was rich (*Silv.*
2. 7. 86) while Argentarius said he was poor (*Anth. Pal.* 9. 229. 3 = Gow-Page, l. 1429).
Epigrammatists since Leonidas had laid claim to poverty, and in any case on our theory
there was a generation intervening.

[61] Small, op. cit. (n. 51), 69f.; Gow-Page, op. cit. 1. xlvf.

[62] C. Cichorius, *Römische Studien* (1922), 361f.

irreverent cynic of whom the elder Seneca commented 'multa con-tumeliose interponebat'.[63] The epigrammatist shows an ingenious crudity worthy of Martial | himself;[64] he dwells on the unromantic and commercial aspects of sex without any of the sentiment that his subtler predecessors (such as Philodemus) had blended with their wit. He is a truly Roman punster, particularly on proper names:[65] if the girl who once was a Σικελή[66] is now an Αἰτωλή he himself is a Μῆδος; when Pyrrha passes he exclaims to his text of Hesiod ἔργα τί μοι παρέχεις;[67] if Philostratus cannot sleep with Antigone he can always sleep with ἀντία γούνατα.[68] His pithy phrases and fondness for antithesis have been connected with the *schemata minuta* of the declaimer.[69] His epigrams were epigrams in the modern sense, with the sting in the tail; here again there is a link with the 'terminal *sententia*'[70] of declamation, and of Lucan.

The qualities of Argentarius may be illustrated by one epigram out of three dozen:[71]

> Μήνη χρυσόκερως, δέρκῃ τάδε, καὶ πυριλαμπεῖς
>   ἀστέρες οὓς κόλποις Ὠκεανὸς δέχεται,
> ὥς με μόνον προλιποῦσα μυρόπνοος ᾤχετ' Ἀρίστη,
>   ἑκταίην δ' εὑρεῖν τὴν μάγον οὐ δύναμαι;
> ἀλλ' ἔμπης αὐτὴν ζητήσομεν· ἢν, ἐπιπέμψω
>   Κύπριδος ἰχνευτὰς ἀργυρέους σκύλακας.

Here the forlorn lover's address to the heavenly bodies is made an occasion for point rather than feeling. When the fiery stars are received in the gulf of Ocean, there is not only an antithesis between fire and water but an implicit contrast with the less welcoming κόλπος of the poet's beloved.[72] Ariste is called a witch not simply for her

---

[63] *Cont.* 9. 3. 12–13: he swore 'per manes praeceptoris mei Cesti' while Cestius was still alive.

[64] Small, op. cit. (n. 51), 95 f.; *Anth. Pal.* 5. 104, 105, 116; 9. 554; *Anth. Plan.* 241 = Gow-Page, ll. 1323 f., 1329 f., 1345 f., 1485 f., 1503 f.

[65] Small, op. cit. (n. 51), 87; Del Re, op. cit. (n. 60), 193. Note esp. *Anth. Pal.* 9. 229. 5 f. = Gow-Page, ll. 1431 f. (the flagon is presented as an aged *hetaera*): αἴθ' ὄφελες καὶ ἄμικτος ἀνύμφευτός τε παρείης ἄφθορος ὡς κούρη πρὸς πόσιν ἐρχομένη.

[66] *Anth. Pal.* 5. 63. For the apparent pun on Latin *sic* (= 'yes') cf. R. Keydell, *Hermes*, 80 (1952), 497 f. (rejected by Gow-Page, l. 1311).

[67] *Anth. Pal.* 9. 161 = Gow-Page, ll. 1369 f.

[68] *Anth. Pal.* 11. 320 = Gow-Page, ll. 1491 f.

[69] Sen. *Cont.* 9. 2. 22; Small, op. cit. (n. 51), 77, 112; cf. Bonner, *Roman Declamation*, 65.

[70] The phrase is used by S. F. Bonner, *AJP* 87 (1966), 264 f.

[71] *Anth. Pal.* 5. 16 = Gow-Page, ll. 1301 f.

[72] For similar puns cf. Philodemus, *Anth. Pal.* 5. 107. 8 (= Gow-Page, l. 3195) and 10. 21. 8 (= Gow-Page, l. 3253).

bewitching qualities (Gow-Page) but because she has worked a dis-
appearing trick, not on the moon (as witches often do) but on herself.
Then with a characteristically cynical climax the poet promises to send
his silver sleuth-hounds after her: ἀργυρέους is a parody of ἀργούς,
the Homeric epithet for dogs, and balances the golden horn in the first
line (the moon, like the stars, is better off than the poet). Small, op. cit.
(n. 51), 111, and Gow-Page comment that 'silver sleuths' seems to be
an original metaphor for money, but that does not bring out the full
force of the concluding epigram: Argentarius *suo more* is playing on his
own name.[73]

The name encouraged puns. It has been mentioned how Sidonius
wrote of Lucan's widow 'Argentaria pallidat poetas' (*Carm.* 23. 166);
the verb is sometimes altered to *Polla dat*, but *dat* is quite unconvincing, especially as the word is used in a meaningful sense three lines
earlier. In fact *pallidat*[74] is correctly formed from *pallidus* (cf. *fluidare*,
frigidare, *limpidare*, *lucidare*), makes admirable sense in the context
(above, p. 35), and seems to be in a pointed relationship with *Argentaria* (cf. Hor. *Serm.* 2. 3. 78: 'argenti pallet amore'); either silver is
regarded as pale in colour, or perhaps rather its *nitor* is contrasted with
the poets' pallor.[75] Then again, Argentaria wished the *genethliacon*
'imputari sibi' (above, p. 32); the verb is often used metaphorically in
the Silver Age,[76] but here the primary commercial sense of 'debit'
makes a play on words with *Argentaria*. And now let us turn to the wife
of Pollius: it will be remembered how Statius says 'Your wealth is not
hidden away and stifled in a sterile coffer (*arca*), nor is your mind
racked by the loss (*dispendia*) of usurious interest (*faenoris*); your
capital (*census*) is placed on view, and you have learned how to employ
it with discretion'.[77] Here there is a series of banking terms addressed
not to a man, who might have had commercial interests, but to a
woman, who clearly had not. This | passage provides the central argu-
ment for the identification of Pollius's wife with Lucan's widow: it
would be a curious paradox if Statius in one and the same book
addressed two Pollae who were similar in age, charm, and benevolence

[73] The point is noted somewhat tentatively by Del Re, op. cit. (n. 60), 185.
[74] The verb is also found at Mutianus, *Chrysost. Hom.* 28, p. 420 (information derived
from the *Thesaurus* by Dr N. M. Horsfall).
[75] For another pun cf. perhaps *Silv.* 2. 7. 81 (above, p. 32), where 'nec solum dabo
carminum nitorem' may imply 'sed etiam Argentariae'.
[76] Cf. 2. 7. 30 'Lucanum potes imputare terris'.
[77] 2. 2. 151f., cited above, p. 31.

to poets, and applied the vocabulary of banking to the one who was
not an Argentaria.

Puns on proper names are familiar in Latin from Plautus to
Augustine, and even in the Silver Age Seneca dedicates his *De Bene-
ficiis* to Liberalis and his *De Tranquillitate Animi* to Serenus.[78] As for
Statius himself, Vollmer quotes instances of word-play involving places
(on 1. 1. 6, etc.), but he fails to observe similar puns on the names of
people, and in particular of the addressees of the poems. As the point
is crucial for the thesis of this paper, an extended list may be
attempted; some items in isolation may seem far-fetched, but the
clearer cases support the less obvious. 1. *praef.* 'Stella ... in studiis
nostris eminentissime' (for *eminere* of heavenly bodies cf. *TLL* 5. 2. 491.
49 f.). 1. 2. 81 (also on Stella) 'quantos iuvenis premat anxius ignes' (cf.
Virg. *Aen.* 4. 80 f. 'lumenque obscura vicissim luna premit'); 212 f. 'ire
polo nitidosque errare per axes visus'. 1. 3. 1 f. 'cernere facundi Tibur
glaciale *Vopisci* si quis et inserto *geminos* Aniene penates ... potuit' (a
vopiscus was somebody whose twin had died at birth). 2. *praef.* 'Melior,
vir optime' (cf. perhaps also 2. 3. 70 f. to the same man 'optimus idem
promere[79] divitias opibusque immittere lucem'). 2. 3. 76 f. 'situm
fugitura tacentem ... gloria Blaesi' (*blaesus* means 'stammering'; cf. also
Vollmer on 2. 1. 201). 2. 6. 10 'sed famulum gemis, Urse, pium'; 14 f.
'hominem gemis, ... hominem, Urse, tuum' (cf. Hor. *Epod.* 16. 51 'nec
vespertinus circumgemit ursus ovile'). 2. 6. 93 f. 'quid terga dolori,
Urse, damus?' (perhaps suggesting the ring-master's whip;[80] the plural
is sympathetic). 2. 6. 105 (the dead Philetos will instruct the next
delicatus) 'similemque docebit amari' (*amori* of the MS is nonsense, and
amari makes the verbal play sharper than *amorem*). 3. *praef.* 'Maecium
Celerem ... quia sequi non poteram sic prosecutus sum' (noticed for
once by Vollmer). 3. 2. 125 (also to Celer) 'turmas facili praevertere
gyro'. 4. 5. 33 f. 'quis non in omni vertice Romuli reptasse dulcem
Septimium putet?' (with a play on the seven hills). 4. 6. 3 f. 'rapuit me
cena benigni Vindicis' (an oxymoron). 4. 6. 88 'felix dominorum
stemmate signum' (it has just been mentioned that the statuette had
belonged to Sulla). 4. 7. 9. 'Maximo carmen tenuare tempto'. In 2. 2. in
particular there are several allusions to the happiness of Pollius Felix

---

[78] See M. T. Griffin, op. cit. (n. 52), 319 n. 5.

[79] *promere*, Madvig; *comere*, cod., edd.

[80] See J. M. C. Toynbee, *PBSR* 16 (1948), 36 with pl. x, fig. 29; *Animals in Roman Life
and Art* (1973), 96 f. For *dare terga* cf. Ov. *Fast.* 2. 445 f. 'terga ... percutienda dabant';
TLL 5. 1. 1668. 58 f.

(the adjective *felix* is found at 23, 107, 122). If there is a pun at the end of the poem on the name *Argentaria* it would produce a perfect balance, especially as the lines in question repudiate an *infelix arca* (151).

If the two Pollae are identical several agreeable consequences may be noted, even if these further points are not unambiguous enough to be used as contributory arguments. It has already been mentioned that in the preface to his second book Statius describes Lucan's widow as *rarissima uxorum* (above, p. 32); perhaps he is making an oblique reference to the two marriages, a procedure that would be perfectly acceptable to ancient taste. Then again, our identification would give more coherence to the arrangement of the book (though all such schematizing tends to be dangerously subjective):[81] the subjects are (1) Melior's *delicatus*; (2) Pollius and Polla; (3) Melior again; (4) and (5) short poems, the former to Melior; (6) Ursus's *delicatus*; (7) Lucan and Polla. After the opening poem to Melior (to whom the preface is addressed), Polla is given the two places of honour; and just as (6) balances (1) (both are *epicedia* for *delicati*), so (7) would balance (2). Another point may be provided by the invocation to Hercules, for whom Pollius has built a shrine at his Surrentinum (3. 1. 158f.):

> indulge sacris, et si tibi poma supersunt
> Hesperidum, gremio venerabilis ingere Pollae;
> nam capit et tantum non degenerabit honorem. |

The apples of the Hesperides are always regarded as golden from the time of Hesiod,[82] so there might be another instance of word-play if the lady was regularly known as Argentaria. In moralizing discourse gold was regarded as superior to silver, as in the Golden Age, or Plato's allegory of the metals (*Rep.* 415a–c); Statius may be suggesting that in spite of her materialistic name 'Argentaria', Polla's character is pure gold.[83]

Another argument has more independent force. In his address to Polla Pollii at the end of 2. 2, Statius praises the lady's serenity (148f.):

---

[81] For one over-elaborate attempt see H. Cancik, *Untersuchungen zur lyrischen Kunst des P. Papinius Statius* (*Spudasmata*, 13; 1965), 19f.

[82] *Theog.* 215 with West's note.

[83] A similar contrast may be implicit at Suid. 2. 584. 12f. (cited by Vollmer): τὰ τρία μῆλα, ὅ ἐστι τὰς τρεῖς ἀρετάς, τὸ μὴ ὀργίζεσθαι, τὸ μὴ φιλαργυρεῖν, καὶ τὸ μὴ φιληδονεῖν. So also the Byzantine poet Meliteniotes, εἰς τὴν σωφροσύνην, 2072f., cited by A. R. Littlewood, *HSCPh.* 72 (1967), 170.

⟨cui non⟩ praecordia curae,
non frontem vertere minae, sed candida semper
gaudia et in vultu curarum ignara voluptas.

vertere is a certain conjecture for *vescere* of the Matritensis,[84] but it is oddly misinterpreted by Vollmer, D. A. Slater (in his translation), and Frère-Izaac's Budé edition: these scholars suppose that Polla has not threatened other people, which seems faint praise for so gracious a person. In fact the meaning must be 'whose brow no menace has dismayed' (Mozley). Though *minae* can sometimes be used in a general way of menacing circumstances,[85] the word at first sight seems unsuited to a prosperous lady living quietly on the Bay of Naples. But if Polla was Lucan's widow, Statius could be alluding with tactful reticence to her demeanour in the aftermath of the Pisonian conspiracy twenty-five years before: under the tyrant's threats[86] she kept the *idem semper voltus eademque frons*[87] commended by the moralists. Then *candida semper gaudia* comes back to the present again; as suits her husband's philosophy (126, *exemptus fatis*), she does not brood on past sorrows (below, n. 100), but shows in her face an Epicurean *voluptas* and freedom from care.

It may be argued that this Epicurean outlook of Polla Pollii is incompatible with the concluding section of the *Genethliacon Lucani*.[88] Here Statius thinks of Lucan as soaring through the sky, like Pompey's soul in the *Bellum Civile* (9. 3 f.), or as seeing Nero haunted by his mother's ghost;[89] equally un-Epicurean is the prayer that he may return to Polla like Protesilaus for a day (above, p. 34). But after that, though there is no explicit contradiction, the emphasis of the poem begins to change (124 f.):

haec te non thiasis procax dolosis
falsi numinis induit figura,
ipsum sed colit et frequentat ipsum
imis altius insitum medullis ...

---

[84] For other confusions in this MS of *r* and *s* and of *t* and *c* see H. Frère's 1943 edn., xxx and xxxvi.

[85] *TLL* 8. 993. 80f.; usually 'fortune' or something similar is mentioned in the context. For an absolute use cf. Sen. *Epist.* 104. 22 'animum indurari et adversus minas erigere'; yet that passage is Stoic, and the heroics are addressed to a man.

[86] Cf. Hor. *Carm.* 3. 3. 3f. 'non vultus instantis tyranni mente quatit solida'; Epictet. 1. 29. 5.

[87] Cic. *Off.* 1. 90. Cf. *Silv.* 3. 5. 11: 'dic tamen unde alia mihi fronte et nubila vultus', where *alia*, the Aldine's conjecture for *alta*, is rightly supported by Håkanson, op. cit. (n. 17), 95.　　　　　[88] 2. 7. 107f., discussed by V. Buchheit, *Hermes*, 88 (1960), 231f.

[89] 2. 7. 118f.; cf. *Octavia* 619f.; Suet. *Ner.* 34. 4.

Unlike Laodamia[90] in the Euripidean *Protesilaus*, Polla dedicates no
Bacchic rites to her dead husband. The Loeb editor talks of her mystic
communion with the spirit of the departed, but though *colit* and
frequentat are religious words (like 135, *adoret*), they are used here in a
pointedly secular sense.[91] This rejection of superstition, combined with
a dangerously ambiguous use of religious language, is well suited to an
Epicurean environment, as it is reminiscent of the way that the Epi-
cureans talked about their founder.[92] |

The same sort of outlook is shown by Statius in the lines that follow
(128 f.):

> ac solacia vana subministrat
> vultus, qui simili notatus auro
> stratis praenitet incubatque somno
> securae. procul hinc abite, Mortes . . .

In the Euripidean play[93] Laodamia had found consolation in a statue of
her dead husband, but though Polla uses such material props,[94] in her
case they are subsidiary (*subministrat*) and superfluous (*vana*). The
early editors took *securae* with *mortes*, but though this gives an elegant
word-order,[95] it makes no sense; Phillimore's *obscurae* would be some
improvement, *obscenae* ('ill-omened') perhaps better still. But in fact
J. F. Gronovius (1653) was probably right to join *securae* to the
previous sentence; though the strong pause after the third syllable of
the line is very unusual, it marks the adjective as a climax.[96] Polla is
secura because of her inward serenity: the word suggests the Epicurean

[90] *Silv.* 3. 5. 49 'fecerunt maenada planctus'; Philostr. *Imag.* 2. 9; cf. also the Bacchic
symbols on the Vatican sarcophagus illustrated at Roscher, *Lex.* 3. 3170. For the Euripidean source see n. 93 below.

[91] For parallels see Vollmer, ad loc.; add Thuc. 2. 43. 3: ἄγραφος μνήμη παρ᾽ ἑκάστῳ
τῆς γνώμης μᾶλλον ἢ τοῦ ἔργου ἐνδιαιτᾶται; Lucan 9. 71 f. 'non imis haeret imago
visceribus?' (Cornelia to Pompey).

[92] Pease on Cic. *Nat. Deor.* 1. 43; W. Schmid, *RAC* 5. 746 f.

[93] Presumably the source of Hygin. 104; Ov. *Her.* 13. 152 f.; *Rem.* 723 f.; see further
M. Mayer, *Hermes*, 20 (1885), 101 f.; *RE* 23. 934 f.; more sceptically H. Jacobson, *Ovid's
Heroides* (1974), 195 f. Euripides's reservations about the passionate Laodamia (Mayer,
114) are echoed by the middle-aged Wordsworth, *Laodamia* 74 f. 'the gods approve | The
depth, and not the tumult, of the soul'.

[94] For similar likenesses of the dead cf. Eur. *Alc.* 348 f.; E. K. Borthwick, *CPh.* 64
(1969), 173 f. They were used even by the Epicureans; cf. Plin. *NH* 35. 5 'Epicuri voltus
per cubicula gestant'; Origen, *Cels.* 7. 66; N. W. DeWitt, *Epicurus and his Philosophy*
(1954), 100 f.

[95] V. Buchheit, who accepts the punctuation (op. cit. 239), cites *Priap.* 8. 1 'matronae
procul hinc abite castae'; Mart. 11. 6. 6 'pallentes procul hinc abite curae'.

[96] As Mr C. W. Macleod points out.

ideal. It also coheres with several passages from the poem on the
Surrentinum: 2. 2. 71, 'expers curarum' (Pollius); 149, 'curarum ignara
voluptas' (Polla); 143, 'discite securi' (Pollius and Polla).

The next four lines bring the poem to a close (132f.):

> haec vitae genitalis est origo.
> cedat luctus atrox genisque manent
> iam dulces lacrimae, dolorque festus
> quidquid fleverat ante, nunc adoret.

Here *haec* (picking up *hinc*) refers to the birthday rather than the bed
(Lucan's marriage is not under discussion); by the normal Latin
practice the word is attracted to the gender of the predicate. The day is
the *genitalis origo* of life (in its most meaningful sense *vitae* needs no
adjective); editors prefer the early conjecture *genialis* (to be taken with
vitae), but this gives a less convincing word-order and loses the allusion
to *genethliacon*, the title of the poem (cf. 2. 3. 62, 'genitali luce'; 5. 5. 70,
'genitali carmine'). The birthdays of the dead were sometimes
celebrated in antiquity,[97] but the practice was particularly important
for the Epicureans,[98] and such an association is encouraged by the
Lucretian phrase *genitalis origo*.[99] The adjuration to stop mourning,
though the right conclusion for any *epicedium*, here again suits an
Epicurean house; for *dulces lacrimae* cf. Metrodorus's consolation to his
sister, 'esse aliquam cognatam tristitiae voluptatem, hanc esse ca-
ptandam in eiusmodi tempore'.[100] And though such an attitude might
be shared by other schools,[101] *dolor festus* is more specifically Epicurean: it describes exactly the εὐωχία[102] with which Epicurus himself
wished to be remembered. Alike in its commitment to life and its

---

[97] Sen. *Epist.* 64. 9; Plin. *Epist.* 3. 7. 8 (Silius and Virgil); Juv. 5. 37 'Brutorum et Cassi
natalibus', with Mayor's note; *RE* 7. 1137f.; *RAC* 9. 219f.

[98] *Vita* 18; Cic. *Fin.* 2. 101.

[99] 5. 176, 324,1212 (admittedly all referring to the creation of the world).

[100] Sen. *Epist.* 99. 25; J. M. Rist, *Epicurus* (1972), 136. The Epicureans used memory
very selectively to keep life from disintegrating into a series of moments; cf. Epicur. fr.
138 ἀντιπαρετάττετο δὲ πᾶσι τούτοις (the pain of his death-bed) τὸ κατὰ ψυχὴν χαῖρον
ἐπὶ τῇ τῶν γεγονότων ἡμῖν διαλογισμῶν μνήμῃ; 213 ἡδὺ ἡ φίλου μνήμη τεθνηκότος;
436–7; *Ep. Men.* 122; *Sent. Vat.* 17. 55 θεραπευτέον τὰς συμφορὰς τῇ τῶν ἀπολλυμένων
χάριτι; Cic. *Fin.* 2. 104–5; Plut. *Non posse suaviter vivi secundum Epicurum*, 1097 f. τῇ μετὰ
δακρύων ἰδιοτρόπῳ ἡδονῇ (I owe this reference to Mrs P. G. Fowler).

[101] Sen. *Epist.* 63. 5 (citing the Stoic Attalus) 'sic amicorum defunctorum memoria
iucunda est quomodo poma quaedam sunt suaviter aspera'.

[102] Philodemus, περὶ Ἐπικούρου, p. 70 Vogliano (*Epicuri et Epicureorum scripta*, 1928):
εὐωχεῖσθαι; A.-J. Festugière, *Épicure et ses dieux* (1946), 33f. (= 22 in English edn.);
W. Schmid, *RAC* 5. 748f.

celebration of lost | blessings, the end of the *Genethliacon* turns out to be very appropriate for the wife of an Epicurean; as in the poem on the Surrentinum, the moral system is shown as still an influence on real human situations.

Argentaria Polla was not herself a person of great importance, but if the theses of this paper are correct, she may provide a clearing-house for some of the literary currency of the Silver Age. M. Argentarius had cross-fertilized Greek and Latin, in prose and in verse; and she was patron to the Neapolitan Statius, whose *Silvae* owe so much to contemporary Greek *epideixis*. Argentarius had developed a new type of cynical and pointed epigram, and she lived to befriend Martial; he had used a broken-up Asianism for his Latin declamations, and she married into the house of the Annaei.[103] Above all, as wife of Lucan and benefactress of Statius she linked the two dominating poets of the century; it is easy to forget that though they wrote a generation apart, they were more or less contemporaries. They present a striking series of contrasts: Stoics and Epicureans, *Bellum Civile* and *Bellum Germanicum*,[104] precocious maturity and premature elderliness,[105] brash Corduba and effete Naples. Statius professed reluctance to praise Lucan in hexameters (2. praef.), but technically he had nothing to fear from the relentless thump of his predecessor's lines, the *pingue quiddam* that Cicero had already deplored in the Corduban school of poets (*Arch.* 26; Sen. *Suas.* 6. 27). But though his glitter had more warmth than is sometimes realized (as can be seen from the poems under discussion), he lacked authority and conviction: while Lucan had denounced the corruption of power in terms that make even Tacitus seem a timeserver, Statius charmed[106] his rich friends with pleasant fancies about Nereids stealing grapes. But in his social and historical circumstances that was understandable. When he heard the Siren singing on the cliffs of Surrentum, she could have taught him from her own story to watch the storm from the shore: τὸ κολακεύειν καὶ κεχαρισμένα λέγειν Σειρήνων ἐστίν.[107]

---

[103] For the influence of declamation on Seneca's style cf. E. Norden, *Die Antike Kunstprosa*² (1909), 1. 205 f. (citing Argentarius), 309 f.

[104] Cf. Morel, *Frag. Poet. Lat.* 134 (= Schol. Vallae on Juv. 4. 94).

[105] *Silv.* 3. 5. 40 f.; 4. 4. 70 'vergimur in senium'; 5. 2. 158 f.

[106] Cf. Juv. 7. 83 f. 'laetam cum fecit Statius urbem promisitque diem'.

[107] Origen, *Cels.* 2. 76.

4

Virgil's Fourth *Eclogue*:
Easterners and Westerners

It has often been pointed out that there are two main schools of thought about the Fourth *Eclogue*.[1] Some, such as Norden,[2] have looked for analogies in the religions of the East, notably in Jewish hopes for a Messiah or Χριστός. Others have seen the poem in essentially Western terms, as a reasonably normal representation of a tradition that goes back to Hesiod and Theocritus; on this side Jachmann's article[3] has been particularly influential. As an easy method of reference Norden's party are here called 'Easterners' and Jachmann's 'Westerners'. It will be remembered that in the strategic debates of the First World War the Easterners preferred large-scale diversions through unfamiliar terrain to concentrated attacks on heavily manned positions for limited gains. They underestimated the difficulties of the logistics and the vulnerability of exterior lines, but their imagination was rewarded in unintended ways, and though they failed to reach the Golden Horn they played their part in the liberation of Jerusalem. It will be convenient to examine the poem section by section, and, as only some aspects can be covered, to assess the strength in particular of the Easterners' case.

> Sicelides Musae, paulo maiora canamus.
> non omnes arbusta iuvant humilesque myricae.
> si canimus silvas, silvae sint consule dignae.   (1-3)

A shorter version of this paper was given as a special lecture in the University of London on 21 Oct. 1977. I owe much to the colleagues and graduate students who took part in a class on the subject in Oxford the previous term: Colin Clarkson, Kathleen Coleman, Anna Crabbe, Malcolm Davies, Don Fowler, Jasper Griffin, Nigel Kay, Perilla Kinchin, Peta Moon (now Mrs Fowler), Donald Ringe.

[1] The bibliography is vast; for general surveys of the poem cf. K. Büchner, *RE* 8A. 1195 ff.; H. Hommel in *Wege zu Vergil*, ed. H. Oppermann (1966), 368 ff., G. Williams in *Quality and Pleasure in Latin Poetry*, ed. T. Woodman and D. West (1974), 31 ff.

[2] E. Norden, *Die Geburt des Kindes* (1924).

[3] G. Jachmann, *Annale della scuola normale di Pisa*, 21 (1952), 13 ff.

These three lines form a proem in the Western tradition.[4] A pastoral note is struck in the first two words by the allusion to a refrain of 'Moschus' (3. 8 Σικελικαὶ ... Μοῖσαι), but though Virgil promises grander themes, the urbanity of *paulo* (pointedly incongruous with the more poetical *canamus*) suggests the manner of Cicero rather than of John the Divine. Even if the lowly tamarisks are rejected, the very literary play on *humilitas* encourages no inflated expectations. By admitting that he sings of woods Virgil shows that he is still writing within the bucolic genre, and though they are woods with a difference, they owe their special character not to Eastern mysticism but to the solemnities of Roman public life.

> Ultima Cumaei venit iam carminis aetas;
> magnus ab integro saeclorum nascitur ordo.
> iam redit et virgo, redeunt Saturnia regna;
> iam nova progenies caelo demittitur alto.
> tu modo nascenti puero, quo ferrea primum
> desinet ac toto surget gens aurea mundo,
> casta fave Lucina, tuus iam regnat Apollo.   (4–10)

After the restrained bucolic invocation, the emphatic *ultima* suddenly transports us to the world of eschatology. The *Cumaeum carmen* has nothing to do with Hesiod's descent from the Asiatic Cyme (Probus): 'to say that the last of that poet's ages has come is extremely stale news'.[5] The expression must refer to the Sibylline oracles (Servius), which in this context cannot mean the Western collection destroyed on the Capitol in 83 BC, and later imperfectly replaced from a variety of sources;[6] these seem to have dealt with prodigies and sacrifices, and access to them was controlled by the quindecimviri. 'Cumaean' must be used for 'Sibylline' in an extended sense, and refer to one of the unofficial sorts of oracle so prevalent in the period; but while ordinary Greek Sibyls might offer time-schemes and prophecies of doom, they could not so easily accommodate a child whose appearance would regenerate | the world (see below on line 8). The case is different with the Eastern Sibylline oracles[7]

[4] *Rhet. ad Herenn.* 1. 7 'attentos habebimus si pollicebimur nos de rebus magnis novis inusitatis verba facturos'.

[5] H. J. Rose, *The Eclogues of Vergil* (1942), 177.

[6] Rzach, *RE* 2A. 2105 ff.; H. Diels, *Sibyllinische Blätter* (1890).

[7] Texts by Rzach (1891), Geffcken (1902), Kurfess (1951). See further Rzach, *RE* 2A. 2117 ff.; V. Nikiprowetzky, *La Troisième Sibylle* (1970); P. M. Fraser, *Ptolemaic Alexandria* (1972), 1. 708 ff., 2. 989 ff.; J. J. Collins, *The Sibylline Oracles of Egyptian Judaism* (Society of Biblical Literature, Dissertation Ser. 13, 1974), summarized in *Bulletin of Institute of Jewish Studies*, 2 (1974), 1 ff. For their influence on Virgil, cf. F. Marx, *Neue Jahrb.* 1 (1898), 121 ff.; H. Jeanmaire, *La Sibylle et le retour de l'âge d'or* (1939).

produced by the Hellenized Jews of Egypt, and Lactantius was surely right to see a similarity to Virgil (*Inst.* 7. 24. 12), though it must still be determined whether the eclogue draws directly on such a Jewish oracle or on a pagan Eastern production of the same general type (Norden's theory). Before we consider correspondences in detail, it is important to record a general resemblance of literary form: both the eclogue and the oracles offer an unusual blend of the Hesiodic, the eschatological, and the political.[8] The anti-Roman stance of much Jewish apocalyptic is not a decisive argument against a connection (in spite of Norden, op. cit., 53); Virgil could have reversed any such tendency in his model, just as he does with the pessimism of Catullus 64.

But could Virgil have known the Eastern Sibylline oracles? The surviving collection presents difficult problems of chronology:[9] pagan, Jewish, and Christian elements seem to have been jumbled by the wind, plagiarism is a normal principle of composition, and *vaticinia post eventum* obscure the historical sequence. The bulk of the third book, which is the oldest and for our purposes the most important, has recently been assigned by Nikiprowetzky to 42 BC (n. 7), but it is implausible to give a unified origin to so amorphous a conglomeration, and there is much more to be said for the orthodox view that places the early strata in the middle of the second century BC.[10] The book seems to have mainly an Egyptian provenance (so far as any indications are given), and the reign of Cleopatra must have encouraged the Roman interest in such oracles.[11] Alternatively it has been supposed that the poet learned about the Jews from Pollio,[12] who met Herod

---

[8] There are also some stylistic resemblances (R. G. Austin, *CQ* 21 (1927), 100 ff.; I. M. Du Quesnay, *Papers of the Liverpool Latin Seminar*, 1976 (*Arca* 2), 77 ff.), but they are mainly either Hesiodic or typical of oracles in general; Virgil's end-stopped and sometimes rhyming lines (5 ff., 50 ff.) suggest the hypnotic rhythms of an incantation, but they have less in common with the Sibyl than with the Parcae of Catullus 64. On the other hand it seems significant that the groups of seven lines (4 ff., 11 ff., 46 ff., 53 ff.) can be paralleled at *Orac. Sib.* 3. 227 ff.

[9] J. Geffcken, *Komposition und Entstehungszeit der Oracula Sibyllina* (1902); Fraser, loc. cit.; Collins, op. cit. 21 ff.

[10] Cf. esp. 3. 608 ff. ὁππόταν Αἰγύπτου βασιλεὺς νέος ἕβδομος ἀρχῇ τῆς ἰδίης γαίης ἀριθμούμενος ἐξ Ἑλλήνων ἀρχῆς ἧς ἄρξουσι Μακηδόνες ἄσπετοι ἄνδρες. Cleopatra VII (not an ancient title) could not possibly be described in this way; probably the oracle refers to Ptolemy Philometor, the seventh Macedonian ruler of Egypt, and a pro-Jew (cf. Collins, op. cit. 29 ff.).

[11] Cf. W. W. Tarn, *JRS* 22 (1932), 135 ff.; Collins, op. cit. 61 ff. Horace's sixteenth epode may show some influences (D. Ableitinger-Grünberger, *Der junge Horaz und die Politik* (1971), 73 f.); compare also line 10 with *Orac. Sib.* 8. 41 (a Christian denunciation of Rome) καὶ τὰ θέμειλα λύκοι καὶ ἀλώπεκες οἰκήσουσιν.

[12] F. Marx, op. cit. (n. 7), 124 ff.; L. H. Feldman, *TAPA* 84 (1953), 73 ff.

when consul in 40 (and later gave hospitality to his sons);[13] amid the hectic intrigues of the year, when a Parthian protégé ruled in Jerusalem and Herod received his kingdom in Rome, eastern prophecies would have attracted particular attention. But while Pollio's versatile tastes might have suggested the direction of the eclogue, Virgil cannot have seen much of him during the troubles of his consulship; and though Herod's visit was a spectacular occasion, it probably came too late to influence the poem significantly except by giving an extra topicality to Jewish matters. Virgil must have expected from his readers a familiarity with Sibylline oracles of the relevant type, and they are more likely to have associated them with Cleopatra and Egypt than with Herod and Judaea.

To turn now to the details, the Easterners may help with the chronological problems of lines 4 and 5. Servius comments that 'last' means 'tenth', and the extant Sibylline oracles often mention ten ages;[14] but as more than one system was possible, it is pointless to pursue what the poet has left unspecified. It is more important to decide whether the *ultima aetas* is the predecessor of the Golden Age (6) or the Golden Age itself.[15] The former view can hardly be right: *iam* here would have a different reference from *iam* in lines 6 and 7, and the *ultima aetas* would either last a very short time or take a very long time to be recognized. This conclusion seems to be supported by the stereotyped form of eschatological proclamation: 'the time has come'.[16] The perfect *venit* is not seriously contradicted by the present tenses below: the last age has arrived, and so various things are happening or about to happen.

Line 5 offers a different time-scheme. In the first place a *saeculum*[17] is a Western concept, not a period of the world (like *aetas*) but the maximum age of a man; the doctrine was topical, as one Vulcacius had announced the tenth or last *saeculum* in 44 BC,[18] and by another calculation the new age began in 39,[19] only a month or two after the

---

[13] Joseph. *AJ* 14. 388, 15. 343. The relationship with Herod suits Asinius Pollio's cosmopolitan interests (cf. his later patronage of Timagenes).

[14] Jeanmaire, op. cit. (n. 7), 100 ff.

[15] B. Gatz, *Weltalter, goldene Zeit und sinnverwandte Vorstellungen* (*Spudasmata* 16; 1967), 93 ff. At *Orac. Sib.* 4. 47 the tenth age is a time when felicity is achieved.

[16] Gal. 4: 4 ὅτε δὲ ἦλθεν τὸ πλήρωμα τοῦ χρόνου; Mk. 1: 15 πεπλήρωται ὁ καιρός; Jn. 4: 23 ἔρχεται ὥρα καὶ νῦν ἐστιν. As Norden points out, ideas found in both Paul and Mark are deeply rooted (op. cit. 33).

[17] Nilsson, *RE* 1A. 1709 f.; S. Weinstock, *Divus Julius* (1971), 191 ff.

[18] Serv. Auct. *Ecl.* 9. 46; cf. Censorinus 17. 6 'nonum et decimum superesse, quibus transactis finem fore nominis Etrusci'.

[19] S. Sudhaus, *RhM* 56 (1901), 38 ff.

purported time of writing (below, p. 57). Secondly, the system here is
not simply linear (as in the previous line), but involves a cyclic element:
ab integro nascitur[20] alludes to the παλιγγενεσία[21] of the Stoics and
others. On the other hand, *magnus saeclorum ordo* cannot directly
represent the Stoic *magnus annus*[22] (where *magnus* marks a contrast
with the solar year); nor is the apparent identity of the *ultima aetas* with
the new age compatible with the Stoic view that the old cycle ends in
κατακλυσμός and ἐκπύρωσις; nor indeed is Virgil thinking of a cycle
in the full sense, as there is no suggestion that the new Golden Age will
be displaced in turn. It is sometimes supposed that the poet has
inconsistently juxtaposed a linear Hesiodic system with a cyclic Stoic
one; yet lines 4 and 5 belong closely together (as do 6 and 7), and
though Virgil's syncretism sometimes produces inconsistencies, they
should not be as blatant as is suggested here. It may therefore be
relevant that | in Jewish and Christian eschatology the Messianic age is
sometimes represented as the end of the old series (corresponding to
the seventh day in *Genesis*), sometimes as an additional 'day' (compared by Christians to the Sunday of the resurrection);[23] sometimes
the two systems are harmonized (the same period is regarded as both
an end and a beginning,[24] or the terrestrial 'millennium' is followed by
an eternal heavenly kingdom), sometimes they are uneasily juxtaposed.[25] But when the new creation is complete there is no second
deterioration, exactly the situation that seems to be implied in the
eclogue. As Virgil's confusing time-scheme bears some resemblance to
the Jewish system, and as he has just proclaimed his dependence on
the Sibyl, it seems possible that a Jewish oracle is one of the sources of
his chronology.

The sixth line is claimed by the Westerners, but it owes more to the
Eastern tradition than is sometimes realized. The Virgo is obviously
the Δίκη of Aratus, who left the earth apparently for good (*redit* is

[20] Cf. Sen. *Nat. Quaest.* 3. 30. 8 'omne ex integro animal generabiter dabiturque terris
homo inscius scelerum et melioribus auspiciis natus'.

[21] See Kittel–Friedrich, *Theologische Wörterbuch zum Neuen Testament*, 1. 685ff.

[22] B. L. van der Waerden, *Hermes*, 80 (1952), 129ff.; Pease on Cic. *Nat. Deor.* 2. 51.

[23] E. Schürer, *Geschichte des jüdischen Volkes* 2⁴ (1907), 636ff.; J. Daniélou, 'La Typologie
millénariste de la semaine dans le christianisme primitif', *Vig. Christ.* 2 (1948), 1 ff.

[24] 2 Baruch 74. 2 'From that time is the consummation of that which is corruptible
and the beginning of that which is not corruptible', [Barnabas], *Epist.* 6. 13 δευτέραν πλά-
σιν ἐπ' ἐσχάτων ἐποίησεν. λέγει δὲ κύριος· ἰδού, ποιῶ τὰ ἔσχατα ὡς τὰ πρῶτα (Kirsopp
Lake, *Apostolic Fathers* (Loeb edn., 1975), 1. 362).

[25] [Barnabas] 15. 5–9; the inconsistency is pointed out by H. Windisch in his commentary (*Handbuch zum Neuen Testament, Ergänzungsband*, 1920), 384.

paradoxical), and was translated to the sky as Parthenos[26] (the Latin name similarly suggests an astronomical reference). But even where Virgil depends ultimately on Greek didactic, his words can often be harmonized with the Sibylline poems, which themselves were written in the Hesiodic manner: thus it is highly relevant that an oracle from the time of Cleopatra describes the return of Justice from the stars and the consequent cessation of bloodshed and strife.[27] There is indeed something oracular about the allusive reference to the Virgin, and her juxtaposition with the young child; and though nobody now accepts the naïve formulation of Philargyrius 'id est Iustitia vel Maria', the word might derive some of its resonance from Jewish prophecies that mention a κόρη (below, p. 65). The case is much clearer with 'redeunt Saturnia regna': though Hesiod assigned the Golden Age to the time of Saturn (*Op.* 111), the notion of its return is unparalleled in the Western tradition before Virgil.[28] It is therefore extremely significant that a passage in the third book of Sibylline oracles describes a future age of abundance and peace in terms traditionally applied to the past (3. 744 ff.):

> γῆ γὰρ παγγενέτειρα βροτοῖς δώσει τὸν ἄριστον
> καρπὸν ἀπειρέσιον σίτου οἴνου τ᾽ ἰδ᾽ ἐλαίου . . .
> πηγάς τε ῥήξει γλυκερὰς λευκοῖο γάλακτος·
> πλήρεις δ᾽ αὖτε πόλεις ἀγαθῶν καὶ πίονες ἀγροὶ
> ἔσσοντ᾽. οὐδὲ μάχαιρα κατὰ χθονὸς οὐδὲ κυδοιμός.[29]

Here the pessimism of Hesiod is alleviated by an apocalyptic vision of Paradise Regained, exactly the development that we find in the eclogue.

Line 7 is also claimed by the Westerners. Yet the *nova progenies*[30] that descends from heaven is not quite a race of men in the Hesiodic mould; it is clearly contrasted with the *gens aurea* that arises over the whole world (9 *surget*). *progenies* ('stock') is admittedly more general

[26] Arat. *Phaen.* 133 ff., Virg. *Georg.* 2. 473 f.; Ov. *Met.* 1. 149 f.; Symm. *Or.* 3. 9 'dicerem caelo redisse Iustitiam'.

[27] 3. 373 f. εὐνομίη γὰρ πᾶσα ἀπ᾽ οὐρανοῦ ἀστερόεντος ἥξει ἐπ᾽ ἀνθρώπους ἠδ᾽ εὐδικίη, μετὰ δ᾽ αὐτῆς ἡ πάντων προφέρουσα βροτοῖς ὁμόνοια σαόφρων, Collins, op. cit. (n. 7), 57 ff. The theme of ὁμόνοια suited the Western situation in 40 BC when *concordia* was the watchword (*ILS* 3784, Weinstock, op. cit. (n. 17), 262 f.).

[28] Gatz, op. cit. (n. 15), 25; V. Schmidt, *Redeunt Saturnia Regna* (Diss. Groningen, 1977), 56 ff. The use of the theme in imperial panegyric is modelled on Virgil (Gatz, op. cit. 138 f.).

[29] The line is reminiscent of Aratus (*Phaen.* 109 κυδοιμοῦ, 131 μάχαιραν).

[30] *nova* balances *ab integro* above; the child corresponds to the age. Norden (op. cit. 47) calls attention to the importance of newness in the world of the New Testament.

than *puero* below, in that it contains the suggestion of future descendants, but Virgil's attention is concentrated on the supernatural origin of the child himself. In the same way *caelo demittitur* implies not a general descent but a special mission, as when Juno in the *Aeneid* sends Iris from Olympus.[31] The belief that the soul is from heaven is attested in Greek philosophy from the fifth century, and is applied by Cicero especially to rulers;[32] so Virgil's reference, if it had appeared in isolation, could be explained entirely on Western lines. But in view of the other borrowings in this part of the poem, it becomes relevant to record a Sibylline parallel here also: when an early section of the extant oracles describes a 'king from the sun',[33] it is probably referring not to the East but to the sky, a conclusion that is supported by a similar passage (though it also has been disputed) in the Egyptian 'Oracle of the Potter'.[34] It is true that according to orthodox Jewish monotheism the Messiah seems to have pre-existed only in a very notional sense,[35] but the doctrine might have been extended under alien influences. With the later enhancement of his status the Christian view was formulated of a divine descent from heaven;[36] yet even this can be paralleled to some extent in the Hermetic Corpus, where Isis and Osiris are lent to earth for a while[37] (it is hard to believe that this is

[31] Virg. *Aen.* 4. 694 'Irim demisit Olympo'; *Corp. Herm.*, *Kore Kosmou* fr. 24. 4 καταπέμπονται δὲ ἐκεῖθεν εἰς τὸ βασιλεύειν . . . αἱ ψυχαί. Some compare Lucr. 2. 1153 f., but that is irrelevant (Norden, op. cit. 48).

[32] Cic. *Rep.* 6. 13 'hinc profecti huc revertuntur'; Hor. *Carm.* 1. 2. 45 'serus in caelum redeas', A.-J. Festugière, *La Révélation d'Hermès Trismégiste*, 3 (1953), 27 ff.; A. D. Nock, *Essays in Religion and the Ancient World* (1972), 2. 935 ff.

[33] 3. 652 καὶ τότ᾽ ἀπ᾽ ἠελίοιο θεὸς πέμψει βασιλῆα (cited tentatively by Norden, op. cit. 147). Jachmann (op. cit. 43 f.) thinks that this refers to a king from the East like Cyrus in Isaiah (41: 2 ἀφ᾽ ἡλίου ἀνατολῶν); cf. also the kings in the Oracle of Baalbek (§ 180, ed. P. J. Alexander, 1967). Norden (op. cit. 55) also cites 3. 286 καὶ τότε δὴ θεὸς οὐρανόθεν πέμψει βασιλῆα, but there the correct reading seems to be οὐράνιος.

[34] Collins, op. cit. 40 ff., citing *P. Oxy.* 22. 2332. 63 ff. καὶ τότε ἡ Αἴγυπτος αὐξηθήσεται ἐπὰν ὁ τὰ πεντήκοντα πέντε ἔτη ἀπὸ Ἡλίου παραγενόμενος ἀγαθῶν δοτὴρ καθεστάμενος ᾖ ὑπὸ θεᾶς μεγίστης (interpreted otherwise by Jachmann, op. cit. 42), *OGIS* 90 υἱοῦ τοῦ Ἡλίου (the Rosetta Stone on Ptolemy V).

[35] Strack–Billerbeck, *Kommentar zum Neuen Testament*, 2 (1924), 333 ff.; G. Vermes, *Jesus the Jew* (1976), 138 f. Some have seen a reference to a pre-existent Messiah in Enoch 70. 1 (S. Mowinckel, *He that Cometh* (English edn., 1956), 370 ff.); but the relevant section (the 'Book of Parables') has not appeared at Qumran, and is dated by the latest editor to the Christian era (J. T. Milik, *The Book of Enoch* (1976), 91 ff.).

[36] 1 Cor. 15: 47 ὁ δεύτερος ἄνθρωπος ἐξ οὐρανοῦ; Jn. 3: 13 ὁ ἐκ τοῦ οὐρανοῦ καταβάς; *Orac. Sib.* 8. 458 οὐρανόθεν δὲ μολὼν βροτέην ἐνεδύσατο μορφήν (could the first half of the line have come from a pre-Virgilian oracle?).

[37] *Kore Kosmou* fr. 23. 62 ff. (cited by Nock, op. cit. 2. 937 f.); note esp. 64 ὁ μόναρχος θεός . . . τὸν μέγιστόν σου πρὸς ὀλίγον ἐχαρίσατο πατέρα Ὄσιριν καὶ τὴν μεγίστην θεὰν Ἶσιν ἵνα τῷ πάντων δεομένῳ κόσμῳ βοηθοὶ γένωνται, 69 ταῦτα πάντα ποιήσαντες, ὦ

simply a retort to Christianity). The question that now presents itself is this: could Virgil's Sibylline source have marked an intermediate stage between the 'king from the sun' and the fully developed Pauline | theory? If the notion appears fanciful let us formulate it another way: if we assume for the moment what has still to be established, that these lines are modelled on a Messianic oracle, would it not be strange if the child's descent from the sky had nothing to do with similar doctrines about the Messiah?

This brings us to the *nascens puer*,[38] who must surely have been mentioned in the 'Cumaean song': what is his relationship to the infant of the Gospels?[39] The ages of faith believed in a prophecy,[40] the age of scepticism would prefer a coincidence; neither explanation is satisfactory. Semi-divine children are familiar from traditional Greek religion, and human 'saviours' were common in Hellenistic kingdoms, but here we have a baby who will not just rule a nation or benefit mankind but in some sense regenerate the world. The idea of an infant god was widespread in the Near East, and as we seem to be moving in an Egyptian context the cult of Isis and the baby Horus (the Greek Harpocrates) may ultimately be relevant, but Horus was not a saviour in the real sense. Bultmann,[41] who made this point against Norden, looked farther east, but we are less concerned with the remote origins of such beliefs than with Virgil's immediate source. As so many features of the eclogue (some still to be mentioned) are compatible with a Jewish prototype, it is natural to associate the child with Messianic doctrines (it must be emphasized here as elsewhere that the arguments are not so much deductive as mutually supporting). The nativity stories of Matthew and Luke (not in Paul or Mark) are usually regarded as a comparatively late accretion to the tradition: how then are we to explain the infant of the eclogue a generation before the birth of Christ? Perhaps the most promising prototype is the Emmanuel of Isaiah 7: 14 ἰδοὺ ἡ παρθένος ἐν γαστρὶ ἕξει καὶ τέξεται υἱόν, καὶ καλέσεις τὸ ὄνομα αὐτοῦ Ἐμμανουήλ (in this context the Old

τέκνον, Ὄσιρίς τε κἀγώ, τὸν κόσμον πληρέστατον ἰδόντες ἀπῃτούμεθα λοιπὸν ὑπὸ τῶν τὸν οὐρανὸν κατοικούντων.

[38] *nascenti* refers to the critical moment of birth, not the months of pregnancy (thus P. Corssen, *Philologus*, 81 (1925), 42); when an epithalamium mentions Lucina, it is not thinking of ante-natal care (see also p. 71).

[39] Norden, op. cit. 76 ff.; G. Erdmann, *Die Vorgeschichten des Lukas- und Matthäus-Evangeliums und Vergils vierte Ekloge* (Göttingen, 1932).

[40] Cf. P. Courcelle, *REA* 59 (1957), 294 ff.

[41] *Theologische Literaturzeitung*, 49 (1924), 321, contradicting Norden, op. cit. 73 f., 113.

Testament must naturally be quoted from the LXX). Though not in origin a Messiah, Emmanuel influenced later Messianic speculations, and Isaiah's verse is cited in Matthew's infancy narrative (1: 25) as a prophecy of the birth of Jesus.

It is necessary at this point to consider how the baby's influence will operate. The echo of 5 *saeclorum nascitur ordo* underlines the poem's organizing principle: the life of the world moves in harmony with the life of the child. *quo* implies not a deliberate achievement but an automatic consequence ('with whom'). The baby inaugurates the age not by anything he does but because he is there: it is misleading for Carcopino to compare the cock-crow that marks the rising sun,[42] for if there is no baby the day will not dawn. This strange notion well suits the Western situation in 40 BC, when the child of a dynastic marriage might bring peace by his mere existence (see below), but its origins are religious, no doubt being ultimately derived from the sympathetic magic by which seasons were revolved and vegetation renewed. Norden cited the Alexandrian festival of Helios when the initiates proclaimed ἡ παρθένος τέτοκεν, αὔξει φῶς[43] and though his account contains much that is uncertain, this sentence at least shows the concept that underlines Virgil's *quo*. It will be objected that so passive a role does not suit the triumphant Messiah of contemporary Jewish eschatology; on the other hand, the original Emmanuel of Isaiah 'becomes a sign simply by being born',[44] and this view of him may have survived later developments. In much Christian as well as pre-Christian theology the effect of the Messiah seems to be automatic (i.e. not directly related to his teaching and example), and even today when a Greek congregation hails the risen Christ, it may greet the good news not just as a promise of future immortality but as an immediate and actual regeneration of the world.

Lucina in line 10 reminds us of the eclogue's affinities with Western epithalamium,[45] perhaps also of Eilytheia's part in secular rites;[46] yet her role here is completely subordinate to her brother's. *tuus iam regnat*

[42] *Virgile et le mystère de la IVe Églogue* (1943), 29.

[43] Op. cit. 24 ff.; H. Usener, *Das Weihnachtsfest*² (1911), 27 ff.; R. Kittel, *Die hellenistische Mysterienreligion und das Alte Testament* (Beiträge zur Wissenschaft vom Alten Testament, NS 7; 1924), 21 ff. The festival of Helios attested for 25 Dec. is probably to be conflated with that of Aeon attested for 6 Jan. (the later Epiphany); see further Tarn, op. cit. (n. 11), 144 f., who is very sceptical about Norden's interpretation.

[44] Mowinckel, op. cit. (n. 35), 116.

[45] Stat. *Silv.* 1. 2. 269 ff.; D. A. Slater, *CR*, 20 (1912), 114 ff.

[46] Hor. *Carm. Saec.* 14; *ILS* 5050. 117; Zosimus, *Hist. Nov.* 2. 6. 9 (H. Diels, op. cit. (n. 6), 134).

Apollo is not simply a parenthetic encouragement (as seems always to be assumed), but the apodosis of the sentence and climax of the section: 'provided that Lucina helps the birth' (i.e. *modo* points forward, not backwards), 'Apollo is as good as reigning' (on this interpretation *iam* refers to the new age as in lines 4, 6, and 7). This confirms that Apollo's reign is not, as is often supposed, the penultimate age or even a transitional period, but begins with the baby's birth; it is not distinct from *Saturnia regna*, but expresses the same idea in modern, non-Hesiodic terms. Virgil was perhaps aware of a neo-Pythagorean view, apparently of Eastern origin, that assigned the last age to Apollo,[47] but it may be more relevant that the Sibyl assigned it to the sun: Servius explains that this means Apollo, which he would not have had to do | if he had simply fabricated his information out of Virgil's text.[48] It would certainly be anachronistic to explain the allusion on Western lines as a tribute to Octavian; it might be better to look at Antony, whose connection with such beliefs can be shown later by Alexander Helios,[49] his son by Cleopatra. Of course, Virgil's Apollo is harmonized with traditional Roman religion in a way that would have been impossible for Sol at this date, and he has associations of civilization and peace that suit the Western political situation.

> teque adeo decus hoc aevi, te consule, inibit,
> Pollio, et incipient magni procedere menses.
> te duce, si qua manent sceleris vestigia nostri,
> inrita perpetua solvent formidine terras.
> ille deum vitam accipiet, divisque videbit
> permixtos heroas et ipse videbitur illis,
> pacatumque reget patriis virtutibus orbem.　　(11-17)

This section must be explained primarily on Western lines, but not so exclusively as is often supposed. *decus hoc aevi* cannot refer to the baby (though the personified use of *decus* is common in Roman panegyric):[50] this would not suit *inibit*,[51] or lead well to the temporal

---

[47] Serv. Auct. ad loc. 'nonnulli etiam ut magi aiunt Apollinis fore regnum' (his gloss that this may refer to a final conflagration is irrelevant to the poem); Carcopino, op. cit. 52 ff.; Rose, op. cit. (n. 5), 174 ff.

[48] 'dixit etiam quis quo saeculo imperaret et solem ultimum, id est decimum, voluit; novimus autem eundem esse Apollinem.' Augustan poets did not directly identify Apollo with the sun, but Virgil could be influenced here by Sibylline conventions; cf. the extant oracle attributed to 17 BC (Diels, loc. cit. (n. 46), lines 16 f.) Φοῖβος Ἀπόλλων ὅστε καὶ ἠέλιος κικλήσκεται.

[49] Tarn, op. cit. (n. 11), 144 ff.

[50] Ov. *Her.* 15. 94 'o decus atque aevi gloria magna tui'; *TLL* 5. 1. 243. 6 ff.

[51] Cf. Serv. ad loc. 'inchoabit, exordium accipiet, scilicet saeculum'; *TLL* 7. 1295. 49 ff.

incipient procedere menses, or produce a correspondence between the age (11-12) and the child (15-17) to balance the similar correspondence in the preceding section (4-5 and 8-10). On the other hand, Norden was too mystical when he suggested that the new century is the glory of all time (op. cit. 41): eternity is too vast to be embellished by one of its own subdivisions. Yet perhaps he was right that *aevi* is 'eternity' as opposed to *saeculi* or even *aetatis*; 'this glory everlasting' presumably means *aeternum Apollinis regnum* (another reason for thinking that *tuus iam regnat Apollo* is the climax of the preceding sentence). Virgil has given us an Eastern analogue of such slogans as *gloria saeculi*;[52] his expression may even be modelled on something in the Sibylline oracles on the lines of εὐφροσύνην αἰῶνος,[53] 'eternal joy'. In the same way *magni* ... *menses* has a more portentous note than is sometimes realized (the adjective is found in the eclogue also at lines 5, 22, 36, 48, 49). *menses* cannot refer to subdivisions of the Stoic great year (the metaphor is pointless unless it is applied to a cycle), or directly to the pregnancy of the baby's mother (as at line 61); rather it describes a corresponding cosmic parturition, and when combined with the contrasting *aevi* suggests that the splendour of eternity will soon be only a few months distant.

The emphatic *te ... consule* makes a thought-provoking contrast with *decus hoc aevi* by connecting the political with the cosmic time-scale. Norden (42 f.) thought that the poem was written for Pollio's assumption of office at the beginning of 40, and hence was an early specimen of a type of panegyric later familiar in both prose and verse.[54] But Pollio could not have been associated with peace at the beginning of the year, when the Perusine War was approaching its tragic conclusion, or during the summer, when his friend Antony was expected to invade Italy, or indeed at any time till the Treaty of Brundisium in

(on *ex ineunte aetate* and similar expressions). It is argued on the other side that 15 *ille* needs a recent point of reference; but for the stereotyped *ille* (here contrasted with *te*) see p. 60.

[52] The legend 'gloria novi saeculi' is found on coins of Gratian (H. Mattingly *et al.*, *Roman Imperial Coinage* 9. 54); significantly he was addressed by Symmachus (*Or.* 3) in terms borrowed from the eclogue (see below, nn. 100, 111). The genitive *aevi* indicates concomitance, not identity; Virgil's commentators are wrong to compare Plautine expressions like *monstrum mulieris*.

[53] 3. 786 (= 3. 771 αἰώνιον εὐφροσύνην); the phrase looks like a Hebraism (Ecclesiasticus 2. 9 εὐφροσύνην αἰῶνος, 17. 12 διαθήκην αἰῶνος). The first Sibylline passage was understood by Norden to refer to the divine child (op. cit. 147), inconsistently with himself (57) and quite wrongly (L. Deubner, *Gnomon*, 1 (1925), 164; Jachmann, op. cit. 45 f.). For the use of *aevi* cf. also *Sil.* 3. 480 'aevi glacie' ('eternal ice').

[54] For the characteristics of such poems see Du Quesnay, op. cit. (n. 8), 43 ff.

the autumn, the supreme achievement of his distinguished career.[55] If the poet's language suggests an inauguration it is not the consul's but the baby's and the age's, and an extension of the sort of thing said in Eastern inscriptions about rulers' birthdays.[56]

Lines 13 f. belong to the Westerners. *duce* is a political term, glossed by Servius as *auctore*;[57] this dates the poem not just to 40 but to the context of the Treaty. *sceleris* here means the crime of civil war, though a Sibylline prototype could have combined Eastern notions about deliverance from sin with Hesiodic language about the wickedness of the Iron Age. *perpetua formidine* would suit both a religious litany and the historical reality, when the chain of calamity must have seemed never-ending and inescapable. *si qua manent vestigia* is appropriate to prophetic utterances about expiation (for instance Sibylline oracles of the Western type); the phrase suggests in three different ways that the trouble is now virtually over (Virgil says *manent*, not *manebunt*), and would have been nonsensical at any time before the Treaty was signed. One of the main provisions was the dynastic marriage of Antony and Octavia, from which a | child might be conceived with luck before the end of the year.[58] When a poem addressed to Pollio within two months of his Treaty talked of a baby who would bring peace and rule the world, it would have been impossible for a contemporary not to think of the purpose of the recent wedding;[59] by the end of the year Octavian's earlier marriage to Scribonia was unimportant,[60] and Pollio must have deplored that alliance. Of course Virgil speaks inexplicitly, as a sensible oracle should, and the implications of the poem were forgotten when the baby turned out a girl,[61] and especially when Octavian and Antony quarrelled.

Lines 15 ff. again seem to belong to the Westerners, but here there

[55] Tarn, op. cit. (n. 11), 151 ff.; Du Quesnay, op. cit. 48. The latter still sees a celebration of Pollio's entry into office, but in spite of his prolonged absence from Rome he was *consul ordinarius* from the beginning of the year.

[56] *OGIS* 458. 40 f. (on Augustus) ἦρξεν δὲ τῷ κόσμῳ τῶν δι' αὐτὸν εὐαγγελιῶν ἡ γενέθλιος ἡμέρα τοῦ θεοῦ.

[57] *dux* and *auctor* are sometimes combined in Cicero (*TLL* 5. 1. 2317. 58 ff.).

[58] It is clear from Virgil's language in 11 f. (where *inibit* precedes *menses*) that the new age is connected with Pollio by the conception rather than the birth of the child.

[59] The wedding of Catullus 64 (to which the eclogue is to some extent a rejoinder) ends with sinister prophecies of the birth of Achilles.

[60] It is not even plausible to see an ambiguous allusion to both marriages (thus K. Witte, *WS* 43 (1923), 43 f.; G. Williams, op. cit. (n. 1), 45).

[61] The elder Antonia was born by the autumn of 39 (Plut. *Ant.* 33. 3). This goes some way towards refuting the story that at the time of her marriage Octavia was pregnant by her dead husband Marcellus (Dio 48. 31. 4); cf. *RE* 17. 2. 1860.

are greater ambiguities. As parallels to *ille deum vitam accipiet* commentators cite expressions for 'living like gods',[62] but *accipiet* implies the grant of a more clearly defined status, and in that case Virgil means (or at least suggests) something more than earthly felicity (this argument should be closely scrutinized, as much depends on it). The next clause in isolation might refer to the θεοξενία,[63] by which the gods entertained favoured mortals in the Golden Age and later Greek cult, but an anticlimax is avoided if it again refers to the future immortality of the child (the mention of heroes may hint obliquely that he will enjoy a similar position). Such immortality can be explained entirely in terms of early Greek mythology and Hellenistic ruler-cult, so it will probably be thought over-speculative to look beyond Virgil's normal sources. Yet once it is accepted that the poet is drawing on Eastern eschatology, the same sort of question arises as with the descent from the sky (7): might he have transmuted to Western terms something about the ultimate ascension of the Messiah?[64] There seems to be no clear authority for such a view in orthodox Judaism, but the Christian doctrine must link up somehow with similar beliefs in other religions. Could Jews of the Diaspora have ventured, even before the birth of Christ, to give the Messiah a celestial destiny? Before dismissing such a notion out of hand, we must consider the implications of line 17.

Here we are met by further difficulties of interpretation, or rather calculated ambiguities; these may be accepted in oracles (though not indiscriminately in other sorts of poetry) even when one meaning seems more obvious than the other.[65] Thus *patriis virtutibus* from a linguistic point of view goes most easily with *pacatum* (which is improved by a supplement)[66] rather than with *reget* (which is not); yet in a panegyric it is natural to say that somebody will repeat the deeds of his father,[67] and particularly in a poem that has affinities with

[62] Hes. *Op.* 112 ὥστε θεοὶ δ' ἔζωον ἀκηδέα θυμὸν ἔχοντες, Ter. *HT* 693 'deorum vitam apti sumus'.

[63] Hes. fr. 1. 6 M–W ξυναὶ γὰρ τότε δαῖτες ἔσαν, ξυνοὶ δὲ θόωκοι ἀθανάτοις τε θεοῖσι καταθνητοῖς τ' ἀνθρώποις (cf. Gatz, op. cit. (n. 15), 36f.); for later cult cf. Nock, op. cit. (n. 32), 586f. Virgil cannot be thinking simply of renewed visits by the gods to earth (Catull. 64. 384ff., 407f.), for then they would see everybody they met.

[64] Cf. Jn. 6: 62 ἐὰν οὖν θεωρῆτε τὸν υἱὸν τοῦ ἀνθρώπου ἀναβαίνοντα ὅπου ἦν τὸ πρότερον.

[65] The natural interpretation was the wrong one at Enn. *Ann.* 179 'aio te, Aeacida, Romanos vincere posse'.

[66] Cf. Ov. *Her.* 9. 13 'respice vindicibus pacatum viribus orbem' (of Hercules).

[67] Theoc. 17. 13 ἐκ πατέρων οἷος μὲν ἔην τελέσαι μέγα ἔργον; Stat. *Silv.* 4. 7. 43 'crescat in mores patrios'.

epithalamium.[68] In the same way *patriis* can be interpreted as equivalent to *patrum*, 'ancestors', but more particularly as *patris* ('Antony' to contemporaries). *pacatum* suits the Roman context, where *pax* was associated with *victoria*, but peace-making in a more beneficent sense was ascribed to Hellenistic rulers; the same variation of emphasis is found in Messianic writing.[69] Perhaps Antony will pacify the world in the old-fashioned Roman sense, but the baby will rule it as a peace-maker (εἰρηνοποιός).

Another obscurity seems particularly significant. In a Roman context one naturally assumes that the child's future domain is an earthly one; but as the first clause in the series points to a future immortality (see above on *accipiet*), and as it can easily carry the second clause with it, the obvious interpretation of the third clause involves an anticlimax. The awkwardness would be explained, though not indeed avoided, if we could suppose that Virgil is reverting to his Sibylline oracle, and that it referred at this point to an eternal kingdom. Norden well compared Luke 1: 32–3 (Gabriel to Mary) οὗτος ἔσται μέγας καὶ υἱὸς Ὑψίστου κληθήσεται, καὶ δώσει αὐτῷ Κύριος ὁ Θεὸς τὸν θρόνον Δαυὶδ τοῦ πατρὸς αὐτοῦ, καὶ βασιλεύσει ἐπὶ τὸν οἶκον Ἰακὼβ εἰς τοὺς αἰῶνας καὶ τῆς βασιλείας οὐκ ἔσται τέλος.[70] The significance of the parallel lies in more than the hieratic series of future tenses; here we have a conflation of the temporal and eternal kingdoms such as seems to be presupposed by Virgil's line. This conflation was natural among Jews who hoped for a Davidic Messiah, which is how Jesus is regarded in the infancy narrative of Luke and even more conspicuously in that of Matthew; as these two gospels are independent of one another, this feature must go back to a common source of the extant accounts. Indeed, Professor Raymond E. Brown in his illuminating book on the nativity considers that 'the idea of an annunciation of the birth of the Davidic Messiah ... may have already existed in pre-Christian Judaism'.[71] |

Annunciations in the developed sense were an Eastern phenom-

---

[68] Cf. Catull. 64. 348 and 357 (the future *virtutes* of Achilles.

[69] Contrast *Orac. Sib.* 3. 373 f. (n. 27) with 3. 653 ὃς πᾶσαν γαῖαν παύσει πολέμοιο κακοῖο. See further H. Windisch, *Zeitschrift f. Neutest. Wiss.* 24 (1925), 240 ff. (linking pagan and Christian concepts), Mowinckel, op. cit. (n. 35), 176 f.

[70] Norden, op. cit. 125 f., following F. Boll, *Aus der Offenbarung Johannis* (1914), 12 f. They also cited Hephaestion 65. 17 Engelbrecht (= 1 p. 28 Pingree) ἐκ θεῶν σπαρήσεται καὶ ἔσται μέγας καὶ μετὰ θεῶν θρησκευθήσεται καὶ ἔσται κοσμοκράτωρ καὶ πάντα αὐτῷ ὑπακούσεται (though nothing in Virgil corresponds to the naïve καὶ found here and in Luke).

[71] *The Birth of the Messiah* (1977), 310 f.

enon. Norden divined that Gabriel's prophecy was derived from the acclamation of Egyptian god-kings, but he did not discuss more immediate models in the LXX: see Gen. 16: 11 καὶ τέξῃ υἱόν, καὶ καλέσεις τὸ ὄνομα αὐτοῦ Ἰσμαήλ . . . οὗτος ἔσται ἄγροικος ἄνθρωπος, 17: 19 τέξεταί σοι υἱόν, καὶ καλέσεις τὸ ὄνομα αὐτοῦ Ἰσαάκ, Judg. 13: 5 (Samson), 1 Chron. 22: 9 (Solomon) ἰδοὺ υἱὸς τίκτεταί σοι. οὗτος ἔσται ἀνὴρ ἀναπαύσεως . . . οὗτος οἰκοδομήσει οἶκον τῷ ὀνόματί μου, Isa. 7: 14 (so Mt. 1: 21-3, Lk. 1: 13-17). οὗτος in such passages corresponds to *ille* in the eclogue; one may compare the 'Er-Stil' that Norden analysed elsewhere in the praises of gods.[72] The annunciations in the early Greek poets are rudimentary by comparison;[73] it is therefore all the more striking when the Theocritean Tiresias prophesies about Heracles[74] (24. 73 ff.) in terms that recall the pattern[75] of the Old Testament and of Luke. He says to Alcmene θάρσει (she is alarmed by the episode of the snakes), which might be an adaptation of the reassurance normal at epiphanies (Lk. 1: 29 μὴ φοβοῦ, Μαριάμ); he calls her ἀριστοτόκεια γύναι, following the form of Jewish annunciations in addressing the fortunate parent by a relevant periphrasis (Lk. 1: 28 χαῖρε κεχαριτωμένη); he proceeds σέβας δ᾽ἔσῃ Ἀργείαισι (a shame-culture's equivalent of Lk. 1: 42 εὐλογημένη σὺ ἐν γυναιξίν); he prophesies τοῖος ἀνὴρ ὅδε μέλλει ἐς οὐρανὸν ἄστρα φέροντα ἀμβαίνειν τεὸς υἱός (an ascent that corresponds to Virgil and Luke more than to anything in the LXX); he leads up to the climax γαμβρὸς δ᾽ ἀθανάτων κεκλήσεται, where the very pagan γαμβρός (rather than υἱός) recalls the last line of the eclogue, but κεκλήσεται (though it can be paralleled at Hom. *Od.* 7. 313 ἐμὸς γαμβρὸς καλέεσθαι) in the context of an annunciation seems remarkably close to the Jewish formula (Isa. 7: 14, Lk. 1: 32 υἱὸς ὑψίστου κληθήσεται, etc.). The Theocritean passage suggests that though the Greek and Graeco-Jewish cultures of Alexandria were curiously separate, the LXX might have had some

---

[72] *Agnostos Theos* (1913), 163 ff.

[73] Hom. *Od.* 11. 248 f. χαῖρε, γύναι, φιλότητι· περιπλομένου δ᾽ ἐνιαυτοῦ τέξεις ἀγλαὰ τέκνα; Orac. ap. Hdt. 5. 92 β. 2; Pind. *P.* 9. 59 ff. τόθι παῖδα τέξεται . . . θήσονταί τέ νιν ἀθάνατον.

[74] Without noticing the Theocritean annunciation Friedrich Pfister cited other parallels between Heracles and Christ, which led him to posit influence on the prototype of the Gospels by a Stoic–Cynic biography of the Greek hero (*Archiv für Religionswissenschaft*, 34 (1937), 42 ff.). The issues seem much more complex than he suggests; one must not think of a lost source that will explain all, but of a society where many people variously combined in their patterns of thought the most diverse cultural traditions.

[75] R. E. Brown, op. cit. 155 ff., gives a valuable analysis of Jewish annunciations, but he does not include pagan material.

influence on Hellenistic poetry,[76] whether directly or indirectly. Borrowings in the other direction were obviously easier, especially two centuries later, and one asks whether Virgil's Sibylline model could have been coloured in turn by Hellenistic panegyrics on divine Ptolemaic infants.

> at tibi prima, puer,[77] nullo munuscula cultu
> errantis hederas passim cum baccare tellus
> mixtaque ridenti colocasia fundet acantho.
> ipsae lacte domum referent distenta capellae
> ubera, nec magnos metuent armenta leones.
> ipsa tibi blandos fundent cunabula flores.
> occidet et serpens, et fallax herba veneni
> occidet; Assyrium vulgo nascetur amomum.   (18-25)

The fragrant and unusual *munuscula* of this section mark the special position of the baby, just like the frankincense and myrrh of the Magi (Mt. 2: 11), but no close relationship can be posited, as the evangelist's story is obviously Eastern. Virgil's flowers, on the other hand, belong to the Western tradition, where they are a property of pastoral from Theocritus to Milton, and a conventional decoration of houses at the birth of a child; in particular the infant Bacchus was surrounded by ivy,[78] Iamus and Hermes covered in blossoms, while Delos flowered in gold for Apollo. The oriental colocasia and baccar are derived from no Sibylline prototype, but are mentioned from the Roman standpoint as exotic plants, possibly with Dionysiac or even Antonian associations;[79] similarly *amomum* below (25) had been linked with the Golden Age in an earlier eclogue (3. 89), and the supposed derivation of its name ('blameless') suggests a contrast with deceitful snakes and plants. The baccar grows with as little cultivation as the ivy, and the colocasia and amomum are unfamiliarly profuse (*fundet, vulgo*); such spontaneous abundance was a feature of the Golden Age from the time of Hesiod,

---

[76] For other alleged influences of the LXX on Callimachus and Theocritus see the discussion by P. M. Fraser, op. cit. (n. 7), 2. 1000ff.

[77] There is no particular significance in the parallel at Lk. 1: 76 καὶ σὺ δέ, παιδίον, προφήτης Ὑψίστου κληθήσῃ (G. Erdmann, op. cit. (n. 39), 32); an alteration of third-person statement and second-person address is natural in genethliacon, and indeed in other types of panegyric.

[78] Eur. *Phoen.* 651ff.; Philostr. *Imag.* 1. 14. 3; Nonn. *Dionys.* 9. 12 (cf. also Dionys. Periegetes 941 τῷ καὶ γεινομένῳ κηώδεα φύετο πάντα). For Iamus cf. Pind. *O.* 6. 55, for Hermes cf. Philostr. *Imag.* 1. 26. 2, for Apollo cf. *H. Ap.* 135ff., Call. *H.* 4. 260ff.

[79] Baccar must have been associated with Bacchus, colocasia came from Egypt (cf. Serv. ad loc., W. T. Thiselton-Dyer, *JPh.* 34 (1918), 299ff.), ivy was Dionysiac.

though as such it naturally merges in a Sibylline context.[80] The situation is less conventional in line 23 where the cradle produces flowers of its own accord,[81] but commentators fail to note that even this miracle is recorded of the birth of Dionysus.[82] The cradle is not just the place of birth (as Servius and others have suggested), but has ritual parallels in the Dionysiac λίκνον; in the same way the Christian manger (a food-trough rather than a *praesaepe*) not only developed a sacred significance[83] but may have had antecedents in cult.[84] The common source can ultimately be found in the Near Eastern worship of divine infants. |

The animals of the section suit the pastoral setting no less than the flowers. The homing goats are derived from Theocritus,[85] though the context there is quite different; the parallel in Horace's sixteenth epode may be ignored, as that poem's Theocritean element is mediated through Virgil.[86] It is significant that the goats bring their milk not simply to the baby (there is no *tibi*); there is an alternation not only of flowers and animals, but of the local and the universal, the cradle and the world.[87] This variation does not detract from the importance of the child, but on the contrary underlines his superhuman status. In the same way in bucolic poetry all nature mourns for Daphnis; though it is true that the Messiah's influence is often portrayed as universal (cf. 9 *toto ... mundo*), Virgil's formulation here surely owes more to Theocritus than the Sibyl.

An Eastern interpretation is more naturally encouraged by the following reference to the cattle and the lions (22). Virgil is not thinking of a total absence of wild animals (as is often supposed) but of their pacific behaviour;[88] this is the more vivid explanation (especially

---

[80] Hes. *Op.* 117f., Gatz, op. cit. (n. 15), 229; *Orac. Sib.* 1. 297f.

[81] *ipsa* must mean *sua sponte* to balance 21 *ipsae*; this is misunderstood by Jachmann, op. cit. 58f.

[82] Nonn. *Dionys.* 7. 344f. καὶ αὐτοφύτοισι πετήλοις ὅρχατος ἀμπελόεις Σεμέλης περιδέδρομεν εὐνήν (cf. 10. 171ff.).

[83] Usener, op. cit. (n. 43), 286ff.; R. Berliner, *Die Weihnachtskrippe* (1955).

[84] The φάτνη at Lk. 2: 7 is clearly regarded as important (Brown, op. cit. (n. 71), 418ff.), but its motivation is not very clear; it ought to be a substitute for a cradle, not for 'room in the inn'. At *Protevangelium Jacobi* 22. 2 the trough turns up for a different purpose, to hide Jesus from Herod. Did the prop exist before the play?

[85] Theoc. 11. 12 (when the love-lorn Cyclops neglects his work) πολλάκι ταὶ ὄιες ποτὶ τωὔλιον αὐταὶ ἀπῆνθον (αὐταί = *ipsae*). [86] B. Snell, *Hermes*, 73 (1938), 237ff.

[87] Klouček obscured this simultaneous action when he transposed 23 to follow 20 (which is made unattractive in any case by the repetition of *fundere*). The disjointedness of Virgil's arrangement suggests a feature of the bucolic style.

[88] It is sometimes argued that 24 'occidet et serpens' implies that the lion will also perish (S. Sudhaus, *RhM* 56 (1901), 47). In fact *et* may join *serpens* and *herba* (in spite of

in view of *magnos*),[89] is supported by Horace's imitation (below, n. 92), and coheres with the general view of the Golden Age as a time of vegetarianism.[90] Yet peace among animals is not directly ascribed to the Golden Age before our poem,[91] though it is mentioned in similar contexts very soon after;[92] the tame beasts of Empedocles (fr. 130 D-K) are not quite the same (their relation to man is emphasized rather than to each other), nor are proverbial adynata of the type πρίν κεν λύκος οἶν ὑμεναιοῖ.[93] Under these circumstances it becomes relevant to compare the passage from Isaiah where the calf and the young lion lie down together and the child plays on the hole of the asp (11: 6-9). The resemblance of the eclogue is increased by the reference to snakes; though the poet, unlike the prophet, makes them disappear altogether, he may have been attracted by the dire oracular *occidet*, especially when it is combined with the paradoxical *serpens* ('the creeping one will fall'). Yet it is not easy to suppose that Virgil had direct knowledge of the Hebrew scriptures or even of the LXX. Those who posit such curious learning still have to explain how the area of discourse could have been intelligible to the eclogue's readers.

The case is very different with the close paraphrase of Isaiah in an early section of the Sibylline Oracles (3. 788 ff.):

> ἠδὲ λύκοι τε καὶ ἄρνες ἐν οὔρεσιν ἄμμιγ᾽ ἔδονται
> χόρτον, παρδάλιές τ᾽ ἐρίφοις ἅμα βοσκήσονται·
> ἄρκτοι σὺν μόσχοις νομάδες αὐλισθήσονται·
> σαρκοβόρος τε λέων φάγεται ἄχυρον παρὰ φάτνῃ
> ὡς βοῦς· καὶ παῖδες μάλα νήπιοι ἐν δεσμοῖσιν
> ἄξουσιν· πηρὸν γὰρ ἐπὶ χθονὶ θῆρα ποιήσει.
> σὺν βρέφεσίν[94] τε δράκοντες ἅμ᾽ ἀσπίσι κοιμήσονται
> κοὐκ ἀδικήσουσιν· χεὶρ γὰρ θεοῦ ἔσσετ᾽ ἐπ᾽ αὐτούς.

the repetition of the verb); for a somewhat similar schema cf. 6 'iam redit et Virgo, redeunt Saturnia regna' (for parallels see Wagner's note).

[89] H. Wagenvoort, *Studies in Roman Literature, Culture and Religion* (1956), 8.

[90] K. Barwick, *Philol.* 96 (1943), 36 f.

[91] Gatz. op. cit. (n. 15), 165 ff.

[92] Cf. *Georg.* 1. 130; Hor. *Epod.* 16. 33 'credula nec ravos timeant armenta leones', *Carm.* 1. 17. 8 f., 3. 8. 13.

[93] Ar. *Pax* 1076, H. Kenner, *Das Phänomen der verkehrten Welt in der griechisch-römischen Antike* (1970), 63 f. There is a much closer parallel to Virgil at Theoc. 24. 86 f. (on the deification of Heracles) ἔσται δὴ τοῦτ᾽ ἆμαρ ὁπηνίκα νεβρὸν ἐν εὐνᾷ καρχαρόδων σίνεσθαι ἰδὼν λύκος οὐκ ἐθελήσει (cited by M.-J. Lagrange, *Rev. Bibl.* 40 (1931), 613 f.); but that passage seems to be an interpolation (see the commentaries of Gow and Dover).

[94] Isa. 11: 8 mentions a παιδίον νήπιον in the singular, which some have connected with an infant Messiah, but the extant oracle rightly regards the reference as general.

It is particularly important that both the Sibyl and the eclogue set the scene in the future: 'peace among animals' might in isolation be regarded as a coincidence (for though unparalleled before Virgil, the theme fits Western notions easily enough), but the coincidence becomes very considerable when one takes into account the prophetic nature of both passages and Virgil's acknowledged debt to the Sibyl. It is particularly significant that Isaiah's account of the animal peace comes only four chapters later than his mention of the baby Emmanuel (above p. 54); whatever the doubts of modern scholars, the Jewish composers of the Sibylline oracles are not likely to have dissociated these two chapters. Of course if Virgil were relying only on our form of the Sibylline oracle, Emmanuel (who is not there mentioned) would become irrelevant; but the text was exceptionally fluid, and it is clear that the poet was using an oracle that is now lost. The miraculous child and the animal peace are in both Isaiah and Virgil, but only the animal peace in the Sibyl; it would avoid an awkward coincidence if we could suppose that Virgil's version of the Sibyl made some allusion to the child. |

In this connection some attention should be given to the lines of the Sibyl that immediately precede the passage on the animals (3. 785ff.):

εὐφράνθητι, κόρη, καὶ ἀγάλλεο· σοὶ γὰρ ἔδωκεν
εὐφροσύνην αἰῶνος ὃς οὐρανὸν ἔκτισε καὶ γῆν.
ἐν σοὶ δ᾽ οἰκήσει· σοὶ δ᾽ ἔσσεται ἀθάνατον φῶς.

At the most obvious level the κόρη is the 'Daughter of Zion', i.e. Jerusalem itself; the passage is modelled on Zach. 2: 10 τέρπου καὶ εὐφραίνου, θύγατερ Σίων, διότι ἰδοὺ ἐγὼ ἔρχομαι καὶ κατασκηνώσω ἐν μέσῳ σου, λέγει κύριος (cf. also Zach. 9: 9, Zeph. 3: 14, Jer. 31 (38) 4 ἔτι οἰκο-δομήσω σε καὶ οἰκοδομηθήσῃ, παρθένος Ἰσραήλ). Yet in the Sibyl's Isaian context the words might have referred ambiguously, or later been taken to refer, to the virgin mother of the new Emmanuel (cf. Isa. 7: 14, cited above, p. 54). οἰκεῖν not only suits God's habitation of Zion (like κατασκηνώσω cited above), but was later used by Christians of the 'dwelling' of the Pneuma within an individual (1 Cor. 3: 16, Rom. 8: 9); the Sibyl's remark about spiritual habitation might be the sort of thing that led to the evangelists' more physical account of the Messiah's conception. It is important to note that without using the Sibylline passage some theologians have suggested that the Virgin in Luke's nativity actualizes things said in the Old Testament about the Daughter of Zion.[95]

[95] See A. G. Hebert, *Theology*, 53 (1950), 403 ff.; R. Laurentin, *Structure et Théologie de Luc I–II* (1957), 64 ff., 159 ff.; and on the other side R. E. Brown, op. cit. (n. 71), 320 ff.

Such a theory may seem fanciful at first sight, but it makes sense of 2: 35 καὶ σοῦ δὲ αὐτῆς τὴν ψυχὴν διελεύσεται ῥομφαία, ὅπως ἂν ἀποκαλυφθῶσιν ἐκ πολλῶν καρδιῶν διαλογισμοί[96] (the two clauses must be taken together if the characteristically Semitic balance of the passage is to be maintained, yet 'many hearts' is difficult to understand if a single individual is being talked about). It is not of course being suggested here that Luke or his source is drawing on the extant version of the Sibyl, but that a late refabrication of the Sibyl's lines, where the birth of the Messianic child was made explicit, might have exemplified some of the ideas that lie behind the evangelist's account.

> at simul heroum laudes et facta parentis
> iam legere et quae sit poteris cognoscere virtus,
> molli paulatim flavescet campus arista,
> incultisque rubens pendebit sentibus uva,
> et durae quercus sudabunt roscida mella.
> pauca tamen suberunt priscae vestigia fraudis,
> quae temptare Thetim ratibus, quae cingere muris
> oppida, quae iubeant telluri infindere sulcos.
> alter erit tum Tiphys et altera quae vehat Argo
> delectos heroas; erunt etiam altera bella,
> atque iterum ad Troiam magnus mittetur Achilles.   (26–36)

The Easterners fail in their attempt to claim this section. *at simul* (ἀλλ' ὁπόταν) suits the manner of prophecies in general and is not simply Sibylline: oracles regularly follow the pattern 'when A then B'. The childhood of the θεῖος ἀνήρ is often said to foreshadow his future qualities,[97] but when the boy of the eclogue gets his moral education from books, that sets him firmly in the world of reality.[98] The Greek *heroum laudes* leads to the Roman *facta parentis*,[99] which must allude to

---

[96] See esp. P. Benoit, *Catholic Biblical Quarterly*, 25 (1963), 251 ff. Some have seen here a borrowing from *Orac. Sib.* 3. 316 ῥομφαίη γὰρ σεῖο διέρχηται διὰ μέσσον (Erdmann, op. cit. (n. 39), 13), but the resemblance shows no more than a common attitude to the LXX (Ez. 14: 17, combined in Luke's case with Ps. 21: 21, 36: 15).

[97] Lk. 2: 52 καὶ Ἰησοῦς προσέκοπτεν ἐν τῇ σοφίᾳ καὶ ἡλικίᾳ καὶ χάριτι παρὰ θεῷ καὶ ἀνθρώποις, L. Bieler, ΘΕΙΟΣ ΑΝΗΡ, 1 (1935), 34 ff.

[98] Plut. *Cat. Mai.* 20. 5 καὶ τὰς ἱστορίας δὲ συγγράψαι φησὶν αὐτὸς ἰδίᾳ χειρὶ καὶ μεγάλοις γράμμασιν ὅπως οἴκοθεν ὑπάρχοι τῷ παιδὶ πρὸς ἐμπειρίαν τῶν παλαιῶν καὶ πατρίων ὠφελεῖσθαι. Norden is quite unconvincing when he cites parallels for 'das lesende Götterkind' (134 ff.).

[99] Those who deny the parentage of any individual statesman would find advantages in the variant *parentum*, but the singular is supported by the *testimonia* of Nonius (521 L), Servius, and Eusebius (πατρός τε μεγίστου). Carcopino (op. cit. (n. 42), 27 n.) considers that *parentis* might be a Christian interpolation, but the reading of Nonius tells against him; if anything, *parentum* might have been interpolated when the original reference was lost.

the *res gestae* of a historical person rather than to the πράξεις of a god; in the same way *virtus* points unequivocally to the ideals of Virgil's own society. The spontaneous abundance of the Golden Age (28–30) belongs to the Western tradition,[100] and though the transference of the description to the future is most easily paralleled in the Sibyl (p. 52), Virgil's rhythm and colouring are more reminiscent of Catullus. If the soft yellowing bristles of the corn correspond to the first down of adolescence, the symbolism is derived from Greek erotic poetry rather than Jewish apocalyptic, and when nature matures with the development of the boy, though the notion is mystical it is certainly not Messianic. Norden compares the rites of the Egyptian Aeon (op. cit. 42 ff.), but the agricultural setting might suggest a less abstract year-spirit; even | if the infant 'saviour' is derived from a Sibylline oracle, his gradual growth seems to come from other models. But though Jachmann was presumably right to see here a Virgilian elaboration (op. cit. 58 ff.), there is no serious inconsistency with the appearance of the Golden Age in 18 ff.: the smiling flowers and security from snakes are appropriate for a child, the young man enjoys a gradual extension of nature's bounty, but complete deliverance from work comes only to the fully adult.

The references to navigation and agriculture in the next sentence suit Western accounts of the Iron Age, while the Argo recalls the fall from innocence in Catullus 64. The reasons for this interlude have been much debated. Some have thought that Virgil is reversing the Hesiodic sequence to produce a new race of heroes, some that he is repeating it on the lines of a Stoic cycle;[101] neither theory can be made to fit, as the Golden Age starts coming at the birth of the child and is completed at his maturity. Others have compared Jewish eschatology, where the Messiah must destroy the wicked before the age of peace can begin; but Virgil seems to have moved out of this range of ideas, and there is no close analogy in the Sibylline passage where foreign kings lead a counter-revolution.[102] In fact the interlude of war balances the turbulence of youth, and makes a bridge between the innocence of childhood and the felicity of middle age. The retrogression may seem out of line with what has gone before, but Virgil is too good a Roman

---

[100] The open *campus* does not usually produce grain; cf. the elaboration by Symmachus, *Or.* 3. 9 'nunc mihi in patentibus campis sponte seges matura floresceret'.

[101] For the former view cf. Rose, op. cit. (n. 5), 184; for the latter cf. Serv. *Ecl.* 4. 34 'videtur tamen locus hic dictus per apocatastasin'.

[102] *Orac. Sib.* 3. 663 f., cited by Norden, op. cit. 147 and G. Erdmann, op. cit. (n. 39), 85, but rejected by Jachmann, op. cit. 40 ff.

to accept the eschatological myth without qualification: manly achievements were naturally predicted in the epithalamium and genethliacon, and true *virtus* seemed impossible in a paradise where there was nothing to do. The second Troy is clearly not Rome (which is thus represented in the Sibylline Oracles), but presumably Parthia: in the context of 40, when Syria and Cilicia had so recently been over-run, a reference to contemporary Western aspirations is hard to avoid. The new Achilles who is to be dispatched[103] to the wars cannot be Antony; though he claimed descent from the original Achilles, he must not wait so long for his triumphs. Surely he is the child himself,[104] who should be allowed to repeat the *facta parentis* (26) with *facta* of his own (54): here as elsewhere Virgil is contradicting Catullus, who had seen Achilles as a man of blood.[105]

> hinc, ubi iam firmata virum te fecerit aetas,
> cedet et ipse mari vector, nec nautica pinus
> mutabit merces; omnis feret omnia tellus.
> non rastros patietur humus, non vinea falcem;
> robustus quoque iam tauris iuga solvet arator,
> nec varios discet mentiri lana colores,
> ipse sed in pratis aries iam suave rubenti
> murice, iam croceo mutabit vellera luto;
> sponte sua sandyx pascentis vestiet agnos.   (37–45)

The description of the child's maturity also conforms to the Western tradition. The absence of navigation follows Hesiod and Aratus,[106] not Eastern apocalyptic: the sea that was no more in Revelation represents the primeval anarchy of the world, and has nothing to do with Graeco-Roman ideas on the corrupting influence of commerce.[107] The disappearance of work and the automation of the Golden Age are also conventional (n. 80), and though the transference of the theme to the future suits the Sibyl,[108] the actual phraseology recalls Lucretius and especially Catullus (64. 38 ff.). On the other hand, the sweetly blushing ram is a novel embellishment of the topic: Virgil has characteristically transmuted a piece of Etruscan antiquarianism recently translated by

[103] *mittere* is a Roman technicality for dispatching a general to the wars (*TLL* 8. 1183. 55 ff.).

[104] Tarn, op. cit. (n. 11), 155.   [105] 64. 348 ff., J. C. Bramble, *PCPS* 16 (1970), 25 f.

[106] Hes. *Op.* 236 f.; Arat. 110 f.; Gatz. op. cit. (n. 15), 229. Virgil's *et ipse* suggests the sea's irresistible magnetism for the merchant.

[107] Rev. 21: 1 καὶ ἡ θάλασσα οὐκ ἔστιν ἔτι, G. B. Caird's commentary (1966), 262.

[108] 7. 146 f. (a late section) οὐκέτι τις κόψει βαθὺν αὔλακα γύρῳ ἀρότρῳ, οὐ βόες ἰθυντῆρα κάτω βάψουσι σίδηρον (Kurfess gives Jewish parallels).

Tarquitius.[109] His sentimental and humorous[110] fantasy, which does not deserve the scorn of the critics, makes an agreeable contrast with the monstrosities of Daniel and Revelation. |

> 'talia saecla' suis dixerunt 'currite' fusis
> concordes stabili fatorum numine Parcae.
> adgredere o magnos (aderit iam tempus) honores,
> cara deum suboles, magnum Iovis incrementum!
> aspice convexo nutantem pondere mundum,
> terrasque tractusque maris caelumque profundum;
> aspice, venturo laetentur ut omnia saeclo!   (46–52)

From one point of view this passage belongs to the Western tradition, as it is a rejoinder to the sinister epithalamium of the Parcae at the wedding of Peleus and Thetis (n. 105). The first line obviously echoes the Catullan refrain 'currite ducentes subtegmina, currite fusi' (64. 327); Virgil like his model is addressing the spindles, not (as is often thought) the centuries.[111] The section is framed by references to *saecula* (46 and 52), which do not appear in Catullus, but though this suits Virgil's preoccupation with time-schemes, the idea is now expressed in Roman terms. The same is true of *stabili . . . numine*: the movement predicted by the Parcae (*currite*) is fixed immovably by divine decree, just as in Horace's *Carmen Saeculare* (25 ff.).

The following lines are more portentous,[112] and go far beyond the sentimental hopes of Graeco-Roman epithalamium. At first sight *adgredere . . . honores* seems to suggest the assumption of a public career, and to refer therefore to the boy's maturity; the reader is allowed this escape-route if he wishes to take it.[113] But *aderit iam tempus* has an eschatological ring (see above on 4), and the development of events would be disrupted if the words referred to anything but the birth. In that case *magnos* is a sacral word (like *o*) masquerading as political, and

---

[109] Macrob. *Sat.* 3. 7. 2 'purpureo aureove colore ovis ariesque si aspergetur, principi ordinis et generis summa cum felicitate largitatem auget', Serv. Auct. ad loc., H. Wagenvoort, *Mnem.* 15 (1962), 139 ff.; for Tarquitius see J. Heurgon, *Latomus*, 12 (1953), 402 ff.

[110] Hor. *Serm.* 1. 10. 44 'molle atque facetum'.

[111] *talia*, which associates the Parcae with the preceding prophecies, would be unacceptably vague for a vocative. For the internal accusative *saecula* cf. again the imitation of Symmachus, *Or.* 3. 9 'iamdudum aureum saeculum currunt fusa Parcarum'.

[112] This portentousness might seem to support the view that 48–52 should be assigned to the Parcae (thus Kurfess, *Phil. Woch.* 58 (1938), 815 f.), who otherwise have little to say. But it is strange that they should address the baby rather than the parents or the world, and as *adgredere* and *aspice* lead up to *incipe*, these imperatives should all be spoken by the poet.

[113] It makes 53 *tum* easier; yet see below, n. 125.

honores refers not to future magistracies but to more immediate homage; like the adoration of the Magi, this alone marks out the baby as superhuman. The movement of the poem as the birth approaches recalls the Hellenistic poets' practice of describing a ceremony in a running commentary, but it would be misleading here to speak simply of a literary technique. With his feeling for the spirit as well as the externals of religion Virgil has suggested not a pageant but a vigil, not a commemoration but an experience (n. 43). This feature seems neither Roman nor Jewish, but belongs to the world of mystery cults.

The sonorous acclamation of line 49 adds to the religious atmosphere, but it would be dangerous to assume that Virgil took it over from a Sibylline model: though the emphatic σπονδειάζων can easily be paralleled in the Sibyl, it is more probably suggested by Catullus 64. Norden compared *cara suboles* with God's address to Christ, σὺ εἶ ὁ υἱός μου ἀγαπητός, (Mk. 1: 11), but the meaning there is something like ἐκλελεγμένος,[114] and *cara* has far more sentimental associations. Munro[115] even interpreted *magnum Iovis incrementum* as 'promise of Jupiter to be'; but though Roman emperors could later be called 'Jove', such a reference seems impossible at this date, especially after *deum*. The homely *incrementum* is used of additions to a flock or with some tenderness of human offspring,[116] yet there are also difficulties about translating 'child of Jupiter'; this is repetitive after *deum suboles*, and the portentous *magnum* implies that the augmentation will be great rather than just the baby.[117] Perhaps on the surface we are allowed to understand 'great offspring of Jupiter', but once we see the force of *magnum* we are encouraged to think of the destiny of a hero: the child will be a 'great addition' to the divine family, just like Hercules or the Dioscuri.[118]

Lines 50-2 transport us from the infant to the firmament. The world

---

[114] Norden, op. cit., 132. 'Son of God' was not in fact a regular appellation of the pre-Christian Messiah; cf. Strack–Billerbeck on Rom. 1: 3; O. Cullmann, *The Christology of the New Testament* (2nd English edn., 1963), 272 ff.; G. Vermes, *Jesus the Jew* (n. 35), 197 ff.

[115] Cited by J. B. Mayor, *Virgil's Messianic Eclogue* (1907), 111 ff. Cf. Ov. *Met.* 3. 103 'vipereos dentes, populi incrementa futuri'; Apollonides, *AP* 9. 287. 6 (on Tiberius) Ζῆνα τὸν ἐσσόμενον.

[116] Serv. ad loc. 'et est vulgare, quod bucolico congruit carmini'; T. Frank, *CPh.* 11 (1916), 334 ff.; Norden, op. cit. 129 ff.; Carcopino, op. cit. (n. 42), 88 ff.

[117] Büchner, *RE* 8A. 189, citing *Paneg. Lat.* 4(10). 37. 5 'Constantine Caesar, incrementum maximum boni publici'.

[118] Liv. 1. 7. 10 'aucturum caelestium numerum'; Virg. *Aen.* 8. 301 'decus addite divis' (both of Hercules), *Ciris* 398 'cara Iovis suboles, magnum Iovis incrementum' (of the Dioscuri; the singular suggests 'augmentation', rather than 'children').

conventionally shook in response to Zeus,[119] and objects nodded and swayed at the epiphany of a god,[120] but cosmic manifestations at the birth of a baby go beyond the Western precedents. When Theognis[121] describes Apollo's birth, the land rejoices and the sea laughs, but when the theme is taken over by a Christian Sibylline oracle the whole universe exults (8. 474f.): τικτόμενον δὲ βρέφος ποτὶ ἔπτατο γηθοσύνη χθών, οὐράνιος δ' ἐγέλασσε θρόνος καὶ ἀγάλλετο κόσμος.[122] Gladness was the predominant emotion on such occasions: the angel of the evangelist brings tidings of great joy,[123] and at the coming of the Kingdom of God John the Divine hears a voice crying εὐφραίνεσθε, οὐρανοί.[124] So in these lines at least it is plausible | that Virgil had an Eastern antecedent, and possible that he had a Sibylline one; τικτόμενον βρέφος is the Greek for *nascens puer* (Norden, op. cit. 149), and may suggest a common source in an earlier Jewish oracle.

> o mihi tum longae maneat pars ultima vitae,
> spiritus et quantum sat erit tua dicere facta:
> non me carminibus vincet nec Thracius Orpheus
> nec Linus, huic mater quamvis atque huic pater adsit,
> Orphei Calliopea, Lino formosus Apollo.
> Pan etiam, Arcadia mecum si iudice certet,
> Pan etiam Arcadia dicat se iudice victum.   (53-9)

'May I live to describe the day' was a conventional thought in panegyric[125] that particularly suited eulogies of the young,[126] but it can hardly be a coincidence that similar hopes are found in eschatological writings and particularly in the Sibylline oracles.[127] On the other hand, lines 55-9 with their singing match and Arcadian umpires revert to the pastoral tradition, and it is pointless to seek a mystical significance in bards of the countryside like Orpheus and Linus. The repetition of

[119] Hes. *Theog.* 839ff.; Catull. 64. 205f.; Hor. *Carm.* 1. 34. 9ff.

[120] Call. *H.* 2. 1ff.; Virg. *Aen.* 3. 90f.; Pfister, *RE* Suppl. 4. 319.

[121] Theogn. 9f. ἐγέλασσε δὲ γαῖα πελώρη, γήθησεν δὲ βαθὺς πόντος ἁλὸς πολιῆς.

[122] For such portents, cf. ps.-Callisthenes (on the birth of Alexander) ὥστε τὸν πάντα κόσμον συγκινηθῆναι; *Protevangelium Jacobi* 18. 2 (an unnatural stillness at the birth of Jesus), Norden, op. cit. 58n.

[123] Lk. 2: 11, Norden, op. cit. 57f.   [124] Rev. 12: 12, echoing Isa. 44: 23.

[125] Cf. *Ecl.* 8. 7f. 'en erit umquam ille dies mihi cum liceat tua dicere facta?' As *tum* in our passage suits this pattern, it should not be changed to *tam*; though the new age begins immediately, Virgil looks forward to its full development.

[126] See Hor. *Epist.* 1. 4. 8ff., Pers. 2. 37ff. for nurses' prayers for their charges.

[127] *Orac. Sib.* 3. 371f. ὢ μακαριστός, ἐκεῖνον ὃς ἐς χρόνον ἔσσεται ἀνήρ ... (just before the passage on εὐνομίη cited above, n. 27), 4. 192; *Psalm. Sal.* (1st cent. BC) μακάριοι οἱ γινόμενοι ἐν ταῖς ἡμέραις ἐκείναις; Lk. 2: 30 (the 'Nunc Dimittis') ὅτι εἶδον οἱ ὀφθαλμοί μου τὸ σωτήριόν σου; Erdmann, op. cit. (n. 39), 45.

these names in different cases suggests the bucolic idiom, as does the Greek accidence of *Orphei* and the feminine caesura in 57; in the same way the verbal juggling of 58–9 belongs to the style that Theocritus had established with the opening lines of his first idyll. The reference to Pan is an echo of Moschus[128] that balances the invocation of the first line. The dread voice[129] of Eastern apocalyptic has now given place to more familiar melodies.

> Incipe, parve puer, risu cognoscere matrem
> (matri longa decem tulerunt fastidia menses).
> incipe, parve puer: qui non risere parentes,
> nec deus hunc mensa, dea nec dignata cubili est.   (60–3)

With the birth of the child, the eclogue once again becomes enigmatic. The humanity of the scene shows a truly Italian sentiment (cf. Catullus 61. 212f.), and suggests that a real baby is meant rather than some vague abstraction; the mother is presumably Octavia, whose patronage of letters may be significant.[130] No mystical reason[131] need be sought for the ten months of pregnancy, for the inclusive method is often used in such contexts. On the other hand, ordinary children do not smile till they are forty days old;[132] it is only a Wunderkind like Dionysus[133] or Zoroaster[134] who does this on the day of his birth. The Westerners may claim that the exact date is unspecified, but there is less point in stressing the months of pregnancy if there is a significant gap between the birth and the laugh. The right answer may once again be that the ambiguity is deliberate: if we choose to be hard-headed Westerners we need see no more than an encouragement to hurry up and show signs of personality, but for the reader who had understood the message of the poem there is a hint that the infant is out of the ordinary. Such a transcendental note is quite compatible with the domesticity of the

---

[128] 3. 55f. Πανὶ φέρω τὸ μέλισμα; τάχ' ἂν καὶ κεῖνος ἐρεῖσαι τὸ στόμα δειμαίνοι μὴ δεύτερα σεῖο φέρηται.

[129] Milton, *Lycidas* 132; he understood the mixing of the genres (Johnson did not).

[130] C. Cichorius, *Römische Studien* (1922), 277 ff.

[131] Carcopino, op. cit. 94 f., 225 ff., contradicted by Norden, op. cit. 61 n., P. Fabia, *REA* 33 (1931), 33 ff., *TLL* 8. 749. 54 ff.

[132] Arist. *Hist. An.* 587ᵇ5 ff.; Antigonus, *Hist. Mir.* (Keller, *Rer. Nat. Script.* 42) τῇ δὲ τεσσαρακοστῇ προσλαμβάνειν τὸ γελαστικὸν καὶ ἄρχεσθαι ἐπιγινώσκειν μητέρα; Censorin. *Natal.* 11. 7; Lydus, *Mens.* 4. 21 (p. 85 W).

[133] Nonn. *Dionys.* 9. 35f. καὶ πόλον ἐσκοπίαζεν ἀήθεα, θαμβαλέος δὲ πατρῴην ἐγέλασσεν ἴτυν δεδοκημένος ἄστρων.

[134] Plin. *Nat.* 7. 72, Norden 65 ff.; for more remote analogies cf. D. R. Stuart, *CPh.* 16 (1921), 216 ff.

scene; if Isis and Harpocrates touched the hearts of men, it was because they combined the human with the divine.

The poem ends with another enigma, though not where commentators have found it: it is clear from the structure and sense of the passage that the baby is doing the laughing and not the parents (that is to say, the *cui* of Virgil's manuscripts is impossible against the *qui* implied by Quintilian 9. 3. 8).[135] The last line is more difficult. Norden pointed to Eastern legends where the hero receives a divine bride,[136] and nearer home to the Dionysiac mysteries, where the god was acclaimed as a bridegroom;[137] but though this range of ideas may ultimately lie behind Virgil, we need not assume that he is imitating a Sibylline or other mystical prototype. It is simpler to suppose that he is recalling the story of Heracles, who feasted with Zeus and took Hebe to wife;[138] yet even to this it might be replied that the poet's general | formulation (with its implication that every good baby ought to smile) does not suggest so special a privilege. Warde Fowler[139] got round the difficulty by referring to the Roman custom by which at the birth of upper-class children a table was placed for Hercules in the atrium and a bed for Juno; Virgil would then be suggesting a nurses' saw to the effect that the unsmiling baby comes to no good. On the other hand, it seems likely that a bed was placed for Juno only at the birth of a girl,[140] which would make the last words of the poem surprisingly irrelevant; and *dignata cubili est* surely points to something more than an antiquarian symbol. Perhaps one could propose a compromise, or rather recognize another oracular ambiguity; at a superficial level Virgil may be alluding to a nursery saying (this would explain the generalization of *qui non*), but by his form of words he has ensured that the reader will think primarily of superhuman destiny.

Virgil claims at the beginning of the eclogue to be drawing on the

[135] Norden, op. cit. 62n. It is not so certain that *parentes* must be changed to *parenti*; the more general formulation has some attractions. *ridere* with the accusative may describe amusement rather than derision (cf. Ov. *AA* 1. 87 'hunc Venus ... ridet'), and the crowing of babies betrays a robuster emotion than benevolence; thus the infant Dionysus laughed at the stars (above, n. 133).

[136] Norden, op. cit. 68ff.; he regarded the symbolical marriage of Christ at Rev. 19: 7 as an attenuated version of this myth.

[137] Firm. Mat. *De Errore Prof.* 19 νύμφιε χαῖρε.

[138] Hom. *Od.* 11. 602f.; Pind. *N.* 1. 71f.; Theoc. 24. 84 (above, p. 61).

[139] *Virgil's Messianic Eclogue* (n. 115), 75ff., citing Schol. Bern. ad loc. 'Iunoni Lucinae lectus, Herculi mensa'.

[140] Cf. Hesychius στέφανον ἐκφέρειν· ἔθος ἦν, ὁπότε παιδίον ἄρρεν γένοιτο παρὰ Ἀττικοῖς, στέφανον ἐλαίας τιθέναι πρὸ τῶν θυρῶν· ἐπὶ δὲ τῶν θηλειῶν, ἔρια διὰ τὴν ταλασίαν (I owe this reference to Mr S. G. Pembroke).

Sibyl, and he ought to be believed. So many features suit the Eastern oracles that cumulatively they seem decisive, the proclamation of the eschatological period, the ambiguous chronological system, the descent of Justice from the stars, the return of the Golden Age, the prayer to share in the coming felicity, the pervasive blend of the Hesiodic and the prophetic. As the animal peace in particular points to a Jewish oracle, so too should the infant saviour, especially as both pictures are found in the same area of Isaiah. The association of the Messiah with Emmanuel might have proved attractive to the Hellenized Jews of Egypt, who could have been influenced by Greek legends as well as by indigenous cults. It may be significant that though the infancy narratives of the Gospels are basically Jewish, some features suggest a Hellenistic origin,[141] the virgin birth[142] (apparently encouraged by the LXX's translation of Isaiah 7: 14), the mystical Pneuma (paralleled in Philo),[143] the curiously literal notion (however muted) of divine parentage, one might add more subjectively the naïve realism of the Greek Luke's pastoral scene, so imaginatively contrasted (just as in Virgil) with the cosmic revolution it portends. Hellenized Jews of the less sophisticated sort are still rather shadowy people: one would be glad to know more about how they formulated the eschatological message in the pre-Christian period. The extant Sibylline oracles provide one dismal answer, but if Virgil's source had caught more of the Greek spirit, it might have given the abstract and colourless myth a more human aspect, such as later appeared also in parts of Luke's nativity story.

In the end the learning and the vision of the Easterners give no more than a background to the interpretation of the eclogue.[144] Virgil has no interest in Jewish eschatology for its own sake, but is ingeniously adapting it to Western modes of thought (a process that has continued over the centuries to our own day); if we read between the lines the true saviour is not an alien Messiah but a Roman boy, who will owe his existence to an imaginative political achievement and bring the world a peace based on the realities of Western imperialism.

[141] M. Dibelius, 'Jungfrauensohn und Krippenkind', *SHAW* 22 (1932), 4. Abh. (= *Botschaft und Geschichte* (1953), 1. 1 ff.

[142] Dibelius, op. cit. 42 ff.; R. Bultmann, *The History of the Synoptic Tradition* (1963), 291 f. (= 316 in 3rd German edn.).

[143] Norden, op. cit. 78 f.; Dibelius, op. cit. 31 f.

[144] For criticisms of Norden's approach see L. Deubner, *Gnomon*, 1 (1925), 160 ff. (in his review of W. Weber, *Der Prophet und sein Gott*); Jachmann, op. cit. 13 ff. Yet there is also much to criticize in the Westerners' underestimation of this supremely beautiful poem.

If the poem expresses itself in allegories, that suits the general pattern of the book as well as the ambiguous manner of prophetic writing; in the *Aeneid* Virgil was to use other mythological forms to convey a modern message. It could fairly be urged against Norden that instead of interpreting the poet's symbols in a Western political context, he was lured into the mists of oriental religion (though without saying enough about the Sibyl, who alone can guide us through the murk); but even if he failed to give a satisfactory account of the poem, his book is salutary in other directions. In the first place, as a Jew he was able to see Christianity historically, that is to say as a Jewish heresy centring on a Messiah (as its name shows); seeing that the inter-Testamental period is of such critical importance, the uncertain evidence of the eclogue may in fact deserve more attention than he gave it. Secondly, he refused to detach the Greek Bible from the main body of classical literature, but applied his unique ear for form to both impartially (as in the *Kunstprosa* of his youth, where St Paul rubs shoulders with Antiochus of Commagene). These questions of form are so crucial in New Testament studies, and the analyses of the theologians have such far-reaching implications, that more classical scholars ought to follow the Easterners' example. War is too serious a business to be left entirely to the generals.

5

Notes on the Text of Catullus

THE text of Catullus is notoriously corrupt, and though much has
been healed, something remains to be done. An article may still be
useful if it encourages scepticism and speculation.[1] I have found
Baehrens the best commentator for this particular purpose; for information about the manuscripts I rely on Mynors. The text printed is
that of V where I wish to discuss it, but it is sometimes silently altered
where I do not. Textual variants are mentioned only where they are
relevant to the argument.

> Passer, deliciae meae puellae,
> quicum ludere, quem in sinu tenere,
> cui primum digitum dare appetenti
> et acris solet incitare morsus,
> cum desiderio meo nitenti   5
> carum nescioquid lubet iocari,
> et solaciolum sui doloris,
> credo, [ut] cum gravis acquiescit (-et *V*) ardor:
> tecum ludere sicut ipsa possem
> et tristis animi levare curas.   10
>
> (Catullus 2. 1–10)

Lines 5–6 are generally interpreted 'when it is pleasing to my radiant
love . . .'. J. S. Phillimore doubted the possibility of personal *desiderium*
in an oblique case, and reasonably asked for a parallel;[2] Fordyce tried
to meet the challenge by citing 104. 1 'credis me potuisse meae
maledicere vitae?', but *vitae* is an insufficient analogy for more abstract
words like *desiderio* and *voluptati*. And there is a more clear-cut
objection to the traditional explanation: *nitens*, which appeals to the

---

[1] Parts of this paper were read to the Cambridge Philological Society on 2 March
1978, and parts earlier in the University of Manchester. I am grateful to all those in both
places who helped me to clarify my views.

[2] *CPh.* 5 (1910), 217.

---

eye, is the wrong sort of word to agree with *desiderium*.[3] Catullus might call the girl 'my great desire' because desire in the primary sense can be great (cf. Hor. *Carm.* 1. 14. 18 'nunc desiderium curaque non levis'), but not 'my red-haired desire' and not *desiderium nitens*. Therefore *desiderio* is not dative but ablative, and the meaning is 'to her shining with longing for me';[4] commentators do not notice Anacreon, *PMG* 444 πόθῳ στίλβων (of Ἔρως παρθένιος). It now becomes clear that *nitens* refers not to beauty in general but to sparkling eyes; when Juvenal says of Lesbia 'turbavit nitidos exstinctus passer ocellos' (6. 8), he is combining allusions to Catullus 2 and 3.

This conclusion encourages a more tentative reinterpretation of line 7: the girl | offers her finger to the bird (*a*) in happy moments and (*b*) 'as a solace for her pain'. That is to say, *solaciolum* follows *solet incitare morsus* as an 'accusative in apposition to the sentence'; *sui* can now be retained as it refers back to *puella*, the subject (understood) of *solet*. This explanation was excluded so long as *desiderio* was understood in a personal sense; for after it had displaced *puella* as the logical subject of 5-6, it was impossible to find a point of reference for *sui*. It may be thought unnatural to have such an accusative after a *cum* clause has intervened; yet cf. Tac. *Hist.* 4. 19. 1 'pretium itineris donativum, duplex stipendium, augeri equitum numerum, promissa sane a Vitellio, postulabant, non ut adsequerentur sed causam seditioni'.

I am not here primarily concerned with 8, but quote it to show how the lines go in pairs: like Munro I look for a clear contrast between *dolor* and *ardor*. The omission of *ut* is due to Baehrens,[5] the present *acquiescit* to Ellis.

> quare, quidquid habes boni malique,
> dic nobis: volo te ac tuos amores
> ad caelum lepido vocare versu.   (6. 15-17)

Catullus cannot 'call' anybody to the sky unless he is already there himself. He cannot even be referring to his own immortality as a poet, as that has yet to be achieved; mock-heroic exaggeration is not plausible in this mundane context. Baehrens, who saw the difficulty, was as often better at diagnosis than treatment. His *ad cenam* suggests a

---

[3] This point is seen by J. P. Postgate, who talks of the added offence in *nitenti* (*CPh.* 7 (1912), 1). Phillimore and Postgate are not refuted by E. U. Fay, *CPh.* 8 (1913), 301-3.

[4] The above interpretation is one of several heard simultaneously by S. Baker, *CPh.* 53 (1958), 243-4; as he thinks that *cum* has hints of the preposition, his article is unrewarding.

[5] See also H. Offermann, *Eranos*, 73 (1975), 58-60.

nineteenth-century obsession with etiquette: Catullus cannot ask the *febriculosum scortum* to dinner unless he is told what name to put on the invitation.

The line must refer to the poet's power to confer immortality: here the name of the *laudanda* really is necessary. The contrast between the slight *lepido* and the grand *caelum* is effective, and brings out exactly what Catullus did for his friends. Read *levare*. Cf. Prop. 3. 1. 9 'quo (versu) me Fama levat terra sublimis', Hier. *In Os.* 1. 1. 5 (*PL* 25. 823c) 'cur Socratem ad caelum levent', Ven. Fort. *Carm.* 4. 10. 6 'quem ... fama sub astra levat', *TLL* 70. 1234. 63 ff., Pind. *I.* l. 64–5 εὐφώνων πτερύγεσσιν ἀερθέντ' ἀγλααῖς Πιερίδων, *N.* 8. 41–2 (ἀρετά) ἐν σοφοῖς ἀνδρῶν ἀερθεῖσ' ἐν δικαίοις τε πρὸς ὑγρὸν αἰθέρα.

> hic illa, ut decuit cinaediorem,
> 'quaeso' inquit 'mihi, mi Catulle, paulum
> istos commoda: nam volo ad Serapim
> deferri.'   (10. 24–7) |

Plautus might perhaps have scanned imperatival *commoda* as a dactyl, but not Catullus. Though *brevis brevians* was a phenomenon of spoken Latin, it is only found in classical poetry with a few common words; the use of *puta* as a pyrrhic to mean 'for instance' (Pers. 4. 9) is not a parallel. In the absence of other instances from epigram or satire, the prosody cannot be defended by the *oratio recta*, and still less by the social position of the speaker.

commodum enim (Hand) and *commode enim* (Munro) are not only unsatisfactory in sense but give an unparalleled elision at this place in the line; it has also been observed that in the polymetrics Catullus uses *enim* only after *est* (12. 8 and 35. 17). One is reluctant to cut across *nam volo ad Serapim*, which gives a convincing movement (though Passerat's *iam* is agreeably impatient). Munro's final thought was *da modo*, but this phrase is wrongly placed at the end of a sentence.

Ellis considered taking *commoda* as neuter plural in the sense of 'loans'; 'perquisites' would be more promising, as the word is used euphemistically of the rewards of military service.[6] The apposition with *istos*, which Ellis was ready to consider, is impossible on either hypothesis. *ista* would be easy but unsatisfactory: O. Skutsch has pointed out that in this part of the book (poems 2 to 26) Catullus does not give his hendecasyllables a trochaic base.[7] On the other hand, *istaec*

---

[6] Cic. *Phil.* 5. 53; Planc. *Fam.* 10. 24. 2; Ov. *AA* 1. 131 'Romule, militibus scisti dare commoda solus'; *TLL* 3. 1928. 78 ff.

[7] *BICS* 16 (1969), 38, developing observations by M. Zicàri, *SIFC* 29 (1957), 252–3.

might be worth considering (at 67. 37 R restores the form for *iste*); a corruption from *istec* to *istos* does not seem excessive in a context where the next word begins with *c*, and in a tradition where *e* and *o* are often confused. But one can hardly say *istaec commoda* without a verb to mean 'give me your perquisites'; such an accusative may be used in shouting for water or selling figs, or in an impassioned exclamation like 38. 7 'paulum quidlibet allocutionis' or 55. 10 'Camerium mihi, pessimae puellae', but it is too peremptory for our passage and unsuited to a word as abstract as *commoda*.

commoda cannot be governed by *quaeso*, which in classical Latin does not take an accusative of the thing sought;[8] on the other hand, *quaero* seems possible. For the combination with *mihi* cf. 58 b. 9–10 'et multis languoribus peresus essem te mihi, amice, quaeritando' (though the old conjecture *mi amice* should be noted); so *velle sibi, poscere sibi, postulare sibi.* For the separation of the enclitic pronoun by *inquit* cf. 18 '"non" inquam "mihi tam fuit maligne"'.[9] So the sentence now runs '"quaero" inquit "mihi, mi Catulle, paulum istaec commoda"', 'I require your perquisites, darling, for a few minutes'. The speech is not absurdly peremptory (as it would be without a verb), but silkily imperious, *ut decuit cinaediorem.*

> omnia haec, quaecumque feret voluntas
> caelitum, temptare simul parati ...   (11. 13–14)

Catullus has just mentioned all the places where Furius and Aurelius might go as | his *comites*. But though these are well summed up by *omnia haec*, the resumptive pronoun does not seem compatible with the indefinite *quaecumque*. And though the will of the gods may bring death and disaster, it cannot bring the Alps, the Rhine, and the Britons.

Friedrich separates *quaecumque* from *omnia haec*; the relative clause now means 'no matter what the gods bring'. This use of *quaecumque* without an antecedent is explained by Housman[10] on Prop. 1. 21. 9–10 'et quaecumque super dispersa invenerit ossa montibus Etruscis, haec sciat esse mea'. But our passage is much more difficult in two respects: *haec* immediately precedes *quaecumque*, and it is too tempting to connect *omnia* with the generalizing relative pronoun.

---

[8] Enn. *Trag.* 112 J 'liberum quaesendum causa' is legal and already archaic.

[9] Pointed out by O. Skutsch, *BICS* 23 (1976), 19. However, in the passage under discussion he observes that *mihi* cannot go with *quaeso*, which is autonomous, nor with *commoda* (which he regards as imperative) as it would then be too emphatic; accordingly he takes it with *inquit*.

[10] *JPh.* 21 (1893), 184 = *Classical Papers*, 294–5 (with 635); he also cites Lucr. 1. 670–1.

Quinn gives another explanation: 'C.'s friends are ready to face not only all those things (*omnia haec*) which have been mentioned, but whatever the gods have in store for C.'. So R. O. A. M. Lyne:[11] '*quaecumque* would naturally agree with *haec*, but Catullus has a surprise. It must be paratactic . . .; while *haec* looks back, *quaecumque* looks onward, enlarging.' But the surprise is an unpleasant one: an *asyndeton bimembre* is particularly unexpected in a place where *quaecumque* is naturally taken with *omnia*.

Ellis considered *quocumque*, comparing Hor. *Carm.* 1. 7. 25 'quo nos cumque feret melior fortuna parente', but it makes all the difference that Catullus has no accusative *nos*. If Friedrich's interpretation is to be accepted one might consider *quodcumque*, which would now be successfully detached from *omnia haec*. Dr J. Diggle cites in favour of this view Enn. *Ann.* 197 'quidve ferat fors', Ter. *Phorm.* 138 'quod fors feret feremus'; as he points out, such heroics suit the grandiloquence of *voluntas caelitum*. But I prefer to try *quacumque*; *feret* is now intransitive and means 'bears', 'tends', 'goes' (*OLD* s.v. *fero*, 31). The usage is more prosaic than the transitive construction (cf. phrases like 'ut mea fert opinio'), but it is attested with *voluntas* even in poetry: cf. Lucr. 3. 44 'si fert ita forte voluntas', Virg. *Aen.* 6. 675, Manil. 5. 495–6 'qua fert cumque voluntas praecipitant vires' (both verbs are presumably intransitive), a passage actually cited by Ellis in support of his *quocumque*.

An indefinite relative clause indicating 'way by which' fits contexts that refer to leading and following,[12] especially where loyalty is emphasized: cf. Hdt. 1. 151. 3 τῇσι δὲ λοιπῇσι πόλισι ἔαδε κοινῇ ῎Ιωσι ἕπεσθαι τῇ ἂν οὗτοι ἐξηγέωνται, 6. 74. 1 ὅλλους τε ὅρκους προσάγων σφι ἦ μὲν ἕψεσθαί σφεας αὐτῷ τῇ ἂν ἐξηγῆται. Such an oath suits the *comites Catulli*, who are ready to go with him anywhere in the footsteps of Crassus and Caesar; *quacumque* points to the alternative destinations suggested in the first three stanzas of the poem (*sive... sive... seu ... sive... sive*). The poet asks of his comrades not so much endurance as versatility (cf. *temptare*), as emerges in particular from the nature of their mission. This idea is supported by *quacumque* better than by *quaecumque* or *quodcumque*. |

O colonia, quae cupis ponte ludere longo,
et salire paratum habes, sed vereris inepta

[11] *Experiments: Nine Essays on Catullus for Teachers*, ed. C. Greig (Cambridge Schools Classics Project, 1970), 25.
[12] Hom. *Il.* 15. 46; Hes. *Op.* 208; Herodas 5. 43 (with Headlam's parallels).

> crura ponticuli axulis stantis in redivivis,
> ne supinus eat cavaque in palude recumbat.   (17. 1–4)

redivivus is applied by Cicero and Vitruvius to building-stone that has been reused. Editors quote Festus 334 L (= 273 M) 'ex vetusto renovatum', but this gives the wrong emphasis for our passage; Catullus should say nothing to suggest that the bridge is as good as new. Yet the word by origin probably means 'cast-off' (cf. *reduviae* of the skin of a snake), and does not necessarily imply later use.[13] In the fourth century AD it was falsely connected with a second life, but it cannot be demonstrated that this implication was felt as early as Catullus.

But even if *redivivis* cannot be proved wrong, *recidivis* might be considered.[14] This word came to be applied to a new growth (apparently because of the agricultural *recidiva semina*), but in origin it was derived from *cadere* (like *cadivus*). In our passage 'back-sliding' makes an effective contrast with *stantis*; it also leads to *supinus* and *recumbat* (as Professor Kenney observes).

Niall Rudd has convincingly suggested that Catullus gives the bridge anthropomorphic features that match the physical decrepitude[15] of his victim. *redivivis* does nothing to help this association (and if connected with *vivus* would be an actual hindrance): *recidivis*, on the other hand, would strongly reinforce it. The change would be minimal even in an author with a sounder manuscript tradition.

> cartae regiae, nove (novi *cod. det.*) libri,
> novi umbilici, lora rubra, membranae,
> derecta plumbo et pumice omnia aequata.   (22. 6–8)

novi libri is too unspecific compared with the other items (of course the publication was new), and the comprehensive term should not come second on the list. Kroll saw the difficulty but lamely commented 'ohne den Verszwang hätte C. sie vor den *chartae regiae* genannt'. Attempts to explain *libri* as a genitive are equally futile.

Read *bibli*; Catullus is describing royal sheets of new papyrus

---

[13] See L. Lange, '*Redivivus* und *recidivus*', in *Studien zur griechischen und lateinischen Grammatik*, ed. G. Curtius and K. Brugman, 10. 2 (1878), 225–55 (I owe this reference to Professor Kenney).

[14] *irrecidivis*, presumably in the sense of 'unreviving', was implausibly proposed by J. F. Gronovius and Heinsius.

[15] *TAPA* 90 (1959), 238–42, repr. in K. Quinn, *Approaches to Catullus* (1972), 166–70. For sexual hints in the poem see also H. Akbar Khan, *CPh.* 64 (1969), 88–97 (greatly exaggerated); J. Glenn, ibid. 65 (1970), 256–7.

(genitive). The word is first attested in Latin a century later (Luc. 3. 222–3 'nondum flumineas Memphis contexere biblos noverat'); but as the Greek term was a natural one for the book-trade, there is no difficulty about its use in this informal poem. As *biblus* was feminine (like βύβλος), V's *nove* (the medieval spelling of *novae*) is now seen to be correct.

Alternatively, it has been suggested to me that one might interpret *novae bibli* as a nominative; a series of short parallel phrases is thus produced, and *novae* exactly | balances *novi* in the next line. On the other hand, *biblus* refers primarily to the material rather than the book (*TLL* 2. 1959. 5ff.), and the plural at this date might suggest papyrus stalks (as in Lucan, loc. cit.); it is only much later that one finds glosses like *bibli libri* (*CGL* 4. 601. 2). Moreover, if *novae bibli* is part of the first phrase, the contrast with 5 *palimpsesto* is much sharper (I owe this point to Professor Kirk). Certainly it would be impossible to take *cartae regiae* as genitive and *novae bibli* as nominative; the word-order is not easily justified and in the present context far too misleading.

Catullus nowhere else ends a scazon with a word like *libri*, where the spondee is only produced by an artificial lengthening before mute and liquid; on the other hand, *bl* lengthens automatically at its rare occurrences in classical Latin,[16] as it normally does in Greek.[17] But no canon can be established even for Republican poets (cf. Matius, fr. 12 'labra conserens labris'), and there are several intances of artificial lengthening at the ends of Martial's scazons (including 10. 100. 2 *libro*). There is less ambiguity in Greek scazons, as the Ionic of Hipponax usually lengthens before mute and liquid; in this he is followed by Callimachus and to a considerable extent by Herodas.[18]

> Poetae tenero, meo sodali,
> velim Caecilio, papyre, dicas
> Veronam veniat, Novi relinquens
> Comi moenia Lariumque litus.
> nam quasdam volo cogitationes   5
> amici accipiat sui meique.   (35. 1–6)

6 *amici mei* is explained in two ways. Some think that it refers to Catullus himself; but though Horace calls himself *noster* in the sense of 'our hero' (*Serm.* 2. 6. 48), 'my friend' cannot possibly mean 'me', especially where it adds nothing to the straightforward *amici sui.*

---

[16] Housman, *Classical Papers*, 626, describes Ellis's *tăblam* at 63. 9 as a false quantity.
[17] For exceptions see Denniston on Eur. *El.* 1014.
[18] See I. C. Cunningham's edn. (1971), 215.

Others argue that Catullus is referring to some unnamed third party, whose identity will be obvious to Caecilius. This is to ignore the conventions of this type of poetry, which in spite of its air of intimacy is written for a public audience: it would be inartistic in the extreme to introduce an unintelligible allusion that is not elucidated in the rest of the poem.

I suggest *sui tuique*; authors are notoriously well-disposed to their own writings, and Catullus is addressing his poem as if it were a human intermediary (cf. Cic. *Att.* 4. 2. 5 'interventu Varronis tui nostrique'). I have also considered *tui suique*, which gives the more conventional word-order, but the greater courtesy is due to Caecilius, the real recipient of the poem. After *amici* has preceded, *sui* is the expected possessive and *tui* a humorous climax.

It does not seem to have been noticed that Ausonius begins a poetical letter in | similar terms: 'perge, o libelle, Sirmium et dic ero meo ac tuo ave atque salve plurimum' (*Epist.* 16. 2. 1–3 Schenkl = 12, p. 239 Peiper). The recipient of this poem, the magnificent Sex. Petronius Probus (cos. 371),[19] was 'a luminary of literature and oratory',[20] the addressee of the *Ora Maritima* of Avienius and of half a dozen letters from Symmachus (1. 56–61), the part-author of a book of verse dedicated to Theodosius (*Anth. Lat.* 1. 783), the father of the Probinus and Olybrius who were celebrated in Claudian's first poem (1. 31–60). An inscription from Verona suggests that this was his native city;[21] when the *Historia Augusta* describes how the descendants of the Emperor Probus 'vel odio vel invidiae timore Romanam rem fugerunt et in Italia circa Veronam ac Benacum et Larium atque in his regionibus larem locaverunt' (*Prob.* 24. 1), this is clearly an attempt to flatter the Probi of the writer's own day.[22] A man with the Veronese origin and literary tastes of Petronius Probus must have been alert to see allusions to Catullus; if he had estates at Lakes Benacus and Larius that would increase his awareness (the reference to his headquarters at Sirmium might even make a playful contrast with Sirmio). Both Catullus and Ausonius ask the personified poem to carry a message to

---

[19] For Petronius Probus see Amm. Marc. 27. 11; *RE* 1. 2205–7; *Prosopography of the Later Roman Empire*, I. 736–40; J. Matthews, *Western Aristocracies and Imperial Court* (1975), 37–8, 98, 186–7 (his patronage of Ambrose), 195–7 (his mausoleum in St Peter's).

[20] *CIL* 6. 1751 = *ILS* 1265 'litterarum et eloquentiae lumini'.

[21] *CIL* 5. 3344 = *ILS* 1266 'disertissimo atque omnibus rebus eruditissimo patrono'.

[22] When the writer of the *Historia Augusta* says that a prophecy promising greatness to later Probi has not yet been fulfilled (*Prob.* 24. 3 'sed adhuc neminem vidimus'), 'what he is up to is clear. A joke—and the flimsy pretence that he is writing in an earlier age' (R. Syme, *Ammianus and the Historia Augusta* (1968), 164).

a friend (*dicas*, *dic*), and both use two possessive pronouns to express
the friendly relationship. Ausonius has capped his model[23] by showing
the deference due to the great Probus ('ero meo ac tuo'), but there
would be no point in the imitation if Catullus had been referring to a
totally irrelevant third party.

> non tuus levis in mala
> deditus vir adultera
> procatur pia persequens
> a tuis teneris volet   100
>   secubare papillis.   (61. 97–101)

In line 99 Calphurnius proposed *probra turpia*, and this has generally
been found acceptable. *turpia* is certain, *probra* less so. The word can of
course mean not just 'reproaches' but 'acts worthy of reproach' (like
ὀνείδη), but the extended sense does not suit all contexts equally well
(a general principle that we have already met at 2. 5 *desiderio*). *probra
turpia persequens* would naturally suggest not a career of dishonour but
a morbid delight in receiving insults or a thoroughgoing search for
rude expressions; though Catullus himself says 'a turpi mentem
inhibere probro' (91. 4), that phrase is unambiguous.

The possible neuter plurals cannot be many. *facta* would be feeble;
furta is better,[24] but perhaps too euphemistic for *turpia* and *persequens*.
The plain-spokenness of *stupra* would suit; the word is not too low in
style for Horace's *Odes* (4. 5. 21) and Ovid's *Metamorphoses* (2. 529),
and the assonance with *turpia* is forceful rather than clumsy. |

But how can the corruption be explained? *proca* might be derived
from the end of *stupra*, but the loss of letters at the beginning of the
line seems curious. Or perhaps *stupra turpia* was read as *stupratur pia*;
then somebody might have interpolated the innocuous and unmetrical
procatur pia, 'the pious woman is courted' (cf. *CIL* 13. 7550 'ille te
sponsus procat'). But an interpolator so well-intentioned and so
muddled is more likely to have been medieval than ancient, and such a
person would not readily have thought of *procare* with the accusative.
So the safest course is to obelize *proca*.

> quae tuo veniunt ero,
> quanta gaudia, quae vaga   110
> nocte, quae medio die

---

[23] Schenkl in his edition of Ausonius records six imitations of Catullus (though not
this one).

[24] Cf. Eubulus 67. 8–9 καὶ μὴ λαθραίαν κύπριν αἰσχίστην νόσων πασῶν διώκειν (I owe
this reference to Mr R. Hunter).

> gaudeat! sed abit dies:
> prodeas nova nupta. (61. 109–13)

There are two things wrong with this passage: *medio* belongs to a different category from *vaga*, and *die* is pointlessly picked up by *dies*. Both faults can be cured by changing *medio* to *emerito*,[25] 'when the day has done his work'. For this use of the word cf. Ov. *Fast.* 4. 688 'dempserat emeritis iam iuga Phoebus equis', Stat. *Theb.* 1. 336–7 'emeriti . . . Phoebi'; at Sen. *Ag.* 908–9 'stat ecce Titan dubius emerito die suane currat an Thyestea via' Tarrant proposes *e medio die*, the reverse of what is suggested here. For the strong elision 'quae emerito' cf. 130 'hodie atque heri', 165 'Tyrio in toro', 215 'Manlio et'.

emerito, with its suggestion of doing a stint and getting an honourable discharge, is contrasted with the flightiness of vagabond night. The second relative clause now refers to the same period as the first, but by way of climax hints that the hour is near; the point is then brought out explicitly by *abit dies*. Editors assume that Catullus is talking about love-making in the siesta (Catull. 32, Ov. *Am.* 1. 5), but a reference to the coming night is better suited to the genre; Paris in *Iliad* 3 might be guilty of such behaviour (Plut. *Quaest. Conv.* 655a ὡς οὐκ ἀνδρὸς ἀλλὰ μοιχοῦ λυσσῶντος οὖσαν τὴν μεθημερινὴν ἀκρασίαν), but it has no place in an epithalamium. In a serious celebration of married love, day must first run its course: 'Now welcome night, thou night so long expected, | That long daies labour doest at last defray'.[26]

> ut aput nivem et ferarum gelida stabula forem,
> et earum omnia adirem furibunda latibula. (63. 53–4)

The two ionics a minore at the beginning of 54 have no anaclasis; though this rhythm is possible in galliambics, there is no other instance in this poem. What is | more, *omnia* is pointless in itself: why should Attis tour all the lairs? L. Mueller's *opaca* heals both these faults but leaves a third: *earum* is avoided in verse[27] (except in Lucretius and Horace's satires), and here seems too emphatic.

For *earum omnia* I have tentatively considered (*h*)*arundinosa*; in all Latin this word occurs only at 36. 13 'Cnidumque harundinosam'. For reeds as a lair cf. Claud. 24. 305–6 'defensus arundine Rheni vastus

---

[25] I have an uncomfortable feeling that I have met this conjecture somewhere, but I am unable to trace its source.

[26] Spenser, *Epithalamium* 315–16.

[27] B. Axelson, *Unpoetische Wörter* (1945), 72. The position of *earum* is inadequately supported by 64. 122 'ut eam devinctam lumina somno'.

aper'; Sinon and Moses used similar hide-outs. There is no serious
objection to reeds on Ida, which was a large area with many foun-
tains; Catullus below associates it with the 'aper nemorivagus' (72).

Yet I feel some difficulty about the lack of a genitive; as 53 *ferarum*
belongs only to the second member, it seems unnatural to continue its
influence. We are now threatened by a real dilemma: the absence of
earum is as objectionable as its presence. But perhaps Attis is going not
to the animals' lairs but to his own; *adire* sometimes suggests boldness,
but not necessarily so here. In view of the feminine adjective it makes
more sense if he is not too adventurous in approaching wild animals'
dens (53 may simply mean 'make my home in the snow and the cold
country inhabited by beasts'). But this interpretation may be incompatible with *furibunda*, which suggests manic behaviour; the word is used
at 31 of the earlier phase before Attis has seen the light. As *fugibunda* is
not attested one might consider something like *tremibunda* (note the
preceding *-irem*).

> ego gymnasi fui (sui *X*) flos, ego eram decus olei. (63. 64)

The change of tense from *fui* to *eram* is wasteful and meaningless
(see Baehrens); it is no use quoting instances of tense-variation where
the verb also changes. The alliterative *fui flos* is so crisp and satisfying
that one turns one's first attention to *eram*; but no suitable substitute
presents itself (the *i* of (*h*)*eri* is of too indeterminate a quantity to be
allowed in this position). Baehrens proposed *mei* for *fui*, but this lacks
edge; Nencini's *tui* is worse. I have considered *prius* but prefer *suus*
('the very own flower'). If that is right, it would mean that X's *sui* was
the reading of V; for the familiar confusion of *s* and *f* cf. 14. 16, 68. 79,
68. 130.

> roseis ut hinc labellis sonitus . . . adiit
> geminas deorum ad aures nova nuntia referens . . .   (63. 74–5)

adiit does not explain the case of *labellis* and is uneconomical with
75 *ad*; it was emended by the Itali to *abiit*. Bentley's supplement *citus* is
palaeographically neat, but would suit the arrival of the news (he
retained *adiit*) better than its departure (Attis is not wishing to be
heard); from this point of view Ahlwardt's *vagus* or Giri's | *miser*
(balancing 49 *miseriter*) might be an improvement. For V's impossible
hinc the Itali proposed both *huic* and *hic* (nominative); the latter
avoids the slight clumsiness of *huic labellis* ('minus onerat constru-
ctionem' Baehrens).

deorum presents a more interesting puzzle; the only god in question is Cybele. For the generalizing plural editors quote 63. 68 'ego nunc deum ministra et Cybeles famula ferar?' (where see Friedrich's note); the masculine is used in such plurals even where a woman is meant. The usage is discreet and euphemistic (as people say 'headquarters' when they mean 'the boss'), but the plural remains a plural; in the absence of further specification the gods' two ears come in very awkwardly. Lachmann proposed 'geminas matris ad aures'; but Cybele was not Attis's mother, and ionics without anaclasis are attested in the poem only at the corrupt 54 (see above). Ahlwardt proposed 'matris deorum ad aures'; but the double genitive sounds clumsy, and *geminas* is convincingly paralleled. In place of *deorum* we need another elided genitive, but a suitable genitive singular in *-ae* is not easily found (Munro's *deae tam* and Riese's *deae tum* are best forgotten).

The difficulty would be diminished, even if not removed, by reading *erorum* (or *herorum*, as the word would be spelt in this tradition); Catullus calls Cybele an *era* at lines 18 and 92. Plural *eri* of a singular mistress is much easier than plural *dei* of a singular goddess: the former, unlike the latter, describes a relationship to Attis, and so defines precisely who is meant. 'Plural for singular' is particularly well attested with words referring to the family (thus *liberi* is often found of a single child);[28] for 'masters' cf. Eur. *Hipp.* 287 οἷα πέφυκα δυστυχοῦσι δεσπόταις (Phaedra), *Med.* 61, *Andr.* 391. See especially Catull. 68. 75–8 'inceptam frustra, nondum cum sanguine sacro hostia caelestis pacificasset eros. nil mihi tam valde placeat, Ramnusia virgo, quod temere invitis suscipiatur eris'; here *eros* may refer not to the gods of marriage (as editors assume), but be a sinister euphemism for Venus herself. The legend is not elucidated precisely elsewhere, but Eustathius mentions Aphrodite's later anger (*Il.* 2. 700, p. 325).

> dona ferunt prae se, declarant gaudia vultu.
> deseritur †siros (syros *X*), linquunt Pthiotica Tempe 35
> Crannonisque domos ac moenia Larisaea,
> Pharsalum coeunt, Pharsalia tecta frequentant. (64. 34–7)

siros was changed in the fifteenth century to *Scyros*, and by Meineke to *Cieros*; the former has recently been championed by G. Giangrande.[29] But in this carefully structured passage the passive *deseritur* also requires scrutiny; the variation of voice in 32–3 and 38–40 (cited below) is not a defence. We look for a word to balance *linquunt* exactly,

---

[28] Kühner–Stegmann I. 87; J. Wackernagel, *Vorlesungen über Syntax*, I (1926), 95.

[29] *LCM* 1 (1976), 111 (developing Ellis's arguments on Pelasgians).

just as *ferunt prae se* balances *declarant*, and *coeunt* balances *frequentant*. Perhaps one might try *destituunt* with an accusative place-name; a verb |
for 'leaving in the lurch' is acceptable in a context that goes on to describe the abandonment of agriculture. If a syllable was left out, *deseritur* might seem the easiest way of restoring the metre.

> rura colit nemo, mollescunt colla iuvencis,
> non humilis curvis purgatur vinea rastris,
> non glebam prono convellit vomere taurus,   40
> non falx attenuat frondatorum arboris umbram,
> squalida desertis rubigo infertur aratris.   (64. 38–42)

This description owes its beauty to a wonderfully precise series of verbs: *mollescunt, purgatur, convellit, attenuat*. The positive *infertur* in the last line should mark the climax, but it seems by comparison vague and inert. Commentators see a military metaphor, which might cohere with *desertis*, but one would prefer something that reinforces *squalida rubigo* by appealing to the eye or the touch. Perhaps *increscit* would suggest the required scaliness; cf. Ov. *Met* 4. 577 'durataeque cuti squamas increscere sentit'.

> sic nimis insultans extremo tempore saeva
> fors etiam nostris invidit questibus auris.   (64. 169–70)

saeva is taken as an attributive adjective with *fors*. But the participial clause must make a colon, and if it includes *fors*, the break then comes at a very awkward place. By Virgilian canons it would be illegitimate for an adjective at the end of one line to be followed by its monosyllabic noun at the beginning of the next, especially where this in turn is followed by a pause. It is not clear that in this end-stopped poem the practice of Catullus was very different.

To meet the difficulty one might try to take *saeva* with *insultans*; but though 'arduus insurgens' (Virg. *Aen*. 11. 755) is a familiar poetic locution,[30] the word-order *insultans... saeva* causes serious doubts. It would perhaps be a little easier if we took *nimis* closely with the adjective; for this hyperbaton cf. Cic. *De Or* 2. 288 'sed haec ipsa nimis mihi videor in multa genera digessisse', *Pis.* 17 'cui nimis videtur senatus in conservanda patria fuisse crudelis'.[31] If *saeva* still seems too difficult, the problem could be solved by reading *saeve* (to be taken closely with *nimis*); Catullus uses adverbs more freely than later poets.

The conventional view of our passage may seem to be supported by

---

[30] Kühner–Stegmann, I. 237.
[31] See further C. F. W. Müller, *RhM* 55 (1900), 636–7; E. Fraenkel, *Horace* (1957), 84–5.

64. 246–7 'sic funesta domus ingressus tecta paterna morte ferox
Theseus' (where Kroll compares 'saeva/fors').[32] But though *morte* does
not present the particular difficulty of a monosyllable followed by a
pause, its juxtaposition with *ferox* produces an | unfortunate ambiguity.
There is something to be said for the idea of Marcilius, who read
paternae (with *domus*) and *Marte* (with *ferox*); for the latter collocation
cf. Ov. *Pont.* 2. 9. 45 'Marte ferox et vinci nescius armis', Luc. 2. 590
'Marte feroces'. Having slain the Minotaur, Theseus came galumphing
back (Naxos was only an interlude); cf. Liv. 1. 25. 11 'geminata victoria
ferocem', Sen. *HF* 57 'rupto carcere umbrarum ferox'.

> cuius iter caesis (cessis *O*) angustans corporum acervis,
> alta tepefaciet permixta flumina caede.
>
> (64. 359–60)

Achilles will choke the Scamander with piles of corpses. *caesis* can be
explained as a hypallage for *caesorum*, which would be legitimate with
corporum.[33] But doubts arise when the word is followed by *caede* without any clear rhetorical pattern; the shift of meaning from 'cut down'
to 'blood' does not help.

Baehrens proposed *celsis*, which is very close to *cesis*. The word
seems too grand for heaps of bodies, but the grandeur might be suitably ironic; the variation to *alta* in the next line is justifiable, as the
deep gore would correspond to the high heaps. It might be objected
that *celsis* is infelicitously repeated at 363 'cum teres excelso coacervatum aggere bustum'; but Achilles's own tomb could appropriately
recall his mounds of dead (thus *acervis* is picked up by *coacervatum*).

Yet I should prefer *densis* (*dēsis*), which would refer to the same
dimension as *angustans* and a different one from *alta* (rather than the
other way round). *densas... aristas* has already occurred at 353, but in
this sinister incantation there is an effective repetition of key words (to
be distinguished from the banality of *caesis... caede* in one sentence):
cf. *corpora* (355, 359), *caede* (360, 368), *acervis* (see above). For the grue-
some scene cf. Juv. 10. 185–6 'cruentis fluctibus ac tarda per densa
cadavera prora'.

> saepe in letifero belli certamine Mavors
> aut rapidi Tritonis era aut Amarunsia virgo   395
> armatas hominum est praesens hortata catervas.   (64. 394–6)

---

[32] Kroll also cites 64. 288–9 'altas fagos ac recto proceras stipite laurus'; but here *fagos*
is a more substantial word and only one colon is involved.

[33] Cf. Liv. 22. 48. 4 'inter acervos caesorum corporum'.

rapidi is conspicuously unsuited to the Libyan Lake Triton, which is described as a marsh by Lucan (9. 343) and the elder Pliny (5. 28). Editors more plausibly quote Pausanias on the river Triton in Boeotia (9. 33. 7): ῥεῖ δὲ καὶ ποταμὸς ἐνταῦθα οὐ μέγας χείμαρρος· ὀνομάζουσι δὲ Τρίτωνα αὐτόν, ὅτι τὴν Ἀθηνᾶν τραφῆναι παρὰ ποταμῷ Τρίτωνι ἔχει λόγος, ὡς δὴ τοῦτον τὸν Τρίτωνα ὄντα καὶ οὐχὶ τῶν Λιβύων. In that case Catullus is indulging a perverse Alexandrian taste for obscure variations on familiar legends. |

But the poet is more concerned with the prowess of Athene than with the torrents of Boeotia: perhaps he wrote *rapida* (nominative).[34] The adjective is not used of fleet-footed people, but the case is different with the onrush of a goddess; in particular it might represent θοῦρις, which is applied by Homer to the aegis, and by Nonnus to Athene herself (*Dion.* 48. 799). The lengthening of the final syllable before a mute and liquid in the following word might be defended as an imitation of Greek heroic poetry (note the proper name); it is otherwise attested in Catullus only in pure iambics (4. 9, 4. 18, 29. 4), though similar lengthening before *sp-* and *st-* is found in grander poems (63. 53, 64. 186). Yet as the irregularity was exposed to corruption it is also worth citing 63. 50 'patria o mei creatrix, patria o mea genetrix'; here *mea creatrix* (A. Guarinus) produces a variation in prosody[35] that is much more elegant than the variation in syntax.

> ignaro mater substernens se impia nato
> impia non verita est divos scelerare penates.   (64. 403-4)

Editors decline to punctuate, with good reason. Kroll talks of the epanalepsis of *impia*, but one would like to see another place where an adjective in a participial clause is repeated with the main verb. Alternatively we could put commas after *nato* and the second *impia*; but though the epanalepsis is now cured, the adjective is separated from the clause with which it should be particularly associated.

Perhaps the first *impia* should be changed to *improba* (abbreviation of *pro* might have helped the corruption); for confusion between the two words see *TLL* 7. 620. 65. At 14. 7 'qui tantum tibi misit impiorum' there might be something to be said for *improborum*. Editors see a contrast with *pii vates*, but instead of this artificial joke one expects a more general word for rascals.

---

[34] I cannot trace the source of this conjecture, but doubt whether it is my own.
[35] See Nisbet and Hubbard on Hor. *Carm.* 1. 32. 11, with bibliography there cited.

> estne novis nuptis odio Venus? anne parentum
>   frustrantur falsis gaudia lacrimulis,
> ubertim thalami quas intra limina fundunt?
>   non, ita me divi, vera gemunt, iuerint.   (66. 15-18)

Perhaps brides spoil their parents' joy by only pretending to cry. But
the parents cannot be disappointed unless they witness their daughter's tears; and they are not present in the bridal bedroom, where the
tears are shed. It is no use saying that their happiness is in some ideal
sense nullified by matters outside their knowledge; *falsis* implies
deception (the text is supported by *vera* below), and in the context the
persons deceived can only be the parents.

Friedrich saw the difficulty, and came up with a characteristic
answer. The | *thalamus* is the girl's bedroom in her father's house:
'hier im Zimmer der zur Deductio geschmückten Braut, haben sich
Vater und Mutter eingefunden; hier weint sie die bittern Tränen . . .'.
He develops this scene at some length, but does not pause to
consider that after *novis nuptis* the *thalamus* can only refer to marriage.

Baehrens had given a terser solution: 'intra, dum limen supergredi
verentur'. But *intra limina* cannot mean 'in the doorway'; a Roman
limen was such a physical and psychological barrier that the phrase can
only mean 'inside the room'. *extra* is one's first thought, but not necessarily the right one. Perhaps Catullus wrote *citra limina* (cf. Ov. *Met.*
7. 238 'constitit adveniens citra limenque forisque'): brides weep on
this side of the threshold, but no farther.

> namque ego non ullo vera timore tegam,
>   nec si me infestis discerpent sidera dictis,
>   condita quin (qui *V*) vere pectoris evoluam. (66. 72-4)

vere is not an adverb naturally found with *evolvere*, which is not
primarily a verb of speaking. So editors accept the early conjecture
veri, but that still involves an imprecision that seems uncharacteristic
of Catullus. Doubts about both *vere* and *veri* are greatly increased by
the occurrence of *vera* two lines above; this circumstance diminishes
the force of the parallels at 64. 198 'quae (querellae) quoniam verae
nascuntur pectore ab imo', Lucr. 3. 57-8 'nam verae voces tum demum
pectore ab imo eliciuntur'. These passages might rather suggest *imi* in
Catullus (which also suits *condita* and *evoluam*); if *quin imi* was conflated to *qui*, the transmitted reading, then *vere* might have been interpolated to restore the metre. When a constellation called 'Coma' talks

about its *pectus*, the absurdity must be intentional, and this would be
underlined by *imi*.

> quod cum ita sit, nolim statuas nos mente maligna
>   id facere aut animo non satis ingenuo,
> quod tibi non utriusque petenti copia posta est:
>   ultro ego deferrem, copia siqua foret.   40
>   (68. 37–40)

39 *utriusque* is supposed to refer back to 10 'muneraque et Musarum
hinc petis et Veneris'. But the gifts of the Muses and Venus are one and
the same; Catullus is not being asked to provide a poem and a girl (he
cannot do the latter from Verona), but to write something serious and
beautiful about life and love (such as 68 in fact is).[36] But if only one gift
is involved, *utriusque* becomes very difficult; Catullus cannot be
humorously distinguishing the two aspects of his friend's hendiadys, as
it came too far back for the reference to be intelligible. I suggest
hucusque,[37] 'up till now'. |

39 *copia* also seems a little strange; one would expect a contrast
between the larger stock on which Catullus might draw (40),[38] and the
particular specimens that he selects for his friend. I have considered
exempla (*exēpla* is not too far from *copia*, given the appearance of the
latter word twice in the context and the common confusion of *e* and *o*
in this tradition). We now need an active verb to replace *posta est*
(which has rightly been doubted even with *copia*); I prefer *paravi* to
posivi (if *exempla* was once corrupted, rewriting was necessary to save
the sense and metre). That gives us 'quod tibi non hucusque petenti
exempla paravi'; I should also prefer *nulla* for *non*, though one must
feel some diffidence about changing four words in the line.

> non possum reticere, deae, qua me Allius in re
>   iuverit, aut quantis iuverit officiis.   (68. 41–2)

[36] The poem is probably addressed to L. Manlius Torquatus, praetor 49 (*RE* 14. 1203–
7); 'Allius' in the more public second part would then be a 'cover-name'. Hortensius
described Torquatus as ἄμουσος ἀναφρόδιτος ἀπροσδιόνυσος (Gell. 1. 5. 3); this may
be the rebuttal of some claim of his own to be a protégé of Venus and the Muses
(Gellius's comment, *subagresti . . . ingenio*, is an unlikely story about the Torquatus of the
De Finibus). Cf. also 61. 191–2 'neque te Venus neglegit'.

[37] After writing this article I found that Weber (cited in Merrill's Teubner edition) had
proposed *non ulla usque*. But it is more courteous for Catullus to mention his own failure
'so far' (*hucusque*) rather than his friend's continuing entreaties (*usque*).

[38] Cf. also 33 'nam quod scriptorum non magna est copia apud me'. This is generally
taken to refer to previous *scriptores*, but there are advantages in thinking of Catullus's
own *scripta* (thus Quinn); *copia* would then have the same reference at the beginning and
end of this group of lines (33–40).

Baehrens and Kroll defended the repetition of *iuverit*, but Riese more plausibly looked for a change of verb; Cornelissen proposed *foverit* in the second clause.[39] Without knowing of this conjecture, Ellis in his Oxford text records a possible imitation in Agius, *Epicedium Hathumodae* (AD 874), 73-4.

> vos melius nostis quanto me semper amore,
> quantis incolumis foverit officiis.

Cornelissen was not aware of this passage when he made his conjecture, and the resemblance is regarded as simply a coincidence by Traube in his text of Agius.[40] But *foverit* suits admirably the context of Catullus: after the severely objective *iuverit* the poet describes more warmly the kindnesses of his friend. Agius surely deserves further investigation.

In fact his elegy includes other parallels to Catullus 68 that are not noticed by Traube or Ellis:

Agius 57-8	quae nostrae dulcedo simul vel gloria vitae in qua sunt una perdita tanta bona?
Catull. 68. 158	a quo sunt primo †omnia[41] nata bona (bono *V*).
Agius 71-2	nam minime, veluti est dignum, nunc dicere possum quanta ego vobiscum commoda perdiderim.

Catull. 68. 21-3	tu mea tu moriens fregisti commoda, frater,
	  tecum una tota est nostra sepulta domus,
	  omnia tecum una perierunt gaudia nostra.

As the three parallels occur within twenty lines of Agius and a single poem of Catullus, they cannot be brushed aside as a coincidence, or even as commonplaces | of the genre; so Cornelissen's forgotten *foverit* should be put in the text. The abbess Hathumoda and the Epicurean 'Allius' must have cherished their friends in very different ways, but the *vox humana* survived the centuries: 'sed dicam vobis, vos porro dicite multis'.

Agius[42] was a monk at Corvey on the Weser, and his knowledge of Catullus 68 raises questions that I am unable to answer. The codex

---

[39] *Mnem.* NS 6 (1878), 307 'iteratio v. *iuverit* aliquantum displicet'.

[40] *Poetae Latini Aevi Carolini*, 3. 373.

[41] The hiatus is implausible (G. Goold, *Phoenix*, 12 (1958), 108). *tanta* in Agius might suggest 'a quo sunt primo plurima nata bona'; *plurima* (which would echo 153 'huc addent divi quam plurima') could have fallen out after *primo*. Alternatively one could try *sunt uno plurima* (cf. *una* in Agius) or *sunt primo tot mihi*.

[42] M. Manitius, *Geschichte der lat. Lit. des Mittelalters*, I (1911), 581-2; *Poet. Lat. Aev. Car.* 3. 369-88, 4. 937-43; P. Lehmann, *Corveyer Studien* (*ABAW* 30. 5; 1919), 4-9.

Thuaneus (Paris. lat. 8071), which contains poem 62 among miscel-
laneous other authors, was written in France in the ninth century. It
was copied from the manuscript now identified as Vind. lat. 277,[43]
which is known mainly for Grattius and the *Halieutica*; this was written
in the eighth or ninth century, probably in France but possibly in
Germany.[44] The latter manuscript was brought from France by San-
nazaro about 1502 (possibly 'e Turonibus'),[45] and B. L. Ullman[46] sees a
possible descent from a book of verse lent by Gregory of Tours to
Venantius Fortunatus between 573 and 576 (*Carm.* 5. 8b); he compares *Carm.* 6. 10. 6 'per hiulcatos fervor anhelat agros' with Catull.
68. 62 'aestus hiulcat agros' (interestingly from the very poem under
discussion). He mentions some fainter resemblances to Catullus in
Carolingian writers; most of these are worth nothing,[47] but in view of
the evidence from Agius one cannot disregard the similarity of Catull.
40. 5 'an ut pervenias in ora vulgi?' and Heiric, *Allocutio ad librum* 29 'et
ni proripias in ora vulgi' (*Poet. Lat. Aev. Car.* 3. 437). This passage
suggests that acquaintance with Catullus, in however limited a sense,
might have extended beyond poems 62 and 68, and Ullman believes
that the Veronensis itself came from Northern Europe.

> nec tenuem texens sublimis aranea telam
> in deserto Alli nomine opus faciat.   (68. 49–50)

Spiders spin their webs in the rafters; commentators cite Hes. *Op.*
777 ἀερσιπότητος ἀράχνης, Ov. *Am.* 1. 14. 7–8 'vel pede quod gracili
deducit aranea filum cum leve deserta sub trabe nectit opus' (note
especially *deserta*). Yet the picture in Catullus is unclear: *imagines* were
displayed in the atrium where they became black with soot (Cic. *Pis.*
1), but there seems to be no evidence that they were stored in the roof.
Fordyce talks of an abandoned monument (cf. Prop. 2. 6. 35 'velavit
aranea fanum'), but it is awkward to think in our passage of a lofty edi-
fice; the tomb of Caecilia Metella has suffered little from the ravages of
spiders. And besides encouraging too visual an interpretation, *sublimis*
is too grand[48] a word to be used naturally of the insect.

[43] H. Schenkl, *JKPh.* suppl. 24 (1898), 387–414; J. A. Richmond, *The Halieutica ascribed
to Ovid* (1962), 1–2.
[44] E. A. Lowe, *Codices Latini antiquiores*, 10 (1963), 1474.
[45] R. Sabbadini, *Scoperte* (1905), 139–40, 165–6.
[46] *Studi in onore di L. Castiglioni*, 1027–57.
[47] Agius, op. cit. 417, uses the word *femella*, which occurs in classical Latin only at
Catull. 55. 7; yet as Ullman points out, the word lies behind old French 'femelle' (whence
'female').
[48] See Brink on Hor. *AP* 165.

I propose *subtilis*. The word suits 'the spider's touch, how exquisitely fine', especially as it is etymologically connected with *tela*; the words in the line now reinforce each other in a manner familiar from Catullus 64. It is a commonplace that time works its attrition through slight but persistent agencies; cf. Lucr. 1. 326 | 'vesco sale saxa peresa', Ov. *AA* 1. 473 'ferreus adsiduo consumitur anulus usu'. This notion is found in the corresponding passage at the end of our poem (149–52): 'hoc tibi, quod potui, confectum carmine munus pro multis, Alli, redditur officiis [cf. 42 officiis], ne vestrum scabra tangat rubigine nomen haec atque illa dies atque alia atque alia'. *subtilis* would suggest something of the same idea: the spider, like rust and time, does ill by stealth.

> qualis in aerii perlucens vertice montis
> > rivus muscoso prosilit e lapide,
> qui cum de prona praeceps est valle volutus
> > per medium densi⁴⁹ transit iter populi,   60
> dulce viatori salso⁵⁰ (basso *V*) in sudore levamen
> > cum gravis exustos aestus hiulcat agros.   (68. 57–62)

perlucens normally means 'transparent', but this is not the conventional epithet of a mountain torrent (note *vertice*); Baehrens explains the word as *limpidus*, but this blurs the precision of the prefix. Ellis talks of the glimmer of the rivulet and compares διαγλαύσσειν, but *per-* cannot mean 'between' where no background is specified; the *OLD* cites Plin. *Nat.* 18. 358 'cum carbo vehementer perlucet', but that passage refers to incandescence. I suggest *praelucens*, 'shining out'; the word is used absolutely at Sen. *Cont.* 1. 6. 4 'auro puro fulgens praelucet Capitolium'. *prae-* is better suited than *per-* to the scale of landscape implied by *vertice*; Baehrens comments 'si de aquis longe splendentibus cogitandum esset, flagitaretur verbum simplex *lucens*', but he does not consider changing the compound. It may not be necessary to alter *in* to *ab*, as Catullus is mentally up the mountain and not looking at it from miles away; this is shown by the detail of *muscoso . . . lapide*.

The simile and its successor (on deliverance from storm) go primarily with what follows (the relief provided by Allius), not with what

---

⁴⁹ *densi* gives an odd impression of traffic-jams (as Haupt and Baehrens saw), and even *multi* (cf. Call. *Ep.* 28. 2) seems unsuited to this remote highway. Perhaps Catullus wrote *properi*; if the word was once corrupted to *populi*, anything might then have happened.

⁵⁰ Editors prefer the early proposal *lasso*, but the elided adjective ought to combine with *sudore* rather than with *viatori*. Baehrens's *salso* (cf. Virg. *Aen.* 2. 173–4 'salsus . . . sudor') gives a good contrast with *dulce*.

precedes (Catullus's tears); the two images are combined by earlier poets[51] in similar contexts (a good case to remember when people doubt the relevance of parallels). But the analogy extends beyond *levamen* to the whole situation: *prosilit* and *praeceps* suggest a friend bounding forward (cf. 65. 22 'dum adventu matris prosilit') and rushing to the rescue; *salso in sudore* (if Baehrens's conjecture is right) would answer to 56 *tristi imbre* (of the poet's salt tears); *gravis aestus* and *exustos* not only recall the elegists' comparison of love and heat, but correspond to the earlier description of Catullus's own burning (52 *torruerit*, 53 *arderem*, 54 *Thermopylis*). In this sequence *praelucens* has a function that *perlucens* lacks: Allius's unexpected offer flashes out like a mountain cataract with the first promise of relief. |

> hunc metuunt omnes, neque mirum: nam mala valde est
>   bestia, nec quicum bella puella cubet.
> quare aut crudelem nasorum interfice pestem,
>   aut admirari desine cur fugiant.

$$(69.\ 7\text{--}10)$$

hunc is Rufus's smell of goat. Catullus plays on the two meanings of *hircus* by regarding it as a real animal: it lives *valle sub alarum*, it is called *trux caper*, *mala bestia*, *crudelem pestem* (like some monstrous creature of legend), everybody fears it and runs from it, no pretty girl could sleep with it. *interfice* may seem to sustain the image, but so unequivocal a word is awkwardly juxtaposed with *nasorum*: the former suits only the goat, the latter only the smell. Ellis, who seems to sense the problem, points out that the verb can be applied to bread (Lucil. 1157 M) and harvests (Virg. *Georg.* 4. 330), but 'kill that smell' was surely not a Latin locution.

Perhaps *intercipe* might be considered; it primarily suggests cutting off the smell, but could also be used euphemistically of eliminating the beast (cf. Colum. 9. 3. 4 of bees 'saepe morbis intercipiuntur'). Catullus affects a concern for the public at large (7 *metuunt omnes*, 10 *fugiant*), but is actuated by sexual jealousy (cf. 1–4); there is still much to be said for the view that he is addressing Caelius Rufus.[52] He has no wish to cure his rival's alleged complaint, but only to see that he breaks off physical contact with the one *puella* who matters.

[51] Aesch. *Ag.* 900–1 κάλλιστον ἦμαρ εἰσιδεῖν ἐκ χείματος, ὁδοιπόρῳ διψῶντι πηγαῖον ῥέος; Asclepiades, *AP* 5. 169. 1–2.

[52] T. P. Wiseman, in his interesting reappraisal of these problems, argues that the malodorous and gouty Rufus cannot be identical with a dancer as accomplished as Caelius (*Cinna the Poet* (1974), 106–7). Yet ancient invective sometimes derived its appeal from its inappropriateness: why was Socrates said to accept fees for his tuition?

> aemulus iste tuus, qui vestrum exercet amorem,
>> mirifice est a te nactus utrumque malum.   (71. 3-4)

Catullus is talking about the gout and disagreeable smell of an unnamed friend's unnamed rival. 4 *a te* must be corrupt: the complaints in question are not infectious. Schoell[53] solved the problem by *apte* (*abte* might be the intermediate stage); Catullus goes on to explain why the punishment fits the crime. *mirifice* would be used with another adverb like θαυμασίως ὡς.

Line 3 is also difficult. The successful rival may be said to 'carry on' the love affair that belongs to the loser, but plural *vestrum* (which naturally includes the lady) is incompatible with this interpretation. Nor is it convincing to take *vestrum* as equivalent to *tuum*; though this very rare usage is attested in Catullus,[54] it is confusing so soon after *tuus* in a context where a woman is also involved. Because of these difficulties Kroll asked whether *exercet* might mean 'disturbs'; but in a poem about rivalry it obviously refers to a take-over.

nostrum is an early conjecture (the corrector of G); n̄r̄m and ū̄r̄m are easily confused (cf. 26. 1, 55. 22). But this does little good unless we also emend *tuus* to *meus*; the former might well have been interpolated after *nostrum* had been corrupted to *vestrum* and *apte* to *a te*. The rival is presumably Rufus, who is reviled | in similar terms in 69; as sometimes happens elsewhere, a pair of parallel poems is separated by one on a different subject. If Catullus is writing about himself, that explains why he is so virulent, and why the poem has no addressee.

> credo, sic mater, sic liber avunculus eius,
>> sic maternus avus dixerat atque avia.   (84. 5-6)

liber is hard to justify as an attributive adjective referring to a social status; *libertinus* would be expected. And though allegations of servile origin are common in invective, they are not made so circuitously; what is said about the uncle is too obscure to be an acknowledged fact and too indirect to be a malicious fiction. Catullus neither knows nor cares about the maternal relatives of Arrius, but he supposes with some confidence (*credo*) that they all spoke alike. He concentrates on the mother's line (as happens elsewhere in invective) because of its greater obscurity; it is quite wrong to quote Cicero on the conservatism of women's speech.

[53] *NJPhP* 121 (1880), 486. See now also R. A. Kaster, *Philologus*, 121 (1977), 308–12, who reports that *apte* was already conjectured in a MS.

[54] Housman, *CQ* 3 (1909), 244–8 = *Classical Papers*, 790–4, citing 39. 20, 99. 6.

The same line of argument can be used against any adjective that differentiates the uncle from the rest of the family. If he was a *gibber* or hunchback, Catullus would not have known, and the insult diverts us from the uniformity of the family in the only circumstance that matters. If he was a *Cimber* (Heinsius) or an *Umber* (Riese), it is not clear why the grandparents were not; special circumstances might exist in a particular case, but these would be unfamiliar and irrelevant. An ἀπὸ κοινοῦ construction is equally impossible: such artificialities do not suit the simplicity of a lampoon, and even the most mannered poet would not give the adjective to the second item in a sequence of four.

If this reasoning is correct, the missing word describes neither a particular characteristic of the uncle nor a general characteristic of the family. Therefore it is not an adjective at all. It cannot be a noun, pronoun, preposition, conjunction, interjection, or verb (for *dixit* would be fatuous). It must surely be an adverb; there is no artificiality now about an ἀπὸ κοινοῦ construction. Wick proposed *libere*, which makes no sense and produces an unconvincing elision. I suggest *semper*, a word natural in invective and particularly so here: the family were all alike in their misuse of aspirates, and this misuse was persistent.

> Zmyrna †canas Satrachi penitus mittetur ad undas,
> Zmyrnam cana diu saecula pervoluent.   (95. 5–6)

The unmetrical *canas* was altered to *cavas* in the fifteenth century; the conjecture has proved generally acceptable, but the parallels are less satisfactory than is supposed. The adjective can refer to engulfing waters (cf. 17. 4 'cavaque in palude | recumbat'), but such a notion is irrelevant here: Cinna's poem is not going to be thrown in. When Virgil says 'cava flumina' (*Georg.* 1. 326), he is describing hollow river-beds; but while *flumina* can include the banks, *undae* cannot. Ovid says 'qua cava de Stygiis fluxerat unda vadis' (*Ibis* 226), but that water flows from underground. Lucan says 'dexteriora petens montis declivia Thybrim unda facit Rutubamque cavum' (2. 421–2), but there the adjective suggests the channel of a mountain torrent. On the other hand, the actual appearance of the Cypriot Satrachus is irrelevant, as neither Catullus nor his readers can have known a thing about it.

canas has clearly jumped from the line below, and in such circumstances palaeographic considerations should not be given undue weight. The right adjective should support the thought rather than appeal to the eye; picturesque detail is out of place in an epigram of this kind. *brevis* might give a possible sort of sense; there would then be a contrast between the great masterpiece and the small river. I suggest rather *suas*, which goes better with *penitus*: the poem will be sent even to the exotic places from which Zmyrna herself came. Parthenius mentioned the river (*Etym. Gen.* s.v. Ἀῶος), and his influence on Cinna is established:[55] the *Zmyrna* must have described the stream. *suas* would underline the compliment; the degree of emphasis imposed by the hyperbaton is now seen to have point.

Anybody who tries to emend the text of Catullus will sometimes find that others have been there first. A few such conjectures may be worth reviving, particularly if they are in danger of disappearing from view. I give first the reading of V, but have sometimes modified it to include agreed corrections. 51. 9–10 'tenuis sub artus flamma demanat': *dimanat* Statius (*tenuis* and *sub* suit the idea of diffusion). 61. 125–7 'satis diu lusisti nucibus: lubet iam servire Talasio': punctuate after *lusisti* with Owen, *CR* 4 (1890), 312 (nuts cannot symbolize immaturity as well as fertility), and read *iuvet* with Busche, *NJPhP* 149 (1894), 395 (the *concubinus* is not in the least pleased). 63. 5 'devolsit iletas acuto sibi pondera silice': *icta* Statius. 63. 85 'ferus ipse sese adhortans rapidum incitat animo': combine Schwabe's *rabidum* (the words are virtually interchangeable) with *animum* of the Itali (*sese* goes well only with *adhortans*). 64. 108–9 'illa procul radicitus exturbata prona cadit': *exstirpata* ed. Ald. 2 of 1515 (pointed with *radic*-). 64. 237 'cum te reducem aetas prospera sistet': *lux prospera* Baehrens (he rejects his idea as too remote, but perhaps *lucx* fell out after *ducē*, and *aetas* was interpolated from 232); *lux* suggests the day of deliverance (a period of time is not wanted), and hints at the 'first beam glittering on a sail'. 64. 288–9 'namque ille tulit radicitus altas fagos': *radicibus* L. Herrmann[56] (can trees be carried *radicitus*?). 64. 308 'candida purpurea talos intinxerat ora' (*incinxerat* G): *intexerat* Scaliger (cf. 307 *complectens undique*). 66. 31 'quis te mutavit tantus deus?': *tantum* cod. det. 68. 142 'ingratum tremuli tolle parentis onus': *opus* Postgate (*ingratum* means 'disagreeable to others', cf. 137 *molesti*). 88. 7 'nam nihil est quicquam sceleris, quo prodeat ultra': *prodeat, ultra* Palmer (though his *quisquam* is | not necessary). 107. 3–4 'quare hoc est gratum nobis quoque carius auro quod te restituis, Lesbia, mi cupido': *quoque, carior* Walker (cited

[55] W. Clausen, *GRBS* 5 (1964), 190–1.
[56] *Les Deux Livres de Catulle* (1957); yet as the reading is ignored both in the apparatus and the translation, it must be counted a happy accident.

in Postgate's *Corpus*). Though I have taken the more obvious precautions, some of the other proposals in this paper may well have been anticipated (see especially on 61. 111 and 64. 395); a repertorium of conjectures on Catullus would be of great assistance.

6

Elegiacs by Gallus from Qaṣr Ibrîm

[THIS chapter contains sections IV–VIII of the *editio princeps* of the Gallus papyrus, *JRS* 69 (1979), 140–55; section IV was written in collaboration with P. J. Parsons. Section I by R. D. Anderson (ibid. 125–6) described the discovery of the papyrus in 1978 at Qaṣr Ibrîm, 150 miles south of Aswan. Section II by P. J. Parsons (ibid. 126–38) gave a description of the papyrus, a discussion of its date, and a detailed account of its format (the sections were separated after lines 1, 5, and 9 by H-shaped signs), its interpunction, its orthography, and its hand. Section III by P. J. Parsons (ibid. 138–9) gave a transcript of the papyrus with comments on the uncertain letters.]

IV. TEXT, TRANSLATION, AND COMMENTARY

	Col. i	Col. ii
1	tristia ṇequiṭ[ia . . . .]ạ Lycori tua.	[
		[
2	Fata mihi, Caesar, tum erunt mea dulcia, quom tu	. . [
3	maxima Romanae pars eri⟨s⟩ historiae	[
4	postque tuum reditum multorum templa deorum	
5	fixa legam spolieis deivitiora tueis.	
		Qui . [
6	. . . . .] . . . . . ṭaṇdem fecerunt ç[ar]mina Musae	[
7	quạe pọssem domina deicere digna mea.	
8	. . . .] . ạtur iḍẹm tibi, non ego, Vịsce	
9	. .] . . . .] . Kato, iudice te vereor.	
10	] . . . [	] .
11	] . . . [	] . Ṭyria
12		] .

(*a*) . . . . sad, Lycoris, by your misbehaviour.

(*b*) My fate will then be sweet to me, Caesar, when you are the most important part of Roman history, and when I read of many gods' temples the richer after your return for being hung with your trophies.

(*c*) At last the . . . Muses have made poems that I could utter as worthy of my mistress. . . . . the same to you, I do not, Viscus, I do not, Cato, fear . . . ., even if you are the arbiter.

(*d*) . . . Tyrian . . .

Col. i

1　　The last line of an epigram or elegy addressed to Lycoris.

ņequiṭ[*ia*: the reading is inevitable, though the traces which represent *n* are anomalous. *nequitia* is the quality of the *nequam* or good-for-nothing, and hence attributed to self-indulgent young men in comedy and Cicero. The word is not found in Catullus or Tibullus, but is applied by Propertius to Cynthia (1. 15. 38 'nec tremis admissae conscia nequitiae', 2. 5. 2 'et non ignota vivere nequitia'); its moralizing tone suits reproaches to a mistress of whom better things might have been expected. For the distribution *nequitia . . . tua*, cf. Prop. 3. 10. 24; Hor. *Carm.* 3. 15. 2; Ov. *AA* 2. 392. For similar complaints cf. Cat. 11. 22 'illius culpa', 75. 1 'tua . . . culpa'. The line confirms what is already clear from Virgil's tenth eclogue, that Gallus wrote 'subjective' love-elegy: thus F. Jacoby, *RhM* 60 (1905), 72 f., contradicted by A. Rostagni, *RFIC* 63 (1935), 253.

. . . .]*ạ*: the last letter must be a short vowel; and of short vowels only *a* suits the trace. Allowing for this, and assuming that [*IA* is correctly restored at the beginning of the gap, there remains space for some three or four letters. In principle one could look for (*a*) an epithet of Lycoris; (*b*) a noun belonging to *tristia*; (*c*) a participle belonging to *tristia*. Against (*a*) it could be said that Lesbia, Delia, Cynthia, and Corinna are never addressed with any epithet except *mea* and *nostra*, which will not fit here; and that the construction becomes top-heavy if *nequitia* depends on *tristia*, and *tristia* in turn on a noun in the line before. Under (*b*) the possibilities include *fat*]*a* (a little short; but not excluded, given the irregularities of letter-size and letter-spacing). This looks forward attractively to the next poem (see below, p. 120), though the repetition is in no way essential; for the combination with *tristia* cf. *TLL* 6. 369. 23 f. Under (*c*), *fact*]*a* would suit the space and the grammar; one might supplement the hexameter *exempli gratia* 'tempora sic nostrae perierunt grata iuventae'. If *facta* is read in the pentameter, *fata* would not suit the hexameter well, as the word's melancholy tone would anticipate too much the idea of *tristia facta*. |

Lycori: on her name see p. 117, on her history p. 126. This is the normal classical vocative for such Greek names, though Plautus and

Terence use -*is* (Neue-Wagener, *Formenlehre*, 1. 443 f.). Lycoris need
not be thought of as actually present (cf. Virg. *Ecl.* 10. 46 f., cited below,
p. 127); for this type of dramatic monologue cf. W. Abel, *Die Anrede-*
formen bei den römischen Elegikern (1930), 120; K. Quinn, *Latin Explora-*
tions (1963), 84 f.; M. Hubbard, *Propertius* (1974), 33.

tua: the word in this position need have no emphasis, but it may
derive some from a part of *meus* or *ego* in the previous hexameter; cf.
the contrasts between the first and second persons in the following
epigrams (below, p. 119).

2–5   Epigram addressed to Caesar. See *JRS* 69 (1979), pl. V. It is
suggested below (p. 125) that the poet is referring to Julius Caesar and
his anticipated Parthian triumph, not to Octavian and his triumph over
Cleopatra.

fata mea is the subject, *dulcia* the predicate; the hyperbaton, perhaps
characteristic of Gallus, throws emphasis on *mea. fata* is not here a
neutral word for 'fortune', but has a melancholy note (appropriate to
elegy). Gallus is unhappy because of Lycoris's behaviour, perhaps also
because Caesar is leaving him behind: the quatrain seems to derive
part of its meaning from its context in the book (below, p. 120).

Caesar... tu is set against *mihi... mea*. Roman poets often draw a
contrast between themselves and their grand friends, particularly at
the end of a poem (Nisbet–Hubbard on Horace, *Carm.* 2. 16. 37); for
the application of the motif to victories and triumphs cf. Virg. *Georg.*
4. 559 f. (the end of the whole work): 'haec super arvorum cultu
pecorumque canebam et super arboribus, Caesar dum magnus ad
altum fulminat Euphraten bello ...'; Tib. 1. 3. 1 f.: 'ibitis Aegaeas sine
me, Messalla, per undas, ... me tenet ignotis aegrum Phaeacia terris';
Prop. 3. 4. 21 f.: 'praeda sit haec illis quorum meruere labores; me sat
erit Sacra plaudere posse via' (see below, p. 125, for other resemblances in this poem); Hor. *Carm.* 4. 2. 45 f. (the poet adds his voice at
the triumph of Augustus). Sometimes the writer looks forward to the
day when he can enjoy and celebrate the great man's achievements:
cf. Virg. *Ecl.* 4. 53 f.: 'o mihi tum longae maneat pars ultima vitae,
spiritus et quantum sat erit tua dicere facta'; Prop. 2. 10. 19 f. (on
Augustus and Parthia): 'haec ego castra sequar: vates tua castra
canendo magnus ero: servent hunc mihi fata diem'; 3. 4. 12 f. (on the
same subject): 'ante meos obitus sit, precor, illa dies qua videam spoliis
oneratos Caesaris axis' (below, p. 125). These passages suggest the
idea 'may I see before I die', but *fata* in Gallus does not mean 'death':

this would impair a convincing contrast between present misery and future happiness, and involve the odd notion that the poet will die in the moment of reading of Caesar's triumph (for the temporal relation of these clauses see below on 4–5).

tum: 'then and then only'. On the prosody of *tum erunt* see below, p. 118. Dr Lyne suggests *tum, Caesar, erunt*, but the hiatus should not be rejected in a poet of the period.

dulcia makes a pointed contrast not only with *fata* but with 1 *tristia*; cf. Virg. *Ecl.* 3. 80–2: 'triste' . . . dulce'.

quom: on the orthography see P. J. Parsons, *JRS* 69 (1979), 132.

3 *maxima*: a true superlative: Caesar must already be 'very great'. On the orthography see Parsons, ibid.

pars: the *p* is badly damaged, and the interpunct after the word has disappeared, but the restoration is certain; cf. Prop. 1. 6. 34 'accepti pars eris imperii'; 1. 21. 4 'pars ego sum vestrae proxima militiae'; *Carm. de bello Aegyptiaco* 24 f. Baehrens (3. 5 f., ed. Garuti): 'cum causa fores tu ma[xi]ma [be]lli, pars etiam im[per]ii'; Virg. *Aen.* 2. 6 'et quorum pars magna fui'; 10. 427; Val. Max. 8. 13 ext. 4: 'Asinius etiam Pollio, non minima pars Romani stili'.

eris: an emendation; the scribe certainly wrote *erit*, by assimilation to the predicate *pars*. It is useless to suggest that *tu* is the predicate ('the greatest part of Roman history will be—you'); this gives an impossible word-order, and destroys the contrast between 'I' and 'you' that gives coherence to the quatrain, and indeed to all nine verses.

historiae refers to historiography, not to the events themselves. The word is found at this place in the pentameter five times in Propertius; cf. especially 2. 1. 16 'maxima de nihilo nascitur historia' (undercutting the serious associations of the word); 3. 4. 10 'ite et Romanae consulite historiae' (for the importance of this parallel see below, p. 125). For the collocation with *Romanae* cf. also [Virg.], *Catal.* 11. 6; Val. Max. 1. 7. 6; Mart. 14. 191. 2 'primus Romana Crispus in historia'. It was given to few to be read about in their lifetime (cf. Virg. *Ecl.* 4. 26 f. 'facta parentis iam legere'), but Eastern wars since Alexander were an obvious subject for instant historiography: thus Lucullus was celebrated by himself, Pompey by Posidonius, Antony later by Dellius. Gallus says nothing to suggest that Caesar might be his own historian.

4–5 It is not possible to regard *templa legam deivitiora* as on all fours with *fata tum erunt dulcia* (note the co-ordinating *-que*). Therefore the couplet is still under *quom*; this underlines the relationship of *legam* to *historiae* (see below), and provides a balance of *tu* . . . *tuum* . . . *tueis*.

Anaphora of *tu* | is particularly familiar from hymns (E. Norden, *Agnostos Theos* (1913), 149 f.), but is suited to panegyrics in general.

postque tuum reditum: the phrase has an official tone; for the formalities on a return from the wars cf. T. E. V. Pearce, *CQ* 20 (1970), 313 f.; S. Weinstock, *Divus Julius* (1971), 289 f. *tuum* is given emphasis by its position before *reditum*; the rhyme might seem inelegant by Ovidian standards.

fixa legam: much depends for the historical context on the exact interpretation of these words. We take *fixa* to mean 'hung' (with spoils), not 'founded'; and *legam* to mean 'I shall read', not 'survey' or 'go round'.

figere is the *vox propria* for attaching arms to a wall (*TLL* 6. 710. 53 f.; 711. 30 f.). Normally one would say 'spolia in templis figere'; 'parietem clavo figere' is also natural (where 'nail' is clearly instrumental), but an ablative of the thing fastened (*spolieis*) is more difficult. Yet the inversion can be regarded as an instance by the poetic locution found at Virg. *Aen.* 4. 506 'intenditque locum sertis' (where Servius comments 'et est hypallage, intendit serta per locum'); the phenomenon was called by Norden 'Objektsverschiebung' (on *Aen.* 6. 884 f.). For a relevant parallel cf. Val. Fl. 1. 836 f. 'galeis praefixa rotisque cui domus' (whereas Virg. *Aen.* 11. 778 has the normal 'templis praefigeret arma'). The construction is a little more difficult with *figere* than with *praefigere*, but the former use may have been influenced by the latter; thus Tib. 1. 7. 50 'tempora funde mero' may be a development of the use of *perfundere* with the ablative.[1]

Alternatively one might try to see in *fixa . . . templa* a reference to building; the foundation of a new temple (Mars Ultor) may have figured in Julius Caesar's victory programme, and the rebuilding of others in Octavian's. *figere* can be used to mean 'figendo construere' (*TLL* 6. 712. 77 f.), but the instances cited suggest literal and metaphorical stability (*moenia*), the settling of a fixed abode (*larem, sedem, domicilium*), the fastening of a cross in the ground, a pipe in the wall, or a nest in the eaves. The word could also be applied to the fixtures that marked out a *templum* or consecrated area (Fest. 146 L 'itaque templum est locus ita effatus aut ita septus ut ex una parte pateat, angulosque adfixos habeat ad terram'; 476 '(stellam) . . . quae ex lamella aerea adsimilis stellae locis inauguratis infigatur'); but if Caesar was only going to start building after his return, there was no place to

---

[1] (= n. 108) See the excellent discussion by H. Tränkle, *Die Sprachkunst des Properz und die Tradition der lateinischen Dichtersprache* (*Hermes* Einzelschriften, 15; 1960), 66 f.

put his trophies and *deivitiora* loses all point. Neither could *fixa* be used like *fulta* for the repair of temples; it is true that Propertius says 'fixa toro cubitum' (1. 3. 34) where one might expect the weaker *fulta*, but in our passage the word would need elaboration if it was to be intelligible (especially in view of the collocation with *spolieis*).

legam is naturally interpreted 'read', to balance *historiae* in the parallel clause; there is a conventional contrast between making history and simply reading about it (cf. Cic. *Man.* 28 'plura bella gessit quam ceteri legerunt'; *Fin.* 5. 52; Sall. *Jug.* 85. 13 'quae illi audire aut legere solent, eorum partem vidi, alia egomet gessi'). One could say *legere librum* but not *legere templum* (there is no analogy at Cic. *Senec.* 21 'sepulcra legens', since reading tombstones is a more regular activity than reading temples). Therefore we must understand *templa fixa legam* or more probably *templa deivitiora legam* (see below). Propertius seems to have remembered our passage at 3. 4. 16 'titulis oppida capta legam' (for other parallels in the context cf. p. 125); though he will be absent from the Parthian War, he hopes to be present at the triumph and to read of victories on the placards. But Gallus, in his disappointment at being left behind (below, p. 128), is emphasizing his isolation from Caesar's victories: he will not even be present at the triumph, but will read about it afterwards in the history-books.

Alternatively one might consider the meaning 'go round' (Virg. *Ecl.* 8. 7 'sive oram Illyrici legis aequoris'); but this nautical usage is too specialized to be natural here, as well as losing all contrast with *historiae* in the parallel clause. *legere* also has the very rare meaning 'survey' (Virg. *Aen.* 6. 754f. 'unde omnis longo ordine posset adversos legere'; Sil. 12. 569; *TLL* 7. 1. 1128. 19f.); but even here the primary notion is one of traversing (as of a general reviewing his troops), and there is no idea of 'merely looking on' to set against the making of history. The parallel from Propertius also tells against these artificial interpretations.

spolieis: for the orthography see *JRS* 69 (1979), 132. As Gallus is talking of victories, the word must be used in its proper sense of captured arms, which could be attached to temple walls. *deivitiora* seems to imply gold and silver *manubiae* in a wider sense, but these were less suitable for attaching to walls. Perhaps Gallus is suggesting that the trophies of war are a more splendid decoration than the ornaments that were in the temples already: the true riches are the battered emblems of victory. For dedications in temples cf. *RE* 3 A. 1844; for hopes of despoiling the Parthians see below, p. 125.

deivitiora: for the use in dactylic poets of the long form (as opposed to *ditiora*, etc.) cf. Lucr. 5. 1115; Ov. *Her.* 15 (16). 34; *Met.* 6. 452; *Pont.* 3. 4. 110. Ovid, but not Propertius, often has | neuter plural comparatives at this place in the pentameter (in the *Amores* alone cf. 2. 5. 50; 2. 6. 40; 2. 9. 10; 2. 17. 14; 3. 4. 10; 3. 6. 66; 3. 7. 8; 3. 7. 66).

The meaning is not 'hung more richly' (predicative adjective); *fixa* and *deivitiora* belong to different areas of discourse (you cannot say 'nail up opulently'). The word might be appositional (= πλουσιώτερα ὄντα); but if it is taken in isolation it is too short to make a fresh colon; and if it is combined with *spolieis tueis* (cf. Ov. *Met.* 2. 77 'delubraque ditia donis'), then *fixa* becomes unintelligible (even if *spolieis tueis* is taken ἀπὸ κοινοῦ with both *fixa* and *deivitiora*, it would be an unusual situation if neither *fixa* nor *deivitiora* were complete without the supporting ablative). It remains to intepret 'I shall read of temples the richer for being hung with your trophies'; this also gives *legam* a plausible construction (see note above). The word-order is admittedly very artificial, but the neoteric Gallus may have experimented with arrangements that his successors declined to follow (cf. p. 119).

The theory of an interlaced word-order is supported by *post tuum reditum*, which is most pointed if taken with *deivitiora*: the temples will be even richer than they were before (the temporal phrase derives emphasis from its position at the beginning of the couplet). It is banal by comparison to draw a contrast between a first stage, when Caesar becomes *maxima pars Romanae historiae*, and a second stage, when the temples are hung with spoils (or Gallus reads that they are). The argument ought to run 'My lot will be sweet when Caesar becomes the subject of history and I can read about his trophies'; if *legam* balances *historiae* (as suggested above), there is no sharp temporal distinction between the two clauses.

6–9   Epigram addressed to the critics, Viscus and Valerius Cato. For the occurrence of such a poem near the end of a book, see below, p. 121.

6 . . . . .] . . . . . : the traces are tenuous: see *JRS* 69 (1979), pl. VI. First, a heavy point of ink just above the upper level (the lighter trace visible to the left is mud stuck to the surface of the papyrus), then immediately spots of ink aligned vertically (so that we might be dealing with the vertical of e.g. *I* or *L*, with its hook to the left at the top). Then two points of ink at middle height; to the left of the first point, at base-level, perhaps another point (so that the two could

represent an oblique sloping down from right to left); the second point itself looks as if it might come from an oblique sloping down from left to right. Then a short horizontal at the upper level, and slightly further right a short thick horizontal at base-level. Then perhaps the upper and lower parts of a vertical. Then perhaps an oblique sloping down from left to right. To the right of this, and higher up, anomalous traces suggesting the left-hand half of an oval, the top arc extended to the right, a horizontal cross-bar half-way down. These last traces are especially difficult. The highest trace stands well above the expected upper level. One way out is to treat this as stray ink (cf. the inexplicable blots above *TA* of *tandem*), although there is a lot of it. Another is to take it as part of a superscript letter (an addition which could not, like the *T* in 4 *post*, be squeezed into the line).

The sense suggests some possible patterns. (i) An epithet for *carmina*. Any such epithet will end in a short *a*; therefore something else would have to stand between it and *tandem*. Patterns: *dulcia iam*, *blanda mihi*. (ii) An epithet for *Musae*. Any such epithet will end in *-ae* or *-es*. Patterns: *Castaliae, Aonides*; *haec Latiae, haec dulces*, etc. (iii) A series of short words like *en mihi iam*.

(i) is less plausible in sense; an epithet is unnecessary and perhaps undesirable when *quae possem* characterizes the poems. Nor have we found a reading which suits this pattern. *mihi* was not written. *iam* was probably not written (*A* would be unusually wide, *M* unusually narrow; it would be necessary to ignore the high horizontal trace to the right of the putative *A*, and the whole group of traces to the upper right of the putative *M*).

(ii) We may begin by looking for *-ae* or *-es* in the traces before *tandem*. (*a*) If the last letter was *S*, the apparent remains of an oblique (sloping down from left to right) before it must be ignored; and also the trace high up to the right of it. This is not satisfactory. (*b*) If the last letter was *E*, the high trace to the right must again be ignored; the oblique traces to the left must either be ignored, or taken as the right side of *A*; but in that case the letters *AE* are written so close that they join, which happens nowhere else in this manuscript. (*c*) if the last letter was *A* (represented by its right side), the whole group of traces to its right might be taken as a suprascript *e*. To this there is an immediate objection, the shape Є; this is quite different from the scribe's tall narrow *E*; it might be conceivable in the Latin cursive of the period (Mallon, *Pal. rom.* pl. ii); but the prolongation of the upper curve more suggests the Greek epsilon. Even if this objection is discounted, more difficulties remain. Before *A* there seem to be traces of an upright (i.e. *I* or a letter with a vertical right side); the smudge to the right of its foot could then be taken as the left foot of *A*. But, even allowing for a small vertical crease in the papyrus, the feet of *A* and the preceding letter would be unexpectedly close to one another. If again this objection is discounted,] . *atia*ᵉ might be considered; this naturally points to *Latiae* (Germ. *Arat.* 15; Lucan 9. 983, etc.); but the first trace is too close to be the top of *L*; and if it were, the preceding space (even allowing for an enlarged and spaced initial on the scale of line 2) is substantially too long for *haec.* |

(iii) Mr P. G. McC. Brown suggests *haec mih*]*i̢ vi̢x*. His *vix* looks possible, except that the highest traces at the end must be taken as stray ink. If *haec mih*]*i̢* is too long, we might consider *en mih*]*i̢*.

tandem: a natural expression of relief at the completion of a book; it gives little clue to the time taken to compose it (below, p. 128).

fecerunt: cf. Virg. *Ecl.* 3. 86 'Pollio et ipse facit nova carmina'; 7. 23; Prop. 2. 8. 11; 2. 34. 79; *TLL* 6. 91. 9f. By the old belief the poet utters what the Muses put in his head (Hom. *Il.* 2. 485 f., etc.). *fecerunt* is unconventional in such a context, and to a Roman reader would inevitably suggest ποιητής (not used of poets in early Greek); the Muses of Gallus provided craftsmanship as well as inspiration.

Musae: Gallus described elsewhere his initiation by the Muses (below, p. 123), and Lycoris derived her name from Parnassus (p. 117).

7 *possem*: for the imperfect subjunctive after a true perfect see Kühner–Stegmann, 2. 179. Gallus is not implying that his hope is now inapplicable.

domina: the word is used of an *amica* by Lucilius 730 M, and therefore must have had popular currency as early as the second century. Though the sense becomes common in Augustan poetry (Nisbet–Hubbard on Hor. *Carm.* 1. 33. 14; 2. 12. 13), its ascription to Catullus rests on a mistake (see L. P. Wilkinson, *CR* NS 20 (1970), 290); it would be intriguing if the masterful Gallus introduced the colloquialism to elegy with reference to a freedwoman. For *domina . . . mea* with this distribution in the pentameter, cf. Prop. 1. 4. 2; 3. 5. 2.

deicere digna: not 'call worthy' (which limits the poet's role too much), but 'utter as worthy' (which makes a pointed contrast with *fecerunt*); for *dicere* of poetry cf. Virg. *Ecl.* 6. 5 'deductum dicere carmen'; 10. 3 (below, p. 122); Prop. 1. 9. 9; *TLL* 5. 1. 977. 65f. For poems 'worthy of the recipient' cf. Lucr. 3. 420 'digna tua pergam disponere carmina vita' (*cura* Lachmann, *mente* Müller); Virg. *Ecl.* 4. 3;

Culex 10 'ut tibi digna tuo poliantur carmina sensu'. For the collocation of words cf. Virg. *Ecl.* 9. 35 f. 'nam neque adhuc Vario videor nec dicere Cinna digna' (pointed out by Professor J. Van Sickle).

8] *.atur*: of *t* the characteristic top and stem; before it, part of an oblique sloping down from left to right, *A* or *M*, *A* in context more likely (and a trace perhaps remains of its left foot, moved downwards and leftwards by the dislocation of the papyrus; but this may be dirt adhering to the surface); before this, indeterminate traces of ink or dirt; before that the papyrus is stripped.

idem: of *D* the right side is partly lost, partly covered by a crack in the papyrus (apparently not *T*; the left-ward projection of the cross-bar from the upright would be short, even in comparison with *T* of *tibi*; and the right-ward part does seem to begin a curve down); of *E* only fragments remain, all consistent with *E* except the short oblique, descending from left to right, at the upper level, which gives the appearance of a triangular peak (suited only to *O*); but this oblique, under the microscope, shows a different texture and may be taken as mud adhering to the surface.

The reconstruction of the broken word depends on the structure of the couplet as a whole. Two things seem certain (*a*) The clause or sentence ends after, not before, *tibi*. For (i) the emphatic *non ego* should begin its clause; (ii) when a hexameter ends with two disyllables, these are commonly preceded by a monosyllable, and that monosyllable by a pause at the bucolic diaeresis (J. Soubiran, *Pallas*, 8 (1959), 37 f.). (*b*) The beginning of 9 must have contained a negative which, by taking up *non*, linked the vocatives *Kato* and *Visce*.

As to (*a*), cf. Virg. *Ecl.* 7. 7 'atque ego Daphnin'; 8. 102 'his ego Daph-nin'; and especially 2. 25 f. (Corydon to Alexis): 'nuper me in litore vidi, cum placidum ventis staret mare. non ego Daphnin iudice te metuam, si numquam fallit imago'. In view of *non ego*, *iudice te* and *metuam*, one poet seems to have influenced the other; as the rhythm is characteristic of the *Eclogues*, and is found three times in conjunction with the name of Daphnis, the priority should perhaps be given to Virgil, in which case we may have new evidence for the dating of the second eclogue.[2]

---

[2] The second eclogue is assigned to 45 by C. G. Hardie, in *The Ancient Historian and his Materials* (*Essays in honour of C. E. Stevens*), ed. B. Levick (1975), 111: Virgil says to Pollio 'accipe iussis carmina coepta tuis' (*Ecl.* 8. 11 f.), and Pollio was absent from Italy during the relevant years except for the latter part of 45. Mr J. C. Bramble suggests that *Ecl.* 2. 24 'Amphion Dircaeus in Actaeo Aracyntho' may be derived from Gallus; he points not just to the neoteric rhythms but to Prop. 3. 15. 39 f., where Dirce, Amphion, and Aracyn-thus are mentioned in the same context.

In 8–9 Gallus emphatically denies that he has anything to fear from
the critics; one suspects that 8 began with a conditional clause, in
which he expressed the prerequisite for this critical acclaim. *idem*
cannot refer to the plural *carmina*, but it could take up the idea that the
poems are worthy of Lycoris. Thus one pattern of restoration would be
'quodsi iam videatur idem tibi' ('if the critics agree that the poems are
worthy of Lycoris'); this supplement suits the space (given the other
EI spellings, *quodsei* might be expected; this looks a little long, but
cannot be ruled out). More pointed would be 'quae si iam testatur (or
confiteatur) idem tibi' ('if only Lycoris agrees that the poems | are
worthy of her, I fear nothing from the critics'). For a similar movement
of thought, cf. Mart. 3. 2. 12 (to his book): 'illo vindice,[3] nec Probum
timeto'; Auson. *Ecl.* 1. 17 f. (p. 86 Peiper): 'ignoscenda teget, probata
tradet: post hunc iudicium timete nullum' (the end of a dedication-
poem); Naucellius, *Epigr. Bob.* 57. 1 f. (see W. Speyer, *Naucellius u. sein
Kreis* (Zetemata, 21, 1959), 77 f.): 'si Pergamenis digna canimus paginis,
teque adprobante, columen urbis, Attice, nihil Latinos demoror librar-
ios quin inter orsa vetera nostra sint quoque, victura in aevum et in
nepotum posteros'; Sidon. *Carm.* 24. 15 (an envoi): 'hic si te probat,
omnibus placebis'. For the mistress as the only critic who matters cf.
Prop. 2. 13. 14 'domina iudice tutus ero'; the context is full of Gallan
echoes (below, p. 122). Yet it may be argued that though Gallus can
address both Lycoris and the critics, Lycoris does not so naturally
address the critics; from this point of view the first supplement is
perhaps preferable.

Visce: the letter after *V* was narrow; nothing survives except the top,
a very short horizontal tilted down to the right; *E* and *I* are the only
possibilities. *vesce* imperative is out of court (the active form is quoted
first from Tertullian). *vesce* vocative or (unattested) adverb could not
be ruled out, if the context backed them. But *Visce* fits so well among
the critics that we do not hesitate to print this reading.

The Visci (*RE* s.v. 'Vibius', 68) are mentioned as literary critics by
Horace, *Serm.* 1. 10. 81 f. (about 35 BC): 'Plotius et Varius, Maecenas
Vergiliusque Valgius et probet haec Octavius optimus atque Fuscus et
haec utinam Viscorum laudet uterque'. Ps.-Acro comments ad loc.:
'Visci duo fratres fuerunt, optimi poetae (perhaps not true), alii criticos
dicunt ... pater eorum Vibius Viscus, quamvis et divitiis et amicitia
Augusti usus esset, tamen in equestri ordine perduravit, cum filios suos

---

[3] There is no reason to emend to *iudice* in view of 2 'festina tibi vindicem probare'.

senatores fecisset'. If this information is accurate, it might suit best a date of 35–30; if Viscus was already a critic in 45, his father is likely to have been born by 100, in which case he was rather an elderly *amicus* of Octavian's (though ancient commentators talk freely of 'Augustus' before 27 BC, this does not wholly remove the awkwardness).

The family may have come from Cisalpina; an inscription of 8 BC (*CIL* 5. 4201) records a Vibius Viscus at Brixia, perhaps also the home town of Cinna. Horace includes the brothers among the critics of whom he approves, and mentions Viscus (Thurinus) elsewhere along with the old-fashioned Varius (*Serm.* 1. 9. 22; 2. 8. 20). But there are dangers in drawing the party lines too sharply; Virgil had a foot in both the neoteric and the classicizing camps, and even Gallus cultivated both Pollio and Cicero (below, n. 42).

9 ..] . . . . | . : see *JRS* 69 (1979), pl. VI: the first five traces are hopelessly damaged; the sixth is apparently a short oblique, descending from left to right, a little above base-level (i.e. an interpunct; or from the right side of *A*, *K*, *M*, *R*, *X*); then what looks like a damaged *L*, the base sloping down rather sharply, followed by an interpunct or part of a vertical (too close to be *LI*), the whole might be *V* (the surface is damaged enough to explain the ink missing at the top and foot of the right side); then apparently *P* (*D* could also be considered, since surface-damage would easily explain the gap at the bottom right; but the angle of slope at the top would be noticeably more acute than in any other example of the letter); then apparently *L*, with the back-hook at the top damaged; then three points of ink vertically aligned, and further right a short oblique, descending from left to right, a little above base-level (if this is an interpunct—and it is in shape and placing just like the interpunct after *Kato*—then the traces before must belong to a very narrow letter, i.e. *E* or *I*; if it is not—in which case the interpunct must have stood higher up, in an area where the surface is now damaged—all the traces might combine in *A*; although it would be unusually narrow, even when the vertical crease which bisects it is smoothed out).

The sense gives limited guidance: *vereor* may have an infinitive or an object or no complement at all. Patterns: (i) 'non certare, Kato'; (ii) (*a*) 'non ego damna, Kato' (penalty), (*b*) 'non Cinnana (non Corydona, non Colophona), Kato' (the works or a work of a rival poet, or the poet himself; if the latter, he must be named indirectly, say by reference to his birthplace, since no Roman poet will fit the metre here, and no Greek poet we can think of will fit into the three or four syllables available); (iii) 'non, venerande Kato'.

Given the palaeographic data, (i) can be excluded; *-are, -ere,* and *-ire* are all impossible. Under (ii) we could consider *-upla* or possibly *-udla* (neuter accusative plural). Gradenwitz lists no words in *-udlus* (*-um*); under *-uplus* (*-um*) only the group of numerical adjectives. Of these only *quad]rupla* suits the first significant trace; and in fact *non quad]rupla* would fit the space available at the line-beginning. This reading, then, would be acceptable palaeographically (except for the doubt about the width of the final *A*), grammatically, and metrically (if *DR* and *PL* can both make position in a word so prosaic). Under (iii) we could try *non, quad]ruple Kato*; the final *-e* is perhaps more satisfactory palaeographically than *-a*. But what could these supplements possibly mean?

quadrupla ought to refer to 'fourfold penalties'; for this form of exemplary damages see | J. M. Kelly, *Roman Litigation* (1966), 153 f. For the unusual plural (perhaps justified by the plurality of critics) one may compare from late Latin *centupla* and *dupla* (*TLL* 3. 830. 69; 5. 1. 2283. 15 f.). The technicality is more appropriate to epigram than elegy, but Gallus in some respects seems to have been nearer Catullus than Propertius; a book may be begun (or presumably ended) by a slighter piece in a lower style (A. Cameron, *CQ*, NS 20 (1970), 119 f.), and a whimsical facetiousness suits such contexts (cf. the choliambic proem to Persius). Legal puns are common in Latin poetry, and are perhaps particularly appropriate to a public man like Gallus; for plays on the legal and literary senses of *iudex* (much more natural than with κριτής) cf. Sidon. *Carm.* 22. 5 'quandoquidem Baccho meo iudicium decemvirale passuro tempestivius quam convenit tribunal erigitur'; 23. 266 f. 'tamquam si Arcitenens novemque Musae propter pulpita iudices sederent'.

The difficulty is to see how 'fourfold penalties' can be transferred to a literary context. It may be worth observing that an action for *quadruplum* was established by the praetor's edict for *furtum manifestum* (Gaius, *Inst.* 3. 189); de Zulueta comments 'in cases (easily conceivable) where the prisoner's guilt was seriously disputed one' does not see why the magistrate should not have referred the question to a *iudex*'. Gallus would then be playing on *furtum* in the sense of plagiarism (a preoccupation of critics in Virgil's day); cf. Mart. 1. 53. 3 'quae tua traducit manifesto carmina furto' . . .; 11 f. 'indice non opus est nostris nec iudice libris: stat contra dicitque tibi tua pagina "fur es"'. Gallus does not fear penalties for plagiarism once it is agreed that the Muses have inspired him (or if the emphasis is put on the relative clause, because what was adequate for Lycoris could not have been said before to any other woman); it would add piquancy to the allusion if he is here contriving a *furtum* from Virgil's second eclogue (see above, 8 n.). Yet when all is said and done, the reference remains obscure; it is not as if fourfold penalties were imposed on only one possible occasion.

quadruple Kato is even more difficult. One might imagine that somebody called Cato Uticensis 'Bicato' (on the lines of *Sesculixes*) to indicate that he was twice as bad as the Censor; Gallus then calls Valerius Cato 'fourfold Cato' to suggest that he is even more severe (cf. Sidon. *Carm.* 9. 338f. 'sed nec turgida contumeliosi lectoris nimium verebor ora, si tamquam gravior severiorque nostrae Terpsichores iocum refutans rugato Cato tertius labello narem rhinoceroticam minetur'). But even if *quadruple* can be regarded as the equivalent of *quadruplex* (cf. Suet. *Tib.* 34 'consuerat quadriplam strenam et de manu reddere'), it is difficult to think of any satisfactory supplement in the previous line (on this hypothesis presumably a *ne* clause).

Mr G. O. Hutchinson (Balliol College, Oxford) has suggested a quite different, and most ingenious, line of attack: to write *plakato = placato*. We find two difficulties here. (i) The spelling *-ka-* is in itself perfectly possible (examples are collected by Dessau, *ILS* 3. 2. 823). But if the discrepancy between *ka* here and *ca* in i. 6 is significant, then it is most likely to signify that *ka* begins a proper name or one of a limited number of common nouns (*JRS* 69 (1979), n. 77). On the other hand, the discrepancy may be simple inconsistency, from which no argument can be drawn. (ii) Much more serious is the difficulty of reconstructing the sentence round *plakato*. *Plakato iudice te* cannot be taken together; the word-order would be impossible. Theoretically, one might consider a pattern like 'sei Caesar testatur idem tibi, non ego, Visce, | Caesare plakato iudice, te vereor'. But it is highly artificial to separate *te* from *iudice* (especially in view of Virg. *Ecl.* 2. 27), *plakato* does not well suit the arbitrating function of the *iudex*, and it is difficult to find an opening name to fill the gap (*Caesare* looks too short; and although the trace immediately before *PLA* might well represent an interpunct, the trace before that slopes down too much to suggest the base of *E*).

Since none of these approaches gives a satisfactory solution, there is a strong possibility that the traces should be read in some other way. One might cut the knot by reading *L* instead of *P* (in that case the top stroke must be stray ink or mud, though it looks solid enough under the microscope).] . *VLLE* · leads nowhere. But] . *VLLA* [·] would allow e.g. *non vetera*] *ulla* or *non Graeca*] *ulla* (*non scripta*] *ulla* looks too long, besides being very tame). Ideally one would like a reference to a rival poetry-book: this would suit the discriminating function of the critic (see below on *iudice*), and especially the parallel at Virg. *Ecl.* 2. 26 f. 'non ego Daphnin iudice te metuam'. Thus *Serpulla* or 'Thyme-plants' could be a humorous allusion to the homeliness of the *Bucolics* (2. 11 'alia serpyllumque herbas contundit olentis'), or even the title of Virgil's earliest collection, indicating rusticity, fragrance, *humilitas*, and inconsequentiality (from *serpere*); the spelling is attested in manu-scripts of Cato, the plural at Virg. *Georg.* 4. 31. This particular supple-ment looks at least a letter too short, and the *P* does not suit the meagre traces; but it has been left on the record as a possible guide to further speculation.

In view of all the difficulties, we have further considered the possibil-ity that the penultimate letter is not *L* but *I* or *T*. The length of the base-stroke tells strongly against this, and in any case this approach has suggested no satisfactory supplement.

Kato: P. Valerius Cato, the poet and critic (*RE*, 'Valerius' 117, Schanz–Hosius, 1⁴. 287 f.). He came from Gaul, probably Cisalpina (Suet. *Gramm.* 11), like so many writers of the period. He | was still a *pupillus* (not more than 14) in the *Sullanum tempus* (Suet. ibid.), i.e. he was born not earlier than 96 BC; as he is said to have lived to an impoverished old age (Bibaculus, fr. 1. 8, 'ad summam ... senectam'), his mention here does little to date the epigram. He himself wrote learned poems called *Dictynna* and *Lydia*, which were admired by such neoterics as Cinna (fr. 14) and Ticidas (fr. 2). The epigrams of Bibacu-lus seem bantering rather than hostile (fr. 1. 1 'mei Catonis'). One of these, which belongs to the time of his impoverishment, is addressed to a Gallus (fr. 2. 1 f. 'Catonis modo, Galle, Tusculanum tota creditor urbe venditabat'), and the new papyrus gives some support to the idea that this is the poet (*RE* 4. 1345); perhaps *summam senectam* in the parallel epigram is humorous exaggeration.

Cato had a great influence on aspiring poets; cf. Suet. loc. cit. 'docuit multos et nobiles, visusque est peridoneus praeceptor, maxime ad poeticam tendentibus, ut quidem apparere vel his versiculis potest: "Cato grammaticus, Latina Siren, qui solus legit ac facit poetas"' (Bibaculus?, fr. 17). Cato perhaps 'made poets' not by coaching un-naturally precocious schoolboys (as Suetonius interprets), but by his influence on what was written and read (a Siren is like a Muse); *legit* in the sense of 'chooses' suits the discrimination of the critic, and this

view is supported by the new papyrus (cf. below on 9 *iudice*). Such
activity was characteristic of *grammatici* (cf. Hor. *Epist.* 1. 19. 40);
Caecilius Epirota, who was befriended by Gallus, actually added Virgil
to the curriculum (Suet. *Gramm.* 16, citing Dom. Mars. fr. 3 'Epirota,
tenellorum nutricula vatum'). Even in his edition of Lucilius, Cato
could not resist making improvements (cf. the badly fitting lines
prefixed in some MSS to Hor. *Serm.* 1. 10 'Lucili quam sis mendosus
teste Catone, defensore tuo, pervincam qui male factos emendare
parat versus');[4] it is a curious coincidence that Viscus appears later in
the same satire (8 n.), but perhaps an interpolator has fastened on
Horace another piece of criticism from the same period. Valerius Cato
used to be regarded as the moving spirit behind the whole neoteric
movement; though scholars now show greater caution,[5] the new
papyrus suggests that this reaction should not be carried too far.

  iudice: a literary critic or κριτής, who as in Alexandria might also be
a grammarian; cf. *TLL* 7. 2. 602. 53 f. (and for *iudicium*, ibid. 615. 76 f.).
Such a person might read poems for his friends, suggest improvements, and give moral support; cf. Hor. *Serm.* 1. 10. 81 f. (cited above
on 8 *Visce*), *Epist.* 1. 4. 1 'Albi, nostrorum sermonum candide iudex',
Ars P. 438 f. on Quintilius (with Brink's note); Ov. *Pont.* 2. 4. 13 f. But he
also had the more independent function of setting up standards,
making comparisons (for σύγκρισις in criticism cf. Ar. *Ran.*; Hor.
Carm. 2. 13. 30 f., with A. La Penna, *Maia*, 24 (1972), 208 f.), and form-
ing a canon of classics (ἐγκρίνειν); cf. above, 8 n.; Furius Bibaculus(?) fr.
17 (cited above on 9 *Kato*); Hor. *Carm.* 1. 1. 35 'quodsi me lyricis
vatibus inseres' (the end of the programmatic poem); Auson. *Ludus
Septem Sapientum* 3 f. (p. 169 Peiper): 'aequanimus fiam te iudice, sive
legenda sive tegenda putes carmina quae dedimus'; Claud. 6. 18; Sidon.
Carm. 3. 7 f., 8. 12 f. (for further parallels see W. Speyer, op. cit. [8 n.],
80 f.). The shepherds' songs of the *Eclogues* with their competitive-
ness and their umpires reflect the rivalries of real poets; for the use of
iudice cf. 4. 58: 'Pan etiam Arcadia mecum si iudice certet'. This
parallel suggests that Gallus is regarding Viscus and Cato as potentially hostile (even if only as a joke); Servius sees this nuance at *Ecl.*
2. 27 (cited on 8), where he comments '*te* autem *iudice* ac si diceret

---

  [4] The lines are assigned to a first edition by G. L. Hendrickson, *CPh.* 11 (1916), 249 f.;
12 (1917), 77 f.; their authenticity is rejected by E. Fraenkel, *Hermes*, 68 (1933), 392 f. =
Kleine Beiträge, 2 (1964), 199 f.
  [5] R. P. Robinson, *TAPA* 54 (1923), 98 f.; N. B. Crowther, *CPh.* 66 (1971), 108 f.; T. P.
Wiseman, *Cinna the Poet* (1974), 53.

qui meam respuis pulchritudinem"'. For the discriminating function of critics see further M. Puelma Piwonka, *Lucilius und Kallimachos* (1949), 126 f.; R. Pfeiffer, *History of Classical Scholarship from the Beginnings to the End of the Hellenistic Age* (1968), 203 f.

vereor: the verb well suits *verecundia* for rival poems, but it could also be used (like *timeo*) of a punishment.

11   *Tyria*: not *Syria*, it seems; the stem of the first letter is straight, and remains of the cross-bar can be seen projecting to the top left of it. Before that, a high interpunct, and an oblique foot suited to *A*, *R*, etc. *Tyrius* is common in the elegists (though never at the end of the pentameter), mostly of purple-dyed fabrics; it could qualify e.g. *concha* (Prop. 4. 5. 22), *vestis* (cf. Prop. 3. 14. 27, Tib. 1. 7. 47), *palla* (Tib. 3. 8. 11). The context is totally obscure, but it might have dealt with triumphs (real or metaphorical) rather than with the finery of Lycoris: cf. Virg. *Georg.* 3. 17 (of the poet-*triumphator*): 'Tyrio conspectus in ostro'.

12   After this line, a lacuna of unknown length. |

Col. ii

1–4 Line 3 certainly was a hexameter, so that 4 must be a pentameter. Presumably 1–2 contained another couplet; although, since nothing survives, there could in principle have been (say) a heading in two lines, followed by the single distich 3–4.

5 *qui . [*: the possibilities include *quiḍ* and *quiṇ*.

V. THE POET

The author was Cornelius Gallus, as is opportunely shown in the first line by the vocative *Lycori*. His famous love-elegies were addressed to Lycoris, as is already clear from Virgil's tenth eclogue, and the names are regularly linked by Augustan and later poets.[6] Servius says that she was the courtesan Cytheris, the freedwoman of Volumnius (*Ecl.* 10. 1); by the usual principle the pseudonym was metrically equivalent.[7] Lycoreia was a place on Parnassus and Lycoreus a cult-title of Apollo,

---

[6] Prop. 2. 34. 91; Ov. *Am.* 1. 15. 30, *AA* 3. 537, *Trist.* 2. 445; Mart. 8. 73. 6. See Schanz–Hosius, 2⁴, 171; *RE* 12. 218.

[7] Established by Bentley on Hor. *Carm.* 2. 12. 13; cf. Lesbia and Clodia, Perilla and Metella, Delia and Plania, Cynthia and Hostia (Apul. *Apol.* 10).

notably in his poetical aspects.[8] Therefore 'Lycoris' suggests that the lady was a devotee not just of Aphrodite of Cythera but of Apollo and learned poetry; perhaps she was the poet's inspiration no less than the Muses.[9] Therefore the name was invented by Gallus himself, who is known to have shown an interest in Apollo and Helicon;[10] Propertius and Tibullus were to use cult-titles of the same god when they called their mistresses 'Cynthia'[11] and 'Delia' (not girls' names in the ancient world). Later instances of 'Lycoris' are obviously derived from Gallus himself.[12]

It might be objected that another poet could have addressed Lycoris, but a rival lover would not have used the name created and made famous by Gallus. Nor is it natural to suggest a rhetorical apostrophe by a third party ('and you, Lycoris, brought sorrows to Gallus by your immorality'); the line in question precedes two personal epigrams (for the unity of structure see p. 120), and is surely more than an illustrative *exemplum*. Gallus could reproach his mistress for her *nequitia*, but this was less appropriate for others in the days of his power, while in the years immediately after his death nobody would wish to mention his name very much (below, p. 130). The subject-matter amply supports the authorship (war, the Muses, a cultivated and capricious mistress), and the style also suits (see below). *Neget quis carmina Gallo?*

VI. METRE AND STYLE

The metre suits a poet writing between Catullus and Propertius. 2 *tum erunt* gives a 'prosodic hiatus' of a type hitherto unparalleled in elegy; for similar instances after -*m* in hexameter poets cf. Lucr. 2. 681 'cum odore', 3. 394 'quam in his', 3. 1082 'dum abest', 6. 276 'cum eo', Hor.

---

[8] *RE* 13. 2382f.; Call. *H. Ap.* 18f.: ὅτε κλείουσιν ἀοιδοὶ ἢ κίθαριν ἢ τόξα, Λυκωρέος ἔντεα Φοίβου (with F. Williams's note); Euphorion fr. 80. 3 (a poet notoriously imitated by Gallus).

[9] Cf. Prop. 2. 1. 3f. (programmatic): 'non haec Calliope, non haec mihi cantat Apollo; ingenium nobis ipsa puella facit' with W. Stroh, *Die römische Liebeselegie als werbende Dichtung* (1971), 55f.; Mart. 8. 73. 6 'ingenium Galli pulchra Lycoris erat' (the motif may be derived from Gallus himself).

[10] Virg. *Ecl.* 6. 64f. (cited p. 123). Cf. also *Ecl.* 10. 11f. 'nam neque Parnasi vobis iuga, nam neque Pindi ulla moram fecere neque Aonie Aganippe'; this would have an extra point if Gallus had mentioned Parnassus as well as Helicon.

[11] The cult-title suggested especially the learned poetry of Callimachus; cf. W. Clausen, *AJP* 97 (1976), 245f. and 98 (1977), 362.

[12] Hor. *Carm.* 1. 33. 5; Mart. 1. 72. 6; 102. 1; 3. 39. 2; 4. 24. 1; 62. 1; 6. 40. 1; 7. 13. 2; Maxim. *Eleg.* 2. 1.

Serm. 2. 2. 28 'num adest', J. Soubiran, *L'élision dans la poésie latine* (Études et commentaires, 63; 1966), 374. Quadrisyllabic pentameter-endings like 4 *historiae* are particularly abundant in the first book of Propertius; trisyllabic endings like 3 *vereor* and 11 *Tyria* occur about 50 times in Catullus and over 30 times in Prop. 1 (R. Atkinson, *Hermathena*, 1 (1874), 276f.). No problems are presented by hexameter-endings such as 2 *quom tu* (cf. Prop. 2. 18. 19, 2. 33. 23) or 8 *non ego, Visce* (cf. note ad loc.). The repeated central molossi (4 *multorum*, 6 *fecerunt*) give a heavy and slightly old-fashioned effect.

The style also fits the personality of Gallus and his time of writing. The poet's | vocabulary has an impressive simplicity, suitable to a forth-right man of action (note especially 6f.); he does not avoid prosaic and semi-technical words (3 *historiae*, 4 *reditum*, 9 *iudice*, possibly even *quadrupla*). Among archaic features one may mention (in addition to the metrical oddities) the alliteration of 7 *domina deicere digna*. These short poems may have been less exquisite than the elegies proper, but they are more elaborate than the epigrams of Catullus. Gallus has a taste for antithesis (note 1 *tristia . . . 2 dulcia*, as well as the repeated contrasts between the first and second persons); this was already exemplified in the one previously existing fragment (1 Morel 'uno tellures dividit amne duas'). In four out of five pentameters the two halves end with a rhyming noun and adjective (for the same arrangement without rhyme cf. 'tellures . . . duas' cited above); this pattern,[13] already well attested in Catullus, is particularly common in the first two books of Propertius (cf. notably 1. 1 and 2. 34), and may have been developed by Gallus himself under the influence of Hellenistic poets (cf. Call. *H.* 5; Hermesianax, fr. 7 Powell).[14] For other greater or lesser artificialities of word-order cf. 2 *mea*, 4–5 *post tuum reditum . . . deivitiora* (this one seems contorted to the point of obscurity), and 9 (where there may be an ἀπὸ κοινοῦ accusative in the second of two parallel clauses). This combination of austere diction and involuted arrangement may help to explain Quintilian's judgement, 'durior Gallus' (*Inst.* 10. 1. 93).

[13] For such hyperbaton in pentameters and hexameters see B. O. Foster, *TAPA* 40 (1909), 32f. (Propertius); M. Platnauer, *Latin Elegiac Verse* (1951), 49; H. Patzer, *MH* 12 (1955), 77f.; C. Conrad, *HSCP* 19 (1965), 195f.; J. B. Van Sickle, *TAPA* 99 (1968), 487f. (Catullus 65); B. Wohl, *TAPA* 104 (1974), 385f. (Tibullus).

[14] O. Skutsch had already suggested that the sandwiched word-order of 'raucae, tua cura, palumbes' originated with Gallus (*RhM* 99 (1956), 198f.).

VII. THE LITERARY FRAMEWORK

The papyrus contains (*a*) one pentameter on the *nequitia* of Lycoris; (*b*) two elegiac couplets on Caesar and his trophies; (*c*) two couplets on the merits of the poet's *carmina* in relation to Lycoris and the critics; (*d*) a lost poem of unknown length of which only one word survives; (*e* and *f*) traces in the second column of six lines, of which the last two belong to a new poem. After each of (*a*), (*b*), (*c*) and (*e*) there is a significant gap with a sign to mark the division (*JRS* 69 (1979), 129). It is surprising to find several consecutive epigrams in a book of elegies; even if the surviving collection of Catullus is due to the poet, it has none of the unity imposed by line 6 of the papyrus, 'fecerunt carmina Musae'. In the Augustan age Macer wrote a book of quatrains (Quint. *Inst.* 6. 3. 96 'ut Ovidius ex tetrastichon Macri carmine librum in malos poetas composuerit'), as did Ausonius in his *Tetrasticha de Caesaribus* (cf. also the *Dittochaeon* in hexameters attributed to Prudentius), but these were self-contained works. A closer though still imperfect analogy is the first book of Propertius, which ends with two ten-line poems of an autobiographical character.

It is noteworthy that the epigrams in the papyrus have thematic connections. The last part of (*a*) apparently commented on the poet's sad lot (*tristia*); this is picked up in (*b*) by *fata… dulcia*. (*b*) seems very bald unless it is seen in a wider context: it should be stated explicitly somewhere that Gallus is not joining Caesar's campaign. Lycoris is mentioned with disapproval in (*a*) and admiration in (*c*): the discrepancy seems piquant rather than awkward. Above all there is a persistent antithesis between the first and second persons, which is applied in (*a*) to Lycoris, in (*b*) to Caesar, in (*c*) to the critics. This contrast is underlined by accumulation (2 *mihi… mea*), anaphora (2–5 *tu, tuum, tueis*), hyperbaton (2 *fata… mea*, 4 f. *postque tuum reditum… deivitiora*), by the emphatic use of pronouns (2 *tu*, 8 *ego*), by the placing of the pronoun or pronominal adjective at the end of the line (four times out of nine) or of the adjective before the noun (4 *tuum reditum*). The surviving epigrams seem to have been composed as a sequence[15] dealing in turn with the ruling passions and dominating personalities of the poet's life.

[15] The fragments would seem more effective if they could be regarded as sections of one complex poem (the connections in elegy are often loose, and Propertius sometimes divides into quatrains), but the layout of the book tells against such a hypothesis (*JRS* 69 (1979), 129 f.).

The physical form of the papyrus gives no indication of the fragment's position within the roll, but the contents suggest that it came near the end; though (*c*) was followed | by further lost epigrams,[16] it contains elements appropriate to a *sphragis*,[17] the personal declaration that concludes a poem or a collection of poems. Its character is sufficiently shown by 6 *tandem fecerunt carmina Musae*: the perfect *fecerunt* corresponds to Horace's 'exegi monumentum' (*Carm.* 3. 30. 1) or Ovid's 'iamque opus exegi' (*Met.* 15. 871), whereas a *prooemium*, even if it is written late in the day, professes to look to the future (Hor. *Carm.* 1. 1. 36 'sublimi feriam sidera vertice'). The Muses are appropriately given credit for the literary achievement, just as in Horace's sphragis;[18] on the same principle they are mentioned at the beginning not only of archaic Greek poems but of Hellenistic and Roman collections.[19] But again as in Horace, the recognition of the debt is combined with an affirmation of pride (*digna*) that contrasts with the diffidence of a preface. When Gallus addresses in turn the important figures in his life, the list of acknowledgements suits the end of a collection: thus Propertius (2. 34. 61 f.) and Ovid (*Am.* 1. 15) recall the poets they admire, Marcus Aurelius pays tribute to the people who have influenced him (book 1 is either a preface or a misplaced epilogue), while Sidonius in his *envoi* asks his book to pay a round of calls on sympathetic friends (*Carm.* 24. 75 f.). The appeal to the critics in particular may be paralleled by the end of Horace's tenth satire (see note on 8 *Visce*) and first ode (see note on 9 *iudice*, citing also material from late Latin).

The new fragment could even have influenced the end of Virgil's eclogue in honour of Gallus (10. 70 f.):

> haec sat erit, divae, vestrum cecinisse poetam,
> dum sedet et gracili fiscellam texit hibisco,
> Pierides: vos haec facietis maxima Gallo.

While Gallus claimed that the Muses had made him songs worthy of Lycoris, Virgil asks them at the same place in the book to make his

[16] It is of course possible that the book ended in the lost lower position of column i, but apart from the natural assumption that the book and the roll coincide, there would be no room for a heading at the top of column ii, unless the poem following consisted of no more than a single couplet.

[17] W. Kranz, *RhM* 104 (1961), 3 f., 97 f. = *Studien zur antiken Literatur und ihrem Fortwirken* (1967), 27 f.; Nisbet–Hubbard on Horace, *Carm.* 2, 335 f.

[18] *Carm.* 3. 30. 14 f. 'sume superbiam quaesitam meritis et mihi Delphica lauro cinge volens, Melpomene, comam'; Kranz, op. cit. 5. For the pretensions of elegiac poets cf. Hor. *Epist.* 2. 2. 92 (apparently on Propertius) 'caelatumque novem Musis opus'.

[19] Nisbet–Hubbard on Horace, *Carm.* 1. 1. 33; F. Cairns, *Mnem.* 22 (1969), 155 f.

songs great for Gallus. *fecerunt* in the epigram could lie behind *facietis* in the eclogue, even if the latter is used in a different sense. If this speculation were correct, the new fragment would antedate the eclogue (which *ex hypothesi* caps it), i.e. it would be written before 39 (below, p. 127).

It perhaps helps our theory that the end of the tenth eclogue is an echo of the beginning (2f.): 'pauca meo Gallo sed quae legat ipsa Lycoris carmina sunt dicenda' (by the principle of ring-composition *pauca Gallo* is balanced by *maxima Gallo*). When an erotic motif in the eclogue is later repeated in Propertius, scholars have reasonably suspected a common source in the earlier elegist, and such a parallel is forthcoming here in a passage that is otherwise important for Gallus (Prop. 2. 13. 3 f.):

> hic (Amor) me tam gracilis vetuit contemnere Musas,
>   iussit et Ascraeum sic habitare nemus,
> non ut Pieriae quercus mea verba sequantur,
>   aut possim Ismaria ducere valle feras,
> sed magis ut nostro stupefiat Cynthia versu:
>   tunc ego sim Inachio notior arte Lino . . .
>
> me iuvet in gremio doctae legisse puellae,   11
>   auribus et puris scripta probasse mea.
> haec ubi contigerint, populi confusa valeto
>   fabula: nam domina iudice tutus ero.

When he introduced Lycoris at the beginning of his book, Gallus is likely to have explained her learned pseudonym (above, p. 117) by associating her with Apollo and the Muses: in such a context he could have asked for her approval of his verses (as at *Ecl.* 10. 2 'legat', Prop. 2. 13. 7 'stupefiat', cf. 1. 7. 11 'me laudent doctae solum placuisse puellae'). In | the new papyrus he may even claim to have won her approval (above, 8 n., citing Prop. 2. 13. 14 'domina iudice'); the beginning and end of the book would then balance, just like Virgil's imitation in the tenth eclogue. It may be relevant that the Propertian *auribus puris* (above, 2. 13. 12) can be paralleled from the sphragis of Posidippus, where the poet says to the Muses of Helicon εἴ τι καλόν, Μοῦσαι πολιήτιδες, ἢ παρὰ Φοίβου χρυσόλυρεω καθαροῖς οὔασιν ἐκλύετε Παρνησοῦ νιφόεντος ἀνὰ πτύχας.[20] Perhaps Propertius derived this theme from Gallus, who could have given the discriminating ears to Lycoris, the new Muse of Parnassus (above, p. 118).

[20] H. Lloyd-Jones, *JHS* 83 (1963), 75f.

It will be objected that this is to multiply entities beyond necessity: Propertius might have imitated Posidippus directly, or simply used a Hellenistic commonplace. Yet the Gallan origin of the passage is supported by the central section of Virgil's 'Song of Silenus' (*Ecl.* 6. 64f.), which deals explicitly with Gallus and the Muses; here, as in the lines cited from Propertius, we find the Hesiodic Ascra, a poetical Linus, and mountain trees drawn by real verses (as opposed to the mythological song of Orpheus):

> tum canit errantem Permessi ad flumina Gallum
> Aonas in montis ut duxerit una sororum,
> utque viro Phoebi chorus adsurrexerit omnis;
> ut Linus haec illi divino carmine pastor
> floribus atque apio crinis ornatus amaro
> dixerit: 'hos tibi dant calamos, en accipe, Musae,
> Ascraeo quos ante seni, quibus ille solebat
> cantando rigidas deducere montibus ornos.
> his tibi Grynei nemoris dicatur origo,
> ne quis sit lucus quo se plus iactet Apollo'.

It was observed long ago that Gallus himself[21] must have described his initiation by the Muses of Helicon[22] (the pejorative *errantem* is more likely to have originated with him than with Virgil); this interpretation was reinforced when the opening of the eclogue (6. 3f. 'cum canerem reges et proelia . . .') was shown to derive from the same source as the initiation, namely the prologues to the *Aetia* of Callimachus.

The ascent of Gallus from the stream of Permessus (at the foot of Helicon) to the heights of the Muses has plausibly been taken to describe a change from love-elegy (note *errantem*) to learned aetiological poetry (the Grynean grove was a subject of Gallus's model Euphorion); scholars compare Prop. 2. 10. 25f. (on his inability to write on Parthia): 'nondum etiam Ascraeos norunt mea carmina fontis, sed modo Permessi flumine lavit Amor'. If that is right, Gallus went through the same kind of development as Propertius, who moved from the programmatic 1. 1 and 1. 2 on Cynthia and her accomplishments to the more pretentious initiation of 3. 1. 1f. ('Callimachi manes et Coi sacra Philitae, in vestrum, quaeso, me sinite ire nemus'), which was followed in turn by the aetiological poems of the fourth book. However,

---

[21] R. Reitzenstein, *Hermes*, 31 (1896), 194f.; F. Skutsch, *Aus Vergils Frühzeit* (1901), 34f.; D. O. Ross, Jr., *Backgrounds to Augustan Poetry: Gallus, Elegy, and Rome* (1975), 20f.
[22] R. Pfeiffer, *Hermes*, 63 (1928), 302f. = *Ausgewählte Schriften* (1960), 98f.; W. Wimmel, *Kallimachos in Rom* (Hermes Einzelschriften, 16; 1960), 142f.

Propertius complicates the issue in 2. 13 (cited above) by adapting his prototype: he says there in effect 'whatever Gallus may have thought, *my* love-poetry does scale the heights'.[23] If this analysis is correct, the scene-setting of that elegy is derived from the later *prooemium* of Gallus (Ascra, Linus, sacred woods, just as in *Eclogue* 6), but Cynthia's critical discrimination from the earlier love-poetry (12 'auribus puris', 14 'domina iudice'). Though nothing can be proved, the *prooemium* of the first book would be an appropriate setting, and an appropriate counterpart to the new epigram.

VIII. THE HISTORICAL CONTEXT

Who is Caesar and what is the campaign? It will be undertaken primarily against foreign enemies; however lax the old observances might have become, nobody was likely | to describe a future victory in civil war by promising Roman spoils in Roman temples. It will mark a decisive stage in the victor's career; only afterwards will he be called 'maxima pars Romanae historiae'. The former of these considerations seems to rule out the Munda campaign of 45, though the ensuing triumphs were in fact spectacular.[24] The latter tells against even as important an undertaking as the Illyrian wars of 35-3.[25]

The wars of 31-30 are more promising, as they were waged from the start against Cleopatra, and followed by a conspicuous enhancement of Octavian's power. But in 32, before the battle of Actium, or late 31, before the invasion of Egypt, Gallus would not have known that he was going to be left there as Prefect (the consequence surely of his military success); he would expect to take part in any triumph, not to read about it from afar. It would be better to consider a date in 30-29, when plans were being made for Octavian's return. This hypothesis provides a simple explanation for Gallus's puzzling absence from the triumph, namely his prefecture; but it seems tactless to imply in the aftermath of victory that he will be sad till he reads of the triumph in the histories (cf. 2 *tum erunt*). From this point of view it is more natural to assume that the victory itself still lies in the future.

This dilemma sends us back from Octavian to Julius, and from

[23] Ross, op. cit. (n. 21), 109, does not admit that Propertius is contradicting Gallus; he thus concludes that the latter's personal poetry was a later development.

[24] Plut. *Caes.* 56. 4; S. Weinstock, *Divus Julius* (1971), 197f.

[25] J. J. Wilkes, *Dalmatia* (1969), 46f. Those who wish to assign the new poems to this period may claim support from the allusion to Viscus (above, p. 112); on the other hand, the chronology of Lycoris raises problems (p. 126).

realized victories to the war that never happened. A campaign against Parthia had long been envisaged, and serious preparations began after Caesar's return from Spain in 45;[26] a poetical allusion by Gallus is entirely natural in view of Caesar's literary bent and the panegyrics of his Gallic Wars by Furius Bibaculus and Varro Atacinus.[27] An army of 16 legions and 10,000 cavalry was mobilized (App. *Civ.* 2. 110/460), large forces were transported across the Adriatic, popular enthusiasm was stimulated (Dio 43. 51. 1); a campaign of three years was contemplated, beginning with an attack on the Dacian Burebista, and ending (or so it was reported) with a vast movement from the Caspian to the Danube and Gaul. These megalomaniac ambitions must have influenced the conspirators, who included such experienced campaigners as Cassius and D. Brutus (the former had restored the situation after Carrhae); and Caesar was assassinated three days before he was due to depart. By then Gallus might already have issued his poetry-book; as has been seen above (p. 121), the language of the papyrus suggests that he is nearing the end.

If Caesar's gamble had come off, he would have achieved a dominance in the histories more complete than after Munda. Even the victor's party might have represented the civil wars as a mere preliminary to an Eastern campaign; so Horace was to say of his successor 'praesens divus habebitur Augustus adiectis Britannis imperio gravibusque Persis' (*Carm.* 3. 5. 2 f.). The dedication of spoils was a particularly fitting punishment for the Parthians, who were presumed to have hung the Roman standards in their own temples.[28] The theme is taken up in the next generation by Virgil, *Aen.* 1. 289 (of Augustus, not Julius) 'spoliis Orientis onustum', Prop. 3. 12. 3 'spoliati gloria Parthi', 4. 6. 80 'reddat signa Remi, mox dabit ipse sua'. Particularly important is 3. 4 ('arma deus Caesar'), which seems to have been influenced by Gallus: the Parthian trophies will grow accustomed to the Capitoline temple (6 'assuescent Latio Partha tropaea Iovi'), the Roman armies are to provide material for the historian (10 'ite et Romanae consulite historiae'), the poet hopes to see Augustus's chariots laden with spoils (13 'spoliis oneratos Caesaris axis'), but he

---

[26] E. Meyer, *Caesars Monarchie*[3] (1922), 474 f.; M. Gelzer, *Caesar* (1960), 298 f. (= 322 f. in English edn., 1968); S. Weinstock, op. cit. (n. 24), 130 f., 340 f. I exclude consideration of a Parthian campaign under Octavian: a suitable context is hard to find, Gallus would be more aware of the realities than Horace or Propertius, and anything that minimizes present achievements (2 *tum erunt*) comes badly from the Prefect of Egypt.

[27] Schanz–Hosius, 1[4]. 163, 313, 349 f.

[28] Hor. *Epist.* 1. 18. 56, *Carm.* 4. 15. 7 f.

himself will play an inactive part (15 'inque sinu carae nixus spectare puellae'), and simply read about the distant victories from the placards in the procession (16 'titulis oppida capta legam'). This parallel does a little to support one's impression that Gallus is talking not of the victory over Cleopatra, to which he had contributed so much, but of a victory over the Parthians, to which he would contribute nothing.

The next step is to consider how a date in 45–4 fits the story of Cytheris. She first | appears in Antony's retinue in May 49, reclining behind the lictors in an open litter, and greeted as Volumnia by respectable burghers; her demeanour made a deep impression on Cicero, who describes it not only in two contemporary letters but five years later in the *Second Philippic*.[29] On Antony's return to Brindisi from the Thessalian campaign at the end of 48, she was there to welcome him (*Phil.* 2. 61); Cicero was also in Brindisi at the time, and in January 47 he had to calm down Terentia,[30] who predictably resented the mistress of the new man of power. In the same year Antony divorced his cousin Antonia (Plut. *Ant.* 9. 2), and in due course married Fulvia, who was not the woman[31] to tolerate a flamboyant *paelex*. When late in 46 Cicero saw Cytheris at the dinner-table of her *patronus* Volumnius[32] (at a time when Antony was in Italy), she may have gone back to her old lover: the ingratiating Volumnius appears later as a protégé of Antony (*RE* 9 A, 878f.), and presumably had lent him the lady in the first place. When Antony returned from Narbo in the autumn of 45, Cicero tells how he promised Fulvia to have no more dealings with Cytheris;[33] but as the whole account is imaginatively overdrawn, it does not prove that the association had continued till that time. Cicero's memories of 49–8 would be enough to suggest the detail, as they did in June 44 when he calls Antony 'Cytherius' (*Att.* 15. 22).

Even if Gallus was too ambitious to appropriate Antony's mistress, he might have begun a relationship as early as 47. His moods must have extended from admiration to disillusionment: *nequitia* in the papyrus confirms Virgil's more discreet phraseology (*Ecl.* 10. 6 'sollicitos Galli dicamus amores'). Virgil describes how Lycoris went off through the snows with a soldier, presumably a person of distinction

---

[29] *Att.* 10. 10. 5, 10. 16. 5, *Phil.* 2. 58.

[30] *Fam.* 14. 16; Shackleton Bailey rightly identifies this Volumnia with Cytheris.

[31] Plut. *Ant.* 10. 3 γύναιον . . . ἄρχοντος ἄρχειν καὶ στρατηγοῦντος στρατηγεῖν βουλό-μενον.

[32] *Fam.* 9. 26. 2 'infra Eutrapelum Cytheris accubuit. "in eo igitur" inquis "convivio Cicero ille quem aspectabant, cuius ob os Grai ora obvertebant sua?"'

[33] *Phil.* 2. 77 'sibi cum illa mima posthac nihil futurum'.

(10. 23 'perque nives alium perque horrida castra secuta est'); even if Servius had not told us, we could posit from the imitation in Propertius (1. 8) a pastiche of Gallus himself (*Ecl.* 10. 46f.):

> tu procul a patria (nec sit mihi credere tantum)
> Alpinas, a dura, nives et frigora Rheni
> me sine sola vides. a, te ne frigora laedant,
> a tibi ne teneras glacies secet aspera plantas.

The date of this episode is difficult to determine, but as it seems to have been historical, it deserves more discussion than it usually receives. Commentators refer to Agrippa's crossing of the Rhine in 39 or 38,[34] but the eclogue itself can hardly have been written later than 39;[35] unfortunately not much is known of operations in Gaul during the preceding years, and the mention of the Rhine need not be literal. When Servius says that the other man is Antony (*Ecl.* 10. 1), the story does not easily fit his career, and as it is an obvious guess, there is no need to think with Leo of L. Antonius.[36] One possibility is Volumnius himself, if he can be identified with the man who in 43[37] became *praefectus fabrum* to Antony (proconsul of Cisalpine and Transalpine Gaul). Another candidate might be D. Brutus, who defeated the Bellovaci (between the Somme and the Seine) in 46 (Liv. *Per.* 114), and travelled back with Caesar from Narbo in the autumn of 45 (Plut. *Ant.* 11. 2); when a late authority states that M. Brutus was one of Cytheris's lovers (*Vir. Ill.* 82. 2), there could be a confusion with his less austere namesake.[38]

When Lycoris goes off with her officer, Gallus is in the thick of the fray (*Ecl.* 10. 44f.):

> nunc insanus amor duri me Martis in armis
> tela inter media atque adversos detinet hostis. |

Though the time-scheme of the eclogue is misty, these adventures must be simultaneous: there is a conflict between Mars and Venus, and the true madness is the love of war.[39] Some interpreters set the scene

---

[34] Dio 48. 49. 3; *RE* 9 A. 1233f.; *MRR* 2. 389.

[35] Mr I. M. LeM. DuQuesnay has observed that the *Eclogues* should have been completed in 39: Maecenas, who took up Virgil no later than 38, is mentioned nowhere in the book. There is no justification for the view that the eighth poem belongs to 35.

[36] *Hermes* 37 (1902), 19 = *Ausgewählte Kleine Schriften*, 2 (1960), 34.

[37] Nep. *Att.* 12. 4; *RE* 9 A. 875f.

[38] D. Brutus was the son (or perhaps stepson) of the cultured but notorious Sempronia (Sall. *Cat.* 25).

[39] This is true even if *Martis* is taken primarily with *armis* (as the word-order naturally suggests). Gallus is not with Lycoris in imagination (thus Servius), but on a separate expedition; this is shown by *nunc*, *detinet*, and the contrasting *tu* in 46.

in the aftermath of Philippi in late 42, but they attach too geographical an interpretation to the poem's Arcadian scenery:[40] Gallus was not enjoying long leave in the Peloponnese, and he would have been more conscious of Cytheris's whereabouts if he was based in the West. One possibility is the war of Munda[41] in early 45, which was a good time for him to impress Pollio; he seems to have served under him in Spain in 44,[42] as he did in Cisalpina in 41 (perhaps as *praefectus fabrum*).[43] It might, however, be argued that *Ecl.* 10. 46 'tu procul a patria' implies that Gallus himself is nearer home than Cytheris. Perhaps he was manœuvring with Pollio in the Perusine War in the winter of 41-40 (though *hostis* now seems rather strong); in that case the tenth eclogue could imitate a book of Gallus later than the one under discussion.

If the first book was completed at the end of 45, that allows Gallus perhaps two years of Lycoris to celebrate; this is less than might have been wished, but *tandem* in the papyrus does not prove that the association was a long one, and so practical a man may have composed more expeditiously than poets with less to do. When he implies his exclusion from even a view of the Parthian triumph, that points to a prolonged absence from Rome in the West; one might guess that with his administrative capacities he was involved with Caesar's colonies in Spain or Narbonensis (just as in 41 he was to assist Pollio in settling veterans in Cisalpina). The new community of Forum Iuli (Fréjus) belongs to this period,[44] though the *colonia* may have been founded a decade later by Octavian;[45] as Gallus himself came from the district[46] (Jerome misleadingly calls him 'Foroiuliensis'), his local knowledge and influence would have been invaluable (as in the case of Alfenus Varus at Cremona in 41). The speculation would hardly be worth making if it did not provide a possible explanation for another diffi-

[40] F. Leo, op. cit. (n. 36), 18 f.; H. J. Rose, *The Eclogues of Virgil* (1942), 106 f.

[41] For Pollio's presence in Spain in 45 (before his late praetorship) cf. J. André, *La Vie et l'œuvre d'Asinius Pollion* (1949), 16 (citing Suet. *Jul.* 55. 4).

[42] Pollio writes from Spain to Cicero in June 43 that he can borrow one of his tragedies from Gallus (*Fam.* 10. 32. 5), a sign that the two men had been recently together (cf. also 10. 31. 6 of March). The episode shows that Gallus was already regarded by Pollio as a literary man.

[43] R. Syme, *Roman Revolution* (1939), 252 n. 4; Gallus has since turned up with the same title in Egypt (see next paragraph).

[44] Plancus ap. Cic. *Fam.* 10. 15. 3, 10. 17. 1 (both of 43 BC); *RE* 7. 69.

[45] J. Kromayer, *Hermes*, 31 (1896), 12 f.; R. Syme, *CQ* 32 (1938), 40 f.; F. Vittinghof, *Römische Kolonisation und Burgerrechtspolitik unter Caesar und Augustus* (= Abh. der Akad. der Wiss. Mainz, 1951), 67 n. 3.

[46] The place in Narbonensis was far more important than others of the same name, see R. Syme, *CQ* 32 (1938), 39 f.

culty. Fifteen years later, when he was about to become Prefect of Egypt, Gallus made a proud boast in bronze letters (later removed) on the obelisk that now stands in front of St Peter's: 'iussu Imp. Caesaris Divi f. C. Cornelius Cn. f. Gallus praef. fabr. Caesaris Divi f. Forum Iulium fecit'.[47] The inscription presumably refers to what was later called the Forum Augusti (Σεβαστὴ Ἀγορά) at Alexandria,[48] but it is a very odd coincidence that the man from Forum Iuli should make a Forum Iulium. One scholar suggests that Jerome's source depended on a garbled account of the inscription,[49] another speaks more convincingly of nostalgia;[50] but with his literary perceptions and flair for austere epigraphic self-advertisement,[51] Gallus might have intended something more specific. Perhaps he is recalling that as the representative of the now deified Julius he had previously 'made' Forum Iuli at the other end of the Roman Empire.

In view of the obscure chronology of the tenth eclogue, we cannot be sure that Lycoris ever went back to Gallus; in the sixth eclogue (which shortly preceded the tenth) he seems already to have turned to more mythological forms of poetry (above, p. 123). As he progressed in his official career, he may have abandoned verse altogether (another reason for doubting a reference to the Illyrian campaign); Propertius in his first book writes 'neoteric' elegies to a Gallus who is not the poet (there is a reference to his *nobilitas* and | *imagines*)[52] without apparently any danger of confusion. By 30 BC Cytheris was probably over forty, but the contrast between 1 *tristia* and 2 *dulcia* implies that her misbehaviour has been recent, the language of line 7 does not naturally suggest a long-dead romance (contrast Prop. 3. 24), and 6 *tandem* would be uncharacteristically modest a decade after the *Amores* had been celebrated by Virgil. Complaints about the lady's *nequitia* would not have suited Gallus's public position at a time when Alexandrian immorality was being denounced; it would have been a particular embarrassment that she had been Antony's mistress twenty years earlier, and hilariously depicted as such in Cicero's classic invective. An established statesman might employ his leisure scribbling *nugae*, but

[47] For bibliography see H. Volkmann, *Gymnasium*, 74 (1967), 501 f.; P. M. Fraser, *Ptolemaic Alexandria*, 2 (1972), 97.

[48] Fraser, op. cit. 2. 96.

[49] F. Bömer, *Gymnasium*, 72 (1965), 8 f.

[50] E. Hartmann, *Gymnasium*, 72 (1965), 3.

[51] Dio 53. 23. 5 καὶ τὰ ἔργα ὅσα ἐπεποιήκει ἐς τὰς πυραμίδας ἐσέγραψε; see *ILS* 8995 = *OGIS* 654.

[52] Prop. 1. 5. 23 f.; M. Hubbard, *Propertius* (1974), 25; R. Syme, *History in Ovid* (1978), 99 f.

editing a book of love-elegies was a different matter, and the take-over
of Egypt required ostentatious attention from a new man in his first
great office.

But even if he wrote no more verse, he must have become a living
legend. The papyrus was found at the southern frontier of Egypt, just
beyond the area where the poet himself had campaigned; one recalls
the interest in literature shown by the *comites* of Memmius and
Tiberius.[53] If the Romans at Carrhae transported Milesian tales in their
baggage (Plut. *Crass.* 32. 3), a lonely officer might treasure romantic
elegies on love and war, written in his youth by the Prefect of the
province. When Gallus was dismissed and driven to his death (27 or
26), there was no immediate censorship of his writings: the book found
its way to Qaṣr Ibrîm, which was only occupied in 25 or 24. But when
the fort was evacuated, perhaps only a few years later, it was dropped
on the rubbish-dump: Gallus was now disposable.

The episode was an omen. There was no formal burning of the
books:[54] Propertius and Ovid pay discreet tributes,[55] and over a century
later Quintilian still knows the elegies. But when Servius says that
Virgil withdrew 'laudes Galli' at the end of the *Georgics*, the story (at
least in a modified form) is less fantastic than is usually now supposed:[56] considering the stature of the man, too little is said of his
achievements and his fall. Apart from his victory over Antony and
prefecture of Egypt, he had developed a type of poetry unknown to the
Greeks that gave a new direction to Latin literature (*Eclogues* and
Epodes as well as elegies). His sentiment was transmitted and perhaps
exaggerated by Virgil and Propertius, but the new fragments hint
tantalizingly at a more authoritative and realistic voice: his successors
also talk of infidelity in a cold climate (Prop. 1. 8. 7 f.), the conflict of
duty and happiness (that obsession of the early Augustans), and the
prospect of despoiling the Parthians,[57] but for Gallus such themes

[53] Cat. 28 and 47; Hor. *Epist.* 1. 3. 6 f.

[54] For the alleged *damnatio memoriae* see J.-P. Boucher, *Caius Cornélius Gallus* (1966),
56 f.

[55] Prop. 2. 34 B. 91 f.; Ov. *Am.* 1. 15. 29 f., 3. 9. 63 f. 'tu quoque, si falsumst temerati
crimen amici, sanguinis atque animae prodige Galle tuae'.

[56] W. B. Anderson, *CQ* 27 (1933), 36 f.; E. Norden, *Sitzungsb. der Preuss. Akad. der Wiss.*
(1934), 627 f. = *Kleine Schriften* (1966), 469 f.; J. Griffin, *G & R* 26 (1979), 74 f. But
revisions are possible in principle (cf. Ovid's *Amores* and *Metamorphoses*), and only a few
lines need have been excluded.

[57] When the Augustan poets talk of Parthian expeditions, their political realism has
been variously regarded (P. A. Brunt, *JRS* 53 (1963), 170 f.; R. Syme, *History in Ovid*,
186 f.); imitation of Gallus would not be a total explanation, but would help to account for
the degree of interest shown by Propertius. The political element in the elegies of Gallus

sprang from experience. It is deeply satisfying that the Egypt Exploration Society should have recovered this papyrus, two thousand years after it was jettisoned, from the limits of the province which the poet conquered and ruled. His literary fame, said Ovid, would reach as far as his military commands, and last longer:[58]

> Gallus et Hesperiis et Gallus notus Eois
> et sua cum Gallo nota Lycoris erit.

was divined by the Renaissance forger of *Anth. Lat.* 914 (even if his Roman history left much to be desired): '(Lycoris) pingit et Euphratis currentes mollius undas victricesque aquilas sub duce Ventidio qui nunc Crassorum manes direptaque signa vindicat Augusti Caesaris auspiciis'.

[58] *Amor.* 1. 15. 29 f. *Lycoris* is the poetry-book as well as the actress; *nota* is not only 'famous' but 'notorious'.

7

Aeneas Imperator: Roman Generalship in an Epic Context

A lecture to the Virgil Society, January 1980

AENEAS is a man of many facets. He is a second Ulysses, *immersabilis* if not *versutus*, with intermittent hints of Achilles, Hercules, and other heroes. He is a Stoic exemplar, willingly obedient to the fates, and painfully growing in authority on his pilgrimage. He is a proto-Augustus, carrying the destiny of his nation on his shoulders, and pre-figuring the political ideology of Virgil's own patrons. In this paper I shall consider him as he undertakes one of the most important func-tions of Roman government, republican or imperial, the command of an army. The *Aeneid* is like a great novel of war and politics, and the poet can help the historian not so much by describing institutions as by making attitudes come alive. As the relevant material is scattered, I shall proceed book by book in the chronological order of the events described, that is to say beginning with Book 2.

At the fall of Troy Virgil must establish three things about Aeneas. In the first place it must be made clear that the disaster was not his fault. In Homer he appears as a prudent soldier and a wise statesman,[1] apparently second in esteem only to Hector himself, and after Hector's death his position in the hierarchy ought to have been improved. But in Virgil he is consulted neither on the horse nor the serpents, when the enemy attacks he does not know what is happening, and Panthus has to tell him that the war is lost (324 ff.). There was a very literal lack of *vigilantia*, one of the suspicious Romans' most prized virtues, but though Aeneas uses first person plurals to describe what the Trojans did, he does not seem to admit any individual responsibility. There is an implicit moral on the dangers of oligarchy and plutocracy, where a

---

[1] G. K. Galinsky, *Aeneas, Sicily, and Rome* (1969), 20 ff., 36 ff.; N. Horsfall, *CQ* 29 (1979), 372 f.

Proceedings of the Virgil Society, 18 (1978–80), 50–61.

leaderless nation listens to uninformed voices, and nobody is in overall charge. Such a lesson would seem a natural one in Augustan Rome, and it is worth remembering that in Horace's third Roman Ode, Troy has been thought to suggest the fallen Republic.

Secondly, Virgil must emphasize Aeneas's courage. It could be held against him that he had survived his city, and Turnus touched a sore point when he called him *desertorem Asiae* (12. 15). That is why Virgil makes him organize resistance, though only at a local and subordinate level: he takes up arms without regard for consequences (314 'arma amens capio, nec sat rationis in armis'), if he had been fated to fall he deserved it by his actions (433 f. 'si fata fuissent ut caderem meruisse manu'), he emphasizes several times his own *furor* or loss of control | (316, 588, 595). He even takes a leaf out of his enemies' book and stoops to disguise (390 'dolus an virtus quis in hoste requirat?'), but it is made clear by what happens that such subterfuges did no good in the long run: like other successful imperialists the Romans were under the illusion that they themselves fought according to the rules (Liv. 1. 53. 4 'minime arte Romana, fraude ac dolo'). The climax comes in the disputed passage where he considers killing Helen at the altar, a scene that is Virgilian[2] not only in style but in imaginative power and psychological appropriateness (extending beyond the immediate context to the epic as a whole). There is a conflict here between the passionate and the reasoning parts of the soul, and it suits the Augustan ideal that rationality prevails.

Thirdly, Virgil must confirm the legitimacy of Aeneas's *imperium*; he cannot like de Gaulle appoint himself. In the *Iliad* Achilles had taunted Aeneas with wishing to succeed Priam, an ambition that seemed absurd as long as the king was in good health and had living sons (20. 180 ff.). Now the changed situation must be formally recognized. Aeneas is entrusted with the Penates by Hector's ghost (293 ff.), and they are brought by Panthus to the house of Anchises (320 f.), who carries them from the fallen city (717). The party does not leave without explicit instructions from Venus Genetrix (619 f.). Above all, when the flame plays round the head of Iulus (682 ff.), the spontaneous phenomenon provides an excellent instance of *auspicia oblativa*, and when Anchises with Roman prudence insists on a double-check, they

[2] R. G. Austin, *CQ* 11 (1961), 185 ff.; otherwise G. P. Goold, *HSCPh.* 74 (1970), 101 f.; C. E. Murgia, *CSCA* 4 (1971), 203 ff. Opponents of authenticity may stress too much the difficulties of the transmission; the lines are far too good to have been written later than the 1st cent. AD, and though we cannot show how they survived, any view of their authorship presents some problems.

are promptly converted by celestial phenomena into *auspicia impetra-tiva*.[3] All this corresponds to the taking of the omens when a Repub-lican general sets out to war.

At this point we are faced by a constitutional puzzle: who has *imperium maius*? The taking of the omens by Anchises might suggest that the expedition was begun under his own *ductu auspiciisque*, but such a conclusion is belied by his words 'nec, nate, tibi comes ire recuso' (2. 704), as well as by the traditional form of the legend. Aeneas reports prodigies to his father (3. 58f., 179), as M. Caedicius did to the magistrates in Livy (5. 32. 6, cf. 2. 36. 7), but Anchises may be acting rather as a priest; by the Roman system religious authority was vested in suitable statesmen (cf. Laocoön and Panthus), who interpreted the divine will more sensibly than whole-time professionals like Calchas or Tolumnius (12. 258ff.). Anchises is supported by *delecti proceres* (58), not a council of war on the Homeric model (it is only the Latins who give scope to a politician like Drances), but an advisory *consilium*; as the institution was found in many spheres of Roman life, the old man may be represented as *pontifex maximus* rather than *imperator*. Apart from his interpretation of religious phenomena, Anchises determines the successive stages on the journey;[4] Aeneas is thus absolved from responsibility for the wanderings, and in particular for the abortive settlement in Crete (100f.). On the other hand, it is Aeneas who organ-izes the details of administration (137 'iura | domosque dabam') and commands in the battle against the Harpies (234ff.), from which his father is excluded by age and infirmity. The allocation of *provinciae* between father and son corresponds to nothing in historical Roman practice; elderly rulers presented no problem under the Republic, when middle-aged consuls were annually replaced, and in the Prin-cipate the issue first becomes important with the declining years of Tiberius. Rather the situation reflects a vision of primitive society: Anchises occupies a position somewhere between Laertes,[5] who seems to have abdicated, and Priam, who remains in nominal control even though Hector commands in battle. With the death of Anchises at the end of the third book (709ff.) the anomaly is removed, and Aeneas assumes the undivided authority that *pietas* had kept him from usurping.

When we first meet Aeneas off Carthage, he is shivering in the

---

storm (1. 92 'extemplo Aeneae solvuntur frigore membra'). His sufferings are modelled on those of Odysseus (Hom. *Od.* 5. 297, 5. 472) but
such weakness is much more conspicuous[6] at the beginning of the
epic. Conventional panegyrics of generals emphasized their endurance
as much as their courage,[7] and particularly their indifference to the
elements, but Virgil is more interested in the Aristotelian distinction
between fortitude and insensibility (*Eth. Nic.* 1115^{b}24 ff.). Augustus
himself was surprisingly susceptible to cold, and wore four tunics in the
winter (Suet. *Aug.* 81–2), and though the poet is unlikely to have
intended so specific a reference, he would at least have been aware
that the great man's dominance was more psychological than physical.

The storm is stilled by Neptune with a calm but firm exercise of
authority (1. 132 ff.), that symbolically suggests Roman *imperium*. The
drill of the Trojans on landing is more systematic than anything in
Homer: the lighting of fire and baking of bread (174 ff.) follow the prosaic
priorities of the Roman army (cf. 6. 8 for *aquatio*), even if the stag-hunt
and roast venison belong to traditional epic. The allocution of Aeneas to
his men, though formally modelled on Homeric rodomontade (199 'o
passi graviora', cf. *Od.* 12. 208 ff.) shows a topical awareness of the
anxieties of leadership (209 'spem vultu simulat, premit altum corde
dolorem'). After a typically restless night (305), the cautious commander
sends out *speculatores* (more professional than the 'looking in all directions' at *Od.* 10. 146), and camouflages his fleet under a wooded cliff
(310 ff.). In spite of all the Odyssean disappearing-tricks, the meeting
with Dido is conducted with realistic circumspection, and Aeneas stays
in the background like a Roman *imperator* till he sees how his legate
gets on. There follows top-level diplomacy of the sort that a distinguished personality still could influence in the ancient world: the
negotiation is supported by appeals to traditional ties (619 ff.), military
and political alliance is treated in terms of private *amicitia* (whose
moral component can too easily be underestimated),[8] and though
mutual advantage | is implicit in the understanding (548 ff., cf. 563 f.),
the emphasis is placed on magnanimity and obligation. The spontaneous gifts that conclude the conversations have more binding force
than the interchanges at modern State Visits; the Homeric pattern[9]

---

[6] Serv. auct. ad loc. 'reprehenditur sane hoc loco Vergilius ...' Virgil is defended by
A. J. Gossage, *Phoenix*, 17 (1963), 131 ff.

[7] Xen. *Hell.* 5. 1. 15; Sall. *Cat.* 5. 3; Liv. 21. 4. 6; K. J. Dover, *Greek Popular Morality*
(1974), 163.

[8] P. A. Brunt, *PCPS* 11 (1965), 1 ff.

[9] Finley, op. cit. 120 ff.

would still be valid with foreign potentates, as it surely was in the world of Lawrence of Arabia.

But *amicitia* ought not to have included emotional entanglements; the hint of Cleopatra is unavoidable in a poem written in the decade after her death. Antony might claim precedent in Alexander, who had to deal with the queens of the East, but a Roman *imperator* should have been less cosmopolitan. When the gods give Aeneas new sailing-directions, the *foedus* by which he bound others is superseded for himself; Virgil writes without cynicism, but he has the imaginative sympathy to see how Roman *fides* must have looked to the losers (4. 376 ff.), as to the Samnites after the Caudine Forks. A realistic general knew how to cut his losses (as is shown in Book 3), even if it meant a voyage in winter (4. 313), and the evacuation is planned with the two essentials of secrecy and speed. When Dido looks down from her acropolis she sees no longer productive bees (1. 430 ff.) but ants on the move (4. 404 ff.):

> it nigrum campis agmen praedamque per herbas
> convectant calle angusto; pars grandia trudunt
> obnixae frumenta umeris, pars agmina cogunt
> castigantque moras, opere omnis semita fervet.

There could be no better description of the legalized destructiveness of the Roman army with its requisitioning of corn (*frumentum impera-tum*), organized supply-columns, and discipline on the march; when a centurion said 'go', you went.

The celebrations in Book 5 suggest national Roman *ludi* rather than regimental sports, but though Aeneas presides from a mound of turf (290) with the affability of a civilian Princeps, military lessons are implicit. The boat-race teaches that opportunities should be seized without running unreasonable risks; these were the methods of Pompey and Augustus (rather than of an *aleator* like Julius Caesar), and it is significant that the reckless Sergestus is the ancestor of the Sergii (121), that is to say of Catiline. The boyish loyalties of Nisus and Euryalus foreshadow their tragic sortie in story-book manner (even if their notion of playing the game was different from Sir Henry New-bolt's); the moral education of the young in ideals appropriate to a military society must have seemed a natural function of the new epic. In the same way the boxing-match idealizes the controlled courage of experience as opposed to the mindless brutality of the prize-fighter: 'vis consili expers mole ruit sua' (Hor. *Carm.* 3. 4. 65). The flame that

ends the archery-contest teaches the validity of omens (as well as
suggesting Caesar's Comet), while the *lusus Troiae* describes the
equestrian exercises of Virgil's own day. |

The military lessons of the games are brought out in practice at the
burning of the boats. Ascanius shows his initiative and discipline by
quelling the riot and awaiting assistance, where a less responsible
officer would have attempted too little or too much; with an aristocratic belief in heredity the Roman governing class gave its favoured
young men rapid promotion, and the first signs of leadership must
have been eagerly welcomed, as in the case of Marcellus. Aeneas's
actions in turn show *pietas* and *consilium*, both desirable qualities in a
Roman commander. After a prayer to Jupiter, which is providentially
heard (cf. 235 ff. in the boat-race), he listens to the experienced Nautes
(709 ff.); a good *imperator* founded cities as well as destroying them,
and those who did not wish to sail further were left behind without
recriminations (contrast the Phocaeans at Herodotus 1. 165. 3). This
readiness to cut knots and not batter heads against brick walls
illustrates the sense of the possible that made the Roman empire last
longer than some others.

The fifth book must have suggested Roman campaigning in another
way; anybody who had read about the First Punic War and experienced the campaigns against Sextus Pompeius would have been
moved in Sicilian waters to patriotic 'home-thoughts from the sea'.
When Aeneas in the storm accepts the advice of Palinurus (26 ff.), we
may recognize the respect for the expert that Octavian must have
shown in his naval wars. It seems significant that both the serene
regatta and the sinister burning of the boats (which was assigned to
various places by the tradition) are set by Virgil at Drepanum
(Trapani), the scene of a famous naval disaster in the First Punic War
(Polyb. 1. 49–51); the Roman commander had thrown the sacred
chickens into the sea ('if they will not eat, let them drink'), and his ill-
fated impiety[10] is implicitly contrasted with the faith and hope of
Virgil's heroes. When Aeneas sacrifices a lamb to the Tempestates
(772), we may compare Octavian's dedications from the same period
(App. *Civ.* 5. 98. 406, *ILS* 3279 'Ara Ventorum'); for a topical parody of
the rite cf. Hor. *Epod.* 10. 23 f., where a goat is promised to the Storm-
Winds for the drowning of Mevius. When Palinurus is washed ashore

---

[10] Pease on Cic. *Nat. Deor.* 2. 7; T. P. Wiseman, *Clio's Cosmetics* (1979), 90 f., 110 f. The
battle is mentioned by F. Della Corte, *La Mappa dell'Eneide* (1972), 96 f., but he sees a
moral simply in the need for fast ships.

on the Lucanian coast, Virgil is likely to have remembered the setback
of 36 BC, when many of Octavian's men, including perhaps Maecenas
and Horace, met a similar experience in the same area.[11] And when a
pyre is built for Misenus (6. 179ff.), who gave his name to Rome's naval
base, Aeneas's timber-felling (more mechanized than in Homer or
Ennius), suggests the deforestation (Strab. 5. 4. 5), familiar to Virgil in
Naples, at the construction of the Portus Iulus.

The Aeneas of the sixth book must make his catabasis alone, but in
the second half of the epic he resumes his position as an *imperator*. The
invasion comes ashore not at the traditional landing-place 'in agrum
Laurentinum' (Liv. 1. 1. 7), but farther north at the mouth of the Tiber;
Virgil is not trying to protect | Aeneas's left flank, but rather to associ-
ate him with the Roman river. A settlement is fortified with *agger* and
fossa on the formidable lines of a Roman camp (159);[12] an allusion to
the Ostian *castrum* has been suspected but is difficult to prove. Legates
are dispatched to King Latinus with a blend of bluff and appeasement
(as was wise in the Trojans' plight). Odysseus may boast 'I captured the
city and killed the men' (*Od.* 9. 40), but like a good Roman *imperator*
Aeneas conserves his outnumbered forces and tries to use *socii* on the
spot.[13] With an instinct for the workings of Roman conquest Virgil
envisages an immediate *foedus* that would include the all-important
right of *conubium* (as shown by the betrothal of Aeneas and Lavinia),
and lead to an ultimate merging of political and religious institutions.

The Trojans showed a Roman assurance in the sanctity of their
foedus, but not surprisingly it proved acceptable only to a section of the
Latins. Historians know that wars originate from deep-seated causes
and trivial occasions, and so it was with the shooting of Silvia's stag.
Allecto plays on natural resentments with the fiendish insight of a
political manipulator, and the crisis escalates[14] in clearly defined stages
to a general mobilization. Aeneas can do nothing for most of the book:
though in all but a technical sense he is the aggressor, as the historical
tradition recognized (Liv. 1. 1. 5, Dion. Hal. *Rom. Ant.* 1. 57. 1, 1. 58. 1),
Roman legalism about the *iustum bellum*[15] required that his posture
should be defensive.

---

[11] Vell. 2. 79. 3; App. *Civ.* 5. 98. 410; Dio 49. 1. 3; E. Wistrand, *Horace's Ninth Epode*
(1958), 16f. = *Opera Selecta* (1972), 304f.

[12] J. Carcopino, *Virgile et les origines d'Ostie*, 2nd edn. (1968), 358ff.

[13] E. N. Luttwak, *The Grand Strategy of the Roman Empire* (1979), 30ff.

[14] E. Fraenkel, *JRS* 35 (1945), 4ff. = *Kleine Beiträge zur klassischen Philologie*, 2 (1964),
151ff.

[15] W. V. Harris, *War and Imperialism in Republican Rome* (1979), 166ff.

In Book 8 the two sides seek to extend their network of alliances (a side of warfare more emphasized in Livy than in Homer). The Latins send a mission to Diomede in Apulia (9 ff.) with a realistic appeal to self-interest (note the historian's *oratio obliqua* at 15 ff.); Aeneas, after agonizing in the night, sees that he can do more by diplomacy than fighting (18 ff.), and resolves to negotiate with Evander in person. His voyage up the Tiber shows Virgil's imaginative awareness of how to penetrate a forested interior. The conversations at the site of Rome begin as usual with expressions of respect and claims to shared antecedents (134 ff., 157 ff.); with a disdain for explicit bargaining characteristic of gentlemanly societies (think of Augustan poets and their patrons), Aeneas suggests the common danger, mentioning his own contribution only as an afterthought (150 f. 'sunt nobis fortia bello pectora'). The next day Evander points out the advantages of an alliance with the anti-Mezentian faction at Agylla (the Caere that was to be so important in the Latin Wars); such interference in the stasis of neighbours was characteristic of Rome as of more recent imperialisms (cf. the Parthian rebellion of 26), but justification is naturally found in the misgovernment of Mezentius. Evander proves his *fides* by sending his son Pallas, and the party ride in splendour from the North Gate like a Roman commander and his *comites* setting out to war: 'stant pavidae in muris matres oculisque sequuntur pulveream | nubem et fulgentis aere catervas' (592 f.).

The removal of Aeneas from the battlefield produces a critical change in the balance of forces (9. 6 ff.) without impugning the martial or other virtues of the hero: Achilles had sulked in his tent out of personal pique, but for a responsible and rational leader diplomacy was an indivisible element of war. Ascanius is left in charge, though Aletes plays the experienced *legatus* (246); the arrangement (derided by Juno at 10. 70) suggests in exaggerated form the aspirations of Marcellus, whose role may have been extended during Augustus's illnesses (he would have been preferred by Maecenas to Agrippa). When the attack comes, the Trojans retreat to their base (9. 38 ff.) as Aeneas had instructed, secure in the knowledge that his commands would be obeyed; the Roman army was to prosper by a combination of threatening attitudes and defensive tactics,[16] which were resolutely maintained in spite of provocation (54 ff.) till the moment for counter-attack. The lesson could be learned from a contemporary prose work, the Hannibalic books of Livy, as well as from Augustus's own policies.

[16] Luttwak, op. cit., 1 ff.

In the middle of the crisis Nisus and Euryalus try to summon help from Aeneas (192 ff.) by breaking out on the unexpected seaward side (238). Unauthorized combat in the Nelson manner played no part in Roman heroics, as the story of Torquatus shows (Liv. 8. 7), so they correctly ask permission from Ascanius. Nisus is mature enough to understand that inner promptings may be delusive (185 'an sua cuique deus fit dira cupido?'), but he is diverted from his mission by a wish for the more obvious forms of military glory. Euryalus, who has been set to guard the rear, is brought down by his own battle-lust (354 'cupidine ferri') and greed for loot (384), and Nisus is also killed in a futile attempt to save him. In the circumstances anything but eulogy would be ungracious, but like a good novelist, Virgil does not always make his moral explicit;[17] older heads would have seen that though magnificent, the escapade was not war.[18] Aeneas is as far away as ever (10. 25 'Aeneas ignarus abest'), and when the light flashes on Euryalus's captured helmet (373 f.), he is betrayed by the childish love of prizes that the pair has already shown in the foot-race (5. 343 ff.).

After the success of his diplomatic initiatives, Aeneas returns in the tenth book to the rescue of the Trojan encampment. The enchanted Odyssean atmosphere is piquantly combined with more realistic elements: the newly acquired *socii* provide the cavalry and the fleet (as was inevitable in Rome's foreign wars), the combined military and naval operations foreshadow the sort of thing that happened at Actium, the Etruscan order of battle (included against the tradition perhaps in deference to Maecenas) is a proper reminder of Etruria's part in the development of Roman power. Turnus naturally tries to repel the invasion before it gets ashore (277 'litora praecipere et venientis pellere terra'); ships smash on sandbanks and soldiers slither down poles. But the dispositions of Aeneas's | D-Day are far from obvious. If the Trojan settlement stretched to the Tiber, why was the disembarkation made on the open beaches against an opposing army? On the other hand, if the Trojan landing-place was not included in the main fortifications, that goes against the principles both of Homeric and Roman warfare. There is also some obscurity about the movements of Evander's cavalry, which is fighting on foot near the Tiber's mouth (10. 362 ff.), and cut off between the settlement and the sea (378 'pelagus Troiamne petemus?'). But we should not read the *Aeneid* any

[17] K. Quinn, *Virgil's Aeneid* (1968), 339 f.
[18] G. E. Duckworth, *AJP* 88 (1967), 129 ff. On the other hand P. G. Lennox defends Nisus, though not Euryalus (*Hermes* 105 (1977), 331 ff.).

more than the *Iliad* for precise topographical detail; Virgil would be less zealous in exploring the Campagna than some of his interpreters.

The interest of the book is not strategic but psychological, and centres round Aeneas's response to the death of Pallas. To understand his agony we must remember the sacred responsibilities of *contubernium*, by which a general took a young man under his wing;[19] 'haec mea magna fides?' says Aeneas (11. 55) and though his self-reproaches are less justified than those of Achilles over Patroclus they make him lash out in the same way. When he promises human sacrifice to Pallas (10. 517ff., 11. 81f.), there is an obvious parallel to the destructive deeds devised by Achilles (*Il.* 21. 27ff., 23. 175ff.), and in a Roman context the idea is a particular abomination (*RE* 15. 955).[20] Though it is true that the slaughter of prisoners was permitted in ancient warfare,[21] Aeneas kills suppliants with barbaric insults (10. 560, 592ff.) that remind us again of Achilles in his rage. The same blind fury is directed against Lausus, though Virgil goes out of his way to emphasize that *pietas* operated on both sides (cf. 10. 822 *Anchisiades*, 824, 826). Some scholars invoke the conventions of heroic and Roman war to suggest that our distaste is a modern anachronism, but this view goes against the whole tenor of the poem, ignores philosophical disquisitions on *ira* and political panegyrics of clemency, and is more objectively refuted by the Homeric parallels. Virgil would read the *Iliad* in a moralizing spirit, which in spite of its unhistorical formulations has more essential truth than is sometimes supposed. Whatever the original form of the saga, in the epic as we have it the wrath of Achilles extended from his feud with Agamemnon to his revenge on Hector, until he redeems himself by receiving Priam at the end of the poem.

In the eleventh book Aeneas shows a more Roman fortitude at the fate of Pallas (which seems to reflect the death of Marcellus in 23), and does not allow his emotions to interfere with his responsibilities. He gives commands to his army with the menacing understatement of a successful soldier (17 'nunc iter ad regem nobis murosque Latinos'); in the manner of the later Roman army, which avoided unconsidered

---

[19] Cic. *Sull.* 34, *Planc.* 27, *Cael.* 73, *Brut.* 105, Serv. *Aen.* 5. 546 '(custodem) secundum Tullium qui dicit ad militiam euntibus dari solitos esse custodes, a quibus primo anno regantur; unde ait de Pallante (8. 515) *sub te tolerare magistro militiam et grave Martis opus*'.

[20] There can hardly be a conscious reference to Octavian's massacre at Perusia (Sen. *Clem.* 1. 11. 1 'Perusinas aras'; Suet. *Aug.* 15; Dio 48. 14. 4); *mactare* is a natural metaphor in Roman political invective, and though something very ugly happened, a solemn sacrifice of 300 senators and *equites* is not to be believed (R. Syme, *The Roman Revolution* (1939), 212).

[21] Harris, op. cit. 50ff.

offensives, he aims at careful material and psychological preparation (18 'arma parate, animis et spe praesumite bellum'). When the Latins ask for recovery of their dead, he receives them with brief but conciliatory words (113 'nec bellum cum gente gero') that are carefully designed to detach them from | Turnus (in which they have their effect); unlike modern ideologists the more rational ancient imperialists knew that the aim of war is peace (Ar. *Eth. Nic.* 1177^{b}5f.), that is to say an advantageous political settlement. Having thus asserted his dominance, Aeneas marches while the enemy is still in disarray (446). While his cavalry fights Camilla in the plain, he makes a sudden swoop through the hills (what hills?); the manœuvre is unconvincing, as the Romans captured cities *sedendo* rather than by surprise thrusts. Turnus lies in wait in a defile, the usual terrain in Livy for Roman disasters, but in his madness abandons the ambush even before he hears of Camilla's defeat. The strange manœuvres on both sides are determined not by military necessity but by the strategy of the poem: Virgil wishes to keep the protagonists apart as long as possible.

The framework of the last book is Homeric, but Roman attitudes sometimes intrude. When Turnus takes up the idea of a single combat the tactics are epic (or Livian), but the tone becomes more realistic when Aeneas promises an *aequum foedus* (189 ff.); and when he is wounded in trying to preserve the truce, the adaptation of the Homeric episode in the *Iliad* (*Il.* 4. 127 ff.) gives him the moral excuse that meant so much to Roman empire-builders. He shows more fortitude over his injury than Menelaus; and when he is treated by Iapyx with his *dictamnum*, a contemporary might think not just of the Homeric leech but of Antonius Musa, who had saved Augustus from more than one illness (for his expertise in pharmacology cf. Galen 13. 463 K). As his resolution grows, Aeneas promises the destruction of the Latin capital in the bleak, authoritative tones of a real *imperator*, which show a Roman confidence in the righteousness of his cause: 'urbem hodie, causam belli, regna ipsa Latini . . . eruam et aequa solo fumantia culmina ponam' (567 ff.). Yet he is talking here not of Mezentius or even Turnus but of kind, bumbling Latinus: there is a disconcerting parallel with Priam and the fires of Troy. With his feeling for Rome's mission and his sense of loyalty to his patrons, Virgil is not making an outright rejection of imperialism. But in Greek tragedy the sack of Troy, however justified, is nothing to boast about (cf. Aesch. *Ag.* 472 'may I not be a sacker of cities'), and in the only comparable Latin work the loss of humanity cannot be unintended.

The plot required that Turnus should die, but he did not have to plead 'ulterius ne tende odiis' (938), and his killing is no more endorsed by the poet than the slaughter in the tenth book. It cannot be justified by appeals to the epic tradition and the Roman laws of war: Aeneas has been built up as a philosophic hero, and no philosopher could commend revenge on impulse. He is actuated not by a sense of honour, as he himself imagines (cf. 11. 178f. for Evander's plea), nor even by a higher necessity (as in his corresponding destruction of Dido), but by a loss of control that reduces him to the level of his enemy:[22] nothing could be more explicit than Virgil's words 'furiis accensus' (12. 946). | The climax is disturbing because it denies us the expected moral ending (as if Virgil were as smug as Livy), not because it is false to human nature or the facts of Roman or more recent history. Though he had so little experience of the world, the poet intuitively understood what it costs to build a city, and at this stage of the epic he had to write what he felt, without regard for the only Man of Destiny on view. In spite of his solid exterior, Aeneas is an unfulfilled hero, clutching at phantoms, pursuing receding shores, issuing from the Gate of Illusions (6. 898), fated to wander but not quite to arrive, not to found his city (*dum conderet*, not *condidit*), but to fall before his time on the barren sand (4. 620), in Stoic terminology sometimes *proficiens* but never *perfectus*. The *imperator* wins his *spolia opima* from Turnus, but the supreme command has eluded him: 'imperare sibi maximum imperium est' (Sen. *Epist.* 113. 30).

---

[22] C. M. Bowra, *G & R* 3 (1933), 17f.; K. Quinn, op. cit. 272f. Aeneas is criticized too much by M. Putnam, *The Poetry of the Aeneid* (1965), 193ff.; too little by B. Otis, *Virgil, A Study in Civilised Poetry* (1963), 381.

8

Sidere Clarior (Horace, *Carm.* 3. 1. 42)

> quodsi dolentem nec Phrygius lapis,
> nec purpurarum sidere clarior
> delenit usus, nec Falerna
> vitis Achaemeniumque costum . . .
>
> (Horace, *Carm.* 3. 1. 41–4)

IN ancient literature handsome or magnificent people are sometimes compared to stars; cf. Horace, *Carm.* 3. 9. 21–1, 'quamquam sidere pulchrior I ille est', with the parallels cited by Nisbet and Hubbard on 1. 12. 47. Some readers may have felt mild surprise at the application of the encomium to purple furnishings. But doubts are soon laid to rest when one considers the hyperbolical character of the passage, as shown by the periphrastic *purpurarum . . . usus* and the extravagant hypallage at *clarior*. Here as elsewhere in the ode Horace is imitating the proem to Lucretius 2, where the ostentation of luxury is depicted with appropriate grandeur:

> neque fulgorem reverentur ab auro,
> nec clarum vestis splendorem purpureai.
>
> (Lucretius, 2. 51–2)

But *sidere clarior* presents a more serious difficulty. Three of the four luxuries in the stanza are characterized by the adjectival form of a proper name (*Phrygius*, *Falerna*, *Achaemenium*), but the purple fabrics have no corresponding epithet. We look for the same stately balance and evocative resonance that we find in two passages of similar content:

> 1. 31. 3–8   non opimae
>   *Sardiniae* segetes feracis,
>
> non aestuosae grata *Calabriae*
> armenta, non aurum aut ebur *Indicum*,
> non rura quae *Liris* quieta
> mordet aqua taciturnus amnis.

3. 16. 33-6   quamquam nec *Calabrae* mella ferunt apes,
               nec *Laestrygonia* Bacchus in amphora
               languescit mihi, nec pinguia *Gallicis*
                   crescunt vellera pascuis ...

Those who wish to defend the *inconcinnitas* will appeal to 2. 9. 1-8:

               non semper imbres nubibus hispidos
               manant in agros, aut mare *Caspium*
                 vexant inaequales procellae
                   usque, nec *Armeniis* in oris,

               amice Valgi, stat glacies iners
               mensis per omnis, aut aquilonibus
                 querqueta *Gargani* laborant
                   et foliis viduantur orni.

There *hispidos* is plausible (see Nisbet and Hubbard ad loc.), though *Istricos* has been proposed; but as the anomaly occurs in the first item on the list, the awkwardness is much less than in the passage under | discussion.

    Instead of *sidere* one looks for an exotic place-name associated with purple. Read *Sidone*; cf. *Epist.* 1. 10. 26 *Sidonio ... ostro*, Virgil, *Aen.* 4. 137 *Sidoniam ... chlamydem* (with Pease ad loc.), (Tibullus) 3. 3. 18, Seneca (?), *Herc. Oet.* 663-4 'nec Sidonio mollis aeno | repetita bibit lana rubores', Statius, *Silv.* 3. 2. 140, Sidonius, *Carm.* 15. 128. Purple was associated particularly with Tyre, but for the substitution of the parallel name cf. Servius, *Aen.* 1. 235 'Didonem Sidoniam dicit, cum sit Tyria, a loci vicinitate', Pease on Virgil, *Aen.* 4. 75, A. J. Bell, *The Latin Dual and Poetic Diction* (1923), 11. The *o* of *Sidone* is normally long, but a short vowel is adequately supported by Silius, 8. 436-7:

               stat fucare colus nec Sidone vilior Ancon
               murice nec Libyco,

Martial, 2. 16. 3 and 11. 1. 2 (cited below); for very uncertain Greek instances cf. Strabo, 16. 2. 13, Dionysius Periegeta, 912 with Eustathius on 117 (the short vowel is well attested with Σιδόνιος, *Sidonius*, *Sidonis*). The unusual metrical feature might well have helped the corruption; this seems to have taken place early, as the transmitted text is supported by Porphyrio's note (not just his lemma).

    Sidone clarior is a compendious comparison for 'more brilliant than the purple of Sidon'; cf. Kühner–Stegmann, 2. 566 f., Hofmann–

Szantyr, 826. The construction is convenient in the comparison of products; cf. 2. 6. 14–16:

> ubi non Hymetto
> mella decedunt, viridique certat
> baca Venafro,

Varro, *Rust.* 1. 2. 6 *quod oleum* (*conferam*) *Venafro?* (by a reverse procedure Silius, 8. 436–7 above, compares Ancon with Libyan *murex*). *Sidon* can be used for purple even where there is no comparison; cf. Martial,

| 2. 16. 3 | quid torus a Nilo, quid Sidone tinctus olenti? |
| 11. 1. 2 (of the book) | cultus Sidone non cotidiana |

(where the oddity of the expression has produced the variant *sindone*).

9

'Great and Lesser Bear' (Ovid, *Tristia* 4. 3)

WHEN Ovid was relegated in AD 8, he left a notorious problem for scholarship. Some attribute his downfall to the *Ars Amatoria*, whose second edition appeared about 1 BC,[1] but that raises questions about the time-lag as well as about the misunderstanding of literature. Others emphasize the disgrace of Augustus's granddaughter Julia, banished for adultery in the same year as Ovid, but doubts remain about the degree of complicity needed to explain the poet's punishment. Again it has been supposed that the domestic scandal masks a political plot, a possibility that has also been canvassed over the disgrace of the elder Julia in 2 BC. Unfortunately the evidence for the various theories is so scattered that it may distract attention from the tone of particular poems, yet in this psychological drama overall impressions ought to count as well as fragments of fact. Here I shall try to interpret a single elegy, *Tristia* 4. 3, looking at it in sections as it comes; though the debate about the exile will not be repeated in detail, a view will emerge at the end about what happened.

> Magna minorque ferae, quarum regis altera Graias,
>   altera Sidonias, utraque sicca, rates,
> omnia cum summo positae videatis in axe,
>   et maris occiduas non subeatis aquas,
> aetheriamque suis cingens amplexibus arcem   5
>   vester ab intacta circulus extet humo,
> aspicite illa, precor, quae non bene moenia quondam
>   dicitur Iliades transiluisse Remus,
> inque meam nitidos dominam convertite vultus,
>   sitque memor nostri necne, referte mihi.   (1–10)

This paper began in a graduate class at Oxford, under the impact of Sir Ronald Syme's *History in Ovid* (1978), and was afterwards read in the University of Reading. I am grateful to all in both places who made suggestions, and especially to Colin Macleod, *in quo multum nuper amisimus*, for his comments on a later draft.

[1] For the date see below, n. 73.

Ovid, in banishment at Tomis, is transmitting messages to his wife by the stars, a fantasy that it is not easy to parallel directly in ancient poetry.[2] The great beast is Ursa Major,[3] also called Arctos, Helice, Septentriones, the Wain, the Plough. The lesser beast is Ursa Minor, Cynosura, Phoenice, the constellation that includes the Pole Star. It was a literary commonplace since Aratus that Greeks navigated by the Great Bear and Phoenicians by the Lesser Bear;[4] here the pedantic allusion (1 f.) helps to distance the heavenly bodies from the human suffering below. The stately period of ten lines, so unlike Ovid's usual end-stopped couplets, suits the majestic spectacle of the skies,[5] just as at the beginning of Catullus's poem on the Coma Berenices (66. 1 ff.).

Ovid chooses these particular constellations first because they belong to the far north,[6] as we are reminded by the Greek name for the Bear: though Tomis (Constanza) has about the same latitude as Rimini, its continental climate combined with the poet's misery to make it seem truly Arctic. Secondly, as Homer already points out, the Bear never sinks in the waters of Ocean:[7] just as these constellations can see everything (*Fast.* 4. 577 f.), so they are available every night for the sending of signals. Thirdly, though they guide storm-tossed mariners, they are untouched by trouble themselves (2 *utraque sicca*);[8] it was sometimes regarded as a punishment for Arctos that she was not allowed to bathe in Ocean,[9] but the emphasis here is on immutability (cf. 15) and immunity from stress. In ancient love-poetry the stars are sometimes sympathetic confidants,[10] sometimes dispassionate observers: the latter attitude suits the lonely mood of the elegy. |

Ovid's theme is developed with the epigrammatic point that he took from declamation and made his characteristic mode of self-expression; there should be no feeling, any more than with Shakespeare, that seriousness and wit are incompatible. In line 4 *occiduas* means 'occidental', but there is a pun on the primary meaning of 'falling' (cf. *Fast.*

---

[2] At Soph. *Trach.* 94 ff. the sun is asked the whereabouts of Heracles (as Mr G. O. Hutchinson reminds me); cf. also Eur. *Med.* 1251 ff.; Enn. *Scen.* 284 ff. V.

[3] *RE* 9A. 1034 ff.; Roscher, *Lex. d. Myth.* 6. 873 ff.; Bömer on Ov. *Fast.* 3. 107.

[4] Arat. *Phaen.* 36 ff.; Pease on Cic. *Nat. Deor.* 2. 106.

[5] Note also the grandiloquent *Graias* (instead of the prosaic *Graecas*).

[6] *Trist.* 2. 190 (with Owen's note); *RE* 9A. 1042.

[7] *Il.* 18. 489 = *Od.* 5. 275; Pease on Cic. *Nat. Deor.* 2. 105; Bömer on Ov. *Met.* 2. 171.

[8] *Trist.* 1. 2. 29, 4. 9. 18; Manil. 1. 610; Sen. *Med.* 404 f.

[9] *RE* 9A. 1044; G. Gundel, *De stellarum appellatione et religione Romana* (1907), 78 f.

[10] Meleager, *Anth. Pal.* 5. 191. 1; *Frag. Grenf.* 11 (p. 177 Powell) ἄστρα φίλα καὶ πότνια Νὺξ συνερῶσά μοι. Contrast Catull. 7. 7 f.

1. 314): the Bears do not wester in the western waves (there is also an antithesis with *summo*). In 4–6 the elements of water, aether, and earth are set against one another by their mention at the beginnings and ends of lines. In 9 the emphatic *meam* corresponds to the reciprocal *mihi* at the end of the couplet as well as to *nostri* at the break in the pentameter; the latter is an elegant variation for *mei*,[11] and is answered by 17 *tui memorem*. 9 *nitidos . . . vultus* is pointedly inappropriate for real bears, whose faces are not glistening but shaggy.[12] The manner of Ovid's verse will elude the reader who disregards such conceits, and so sometimes will matters of substance.

This is the case with line 5, where *suis* is marked as emphatic by its position two words in front of *amplexibus* ('with *its* embraces'); the word balances 6 *vester*, 7 *illa*, 9 *meam*, which are all similarly stressed. There may be a suggestion that the poet is denied *amplexus* of his own, but there is a more significant contrast between the circles that surround the heavenly *arx* (the part of the sky nearest the pole) and the walls that surround the Capitoline citadel.[13] The patterns traced by the two constellations are unimpaired by contact with earth: at least since Plato's *Timaeus* (41–2) and the pseudo-Platonic *Epinomis* (981–5) the stars had been associated with the perfect and the eternal,[14] the ground with corruption and mortality. On the other hand, Remus violated the sanctity of his brother's walls by breaking the continuity of the circuit, always a serious offence for the Romans;[15] it is relevant that *transiluisse* can imply transgression as well as literal jumping, while *Iliades* recalls that Remus's mother also came to ruin by metaphorically overstepping the bounds. Ovid would not allude to these disturbing legends if he were simply seeking a grandiose periphrasis for Rome;[16] rather he is suggesting a comparison between the unchanging perfection of the celestial

[11] Cf. Prop. 1. 11. 5 'nostri cura subit memores a ducere noctes?'; Hor. *Carm.* 3. 27. 14. For memory as a theme in the poems of exile cf. B. R. Nagle, *The Poetics of Exile* (Collection Latomus, 170; 1980), 92 ff.

[12] At *Pont.* 1. 5. 74 'aspicit hirsutos comminus Ursa Getas' the epithet appropriate to the bear is applied to the inhabitants of the North.

[13] It is hardly relevant in this context that Romulus excluded the Capitoline from his walls (Tac. *Ann.* 12. 24. 2; *RE* 21. 2. 1872).

[14] M. P. Nilsson, *HTR* 33 (1940), 1 ff. = *Opuscula Selecta*, 3 (1950), 31 ff. (with 255 ff.); E. Fraenkel, *CQ* 36 (1942), 10 ff. = *Kleine Beiträge*, 2 (1964), 37 ff.; S. Weinstock, *Divus Julius* (1971), 371 f.

[15] *Dig.* 1. 8. 11 'si quis violaverit muros, capite punitur . . . nam et Romuli frater Remus occisus traditur quod murum transcendere voluerit'; Pease on Cic. *Nat. Deor.* 3. 94; Bömer on Ov. *Fast.* 4. 809; Ogilvie on Liv. 1. 6. 3-7. 3.

[16] Contrast *Trist.* 1. 5. 69 f. 'sed quae de septem totum circumspicit orbem montibus imperii Roma deumque locus'.

order and the primal fault in Rome's institutions, which was deplored
by her critics from Horace to St Augustine.[17] The founder of the city
had killed his light-hearted brother in the supposed interest of
discipline and religion. Is there not an unspoken thought that the new
Romulus is destroying a well-intentioned man for his ill-timed mock-
ery of decorum in the *Ars Amatoria*?

> ei mihi, cur timeam? quae sunt manifesta, requiro.
> cur labat ambiguo spes mea mixta metu?
> crede quod est et vis, ac desine tuta vereri,
>   deque fide certa sit tibi certa fides;
> quodque polo fixae nequeunt tibi dicere flammae,   15
>   non mentitura tu tibi voce refer:
> esse tui memorem, de qua tibi maxima cura est,
>   quodque potest, secum nomen habere tuum.
> vultibus illa tuis tamquam praesentis inhaeret,
>   teque remota procul, si modo vivit, amat.   (11–20)

Ovid now describes only to dismiss his doubts about his wife's affec-
tion; he thus demonstrates his own loyalty while putting in a plea for
sympathy and reassurance. He is | afraid for no definite reason, and
keeps on asking about what is obvious; his anxiety is reiterated by *labat*
(undoubtedly the right reading),[18] *ambiguo* and *spes mea mixta metu* (12).
But as his wife's faithfulness is sure, he himself should have sure faith;
though the meaning of *fides* shifts in emphasis, the chiasmus of 14
underlines its reciprocity. The stars are too remote to help in spite of
their appearance of constancy (15),[19] and he will receive more reliable
messages from an inner voice: here he recalls the passage where
Lucretius asserted the supremacy of human reason.[20] Such soliloquies
of the irresolute mind were characteristic of the *Heroides*, where no
response was possible; they are particularly common in Seneca's
tragedies,[21] from where they flowed to Shakespeare, and as the feature

---

[17] *Epod.* 7. 17 ff. 'sic est: acerba fata Romanos agunt scelusque fraternae necis, ut
immerentis fluxit in terram Remi sacer nepotibus cruor'; Tert. *Nat.* 2. 9; Min. Fel. 25. 2;
Aug. *CD* 3. 6; H. Wagenvoort, *Studies in Roman Literature, Culture and Religion* (1956),
169 ff.; H. Fuchs, *Der geistige Widerstand gegen Rom* (1964), 86 f. Ovid tactfully reserves any
criticism for Remus, but for somebody of his temperament it must have been Romulus's
conduct that raised doubts.

[18] Cf. *Her.* 9. 42, 13. 124, 17. 178 'labant'.

[19] *fixae flammae* is an oxymoron, as flames normally flicker (Virg. *Ecl.* 8. 105 'tremulis
... flammis'), but the point is purely verbal: the noun has no implication of uncertainty.

[20] 1. 737 ff. 'ex adyto tamquam cordis responsa dedere sanctius et multo certa ratione
magis quam Pythia quae tripode a Phoebi lauroque profatur'; Ov. *Trist.* 1. 9. 51; Housman, *Last Poems*, 25. 6 'the heart within, that tells the truth and tells it twice as plain'.

[21] See Tarrant on Sen. *Ag.* 132 ff.

is also found in the *Medea* of Euripides, Ovid's own *Medea*[22] may have
been an intermediate link.

> ecquid ubi incubuit iusto mens aegra dolori,
>   lenis ab admonito pectore somnus abit?
> tunc subeunt curae, dum te lectusque locusque
>   tangit et oblitam non sinit esse mei,
> et veniunt aestus, et nox inmensa videtur,   25
>   fessaque iactati corporis ossa dolent?
> non equidem dubito quin haec et cetera fiant,
>   detque tuus maesti signa doloris amor,
> nec cruciere minus quam cum Thebana cruentum
>   Hectora Thessalico vidit ab axe rapi.   (21–30)

Ovid now turns from addressing the stars and himself to addressing
his wife directly, and again as in the love-elegies he aims not just to
describe but to persuade.[23] As he professes to be lying awake at night,
he plausibly imagines his wife's insomnia: 21 *incubuit* implies both
reclining and brooding. 24 *tangit* not only means 'touches the heart'
but recalls the physical contact of the past,[24] as does the discreet
lectusque locusque.[25] Such passages should discourage us from under-
estimating the emotional content of Roman marriage;[26] though few
writers have Ovid's excuse for breaking the conspiracy of silence, other
hints may be found in Catullus's epithalamium to Manlius (61),
Lucan's lines on Pompey and Cornelia (5. 805 ff.), and especially from
the subtle scene where the widowed Dido feels the reawakening of
love.[27] The next couplet (25–6) significantly recalls the conventional
agonies of the frustrated lover;[28] *inmensa* perhaps suggests not just the

---

[22] One is tempted to suggest that Tomis was chosen for Ovid's banishment because it
was where Medea chopped up her brother (cf. *Trist.* 3. 9); sadistic merriment is the
prerogative of autocrats. Perhaps the elder Julia was sent to Rhegium because her
promiscuity and unfilial behaviour recalled Scylla (for whom see Lyne on *Ciris* 67 ff.), and
Cassius Severus to Crete (Tac. *Ann.* 4. 21. 3) because his gibes were regarded as lies.

[23] W. Stroh, *Die römische Liebeselegie als werbende Dichtung* (1971), 250 ff.; Nagle, op. cit.
(n. 11), 43.

[24] Cf. *Her.* 10. 53 'et tua, quae possum, pro te vestigia tango'.

[25] Cf. *Met.* 11. 472; Plaut. *Amph.* 513 'prius abis quam lectus ubi cubuisti concaluit
locus'.

[26] R. O. A. M. Lyne, *The Latin Love Poets* (1980), 18 'for ladies tradition prescribed
knitting'.

[27] Virg. *Aen.* 1. 722 'iam pridem resides animos desuetaque corda'. See also Prop.
2. 6. 32 (which surely reflects the attitudes of marriage) 'orgia sub tacita condita laetitia'
(where *orgia* is Ruhnken's conjecture for *iurgia*).

[28] There is a close reminiscence of *Am.* 1. 2. 3 f. 'et vacuus somno noctem, quam longa,
peregi lassaque versati corporis ossa dolent'. See further Nisbet–Hubbard on Hor. *Carm.*
1. 25. 7.

'long night' of the commonplace but the vastness of the cosmos and the contrast with the narrow bed. When Ovid continues '*I* don't doubt that *your* love shows tokens of sorrow', it is clear from the emphasis on the pronouns that he infers his wife's distress from his own; with a man's self-centredness he is thinking primarily of himself.[29] Mental suffering (as in 21) merges with physical pain (the five words of 26 support one another): when Hector was dragged behind Achilles's chariot (while still alive, according to post-Homeric accounts), Andromache felt the torture;[30] (*cruciere* is bound to *cruentum* by the alliteration). Again as in his love-poetry, Ovid relates his calamity to the paradigms of myth: Hector and | Andromache were examples of marital fidelity,[31] Achilles a warning against the inhumanity of anger. The epithets *Thebana* and *Thessalico* (again connected by the alliteration) are not just metrically convenient periphrases, but give the allusion dignity and detachment.

> quid tamen ipse precer dubito, nec dicere possum
>   affectum quem te mentis habere velim.
> tristis es? indignor quod sim tibi causa doloris:
>   non es? at amisso coniuge digna fores.
> tu vero tua damna dole, mitissima coniunx,   35
>   tempus et a nostris exige triste malis,
> fleque meos casus: est quaedam flere voluptas;
>   expletur lacrimis egeriturque dolor.   (31–8)

Ovid now purports to show his anxiety by a further display of irresolution, though here it assumes another form (31–4): whether his wife is sorrowful or not (cf. *Trist.* 3. 3. 26 ff.), he takes it amiss. In 35 his pretended self-sufficiency begins to weaken when he tells her to grieve at her own loss; *mitissima*, which is opposed to 33 *tristis* and 36 *triste* (they are words of taste like 'mild' and 'bitter'), encourages her actually to show the tender-heartedness that she is represented as possessing. In 36 he compromises further by speaking of joint troubles: between 35 *tua* and 37 *meos*, which are emphatic and balancing, *nostris* seems to fit best if it is not equated with *meis* (as the translators suppose) but rather applied to both parties. Then at 37 he reveals his true wish and asks her to weep at *his* sorrow, though he justifies himself by the

---

[29] As Mrs S. Hockley has emphasized to me.
[30] For Andromache's participation in Hector's sufferings cf. Hom. *Il.* 22. 463 ff., 477 ff.; Enn. *Scen.* 100 f. V.
[31] For such *exempla* in the poetry of exile cf. Nagle, op. cit. (n. 11), 76 f.

commonplace that weeping can be a kind of pleasure;[32] (*voluptas* is opposed to the *dolor* that has dominated the poem since line 21). In 38 he makes the further excuse that grief is alike glutted and evacuated by tears (the verbs make yet another pointed antithesis): *egeritur*,[33] which is sometimes used of the body's waste products, recalls the Aristotelian theory of catharsis, and suggests that a medical interpretation of that word[34] may have seemed natural to the poet.

> atque utinam lugenda tibi non vita sed esset
>   mors mea, morte fores sola relicta mea: 40
> spiritus hic per te patrias exisset in auras,
>   sparsissent lacrimae pectora nostra piae,
> supremoque die notum spectantia caelum
>   texissent digiti lumina nostra tui,
> et cinis in tumulo positus iacuisset avito,   45
>   tactaque nascenti corpus haberet humus;
> denique, ut et vixi, sine crimine mortuus essem:
>   nunc mea supplicio vita pudenda suo est.   (39–48)

Ovid now carries his *querimoniae* further and wishes that he had died rather than been exiled,[35] and he imagines how his wife would have mourned him; the morbid topic is conventional in elegy,[36] yet here it seems well suited to manipulate his wife's emotions, and through her those of the general reader. In this fantasy the personal bond is emphasized by the repeated contrast of 'I' and 'you' (39–44), but significantly at the return to reality in 48 the accented *mea* is offset only by *supplicio suo*. The section is given unity by other characteristic instances of correspondence and antithesis: the release of the soul to air (41 *spiritus* balances *auras*) is followed by the return of the body to earth (45), a sequence familiar from Greek sepulchral epigram;[37] the reference to place in 41 *patrias* is picked up by 43 *notum*, 45 *avito*, and the whole of 46; 42 *pectora nostra* points to 44 *lumina nostra*, just as 42 *lacrimae...piae* to 44 *digiti...tui*;[38] 45 *avito* is answered by 46 *nascenti* (which also | looks back to 43 *supremoque die*), 45 *cinis* by 46 *corpus*, 47 *vixi* by 47 *mortuus* (so *vita* and *mors* in 39f.), 47 *crimine* by the stronger

---

[32] W. Stroh, op. cit. (n. 23), 32, n. 72.

[33] *TLL* 5. 2. 244. 7ff. See also Juv. 5. 159 'per lacrimas effundere bilem'.

[34] For a summary of the issues see D. W. Lucas's commentary on the *Poetics*, appendix II.

[35] For exile as a form of living death cf. Nagle, op. cit. (n. 11), 23ff.

[36] *Trist.* 3. 3. 29ff.; Prop. 1. 17. 19ff., 2. 13. 17ff.; Tib. 1. 3; Nagle, op. cit. 46ff.

[37] See Luck ad loc., citing esp. A. Dieterich, *Nekyia*² (1913), 106f.

[38] One may again compare Ovid's love-romances (*Her.* 10. 120 'nec mea qui digitis lumina condat erit?').

supplicio in 48. Most significantly of all, 46 *humus* looks back not just to 45 *tumulo* but to 43 *caelum*. The dying eyes that gaze on the sky, like Dido's,[39] recall the spectacle of the constellations in the opening lines,[40] and this suggests a further back-reference from 46 'tactaque nascenti corpus haberet humus' to 6 'vester ab intacta circulus extet humo'.[41] The Bears are eternally immune from the contagion of earth, but a baby is doomed to mortality from the day he is born, when by Roman ritual he is formally placed on the ground.[42]

> me miserum, si tu, cum diceris exulis uxor,
>   avertis vultus et subit ora rubor!   50
> me miserum, si turpe putas mihi nupta videri!
>   me miserum, si te iam pudet esse meam!
> tempus ubi est illud, quo te iactare solebas
>   coniuge, nec nomen dissimulare viri?
> tempus ubi est, quo te (nisi non vis illa referri)   55
>   et dici, memini, iuvit et esse meam?
> utque proba dignum est, omni tibi dote placebam:
>   addebat veris multa faventis amor;
> nec quem praeferres (ita res tibi magna videbar),
>   quemque tuum malles esse, vir alter erat.   60
> nunc quoque ne pudeat, quod sis mihi nupta; tuusque
>   non debet dolor hinc, debet abesse pudor.   (49–62)

Ovid now shows increasing uncertainty about his wife's attitude: the relationship is underlined by a continuing contrast of personal pronouns as well as by a repetition of words like *uxor*, *coniunx*, *nupta*, *vir*.[43] Just as in the last line of the previous section (48), *pudor* replaces *dolor* as the dominant emotion (52, 61, 62): the lady seems to avert her face, and with an excessive regard for public opinion (49 *diceris*, 51, 55) to blush at her position as an exile's wife.[44] Yet Ovid himself has no consciousness of guilt (62), which coheres with what he says so often elsewhere: when he swears to his parents' shades 'errorem iussae, non scelus, esse fugae' (*Trist.* 4. 10. 90), it is difficult not to believe him. He had taken part in no plot, made love to no princess, broken no law (*Pont.* 2. 9. 71), uttered no indiscretion (*Trist.* 3. 5. 47f.), and mocked

---

[39] For this motif see Pease on Virg. *Aen.* 4. 692.
[40] I owe this point to Mr D. P. Fowler.
[41] I owe this point to Mrs S. Hockley.
[42] Suet. *Ner.* 6. 1; Aug. *CD* 4. 11; A. Dieterich, *Mutter Erde*² (1913), 6ff.; *RAC* 9. 116.
[43] 57 *dote* (also used of accomplishments at *AA* 1. 596) may have a witty ambiguity in this context.
[44] For the shameful word *exul* cf. also *Trist.* 5. 11. 2; Cic. *Mur.* 61, *Dom.* 72.

Augustus in no charade;[45] such reprehensible activities all seem
incompatible with his constant emphasis on what he has seen[46] rather
than on what he has done (even other people's conspiracies are heard
of rather than observed). Since the year of his banishment is fixed
independently as also that of the disgrace of the younger Julia,[47] it
seems certain that he was aware of some impropriety, but when he
speaks of his *timor*[48] or embarrassment, that suggests that the mistakes
which made Cotta Messalinus groan (*Pont.* 2. 3. 66) stopped short of
active collusion (cf. *Trist.* 2. 104 'cur imprudenti cognita culpa mihi?').
In his own liberal circle no action was called for, but in the grim last
years of Augustus the delation associated with later reigns was already
a duty.[49]

> cum cecidit Capaneus subito temerarius ictu,
>   num legis Euadnen erubuisse viro?
> nec quia rex mundi compescuit ignibus ignes,   65
>   ipse suis Phaethon infitiandus erat.
> nec Semele Cadmo facta est aliena parenti,
>   quod precibus periit ambitiosa suis.
> nec tibi, quod saevis ego sum Iovis ignibus ictus,
>   purpureus molli fiat in ore pudor.   (63-70) |

In the manner familiar from his love-poetry Ovid now produces
three mythological *exempla*, which illustrate his own case more
precisely than is sometimes realized. Capaneus was scaling the Theban
walls with fire when he was felled to the ground by an unexpected bolt
from heaven; though his behaviour was reckless like Ovid's own,[50]
Evadne did not blush like Ovid's wife (50) but immolated herself on
her husband's pyre (cf. *Trist.* 5. 5. 54). The king of heaven 'checked fire
with fire' (the words repeat *Met.* 2. 313) when he blasted Phaethon
from the chariot of the sun; the emperor of the world curbed passion,[51]
that is to say love-poetry, by burning[52] the offending poems. Semele
was struck down because of her pretensions, and Ovid could attribute

---

[45] Cf. R. Syme, *History in Ovid* (1978), 219f.
[46] *Trist.* 2. 103, 3. 5. 49f., 3. 6. 28; J. C. Thibault, *The Mystery of Ovid's Exile* (1964), 27ff.
[47] Tac. *Ann.* 4. 71. 4; Syme, op. cit. (n. 45), 37f., 207f.
[48] *Trist.* 4. 4. 39, cf. *Pont.* 2. 2. 17.
[49] See esp. Syme, op. cit. (n. 45), 214, for the suspicious atmosphere of the period.
[50] Cf. *Trist.* 5. 3. 29f. 'illo nec levius cecidi quem magna locutum reppulit a Thebis Iuppiter igne suo' (*suo* points a contrast with the fire that Capaneus carried).
[51] For *ignes* of love-poetry cf. *Trist.* 4. 10. 45 'saepe suos solitus recitare Propertius ignes'. *compescere* suits alike checking a fire (Plin. *Epist.* 10. 33. 2) and curbing licentiousness.
[52] For the burning of bad poetry cf. Nisbet–Hubbard on Hor. *Carm.* 1. 16. 3.

his own disaster to his literary ambition;[53] on the other hand, it is implied by 67 *aliena* (which characteristically balances 68 *suis*) that he himself may be estranged from his wife (cf. 66 *infitiandus*). In 69–70 he makes it explicit that he too was struck by the fire of 'Jove'; he thus suggests the unexpectedness,[54] the ferocity (*saevis*), and the capriciousness of his punishment, while not denying that Augustus had the right, or at any rate the authority, to punish. The metaphor is a persistent one in the exile poetry,[55] and it is hard not to recognize it at *Met.* 15. 871 f. 'iamque opus exegi quod nec Iovis ira[56] neque ignis nec poterit ferrum nec edax abolere vetustas' (if one can postulate a revised edition after the decree of banishment):[57] Ovid says elsewhere of his own genius 'Caesar in hoc potuit iuris habere nihil' (*Trist.* 3. 7. 48). At the end of the section Ovid contrasts his wife's gentleness (70 *molli*) with the savage treatment he has received; the abstract *pudor* combines well with the alliterative *purpureus* just as in the *Amores* (2. 5. 34), and effectively rounds off this part of the poem (49–70 belong together).

> sed magis in curam nostri consurge tuendi,
>   exemplumque mihi coniugis esto bonae,
> materiamque tuis tristem virtutibus inple:
>   ardua per praeceps gloria vadit iter.
> Hectora quis nosset, si felix Troia fuisset?   75
>   publica virtutis per mala facta via est.
> ars tua, Tiphy, iacet, si non sit in aequore fluctus:
>   si valeant homines, ars tua, Phoebe, iacet.
> quae latet inque bonis cessat non cognita rebus,
>   apparet virtus arguiturque malis.   80
> dat tibi nostra locum tituli fortuna, caputque
>   conspicuum pietas qua tua tollat, habet.
> utere temporibus, quorum nunc munere facta est
>   et patet in laudes area lata tuas.   (71–84)

Ovid now exhorts his wife to forget her sensitive feelings and rise from her prostration: *consurge* has a literal dimension (like 21 *incubuit*), but is primarily psychological (high ideals suit the path to glory in 74 as well as the vision of the stars that set the mood of the poem). Once

[53] *Trist.* 3. 3. 74 'ingenio perii Naso poeta meo', *Pont.* 2. 7. 48.
[54] If anybody had predicted that Ovid would be sent to the Black Sea, he would have told him to drink hellebore (*Pont.* 4. 3. 51 ff.).
[55] *Trist.* 1. 1. 72, 1. 3. 11 f. etc. (see de Jonge on our passage).
[56] For Augustus's *ira* cf. Syme, op. cit. (n. 45), 223 ff.
[57] M. Pohlenz, *Hermes*, 48 (1913), 10 ff.

again he shows the egotism of a husband and a poet: *she* is to show her fine qualities in order to defend *him* (the emphatic *nostri* in 71 is here singular in reference and picked up by 73 *tuis*). Like the romantic mistresses of elegy[58] she is to derive her fame from the poems whose subject-matter she will supply: 73 *inple*[59] is a term of rhetoric no less than *exemplum* and *materiam*, and there is a wry reversal of *Amores* I. 3. 19 'te mihi materiem felicem in carmina praebe'. Her task is both difficult (74 *ardua*) and dangerous (*praeceps*), but such is the way to glory: here Ovid gives a new turn to Hesiod's maxim on the uphill path to virtue (*Op.* 290). |

With his new-found conviction the poet next develops a Stoic doctrine expounded in Seneca's *De Providentia* and summed up by the aphorism 'calamitas virtutis occasio est' (4. 6).[60] He reverts in 75 to the paradigm of Hector (cf. 29 f.): nobody would have heard of him but for the proverbial 'Iliad of woes'.[61] Misfortunes can turn Hesiod's lonely path of virtue (cf. 74) into a public highway (76), where all may watch and follow; *publica* should be taken with *via* rather than *mala* (as many suppose), and balances 75 *quis nosset?* and 80 *apparet*. Yet even in his most significant examples (77 f.) Ovid cannot resist the elegance of framing his couplet with a repeated 'ars tua ... iacet'; in line 77 *iacet*, with its suggestion of flatness, makes a clear contrast with *fluctus* (which is also set against *aequore*), and similarly in 78, with its possible meaning of 'lying ill', it seems to make a further contrast with *valeant*. But though the art of Phoebus must be primarily medicine (*Fast.* 3. 827), which is sometimes combined with navigation,[62] it is tempting to suspect a secondary meaning that is relevant to Ovid's own situation rather than to his wife's: poetry[63] as well as medicine may languish from too much well-being. In *The Wound and the Bow* Edmund Wilson exploited the myth of Philoctetes, who owed his pre-eminence in archery to his festering foot, and it might be argued that exile gave Ovid's writing a new seriousness and authority. Though he usually

[58] For such a transference of motifs from the love-poetry cf. *Trist.* 1. 6, 5. 14 (with n. 31 above).

[59] *TLL* 7. 636. 34 ff.; *OLD* s.v. 6.

[60] Cf. also *Trist.* 5. 5. 49 ff. (with further *exempla*), 5. 14. 23 f.; Sen. *Prov.* 4. 4 'gaudeant, inquam, magni viri aliquando rebus adversis, non aliter quam fortes milites bello'; Luc. 8. 74 ff.; Arr. *Epict.* 1. 24. 1 αἱ περιστάσεις εἰσὶν αἱ τοὺς ἄνδρας δεικνύουσαι; A. Bonhöffer, *Die Ethik des stoikers Epiktet* (1894), 24.

[61] For troubles as a subject for song cf. Hom. *Il.* 6. 357 f., *Od.* 8. 579 f.; Eur. *Tro.* 1240 ff.

[62] Pease on Cic. *Div.* 1. 24.

[63] Cf. *AA* 1. 25 'non ego, Phoebe, datas a te mihi mentiar artes' (with a pun on the title of his work), *Trist.* 3. 3. 10 'Apollinea ... arte'; cf. Hor. *Carm.* 4. 6. 29.

regards his misfortune as disadvantageous to poetry, in this elegy he takes a more constructive attitude.[64]

The last six lines of the elegy continue to combine noble sentiments with verbal wit, just as in Seneca. In good times *virtus* lies obscure and inert (as the noun implies energy, 79 *cessat* makes an oxymoron),[65] but in adversity it can no longer be concealed (80 *arguitur* would more usually suggest the detection of weakness). Ovid's fortune gives his socially ambitious wife[66] something to boast about (81): *nostra* is exultantly emphatic (leading to 82 *tua* and 84 *tuas*), and *fortuna* defiantly ironic. She should hold her head high (81 f.) instead of averting her gaze (50); her *pietas* (82) is best shown in fidelity to himself (cf. *Trist.* 1. 3. 86; 5. 14. 28), not in the religiosity of her friends at court. She now has space and scope for the exercise of her glory (84 *area*),[67] not just a *locus* (81) or a *via* (76, also combined with *facta est*); with further point 84 *patet* is opposed to 79 *latet*, and 84 *lata* balances 82 *tollat*. And though making use of misfortune was recommended by moralists,[68] there is a paradox in the wording *utere temporibus* (83), which naturally suggests opportunism and living for the moment. The elegy is not just an exhortation to the lady, but a self-justification to the world; as suits his invocation to the eternal Bears, Ovid has consciously reversed the cynicism of the *Ars Amatoria*.

For the *Ars* was the real cause of his ruin, not simply a convenient cover (cf. *Pont.* 2. 9. 75 f.) or a make-weight on the charge-sheet: if the later *error* had been the primary offence (thus *Pont.* 3. 3. 72), why was Ovid treated more severely than the younger Julia's lover Silanus, who simply got a hint from Augustus to go away and a hint from Tiberius to come back?[69] But the scandal of 8 AD caused the Princeps to relive his agony of 2 BC, when the elder Julia had been the culprit and the victim. She had been a pawn in political strategies since the day of her birth, when her mother was divorced for producing a girl, and when she jumped over the wall, she felt a compulsion not just to defy but to

[64] Cf. *Trist.* 5. 1. 28 'materia est propriis ingeniosa malis'.

[65] For the collocation cf. Cic. *Post Red. in Sen.* 13; Luc. 3. 690.

[66] She was a dependant of Marcia, the cousin of Augustus and wife of Paullus Fabius Maximus, cos. 11 BC and patron of poets (Hor. *Carm.* 4. 1. 10 f.; Syme, op. cit. (n. 45), 135 ff.).

[67] The word yields another pun at *Trist.* 5. 14. 23 'area de nostra nunc est tibi facta ruina', which confirms Ehwald's *facta est* in our passage (the MSS read *ficta est* or *freta es*).

[68] See for instance Plut. *De Tranq. An.* 467a–e.

[69] Tac. *Ann.* 3. 24. 4 'se quoque laetari quod . . . e peregrinatione longinqua revertisset'; Syme, op. cit. (n. 45), 207. Silanus's political importance would not have saved him if Augustus had been mainly concerned about the younger Julia.

desecrate.[70] Augustus saw great damage to his social and dynastic policies, and he did not like being made a fool of by his own daughter; his indignation was perfectly sincere[71] (the charges | were too embarrassing to have been trumped up), and though the episode had political consequences (notably the elimination of Iullus Antonius), there is no certain evidence for an anti-Augustan plot.[72] Livia must have been well satisfied at the disgrace of her stepdaughter, the mother of the princes who had so recently supplanted Tiberius (on merely objective criteria the natural heir), but she would present her motivation to her husband, perhaps even to herself, as moral rather than political. The amiable and thoughtless Ovid, who seems to have been unconscious of these complexities, chose this moment to publish a second edition[73] of the *Ars Amatoria*, embellished by a third book addressed to *puellae*. The Princeps, who read poetry in a literal spirit, characteristically did not caution the poet, but nursed his fury[74] for some eight years and, when the new scandal provided a pretext, loosed his thunderbolt.

When Ovid was relegated, his wife offered to accompany him (*Trist.* 1. 2. 41; 1. 3. 81f.), but it seemed more sensible that she should stay behind to protect the property (*Trist.* 1. 6. 7ff.) and organize support; but when the poet on his sick-bed imagines her arrival at Tomis,[75] he reveals his true wish without daring to mention it directly. He even came to feel, quite unfairly, that she might have done more for him by a direct approach to Augustus (*Trist.* 5. 2. 37) or Livia (*Pont.* 3. 1. 114).[76] Yet for the purposes of our poem, confidence is still the dominating motif, even if there is an undercurrent of anxiety; by the conventions of ancient literature, exhortation does not necessarily imply that the other party needs exhorting.[77] Ovid's banishment produced a series of piquant ironies: the most frivolous and least

---

[70] Sen. *Ben.* 6. 32. 1 (from Augustus's own report) 'forum ipsum ac rostra, ex quibus pater legem de adulteriis tulerat, filiae in stupra placuisse'.

[71] Suet. *Aug.* 65. 2 'abstinuitque congressu hominum diu prae pudore'; Dio 55. 10. 14.

[72] Sen. *Brev. Vit.* 4. 6 'iterum timenda cum Antonio mulier'; Syme, op. cit. (n. 45), 194 (with bibliography). Against a plot see A. Ferrill in *Studies in Latin Literature and Roman History* (ed. C. Deroux), 2 (Collection Latomus, 168; 1980), 332ff.

[73] *AA* 1. 171–228 (which can be dated to about 1 BC) seem to be a later insertion (R. Syme, op. cit. (n. 45), 13ff.), and were presumably added with the independent third book (cf. ibid. 19). If the first edition of the first two books is put back a few years, then Ovid's works are spaced more plausibly (cf. ibid. 18).

[74] Tiberius, who must have resented Julia's behaviour as a slight on himself, was equally unforgiving.

[75] *Trist.* 3. 3. 23 'nuntiet huc aliquis dominam venisse, resurgam'.

[76] Cf. *Pont.* 3. 1. 31ff., 3. 7. 12 'quam proba tam timida est experiensque parum'.

[77] *Trist.* 5. 14. 43ff.; Isoc. 9. 78–9; Nisbet–Hubbard, *Horace, Odes* 2, 3f.

autobiographical of the Roman elegists portrays a family relationship with a particularity unparalleled in ancient poetry; he gives an insight into the nature of power under the Principate which in spite of his necessary discretion is more revealing than anything in Virgil or Horace; he shows greater resolve than a moralist like Cicero under far more formidable persecution (for his adjurations are really saying something about himself). Most curiously of all, and surely deliberately, he professes an Augustan ideal of marriage,[78] even if the celestial pattern is marred by the imperfections of earth.

[78] *Pont.* 3. 1. 73 ff. 'exigit hoc socialis amor foedusque maritum . . .'.

10

Horace's *Epodes* and History

> It was the best of times, it was the worst of times, it was the age of
> wisdom, it was the age of foolishness, it was the epoch of belief, it
> was the epoch of incredulity, it was the season of Light, it was the
> season of Darkness, it was the spring of hope, it was the winter of
> despair.
>
> Charles Dickens, A Tale of Two Cities.

OUR two cities are Rome and Alexandria and the time is the triumvirate, or more precisely the years from 42 BC, when Antony and
Octavian defeated Cassius and Brutus at Philippi, till 31 BC, when
Octavian defeated Antony and Cleopatra at Actium. As in all revolu-
tionary periods men gave way to extremes of hope and despair,
according to their temperament and luck: for every dispossessed
Meliboeus there was a satisfied and grateful Tityrus, or the same
person might oscillate between both moods, like Virgil himself in the
Eclogues and *Georgics*. And as in other times of uncertainty there was a
recrudescence of superstition,[1] often in its less orthodox forms—witch-
craft, astrology, oracle-mongering, eschatology, ruler-cult. When Julius
Caesar was assassinated in 44, the preceding bad weather was treated
ex post facto as a portent of doom (*Georgics* 1. 466-88), but when a
comet appeared during the games in his honour, it was represented
less conventionally as evidence of apotheosis (*Eclogues* 9. 46-9). The
Greek-speaking Jews of the Diaspora composed 'Sibylline' oracles
lamenting the ruin caused by the triumvirate and prophesying the
revenge of the East,[2] or perhaps imagining an infant Messiah, a

---

[1] R. Syme, *The Roman Revolution* (Oxford, 1939), 218, 256, 471-2; id., *Sallust* (Berkeley
and Los Angeles, 1964), 237.

[2] *Orac. Sib.* 3. 52 τρεῖς Ῥώμην οἰκτρῇ μοίρῃ καταδηλήσονται ('three men will ruin
Rome with a piteous fate'); 3. 350-3 ὁππόσα δασμοφόρου Ἀσίης ὑπεδέξατο Ῥώμη |
χρήματά κεν τρὶς τόσσα δεδέξεται ἔμπαλιν Ἀσὶς | ἐκ Ῥώμης, ὀλοὴν δ᾽ ἀποτίσεται ὕβριν
ἐς αὐτήν ('as much money as Rome received from the tribute of Asia, three times as

---

From *Poetry and Politics in the Age of Augustus*, ed. T. Woodman and D. West (Cambridge,
1984), 1-18, 197-200.

conflation of Isaiah's Emmanuel with the semi-divine babies of Greek or Egyptian mythology, who would bring the millennium to the world.[3] By an ingenious transmutation of his sources Virgil in his fourth eclogue applied these fancies to Western aspirations for peace, but not everybody was as optimistic: the other literary genius of the day, namely Sallust, showed how national and personal misfortune sometimes concentrates the mind on realities.

When our tale begins Horace was among the pessimists. The | Republican cause, which he had joined out of youthful idealism, was destroyed at Philippi, and already there may have been a lack of sympathy between the freedman's son and his aristocratic brother-officers.[4] His ambition to write epodes in the manner of Archilochus had its origins in the bitterness of defeat; after the rout he could quote to himself the Greek poet's lines on his shield,[5] which he had discarded in much the same area with an insouciant disregard for heroics, and when the Republican army capitulated in Thasos, he might recall that this was Archilochus's second homeland, which he had compared in his disillusionment to a donkey's spine (21 West). The Archilochus of the ancient tradition was the son of a Thracian slave-woman who lost his property through political folly[6] and gave vent to his misanthropy in virulent iambics, yet in the vicissitudes of war and politics showed a virile resolution and durability. Poets do not choose their personae at random, but to match something that they would like to see in themselves; Horace says of his own desperation, after he had been mellowed by success, 'inopemque paterni | et laris et fundi paupertas impulit audax | ut versus facerem'.[7] Among his political epodes the sixteenth is the most Archilochean, and it will be convenient now to examine it by sections.

much will Asia receive in turn from Rome, and will pay her back for her destructive aggressiveness'); cf. W. W. Tarn, 'Alexander Helios and the Golden Age', *JRS* 22 (1932), 135–43.

   [3] R. G. M. Nisbet, 'Virgil's Fourth Eclogue: Easterners and Westerners', *BICS* 25 (1978), 62 (= above, p. 54).

   [4] *Serm.* 1. 6. 46–8; *Odes* 2. 7. 11–12; R. G. M. Nisbet and M. Hubbard, *A Commentary on Horace's Odes: Book II* (Oxford, 1978), 106.

   [5] Archilochus fr. 5 West; Horace, *Odes* 2. 7. 10.

   [6] See the testimonia at 295 West, esp. (*b*) ἀποβαλόντι τὴν οὐσίαν ἐν πολιτικῇ φλυαρίᾳ ('having lost his property in political foolishness').

   [7] Horace, *Epist.* 2. 2. 50–2. *audax* suggests a desperate recklessness; cf. E. Wistrand, 'Archilochus and Horace', *Entretiens Hardt*, 10 (1963), 262–5 (= id., *Opera Selecta* (Stockholm, 1972), 402–5).

        altera iam teritur bellis civilibus aetas,
          suis et ipsa Roma viribus ruit:
        quam neque finitimi valuerunt perdere Marsi
          minacis aut Etrusca Porsenae manus,
        aemula nec virtus Capuae nec Spartacus acer   5
          novisque rebus infidelis Allobrox,
        nec fera caerulea domuit Germania pube
          parentibusque abominatus Hannibal,
        impia perdemus devoti sanguinis aetas,
          ferisque rursus occupabitur solum.   (16. 1–10)

The epode as a whole has close affinities with Virgil's fourth
eclogue, which celebrated the pact between Antony and Octavian in
the autumn of 40 BC, but we cannot determine its historical context
without making our minds up about priority:[8] is the poet deploring the
Perusine War of 41 or the conflict with Sextus Pompeius that began in
38? On general grounds it is easier to believe that Horace deflated
unrealistic optimism than that his friend reversed the process, and this
view already draws some support from the first line of the epode.
When the overall resemblances of the two poems are taken into
account, this must have some relationship to the opening of the
eclogue (after the | proem), 'ultima Cumaei venit iam carminis aetas'
(4. 4); but whereas the new Sibylline age gave Virgil his organizing
principle, Horace's *aetas* is inexplicit by comparison and therefore
more probably derivative. In that case *iam* is also influenced by the
eclogue; as Virgil is imitating oracles composed by Hellenized Jews, his
iam suggests eschatological proclamations, of the type familiar from
the New Testament, saying that the time has come. The contemporary
Eastern oracles that are the acknowledged source of the eclogue are
hinted at more obliquely in the epode: thus in the second line the pun
on *Roma* (cf. ῥώμη 'strength') and *viribus* is the sort of thing that is
found in the extant 'Sibylline' collection.[9] And when the poet predicts

---

[8] See esp. S. Sudhaus, 'Jahrhundertfeier in Rom und messianische Weissagungen',
RhM 56 (1901), 37–54; B. Snell, 'Die 16. Epode von Horaz und Vergils 4. Ekloge', *Hermes*,
73 (1938), 237–42; K. Barwick, 'Zur Interpretation und Chronologie der 4. Ecloge des
Vergil und der 16. und 17. Epode des Horaz', *Philologus*, 96 (1944), 28–67; D. Ableitinger-
Grünberger, *Der junge Horaz und die Politik* (Heidelberg, 1971), 66–79; and for further
bibliography A. Setaioli, 'Gli "Epodi" di Orazio nella critica dal 1937 al 1972', *ANRW*
2. 31. 3 (1981), 1753–61.

[9] C. W. Macleod, 'Horace and the Sibyl (*Epode* 16. 2)', *CQ*, NS 29 (1979), 220–1 cites
Orac. Sib. 3. 363–4 ἔσται καὶ Σάμος ἄμμος, ἐσεῖται Δῆλος ἄδηλος | καὶ Ῥώμη ῥύμη ('and
Samos will be sand, and Delos invisible, and Rome an alley'); he suggests that ῥύμη may
in fact not be 'an alley' but 'a collapsing ruin' (cf. Horace's *ruit*).

in line 10 that wild animals will repossess the site of the city, his cries
of woe seem to be derived from the apocalypses of the East, where
ruins in the desert were a familiar scene; thus a later oracle announces
to Rome καὶ τὰ θέμειλα λύκοι καὶ ἀλώπεκες οἰκήσουσι (8. 41), 'and
wolves and foxes shall inhabit the foundations'.[10]

> barbarus heu cineres insistet victor et Urbem
>   eques sonante verberabit ungula,
> quaeque carent ventis et solibus ossa Quirini,
>   nefas videre! dissipabit insolens.
> forte quid expediat communiter aut melior pars   15
>   malis carere quaeritis laboribus.
> nulla sit hac potior sententia, Phocaeorum
>   velut profugit exsecrata civitas
> agros atque Lares patrios, habitandaque fana
>   apris reliquit et rapacibus lupis,   20
> ire pedes quocumque ferent, quocumque per undas
>   Notus vocabit aut protervus Africus.
> sic placet? an melius quis habet suadere? secunda
>   ratem occupare quid moramur alite?   (16. 11-24)

The turning of Rome to ashes continues the apocalyptic note, but
though vague and exaggerated Horace's words derive their significance from a real and recent historical catastrophe. In 40 BC the Parthians took advantage of the civil wars to overrun the provinces of
Syria and Cilicia and threaten the empire's whole Eastern position.
Ventidius restored the situation with victories in 39 and (following a
renewed assault) in June 38,[11] but though it would be needlessly
pedantic to place our poem before the first of his campaigns, the panic
might seem less topical after the second, and certainly after his
triumph in November 38. The poet then turns to the Herodotean story
of the Phocaeans | (1. 165), who evacuated their city in 534 BC before
the advance of the Persian Harpagus; commentators fail to underline
the relevance of the story at a time when the Parthians had threatened
to occupy the whole of Asia Minor. Of course Horace introduces an
element of fantasy when he suggests that Rome itself will be
abandoned, but though he speaks as a poet rather than as a historian,

[10] E. Fitzgerald, *Rubáiyát of Omar Khayyám*, 1st edn., stanza XVII 'They say the Lion and
the Lizard keep I The courts where Jamshýd gloried and drank deep'; Ableitinger-
Grünberger, op. cit. (n. 8), 67.

[11] Dio 49. 19-21; T. Rice Holmes, *The Architect of the Roman Empire* (Oxford, 1928),
I. 121-2; N. C. Debevoise, *A Political History of Parthia* (New York, 1938), 114-20; *RE*
8A. 807-14.

his words reflect a genuine mood of alarm. His direct address to the people suits the political arrangement of an early Greek city rather than of Rome, where there was no general *ius agendi cum populo*, but what matters for us is the vivid presentation of an authentic attitude.

> sed iuremus in haec: simul imis saxa renarint   25
> vadis levata, ne redire sit nefas;
> neu conversa domum pigeat dare lintea, quando
> Padus Matina laverit cacumina,
> in mare seu celsus procurrerit Appenninus,
> novaque monstra iunxerit libidine   30
> mirus amor, iuvet ut tigris subsidere cervis,
> adulteretur et columba miluo,
> credula nec ravos timeant armenta leones,
> ametque salsa levis hircus aequora.
> haec et quae poterunt reditus abscindere dulcis   35
> eamus omnis exsecrata civitas,
> aut pars indocili melior grege; mollis et exspes
> inominata perprimat cubilia!
> vos quibus est virtus, muliebrem tollite luctum,
> Etrusca praeter et volate litora.   (16. 25–40)

Horace now urges that the abandonment of Rome should be permanent: the citizens may return only when various *adynata* or impossibilities have occurred. By a characteristically poetic synthesis he combines motifs from a wide range of sources, Herodotus on the Phocaeans (25–6), Sibylline Oracles (27–9),[12] and Archilochus (34 and 39), but his use of Virgil (30–3) gives the historian the crucial *terminus post quem*. The line on the cattle and the lions (33) provides clear evidence, usually disregarded, that he is imitating the fourth eclogue: when Virgil says 'nec magnos metuent armenta leones' (4. 22), his vision of a future peace among the beasts comes not from the epode but from a Jewish Sibylline paraphrase of Isaiah.[13] Horace's description of incompatible matings (30–2) is probably influenced by *Eclogues* 8. 27 'iungentur iam grypes equis' (the poem should be dated to 39);[14] the cruder

[12] For the oracular language cf. *Orac. Sib.* 4. 97–8 (as cited by Strabo 1. 3. 7) ὅτε Πύραμος ἀργυροδίνης | ἠϊόνα προχέων ἱερὴν ἐς Κύπρον ἵκηται ('when Pyramus with its silvery eddies by throwing out a shore comes to holy Cyprus').

[13] Isaiah 11: 6–8; *Orac. Sib.* 3. 788–95; Barwick, op. cit. (n. 8), 54–5; Nisbet, op. cit. (n. 3), 66 (above, p. 64).

[14] Snell, op. cit. (n. 8), 237–9. The eighth eclogue was written shortly before Pollio's return from his province (dated by the *Fasti triumphales* to 39 or 38); Maecenas, who must have become Virgil's patron by the first part of 38, is mentioned nowhere in the book.

tone of *subsidere* and *adulteretur* suggests that the epode is the | imitation, and it is likely in any case that Horace should derive his rustic fancy from the great new bucolic poet of the day.

> nos manet Oceanus circumvagus: heia,[15] beata
>   petamus arva, divites et insulas,
> reddit ubi Cererem tellus inarata quotannis,
>   et imputata floret usque vinea,
> germinat et numquam fallentis termes olivae,   45
>   suamque pulla ficus ornat arborem,
> mella cava manant ex ilice, montibus altis
>   levis crepante lympha desilit pede.   (16. 41–8)

Horace now proclaims his resolve to seek the Happy Isles, where everything grows in abundance without the toil of man. The ancient commentary of 'ps.-Acro' compares an anecdote about Sertorius, who when in revolt in Spain in the 70s envisaged an escape to the *insulae fortunatae* in the Atlantic; the story was told in the first book of Sallust's *Histories*,[16] which also mentioned the automatic bounty of nature, and as the historian gave great prominence to Sertorius (a fellow Sabine), he is likely to have treated the incident not as a peripheral curiosity but as a symbolic rejection of the corruption of Rome. As the time of writing is very close on any assumption (Sallust composed five books between about 40 and 35), it has reasonably been supposed that Horace drew on the great new history of the age, another argument that he is writing after Virgil's fourth eclogue.[17] It has also been observed that Horace's allusion to Catiline and the Allobroges (line 6) may have been influenced by Sallust's recent *Bellum Catilinae*; as in all these matters the issue is not the information itself but its topicality. The theme of recurring civil war could also owe something to Sallust.[18] When Horace says that Rome is collapsing from its own strength (line 2), that is not a poet's formulation but a historian's, which is repeated even by the complacent Livy (*praefatio* 4 'ut iam magnitudine laboret sua'). Perhaps the common source is the *praefatio* of Sallust, who may

---

[15] *arva* of the MSS is explained by the commentators in three ways, all unconvincing. To provoke discussion I have printed Axt's (*h*)*eia* (cited but not supported by W. Dillenburger, *Q. Horatii Flacci Opera Omnia*, 4th edn. (Bonn, 1860), ad loc.), which I thought of independently; for this stirring exhortation cf. Virg. *Aen.* 4. 569; Pers. 5. 132; Stat. *Theb.* 12. 406 (so 'Westward ho!').

[16] Sall. *Hist.* 1. 100–2 Maur.; Plut. *Sert.* 8. 2–9. 1.

[17] G. Schörner, *Sallust und Horaz über den Sittenverfall und die sittliche Erneuerung Roms* (Diss. Erlangen, 1934), 45; Syme, op. cit. (n. 1 (1964)), 285.

[18] For Sallust's emphasis on national disunity cf. *Hist.* 1. 11–12 Maur.; Syme, op. cit. (n. 1 (1964)), 182–3.

have brooded on the nation's self-destruction with the sombre realism
of his imitator Pollio.[19]

> illic iniussae veniunt ad mulctra capellae,
>   refertque tenta grex amicus ubera;   50
> nec vespertinus circumgemit ursus ovile,
>   neque intumescit alta viperis humus;
> nulla nocent pecori contagia, nullius astri   61
>   gregem aestuosa torret impotentia. | 62
> pluraque felices mirabimur; ut neque largis   53
>   aquosus Eurus arva radat imbribus,
> pinguia nec siccis urantur semina glaebis,
>   utrumque rege temperante caelitum.
> non huc Argoo contendit remige pinus,
>   neque impudica Colchis intulit pedem;
> non huc Sidonii torserunt cornua nautae,
>   laboriosa nec cohors Ulixei.   60
> Iuppiter illa piae secrevit litora genti,   63
>   ut inquinavit aere tempus aureum,
> aere, dehinc ferro duravit saecula, quorum
>   piis secunda vate me datur fuga.   (16. 49-66)

The co-operative goats of the Happy Isles (49-50) once again recall
the fourth eclogue (21-2 'ipsae lacte domum referent distenta capellae
| ubera'); the Virgilian passage seems to be derived directly from
Theocritus.[20] Virgil follows immediately with the sentence cited on 33
about the concord of the animals (4. 22 'nec magnos metuent armenta
leones'), that is to say, he takes together what the epode keeps apart; it
is significant that Horace breaks up Herodotus' story of the Phocaeans
in exactly the same way (17-19, 25-6, 35-6), while there is a similar
distribution of the Archilochean allocutions (15-16, 39), the oracular
prophecies about beasts in the city (10, 19-20), and perhaps the
reminiscences of Sallust (see above). The poem ends, as it began, with
a reference to time-schemes; the mention of *saecula* as in the fourth
eclogue reminds us that a new century was assigned by some to 39 BC.
When he calls himself a *vates* in the last line (66), Horace speaks not as
a second Archilochus but as the substitute for an oracle (always
important at Greek colonizations). But unlike the Sibyl of the eclogue,
this prophet sees the good society not as something that is now being

[19] Hor. *Odes* 2. 1. 29-36 with Nisbet and Hubbard, op. cit. (n. 4), 9.
[20] Theoc. 11. 12. πολλάκι ταὶ ὄιες ποτὶ τωὔλιον αὐταὶ ἀπῆνθον ('often the sheep came
of their own accord to the fold'); Snell, op. cit. (n. 8), 240-1.

inaugurated in Rome, but as an unrealizable fantasy to be set before the beginning of history or outside the known world.

The seventh epode reflects similar attitudes to the sixteenth; as the poem is short it may be taken all together.

> quo, quo scelesti ruitis? aut cur dexteris
>   aptantur enses conditi?
> parumne campis atque Neptuno super
>   fusum est Latini sanguinis,
> non ut superbas invidae Carthaginis   5
>   Romanus arces ureret, |
> intactus aut Britannus ut descenderet
>   Sacra catenatus via,
> sed ut secundum vota Parthorum sua
>   urbs haec periret dextera?   10
> neque hic lupis mos nec fuit leonibus
>   numquam nisi in dispar feris.
> furorne caecos, an rapit vis acrior,
>   an culpa? responsum date!
> tacent et albus ora pallor inficit   15
>   mentesque perculsae stupent.
> sic est: acerba fata Romanos agunt
>   scelusque fraternae necis,
> ut immerentis fluxit in terram Remi
>   sacer nepotibus cruor.   (7. 1-20)

As this epode has fewer indications of date than the sixteenth, it is here discussed in the second place, but it was probably in fact written earlier; this is not so much on account of its comparative simplicity (sometimes a deceptive criterion), as because the war that is there already disastrous (16. 1-2) is here only threatening (7. 1-2). That suggests that it was composed in 39 or early 38,[21] when the campaign against Sextus Pompeius is about to begin; the allusion to the Parthian menace (9-10), which is more explicit than in the companion poem, suits such a date (above, p. 164). In that case the reference to war at sea (3 *Neptuno super*) alludes to the previous naval activities between 42 and 39; as *Neptuno* seems to hint at Pompeius, who took the god as his patron, we shall think especially of the operations against him in 40-39 before the Peace of Puteoli. If we refer *Neptuno super* to the main war against Sextus Pompeius (38-36), the poem itself would have to be assigned to the preliminaries of Actium (say 33-32); but Horace's grim

---

[21] See Ableitinger-Grünberger, op. cit. (n. 8), 60-5; Setaioli, op. cit. (n. 8), 1710-12.

pessimism would have been politically impossible when the crusade against Cleopatra was being planned, or indeed at any time after he had entered the circle of Maecenas (see below).

The web of allusion is less complex than in the sixteenth poem, but here too Horace uses a poet's imagination to express genuine historical attitudes. Once more he addresses the crowd with the anachronistic directness of an early Greek poet, and restrains the belligerent citizens as if they were literally drawing their swords. When he turns away in disgust and speaks in the third person of the people's embarrassment (15-16), his words recall Cicero's recent gibe at Antony (*Philippics* | 2. 84 *sudat pallet*), but there is greater significance in the epode's Sallustian manner; the truncated sentences and bald style suggest the historian's sinister brevity. Once again Horace may be echoing something from Sallust's preface to his *Histories* (though the chronology is even tighter than with the other poem); the curse of Romulus, a motif that has been attributed to Timagenes,[22] could have been hinted at in the historian.[23] When the poet describes Rome's exposure to the Parthian menace (7. 9-10), it seems relevant to quote the first 'Sallustian' epistle to Caesar (1. 5. 2): 'quoniam orta omnia intereunt, qua tempestate urbi Romanae fatum excidii adventarit, civis cum civibus manus conserturos, ita defessos et exsanguis regi aut nationi praedae futuros. aliter non orbis terrarum neque cunctae gentes conglobatae movere aut contundere queunt hoc imperium.' Though this composition was surely not written by Sallust,[24] it may have made use of something in the preface to the *Histories*; 'regi aut nationi praedae futuros' was more relevant in 39 than during Caesar's dictatorship, the purported date of the epistle, when the Parthians were relatively quiescent. Certainly if Horace is imitating Sallust, that explains why he is able to speak with such gravity and authority.

The two poems were so impressive and so damaging that Maecenas now intervened. Evidence for the all-important date is found in the sixth satire of the second book: 'septimus octavo propior iam fugerit annus | ex quo Maecenas me coepit habere suorum | in numero' (40-2). The satire mentions as a topical talking-point the allocation of lands to the veterans (55-6), so it probably belongs to the winter of 31-30,

---

[22] H. Wagenvoort, *Studies in Roman Literature, Culture and Religion* (Leiden, 1956), 173-4.
[23] Barwick, op. cit. (n. 8), 64-7; Ableitinger-Grünberger, op. cit. (n. 8), 16.
[24] Syme, op. cit. (n. 1 (1964)), 314-51.

when Octavian demobilized some of his army;[25] if we can assume that the ordinals are inclusive, that seems to put the beginning of the *amicitia* early in 37.[26] Such a date suits the poet's presence as *comes* to his patron in the spring of that year (*Satires* 1. 5 on the *iter Brundisinum*); Maecenas was on the way to negotiate a political settlement (28–9), presumably the pact of Tarentum with Antony, and the croaking of the frogs (14–15) supports the season. Horace had been introduced to Maecenas nine months before he was taken on (*Satires* 1. 6. 61–2); that gives the middle of 38 as a *terminus ante quem*. Five separate paths now converge on the first half of 38 for the composition of the sixteenth epode (and the seventh is unlikely to have been much earlier). The war with Sextus Pompeius, which restarted in the spring of 38, is already proving ruinous; the Parthian invasion has not yet been broken by the decisive victory of June 38; Virgil's fourth eclogue, which must have become known in 39, is a recent masterpiece crying out for rebuttal; Sallust's first book of *Histories* can be | accommodated as a source on the Happy Isles; Horace has not yet been introduced to Maecenas, after which such sceptical poems become much less likely.

The first result of Maecenas's patronage was to trivialize the poet's treatment of war and politics; though his experiences in the campaign against Sextus Pompeius might have seemed suitable for Archilochean touches, they have left no traces on the *Epodes*. In the fourth poem he mocks an upstart *tribunus militum*, but the man is unimportant or even fictitious: Porphyrio is wrong to see a reference to the treacherous Menodorus, who was a commander of fleets. When the tenth poem promises an offering to the storm-winds if Mevius is drowned, that reminds us of Octavian's more creditable dedications to the Venti at Anzio;[27] but characteristically Horace's enemy is not a man of power but simply a bad poet. One is tempted to suggest a more pointed contemporary allusion in the epodes on Canidia's witchcraft (5 and 17); as her name was extremely rare, it would remind everybody of Canidius Crassus (cos. suff. 40 BC), a long-standing opponent of Octavian, who was to put him to death after Actium. Horace says that Canidia asks for the herbs 'quas Iolcos atque Hiberia | mittit vene-

---

[25] Dio 51. 4. 3; Rice Holmes, op. cit. (n. 11), 158–9.
[26] This interpretation could explain the tense of *fugerit*, which at first seems to suit the eighth year better than the seventh. When the end of 31 was approaching, the seventh year since 37 had almost run out, if we count inclusively and by consular years; but if we reckon in terms of anniversaries, then the eighth year (again counted inclusively) was nearly over.
[27] *ILS* 3279; Appian *BC* 5. 98. 406.

norum ferax' (5. 21-2); the latter place-name refers to Georgia in the Caucasus (south of Medea's Colchis), but commentators fail to observe that Canidius conquered Hiberia in 36 on behalf of Antony.[28] This oblique gibe is all that the new Archilochus offers by way of political invective.

As the war of Actium approached, Maecenas presented Horace with a Sabine estate (cf. *Epodes* 1. 31-2), which gave him financial independence. His motives ought to be obvious: he was not just a literary patron with an unusual insight into poets' ways, but one of the inner circle of Octavian's party, a propagandist and power-broker of genius, not least because he was willing to wait. If he divined Horace's price, he required no explicit commitments in return; by giving him freedom to exercise his talent and a property to replace his lost inheritance he bound him by *fides* more securely than by any deal. Horace now finally renounced the angry convictions of his youth to become the ingratiating ironist that the world loves so much; 'imbellis ac firmus parum' (*Epodes* 1. 16) is an odd self-description in the introductory poem of an Archilochean collection. In 37 he had given Maecenas his gratitude and sympathy, but now in moments of crisis more active support would be required. Such an occasion arose in 31 BC.

We come now to a familiar problem: were Maecenas and Horace present at the battle of Actium?[29] The external evidence is ambiguous:[30] Appian implies that Maecenas was in Rome at the time, Velleius proves | nothing one way or another, while the first *Elegia ad Maecenatem*, written in the first century AD, is explicit that its hero was at the battle (1. 45-6):

> cum freta Niliacae texerunt lata carinae,
> fortis erat circa, fortis et ante ducem.

It may be significant that Horace himself suggests that he took part in campaigns later than Philippi:[31] when he claims at the end of his first

[28] Plut. *Ant.* 34. 6; Dio 49. 24. 1; Canidia reappears in *S.* 1. 8.

[29] In favour cf. F. Bücheler, 'Coniectanea', *Index scholarum hib. Bonnae* (1878-9), 13 (= *Kleine Schriften, 2* (Leipzig, 1927), 320-1); E. Wistrand, *Horace's Ninth Epode and its Historical Background* (Göteborg, 1958) (= *Opera Selecta* (Stockholm, 1972), 289-350); against, cf. E. Fraenkel, *Horace* (Oxford, 1957), 71-5. For further bibliography see Setaioli, op. cit. (n. 8), 1716-28.

[30] Appian *BC* 4. 50. 217 τὸν μὲν δὴ παῖδα ὁ Μαικήνας ἐς Ἄκτιον ἔπεμπε τῷ Καίσαρι ('Maecenas sent the son [of Lepidus] to Octavian at Actium'); Vell. 2. 88, where Wistrand, op. cit. (n. 29), 7-9 refutes Fraenkel, op. cit. (n. 29), 71 n.; for varying views on the *Elegiae in Maecenatem* cf. E. Bickel, 'De elegiis in Maecenatem', *RhM* 93 (1950), 113-16; H. Schoonhoven, *Elegiae in Maecenatem* (Groningen, 1980), 39-68.

[31] Wistrand, op. cit. (n. 29), 35-9.

book of epistles 'me primis urbis belli placuisse domique' (1. 20. 23), *belli* is hardly just a reference to Brutus, and when he talks of war-weariness in his ode to Septimius (2. 6. 7–8, perhaps written about 26 BC), that implies relatively recent military service.

More clear-cut evidence is provided by the opening lines of the book of epodes (1. 1–4):

> ibis Liburnis inter alta navium,
> amice, propugnacula,
> paratus omne Caesaris periculum
> subire, Maecenas, tuo . . .

This passage catches precisely the ideology of the period, when traditional patriotism was replaced by oaths of loyalty to the leader, and Horace makes it clear in the rest of the poem that he feels similarly bound to his patron. It is sometimes said that Maecenas meant to join the campaign, but was driven by political necessities to a change of plan; but then it would have been absurd for the poet to leave his protestations unaltered when he published the book, and what is worse to place them at the beginning of the collection. Indeed it seems possible that in spite of the future tense, the opening dedication was written after the event: the two-banked Liburnian galleys played an important part in the mythology of the battle.[32] It is usually supposed that *propugnacula* refers to Antony's towering galleons, which are compared elsewhere to city walls,[33] but the word has a potentially favourable ring (like the 'wooden walls' at Salamis); as Dillenburger (1860) suggested in his edition[34] the contrast may be between Octavian's own heavy ships[35] and the more modest galleys that were appropriate to Maecenas. *inter* suggests comradeship and loyalty (important qualities for the poem) sooner than hostility, while *ibis* suits the whole enterprise[36] better than the moment of attack (the

---

[32] Hor. *Odes* 1. 37. 30 with R. G. M. Nisbet and M. Hubbard, *A Commentary on Horace's Odes: Book 1* (Oxford, 1970), 420.

[33] Plut. *Ant.* 66. 2; Dio 50. 33. 8; J. Kromayer, 'Der Feldzug von Actium und der sogennante Verrath der Cleopatra', *Hermes*, 34 (1899), 40; cf. Pliny, *Nat.* 32. 3.

[34] For the same view of *ibis . . . inter . . . propugnacula* cf. also M. W. Thompson, 'The Date of Horace's First Epode', *CQ*, NS 20 (1970), 332, who, however, refers the poem to the war against Sextus Pompeius. Yet as the collection was published about 30, the introductory epode, with its Liburnian galleys and declarations of loyalty, must point to Actium.

[35] As W. W. Tarn, 'The Battle of Actium', *JRS* 21 (1931), 193 points out, Octavian did not rely on *Liburnae* to bear the brunt of the fighting.

[36] Hor. *Odes* 1. 7. 26 'ibimus, o socii comitesque'; 2. 17. 9–10 'non ego perfidum I dixi sacramentum: ibimus ibimus' (a passage that may allude to Actium).

same is true of the plural *Liburnis*). But it is time to turn to the ninth epode, Horace's main pronouncement on Actium, which will be discussed in sections. |

> quando repostum Caecubum ad festas dapes
>   victore laetus Caesare
> tecum sub alta—sic Iovi gratum—domo,
>   beate Maecenas, bibam,
> sonante mixtum tibiis carmen lyra,   5
>   hac Dorium, illis barbarum,
> ut nuper, actus cum freto Neptunius
>   dux fugit ustis navibus,
> minatus Urbi vincla, quae detraxerat
>   servis amicus perfidis?   (9. 1-10)

We must first ask whether the opening scene is set before or after the battle. *victore laetus Caesare* is contemporaneous with *bibam*, but that does not exclude the possibility that the war has already been won and that Horace is simply waiting for the symposium. Yet such a reading diminishes the poem disastrously: *quando* readily takes on a longing tone, but in the agony of the world it should suggest a patriot's deferred hopes[37] rather than a parasite's impatience for a party. The Caecuban has been set aside not for its own sake but as a symbol of victory, much as in the Cleopatra Ode it could not be produced till the queen was dead (1. 37. 5). It is therefore implausible to posit a situation where victory has been achieved but the poet is still worrying about the celebration.

We may still ask whether in fact Horace was writing before the battle; this is a different kind of question, being concerned not with the poem as it is presented to us but with the processes of composition.[38] Here the reference to Sextus Pompeius's defeat at Naulochus (7-8) perhaps betrays knowledge of Antony's defeat at Actium: *ustis navibus* suits the latter no less than the former.[39] *dux* is paradoxically combined with *fugit* (8) (just as *Neptunius*[40] with *actus freto* in the previous line);

---

[37] Cf. Ar. *Peace* 346 εἰ γὰρ ἐκγένοιτ' ἰδεῖν ταύτην με τὴν ἡμέραν ('would that it were possible for me to see this day').

[38] G. Williams, *Tradition and Originality in Roman Poetry* (Oxford, 1968), 214 regards such questions as misguided. But information about a poet's methods is always interesting and sometimes explains anomalies.

[39] Hor. *Odes* 1. 37. 13 'vix una sospes navis ab ignibus'; F. Wurzel, 'Der Ausgang der Schlacht von Aktium und die 9. Epode des Horaz', *Hermes*, 73 (1938), 372-3.

[40] Perhaps *Neptunius* is a noun ('the Neptunian'); *dux* is then predicative with *fugit*. It is always assumed that *Neptunius* qualifies *dux*; but the intervention of the line-ending is awkward, especially before a monosyllable.

the epigram seems applicable not just to Pompeius but to Antony, whose place was notoriously at the fore in the flight from Actium. But though our suspicions may be aroused, judgement on the time of composition must be reserved till we have examined more of the poem.

We may next ask what the opening lines reveal on Horace's presence at the battle. If he purports to be speaking at Actium, then *sub alta . . . domo* has resonances of home to set against the foreign surroundings, and *sic Iovi gratum* (which seems to comment particularly on *sub alta domo*) suggests that Jove is concerned for the men's return; editors should note the Homeric lines where Athene says to Zeus εἰ μὲν δὴ | νῦν τοῦτο φίλον μακάρεσσι θεοῖσι | νοστῆσαι Ὀδυσῆα πολύφρονα ὅνδε δόμονδε, 'if this is dear to the blessed gods, that wise Odysseus should return to his own home' (*Odyssey* 1. 82–3). On the other hand, if the scene is set at Rome, *sic Iovi gratum* is much less pointed and can imply no more than a general blessing on the celebrations; it cannot refer to *sub alta domo*, as the exact place is now of little interest to the gods. Fraenkel (n. 29), 74 thinks that the venue may be Horace's town-house, but there is nothing in the text to suggest anything so specific, and it is unlikely that Maecenas visited his protégé often, especially in such a crisis. Williams (n. 38), 216 sets the scene at Maecenas's own palace, but that can hardly be so: nobody would say to a friend 'When shall I drink with you in your house?' if he were there already. Fraenkel says that there is nothing to indicate a setting so unusual as Actium, but he admits himself that some Horatian poems (for instance *Odes* 1. 28 on Archytas) only reveal their situation gradually; as elsewhere, he fails to allow for the fact that Augustan poets treated as matters of common knowledge some things that are obscure to us.

> Romanus, eheu,—posteri negabitis—
>   emancipatus feminae
> fert vallum et arma, miles et spadonibus
>   servire rugosis potest,
> interque signa turpe militaria
>   sol aspicit conopium.   (9. 11–16)

These lines vividly demonstrate the organization of opinion that was so decisive a factor in the war of Actium.[41] Antony is simply ignored, while Cleopatra is too abominable to be named. Instead of just freeing slaves, as Sextus Pompeius had done (9–10), Antony's men

---

[41] Syme, op. cit. (n. 1 (1939)), 459–75.

have become slaves themselves. The mosquito-net was a prudent
precaution on that malarial shore, but here it has suggestions of
effeminacy (to balance 12 *feminae*, 13 *spadonibus*); *conopium* is not
simply derived from the Greek word for a gnat, but lies behind English
'canopy'. The indignation of these sentences shows that the present
tenses are not historic; Horace represents the horrors as going on at
the moment of writing. And when he says *sol aspicit conopium*, that is
more convincing if he claims to be present in the area and not just
imagining the scene from Rome.

> †ad hunc† frementes verterunt bis mille equos
>   Galli canentes Caesarem, |
> hostiliumque navium portu latent
>   puppes sinistorsum citae.   (9. 17–20)

The first couplet describes the defection from Antony of Amyntas,
who as a client-king naturally supplied him with cavalry; the episode,
which took place shortly before the main battle, caused the abandonment of the attempt to defeat Octavian by land.[42] *Galli* refers to the
Galatians of Asia Minor, but in conjunction with *Caesarem* the word
reminds us of Julius Caesar's conquest of Gaul: it is a paradox that
while Romans were enslaved to an Eastern queen, Gauls voluntarily
joined Caesar's heir.[43] The crux at the beginning of line 17 is all-
important for the interpretation of the poem: *ad hunc* has by far the
clearest authority, *adhuc* is read by at least one important manuscript,
at huc was found by Cruquius in a *codex Blandinianus*,[44] *ad hoc* and *ad
haec* were proposed by Bentley, *at nunc* by Housman. Several considerations will occur to the critic: the impossibility of referring *hunc*
either to *Romanus* or to *sol*, the oddity of *ad* with the masculine
pronoun, the need to read accusative *frementis* (of horses raring to go).
But for present purposes it will be enough to concentrate on a single
decisive argument: *verterunt* combines well with *huc* 'diverted their
horses this way'), but with other readings it could only mean 'turned in
flight',[45] an interpretation that is incompatible with *canentes Caesarem*.
But if *huc* is correct, it means not just 'to our side' (which would suit a
poet writing in Rome), but quite literally 'in this direction'; if it had

---

[42] Vell. 2. 84. 1–2; Plut. *Ant.* 63. 3; Serv. *Aen.* 6. 612; Kromayer, op. cit. (n. 33), 23–4.

[43] There is also a disregarded pun on *gallus*, 'a cock'; *canere* is the Latin for 'to crow'.

[44] Comm. Cruq. ad loc. 'at Galli canentes Caesarem, id est laudantes, verterunt huc, id
est ad nos transtulerunt, bis mille equos frementes'.

[45] The point is made by W. M. Edwards in A. Y. Campbell, *Horace: Odes and Epodes Re-
edited* (Liverpool, 1953), 160.

undisputed manuscript authority it would show unequivocally that Horace was present at Actium.

The following couplet (19–20) is also important for our view of the poem and the battle; the interpretation depends on four points of detail that have all been accepted by some scholars but perhaps never combined. *portu* means the Ambracian gulf, at whose mouth Actium was situated; it cannot refer to a distant port like Alexandria, as the poet's knowledge does not extend so far (as becomes clear from 29–32). *citae* in conjunction with an adverb of direction (*sinistrorsum*) must be a participle ('set in motion'),[46] not an adjective; if there is an ironic reference to the conventional 'swift ships', it can only be secondary. *navium ... puppes* is an intolerable periphrasis for 'ships' in so concentrated a poem, and therefore refers literally to hulls; in view of the close conjunction of *puppes* with *citae*, Horace seems to mean that the vessels were propelled stern-first (Bentley compared πρύμναν (ἀνα)κρούσασθαι).[47] *sinistrorsum* must have been the nautical term for 'to port',[48] and therefore is used with relation to the ships themselves; it | cannot refer to the viewpoint of Octavian's fleet, or of an observer on the promontory to the north, still less to what somebody in Rome might have thought about his relative position as he gazed in imagination to the south-east.

Horace's lines, when correctly understood, seem to explain the tactics of the battle. The Ambracian gulf[49] is an indentation in the western Greek coast some fifty miles south of Corfu and the modern Albania. Tarn[50] thought that when Antony emerged from the gulf he was intending to encircle Octavian's fleet to the north, Kromayer[51] that he was aiming at a general break-out to the south; the latter view coheres better with his earlier failures (prominent Romans were defecting as well as the Galatians), and is supported by the epode's evidence, which Kromayer failed to use. After Cleopatra and then Antony had fled, other ships would have followed if they had not been outflanked by Octavian; if they were pointing south, and there was no room or time to wheel round, perhaps they turned their sterns to port

---

[46] Cf. *Epod.* 17. 7 'citumque retro solve solve turbinem'; Virg. *Aen.* 8. 642 'citae ... in diversa quadrigae'.

[47] L. Casson, *Ships and Seamanship in the Ancient World* (Princeton, NJ, 1971), 279n.

[48] Plaut. *Rud.* 368–9 'nos cum scapha tempestas dextrovorsum | differt ab illis'.

[49] For maps see J. Kromayer and A. Veith, *Schlachten-Atlas zur antiken Kriegsgeschichte* (Leipzig, 1922); Rice Holmes, op. cit. (n. 11), 147.

[50] W. W. Tarn, op. cit. (n. 35) and id., 'Actium: A Note', *JRS* 28 (1938), 165–8.

[51] Kromayer, op. cit. (n. 33) and id., 'Actium: Ein Epilog', *Hermes*, 68 (1933), 371–8.

and reversed eastwards into the gulf. 'Backing water' was only
attempted over very short distances, and we need not suppose that
many ships executed the manœuvre: when Horace sums up the
shambles in an epigram, he is influenced by the sinister associations of
the Latin adverb. Even so, the degree of detail given by *sinistrorsum* is
probably due to autopsy rather than to a version of Octavian's dispatch
(as Tarn supposed); if it is objected that the tactics and topography of
the battle would be too obscure to the reading public, it must be
remembered that seven hundred senators accompanied Octavian on
the campaign (*Res gestae* 25. 3).

> io Triumphe, tu moraris aureos
>   currus et intactas boves?
> io Triumphe, nec Iugurthino parem
>   bello reportasti ducem,
> neque Africanum, cui super Carthaginem   25
>   virtus sepulcrum condidit.
> terra marique victus hostis Punico
>   lugubre mutavit sagum,
> aut ille centum nobilem Cretam urbibus
>   ventis iturus non suis,   30
> exercitatas aut petit Syrtis Noto,
>   aut fertur incerto mari.   (9. 21–32)

While Horace's shouts of triumph emphasize that the enemies were
treated as foreign, his comparisons with Jugurtha and Carthage
remind | us that they were dangerous, cruel, and African; the former
illustration shows once again the impact of Sallust's monographs, and
perhaps suggests the new esteem of Marius. But scholars have reasonably asked what the poet is exclaiming about: the defection of two
thousand horse and the withdrawal of the enemy fleet seem inadequate reasons in the context. Some have supposed that these are
just the preliminary skirmishes, Quatre Bras rather than Waterloo, and
that Horace has been misled by premature rumours of victory; but the
account of Antony's movements (29–32) corresponds so exactly to his
disappearance from the main battle that it cannot refer to anything
else. Housman[52] suggested that Horace is foreseeing prophetically the
flight of the enemy; but though a poet may visualize the future in
present tenses, a comparison with Jugurtha in the perfect tense makes

[52] A. E. Housman, 'Horatiana', *JPh.* 10 (1882), 195 (= *Classical Papers* [ed. J. Diggle and
F. R. D. Goodyear] (Cambridge, 1972), 7–8); afterwards he changed his mind (reported
by Tarn, op. cit. (n. 50 (1938)), 165 n.), but his later position is not known.

an odd introduction to such a sequence (23–4 'nec Iugurthino parem | bello reportasti ducem'). If the lines were written before the event they are implausibly accurate, and if they were written or simply published afterwards, nobody could know that they were to be understood as a prediction.

In fact *terra marique victus* (27), which must refer to the whole campaign, picks up the earlier reference to cavalry and ships (17–20); there was no later large-scale engagement by land. Where then is the great sea-battle, with its clash of empires and celestial phenomena, as graphically depicted by Virgil (*Aeneid* 8. 675 ff.) and Propertius (4. 6)? Horace may partly be influenced by his anti-heroic Archilochean stance; he is trying to communicate the slow realization of victory, as things happen in real life. But his account corresponds very much to the actualities of this particular battle (which supports the view that he was present): Octavian spent the night on shipboard to prevent further escapes from the gulf,[53] the importance of the enemy withdrawal did not become clear till the next morning, and Canidius's land army did not surrender for some days. The battle of Actium was not so spectacular an occasion[54] as was subsequently represented; even Octavian in his dispatch mentioned only 5,000 dead, and though the figure is variously interpreted,[55] it is not great in view of the large forces engaged and the high stakes involved.

In lines 27–32 the defeated Antony is contrasted with the victorious Octavian: 'conqueror by land and sea' was a formula of panegyric, but here there is evident satire in the substitution of *victus* for *victor*. Like Cleopatra in line 12, the rival leader cannot even be named; the mood of the time is indicated by 27 *hostis*, which goes further than the more general *hostilium* of line 19. *Punico* is not only a conventional | gibe at Antony's magnificence, but significantly picks up 25 *Carthaginem*. The mystery of the enemy's whereabouts well illustrates the elusiveness of sea-power; this is a convincing detail that suits the poet's participation in the battle. *ventis iturus non suis* presents genuine knowledge in a sinister way: from the literal point of view the winds were blowing Antony to Egypt, but they were the same north-westers that had enabled Agrippa to swoop at

[53] Wurzel, op. cit. (n. 39), 363–6 cites Suet. *Aug.* 17. 2 'ut in nave victor pernoctaverit'; Oros. *Adv. Pag.* 6. 19. 10 'reliquum diei cum subsequente nocte in victoriam Caesaris declinavit'; Vell. 2. 85. 6 (the later surrender of the army).

[54] Tarn, op. cit. (n. 35), 182–3; Syme, op. cit. (n. 1 (1939)), 297–8.

[55] Plut. *Ant.* 68. 1; Tarn, op. cit. (n. 35), 177–8; Kromayer, op. cit. (n. 51(1933)), 368–9; Wurzel, op. cit. (n. 39), 367–8.

Actium.[56] With a similar understanding of the strategic issues Horace alludes to Cyrenaica (31 *Syrtis*), where several of Antony's legions were stationed (and ultimately defeated by Gallus), but the treacherous place-name and pejorative description (*exercitatas ... Noto*) are slanted to emphasize the danger to the enemy forces. In the same spirit 32 *incerto* stresses the instability of the sea, to match the shifting Syrtes, while *fertur* ('drifts') makes a climax after *petit*, which at least implies a plan.

It should be clear by this time that Horace has described the changing situation in the form of a running commentary, an established technique of Hellenistic and Roman poetry.[57] The opening section (1–18) presents the period before the battle, while the rest (19–38) describes the latter part of the great day. The close conjunction of 17–18 (the desertion of the Galatians) with 19–20 (the withdrawal of the enemy fleet) is chronologically misleading, but the foreshortening gives tightness to the structure. The developing movement helps the view that Horace is present at Actium rather than awaiting communiqués in Rome: when Fraenkel says that the first reports had just reached Maecenas, he forgets that in the ancient world the news of battles did not arrive piecemeal. But in spite of the illusion of immediacy, the epode cannot really have been written in parts: battles are not the best places for poetic composition, and Horace had more feeling for unity than a Victorian novelist.

> capaciores adfer huc, puer, scyphos
> et Chia vina aut Lesbia,
> vel quod fluentem nauseam coerceat   35
> metire nobis Caecubum:
> curam metumque Caesaris rerum iuvat
> dulci Lyaeo solvere.   (9. 33–8)

With the last section we find ourselves at a celebration on the evening of the day of battle. Fraenkel explains *capaciores* as the common call for bigger cups when the symposium is well advanced (cf. *Satires* 2. 8. 35 'et calices poscit maiores'); but the drinking should not begin till victory is achieved, and the comparative may simply mean | 'larger than usual'.[58]

---

[56] Virg. *Aen.* 8. 682 *ventis et dis Agrippa secundis*, 8. 710 (of the flight) *undis et Iapyge ferri*; Plut. *Ant.* 66. 4. *Noto* (31) is mentioned only as the African storm-wind.

[57] L. P. Wilkinson, 'Horace, *Epode* IX', *CR* 47 (1933), 5–6; Nisbet and Hubbard, op. cit. (n. 32), 310–11.

[58] For the use of the comparative Wistrand, op. cit. (n. 29), 34 cites *Odes* 1. 9. 6–7 *benignius deprome*; add 3. 21. 8 *languidiora vina*, Hom. *Il.* 9. 202–3 μείζονα δὴ κρητῆρα, Μενοιτίου υἱέ, καθίστα, | ζωρότερον δὲ κέραιε ('set down a large-sized mixing-bowl, son of Menoetius, and mix on the strong side'). The naming of the wines in Horace's next line (34) suits the view that the party is just beginning.

Certainly it is difficult to suppose that the party has lasted since the beginning of the poem:[59] though there is 'ring-composition' in the references to drinking at the opening and the close (six lines in each place), Horace could not claim to have spent the whole of the battle, as well as the period before the Galatian surrender (13–16), in one protracted carousal. Fraenkel argues that 35 *nauseam* refers to the consequences of heavy drinking, but though the word sometimes describes a symptom of illness, it does not seem to be recorded of this particular complaint.[60] If it is once conceded that the poet was present at Actium, we may agree with Bücheler that the word bears its primary sense of seasickness;[61] of course on any assumption there is a crude Archilochean realism. Bücheler thought that the drinking is actually set on shipboard, which has literary precedent in Archilochus himself;[62] Fraenkel regards this as impossible in the absence of explicit stage-directions, yet seasickness is normally cured by coming off the boat, it has been noted above that Octavian's fleet was manned all night, and a contemporary reader would have a clearer view than we have of the situation and its possibilities. If Horace's celebration sounds surprisingly civilized, Maecenas's *Liburna* may have been more comfortably equipped than a fighting ship;[63] one recalls Lord Cardigan's yacht at Balaclava.

[59] Thus Williams, op. cit. (n. 38), 215–17, who puts the party in Rome, and C. Bartels, 'Die neunte Epode des Horaz als sympotisches Gedicht', *Hermes*, 101 (1973), 287, who puts it at Actium.

[60] Fraenkel, op. cit. (n. 29) quotes Plin. *Nat.* 23. 43 'merum . . . remedio est . . . et quorum stomachus in vomitiones effunditur', but that passage refers to real illness; cf. R. Hanslik, 'Horaz und Aktium', *Serta Philologica Aenipontana*, 7/8 (1962), 340.

[61] See esp. D. Ableitinger-Grünberger, 'Die neunte Epode des Horaz', *WS*, NS 2 (1968), 85–8, who cites Plin. *Nat.* 27. 52 '[absinthium] nauseam maris arcet in navigationibus potum'. She also shows that *fluens* is a medical term for an illness that involves e.g. vomiting (Celsus *prooem.* 55, *TLL* 6. 1. 975. 46 ff.), and that this might or might not be the case with *nausea* or seasickness (Celsus 1. 3. 11).

[62] Archilochus fr. 4. 6–9 West ἀλλ' ἄγε σὺν κώθωνι θοῆς διὰ σέλματα νηὸς | φοίτα καὶ κοίλων πώματ' ἄφελκε κάδων, | ἄγρει δ' οἶνον ἐρυθρὸν ἀπὸ τρυγός· οὐδὲ γὰρ ἡμεῖς | νηφέμεν ἐν φυλακῇ τῇδε δυνησόμεθα ('But come, go with a mug along the planks of the swift ship, and pull the stoppers from the capacious jars, and draw the red wine from the lees; for neither shall we be able to be sober on this watch'). Archilochus's ship is at sea, as is confirmed by the imitation in Synesius, *Epist.* 32 Hercher = 45 Garyza (see A. Garyza, 'Una variazione archilochea in Synesio', *Maia*, 10 (1958), 66–71); if φυλακή could refer to a blockade (as at Thuc. 2. 69. 1), that would correspond to the situation in Horace's poem.

[63] In peacetime Horace twice mentions luxury-triremes in contexts with hints of Maecenas. See *Odes* 3. 1. 38–40 'neque | decedit aerata triremi et | post equitem sedet atra cura' (does *aerata* suggest a converted warship?); *Epist.* 1. 1. 92–3 'conducto navigio aeque | nauseat ac locuples quem ducit priva triremis' (a commonplace of popular philosophy adapted to a personal situation).

Not enough attention has been paid to the wines, which as usual in Horace have a symbolic significance; we need not ask what in fact was available at Actium. The Chian and Lesbian give a little support to the view that the scene is set in the Greek world. On the other hand, the contrasted Caecuban is one of the finest of Italian wines, which has been explicitly mentioned at the beginning of the poem as the token of victory and home-coming; in view of the 'ring-composition', it is unconvincing for Fraenkel to distinguish the 'Auslese' of line 1 from the ordinary sort of line 36. In fact by calling for Caecuban, Horace is suggesting that victory may already have been won: one may note the tentative *vel*, 'or perhaps rather', as opposed to the previous *aut*, 'or alternatively'. But if the Caecuban has a patriotic rather than a purely medicinal function, then *nauseam* should refer to the sufferings on shipboard rather than the excesses of the celebration itself. The symbolic aspect of the symposium is developed in the last line, where *Lyaeo*, 'the Liberator' (a title of Dionysus, here used of the wine itself) is pointedly combined with *solvere*; Horace is not just thinking of the conventional 'release' of the symposiast but implying that the Caecuban, the token of victory, is bringing liberation from foreign bondage (cf. 11–14).[64] |

Though the *Epodes* lack the Archilochean clarity of vision that can make a remote society seem intensely real, they are of significance to historians on various counts. The seventh and sixteenth poems organize their material in a characteristically poetic way, with few direct facts and many literary motifs, yet they communicate an emotion as Cassius Dio never does; if they do not tell us what actually happened, at least they indicate what it might have felt like at the time. On the other hand, the ninth epode is a primary source of a kind very unusual in poetry; if it is examined closely it seems to yield information, based on personal experience, that is not available elsewhere. But perhaps the book's greatest illumination lies not in Horace's comments on the world but in what he betrays about himself. When he turned to the genre of *iambi*, that was a declaration of his own alienation, yet he ended the decade as a committed supporter of the new regime. It was by such manipulation of men's minds rather than by any exploits at Actium that Octavian's party prevailed.

[64] At *Odes* 1. 37. 1–2 'nunc pede libero | pulsanda tellus', the adjective refers both to agility in the dance and to deliverance from Cleopatra.

11

Sacrilege in Egypt (Lucan 9. 150–61)[1]

ite, duces, mecum (nusquam civilibus armis   150
tanta fuit merces) inhumatos condere manes,
sanguine semiviri Magnum satiare tyranni.
non ego Pellaeas arces adytisque retectum
corpus Alexandri pigra Mareotide mergam?
non mihi pyramidum tumulis evolsus Amasis   155
atque alii reges Nilo torrente natabunt?
omnia dent poenas nudo tibi, Magne, sepulchra.
evolvam busto iam numen gentibus Isim
et tectum lino spargam per volgus Osirim
[et sacer in Magni cineres mactabitur Apis]   160
suppositisque deis uram caput.

GNAEUS POMPEIUS, having heard of his father's assassination, demands vengeance on Egypt; to avoid prejudging any issues, I have followed Housman's text. Already lines 150–2 show the sort of verbal point that Lucan's interpreters usually ignore. Normally in epic one would expect *ite, viri, mecum*, but *duces* suggests the divided command of the Republican party; now leaders have to be urged to follow. *inhumatos condere manes* applies to the shade an expression appropriate to the body (cf. Verg. *Aen.* 4. 34 *manis... curare sepultos*); though *manes* is sometimes used in surprisingly physical contexts (Prop. 2. 13. 32 *accipiet manis parvula testa meos*), the poet is here thinking not just of literal burial but of the repose given by revenge. *semiviri* makes a contrast with the juxtaposed *Magnum* and an oxymoron with *tyranni*. *satiare* means not just 'appease' (J. D. Duff's translation) but more starkly 'gorge'; the collocation of the material *sanguine* with the unsubstantial *manes* recalls the drinking of the ghosts in Homer's Nekyia (*Od.* 11. 23 ff.). |

[1] I owe much to members of a class on Lucan 9, held in Oxford in the autumn of 1984. It is a pleasure to dedicate these interpretations to Professor Borzsák, who has recently made several interesting contributions to the study of Lucan.

Acta Antiqua Academiae Scientiarum Hungaricae, 30 (1982–4), 309–17.

In 153 *Pellaeas arces* is translated by Duff 'the Macedonian city' (i.e. Alexandria), and it is true that *arces* may refer to a city in a general way (*TLL* 2. 739. 63ff.). One might look for something to balance 156 *alii reges* (just as 154 *Alexandri* balances 155 *Amasis*), and Cortius actually proposed *arcas* ('the coffins of the Ptolemies'); but to say nothing of the unattractive homoeoteleuton, an *arca* was much too humble for so magnificent a family (cf. 8. 736 'da vilem Magno plebei funeris arcam'). *arces* is presumably right, as it makes a good hyperbole with *mergam* (Francken insensitively comments 'insolitum'); it also combines pointedly with the juxtaposed *adytis*, as the one word implies 'high up', the other 'deep inside'. In particular it suggests, after 152 *tyranni*, the strategic positions occupied by a despot (*TLL* 2. 739. 44ff.). If a more precise explanation is looked for, *arces* may be a pejorative description of the Βασίλεια or Palaces,[2] the area of Alexandria occupied by the Ptolemaic public buildings; as the name Ἄκρα[3] was given to a fortress within this area, it could have influenced Lucan's choice of word.

There is a parallel to our passage at 8. 692ff., where Lucan declaims against Ptolemy for authorizing Pompey's murder:

> ultima Lageae stirpis perituraque proles,
> degener incestae sceptris cessure sorori,
> cum tibi sacrato Macedon servetur in antro
> et regum cineres extructo monte quiescant,   695
> cum Ptolemaeorum manes seriemque pudendam
> pyramides claudant indignaque Mausolea,
> litora Pompeium feriunt, truncusque vadosis
> huc illuc iactatur aquis.

8. 694 *antro*, like 9. 153 *adytis*, describes the vault where Alexander was buried (both words are used at 10. 19ff., and *penetrali* at Suet. Aug. 18. 1). 695 is referred by recent interpreters to the pyramids of the Pharaohs; but *cineres* does not suit mummified kings, the singular *monte* is puzzling, and it is odd that the word 'pyramids' should be applied not to the Pharaohs, to whom it properly alludes, but only to the Ptolemies (697). In fact 695 alludes to the earliest Ptolemies,[4] the only dynasty relevant at the moment; they still practised cremation,[5] and like the other people in the context were buried in Alexandria.

---

[2] Strab. 17. 1. 8; P. M. Fraser, *Ptolemaic Alexandria* (Oxford, 1972), 1. 14ff.

[3] Fraser, op. cit. 1. 30f.; 2. 98f., n. 225.

[4] H. Thiersch, *Jahrbuch des deutschen archäologischen Instituts*, 25 (1910), 68ff. Cf. already *Adnotationes super Lucanum* (ed. Endt) *alii pyramides volunt esse in Alexandria civitates* (read *civitate*).

[5] Thiersch, op. cit. 57.

Their ashes seem to have been included within Alexan|der's own mausoleum[6] (compare the practice with the relatives of Augustus); *extructo monte* makes a contrast with *antro*, and is elucidated by 10. 19 (Caesar visits Alexander's body) 'effossum tumulis cupide descendit in antrum'. On the other hand, the pyramids of 697 are additional structures built for the last Ptolemies,[7] degenerate persons, in Lucan's opinion,[8] who would be more sympathetic than their predecessors to Egyptian architecture.

To revert to 9. 153, it might be tempting to identify the *Pellaeas arces* with the *mons* of 8. 695 and its surrounding mausolea; this would provide another reference to sacrilege against the dead, the main theme of the passage. But in the present state of our knowledge there is nothing to justify so particular an explanation, and the hint of living tyrants is lost. *arces* is placed next to *adytis* because the Palaces included the area where the monuments were situated: see Strab. 17. 1. 8 μέρος δὲ τῶν βασιλείων ἐστὶ καὶ τὸ καλούμενον Σῶμα, ὃ περίβολος ἦν ἐν ᾧ αἱ τῶν βασιλέων ταφαὶ καὶ ἡ Ἀλεξάνδρου. The precinct is called the Soma[9] by Strabo and ps.-Callisthenes, *Historia Alexandri Magni* 3. 34. 6 Kroll (including the Armenian version), the Sema by Zenobius 3. 94 (*Paroem. Graec.* 1. 81); the former combination looks authoritative, as one manuscript tradition is unlikely to have influenced the other. The name is a strange one, but suggests the veneration felt for the relics of Alexander, which Ptolemy Soter had brought to Egypt to support the legitimacy of his succession.[10] Alexander was mummified, not cremated (Curt. Ruf. 10. 10. 13), and when Augustus touched him he broke off part of his nose (Dio 51. 16. 5); such a burial must have made a unique impression on a Greek city.

At 154 *corpus Alexandri* obviously refers to the actual body, but shows awareness of the position of the Soma among the sights of Alexandria.[11] The founders of cities had the rare privilege of being buried within the walls, and violation of such a tomb portended general calamity;[12] cf. Hor. *Epod.* 16. 13f. 'quaeque carent ventis et solibus ossa Quirini—nefas videre—dissipabit insolens'. There is an

---

[6] Fraser, op. cit. 1. 16; 2. 33 n. 80.

[7] Thiersch, op. cit. 69f.; W. W. Tarn, *Alexander the Great* (Cambridge, 1948), 2. 384f.

[8] See also Strab. 17. 1. 11 ἅπαντες μὲν οὖν οἱ μετὰ τὸν τρίτον Πτολεμαῖον ὑπὸ τρυφῆς διεφθαρμένοι χεῖρον ἐπολιτεύσαντο.

[9] Fraser, op. cit. 1. 15f.; 2. 31ff. nn. 79, 80.

[10] Cf. the bones of Orestes (Herod. 1. 67. 2) and Theseus (Plut. *Cim.* 8. 6).

[11] He must have known Seneca's *De situ et sacris Aegyptiorum*.

[12] For Roman feeling against the τυμβωρυχός cf. Mommsen, *Strafrecht* (Berlin, 1899), 812ff.; *ILS* 8172–258; F. de Zulueta, *JRS* 20 (1932), 184ff.

implicit comparison of Pompeius Magnus with Alexander the Great,[13] whom Lucan loathes because of his own aggressiveness[14] as well as the villainies of the Ptolemies; see the denunciation of | the *felix praedo* at the beginning of the tenth book, especially 22 f. 'sacratis totum spargenda per orbem membra viri posuere adytis'. Such a man deserved to be dumped in Lake Mareotis, on the south of the city he had founded (9. 154 'pigra Mareotide mergam'). *pigra* suggests a sluggish swamp, like the one that Catullus destines for his enemy (17. 10 f.); the adjective may imply an appropriate punishment for Alexander, who, as Lucan himself would admit, was the most *impiger* of mankind (cf. 10. 28 ff.).

At 155 f. Lucan follows two lines on the Macedonian rulers with two corresponding lines on the Pharaohs; *adytisque retectum corpus Alexandri* is balanced by *pyramidum tumulis evolsus Amasis*. The poet is recalling how the Persian Cambyses opened the tomb of Amasis (not strictly a pyramid) and committed outrages on the king's mummy (Herod. 3. 16. 1).[15] If it is objected that Amasis could not suffer this indignity a second time, one may refer to the Egyptian story that the body in question belonged not to the king himself but a substitute (ibid. 3. 16. 5). *evolsus*, 'plucked out', can be paralleled at Verg. *Aen.* 4. 427 'nec patris Anchisae cineres manisve revelli', but a further allusion may be suggested; Cambyses plucked the hair from Amasis's body (Herod. 3. 16. 1 τὰς τρίχας ἀποτίλλειν), and though Lucan uses *evellere* in a different sense, he seems to be recalling the Herodotean equivalent. Similarly when he refers to Cambyses as *vaesanus* (10. 279), he is echoing Herod. 3. 30. 1 αὐτίκα διὰ τοῦτο τὸ ἀδίκημα ἐμάνη, ἐὼν οὐδὲ πρότερον φρενήρης.

The Herodotean analogy may be pursued further. Cambyses was the son and heir of Cyrus, but already in Herodotus is regarded as inferior; for the comparison see also Xenophon, *Cyropaedia* 8. 8. 2, [Lucian], *Macrobioi* 14. Because of Xenophon and others, Cyrus became the subject of uncritical eulogy in the Hellenistic and Roman periods;[16] Cicero claims that he was a model both for Scipio Aemilianus (*QF* 1. 1. 23) and the young P. Crassus (*Brut.* 282), and in composing his own συμβουλευτικόν to Caesar he used the *Cyrus* of Antisthenes (*Att.* 12. 38a. 2 cf. 12. 40. 2). In these circumstances

---

[13] D. Michel, *Alexander als Vorbild für Pompeius, Caesar und Marcus Antonius* (Coll. Latomus, 94; 1967), 35 ff.; S. Borzsák, *Latomus*, 28 (1969), 592 f.

[14] I. Borzsák, *Bull. Assoc. G. Budé* (1980), 68 ff.

[15] I owe this important observation to Mr S. J. Harrison.

[16] R. Höistad, *Cynic Hero and Cynic King* (Uppsala, 1948), 73 ff.; *RE* Suppl. 4. 1162 ff.

Pompey the Great may have been compared with Cyrus the Great (as well as with Alexander), for instance by Posidonius or Theophanes. Both men were conquerors in the East, both were credited with moral virtue and political sagacity, both were killed in distant lands and had their bodies maltreated (Herod. 1. 214. 4).

What is more, both Cyrus and Pompey had degenerate sons; Lucan himself calls Sextus Pompeius 'Magno proles non digna parente' (6. 420). Cassius remarked of the elder brother (who speaks our lines in Lucan) 'scis Gnaeum quam sit fatuus, scis quo modo crudelitatem virtutem putet, scis quam se semper a nobis derisum putet; vereor ne nos rustice gladio velit ἀντιμυκτηρίσαι' | (Cic. *Fam.* 15. 19. 4). A pun seems to be missed here:[17] μυκτηρίζειν with its compounds, like Horace's *naribus uti*, elsewhere refers to sneering (cf. Cassius's *derisum*), but when combined with *gladio* it surely means 'to cut off the nose'[18] (*rustice* suggests a crude reprisal for the sniffs of the sophisticated). Thus when the Ethiopian king Actisanes invaded the Egypt of Amasis and some inhabitants revolted, he cut off their noses and settled them at Rhinocolurus on the Palestinian border, so giving the place its name: see Diod. Sic. 1. 60. 4 ἀποτεμὼν δ' αὐτῶν τοὺς μυκτῆρας (note the noun), Strab. 16. 2. 31. Seneca's version of this story runs 'rex Persarum totius populi nares recidit in Syria, unde Rhinocolura loco nomen est' (*De Ira* 3. 20. 1). Seneca's King of Persia must be Cambyses, the subject of the rest of his chapter, who like Actisanes invaded Egypt during the reign of Amasis. The allusions posited in Lucan and Cassius support one another: it looks as if Gnaeus Pompeius, the vicious son of a great Eastern ruler, had already in his lifetime attracted the nickname 'Cambyses'.[19]

In 9. 156 Pompeius threatens to throw the bodies of the Pharaohs into the Nile (*Nilo torrente natabunt*); in the same spirit the Roman mob shouted *Tiberium in Tiberim* (Suet. *Tib.* 75. 1).[20] The balance with the previous couplet is sustained: *natabunt* makes a contrast with 154 *mergam*, and *torrente* with *pigra. reges . . . natabunt* gives a derisive

---

[17] Plut. *Brut.* 29. 1 calls Cassius φιλοσκώπτην.

[18] αὐχενίζειν and ῥαχίζειν are similar verbs. For such mutilations cf. Verg. *Aen.* 6. 497 'truncas inhonesto volnere naris'; E. Rohde, *Psyche* (Tübingen, 1925), 9th and 10th edn. 1. 322ff.; M. P. Nilsson, *Geschichte der griechischen Religion* (Munich, 1² (1967), 99f.).

[19] The sobriquet would be worthy of Cicero, who annoyed the Pompeian camp with his sarcasms (Cic. *Phil.* 2. 39; Plut. *Cic.* 38. 2–6; Macr. *Sat.* 2. 3. 7–8); in earlier days he called Pompey the Great 'Sampsiceramus' after a minor Eastern potentate (*Att.* 2. 14. 1 etc.).

[20] For similar outrages see Mommsen, op. cit. (n. 12), 988 n. 5; S. Weinstock, *Divus Julius* (Oxford, 1971), 348 n. 1.

picture of mighty kings bobbing about on the surface of the water; in
their mummified state their specific gravity is less than in the days of
their power. As the verb also means 'to swim', there might be a further
suggestion of unathletic Pharaohs battling like Leander against the
current.

We come now to 157 *omnia dent poenas nudo tibi, Magne, sepulchra*;
here Duff translates 'let all their tombs make atonement to Magnus
who has none at all'. His use of the possessive 'their' shows that he
regards the line as a summing-up of 153-6, but after such extravagant
fantasies it comes as an anticlimax. It is much more effective if it looks
forward to 158 ff.: the tombs will be violated not just of kings but of
gods. The argument is made clear if *sepulchra* is followed not by a full
stop (Housman) but by a colon (thus for instance the Budé edition of
Bourgery and Ponchont).

Duff interprets 157 *nudo* as 'unburied' (thus already the *Adnotationes
super Lucanum*); but our passage must be distinguished from such
epigram|matic expressions as 8. 434 *nudae . . . umbrae* and 9. 64 f. *o bene
nudi Crassorum cineres*. When Pompey himself, rather than his ghost or
his ashes, is described as *nudus*, the adjective should be understood
literally; in this account of the maltreatment of the dead, nakedness
adds to the indignity. Shipwrecked sailors and cast-up corpses are
regularly described in this way; cf. Hipponax (?) 115. 5 West γυμνόν,
Lucretius 5. 222 f. 'tum porro puer ut saevis proiectus ab undis navita,
nudus humi iacet', Verg. *Aen.* 5. 871 'nudus in ignota, Palinure, iacebis
harena' (where *nudus* is wrongly interpreted as 'unburied'). When
Pompey was murdered, he had not yet stepped ashore (Lucan
8. 611 ff.); his body was tossed in the sea (698 f., 761), hauled out of the
water (723 ff.), and nearly carried back by the waves (753 f.).

Duff translates 9. 158 'I shall rifle the grave of Isis', but so vague a
paraphrase fails to clarify *evolvam busto . . . Isim*. We may compare
indeed 6. 170 f. 'cadavera plenis turribus evolvit', but there Lucan refers
to rolling corpses downhill (cf. 3. 480 f. 'sed pondere solo contenti
nudis evolvunt saxa lacertis'). In our passage *evolvam* is less forceful
than 155 *evolsus*; the assonance sets one word against the other and so
calls attention to the anticlimax. We look for a verb that suits Isis, just
as *spargam* in 159 suits Osiris; the latter's body was torn limb from limb
by Seth (the Greek Typhon) and distributed round the nomes of
Egypt.[21] *evolvam* can hardly suggest the cylindrical shape of Isis's

[21] Plut. *Is. et Osir.* 18, with the note by J. Gwyn Griffiths (University of Wales Press,
1970), 338.

images, for Lucan is not talking of an image; he must be referring to
the goddess's own mummified body, which by some accounts lay in
the temple-precinct of Ptah (Hephaestus) at Memphis.[22] That may
seem to suit *evolvam* well enough, but a difficulty remains; between 157
nudo and 159 *tectum lino* one looks for a reference to Isis's own dress (I
regard this point as crucial). In such a context *evolvam* should refer not
to rolling the mummy out of its tomb but to unwrapping it from its
winding-sheets.

That leads to the thought that *busto* might be emended to *bysso*, 'fine
linen' (the spelling *busso* is less likely at this date); though the word is not
found in the Latin poets. Lucan is not afraid of such prosaic expressions
as *biblus* (3. 222) and *papyrus* (4. 136), not to mention *bracae* (1. 430).
Byssus,[23] like linen in general,[24] was particularly associated with Isis and
her priests (Apul. *Met.* 11. 3. 5 'bysso tenui pertexta', 11. 24. 2 'byssina
quidem sed floride depicta veste conspicuus'); when Osiris died, she
wrapped his coffin in the material (Diod. Sic. 1. 85. 5). If Lucan knew
Herodotus as well as his account of Amasis suggests, he would remember that *byssus* was regularly used in embalming: λούσαντες τὸν νεκρὸν
κατειλίσσουσι πᾶν αὐτοῦ τὸ σῶμα σινδόνος βυσ|σίνης τελαμῶσι
κατατετμημένοισι (2. 86. 6). *evolvere*, to unroll, is the opposite of
κατειλίσσειν; *involvere* is sometimes used of winding-sheets in Christian
contexts (*TLL* 7. 2. 264. 11 ff.). The demummification of Isis is a drastic
act that balances the treatment of Osiris in the next line; the one is
unwrapped from her *byssus*, and though the other keeps his linen on
(*tectum lino*), his dismemberment is an even worse atrocity. At the same
time the physical violence to the goddess is combined with a cynical gibe
at her spiritual influence (*iam numen gentibus*).

A complication must now be acknowledged. In deriding attempts to
coerce the gods by threats, Porphyry uses words similar to Lucan's: τὸ
γὰρ λέγειν ὅτι τὸν οὐρανὸν προσαράξει καὶ τὰ κρυπτὰ τῆς Ἴσιδος
ἐκφανεῖ καὶ τὸ ἐν Ἀβύδῳ ἀπόρρητον δείξει καὶ τὴν βᾶριν στήσει καὶ τὰ
μέλη τοῦ Ὀσίριδος διασκεδάσει τῷ Τυφῶνι, τίνα οὐχ ὑπερβολὴν
ἐμπληξίας . . .καταλείπει;[25] Threats against the gods are attested in
papyri from Egypt,[26] and if they found their way into Hellenistic

---

[22] Diod. Sic. 1. 22. 2; *RE* 15. 1. 682.   [23] *RE* 3. 1108ff.
[24] Griffiths on Plut. *Is. et Osir.* 4 (op. cit. 270f.) and on Apul. *Met.* 11. 10. 1 (*The Isis-Book*, Leiden, 1975, 192).
[25] *Epistula ad Arebonem* 31 (= 2. 8c Sodano), cited by Iambl. *De Mysteriis Aegyptiorum* 6. 5 and Euseb. *Evang. Praep.* 198a-b.
[26] B. Olsson in ΔΡΑΓΜΑ *M. P. Nilsson Dedicatum* (Lund, 1939), 374 ff.

literary curses,[27] Lucan could have used them for his own purposes; but though his line on Osiris is closely paralleled in Porphyry, his line on Isis is not. 'He will reveal the hidden things of Isis' naturally describes the production of sacred emblems; these may have had a sexual significance in the case of Isis[28] as well as Osiris. Perhaps Lucan misunderstood or wilfully exaggerated his source, so as to transfer to the goddess's own body some discreet expression about τὰ κρυπτά.

Further problems arise at 160 *et sacer in Magni cineres mactabitur Apis*. The preponderance of the manuscript tradition puts the line between 158 and 159; that is certainly wrong, as the passive *mactabitur* disrupts the sequence of *evolvam . . . Isim* and *spargam . . . Osirim*. 160 is placed after 158-9 (as printed above) by the ninth-century Z and by G; this order is supported by Lactantius, who quotes 158-9 together (*Inst. Div.* 1. 21. 21), and by the *Commenta Bernensia*, which quote 160-1 together. Yet as Housman saw, the passive *mactabitur* now comes between *spargam* and *uram*, *Magni* interrupts the vocatives 157 *Magne* and 164 *genitor*, and the sentence straggles unhappily with its repeated *et . . . et . . . que*. Accordingly he followed Bentley in bracketing 160.

In spite of its eminent champions, the deletion cannot be right. As Apis was a bull-god, he is appropriately combined with *mactabitur*; the line makes a very good point for an interpolation.[29] If 160 *in Magni cineres* disap|pears, the balancing *caput* in 161 becomes obscure;[30] it will be recalled that Pompey's head was embalmed (8. 688 ff.) and his body cremated. *Magni* provides a characteristic assonance with *mactabitur*, and there is a grisly suggestion of blood mingling with ash; one may also see a typical antithesis between slaughtering Apis on top of the remains and placing the *dei* under the head. Most strikingly of all, there seems to be another allusion to the sacrilege of Cambyses,[31] who mortally wounded the Apis;[32] normally the bull was disposed of by being drowned in a sacred lake.[33]

The first requisite is to print a full stop after 159 *Osirim*; as has been seen, 157-9 make a unity, and any addition to this sentence is

---

[27] *RAC* 7. 1214 ff.

[28] A. A. Barb, '*Diva Matrix*', *Journal of Warburg and Courtauld Institutes*, 16 (1953), 200 ff. However, this interpretation of Apul. *Met.* 11. 11. 3-4 is very uncertain (see Griffiths, ad loc.). For other mystery religions cf. Clem. Alex. *Protrepticus* 2. 22. 5 (Stählin, p. 17); Nilsson, op. cit. (n. 18), I². 464, 658.

[29] Emphasized to me by Dr D. P. Fowler.   [30] Pointed out by Mr R. G. Peden.

[31] Pointed out again by Mr S. J. Harrison.

[32] Herod. 3. 29; Plut. *Is. et Osir.* 44 with Griffiths, op. cit. 468; *RE* 10. 1818. Artaxerxes III (Ochus) had the Apis for dinner (Plut. *Is. et Osir.* 11).

[33] Griffiths, op. cit. 273 (on *Is. et Osir.* 5).

ineffective. In 160 *et* is now unwanted, but a line can hardly have fallen
out before 160; that would upset the balance between 160 *cineres* and
161 *caput*. Nor should *et sacer* be changed to something like *corniger*, as
the former adjective is the most appropriate that can be found (Cic.
Nat. Deor. 1. 82 'Apim illum sanctum Aegyptiorum bovem'); it adds a
point that *sacer* means not just 'sacred' but 'accursed'. Perhaps 160 *et*
could be emended to *iam*, or even *at* or *nunc* (if 158 *iam numen gentibus*
is thought an obstacle). With the removal of *et* the passage is more
tightly organized, and in a new sentence the passive *mactabitur* and the
genitive *Magni* are no longer seriously disruptive. The corruption
could have originated through the omission of 159 (note the similar
endings at 158 *Isim*, 159 *Osirim*), its insertion in the wrong place after
160, and the alteration of 160's now intrusive *iam* to *et*.

At 161 *suppositisque deis uram caput* Housman refers *deis* to wooden
images; he cites the *Commenta Bernensia* for the explanation 'linea enim
habuerunt simulacra', and emends *linea* to *lignea*. Such a use of *dei* can
easily be paralleled elsewhere; thus Horace says 'paternos in sinu
ferens deos' (*Carm.* 2. 18. 26 f.). But after the extravagances that have
gone before, it makes a better climax if we think of mummified gods,
which in their dry state would make good kindling. Again there would
be an allusion to the atrocities of Cambyses, who burned the mummy
of Amasis; Herodotus explains how impious this seemed to the Egyp-
tians (3. 16. 2–3). There could even be a pun in *suppositis*, which as well
as the primary reference to fire-lighting might suggest that the gods of
Egypt were 'suppositious', i.e. fraudulent interlopers. Lucan is not an
admirer of Egyptian religion; cf. 8. 831 ff. 'nos in templa tuam Romana
accepimus Isim semideosque canes et sistra iubentia luctus et quem tu
plangens hominem testaris Osirim'. The last line suggests that a buried
god was a particular absurdity; the Cretans proved their mendacity
when they talked of the tomb of Zeus (8. 872). |

After a few lines more of rant from Pompeius, Lucan comments 'sed
Cato laudatam iuvenis compescuit iram' (9. 166); as the *Adnotationes
super Lucanum* explain, this means 'et ipse laudavit et ipse compescuit'.
In the same way when Cicero left the Republican army, Pompeius
drew his sword at him, and had to be restrained by Cato (Plut. *Cic.*
39. 1–2). Lucan's summing-up may seem an anticlimax, but the defla-
tion is deliberate; Cato was a man of few words, and in a pointedly
brief reply to one of Cicero's effusions he himself says 'contra con-
suetudinem meam pluribus scripsi' (*Fam.* 15. 5. 3). There is also a Stoic
element, no doubt less historical; anger for a father seems a generous

emotion, but one owes it to oneself to curb it (Sen. *De Ira* 1. 12. 1 'non irascetur sed vindicabit'). This self-regarding self-control is quite distinct from the broad-minded piety of Herodotus, who thought that even strange gods should be respected: πανταχῇ ὦν μοι δῆλά ἐστι ὅτι ἐμάνη μεγάλως ὁ Καμβύσης· οὐ γὰρ ἂν ἱροῖσί τε καὶ νομαίοισι ἐπεχείρησε καταγελᾶν. εἰ γὰρ τις προθείη πᾶσι ἀνθρώποισι ἐκλέξασθαι κελεύων νόμους τοὺς καλλίστους ἐκ τῶν πάντων νόμων, διασκεψάμενοι ἂν ἑλοίατο ἕκαστοι τοὺς ἑωυτῶν (3. 38. 1). This leads to a shocking conclusion that Lucan could never have understood: some men cremate their parents, others eat them, and convention is king (3. 38. 3-4).

Postscript. At 9. 153 D. R. Shackleton Bailey persuades me that *arces* is corrupt (*PCPS* 213 (1987), 88 f.). He proposes *caries* (I have considered *carnes*), but his *Pellaeos cineres* is safer. The earliest Ptolemies were cremated (8. 695; above, pp. 183-4).

12

Review of D. R. Shackleton Bailey (ed.), *Q. Horati Flacci Opera*

In 1985 Teubner of Leipzig published a new text of Horace, edited by Stefan Borzsák, with an apparatus full of trivialities and a very conservative choice of readings (see my review in *Gnomon*, 58 (1986)). Soon afterwards Teubner of Stuttgart produced a rival edition by Professor Shackleton Bailey. In spite of some curiosities this is an important and original work that should interest all Latin specialists and be included in every classical library.

S.B. has not re-examined manuscripts, but though this could contribute to our understanding of early medieval scholarship, it is unlikely to yield anything significant for Horace's text. On the other hand, he has solved the problem of how to present the evidence both fairly and economically (though one regrets the omission of some | nonsensical variants that have solid manuscript support). Klingner posited two families which he called Ξ and Ψ (roughly corresponding to α and β in Wickham–Garrod's OCT), but because of contamination his presentation over-simplified the facts (see Brink on *Ars Poetica*, pp. 12 ff.). Borzsák lists individual manuscripts *seriatim*, but no pattern emerges at all. S.B. uses the symbol Ψ much like Klingner, but breaks the less cohesive Ξ group into its components. He does not cite testimonia, unless to record their readings in places that he recognizes as controversial; in this respect, and in this alone, Borzsák has the advantage. Neither editor regularly mentions the place where conjectures were first made, information that is sometimes hard to find.

S.B.'s text contains a regrettable number of slips, some of which will test the critical powers of the reader. *Carm.* 2. 9. 7 correct *Gargari* to *Gargani*, 3. 1. 20 *cytharaeque* to *citharaeque*, 3. 4. 31 *habenas* to *harenas*, 3. 4. 54 *sed* to *aut*, 4. 2. 15 *tremenda* to *tremendae*, 4. 6. 19 *latentis* to

Classical Review, NS 36 (1986), 227–34, on Shackleton Bailey (ed.), *Q. Horati Flacci Opera* (Bibliotheca Scriptorum Graecorum et Romanorum Teubneriana; Stuttgart: B. G. Teubner, 1985).

latentem; **Serm.** 1. 7. 13 *dirimeret* (unmetrical) to *divideret*, 1. 9. 56 *primos aditus* to *aditus primos*, 1. 10. 24 *dulcior* to *suavior*, 1. 10. 62 *amne* to *amni*, 2. 3. 10 *inclamentque* to *clamentque*, 2. 3. 251 *differe* to *differre*, 2. 3. 291 *indicas* to *indicis*; **Epist.** 1. 1. 76 *quis* to *quid*, 1. 4. 10 *contigat* to *contingat*, 1. 7. 51 *lenius* to *leniter*, 2. 1. 38 *movos* to *novos*, 2. 2. 114 *intra* (a plausible early conjecture, not here recorded) to *inter*, 2. 2. 120 *vehemens* to *vemens* (unless the former is to be pronounced as a spondee); **Ars** 179 *igitur* to *agitur*, 250 *donantque* to *donantve*, 476 *hirundo* to *hirudo*. The layout of the apparatus suggests that the following further corrections should be made in the text: **Carm.** 1. 1. 13 *dimoveas* to *demoveas* (clearly better); **Serm.** 2. 1. 15 *describat* to *describit*, 2. 1. 22 *-que* to *-ve*; **Epist.** 2. 1. 73 *decorum et* to *decorum*. There seems also to be unintended punctuation at **Carm.** 1. 28. 13, 1. 35. 25, 4. 4. 41; **Serm.** 1. 3. 103 (which should read, following Housman, 'donec verba, quibus sensus, vocesque, notarent, | nominaque invenere'), 2. 6. 15; **Epist.** 1. 6. 34, 1. 20. 7.

S.B. makes over 100 proposals of his own, of which he puts over 40 in the text (including significant changes of punctuation); he has defended the more interesting cases in his *Profile of Horace*, 1982 (reviewed *CR* 33 (1983), 23 ff.) and in *HSCP* 89 (1985), 153 ff. Many of his ideas are tentative and others seem over-bold, but he understands that texts may be questioned and suggestions floated even when proof is impossible. He persistently starts from the thought, not the letters, and he has the courage to cut knots, as when he obelizes the notorious *difficile est* at *Ars* 128 (suggesting *praestiterit* in the apparatus). Consider also *Carm.* 4. 5. 31 f. 'hinc ad vina redit laetus et alteris | te mensis adhibet deum'; when he prints *tecta* for *vina* the reader will be surprised, but there is much to be said for his view that *vina* spoils the following libation (he points to the influence of *vitem* in line 30). Among other notable proposals I single out *Carm.* 1. 37. 9 f. 'contaminato cum grege turpium, | morbo virorum' (re-punctuated), 3. 6. 22 'innupta virgo' (*matura* codd.), 3. 17. 3 ff. 'et nepotum | per memores genus omne fastos | auctore ab illo ducet originem' (*ducis* codd., *ducit* D. Heinsius), 3. 20. 7 f. 'tibi praeda cedat, | cedat an illi' (better than Peerlkamp's *maior an illa*, which he prints), 4. 4. 35 'rectique cultus pectora roborat' (for *roborant*, taking *recti* as genitive); **Epod.** 1. 33 f. 'quod aut avarus ut Chremes terra premam | discinctus aut perdat nepos' (*perdam* codd.); **Serm.** 1. 1. 108 f. 'illuc unde abii redeo: nemo est ut avarus | se probet' (citing Lucr. 1. 620 'nil erit ut distet'), 1. 2. 99 'circum addita palla' (for *circumdata*, repeated from 96), 1. 2. 132 'sit',

1. 3. 14 'concha salis pura' (for *puri*), 1. 3. 31 'toga diffluit' (for *defluit*), 1. 7. 23 'ut laudat', 2. 2. 43 'stomachum qui' (in the apparatus), 2. 3. 62 'nunc ego', 2. 5. 55 'quandoque', 'one day' (a surprise for *plerumque*, but let the incredulous look), 2. 7. 102 'nili ego'; *Ars* 171 'spe mancus' (in the apparatus for *spe longus*). |

No less important is the revival of previous proposals: a fair number were not worth mentioning, but many give food for thought, and some are rightly accepted in the text. Bentley, who is disparaged by the inexpert, now comes into his own (cf. S.B.'s *Profile of Horace*, 104 ff., C. O. Brink, *English Classical Scholarship* (1986), 21 ff.); in the apparatus the symbol '(B)' indicates Bentley's choice of reading whether he was the originator or not. Due attention is paid to J. Horkel, *Analecta Horatiana* (1852), whose contribution was perhaps overestimated by Housman (*Classical Papers*, 131), as well as to Housman himself, whose *Horatiana* are too often dismissed as a young man's work (ibid. 1 ff., 92 ff., 136 ff.). A. Y. Campbell's first edition has been used, but apparently not his second (Liverpool, 1953); though most of his ideas are nonsense, he was always ready to admit puzzlement, and even if seldom believed he should be regularly consulted.

I have noted some interesting conjectures that have not been recorded by S.B.: **Carm.** 1. 14. 7 *cavernae* dett., 3. 4. 10 *pergulae* Baehrens (cf. ps.-Quint. *Decl. Mai.* 13. 4 'nutriculam casam'), 3. 4. 32 *Austurii* Wistrand tentatively (*Opera Selecta* (1972), 465 ff., citing *RE* 2. 2592), 3. 8. 17 *paulisper super* Edwards ap. Campbell, 2nd edn., 3. 24. 5 *sic* Bentley, 3. 24. 64 *structae* Campbell, 3. 27. 45 f. *insignem* ... *lacerare frontem et* Campbell, 4. 4. 15 *lactante* anon. ap. Dillenburger, 4. 4. 24 *retusae* Campbell, 1st edn. (this would suit the axes of the Vindelici), 4. 13. 21 *nota quot artium* Housman (or perhaps one could try *et nota quot artium*); **Epod.** 8. 17 *vigent* Edwards ap. Campbell, 2nd edn. (to avoid the tautology with the next line), 15. 16 *pectus* Cornelissen, 16. 41 *eia, beata* Axt ap. Dillenburger (the three explanations given for *arva beata* are all unconvincing); **Serm.** 1. 2. 33 *tenta* anon. ap. Bentley; **Epist.** 1. 1. 78 *crustis* cod. Sangallensis, 1. 2. 31 *inducere somnum* Housman (combined with A. S. Owen's *cessanti* by W. S. Watt, *Eranos*, 79 (1981), 81), 1. 6. 67 *istic* G. Wagner ap. Schütz (S.B. accepts Skutsch's 'si quid novisti rectius, istis | candidus imperti', but the omission of *me* causes doubt); *Ars* 120 *Homeriacum* Bentley. As S.B. has aimed at a radical text, he might have promoted a few more conjectures from the apparatus: **Carm.** 1. 26. 10 *possunt* cod. det., 2. 2. 2 *minuitque* Housman for *inimice* (I have surrendered), 3. 24. 54 *rudi*

Cornelissen (so Varr. *Rust.* 1. 20. 1 of untamed oxen), 3. 25. 13 *rupes*
Muretus, 4. 2. 49 *tuque* dett. (with *procedis*); *Epod.* 1. 5 *sit* Aldus, 11. 4
autpueris Bentley; **Serm.** 1. 2. 86 *Thraecibus* Kiessling, 1. 3. 7 *io Bacchae*
(indistinguishable from the unmetrical *io Bacche*), 1. 3. 42 *victus*
Housman. 1. 3. 107 *creberrima* Campbell, 2. 5. 48 *ut adscribare* Apitz,
2. 6. 103 *arderet* Peerlkamp; **Epist.** 1. 1. 21 *lenta* dett., 1. 1. 91 *viden ut*
Bentley, 2. 1. 115 f. *melicorum ... melici* Bentley, 2. 2. 185 *durus*
L. Müller; **Ars** 45–6 transposed by ed. Britannici, 1516, 65 *palus prius*
Bentley (very elegant), 209 *laxior* Bentley.

Of my own proposals S.B. accepts **Carm.** 2. 15. 13 *probatus* 3. 1. 42
Sidone, as well as the re-punctuations at 2. 13. 1 f. 'ille et nefasto te
posuit die, quicumque, primum' and 2. 18. 32 'erum quid ultra tendis?'
To save space below I list the others (half in my review of Borzsák in
Gnomon 1986, and so too late to be considered by S.B.): **Carm.** 2. 8. 18
haeret, 2. 13. 15 *ultro*, 3. 1. 36 f. *dominoque... fastidioso*, 3. 9. 20 *praelatae-
que*, 3. 14. 11 *labis expertes*, 3. 16. 30 *curta*, 3. 26. 6 f. *lurida ... retusos*,
3. 27. 18 *quo*, 4. 5. 18 *grana*, 4. 10. 5 *filicem* (cf. Pers. 4. 41 of body-hair,
Anth. Pal. 11. 53. 2 οὐ ῥόδον ἀλλὰ βάτον), **Serm.** 1. 2. 40 *dira* (*CR* 16
(1966), 327), 2. 6. 59 *disperit* (following L. Müller's *deperit*), **Epist.**
1. 18. 11 *adrisor*; **Ars** 61 *particulatim*, 320 *pectore*, 433 *adrisor*. I think
that S.B. is right against my published opinions to print at *Carm.* 1. 6. 3
'qua rem cumque' (dett., Bentley), 1. 12. 19 'occupabit' (R. Stephanus),
1. 15. 36 'ignis †Iliacas† domos', 1. 23. 5 f. 'vepris ... l ad ventum' (I am
reluctantly persuaded by Bentley's argument that the season is not the
spring), 1. 28. 24 'capiti †inhumato' (where Peerlkamp's *intumulato* is
plausible). But more often I adhere to the views expressed | in Nisbet–
Hubbard: note especially 1. 7. 7 'undique' (where S.B. accepts Brou-
hier's *indeque*, a combination avoided by the classical poets), 1. 8. 4
'oderit Campum' (where Withof's *deserit* destroys the contrast with
amando), 1. 12. 34 ff. 'an superbos l Tarquini fascis ... an Catonis l nobile
letum' (S.B. obelizes *Catonis*, but for a similar glide cf. N.–H. on 46 f.
'Marcelli ... l Iulium sidus'), 1. 27. 9 f. 'vultis severi me quoque sumere l
partem Falerni?' (where Campbell's *severum* gives little point and a
faulty word-distribution), 1. 27. 19 'quanta laborabas Charybdi' (where
laboras in may suggest 'suffering over' rather than 'suffering from'),
1. 32. 1 'poscimus, si quid ...' (it is a pity to see the return of *poscimur* in
a poem with so many features of a prayer), 2. 3. 9 ff. 'quo ...? quid ...?'
(where the conjectures *qua ... et* are much less lively), 2. 10. 9 f.
'saepius ventis agitatur ingens l pinus' (though *saevius* goes back to the

ancient world, it does not combine convincingly with *agitatur*). I turn
now to more detailed discussions.

Carm. 1. 1. 35f. 'quod si me lyricis vatibus inseres, I sublimi feriam
sidera vertice'. In his apparatus S.B. rewrites the passage, giving
inserens to the Muse; but to include Horace in the canon of the classics
(ἐγκρίνειν) must be the act of the patron to whom the book is
addressed. No invidious distinctions are drawn between the judgement
of Maecenas and the Muses. **1. 4. 7f.** 'dum gravis Cyclopum I Vulcanus
ardens visit officinas'. Instead of the excellent *visit*, S.B. accepts Wade's
versat; he cites Sen. *Phaedr.* 191 'versat caminos' (of Vulcan), but a
factory is not a furnace. **1. 5. 15f.** 'suspendisse potenti I vestimenta
maris deo'. *deo* can be defended against Zieliński's *deae* (cited in the
apparatus), if it is taken as common in gender and referred ambiguously to Venus as well as Neptune (T. E. Kinsey, *Latomus*, 23 (1964),
502ff.). If it is applied exclusively to Neptune, as many insist, the
sustained wit of the poem is impaired. **1. 12. 21f.** 'proeliis audax, neque
te silebo, I Liber'. I am now inclined to follow those who take *proeliis
audax* with *Liber* (rather than with the preceding *Pallas*); the separation of epithets from the vocative name is characteristic of the sacral
style (N.-H. 2. 19. 8n). **1. 20. 9ff.** 'Caecubum et prelo domitam Caleno I
tu bibes uvam: mea nec Falernae I temperant vites neque Formiani I
pocula colles'. S.B. accepts Keller's *bibas* (which avoids confusion with
the future of invitation at 1 *potabis*) and Ensor's *Falerni... collis*. But if
balance is to be the principle rather than variation, that might also
suggest *Caecubo*, which gives an unattractive series of ablatives.
1. 27. 14ff. 'quae te cumque domat Venus, I non erubescendis adurit I
ignibus ingenuoque semper I amore peccas'. S.B. recognizes that *adurit*
(an inference) is not on all fours with *semper peccas* (an admitted fact).
He proposes *semper... pecces*; I have considered *saltem... peccas* (*saltem*
is found once in the *Satires* and six times in Virgil). **1. 35. 21ff.** 'te Spes
et albo rara Fides colit I velata panno, nec comitem abnegat I utcumque
mutata potentis I veste domos inimica linquis'. S.B. accepts Peerlkamp's
sed comitem abnegat, but that does not solve an intractable problem. We
are told in the next stanza that the *vulgus infidum* (which must be
contrasted with *rara Fides*) *retro cedit* (which would be an odd way of
saying 'goes off with Fortune'). We should not think here of false
friends following the current success; that notion does not suit the
Fortuna of Antium or the religious concepts of the day. **2. 20. 17ff.** 'me
Colchus et ... I ... Dacus et ultimi I noscent Geloni, me peritus I discet
Hiber Rhodanique potor'. S.B. obelizes *peritus* as it gets in the way of

the main thrust of the stanza: 'no people so distant and unlettered but will learn Horace's poetry by heart' (*HSCP* 89 (1985), 155). He suggests *remotus*, but that seems less strong than *ultimi*. The word that balances *discet* is perhaps *imperitus*; the closest analogies to the elision are at 2. 3. 6 'seu te in remoto gramine', 4. 10. 6, *Epod.* 5. 9. **3. 2. 1** 'angustam amice pauperiem pati'. S.B. obelizes *amice* and considers *et aeque*, but the adverb may represent Greek ἀγαπητῶς, | 'contentedly'. **3. 2. 13** 'dulce et decorum est pro patria mori'. The first adjective would have seemed false to Cicero (*Fin.* 2. 60ff.) as well as to Wilfred Owen, and it is irrelevant to the poem. Greatly daring, I suggest *dulci decorum est*, which provides an intelligible balance between honour and natural affection; cf. 4. 9. 51f. 'non ille pro caris amicis | aut patria timidus perire', Hom. *Od.* 9. 34 ὡς οὐδὲν γλύκιον τῆς πατρίδος, Cic. *Leg.* 2. 5, Virg. *Aen.* 10. 782 'dulcis moriens reminiscitur Argos', *CIL* 3. 6888, *Acts of the Pagan Martyrs* 11. 41ff. Musurillo κλέος σοί ἐστιν ὑπὲρ τῆς γλυκυτάτης σοῦ πατρίδος τελευτῆσαι. **3. 6. 9ff.** 'iam bis Monaeses et Pacori manus | non auspicatos contudit impetus | nostros et adiecisse praedam | torquibus exiguis renidet'. *nostros* should be obelized; it is weak with *impetus*, and a word balancing *exiguis* should qualify *praedam*. Bentley's *nostrorum* (with *impetus*) meets only the first difficulty; S.B. considers *nostratem* (unlikely) or *Romanam* (not an easy change). I look for an adjective that suits the naïve delight of the Parthians; *praeclaram* could have been corrupted to *praedam*, with consequent interpolation. **3. 11. 30** 'impiae (nam quid potuere maius?)'. S.B. puts *nam* before the bracket, but a pause after the fourth syllable is abnormal (50 'dum favet nox'), and should be admitted only in unambiguous cases; at 1. 12. 31 I am less attracted than S.B. by Lenchantin's 'et minaci (sic voluere) ponto'. **3. 14.** I have written on the text of this poem in *Papers of the Liverpool Latin Seminar*, 4 (1983), 105ff., where I support the following readings: **6** *divis* (not *sacris* with S.B.), **7** *cari* (not *clari* with editors), **11** *male nominatis* = δυσωνύμοις (where S.B. backs Bentley's *male inominatis*), **19** perhaps *vagacem* (Charisius, commended by Brink) for *vagantem*, **22** *cohibente* (Muretus) for *cohibere* (codd., S.B.). **3. 19. 10ff.** 'da, puer, auguris | Murenae; tribus aut novem | miscentur cyathis pocula commodis'. The present indicative *miscentur* does not cohere satisfactorily with *da*, and S.B. accepts *miscentor* (Rutgers), but the status of this passive imperative is questionable (H. Tränkle, *MH* 35 (1978), 57f.). *miscere* in any event seems the wrong word: Horace is talking of total quantities, not of proportions of wine and water. Perhaps *mitescent* (or *mitescant*); on this cold night (8) the cups will grow mellow with the hot wine (6), just like the drinkers themselves. **3. 21. 5** 'quocumque lectum nomine Massicum'. S.B. suspects *nomine*, but it suits the religious parody well; the same Massic could be regarded as suitable for either fun or sleep (2–4). But *lectum* does not combine closely with *quocumque nomine*; hence Bentley's odd *faetum numine* (cited by S.B.). I suggest *laetum* as an extension (appropriate to wine) of the more normal *nomine gaudet*; cf. Eur. fr. 912. 2 f. N² Ζεὺς εἴτ᾽ Ἀίδης | ὀνομαζόμενος στέργεις, Plat. *Crat.* 400e, Cic. *Tim.* 4, Colum. 8. 16. 5 'Sergius Orata et Licinius Murena captorum piscium laetabantur vocabulis'. **3. 24. 1 ff.** 'intactis opulentior | thesauris Arabum et divitis Indiae | caementis licet occupes | Tyrrhenum omne tuis et mare †Apulicum'. *Apulicum* does not scan; the variant *Ponticum* makes no geographical sense; Palmer's *sublicis*, accepted by S.B., gives a suspect word-order if *Tyrrhenum* is kept (Campbell, 2nd edn.); the variant *publicum*, if combined with *terrenum* (Lachmann following the scholia), is at least worth considering. Yet after *Arabum* and *Indiae* one would prefer balancing proper names; the apparatus might mention the poorly attested *mare Punicum*, an old equivalent (Flor. 2. 2. 17) for the *mare Libycum* (for the hyperbole cf. *Carm.* 2. 2. 10 ff.). **3. 24. 19 f.** 'nec dotata regit virum | coniunx nec nitido fidit adultero'. For *fidit* S.B. prints his own *laedit*; I should prefer *fallit* (cf. Ov. *Ars* 1. 310 'sive virum mavis fallere, falle viro'). But *fidit* provides a better contrast with *regit*, and an appropriate paradox (cf. 17 f.): wifely trust is bestowed on a lover. **3. 26. 1** 'vixi puellis nuper idoneus'. S.B. follows Campbell in printing a comma after *vixi*, but 'I have lived my life' impairs the contrast between the past and present; rather compare *CLE* 381. 1 'vixi viro cara'. **3. 27. 23 f.** 'trementis | verbere ripas'. Voyagers | would not be aware of the shaking shore, so S.B. prints his own *costas* (the ribs of a ship); this makes a pun with *verbere*, but without *navis* seems overcompressed. Bentley's *gementis . . . ripas* (*rupes* Cunningham) is mentioned in the apparatus; he aptly compared 2. 20. 4 'gementis litora Bospori', ps.-Quint. *Decl. Mai.* 6. 5 'navigat ergo per horridos fluctus et gementia litora et spumantes scopulos', Claud. 15. 130 (this time of a ship) 'gemens undarum verbere'. **3. 27. 58 ff.** 'potes hac ab orno | pendulum zona bene te secuta | laedere collum'. S.B. accepts from a minor MS *e-/lidere* (which impairs the rhyme), and considers *male* for *bene*; but the euphemism and irony are appropriate. **3. 29. 49 f.** 'Fortuna saevo laeta negotio et | ludum insolentem ludere pertinax'. The *figura etymologica* is found at Ter. *Eun.* 586 f., Boeth. *Cons.* 2. 2. 9 (prose), but does not suit the economical Horace; *ducere*, 'prolong', would cohere with *pertinax*.

4. 4. 57 'duris ut ilex tonsa bipennibus'. Borzsák accepts *tunsa* from an Oxford Queen's College MS (cf. also Keller, *Epilegomena*, 312), and this neglected reading suits not just *bipennibus* but the analogy with Roman resilience. **4. 4. 65** 'merses profundo, pulchrior evenit' (of Rome). S.B. suggests *fortior* or *firmior*, but we have already had *firmior* in 61; perhaps *clarior*. This would suit *enitet*, which is cited from Campbell (Lehrs rather); there may be a suggestion of the sun (cf. Milton, *Lycidas* 168 'So sinks the day-star in the ocean bed ...').

Epod. **1. 19 ff.** 'ut adsidens implumibus pullis avis | serpentium allapsus timet | magis relictis, non, ut adsit, auxili | latura plus praesentibus'. For *praesentibus* (weak after *adsit*) S.B. suggests *precantibus*, not the best word for chicks. Perhaps *poscentibus* (Lucr. 5. 1086 f. of crows) or *petentibus* (less clamorous). **2. 37 f.** 'quis non malarum quas amor curas habet | haec inter obliviscitur?' S.B. reads *malarum Roma quas curas habet* (Scrinerius), but the corrupt word is probably *malarum*, which seems incompatible with the accusative *curas* (L. Müller). I have considered *bonorum quas amor* (cf. φιλοκτέανος); if somebody interpreted this as 'good men' rather than 'possessions', he might well have changed it to *malarum*. **9. 17 f.** '†ad hunc† frementis verterunt bis mille equos | Galli canentes Caesarem' (S.B. obelizes thus). With most proposals (*ad hoc, at nunc*), *verterunt* would imply 'turned in flight', which is incompatible with *canentes*. This points to *at huc* (known to Cruquius), which suggests that Horace was at Actium; see my article in *Poetry and Politics in the Age of Augustus*, ed. T. Woodman and D. West (1984), 9 ff. (above, p. 175). **13. 3 f.** 'rapiamus, amici. | occasionem de die'. S.B. accepts Housman's *Amici* as a proper name, but the ambiguity is impossible in a sympotic poem (cf. *sodales* at *Carm.* 1. 27. 7, 1. 37. 4). **17. 28 f.** 'Sabella pectus increpare carmina | caputque Marsa dissilire nenia'. For the meaningless *increpare* Palmer proposed the unattested *incremare*; S.B. reads his own *et cremare*, but *et* seems padding. Perhaps *macerare*, 'boil'; cf. *Carm.* 1. 13. 8 'quam lentis penitus macerer ignibus', *Ciris* 244 with Lyne.

Serm. **1. 3. 55 f.** 'at nos virtutes ipsas invertimus atque | sincerum cupimus vas incrustare'. S.B. accepts the minor variant *furimus*, commended by Housman on Manil. 5. 660, but it seems too strong for the context. Perhaps *incipimus*, 'we go and smear the untainted vessel'; cf. 2. 3. 128 f. 'populum si caedere saxis | incipias'. **1. 3. 120 ff.** 'nam ut ferula caedas meritum maiora subire | verbera non vereor'. Notoriously the MSS offer *ut* where Latin requires *ne* (Housman, *Classical Papers*, 141 ff.). S.B. reads his own *non moror*, followed by *hoc* at the beginning of the next clause (*HSCP* 89 (1985), 161 f.); he compares *Serm.* 1. 4. 13 'nam ut multum, nil moror'. I have considered *non vincor* 'I am not persuaded that you let off serious offenders too lightly'; cf. 115 'nec vincet ratio hoc', *Epod.* 17. 27 'ergo negatum vincor ut credam miser'. In our passage *vincor ut ferula caedas* would mean *vincor ut credam te ferula caedere*; for the brachylogy cf. Plaut. *Mil.* 187 'ut eum ... verbis vincat ne | is se viderit', Madvig on Cic. *Fin.* 1. 14 (on *adducor*). **2. 3. 147 f.** 'hunc medicus multum celer atque fidelis | excitat hoc pacto'. S.B. comments 'medicum catum malim', but *catus* does not combine well with *fidelis*. Possibly *impiger*, corrupted to *piger* and 'corrected' to *celer*. **2. 6. 93 ff.** 'carpe viam, mihi crede, comes, terrestria quando | mortalis animas vivunt sortita neque ulla est | aut magno aut parvo leti fuga—quo, bone, circa, | dum licet, in rebus iucundis vive beatus'. S.B. prints a full stop at *comes*, in which case the particular injunction might rather suggest *cede* (cf. Virg. *Aen.* 2. 704 'cedo equidem nec, nate, tibi comes ire recuso'); but a full stop at *viam* seems better, as *mihi crede* suits the sententiousness that follows. For *quando* he suggests *cuncta* (to avoid the anacoluthon at *quo... circa* below); at this position in the line I should prefer the Lucretian *quaeque.* **2. 6. 108 f.** 'nec non verniliter ipse | fungitur officiis praelambens omne quod affert'. S.B. with Bentley accepts the less vivid *praelibans* from minor MSS. Bentley's comment misses the humour ('atqui hoc parum *officiose* et *verniliter* facit, si praelambit quodcumque affert'), and his parallels are against him (Lucil. 585 M 'iucundasque puer qui lamberet ore placentas', Juv. 9. 5). **2. 8. 14 f.** 'procedit fuscus Hydaspes | Caecuba vina ferens, Alcon Chium maris expers'. S.B. puts a comma after *Chium*, interpreting *maris* as *virilitatis* with Housman. But Galen says that Ariusian wine from Chios was not mixed with sea-water (10. 833 K); so there seems to be a pun on the two meanings of *maris*.

　　Epist. **1. 1. 4 ff.** 'Veianius armis | Herculis ad postem fixis latet abditus agro, | ne populum extrema totiens exoret harena'. In 6 S.B. reads his own *rediens*, as a famous gladiator would not be defeated *totiens*. But *extrema* suggests that Veianius is not doing too badly; cf. *RE* Suppl. 3. 782, citing *ILS* 5113 'vicit XXI, stans (missus) VIIII, mis(sus) IIII'. **1. 7. 29 f.** 'forte per angustam tenuis vulpecula rimam | repserat in cumeram frumenti ...'. Foxes don't eat corn even in fables (cf. Aesop 24 Hausrath), so S.B. accepts Giangrande's *cornicula*. Crows don't crawl, so Bentley's *nitedula* is better. **2. 1. 211 ff.** 'poeta, meum qui pectus inaniter angit, | irritat, mulcet, falsis terroribus implet, | ut magus, et modo me Thebis, modo ponit Athenis'. S.B. accepts Wakefield's *et*, *magus ut*; but 'witchcraft' in Gorgias refers to the emotional effects of speech (see Brink).

Ars 32 ff. 'Aemilium circa Ludum faber imus et unguis I exprimet et mollis imitabitur aere capillos, I infelix operis summa'. *imus* is obscure (Brink), and should be obelized. S.B. accepts *unus*, which Bentley derived from a citation in John of Salisbury, but that exaggerates the capacities of the man. Perhaps *faber optimus* [*et*]; cf. Cic. *Brut.* 257 'tamen ego me Phidiam esse mallem quam vel optimum fabrum tignarium'. **292 ff.** 'carmen reprehendite quod non I multa dies et multa litura coercuit atque I perfectum decies non castigavit ad unguem'. *Perfectum* (accepted by S.B.) is sense with *quod*, but tame; the variant *praesectum* is difficult with *unguem* (see Brink), but confusing with *quod*. It is also strange that in a passage on literary finish *castigavit* lacks a convincing subject; perhaps *perfector*, which could have been the word for a specialist mason. **464 ff.** 'deus immortalis haberi I dum cupit Empedocles, ardentem frigidus Aetnam I insiluit'. S.B. explains *frigidus* as 'sine animi aestu', and also considers *fervidus*. Others better explain cold blood as a sign of stupidity, probably an Empedoclean doctrine (cf. C. O. Brink, *Phoenix*, 23 (1969), 138 ff.).

The edition ends with a 'Conspectus Metrorum' (following Vollmer and Klingner), and an 'Index Nominum'. The identity of Licinius (*Carm.* 2. 10) is regarded as uncertain, but he was undoubtedly Maecenas's brother-in-law, the patron of the Peripatetic Athenaeus (Nisbet–Hubbard, 2. 152 f., citing Strabo 14. 5. 4). The young Lollius of *Epist.* 1. 2. 1 is as usual assigned the cognomen 'Maximus', though the name was not borne by the consul of 21; perhaps in a poet *maxime Lolli* could | mean *maxime Lolliorum* and refer to the eldest son. It should be made clear that at 2. 11. 2 'Hirpine' is not a cognomen but refers to the geographical antecedents of Quintius.

A review concentrates on points of doubt or disagreement, but it cannot do justice to the many occasions where Professor Shackleton Bailey has made one reader reconsider. It is a privilege and delight to debate with him about these interesting problems.

13

The Oak and the Axe

Symbolism in Seneca, *Hercules Oetaeus* 1618 ff.[1]

TREES are like people. They have a head (*vertex*), a trunk (*truncus*), arms (*bracchia*). They stand tall like a soldier, or look as slender as a bridegroom (Sappho, 115 L–P). Their life moves in human rhythms, which in their case may be repeated: sap rises and falls, hair (*coma*) luxuriates, withers, drops off. Sometimes they are superior and aloof, sometimes they go in pairs, whether as comrades-in-arms (Hom. *Il.* 12. 132 ff., Virg. *Aen.* 9. 679 ff.) or husband and wife (Ov. *Met.* 8. 720). They whisper like lovers (Ar. *Nub.* 1008), embrace, support, cling,[2] and the stricken elm grieves for the vine more than himself (Stat. *Theb.* 8. 544 ff.). When the storm bears down, they suffer, heave, bend, as on Soracte[3] or Wenlock Edge, but though they may take a battering (Hor. *Carm.* 1. 28. 27 'plectantur silvae'), they remain robust ('oaken') and tenacious. Even under the axe they are resilient, like the Romans in the Punic War, and put out new growth (Hor. *Carm.* 4. 4. 57 'duris ut ilex tunsa[4] bipennibus . . .').

The fall of a tree is a thing to remember, as Horace could tell; it all happens so quickly. Now symbols of vulnerability as well as strength, the lofty are laid low, the magnificent decay. Hence epic analogues for a slain warrior (Hom. *Il.* 4. 482 ff., 5. 560, 13. 178 ff.) or a captured city, for the destruction may be cumulative (Virg. *Aen.* 2. 631 'traxitque iugis avulsa ruinam'); further correspondences are developed by Val.

---

[1] A version of this paper was read in Cambridge in 1985 at the Triennial Conference of the Hellenic and Roman Societies. I am glad to dedicate it to a colleague who has taught us all about non-literal meanings in Latin poetry.

[2] For the passions of trees see Achilles Tatius 1. 17. 3–5; E. Rohde, *Der griechische Roman*[2] (1900), 168 n. 2.

[3] For the symbolism of the wood in trouble see my remarks at *JRS* 73 (1983), 239.

[4] With Borzsák I prefer the minor variant *tunsa* to the generally transmitted *tonsa*, which does not contribute to the analogy with Rome.

From *Homo Viator: Classical Essays for John Bramble*, ed. M. Whitby, P. Hardie, M. Whitby (Bristol Classical Press, 1987), 243–51.

Fl. 3. 165 f. 'sic dura sub ictu | ossa virum malaeque sonant sparsusque cerebro | albet ager' (evoking the crack of wood and the scatter of chippings). Catullus (64. 105 ff.) sees the Minotaur as an oak 'in summo quatientem bracchia Tauro' (where *quatientem* suits the man-like wrestler, while *Tauro* hints at the bull), or else as 'conigeram sudanti cortice pinum' (where *conigeram* hints at *cornigeram* and the resinous bark suggests a sweating hide);[5] but Theseus | left him sprawling like an uprooted tree, his branching horns waving in the wind (111 'vanis iactantem cornua ventis'). More derisively the same poet compares a girl-friend's husband[6] to a maimed alder (17. 18 f. 'nec se sublevat ex sua parte, sed velut alnus | in fossa Liguri iacet suppernata securi'); those who suspect a sexual reference[7] (not the commentators) seem for once to be right.

To revert to epic, battle-scenes are sometimes followed by tree-felling for funeral pyres.[8] Homer is matter-of-fact: mass cremation takes a lot of wood. In some of his successors the sound and fury of the scene seems to repeat the violence of the battlefield: the destruction is at once a catharsis[9] and a sacrifice. Thus Ennius accumulates drastic words for overthrow (*Ann.* 175 ff. Skutsch): *caedunt, percellunt, exciditur, frangitur, consternitur, pervortunt.* The human analogy is made more explicit at Virg. *Aen.* 11. 138 'nec plaustris cessant vectare gementibus ornos' (where *gementibus* echoes the groans of the mourners), and

---

[5] Catullus says of his tree 'indomitus turbo contorquens flamine robur | eruit' (107 f.); here I suggest that *indomitum* (a variant without authority) would suit better the analogy with the untamed Minotaur. At 110 'sic domito saevum prostravit corpore Theseus', *saevum* is unconvincing without a noun and does not contribute to the analogy with the tree. I once considered (*ob*)*saeptum*, which would suit alike the labyrinth and the dense forest (cf. 109 'obvia frangens').

[6] Perhaps Catullus 17. 8 'municipem meum' discreetly describes Metellus Celer (the probable husband of Lesbia); as governor of Cisalpina in 62 BC, he might have held an honorary office at Verona, like Piso at Capua (Cic. *Sest.* 19, cf. W. Liebenam, *Städteverwaltung im römischen Kaiserreiche* (1900), 261 ff.). Compare 17. 20 'tantundem omnia sentiens quam si nulla sit usquam', 17. 21 'talis iste merus stupor' (an appropriate gibe at a man called Celer), 17. 26 'mula' with 83. 3 'mule, nihil sentis' (of Lesbia's *vir*), Cic. *Att.* 1. 18. 1 'non homo sed litus atque aer et solitudo mera' (of the lofty and remote Metellus Celer, if the text is sound). It must be admitted that 17. 14 'viridissimo nupta flore puella' would be an exaggeration; Clodia Metelli may have been born as early as 95. See further H. W. Garrod, *CR* 33 (1919), 67 f. (who suggests, but fails to prove, that a *metellus* was a beast of burden), J. W. Zarker, *CJ* 64 (1968-9), 172 ff. (who identifies the *municeps* with Metellus Celer but sees a reference to the sharing of Clodia).

[7] H. Akbar Khan, *CPh.* 64 (1969), 88 ff.; J. Glenn, *CPh.* 65 (1970), 256 f.

[8] G. Williams, *Tradition and Originality in Roman Poetry* (1968), 263 ff.

[9] Gladstone found relief from the Irish question in tree-felling. As Lord Randolph Churchill expressed it, 'the forests labour that the First Lord of the Treasury may perspire'.

especially Stat. *Theb.* 6. 96 f. 'aderat miserabile luco l excidium', 107 'dat gemitum tellus'.

The subject of this paper is the tree-felling in *Hercules Oetaeus*, a play transmitted in the Senecan corpus, but whose authenticity is denied by many. When Philoctetes delivers his messenger-speech on the immolation of Hercules on the mountain (1618–1757), he describes the construction of the pyre that is to receive the suffering hero:

> stat vasta late quercus et Phoebum vetat
> ultraque totos porrigit ramos nemus;
> gemit illa multo vulnere impresso minax
> frangitque cuneos, resilit incussus chalybs
> volnusque ferrum patitur et rigidum est parum.   (1624–8)

Here the huge oak that groans but remains obdurate surely represents the Stoic Hercules himself;[10] for the blunting of the steel *chalybs* compare 151 f. 'nullis vulneribus pervia membra sunt: l ferrum sentit hebes, lentior est chalybs', 1272 f. 'durior saxo horrido l et chalybe voltus'. When the tree falls, the whole wood feels the ruin, and birds are driven from their *sedes* (1629–34); this suggests the panic of the people when their protector is overthrown. 'Aggeritur omnis silva et alternae trabes l in astra tollunt Herculi angustum | rogum' (1637 f.): the criss-cross[11] planks rise skyward, but as so often in the play *astra* also alludes to apotheosis.

The poet is imitating the passage in Sophocles's *Trachiniae* where Heracles gives directions for the construction of his pyre (1195 ff.):

> πολλὴν μὲν ὕλην τῆς βαθυρρίζου δρυὸς
> κείραντα, πολλὸν δ᾽ ἀρσέν᾽ ἐκτεμόνθ᾽ ὁμοῦ
> ἄγριον ἔλαιον, σῶμα τοὐμὸν ἐμβαλεῖν . . .

The commentators note the significance of the trees: the oak was sacred to Zeus (1168 τῆς πατρῴας . . . δρυός), and the wild olive was introduced to Greece by Heracles himself. It has also been observed that 'male' and 'wild' are appropriate to the Sophoclean hero,[12] whose animal savagery appears in his fights with Achelous (517 ff.) and Nessus.[13] It may further be suggested that ἐκτεμόντα, when juxtaposed

---

[10] I owe much to a discussion at my graduate class initiated by Dr D. P. Fowler.

[11] For the *alternae trabes* compare the illustration of Dido's pyre in cod. Vat. lat. 3225 (reproduced for instance in M. R. Scherer, *The Legends of Troy in Art and Literature* (1963), 202).

[12] A. Platt, *CQ* 4 (1910), 166 (after a sober discussion of the propagation of the olive) 'the epithets suit the fierce hero to whom the plant was sacred'.

[13] For the savagery of Heracles cf. C. Segal, *YCS* 25 (1977), 99 ff.

with ἀρσένα, naturally implies 'emasculate' (cf. Soph. fr. 620 P σκάλμη γὰρ ὄρχεις βασιλὶς ἐκτέμνουσ᾽ ἐμούς), just as κείραντα would suit what Delilah did to Samson and Scylla to Nisus; the ruin of Heracles by a woman is a dominating theme of the play.[14] The language of Sophocles is complex and evocative, hinting at more than it says, but even those who reject a double meaning here may grant that the Silver Age would have suspected one. The author of *HO* must be both learned and himself a poet to develop so skilfully an idea that he has seen in the Greek.

The tree in *HO* also recalls a famous Virgilian simile. When beset by entreaties from Dido, Aeneas is as unmoved as a deeply rooted oak that is battered by the winds:

> haud secus adsiduis hinc atque hinc vocibus heros
> tunditur, et magno persentit pectore curas;
> mens inmota manet, lacrimae volvuntur inanes.   (4. 447-9)

In the same way we find at *HO* 1285 'fletum virtus saepe resorbet', and Seneca himself says in prose 'volumus interim ... devorare gemitus: per ipsum tamen compositum fictumque vultum lacrimae profunduntur' (*Helv.* 17. 1). That was cited with other passages from the *philosophica* by E. Ackermann in his defence[15] of the authenticity of *HO*. The Hercules who suffers but does not yield is not only Stoic but Senecan.

A symbolic tree is also found in Seneca's own *Oedipus*, again in a | 'messenger-speech'. Laius is being summoned from the dead to reveal his killer, and Creon describes the sinister scene:

> medio stat ingens arbor atque umbra gravi
> silvas minores urguet et magno ambitu
> diffusa ramos una defendit nemus.
> tristis sub illa, lucis et Phoebi inscius,
> restagnat umor frigore aeterno rigens;
> limosa pigrum circumit fontem palus.   (542-7)

Here the dominating tree suggests Oedipus himself,[16] who enfolds and protects the city, but at the same time oppresses it with his shadow.

---

[14] R. P. Winnington-Ingram, *Sophocles, An Interpretation* (1980), 85 f.

[15] E. Ackermann, *RhM* 67 (1912), 425 ff., following his earlier article in *Philologus*, suppl. 10 (1907), 323 ff.; both still repay study. For the Stoicism of *HO* and the other tragedies see also B. Marti, *TAPA* 76 (1945), 216 ff.

[16] Thus already D. J. Mastronarde, *TAPA* 101 (1970), 314. Earlier in the speech there are two battered trees, one leaning on the other; he sees these as suggesting Tiresias and Manto. For spreading trees as an omen of sovereignty cf. Herod. 1. 108. 1, 7. 19. 1; Soph. *El.* 421 ff.

Though he seems so stately, his life is rooted in pollution, here represented by a chill and slimy bog; for Sophocles the plague had already hints of miasma,[17] but characteristically Seneca uses an image whose only function is symbolic. In the same way *lucis*. . . *inscius* glances at the metaphorical and literal blindness that plays such a part in the Sophoclean story, while *Phoebi* might also allude to the king's neglect of oracles.

Another significant oak appears in Seneca's *Thyestes*, yet again in a messenger-speech, this time describing the crime of Atreus. The scene is set by an *ecphrasis* on the royal palace, which rises like a mountain and looms over the city (643 'urbem premit'). In the centre there is a grove of trees, all suitably dark and sinister;[18] the sun was soon to turn back in horror at Atreus, whose first vowel is long in Latin to suit the blackness of his character.

> arcana in imo regio secessu iacet,
> alta vetustum valle compescens nemus,
> penetrale regni, nulla qua laetos solet
> praebere ramos arbor aut ferro coli,
> sed taxus et cupressus et nigra ilice
> obscura nutat silva, quam supra eminens
> despectat alte quercus et vincit nemus.   (650-6)

Tarrant[19] comments on the last line 'even nature seems to share the Tantalid striving for domination', but in view of the parallel passages we could perhaps go further: the oak that looks down and threatens from on high suggests the megalomaniac Atreus himself (cf. 885 'aequalis astris gradior et cunctos super | altum superbo vertice attingens polum'). Seneca goes on to | describe the nearby spring, which was very different from the sparkling fountains of great Roman houses:

> fons stat sub umbra tristis et nigra piger
> haeret palude: talis est dirae Stygis
> deformis unda quae facit caelo fidem.   (665-7)

Again the symbolism is supported by the parallel with *Oedipus*: at the centre of the glittering palace lurks the pollution of the underworld.

[17] H. Musurillo, 'Sunken Imagery in Sophocles' *Oedipus*', *AJP* 78 (1957), 36ff. For some bibliography on imagery in Greek tragedy see D. H. Porter, *SO* 61 (1986), 19ff.

[18] In Seneca oppressive scenery sometimes corresponds to psychological situations; cf. C. Segal, *A & A* 29 (1983), 180f.

[19] R. J. Tarrant, *Seneca's* Thyestes (American Philological Association, Textbook Series, 11; 1985).

A trunk with another association appears in the messenger-speech in *Phaedra* that recounts the death of Hippolytus. The whole context contains significant images that have recurred through the play:[20] the monster that chases Hippolytus suggests irrational lusts; the man who keeps himself on a tight rein (cf. 450 'effunde habenas') and initially holds his horses (1055 'artis continet frenis equos') is swept to his ruin; the huntsman is enmeshed in a noose of his own harness (1086 'laqueo'), his very instrument of control; the bleeding remnants of his carcass are tracked down by his own pursuing hounds (1108). In particular at the actual moment of disaster Hippolytus is impaled on a stake (1098 ff.):

> tandemque raptum truncus ambusta sude
> medium per inguen stipite erecto[21] tenet;
> haesere biiuges vulnere—et pariter moram
> dominumque rumpunt.

It surely cannot be accidental in this of all plays that the injury is inflicted on the *inguen*,[22] and one suspects a bizarre caricature of Priapus (cf. Hor. *Sat.* 1. 8. 4 'porrectus ab inguine palus'):[23] such is nature's revenge on chastity. The poet thus reverses a conventional antithesis: Ov. *Am.* 2. 4. 31 f. 'ut taceam de me, qui causa tangor ab omni, | illic Hippolytum pone, Priapus erit', *Priapea* 19. 5 f. 'haec sic non modo te, Priape, possit, | privignum quoque sed movere Phaedrae'.

Trees stand as symbols also in Lucan, who has so many affinities with his uncle. Pompey is compared to a venerable oak that is laden with trophies but will fall at the first East wind (1. 135 ff.). The point is less explicit and so more relevant to *HO* at 9. 966 ff. 'iam silvae steriles et putres robore trunci | Assaraci pressere domos et templa deorum | iam lassa radice tenent'; the rotten trunks suggest the decayed majesty of the Trojan kingdom. Even more striking is the Druids' grove at Massilia, which Caesar cuts down to make siege-works (3. 445 f.

---

[20] P. J. Davis, 'Vindicat omnes Natura sibi', in *Seneca Tragicus* (*Ramus Essays on Senecan Drama*, ed. A. J. Boyle, 1983), 114 ff.; A. J. Boyle, 'In Nature's Bonds', *ANRW* 2. 32. 2 (1985), 1284 ff.; C. Segal, *Language and Desire in Seneca's* Phaedra (1986), 73 ff., 176 ff.

[21] *erecto* cod. Treveti: *eiecto* A: *iecto* E: *ingesto* Heinsius (accepted by Zwierlein).

[22] For injury in the offending part cf. *Oed.* 1038 f. (of Jocasta) 'hunc dextra, hunc pete | uterum capacem qui virum et natos tulit' (so *Oct.* 369 ff. and Tac. *Ann.* 14. 8. 5 of Agrippina); R. Heinze, *Vergils epische Technik* (1914), 207 (the boastful Pharus is wounded in the mouth at *Aen.* 10. 322).

[23] Cf. Hor. *Epod.* 12. 19 f. 'cuius in indomito constantior inguine nervus | quam nova collibus arbor inhaeret'; naturally Seneca is less explicit. See further J. N. Adams, *The Latin Sexual Vocabulary* (1982), 23 f.

'gemuere videntes | Gallorum populi');[24] though | he lets in the light, he shows his impatience, ruthlessness, and contempt for established institutions. Here as in *HO* the symbolism is distinctive: we are not given a static image as an analogy to a present happening (like cloudy skies over care-worn symposiasts), but one part of the action points the moral of something more important that has still to take place.

Various forms of foreshadowing are found in ancient literature, though they need more analysis and correlation; as the subject encourages fantasy, any study should proceed from the clear cases to the less clear, and with some sense of historical development. Apart from direct predictions omens are particularly common (significantly in Seneca himself),[25] but they are not always expressly acknowledged as such: thus the Virgilian sea-serpents that swim from Tenedos (*Aen.* 2. 203 ff.) symbolize the invading Greeks. Dramatic irony may allude not just to an existing situation but to future developments: when Medea in the prologue to Seneca's play hopes to scorch Corinth from the chariot of the sun (32 ff.), there is a clear reference to her final departure; when Cassandra's fury is said to collapse like a sacrificial bull (Sen. *Ag.* 776 f.), the chorus's choice of simile points to the king's murder (cf. 898 f.). When Virgil describes Hercules's destruction of Cacus (*Aen.* 8. 184 ff.), in some sense he prefigures the missions of Aeneas and Augustus;[26] one may distinguish the 'typology' of the New Testament, whereby passages in the Old Testament are retrospectively given a prophetic significance.[27] Stories inserted in a narrative may comment on the subsequent action; there are hints of the technique already in Homer,[28] but it is most clearly found in the novelists,[29] notably Apuleius. An *ecphrasis* on a work of art sometimes relates to coming events, as when Europa's basket in Moschus depicts the story

[24] F. Ahl, *Lucan* (1976), 199 f.

[25] Sen. *Thy.* 767 ff.; *Oed.* 337 ff.; N. T. Pratt, Jr., *Dramatic Suspense in Seneca and his Greek Precursors* (Diss. Princeton, NJ, 1939), 95 ff. Stoics believed in portents; cf. Sen. *NQ* 2. 32, Fantham on *Tro.* 368 f.

[26] G. Binder, *Aeneas und Augustus: Interpretationen zum 8. Buch der Aeneis* (1971), 141 ff. For some qualifications and distinctions see J. Griffin, *Latin Poets and Roman Life* (1985), 183 ff.

[27] L. Goppelt, *Typos* (1939 and 1969); G. W. H. Lampe and K. J. Woolcombe, *Essays on Typology* (Studies in Biblical Theology Ser. 1. 22; 1957); D. J. Moo, *The Old Testament in the Gospel Passion Narratives* (1983).

[28] G. Duckworth, *Foreshadowing and Suspense in the Epics of Homer, Apollonius, and Vergil* (Diss. Princeton, NJ, 1933), 24 ff.; B. K. Braswell, *Hermes*, 110 (1982), 129 ff. (Ares and Aphrodite).

[29] J. Tatum, *TAPA* 100 (1969), 487 ff.; B. L. Hijmans and R. Th. van der Paardt, *Aspects of Apuleius' Golden Ass* (1978), 80 ff.; R. L. Hunter, *A Study of Daphnis and Chloe* (1983), 52 ff.

of Io;[30] the description of a gift or an item of booty may recall past tragedies that bode no good for the future (Virg. *Aen.* 1. 650ff., 10. 497ff.).[31] A landscape may suit the happenings that are about to take place in it, as when a flowery meadow witnesses an abduction.[32] A rocky and desolate mountain may symbolize age or endurance, and point to | developments in an ode or an epic, like Horace's Soracte[33] or Virgil's Atlas (*Aen.* 4. 246ff.);[34] in this sense Oeta is an appropriate scene for the agony of Hercules.

It has long been maintained by eminent authorities[35] that *Hercules Oetaeus* was written not by Seneca but by an incompetent bungler. Some of the criticisms concern borrowings from other plays,[36] repetitiveness in vocabulary,[37] a lack of unity and consistency; but these are all Senecan characteristics, even if exaggerated here. Many objections to particular passages dissolve on inspection,[38] and others can be explained by textual corruption (always significant in Seneca) or interpolation. Some anomalies undeniably remain, as they do in most works of literature: scholars cite the scansion of *mihi* as an iambus[39] (perhaps a sign of grandeur), the distribution *caret Hercule* at the end of the

---

[30] P. Friedländer, *Johannes von Gaza und Paulus Silentiarius* (1912), 15; O. Schissel, *Philologus*, 72 (1913), 83ff.; Bühler on Moschus, *Europa* 37-62; R. Peden, *Phoenix*, 39 (1985), 380ff.

[31] G. B. Conte, *RIFC* 98 (1970), 292ff.

[32] C. P. Segal, *Landscape in Ovid's* Metamorphoses (*Hermes* Einzelschriften, 23, 1969); Bühler on Moschus, *Europa* 63-71ff.; Richardson on the *Homeric Hymn to Demeter* 6ff.; J. M. Bremer, *Mnem.* Ser. 4, 28 (1975), 268ff.; C. A. Sowa, *Traditional Themes and the Homeric Hymns* (1984), 135ff.

[33] L. P. Wilkinson, *Horace and his Lyric Poetry* (1951), 129ff.; M. G. Shields, *Phoenix*, 12 (1958), 166ff. See also above, n. 3.

[34] P. McGushin, *AJP* 85 (1964), 225ff.; J. H. W. Morwood, *JRS* 75 (1985), 51ff.; P. R. Hardie, *Virgil's* Aeneid: *Cosmos and Imperium* (1986), 280ff.

[35] F. Leo's edition, vol. 1 (1878), 48ff.; W. H. Friedrich, *Hermes*, 82 (1954), 51ff., repr. in E. Lefèvre, *Senecas Tragödien* (1972), 500ff.; B. Axelson, *Korruptelenkult: Studien zur Textkritik der unechten Seneca-Tragödie* Hercules Oetaeus (1967), 92ff.; O. Zwierlein, *Kritischer Kommentar zu den Tragödien Senecas* (*AAWM*, 1986), 313ff.

[36] A. S. Pease collected 400 parallels to the other plays (*TAPA* 49 (1918), 3ff.), but he thought that their very triviality pointed to subconscious reminiscence by the author rather than painstaking pilfering by a successor.

[37] For repetitions of a leitmotif in Seneca's *Oedipus*, see D. J. Mastronarde, *TAPA* 101 (1970), 291ff.

[38] To mention two of Friedrich's complaints, at *HO* 1394 'sparsus silebo' may be nonsense, but it is Senecan nonsense; at 242 'sub rupe tigris hoste conspecto exilit' the verb means not 'jumped out' but 'jumped up' (as at Cat. 62. 8 'perniciter exsiluere'), and so is compatible with Deianeira's hestitation.

[39] In *HO* the second vowel of *mihi* is long 6 times, and of *tibi* twice, a licence unparalleled in the corpus except for the spurious *Octavia*; yet *tibique* and *sibique* are attested as an amphibrach at *Oed.* 670 and 767.

trimeter (but Euripides shows greater metrical variations), the appearance of *ecce* in the third place in the sentence,[40] the use of *genus*
without qualification for the whole human race (but to accuse this poet
of not knowing Latin is absurd). Statistics of vocabulary show a few
oddities, but the incidence of *ego* is not surprising in an egocentric play,
or of *o* and *ei* in an emotional one. One must certainly register the
frequency of *inquit* (13 times out of 15 in the corpus), but it is no less
noteworthy that *an* appears 26 times in *Troades* and once in *Medea*.

Otto Zwierlein, the latest and best editor of Seneca's tragedies
(OCT 1986), has pronounced firmly against authenticity (see n. 35); he
suggests a second-century date, alleging imitation of Silius. Questions
of priority are notoriously difficult to determine, and on a first
examination of the arguments one's reactions are sceptical. When
Orpheus makes music, birds swoon and drop from the sky (*HO* 1047
'ales deficiens cadit'), Zwierlein thinks this inappropriate to the idyllic
scene, and sees a conflation of Sil. 11. 468 'non mota volucris captiva
pependit in aethra' and 14. 595 'fluxit deficiens penna labente volucris'
(the latter of the plague at Syracuse). But as so often Seneca's
grotesque hyperbole goes one better than the expected | common-
place; if Apollo's lyre could send the eagle to sleep (Pind. *Pyth.* 1. 6 ff.)
and Orpheus himself could hypnotize Cerberus (Virg. *Georg.* 4. 481 ff.),
why should birds on the wing not 'fail' as well as flowing rivers? Later
in the same chorus Zwierlein comments on 1056 ff. 'iuxtaque inpavi-
dum pecus | sedit Marmaricus leo | nec dammae trepidant lupos | et
serpens latebras fugit | tunc oblita veneni'; here he sees an imitation of
Sil. 3. 300 ff. 'Marmaridae, medicum vulgus, strepuere catervis, | ad
quorum cantus serpens oblita veneni, | ad quorum tactum mites iacuere
cerastae'. He gives Silius the priority because he does not like the
African lion to be associated with the Thracian minstrel, but such
global perspectives are quite natural in Seneca; he regards the passage
in *HO* as a conflation of Silius and Sen. *Ag.* 739 'Marmaricus leo', but
the latter citation as soon supports the sequence *Ag.*, *HO*, Silius.

The authenticity of *HO* has recently been championed by Marc
Rozelaar (*ANRW* 2. 32. 2. 1348 ff.); one may note especially his arguments against Friedrich's overrated article. Like Rozelaar I date the
play shortly before Seneca's death in 65; that would explain the
anomalies, the verbosity, the other signs of haste. When the ageing
sage was failing in health and contemplating his own immortality,[41] he

---

[40] Zwierlein, op. cit. (n. 35), 319.

[41] Gibbon says of such Romans 'when they viewed with complacency the extent of

would find an added attraction in the agony of Hercules;[42] he was concerned for a worthy[43] death, and his own last hours were modelled on
Socrates.[44] In particular we may point to the very end of the play,
where the chorus prays to the deified Hercules (1991 ff.):

> nunc quoque nostras aspice terras,
> et si qua novo belua vultu
> quatiet populos terrore gravi,
> tu fulminibus frange trisulcis:
> fortius ipso genitore tuo
> fulmina mitte.

A reappearance of the Nemean lion was an uninteresting contingency,
and anyway beasts don't have faces (Cic. *Leg.* 1. 27); sensible men
regarded Hercules as a saviour not because he protected them from
animals but because he destroyed tyrants (Dio Chrys. 1. 84). At the
beginning of the play Hercules had said to Jupiter 'non est tonandum;
perfidi reges iacent, | saevi tyranni. fregimus quidquid fuit | tibi ful-
minandum' (5 ff.). In the corresponding passage at the end a beast that
Jupiter had failed to destroy begins to have hints of an emperor;
Seneca had no longer the need to be circumspect. |

On one point in particular we may resist the experts: the play, or
anyway most of it, was written by a considerable poet. The author
shows many features of Seneca's style: conceits, *sententiae*, a declaimer's fertility in argument. The multiplication of horrors[45] is
characteristic, as is the geographical and astronomical hyperbole
(what Bottom called 'Ercles' vein'): Pelion is piled on Ossa (1152f.),
Cancer torn from the Zodiac (1218ff.),[46] Danube and Ocean dried by
the sufferer's fever (1365ff.). When Hercules prays to share his ruin

---

their own mental powers . . ., they were unwilling to confound themselves with the beasts
of the field, or to suppose that a being, for whose dignity they entertained the most
sincere admiration, could be limited to a spot of earth, and to a few years of duration'
(*Decline and Fall*, ch. 15).

[42] For Seneca's association of himself with Hercules (and perhaps of his mother with
Alcmena) see M. Rozelaar, *ANRW* 2. 32. 2. 1394ff.

[43] Rozelaar, op. cit. 1400ff. Compare *HO* 1216f. 'iam quis dignus necis Herculeae |
superest auctor nisi dextra tui?' with Sen. *Prov.* 2. 10 'tam turpe est Catoni mortem ab
ullo petere quam vitam'.

[44] Tac. *Ann.* 15. 63; Dio 62. 25; M. T. Griffin, *Seneca* (1976), 370ff. There is a pointed
contrast with the death of Petronius (Tac. *Ann.* 16. 19. 2): 'audiebatque referentes nihil
de immortalitate animae et sapientium placitis'.

[45] For 'deinosis' see H. V. Canter, *Rhetorical Elements in the Tragedies of Seneca* (Univ. Illinois Studies, 10. 1; 1925), 80ff.; J. Smereka, *Eos*, 32 (1929), 615ff.

[46] For cosmic turmoil in Seneca, cf. N. T. Pratt, *TAPA* 94 (1963), 203f., 229f.

with the universe (1149 f.), the megalomaniac self-assertion of the hero is combined with Senecan complacency at the dissolution of the cosmos;[47] when his mortal part is burned (1965 f. 'quidquid in nobis tui l mortale fuerat, ignis evictum tulit'), that again suits Senecan doctrine.[48] In the same way the felling of the oak shows not only a Stoic admiration for the *constantia sapientis* and a Stoic sense of the interaction of man and nature,[49] but a use of symbolism that can be paralleled in undeniably Senecan plays. Minor Latin poets were deficient in imagination and did not think of such things, but Seneca knew better than any Roman how to speak in strong, significant, recurring images.

[47] Compare *HO* 1149 f. 'conde me tota pater, l mundi ruina, frange quem perdis polum' with *Thy.* 830 ff.; *Marc.* 26. 6; *Polyb.* 1. 2; *NQ* 6. 2. 9 'si cadendum est, cadam orbe concusso'.

[48] Sen. *Marc.* 25. 1; A. L. Motto, *Guide to the Thought of L. Annaeus Seneca* (1970), 61 f. For the Stoic belief in creative as well as destructive fire, cf. Pease on Cic. *Nat. Deor.* 2. 40.

[49] K. Reinhardt, *Kosmos und Sympathie* (1926), 111 f.; O. Regenbogen, *Kleine Schriften* (1961), 437 f.

14

Pyrrha among Roses: Real Life and Poetic Imagination in Augustan Rome

Review and discussion of Jasper Griffin,
Latin Poets and Roman Life

THE relation between literature and life concerns both the critic and the historian. The Romantic liked poetry that had in some sense been experienced: hence Fraenkel's remarkable dictum 'Horace never lies' (*Horace*, 456, cf. 199 f.). More up-to-date theorists emphasize the autonomy of the artefact; the poor author becomes a bloodless ghost whose actions and sufferings, even if ascertainable, are thought irrelevant to his product. Scholars of a more empirical temperament will draw distinctions between one writer and another in the use they make of real life; they will not be happy with any formulation that lumps together Lesbia, Cynthia, Dido, the Dark Lady, and the first Mrs Hardy. And when they turn from literary criticism to social history they understand that works of imagination sometimes provide unique insights and sometimes lay particular traps.

Mr Griffin is aware of the complexities in his interesting book, but it is not his purpose to offer any overall view. Five of his chapters are familiar articles in a slightly revised form, five make their first appearance here. Inevitably such a collection has a similarity of approach rather than a unity of structure, so it will be best to deal with each heading in turn. My own position emerges mainly in the discussion, but a few generalizations will be added at the end.

1. *Augustan Poetry and the Life of Luxury* (*JRS* 66 (1976), 87 ff.). In this already influential paper G. shows that the Hellenized life of luxury described by the Augustan poets is not simply a literary convention but is based on Roman reality. Relevant material had been cited by the

Journal of Roman Studies, 77 (1987), 184–90, on Griffin, *Latin Poets and Roman Life* (Classical Life and Letters; London: Duckworth, 1985).

manuals of private antiquities (Friedländer, Marquardt, Blümner), and was not entirely unknown even to commentators on Horace, but it can never have been set out so attractively before. Here we meet wine, perfume, clothes, cosmetics, jewellery, singing and dancing, with an appendix on the specialized skills of the imperial household. In particular we are given Roman evidence for a Graecizing symposium and a sophisticated *demi-monde*.

In G.'s opinion Horace and Propertius describe this world more directly than is sometimes supposed; thus he criticizes a comment of my own (on *Odes* 1. 5), 'Pyrrha herself is the wayward beauty of fiction, totally unlike the compliant *scorta* of Horace's own temporary affairs'. That was over-stated, as the life in question had many gradations; but Horace's anti-romantic attitudes extend consistently from the *Satires* to the *Odes* (cf. 1. 33. 14 ff. on the scolding Myrtale), and we have no reason to associate him with a Lycoris or a Cynthia. But while the poet's personal life-style is a matter for speculation and not ultimately significant, Pyrrha's surround of roses is surely a literary convention (which is not to condemn it); such things are not found in Catullus's short poems, which really do reflect fashionable life as it was. Of course G. recognizes stylization in the *Odes*, just as his opponents would admit a probable authenticity of attitude (notably in the contrast between youth and middle age), but he persistently encourages a more literal reading than contemporaries would have thought plausible. That is not so negligible a matter as is often suggested, as it affects our impression of the character of the poetry; the artificiality of the situation itself says something about Horace's standpoint.

If that proposition is doubted, let us consider some clear-cut cases. In *Odes* 1. 17 Horace urges Tyndaris to leave the violent Cyrus and sing about Penelope in his Sabine valley. G. does not like her to be called 'a dream-figure from pastoral', and quotes material on the *fête-champêtre*, but this is a reversion to Fraenkel's sentimental literalism (*Horace*, 206, 'my dear young lady . . .'); a journey beyond Tibur was no picnic in ancient conditions (for the remoteness of the area cf. *Epist.* 1. 7. 77 ff.), and a glamorous metropolitan *psaltria* would not be interested in Horace's goats. Certainly serenades have been sung till modern times in the Mediterranean world, but when the belated diner-out hurried along the Subura in the rain, did he really pick his way over the prostrate forms of the major Augustan poets? Did Horace really keep up with the loves of his youth so that he could taunt them in the manner of Greek scoptic epigram for their wrinkles and yellow teeth

(*Odes* 4. 13. 10 ff.). Of course he went to parties where women were present, but he did not exchange banter there with the brother of Opuntian Megylla (1. 27. 10 ff.); in so big a city he would not know the relatives of such a person. It would not be at all surprising if he entertained and was entertained by musical girls, but it is unlikely that he sang to them about the green hair of the Nereids (3. 28. 9 ff.). |

G. considers homosexuality in Augustan poetry, and shows that within clearly defined limits it was tolerated by the Romans (see further P. Veyne, *Annales ESC* 33 (1978), 50 ff.); this goes against those who see a Greek literary convention (G. Williams, *JRS* 52 (1962), 42). But there is a special problem at Hor. *Odes* 1. 4. 19 f. 'nec tenerum Lycidan mirabere' (to P. Sestius, cos. 23 BC); such a remark seems inappropriate when addressed to a *princeps civitatis*, who would not be publicly associated with girls either, and is not justified by teasing of Maecenas in an epode (14. 9 ff.). Perhaps the ode in question, though it owes its prominent position to Sestius's consulship, was written long before; its metre has affinities with the epodes. If that be thought an inadequate explanation, perhaps Sestius wrote epigrams himself in the Greek manner.

2. *Propertius and Antony* (*JRS* 67 (1977), 17 ff.). G. takes his text from Prop. 3. 11: 'No surprise if a woman rules my life; Cleopatra tried to conquer Rome'. He shows that though Propertius outwardly supports Augustus, his attitude sometimes seems equivocal: 'if everybody lived the life of pleasure, the sea of Actium would not swirl Roman bones' (2. 15. 41 ff.). He observes that Antony's burial beside Cleopatra would impress susceptible minds, and he concludes that Propertius found in him a paradigm of the great lover.

That goes too far. If the *Monobiblos* was published in 29–28, there was not enough time for Antony's romantic death to make an impact; and Propertius is vindictive about him as well as Cleopatra. As G. himself recognizes, the poet has found a clever way of connecting the battle of Actium with the subject-matter of his poetry; when he mentions Medea and Omphale among women who had dominated their men, it is only by way of wit that Cynthia can be associated with such formidable *exempla*. The tenor of Propertian love-elegy had already been established by Gallus, and it is in him that the significant resemblance to Antony should be looked for: they had more in common than an association with Cytheris. G. is right to observe that if Actium had gone the other way, Propertius would have celebrated Antony; but so would they all.

The most valuable part of the chapter concerns strenuous men of action who were admired also for their pleasure-seeking lives: G. cites Alcibiades and Alexander, Lucullus and Catiline, as well as various eminences in Tacitus. More generalizations might be developed on the nature of charisma, a significant asset in the Republic as well as the Empire: the flamboyant Murena was preferred by the electorate to the high-minded Ser. Sulpicius. If physical magnetism was combined with political power, it would have a potent effect in both public and private life; modern instances could be multiplied from both sides of the Atlantic. When persons of this type were the victims of invective, G. speaks of 'prurient envy', but that was a less important factor than in more egalitarian and hypocritical societies. If the great man moved in a remote enough sphere, his excesses could give drab lives a sympathetic excitement.

3. *Genre and Real Life in Latin Poetry* (*JRS* 71 (1981), 39 ff.). G. begins with some sensible words on the biographical approach to literature: he rejects the old-fashioned way of talking about poets instead of poems, but equally he deprecates any suggestion that the poet's life is irrelevant to his artefact. As one instance of the latter tendency he considers the 'generic' theories associated with Francis Cairns, by which ancient poetry is subdivided into minor categories like 'propempticon' or 'epibaterion' (poem on arrival), each with its standard topics and procedures. G. deplores the exaggerations of the doctrine ('ancient poetry was largely written in a time-free zone'), its scholasticism ('could independent genres become topics of other genres?'), its way of relating literary merit to observance of the rules. He is right to underline that Menander Rhetor, who plays so prominent a part in these discussions, was giving prescriptions for encomia in prose; such an expositor might sometimes draw on the conventions of verse (for instance in flowery speeches at weddings), but he could offer nothing on many of the situations of Augustan poetry (for instance the serenade at the closed door). The name 'eucharisticon' goes back to Statius and 'propempticon' to Cinna, but it is not necessary to determine the date when particular categories were identified; the themes themselves go back to early Greek poetry, long before rhetoric was thought of. It remains true that a rhetorical education must have helped the Augustan poets to improvise fluently within recurring

contexts; such is the fall-back position of I. M. Le M. Du Quesnay in his able defence of the 'generic' approach (*Papers of the Liverpool Latin Seminar*, 3 (1981), 53 ff.).

Some of G.'s particular criticisms seem over-stated. Unfamiliar jargon is always unattractive, but grammar and rhetoric also have their terms of art (like 'accusative' or 'metaphor'), and 'inverse propempticon' is a perfectly sensible description of Horace's epode on Mevius. G. complains of minor categories like *mandata morituri* or 'the poem of gloating', because they fall outside the precepts of the rhetorical theorists; but once we extricate | ourselves from Menander Rhetor (as we surely must), we may find it convenient to label some types of poem that were nameless in antiquity. G.'s strictures should rather be directed against the confusing use of the word 'genre'; this should properly refer to major categories like epic or comedy that were distinguished by a particular function and style, not to minor subdivisions relating primarily to content. In spite of all reservations Cairns has done much to identify commonplaces applicable to particular situations; ancient poetry operates with such commonplaces more than moderns would expect, and though some seem inevitable others need to be pointed out.

To illustrate his approach G. discusses Propertius 1. 3, where the poet returns from a symposium and stands by Cynthia's bed in the moonlight. He rightly rejects Cairns's categorization of this poem as a 'komos' (in which the revelling lover is shut out); as so often with 'generic' interpretations, this 'obliges us to put too much weight on what is not there to the detriment of what is'. But G. himself recognizes in a footnote a number of poems about 'sleeping beauties' (in view of the poet's own comparison, note also the sleeping Maenads of art); when Propertius puts apples in Cynthia's hands one senses a prototype in pastoral or romance where fruit was picked from the branch rather than the sideboard. Commonplaces applied by the Hellenistic poets to mythological characters were transferred by the Roman elegists to themselves; thus when Propertius (1. 18. 22) carves Cynthia's name on trees (in the lady's absence, let it be emphasized), the motif can be traced with others to the Callimachean 'Acontius and Cydippe' (F. Cairns, *CR* 19 (1969), 131 ff.). G.'s Propertius is a romantic aesthete who describes events that might reasonably happen in the life of such a person. More plausibly Paul Veyne sees a virtuoso mimesis of the behaviour and emotions traditionally ascribed to the lover (*L'Élégie érotique romaine* (1983)). No doubt the poet chose a persona that

attracted one side of his personality (in a way that it would not attract
an elderly Stoic philosopher), but he need no more be identified with
the protagonist of his elegies than Virgil with Corydon.

4. *Of Wines and Spirits*. G. is concerned only incidentally with the
realities of viticulture (for which see now N. Purcell, *JRS* 75 (1985),
1 ff.); he deals rather with the central place of wine in the Roman
symposium. Horace's presentation of the institution reflects the ethos
of aristocratic Roman society (O. Murray, *JRS* 75 (1985), 39 ff.), but it
may be less factual than G. would admit: did tired statesmen regularly
drink with the poet to forget their worries about the Cantabrians? G.
says something about Bacchus as a god of poetry as well as wine
(70 ff.). He regards Horace's Bacchic ecstasy (*Odes* 2. 19) as an impassioned claim to supreme literary status, but dithyrambs about
Bacchanals and giants seem irrelevant to the dry distinction of the
Horatian ode; one is inclined to see greater detachment than the
modern world expects in first-person lyrics.

G. observes that Horace's wine-snobbery is not paralleled in the
Hellenistic epigrammatists or even the Roman elegists, who mention
Falernian only to suggest a life grander than their own. One might
illustrate even more than he does the symbolical character of these
vintages. It is not necessary to suppose that the Caecuban that symbol-
ized victory was obtainable at Actium (see my article in *Poetry and
Politics in the Age of Augustus*, ed. T. Woodman and D. West (1984), 17
(above, p. 181), or that Horace really bottled Sabine wine when
Maecenas was cheered in the theatre (*Odes* 1. 20), or that he could
supply Messalla with a vintage of 65 BC—the great man's year of birth, I
suggest, as well as Horace's (3. 21)—still less that he could produce for
Torquatus a Sinuessanum from his ancestor's battlefield (*Epist.*
1. 5. 4 ff., *CQ* 9 (1959), 73). Of course wine could have a sentimental
value in life as well as literature: it has been observed that Opimianum
may have tasted so fine because it commemorated the downfall of
Gracchus.

But in the ancient as in the modern world the symbolism was misunderstood, and Horace was treated as a light-hearted drinking-poet.
When he says 'hoc simul edixi, non cessavere poetae nocturno certare
mero, putere diurno' (*Epist.* 1. 19. 10 f.), he is said to be making a
literary distinction between poets who are temperamentally 'wine-
drinkers' and 'water-drinkers' (though he might himself be regarded as
one of the latter). In fact he may be referring more literally to his

sympotic odes, which have indeed been imitated for the wrong reason
(17, 'decipit exemplar vitiis imitabile').

5. *The Pleasures of Water and Nakedness*. G. provides much entertaining
detail to evoke the delights of water in a hot city. He points out that
Latin literature was concerned with swimming more than Greek
(citing *RE*, Suppl. 5. 847ff.); but that reflects the preoccupations of
urban sophisticates with privileged access to the river or coast. He
comments on the absence | of Leander from Greek literature before
Musaeus; but Strabo knew about Hero's tower (13. 1. 22), and the
recurrence of the theme in Roman poetry and art does seem to point
to a Hellenistic prototype (*RE* 8. 909ff.). He suggests that Cyrene's
grotto in the *Georgics* and the rushing waters of the *Metamorphoses*
reflect contemporary sensibility; here as elsewhere his comments
could have been extended to the *Silvae* of Statius (Z. Pavlovskis, *Man
in an Artificial Landscape*, *Mnem.* suppl. 25 (1973), 16ff.).

Other aspects of the subject do not come within G.'s purview. Since
Horatius kept the bridge, swimming was regarded as useful in war
(Veg. *Mil.* 1. 10), and some of the activity in the Tiber (Hor. *Odes*
1. 8. 8) may in theory at least have been regarded as military training.
Water-sports were not confined to Clodia's *iuventus*; the impeccable
young Trebatius is teased by Cicero for his addiction to swimming
(*Fam.* 7. 10. 2 'qui neque in Oceano natare volueris studiosissimus
homo natandi'), and twenty-five years later as an eminent jurist he was
still going strong (Hor. *Sat.* 2. 1. 7f.). G. alludes to the poetical dreams
where Propertius tries to dive into the sea to rescue Cynthia
(2. 26. 19f.) and Ligurinus swims down the Tiber with Horace in hot
pursuit (*Odes* 4. 1. 37ff.); these fantasies do not belong to the literary
tradition, and if G. is searching for personal experiences they might
repay psychological analysis.

The latter part of the paper is misrepresented by the title: G. is concerned with glimpses of semi-nudity in others, as in descriptions of
bathing or wind-swept heroines. Early Greek poetry did not go in for
this sort of thing, but developments of taste could only be put in
historical perspective by a more detailed discussion of art; to the
Nereids, mentioned in a footnote, add the Anadyomene of Apelles,
removed by Augustus to the temple of Divus Julius. As usual G. averts
his gaze from the more sordid aspects of his subject: for voyeurism see
J. P. Sullivan, *Petronius* (1968), 238ff., N. M. Kay on Mart. 11. 45. 6,
11. 63. One would welcome a systematic discussion on nudity in real

life (as opposed to sentimental literature), as this was one area where traditional Roman *mores* differed from the Greek: cf. Enn. *Scen.* 395 V. 'flagiti principium est nudare inter civis corpora', Cic. *Off.* 1. 129 'nostro quidem more cum parentibus puberes filii, cum soceris generi non lavantur'.

6. Meretrices, *Matrimony and Myth.* G. is not concerned with a general view of Roman prostitution (cf. Herter, *RAC* 3. 1149 ff.), but with the women of elegy, who were not usually portrayed as *meretrices* at all; see R. Syme, *History in Ovid* (1978), 202 on the widows and divorcées of a post-war world. G. talks of the poets' reluctance to mention money, but a Cynthia would not expect payment cash down: like the poets themselves in relation to their patrons, mistresses did better when their recompense was undefined. G. also comments on the absence of the *leno* from elegy, but this again is not just literary romanticism. A girl who could pick and choose would not put herself at the mercy of a Ballio, but she could get moral support from a *vir*, a mother (Tib. 1. 6. 57 ff.), or a small-time *lena*.

When he turns to Roman marriage, G. tends to accept the traditional view that it lacked emotional content. But he does well to cite the epithalamium to Torquatus (Catullus 61), which warns against too schematic an analysis of complex attitudes; here we find subsisting together duty to country and *gens* (71 ff., 205 ff.), fidelity and lifelong devotion (97 ff., 154 ff.), and passionate love within marriage. Peter Gay has forcibly reminded us that the Victorians felt some things that they did not discuss, and so no doubt did the Romans. Arranged marriages (G. 119) may develop strong emotion, as is clear from Queen Victoria herself (to pursue the inquiry no further). Of course the Roman upper classes paid more attention to social and financial suitability than modern sentiment would approve, but so have most societies: the European novel could provide some insights.

G. sees how the imaginary world of mythology may shed light on the realities of Roman private life. He compares Hypermestra's rescue of her husband (Hor. *Odes* 3. 11) with the conduct of Roman matrons in the proscriptions; more could be said about the Laodamia of Catullus 68, who is a paradigm for the poet's ill-omened liaison (cf. C. Macleod, *Collected Essays* (1983), 159 ff.). He finds psychological significance in the pursuits and conquests of Ovid's *Metamorphoses*; for the woman's viewpoint see L. C. Curran in *Women in the Ancient World*, ed. J. Peradotto and J. P. Sullivan (1984), 263 ff. G. says nothing here

about the *Aeneid*, which reveals more than the immaturity of Lavinia
(and even young girls might in time develop wills of their own).
Andromache's second husband reminds us to beware of exaggerated
talk about the virtues of the *univira* (cf. M. Humbert, *Le Remariage à
Rome* (1972), 59f.), Amata shows the part played in matchmaking by
ardent mothers (perhaps just as influential as acquisitive fathers), and
when Dido is captivated by Cupid it is made clear what her marriage
to Sychaeus had been about (1. 721 f. 'vivo temptat praevertere amore
iam pridem resides animos desuetaque corda'). |

7. *Love and Death*. G. produces much fascinating material on the
morbidity of Greek romance and Latin love-elegy. To die of love,
instead of the beloved, in the arms of the beloved, in the very act of
love (see 145 n. 13 on the 'mort de Faure'), to be wept over deliciously
by the beloved, such are some of the fantasies here recorded. G. might
have done even more than he does to trace the historical development
of these themes: Theocritus 1 must have been important, presumably
also Gallus (if his tenor can be deduced from Virg. *Ecl*. 10). At a more
serious level G. deals with Cynthia and her pauper's funeral, epic and
elegiac descriptions of fair women in the underworld, and the eulogies
of wives on tombstones (for the redoubtable Allia Potestas see now
N. Horsfall, *ZPE* 61 (1985), 251 ff.).

The death-wishes of the elegiac lover seem part of his masochistic
self-abasement, but psychological theory is not invoked: are the poets
writing from genuine insight, or are all those *verbera* and *vincula*
simply dead commonplaces? Nor does G. consider the springs of the
Roman relish for killing, which might have led him to a less romantic
presentation of his subject. Walter Burkert has pointed to the sexual
excitement at the climax of hunting or sacrifice (*Homo Necans* (1972),
70 ff. = 58 ff. of the English edition). Roman epic poets show a nasty
sentimentality in describing the deaths of boys in battle (Virg. *Aen*.
9. 433 ff., Stat. *Theb*. 9. 877 ff.). When Horace's Europa imagines herself
being mangled naked by lions (*Odes* 3. 27. 53 ff.), G. himself has sensed
the sadism of the arena (106 ff.). Gladiators were glamorous to women,
like matadors; see K. Hopkins, *Death and Renewal* (1983), 21 f., citing
among other passages *CIL* 4. 4342, 'suspirium puellarum Tr(aex)
Celadus', Juv. 6. 112, 'ferrum est quod amant'. But a reliable assessment
of these issues would require a degree of psychological expertise that is
seldom combined with an understanding of literary conventions.

The chapter ends with a note on the attraction of tombs for sexual encounters. G. suggests that the incongruity of the scene may have produced a *frisson* of its own (one recalls the experiences of Boswell on Westminster Bridge and of Augustus's daughter on the *rostra* (Sen. *Ben.* 6. 32. 1)), but though this element can be found in the Petronian story of the Widow of Ephesus, Martial's *bustuariae moechae* would be less sensitive to atmosphere. As G. himself recognizes, privacy was hard to find in so busy a city (see Ov. *Fast.* 3. 527 for tents at the festival of Anna Perenna); and tombs still offer seclusion in the Rome of Fellini.

8. *The Fourth* Georgic, *Virgil and Rome* (*G & R* 26 (1979), 61 ff.). In this chapter G. considers the point of the Aristaeus and Orpheus episodes at the end of *Georgics*. After dismissing some extravagant theories with the minimum of fuss, he presents a novel version of his own. Observing that Virgil's bees are not associated as elsewhere with poetry, he sees a contrast between the diligence and discipline of the collectivist state and the passion and individualism of the poet. The tension was one that recurs in Augustan literature, and G. brings out Virgil's breadth of understanding without committing the absurdity of making him anti-Augustan.

G. recognizes that the Orpheus digression shows the divergence of style found elsewhere in neoteric epyllion (Catullus 64), but he is surely right to look for something more significant than an artistic balance of opposites. He presents his theory with due caution, but perhaps he puts too much emphasis on the unpoetical nature of Virgil's bees. It might be better to begin with the contrasting temperaments of Aristaeus, who recovers his bees by *experientia* and systematic ritual, and the unpractical Orpheus, with his love of the wilds and unhelpful emotionalism. The Euripidean myth of Amphion and Zethus has some similarities, though there the practical brother was a herdsman (Eur. frr. 178 ff. N², Hor. *Epist.* 1. 18. 41 ff., *RE* 10A. 246). Such a formulation relates the situation less to the tensions of Augustan society (hardly so apparent at the time of writing) and more to the praises of agriculture that were the poem's purported theme. There could then be added the more tentative idea that the organized bees suit the organized beekeeper.

G. adds a short appendix on the reports of Servius that the end of the Fourth *Georgic* (whether the whole Aristaeus episode or only the part about Orpheus) was substituted for *laudes Galli*. He supports the orthodox opinion that the story is incredible; since he wrote his paper this view has been challenged by H. Jacobson, *AJP* 105 (1984), 271 ff. and H. D. Jocelyn, *Atti del convegno mondiale scientifico di studi su Virgilio*, 1 (1985), 431 ff. G. argues that nobody could guarantee success in suppressing an earlier version, but that does not mean that nobody could try; after all, Ovid's *Amores* had a lost first edition, and Virgil's own *juvenilia* disappeared. G. comments that Octavian would have resented eulogies of a subordinate, but even if the *laudes* dealt with politics rather than poetry, he himself could have been given some of the credit; and though he professed sorrow at Gallus's death, it would not be difficult to sense his resentment. More cogently, G. argues for the effectiveness and coherence of the version that we have, but even if we cannot think of alternatives Virgil might have been more | successful. G. mentions the theory of W. B. Anderson (which like his other arguments goes back earlier) that an ancient commentator might have written *in postrema Georgicorum parte* by a slip for *Bucolicorum*; but surely such a writer would have said 'in the tenth Bucolic'. Indeed those who reject the Servian story have their greatest difficulty in suggesting how it originated (see Jocelyn, op. cit.).

One further consideration may be put forward in favour of G. It has been suggested that the story of Orpheus is in some sense a lament for the death of Gallus (R. Coleman, *AJP* 83 (1962), 67 ff.), an implausible theory, as Virgil was too close to the regime to comment sympathetically on its victim. But if we believe that the passage in question conspicuously replaced a panegyric on Gallus, contemporaries familiar with Virgil's taste for allegory might be tempted to see a commemoration of the dead poet; nothing would be gained by the substitution, but matters would be made far worse. Indeed we could speculate further: the whole story of the *laudes Galli* may spring from the misguided attempt by some ancient scholar to see the apparently irrelevant Orpheus as an allegorical representation of Gallus. A less imaginative successor, observing that Gallus is not actually mentioned, might then conclude that something had been excised.

9. *The Creation of Characters in the* Aeneid. The subject of this chapter is not revealed by its title, still less by that of the book where it originally appeared (*Literary and Artistic Patronage in Ancient Rome*, ed. Barbara K. Gold (1982)). In fact G. examines how characters in the epic may foreshadow the actions of historical personages; thus G. Binder in his *Aeneas und Augustus* emphasizes Augustan analogies in *Aeneid* 8. G. criticizes some instances of this kind of interpretation, but by selecting

implausible examples, he sometimes gives too negative an impression. He complains when the boat-race in *Aeneid* 5 is associated with victories in Sicilian waters, fairly pointing out that two of the boats come to grief. But it must surely be relevant that the race is set at Drepanum, the scene of an unforgettable Roman defeat. The impious commander drowned the sacred chickens ('if they will not eat, let them drink'), and Virgil seems to be evoking both contrasts (the peaceful regatta, the piety of the winner) and analogies (the recklessness of the losers, the sinister burning of the boats).

G. is particularly concerned to dissociate Virgil from the so-called 'typology' of the Bible, by which historical events of the Old Testament were thought to foreshadow Christianity. The phenomenon goes further than G. makes clear, and influences the actual presentation of the Gospel narratives even in significant matters (see D. J. Moo, *The Old Testament in the Gospel Passion Narratives* (1983), with literature there cited). The differences in Virgil are obvious: he is writing a work of imagination that in no sense professes to be historical, he is dealing with events that foreshadow rather than those that are foreshadowed, he is not straining for meaningful analogies but is content to hint. G. easily rebuts the absurd view that he was influenced by rabbinical practice; yet here as elsewhere classicists should examine the results of the theologians, if only to bring out distinctions.

G. goes on to give a valuable summary of types of analogy relevant to the characters of the *Aeneid*. He draws the significant parallel with the *Eclogues*, 'where Daphnis both does and does not recall Caesar the murdered dictator'; he points to the prototype in Theocritus 7, where real poets and fictitious goat-herds are similarly blended. He mentions how rulers associated themselves with gods, and poets with their predecessors. He deals with the *exempla* of oratory, made three-dimensional in *Aeneid* 6. He shows how *imagines* at a funeral gave a sense of continuity with the past: an Ahenobarbus was expected to be ferocious, and a Brutus to resist tyranny. Much work remains to be done on the many forms of foreshadowing in ancient literature; one must proceed from the clear cases to the less clear, and with some sense of historical development from one writer to another. In the meantime G. has mapped out some of the ground.

10. *The Influence of Drama.* G. observes that in the search for influences we accept too uncritically the manifestos of the Augustan poets: they exaggerate their debt to fashionable writers like Callimachus, whose

detached wit was remote from their own appearance of involvement, and disregard the literary heroes of the previous generation ('the least interesting of all generations'), whose plays they had studied at school and seen on the stage. He underlines the significance of the many quotations in Cicero from the early Roman poets (note the collection of material in W. Zillinger, *Cicero und die altrömischen Dichter* (Diss. Würzburg, 1911)). The favourite myths, mainly Euripidean, are not always the most familiar to us (for instance the *Alcmeo* and *Telamo* of Ennius, the *Antiopa* and *Iliona* of Pacuvius), and would merit further discussion. |

Similarly G. insists that the elegiac poets must sometimes have been directly influenced by Roman comedy; that remains plausible even if most of the erotic motifs common to Propertius and Plautus can ultimately be traced to New Comedy (cf. N. Zagagi, *Tradition and Originality in Plautus* (Hypomnemata, 62; 1980)). G. sees the reversal of conventional roles that we sometimes find in elegy as typical of Roman comedy rather than Menander; for such themes in Plautus one may add Erich Segal, *Roman Laughter* (1968). This chapter is one of the most salutary in the book: the *cantores Euphorionis* tended to cut off Roman poetry from its roots, and when Cicero contrasts them to their disadvantage with Ennius (*Tusc.* 3. 45 'o poetam egregium'), he is prompted not by the *Annales* but the *Andromacha*.

Mr Griffin's book is a delight to read. He deploys much varied learning, and shows an eye for what is interesting in both primary and secondary sources. He writes with unfailing elegance and good humour, even when rebuking pretentiousness. Above all he offers fresh ideas to learn from or react against.

The title might mislead. The collection is mainly about the Augustans, as the preface makes clear, particularly the *Odes* of Horace and the *Elegies* of Propertius; the *Epistles* and the *Amores* are comparatively neglected, though even the latter describes life more directly. It is clear from his distribution of material that G. is not writing primarily as a social historian, and though he collects valuable *Realien* in several areas, he attempts no appraisal of poetry as a historical source; while it is illuminating both on general attitudes and vivid detail, its situations may be not just fictitious but fantastic, even when described in the first person. He does not as a rule look behind the agreeable scene-setting to the harsher realities, which were probably much the same as those depicted by Martial and Juvenal. The life presented by the poets is treated as largely authentic, sometimes with the thought that it may itself be imitating art. Here as elsewhere the analogy with the Romantics is pressed too far: Augustan poets were more detached and ironic, they had no exaggerated views about the virtues of sincerity and self-expression, and they felt a stronger pull from the literary tradition.

All this matters for the student of poetry even more than for the historian. In stressing reality rather than imagination, G. may give a distorted impression of the character of his authors; Horace and Propertius no less than Virgil would have regarded a close representation of life as too trivial for a serious artist. G. has a fine feeling for the descriptive qualities of Augustan poetry, but there are underlying and largely inherited structures that are less accessible to the modern reader. One is asking him not for a general critical theory (for he is not writing that kind of book), but to define where on the spectrum a few particular poets belong; with his expertise in Homer and Theocritus he is in a better position than most to place Augustan practice in a literary context. It may seem ungrateful to labour this point when we have been given so much, but the history of the subject has a warning for us all. At the beginning of the century cultivated English scholars, repelled by the schematism of more analytic minds, instead of refining the more promising theories made sardonic asides about 'the Higher Criticism', and in so doing cramped the study of ancient literature in this country for a generation.

15

Notes on the Text and Interpretation of Juvenal

Otto Skutsch

viro docto indefesso amico

OVER the years the text of Juvenal has been greatly improved, but doubts keep recurring; some of these were aired in my review of Clausen's Oxford Text in *JRS* 52 (1962), 233 ff. (above pp. 18 ff.). If I return to the problem, it is because there is no room for complacency when manuscripts are known to be unreliable. I have used the texts of Jahn (1851), Housman, Knoche, and especially Clausen, and the commentaries of Ruperti, Mayor, Friedlaender, Duff, and especially Courtney (note also his text, Rome, 1984). In referring to manuscripts I use Clausen's symbols: P, the ninth-century Pithoeanus, is detached from the main stream and relatively 'sincere'; the Φ group, the pick of the herd, is independent of P but has suffered more from rewriting. It is a pleasure to dedicate these remarks to a scholar who has made one of the major contributions of our time to Latin studies.

1. 22–30 cum tener uxorem ducat spado, Mevia Tuscum
      figat aprum et nuda teneat venabula mamma,
      patricios omnis opibus cum provocet unus
      quo tondente gravis iuveni mihi barba sonabat,
      cum pars Niliacae plebis, cum verna Canopi
      Crispinus Tyrias umero revocante lacernas
      ventilet aestivum digitis sudantibus aurum
      nec sufferre queat maioris pondera gemmae,
      difficile est saturam non scribere.

Among Juvenal's reasons for writing satire is the Egyptian Crispinus, who waves a gold ring when fanning himself on a hot day. The scholia comment on 28 'per luxuriam enim anulos aestivos et hiemales

From *Vir Bonus Discendi Peritus: Studies in Celebration of Otto Skutsch's Eightieth Birthday*, ed. N. Horsfall (*Bulletin of the Institute of Classical Studies*, suppl. 51; 1988), 86–110.

invenerat', but Duff among others objected that there is no evidence
that the Romans wore lighter rings in the summer. Housman retorted
'Of course the Romans did not: it was a single Egyptian who did. The
foppery was insufferable precisely because it was unparalleled' (*Classical Papers*, 614). For the foppery of Crispinus he cited 4. 3 f., 'aegrae
solaque libidine fortes | deliciae'.

Those who disbelieve in the lightweight ring interpret *aestivum* as
'in the summer'; for this mock-poetical usage in Juvenal cf. 3. 12 'hic
ubi nocturnae Numa constituebat amicae'; 4. 108 'et matutino sudans
Crispinus amomo'; 6. 118 'sumere nocturnos meretrix Augusta cucullos'; 12. 29 'et matutinis operatur festa lucernis'; 14. 129 ff. 'hesternum
solitus medio servare minutal | Septembri, nec non differre in tempora
cenae | alterius conchem aestivam'. In the first four of these passages
there is exactly the same mock-formal patterning as in our own, with
the adjective coming before the main caesura and the noun at the end
of the line. It is even more significant that the second passage (4. 108)
also refers to Crispinus (a fact concealed by Duff's | abbreviated
citation), and also uses the participle *sudans*. When there are two
legitimate interpretations of *aestivum*, we must choose the one that
coheres with so close a parallel.

At first sight the scholiast's interpretation seems to be supported by
29, *nec sufferre queat maioris pondera gemmae*. To get rid of the dilemma
I have tentatively suggested that the line should be deleted as an interpolation (*JRS* 52: 238); I now wish to make the same point more
firmly. Some who agree with Duff over *aestivum* try to get round the
problem of 29: they interpret not 'Crispinus is wearing a light ring in
the summer', but 'he is wearing a very heavy ring, the biggest that he
can possibly carry'.[1] It may seem an odd coincidence that the line fits
so well the false view of *aestivum*, but the difficulty cannot be decided
without considering the wider context.

Juvenal is saying that people play unnatural roles: a eunuch gets
married, a woman fights in the arena, a low-born barber accumulates a
nobleman's wealth, and an immigrant Egyptian shows off his gold ring.
The point is that a gold ring was the symbol of equestrian rank (Courtney on 11. 129), and Crispinus was a prominent *eques*: cf. 4. 31 ff. (once
again Crispinus) 'purpureus magni ructarit scurra Palati, | iam princeps
equitum, magna qui voce solebat | vendere municipes fracta de merce
siluros'. In our passage, as in the parallel, there is a contrast between

---

[1] Thus A. Gercke, *GGA* (1896), 975; C. Gnilka, *JAC* 8–9 (1965–6), 177 ff.

the man's past and present status: line 29 not only impairs the balance
of purple and gold (which are often combined), but it spoils the hor-
rifying climax of *aurum*. Courtney comments on *aurum*, 'not the plain
gold equestrian ring, since this one has a jewel (29), like a sealing-ring';
but it is precisely the equestrian ring that suits the context.[2]

1. 142-6   poena tamen praesens, cum tu deponis amictus
                 turgidus et crudum[3] pavonem in balnea portas.
                 hinc subitae mortes atque intestata senectus.
                 it nova nec tristis per cunctas fabula cenas;
                 ducitur iratis plaudendum funus amicis.

            145 it *AL*[2]: et *PRVΦ*.

After gorging himself on peacock in solitary splendour the rich man
dies in the bath, to the delight of the poor clients who have been
excluded from his table. A reference to intestacy in 144 is irrelevant, as
was pointed out by Madvig and Housman (*Classical Papers*, 489 ff.); a
rich Roman would make his will when quite young, and the clients are
angry because they have missed a dinner, not because they have
missed a legacy. Housman's 'old age is unattested' also fails to satisfy;
the unattested use of *intestata* is confusing in a context dealing with
death, and it is not specified precisely enough whose old age is in
question. Corelli's *intemptata* is hard to understand, though accepted
grudgingly enough by Courtney. Knoche deleted 144 and the excellent
145; I have myself suggested that 144 should be deleted while 145 is
kept (*JRS* 52: 234). In case anybody was too stupid to see that the rich
man was dead, the interpolator kindly | spells it out; but as elsewhere
with interpolations the plural *subitae mortes* interrupts the vivid particularity of the episode.

I now offer a variation of this solution: read *hinc nova nec tristis per
cunctas fabula cenas*. On this hypothesis the interpolator transferred the
authentic *hinc* to his new line: for somewhat similar cases cf. 7. 191 f.

    [2] Juv. 1. 29 was known to the fifth-cent. Dracontius, *Laud. Dei* 3. 60 ff., 'qui solet
aestivum membris sudantibus ostrum I poscere, deposito confractus murice denso, I cuius
et in digitis non sedit crassius aurum, I et licet exiguae non ferret pondera gemmae, I inter
anhelantes tormenta ultricia flammas I supplicium crudele luens exaestuat ardens'. As the
interpolations in Juvenal were made in antiquity, the parallel is no argument against deletion. Similarly Dracontius, *Satisfactio* 15, 'quidquid agunt homines, bona tristia prospera
prava', imitates Juv. 1. 85 f., which was rightly suspected by Scholte (with *ecquando* in 87);
see the conclusive arguments by E. Harrison, *CR* 51 (1937), 55 f.

    [3] *Φ*'s *crudum* should be preferred to P's *crudus* (which is more repetitive and neces-
sitates *portans*). If the adjective can mean 'raw', and 'with indigestion', and (in medical
writers) the intermediate 'undigested', then in non-medical writers it can mean 'undigested'.

'felix et [sapiens et nobilis et generosus | adpositam] nigrae lunam subtexit alutae' (the deletion is proposed by M. D. Reeve, *CR* 21 (1971), 238); Hor. *Epist.* 1. 18. 89 ff. 'oderunt hilarem tristes tristemque iocosi, | sedatum celeres, agilem navumque remissi, | potores [bibuli media de nocte Falerni | oderunt] porrecta negantem pocula . . .' (thus Pottier and Meineke). The interpolator also added *et* before *nova*, though it is 'no proper link between the general statements in 144 and the statements about one individual in 145 sq.' (Housman, p. xix); A's *it* is poorly attested, and could be an accident or conjecture.

The advantage of retaining *hinc* is that it is paralleled in Juvenal's evident model, Pers. 3. 102f. 'uncta cadunt laxis tunc pulmentaria labris. | hinc tuba, candelae . . .'. That passage also makes an abrupt transition from a heavy meal to a funeral, without explicit mention of the death; *hinc* is more likely to have been borrowed by Juvenal than by the interpolator. It must be conceded that A's *it* provides an effective balance with 146 *ducitur*, but the parallel in Persius seems more significant.

1. 160-8   'cum veniet contra, digito compesce labellum:
             accusator erit qui verbum dixerit "hic est".
             securus licet Aenean Rutulumque ferocem
             committas, nulli gravis est percussus Achilles
             aut multum quaesitus Hylas urnamque secutus:
             ense velut stricto quotiens Lucilius ardens
             infremuit, rubet auditor cui frigida mens est
             criminibus, tacita sudant praecordia culpa.
             inde ira et lacrimae . . .'

The voice of prudence advises Juvenal not to comment on powerful villains. It is safe to write on hackneyed mythological themes, but when Lucilius goes on the war-path as a satirist, people with guilty secrets get angry. Though the text is acceptable as it stands, hesitation on three points may be recorded.

In the first place the reader is pulled up by 161 *verbum*; the pedant in us cannot help noticing that *hic est* is two words. Of course *verbum* is often used of a whole phrase, notably in comedy; cf. for instance, Plaut. *Aul.* 547 'illud mihi verbum non placet "quod nunc habes"'. But such passages may not easily bear the additional nuance 'only a word' (as at Ter. *Andr.* 860 'verbum si addideris'); and that nuance is important in our passage ('if you speak a single word about the man, it will be thought tantamount to prosecuting him in the courts'). If this scruple has any substance, it could be removed by reading ablative *verbo*, which does supply the necessary nuance; cf. Cic. *Rab. Perd.* 8 'ne in tenuissimam quidem suspicionem verbo est umquam vocatus'.

I turn next to 163 *percussus*. The fatal wounding of Achilles seems an appropriate epic theme, and *percutere* an appropriate verb (cf. 15. 66 'vel quo Tydides percussit pondere coxam'); but one aspect causes doubt. The duel between Aeneas and Turnus is described in typically derisive terms, as if the poet were promoting a fight of gladiators,[4] and *urnamque | secutus* is an equally frivolous way of describing Hylas's fall down the well. But when we turn to the middle illustration, there is nothing humorous about *percussus Achilles*; contrast 1. 54 (of Icarus), 'et mare percussum puero' (sandwiched between the equally facetious 'mugitum labyrinthi' and 'fabrumque volantem').

To meet the point I suggest *excussus Achilles*, which would refer to the hero's exposure when he was disguised as a girl on Scyros. *excutere*, 'to shake out', can be used with an accusative either of the object discovered (6. 143 'si verum excutias') or of the person frisked (literally or metaphorically); cf. Cic. *Sex. Rosc.* 97 'non excutio te, si quid forte ferri habuisti, non scrutor'; *TLL* 5. 2. 1312. 8 ff. For a joke about Achilles's early life cf. 7. 211 f. 'et cui non tunc | eliceret risum citharoedi cauda magistri'; for the combination with Hylas cf. Mart. 5. 48. 5 'talis raptus Hylas, talis deprensus Achilles'. The substitution of one prefix for another is common (below on 2. 153 ff.), and *ex-* could have been lost after *est. percussus* would have seemed an easier and more expected word, and it could have been influenced by 1. 54 *percussum* (cited above).

Juvenal's first illustration obviously refers to the *Aeneid*. His third would recall such episodes as Val. Flacc. 3. 535–97; though the famous urn is not in fact mentioned there (Hylas is bathing after hunting), it appears at 1. 219. In the same way *excussus Achilles* might remind the reader of the discovery of Achilles at Stat. *Ach.* 1. 841 ff.; Statius was the outstanding instance of the kind of poet that Juvenal deplored (7. 82 ff.).

I turn thirdly to 165, where *velut* jars a little: the word seems too cautious in this vigorous context where Lucilius blazes and roars (contrast the clear simile at Hor. *Serm.* 2. 1. 39 ff. 'sed hic stilus haud petet ultro | quemquam animantem et me veluti custodiet ensis | vagina tectus'). I suggest *semel*, which could have lost its first syllable after *-se*. 'With sword once drawn' underlines the speed of the wrongdoer's

---

[4] The writer is said to do himself what he describes being done; to the passages cited by Courtney add now G. Lieberg, *Poeta Creator* (1982).

reaction (cf. 4.143 'et semel aspecti litus dicebat echini'), just as *quotiens* underlines its inevitability.

2. 102–3   res memoranda novis annalibus atque recenti
             historia, speculum civilis sarcina belli.

Juvenal is thought to say that Otho's mirror was so disgraceful for a soldier that it should have been recorded in the *Histories* of Tacitus (finished about 109).[5] If so, *annalibus* must be a synonym for *historia*; the *Annals* came too late, and did not deal with the campaigns of 69.

Courtney records without discussion my own interpretation 'a thing that should be recorded while the annals are new and the record is fresh'. For the ablative absolute cf. 6.11 f. 'quippe aliter tunc orbe novo caeloque recenti | vivebant homines'; the coincidence is an odd one if the passage under discussion works differently. I also find it natural to take *res memoranda* as 'a thing to be mentioned' rather than 'a thing that ought to have been mentioned but was not'. Juvenal's point would be that incredible things should be recorded before too much time has elapsed; for somewhat similar remarks cf. 15. 27 f. 'nos miranda quidem sed nuper consule Iunco | gesta super calidae referemus moenia Copti'; Petron. 110. 8 (the story of the widow of Ephesus) 'nec se tragoedias veteres curare aut nomina saeculis nota sed rem sua memoria factam'; Tert. *Apol.* 9. 2 (on Punic infanticide) 'infantes penes Africam Saturno immolabantur palam usque ad proconsulatum †Tiberii, qui ipsos sacerdotes in eisdem arboribus templi sui obumbratricibus scelerum votivis crucibus exposuit, teste militia patris nostri . . .'.[6] If this | interpretation is correct, it would rule out any attempt to see a reference to Tacitus; that would have consequences for the dating of the second satire, which like other second poems in a book may well have come early.

2. 153–9   Curius quid sentit et ambo
               Scipiadae, quid Fabricius manesque Camilli,
               quid Cremerae legio et Cannis consumpta iuventus,
               tot bellorum animae, quotiens hinc talis ad illos
               umbra venit? cuperent lustrari, si qua darentur
               sulpura cum taedis et si foret umida laurus.
               illic heu miseri traducimur.

[5] R. Syme, *Roman Papers*, 3. 1144 f.
[6] The variant *militia patriae nostrae* is preferred by T. D. Barnes, *Tertullian* (1971), 13 f.; so also the postscript to his edition of 1985, 323 ff.

When a Roman homosexual descends to the underworld, the heroes of old would wish to be purified with water sprinkled from a branch of bay. 158 *foret* is too weak to balance *darentur*, Jahn must have felt the difficulty when he punctuated after 159 *illic*, but the word-order is impossible. My first thought was *et si simul umida laurus* (*simul* could easily have been lost between *si* and *umi-*); but the word is not used by Juvenal elsewhere and is not particularly compelling here. I now suggest *adforet* (= *praesto esset*); for the form cf. *TLL* 2. 914. 12 ff., citing Virgil.

The loss or corruption of prepositions or prepositional prefixes may be suspected elsewhere in Juvenal (at 16. 25 'quis tam procul absit ab urbe?' S. T. Collins's *adsit* is certainly right). At 1. 163 I have suggested *excussus* for *percussus*. At 3. 108 'si trulla inverso crepitum dedit aurea fundo', nobody has ever explained *inverso*; I propose *adverso*, which would parody poetical phrases about reverberation (*Epiced. Drus.* 220 'at vox adversis collibus icta redit').[7] At 9. 143 f. 'qui me cervice locata I securum iubeant clamoso insistere circo', the infinitive would suit a chariot better than a litter or even a sedan-chair; I suggest *obsistere*, 'to confront',[8] which combines more pointedly with *clamoso* (*ob-* could have been lost after *-oso*). At 12. 75 'tandem intrat positas inclusa per aequora moles' (the context is cited below), I once considered *exclusa*; but the MSS are supported by Ovid, *Met.* 5. 410 'quod coit angustis inclusum cornibus aequor'. At 12. 104 'belua . . . furva gente petita', one might try *furva e gente*; the omission of the preposition is easier at Hor. *Epod.* 11. 10 'latere I petitus imo spiritus'; *Serm.* 2. 2. 120 'piscibus urbe petitis'. At 13. 230 f. 'missum ad sua corpora morbum I infesto credunt a numine', I suggest that *in sua* would be more normal; note the preceding *-um*.

2. 163–70   et tamen unus
    Armenius Zalaces cunctis narratur ephebis
    mollior ardenti sese indulsisse tribuno.
    aspice quid faciant commercia: venerat obses,
    hic fiunt homines. nam si mora longior urbem
    †indulsit† pueris, non umquam derit amator.

[7] For a useful discussion cf. J. R. C. Martyn, *Latomus*, 44 (1985), 394 ff. (though his explanation of *fundo* is unwarranted). For the mock-poeticism cf. Nero's 'sub terris tonuisse putes', quoted by Lucan in similar circumstances (Suet. *Vita Lucani*).

[8] Cf. 3. 239 f. 'turba cedente vehetur I dives et ingenti curret super ora Liburna'; the image is of a fast galley parting the waves (E. L. Harrison, *CR* 10 (1960), 100 f.). For the symbolism of the litter in Juvenal see R. D. Brown in *Studies in Latin Literature and Roman History*, 3, ed. C. Deroux (Coll. Latomus, 180; 1983), 266 ff.

> mittentur bracae, cultelli, frena, flagellum:
> sic praetextatos referunt Artaxata mores. |

The Armenian prince Zalaces, while a hostage at Rome, was seduced by an officer. 168 *indulsit* was obelized by Housman; before the future *derit*, a future-perfect is expected. Clausen proposed *indulget*, comparing 3. 239 f., 14. 145 ff. (*CR* 1 (1951), 73); but *indulsit* has clearly jumped from 165 *indulsisse* and a repetition of the verb is not wanted. I suggested *induerit* to Professor Courtney, which he mentions in his commentary but not in his 1984 text; 'puts on city ways' would suit the reference to clothing in 169 *bracae*, 170 *praetextatos*. For the accusative (= *urbanitatem*) see Nisbet–Hubbard on Hor. *Carm.* 1. 35. 22; more particularly cf. Ov. *Met.* 10. 105 'exuit hac (pinu) hominem' (with Bömer); *Curt.* 6. 6. 5 'cum illis (spoliis Persarum) quoque mores induerat'; Sen. *Med.* 43 'Caucasum mente indue'; Claud. 7. 157 'indue mente patrem'; *TLL* 7. 1. 1263. 71 ff.

Courtney interprets *referunt* as 'bring back', as if the *mores* were the spoils of war. He considers as an alternative 'recalls' (i.e. 'reproduces', *reddunt*), comparing 1. 66 'et multum referens de Maecenate supino' (add Pease on Virg. *Aen.* 4. 329, Plin. *Epist.* 5. 16. 9 'non minus mores eius quam os vultumque referebat'); this suits the context admirably and is surely right. After *derit* Markland's *referent* seems desirable. A line has probably been lost between 169 and 170 (thus Housman); this allows *sic* to introduce the climax of a tricolon.

3. 1–7   Quamvis digressu veteris confusus amici
          laudo tamen, vacuis quod sedem figere Cumis
          destinet atque unum civem donare Sibyllae.
          ianua Baiarum est et gratum litus amoeni
          secessus. ego vel Prochytam praepono Suburae;
          nam quid tam miserum, tam solum vidimus, ut non
          deterius credas horrere incendia . . .?

Juvenal congratulates his friend on leaving Rome for Cumae, a lonely place but close to the attractive Baiae. Duff commented on 5 *secessus*, 'gen. of definition, like *vox voluptatis*, "the word pleasure". This should not be explained as a gen. of quality; for a noun to which the latter is attached does not take an adjective, whereas *litus* here has *gratum*.' Housman refuted both these propositions (*Classical Papers*, 614 f.); in particular he pointed to such phrases as Hor. *Serm.* 1. 1. 33 'parvola . . . magni formica laboris'. But he admitted that the construction is rare, and he cannot have regarded the interpretation as obvious;

earlier he even considered taking *amoeni secessus* as a nominative plural (*Classical Papers*, 519).

There is in fact a more serious difficulty than the genitive: Cumae was on the coast and had a beach, but it cannot readily be described as being itself a *litus*, especially as important buildings stood on the acropolis (Virg. *Aen.* 6. 42 'Euboicae . . . rupis'). If it is argued that *litus* indicates solitude, that impairs the balance with *ianua Baiarum*, which underlines the *celebritas* of the neighbourhood. The emptiness of Cumae has been mentioned in 2 and 3 (while 6 *solum* refers like *miserum* to Prochyta); but in 4 the emphasis is on positive attractions (*ianua Baiarum, gratum, amoeni*).

I believe that Juvenal wrote *gratum limen amoeni | secessus*, and that the second syllable of *limen* has been swallowed by *ameni*. Now *secessus* would refer to the bay of Baiae; cf. Hor. *Epist.* 1. 1. 83 'nullus in orbe sinus Bais praelucet amoenis'. *secessus* in one of its implications suits a bay (Virg. *Aen.* 1. 159 'est in secessu longo locus' of the harbour at Carthage); the word does not suggest that Baiae was deserted, but simply that people retreated there for holidays (*Hist. Aug.* 27. 19. 5 'abice Baianos Puteolanosque secessus'). The phrase now balances *ianua Baiarum*, and *gratum* suits the welcoming *limen*. It may be added that Cumae was the 'Gateway to Baiae' in more than the metaphorical sense of the travel advertisements. Nearby | still stands the Arco Felice, through which the *via Domitiana* ran on its way to Puteoli and Naples: see Stat. *Silv.* 4. 3. 97 ff. (of a similar arch on this road), 'huius ianua prosperumque limen | arcus, belligeris ducis tropaeis | et totis Ligurum nitens metallis'.

3. 10–20   sed dum tota domus raeda componitur una,
            substitit ad veteres arcus madidamque Capenam.
            hic, ubi nocturnae Numa constituebat amicae
            (nunc sacri fontis nemus et delubra locantur
            Iudaeis, quorum cophinus fenumque supellex;
            omnis enim populo mercedem pendere iussa est
            arbor et eiectis mendicat silva Camenis),
            in vallem Egeriae descendimus et speluncas
            dissimiles veris. quanto praesentius esset
            numen aquis, viridi si margine cluderet undas
            herba nec ingenuum violarent marmora tofum.

Umbricius is leaving Rome for Cumae, and Juvenal says goodbye near the Porta Capena. The articulation of the passage is difficult. At 12 ff. older editors interpreted 'here where Numa dated his girl-friend,

now the grove is rented to Jews'; they were then forced to put a full
stop at 16 *Camenis*, which produces an intolerable asyndeton at 17, *in
vallem Egeriae descendimus*. That is why some moderns put 13–16 in a
parenthesis: 'here where Numa dated his girl-friend (now the grove is
rented to Jews), we went down into the Valley of Egeria'. Others
interpret 'where Numa ... but where now the grove is rented to Jews'
(with only 15–16 in a parenthesis); again the main verb comes at 17
descendimus.

In fact Numa met Egeria not at the gate, as all these punctuations
imply, but some way off at the grove of the Camenae (Liv. 1. 21. 3
'lucus erat quem medium ex opaco specu fons perenni rigabat aqua'). It
is particularly odd that the grove should be described at 13 ff., before
we have reached the Valley of Egeria where it belongs. There is much
to be said for Jahn's neglected view that 12–16 should be placed after
20: 'We went down into the Valley of Egeria and saw the grottoes and
spring. Here where Numa used to meet Egeria, the grove of the spring
is rented to Jews, and the Camenae have fled.' The eviction of the
Camenae and the take-over by aliens are not peripheral themes, but
form a climax that leads well to the rest of the satire. 12, *hic ubi* ...
Numa, is now balanced by 21, *hic tunc Umbricius*: by a piquant irony, at
the very spot where Egeria counselled the king, where now there is
only a shanty town of paupers, Umbricius utters on the state of the
city.[9]

Jahn's transposition had one great disadvantage: the reader was
driven either to admit an abrupt asyndeton between 11, *Capenam*, and
17, *in vallem ... descendimus*, or else to accept a lacuna in the same place
(thus Ribbeck). As a variation I propose, at 10 ff., *sed dum tota domus
raeda componitur una* | (*substitit ad veteres arcus madidamque Capenam*), | *in
vallem Egeriae descendimus*; the parenthesis[10] allows a sensible sequence,
'while the furniture was being loaded, we went for a walk'. *raeda*, which
was ablative with *componitur*, is nominative with *substitit*; the change of
subject is easier if one posits a parenthesis. The tense of *substitit* also |

---

[9] Umbricius was the name of an imperial *haruspex* (*L'Année Épigraphique*, 1930, No.
52 'haruspici Caesarum'), the most expert of Pliny's time (*Nat.* 10. 19), whose dire
prophecies to Galba are described by Tac. *Hist.* 1. 27. 1. Juvenal's friend is hardly to be
identified with this man (unless 3. 44f. 'ranarum viscera numquam | inspexi', puts the
emphasis on *ranarum*); but if he is an imaginary character, his name might suggest a
prophet of doom who would make a contrast with Egeria.

[10] For the possibilities of parenthesis in Latin poetry see M. von Albrecht, *Die Paren-
these in Ovids Metamorphosen und ihre dichterische Funktion* (1964).

suits 'halted' rather than 'stood'; and this is only possible if 11 is detached from *dum domus componitur*.[11]

3. 74–8   ede quid illum
          esse putes. quemvis hominem secum attulit ad nos:
          grammaticus, rhetor, geometres, pictor, aliptes,
          augur, schoenobates, medicus, magus, omnia novit
          Graeculus esuriens: in caelum iusseris ibit.

The subject is the slick versatility of the Greeks. Editors take *ede quid illum esse putes* as an independent sentence, but that leaves its function obscure; the speaker is not asking riddles for their own sake. One would like these words to be linked with what follows as the virtual protasis of a conditional sentence; compare the modern colloquialism 'you name it, he's got it'. But *putes* seems the wrong verb; it is not a matter of guessing the Greek's existing profession, but of asking him to do something unlikely and then finding that he is already an expert.

Heinrich alone saw the drift when he considered *iubes* (in his commentary of 1839), but the indicative is implausible; he cites 3. 296 'ede ubi consistas, in qua te quaero proseucha', but the second part of that line is a direct question. Further, *iubes* is undesirable before 78, *iusseris*; I agree with Courtney that P's *miseris* is a simplification by somebody who failed to understand the construction (*in caelum, iusseris, ibit*). I suggest *ede quid illum | esse velis* (with a comma at *velis* and a full-stop at *ad nos*): 'say what you want him to be, he is it already'. *velis* could have dropped out before *quemvis* and then been replaced by *putes*. The pleonasm of *quid . . . velis* and *quemvis* seems pointed rather than objectionable.

For similar instances of parataxis in Juvenal cf. 1. 155 'pone Tigillinum, taeda lucebis in illa . . .'; 7. 175 ff. 'tempta | Chrysogonus quanti doceat vel Pollio quanti | lautorum pueros, artem scindes Theodori' (where *scindens* of the paradosis is nonsense). For a generally misunderstood passage one may compare Virg. *Ecl.* 4. 8 ff. 'tu modo nascenti puero quo ferrea primum | desinet ac toto surget gens aurea mundo, | casta fave, Lucina, tuus iam regnat Apollo'; I have suggested elsewhere,[12] that *tuus . . . Apollo* is not a parenthetic afterthought but the apodosis to the *modo* clause ('provided that Lucina favours the birth, Apollo is as good as reigning').

[11] I owe much to the discussion of F. Jacoby, *Hermes*, 87 (1959), 449 ff.; he saw the difficulty of a change of subject at 11 *substitit*, and momentarily considered taking 11–16 as a parenthesis (453 n. 1). He himself thought that lines 11–16 were an improved version by the poet introduced into the text by an editor; but we cannot speculate about unintegrated drafts.   [12] *BICS* 25 (1978), 62 (above, p. 56).

4. 45–52

> destinat hoc monstrum cumbae linique magister
> pontifici summo. quis enim proponere talem
> aut emere auderet, cum plena et litora multo
> delatore forent? dispersi protinus algae
> inquisitores agerent cum remige nudo,
> non dubitaturi fugitivum dicere piscem
> depastumque diu vivaria Caesaris, inde
> elapsum veterem ad dominum debere reverti.

The fisherman presents the huge turbot to Domitian as he could not sell it in a police state. To my ear there is something unusual about the word-distribution of 48 f. *dispersi protinus algae | inquisitores*; the genitive *algae* coalesces not with anything in its own line but with the long | *inquisitores* at the beginning of the next line. And though the beaches were full of informers, the *inquisitores* have no place there even as a joke; they would come into action in Rome when the fish was marketed (46 f.). *agerent cum* refers to prosecution in the courts, as commentators recognize, not to remonstrances on the shore; Juvenal is mocking a legal dictum that assigned fish to the emperor (55, 'res fisci est, ubicumque natat') by applying it to worthless seaweed.

I suggest that Juvenal wrote *dispersae . . . algae*,[13] which would give a more attractive word-order. Seaweed is naturally described as being strewn on the beach; cf. Hom. *Il.* 9. 7 πολλὸν δὲ παρὲξ ἅλα φῦκος ἔχευεν; Hor. *Carm.* 3. 17. 10 ff. 'alga litus inutili | demissa tempestas ab Euro | sternet'; Apul. *Apol.* 35. 4 'muscum et algam, cetera maris eiectamenta'. What is 'strewn' by the action of the storm could also be 'scattered'; cf. Val. Flacc. 4. 412 f. (Tisiphone caught in a flood), 'apparent sparsaeque faces disiectaque longe | verbera'. And if the seaweed was once *dispersa*, it would be the duty of the *inquisitores* to track it down (the two words balance). In the same way when a fish is a *fugitivus* (50), they have to ensure its return (52).

4. 119–22

> nemo magis rhombum stupuit; nam plurima dixit
> in laevum conversus, at illi dextra iacebat
> belua. sic pugnas Cilicis laudabat et ictus
> et pegma et pueros inde ad velaria raptos.

The blind courtier Catullus admired the turbot that he could not see; in the same way he applauded the performance of Cilix, who must have been either a gladiator or a boxer. *pugnas* seems too general a word for the context. Duff tentatively translates 'feints', comparing the

---

[13] Graevius proposed *dispersi . . . alni* (of broken-up ships); Ruperti corrected the gender to *dispersae . . . alni* while rightly rejecting the conjecture.

comic *pugnae aliquid dare*, but such passages refer rather to causing trouble; the word still fails to balance the more specific *ictus*. Scholte proposed *pugnos*, but even if Cilix was a boxer, 'fists' and 'blows' would present no clear distinction.

I suggest *punctus*, 'jabs', leading up to the more serious *ictus*. At first sight the former may seem too slight, but cf. Naev. *Com.* 51 'stilo me pupugit in manum'; Liv. 22. 46. 5 'punctim magis quam caesim adsueto petere hostem'.

6. 82–4   nupta senatori comitata est Eppia ludum
             ad Pharon et Nilum famosaque moenia Lagi
             prodigia et mores urbis damnante Canopo.

For *prodigia* I suggested *prodigium* to Professor Courtney, who has recorded it in his commentary; though the conjecture can only be tentative, it is perhaps less pointless than one critic has supposed. Plural *prodigia* would describe not the particular outrage of Eppia's conduct, but the usual outrages of the Romans; *mores*, the less strong word, would then be an anticlimax. Friedlaender and Courtney talk of hendiadys for *prodigiosos mores*, but that term is greatly over-used. On the other hand, if *prodigium* is read, Juvenal would proceed from the particular to the general; *urbis* would then be taken only with *mores*, as suits the word-order.

6. 107–9   praeterea multa in facie deformia, sicut
             attritus galea mediisque in naribus ingens
             gibbus et acre malum semper stillantis ocelli. |

Juvenal describes the disfigurements of a gladiator. Housman expressed surprise that a lump inside the nostrils should be produced by a helmet, and he regarded 108 *que* as superfluous; accordingly he accepted *galeae* (Hadr. Valesius), taking *attritus* as a noun. Courtney thinks that the *gibbus* must have been on the outside of the nose, as Juvenal is referring to visible features (but a swelling inside could cause a bulge outside); he says that *que* combines two points that make the *gibbus* ugly, its irritation by the helmet and its prominence (but that puts too much weight on *mediis*). Some scholars had rightly suspected the otiose *sicut*: Ribbeck proposed *cirrus*, Scholte *vultus*, Buecheler *ficus* (which in medical contexts is used only of piles). I remain convinced by my own *sulcus*, which like ἄλοξ is used of furrows in the skin (*JRS* 52: 235); note also the metaphorical use of *arare*.

It should be noted how *sulcus*, *gibbus*, and *acre malum*[14] balance one another; a failure to appreciate this kind of pointing in Juvenal often produces a faulty text. 6. 137 ff. '*tanti* vocat ille pudicam, |[nec pharetris Veneris macer est aut lampade fervet:]| *inde* faces ardent, veniunt a *dote* sagittae'. Caesennia is admired by her husband because of her money, and Scholte's deletion brings out the relationship of the italicized words. 6. 562 ff. 'nemo mathematicus genium indemnatus habebit, | sed qui *paene perit*, cui *vix* in Cyclada *mitti* | contigit, et parva *tandem caruisse* Seripho'. An astrologer is disregarded unless he has almost been executed, sent to an island as a concession, and at long last released from Seriphus; surely *caruisse* should be replaced by a word that sustains the irony of *paene perit* and *vix mitti*, either Schrader's *latuisse* or my own *iacuisse* ('languished'). The following lines cause equal confusion: 'consulit ictericae lento de funere *matris*, | ante tamen *de te* Tanaquil tua, quando *sororem*|efferat *et patruos*, an sit victurus *adulter*|post ipsam; quid enim maius dare numina possunt?' (6. 565 ff.). The wicked woman consults the astrologer about the deaths of her relatives, but she asks if her lover will live, i.e. recover from an illness (Cic. *Sex. Rosc.* 33 'posteaquam comperit eum posse vivere'); after the triumphant climax at *adulter*, which must have earned a round of applause, 568 is a fatuous appendage, and I urge once more the deletion of the line (*JRS* 52: 235).[15] 7. 134 f. '*spondet* enim Tyrio stlattaria purpura filo |[et tamen est illis hoc utile, purpura vendit] | causidicum, *vendunt* amethystina; *convenit* illi | et strepitu et facie maioris vivere census'. The barrister finds it profitable to make a display of wealth; if 135 is deleted with U and Knoche, we can hear the correspondence of *spondet*, *vendunt*, *convenit*. 8. 199 ff. 'et illic | dedecus urbis habes, nec *murmillonis in armis*|nec *clipeo* Gracchum pugnantem et[16] *falce supina*,|[damnat enim talis habitus sed damnat et odit]| nec *galea* faciem abscondit: movet ecce *tridentem*'. Gracchus fights as a *retiarius*, the most disgraceful of all gladiators, and so carries a trident; if 202 with its pointless ending is deleted (Ruperti), the different pieces of equipment are set against each other.

6. 170–4   tolle tuum, precor, Hannibalem victumque Syphacem
              in castris et cum tota Carthagine migra.
              'parce, precor, Paean, et tu, dea, pone sagittas;

[14] For *acre malum* I might have expected a single Greek medical word, but nothing suitable presents itself. In favour of the transmitted reading Courtney cites Lucr. 3. 252 f. 'nec temere huc dolor usque potest penetrare neque acre | permanare malum'.

[15] For another view see E. J. Kenney, *Latomus*, 22 (1963), 717 f.

[16] My conjecture *et* for *aut* (cf. Cic. *Pis.* 73 'nec . . . scutum et gladium') was anticipated by Lubinus.

> nil pueri faciunt, ipsam configite matrem'
> Amphion clamat, sed Paean contrahit arcum. |

An aristocratic wife is so arrogant that the poet would send her packing with her family's achievements; he goes on to describe how Apollo and Diana punished Niobe for her boasts. 170 *tolle* alludes to the formula of divorce, *tuas res tibi habeto*; cf. 6. 146 'collige sarcinulas', with Courtney, Petron. 79. 11 'res tuas ocius tolle'. It is awkward that *precor* (which does not belong to the formula) is repeated more effectively two lines below (172), where the sacral alliteration protects the text. In the former case Burman proposed *procul*, but I should sooner try *tecum* (which could have fallen out after *tuum*); cf. Ov. *Am.* 1. 8. 66 'tolle tuos tecum, pauper amator, avos'. The repetition of *cum* in 171 seems unobjectionable compared with the repetition of *precor*.

Courtney's note on 16. 9f. mentions a dozen cases of repetition that 'seem ungainly to modern taste', and others could be added. Sometimes I see no awkwardness (1. 73f., 10. 256f., 13. 21f.), sometimes there is real reason to question the text (see below on 6. 471, 10. 192, 12. 91), sometimes the problem may already have been solved: thus Ribbeck deleted 6. 209–11; Castiglioni conjectured *male parvi* at 6. 504 (which seems better than *sibi parvi*, my own first thought); for my account of 16. 17ff., see below, p. 259. I mention briefly a few places where corruption can be suspected rather than proved. 6. 644ff. 'et illae | grandia monstra suis audebant temporibus sed | non propter nummos. minor admiratio summis | debetur monstris quotiens facit ira nocentes | hunc sexum'. Here *summis monstris* rings oddly in itself, as well as seeming repetitive after *grandia monstra*; possibly *noxis*, which would balance *nocentes*. At 7. 175ff. 'merces lautissima' is followed within two lines by 'lautorum pueros'; the adjective is unexpected of a fee, however generous, and is not fully defended by Cic. *Flacc.* 90 'patrimonium satis lautum ... Graecorum conviviis maluit dissipare'. Perhaps *largissima*. 16. 8ff. 'haut minimum illud erit, ne te pulsare togatus | audeat, immo etsi pulsetur, dissimulet nec | audeat excussos praetori ostendere dentes'. The repetition of *audeat* is made less effective by the intervening *dissimulet*; perhaps *excussos studeat* (the civilian is not bold enough to fight the soldier, and not too keen to show his injuries to the praetor).

6. 189–97   hoc sermone pavent, hoc iram, gaudia, curas,
              hoc cuncta effundunt animi secreta. quid ultra?
              concumbunt Graece. dones tamen ista puellis,

> tune etiam, quam sextus et octogensimus annus
> pulsat, adhuc Graece? non est hic sermo pudicus
> in vetula. quotiens lascivum intervenit illud
> ζωὴ καὶ ψυχή, modo sub lodice relictis
> uteris in turba. quod enim non excitet inguen
> vox blanda et nequam?

Juvenal derides women, some of them elderly, who use affected
Greek terms of endearment. On 195 Courtney comments admirably:
'*relictis* is clearly corrupt, as Housman saw. Lascivious words used *in
turba* are not "left under the blanket"; they are inexcusably *impudica*
because they come from an octogenarian who is past intercourse
either in Greek or Latin; and *enim* 196 is senseless as the text stands.
ferendis [Housman's conjecture for *relictis*] does not carry full conviction, but is certainly on the right lines: *modo* will now mean "only",
not "lately".'

I propose *loquendis*, 'you use expressions that should be spoken only
under the blanket'. As *loquendis* suggests words more specifically than
Housman's *ferendis*, 'things endurable', it combines more easily with
uteris (*verbis uti* is a common locution); the emphasis on speech suits
the whole context and leads to *vox* below. For such conversations cf.
Call. fr. 401. 3 | εὐναίους ὀαρισμούς; W. R. Smyth, *CQ* 1 (1951), 74f.,
on Prop. 1. 4. 13 f. 'et quae | gaudia sub tacita dicere veste licet' (though
there the conjecture *ducere* is generally accepted); Kay on Martial
11. 104. 11. The corruption could have been caused by the spelling
locendis and conflation with *lodice*.

6. O. 9–13   quid quod nec retia turpi
>   iunguntur tunicae, nec cella ponit eadem
>   munimenta umeri †pulsatamque arma† tridentem
>   qui nudus pugnare solet? pars ultima ludi
>   accipit has animas aliusque in carcere nervos.

Some *retiarii* fought in a tunic, others in a loin-cloth (12 *qui nudus
pugnare solet*); the former were regarded as *impudici* (Housman, ad loc.),
so the latter kept their gear in a separate locker-room. It is nonsense to
say 'the nets are not joined to the disgraceful tunic'; both sorts of *retiarius* obviously used nets, so *retia* here applies only to the nets of the
nudi. M. D. Reeve comments on the difficulties of the passage without
being sure whether to ascribe them to the reader, the expositors, or
the author (*CR* 23 (1973), 124f.); he talks of the reader 'cursing the

author for using the passive *iunguntur* when he could have spared him
all this trouble by using some active verb co-ordinate with *ponit'*.

It seems to me that the blame rests with the copyists, and that the
author indeed wrote *coniungit* or something of the kind. This could
have been corrupted to *coniungitur* before *tun-*, and *iunguntur* sub-
stituted to restore grammar and metre. The postponement of the
subject to line 12 may have contributed to the confusion; for similar
cases cf. 4. 5 ff. (where 8 should be deleted with Jahn); 6. 287 ff.
'praestabat castas humilis fortuna Latinas I quondam, nec vitiis contingi
parva sinebat I tecta labor somnique breves et vellere Tusco I vexatae
duraeque manus[17] ac proximus urbi I Hannibal et stantes Collina turre
mariti'; here P's *sinebant*, accepted by Housman and Clausen, may have
originated from the assumption that *tecta* was nominative rather than
accusative.

6. 434-7   illa tamen gravior, quae cum discumbere coepit
             laudat Vergilium, periturae ignoscit Elissae,
             committit vates et comparat, inde Maronem
             atque alia parte in trutina suspendit Homerum.

The learned lady compares poets, a regular technique of ancient
criticism. There are parallels for the metaphor of the scales at Hor.
Serm. 1. 3. 72 'hac lege in trutina ponetur eadem'; *Epist.* 2. 1. 29 f.
'Romani pensantur eadem I scriptores trutina'. But in our passage *alia
parte* makes a second ablative less natural; I suggest *trutinae*. For the
word-order cf. Catull. 69. 6 'valle sub alarum'; Virg. *Georg.* 4. 419 'exesi
latere in montis'; Kühner–Stegmann 1. 587 ff. Knoche notes that P
seems originally to have written *trutinam*, but that the first hand changed
this to *trutina*.

6. 467-73   tandem aperit vultum et tectoria prima reponit,
             incipit agnosci, atque illo lacte fovetur
             propter quod secum comites educit asellas
             exul Hyperboreum si dimittatur ad axem. |
             sed quae mutatis induicitur atque fovetur
             tot medicaminibus coctaeque siliginis offas
             accipit et madidae, facies dicetur an ulcus?

The woman who puts packs on her face takes them off for her lover,
and bathes her skin in asses' milk instead. After 468, *illo lacte fovetur*,
the repetition of the verb in 471 is undesirable. Juvenal is not referring

---

[17] The main pauses come after *breves* and *manus*, at the same place in successive lines.
Perhaps *somnique breves* and *duraeque manus* should be transposed.

this time to soothing milk but to sticky plasters; that is shown by 472 f. *coctaeque siliginis offas | accipit et madidae.*

Perhaps *novatur*, which might refer to a second coat of plaster; that would suit 467, *tectoria prima*; 471 ff. *mutatis, tot, coctae. . . et madidae.* The verb may be used of a second ploughing at Cic. *De Or.* 2. 131 'agro non semel arato sed novato et iterato'; *novato et* is omitted by one side of the tradition and doubted by Wilkins, but the clause seems lame without it.

6. 582–91   si mediocris erit, spatium lustrabit utrimque
              metarum et sortes ducet frontemque manumque
              praebebit vati crebrum poppysma roganti.
              divitibus responsa dabit Phryx augur et inde[18]
              conductus, dabit astrorum mundique peritus
              atque aliquis senior qui publica fulgura condit.
              plebeium in circo positum est et in aggere fatum.
              quae nudis longum ostendit cervicibus aurum
              consulit ante falas delphinorumque columnas
              an saga vendenti nubat caupone relicto.

Women of different classes consult different fortune-tellers. In 582–4 the woman of modest station (*mediocris*) goes to the circus, but keeps to either side of the *metae* (these marked the ends of the central *spina*). In 585–7 rich women retain experts from the East. At 588–91 a third category is mentioned (*plebeium. . . fatum*), but difficulties emerge in 588.

First of all the 'plebeian' must be distinct from the *mediocris*, but she is not clearly enough differentiated; one might think that the former is inferior, but she goes to the more central part of the circus, in front of the dolphin-columns in the *spina* itself (590).[19] *positum est*, 'depends on', also pulls the reader up, but can be defended as a satiric joke: 'Juvenal ironically speaks as if destinies were decided and not merely revealed there' (Courtney). On the other hand, *in aggere* seems indefensible, as it belonged to a different part of the city; it is incoherent to say that while the *mediocris* went to the inferior part of the circus, the 'plebeian' went to both the circus and the *agger*, and in particular to the better part of the circus. Finally *aurum* causes a problem; while a few women of lower station might possess a golden necklace, it seems absurd to characterize the whole class this way.

[18] *Indus* (cod. det.) may be the right solution (cf. Housman).
[19] T. P. Wiseman, *PBSR* 48 (1980), 12: 'it is clear that these low-class fortune-tellers are operating inside the Circus, along the *spina* with its columns and dolphins, not in *tabernae* under the seats'.

I propose more strongly than before the deletion of 588, which would remove all these difficulties; now each category is given three lines, without an intrusive full stop in the middle of the third category. The third type of woman is flashier[20] and less respectable than the *mediocris*; she shows off her necklace and changes her lovers. This type is sufficiently characterized by 589, but the interpolator looks for something more explicit; perhaps he did not like a relative clause to begin a sentence. For a comparable case see 14. 7, where I have | suggested that *qui radere tubera terrae* begins a new sentence (*JRS* 52: 237); at 14. 120 the same may be true of *qui miratur opes* (Duff and others have doubted the authenticity of 119).

6. 620–3   minus ergo nocens erit Agrippinae
                       boletus, siquidem unius praecordia pressit
                       ille senis tremulumque caput descendere iussit
                       in caelum et longa manantia labra saliva.

The mushroom that poisoned Claudius was less harmful than the hippomanes that drove Caligula mad, for it only killed one silly old man. 623, *in caelum*, refers to the apotheosis of Claudius (cf. Stat. *Silv.* 3. 3. 77 f. 'nondum stelligerum senior dimissus in axem | Claudius'), but the combination with *descendere* has seemed to some too unsubtle even for Juvenal. Scholte mentions as conjectures *escendere* (in spite of the preceding *capŭt*), *ascendere*, and his own *conscendere*; Castiglioni's *discedere* (cited by Vianello) is an improvement.

I suggest *decedere*, a common euphemism for dying. The humour would lie in the incongruous addition of *caelum* ('to depart this life—for the sky'), and in the conjunction of the emotive verb with *tremulum caput* and *manantia labra*.

7. 50–2   nam si discedas, laqueo tenet ambitiosi
                       consuetudo mali, tenet insanabile multos
                       scribendi cacoethes et aegro in corde senescit.

Should you try to give up writing poetry, you cannot get away from its grip. *consuetudo mali* seems to be a mistaken explanation of *cacoethes*, which in fact is a growth or ulcer (from ἦθος, not ἔθος). *multos* is an anticlimax after *discedas*, which has a general application. For details see Courtney.

Jahn deleted 51, *consuetudo . . . multos*, reading *ambitiosum* in 50; but the metaphor of *laqueo tenet* does not cohere with the medical imagery of *cacoethes* and *aegro*. Housman deleted 50, *laqueo* ... 51, *mali*, but that still leaves *multos* weak; and the first *tenet* coheres better than the second with *discedas*. S. H. Braund follows Jahn's deletion, but reads *ambitioso* with *laqueo* (*Phoenix*, 36 (1982), 162 ff.): this is some improvement, but leaves the unsatisfactory conflation of metaphors.

I believe that 51 has displaced a genuine line, perhaps with consequential patching. (*a*) *consuetudo mali* must go; the subject of *tenet* may be something like *ambitiosum | scribendi studium*. (*b*) The repetition of *tenet* produces a word-pattern paralleled at 6. 585 f. 'dividibus reponsa *dabit* Phryx augur et Indus | conductus, *dabit* astrorum mundique peritus'. On the other hand, the second *tenet* (unlike the first) does not mean *retinet* and does not balance *discedas*. (*c*) *insanabile* is not in itself objectionable, even if a *cacoethes* could often be cured (Cels. 5. 28. 2); but if the rest of the original line has disappeared, it is unlikely that a word in the middle has survived. (*d*) On any assumption *multos* must go; Leo proposed *cultro*, but the word is not attested of a surgeon's knife. (*e*) 52 *scribendi* deserves more scrutiny than it has received; such a genitive would suit the scholiast's view that *cacoethes* was an itch, but less easily the correct view that it was a growth. I have considered *scribenti* or better *scribendo*, which is supported by parallels: Lucr. 4. 1068 f. 'ulcus enim vivescit et inveterascit alendo | inque dies gliscit furor atque aerumna gravescit'; Virg. *Georg.* 3. 454 'alitur vitium vivitque tegendo'.

That leaves us with something like *nam si discedas, laqueo tenet ambitiosum | ⟨scribendi studium, gliscitque atque usque gravescit⟩ | scribendo cacoethes et aegro in corde senescit.* | Needless to say, the supplement is too Lucretian for Juvenal, and only a guide to the possible pattern of the sentence.

7. 165–8   'quantum vis stipulare et protinus accipe: quid do
             ut totiens illum pater audiat?' haec alii sex
             vel plures uno conclamant ore sophistae
             et veras agitant lites raptore relicto.

             haec *PGU Ant. Arov.*: ast haec *FH*: ast *Φ*.

Though the rhetor has had to listen to boring compositions, he has difficulty in collecting his fee; so he says that he would pay good money to see his pupil's father suffer as he has done. *quid do?*, 'what do I have to pay?', is a well-attested idiom,[21] but there is a particular

---

[21] *quid do?* is often paraphrased 'what would I not give', but this is too emphatic for some contexts; the distinction has been elucidated by the Chairman of Lloyds Bank (C. J. Morse, *CR* 6 (1956), 196 ff.).

difficulty in this context: *quantum . . . accipe* when taken by itself does not reveal why the rhetor is offering money, and *quid do . . . audiat?* would be more natural if it preceded the proposed bargain instead of following it. There is something to be said for *quiddam* (cod. Vallae), which is put forward as an original conjecture by W. W. Merry, *CR* 9 (1895), 29 f. The rhetor now says 'accept a certain amount right away'; he pays the agent promptly because he wishes the father to commit himself. The *ut* clause now makes clear the nature of this odd trans-action.

There is also a difficulty in P's *haec alii* . . . (pointed out by Robert Parker, cited by M. D. Reeve, *CR* 33 (1983), 32): if the remark quoted is given to six other sophists, what is left for the first rhetor to say? Dr Parker tells me that he is inclined to accept *Φ*'s *ast alii*, taking *con-clamant* as intransitive ('raise the battle-cry'; he compares 173 'ad pugnam qui rhetorica descendit ab umbra'). But P's reading is sup-ported not just by the kindred *fragmenta Aroviensia* but by the Egyptian *fragmentum Antinoense* of about AD 500; this may be one of the places where P gives a meaningless corruption and *Φ* an intelligible inter-polation. I suggest *hic*, 'hereupon'; this would have the advantage of connecting the sentences more closely than *ast*. The change to *HEC* is minimal.

7. 213-14   sed Rufum atque alios caedit sua quemque iuventus,
               Rufum, quem totiens Ciceronem Allobroga dixit.

       quem *PGU Sang. Σ*: qui *Φ*.

Rufus the rhetor is beaten up by his own pupils. *totiens* would suit an individual's favourite dictum, but less well the random insults of a group; the change of tense at *dixit* is also disconcerting.[22] *quem* must be right, as the oxymoron 'Allobrogian Cicero' suits the patterns of invective; cf. Cic. *Cael.* 19, *Palatinam Medeam*, and for further parallels see my note on Cic. *Pis.* 20; H. Wankel on Dem. *Cor.* 242. The variant *qui* would suit *totiens* much better, but it leaves us with the pointless suggestion that Cicero himself was an Allobrox.

One might think of replacing *totiens* by a participle such as *tundens*, 'thumping', but *dixit* would then surely have to be changed to *dicit*. Or one might try a proper name like *Titius*; then the perfect *dixit* could be retained. I have also considered *Tities . . . dicunt*, of fashionable but unintellectual young men; for the form cf. Prop. 4. 1. 31 'hinc Tities

---

[22] The problem is pointed out by M. D. Reeve, *CR* 33 (1983), 32; he thinks that *totiens* and the change of tense are better suited to a compliment.

Ramnesque viri'; for the thought cf. Hor. *Ars* 342 'celsi praetereunt
austera poemata Ramnes'. If *Tities* was once | corrupted to *toties* (as
would be easy with so rare a word), the number of the verb would have
to be changed; and the perfect could have been introduced at the same
time.

7. 229–32   sed vos saevas inponite leges,
                 ut praeceptori verborum regula constet,
                 ut legat historias, auctores noverit omnes
                 tamquam ungues digitosque suos . . .

Unreasonable demands are made of a *grammaticus*, particularly that
he should know the allusions; Juvenal goes on to mention obscure
mythological lore, the nurse of Anchises and the rest. *ut legat historias*
seems a slight requirement compared with the clauses that precede
and follow. Perhaps *ut sciat*, which would enable us to understand
omnes . . . suos from the next clause; cf. 6. 450 'nec historias sciat omnes'.
Or perhaps *ut legat* has replaced a verb of dactylic shape, for instance
colligat; the compilation of the evidence is part of a scholar's duties.

8. 105–7   inde †Dolabella atque hinc† Antonius, inde
                 sacrilegus Verres referebant navibus altis
                 occulta spolia et plures de pace triumphos.

Extortionate governors used to bring back much booty from their
provinces. 105 does not scan. *inde* means 'a sociis florentibus et modo
victis' (cf. 99); a contrast between different provinces is irrelevant, so
hinc is part of the corruption. Ruperti suggested *Dolabellae* (alluding to
three governors of that name), but Juvenal is combining the defend-
ants in famous republican trials: Cn. Dolabella (procos. Macedonia 80–
78) was prosecuted by Julius Caesar, C. Antonius by Caelius, Verres by
Cicero.

Leo surprisingly proposed *atque inhians Antonius*, but an adjective is
needed rather than a participle. J. Ashton suggested *atque Antonius
ebrius* (cited *CR* 11 (1961), 56); but *ebrius* is not *ebriosus*, and we expect
a reference to extortion. The missing word should come before
Antonius, where the corruption has occurred. It should be a spondaic
word beginning with a vowel or an iambic word beginning with a consonant. Unlike most Latin adjectives it should end with two consonants or *x*.

Knoche's *audax* meets these criteria. As an alternative I suggest
rapax. This would suit well the usual picture of Antonius; it balances
sacrilegus, which is equally appropriate to Verres (Cic. *Verr.* 2. 1. 9 'non

sacrilegum sed hostem sacrorum religionumque'). Juvenal has no inhibitions about using *atque* before a consonant;[23] if a reason for the corruption has to be given, one might suggest confusion with *rarae* at the same place in the line above.

8. 195-7   finge tamen gladios inde atque hinc pulpita poni,
            quid satius? mortem sic quisquam exhorruit, ut sit
            zelotypus Thymeles, stupidi collega Corinthi?

It is better to submit to execution than to be forced to act in an adultery-mime. The *zelotypus* as elsewhere is the jealous husband (Apul. *Met.* 9. 16. 3, 'quendam zelotypum maritum'), and Thymele is his wife. The *stupidus* or buffoon was naturally the husband; see Courtney on 8. 191; Kay on Mart. 11. 7. 1 'stupido . . . marito'; *Hist. Aug.* 4. 29. 2 'cum stupidus nomen adulteri uxoris a servo quaereret' (so Catull. 17. 21 'talis iste merus stupor'). If that is so, his *collega* must be the adulterer; that produces an anticlimax, as the part of the *stupidus* was the more | ridiculous. Courtney comments on 197 that the man takes the part normally played by Corinthus, or that the plot allows for the appearance of two *stupidi*; both these explanations posit untypical situations.

The late J. D. P. Bolton, Fellow of Queen's College, Oxford, once suggested to me in conversation that Juvenal wrote nominative *stupidus*; it may be noted that P. originally had *stupidis*, though the first hand changed this to *stupidi* (thus Knoche). Now the situation is easier to understand; the actor was at one and the same time the *zelotypus Thymeles* and the silly colleague of the lover Corinthus. The lover has the more enterprising role (like Philesitherus in Apul. *Met.* 9. 16-21), and is suitably given a name with suggestions of luxury. The husband is the stooge who reacts inanely to provocation (cf. Hor. *Epist.* 1. 18. 13 f. 'ut puerum saevo credas dictata magistro | reddere vel partis mimum tractare secundas'); so here he is mockingly called the *collega* of the hero.

8. 249-53   hic tamen et Cimbros et summa pericula rerum
             excipit et solus trepidantem protegit urbem,
             atque ideo, postquam ad Cimbros stragemque volabant
             qui numquam attigerant maiora cadavera corvi,
             nobilis ornatur lauro collega secunda.

Though Marius was of humble origin, he defeated the Cimbri; so after the victory he was honoured more than his aristocratic fellow-

---

[23] Juvenal has five cases of unelided *atque* in the third foot; see J. R. C. Martyn, *Eranos*, 72 (1974), 131 ff.

consul. In some circumstances the repetition of *Cimbros* would have been effective: Marius sustained their onset, and soon the carrion crows were flying in their direction. But the addition first of *pericula* and then of *stragem* blunts the point;[24] and no talk of hendiadys gets rid of the difficulty. At 251 Courtney records my ill-considered idea *ad cumulos stragemque*; but *cumulos*, even when combined with *stragem*, seems too unspecific for heaps of corpses. Perhaps *ad stragem tabemque*.

9. 22–5   nuper enim, ut repeto, fanum Isidis et Ganymedem
                 Pacis et advectae secreta Palatia matris
                 et Cererem (nam quo non prostat femina templo?)
                 notior Aufidio moechus celebrare solebas.

Naevolus used to have assignations with married women at temples. *Palatia* must refer to the temple of the Magna Mater on the Palatine.[25] *secreta* has not been satisfactorily explained, as Courtney observes. He cites Lubinus's *sacrata*, comparing Ov. *Ars* 3. 389 'laurigero sacrata Palatia Phoebo' (note also Prop. 4. 1. 3 'stant sacra Palatia Phoebo'). On the other hand, *secreta* gives a suggestion of mystery appropriate to the Magna Mater.

I suggest *advectae secreta Palatia matri*, taking *secreta* as a participle; this would give a sufficient hint of mystery. The dative would allow us to see a conscious parody of Ovid's phrase. It is natural enough to use *Palatia* of Apollo's temple, which like the emperor's palace could almost be identified with the hill; but when the evocative name is associated with the imported Magna Mater, that confirms the satirical tone of the passage. |

9. 104–6   claude fenestras,
                 vela tegant rimas, iunge ostia, tollite lumen,
                 e medio fac eant omnes, prope nemo recumbat.

          tollite *PAKOTZ Sang.*: tollito *GHU*: *om. L.*

Even if the rich man takes every precaution, his guilty secret will out. *tollite* is read by Housman, Clausen, and Courtney, but the plural is unattractively disruptive; in other cases cited for a variation in number, the verbs are not nearly so close together. The variant *tollito* is the

---

[24] Note the similar difficulty at 14. 71 'gratum est quod patriae civem populoque dedisti l si facis ut patriae sit idoneus, utilis agris', where *patriae* is repeated but not *populo*. Housman proposed *ut civis sit idoneus*; I have suggested *ut paci sit idoneus, utilis armis*, with deletion of the following line (above, p. 26).

[25] T. P. Wiseman, 'Cybele, Virgil and Augustus', in T. Woodman and D. West (eds.), *Poetry and Politics in the Age of Augustus* (1984), 125 ff.

most obvious solution; the short -*o* causes no problems in Juvenal.[26]
However, Courtney comments 'apart from *esto* and *memento* the only
-*to* imperative in Juvenal is *sumito* in 8. 134, a probably spurious line
(Lucan also has no -*to* imperatives); therefore *tollito* can hardly be right
here'. This argument in isolation may be over-stated, as some things
happen only once in an author; but the authority of *tollito* is questionable, and the change of form from the other imperatives also causes
surprise.

If *tollito* is rejected, I can only suggest *tolle lucernam*. Admittedly
tollere lumen is a paralleled phrase (Prop. 1. 15. 4 'quantaque sublato
lumine rixa fuit'); but in amatory poetry the lamp plays a part (Prop.
2. 15. 3 'adposita . . . lucerna' with Enk's note).

9. 114–17   illos ergo roges quidquid paulo ante petebas
             a nobis, taceant illi. sed prodere malunt
             arcanum quam subrepti potare Falerni
             pro populo faciens quantum Saufeia bibebat.

Naevolus has asked Juvenal to keep his secrets confidential (93 f.,
101), but Juvenal says that he should address his request to his rich
friend's gossiping slaves. 115 is punctuated as above by all the standard
editions, but after the emphatic *illos* at the beginning of 114, *illi* seems
superfluous. I should prefer to put a semicolon after *taceant*, and to
combine *illi* with *prodere malunt*.

10. 12–18   sed pluris nimia congesta pecunia cura
             strangulat et cuncta exuperans patrimonia census
             quanto delphinis ballaena Britannica maior.
             temporibus diris igitur iussuque Neronis
             Longinum et magnos Senecae praedivitis hortos
             clausit et egregias Lateranorum obsidet aedes
             tota cohors: rarus venit in cenacula miles.

Some men are brought low by their eloquence and strength, but
more by money. I suggest that 15 should perhaps be deleted. The line
seems a clumsy explanation of a vivid *exemplum*; for the comparable
interpolation of historical detail cf. 8. 221 ff. 'quid enim Verginius armis |
debuit ulcisci magis aut cum Vindice Galba, quod Nero tam saeva
crudaque tyrannide fecit?' (where Housman questioned the last line).

igitur seems heavy-handed in the context. Its position in third place
cannot be faulted (cf. 4. 5 'quid refert igitur . . .', 10. 265 'longa dies

[26] R. Hartenberger, *De o finali apud poetas Latinos ab Ennio usque ad Iuvenalem* (Diss,
Bonn, 1911), 92 ff.

igitur'; but the interpolator may have been too fond of the word (as of *ergo*). Compare 6. 209–11; 16. 18 (cited below, p. 259); more doubtfully 13. 100 ff. 'ut sit magna, tamen certe lenta ira deorum est; | si curant igitur cunctos punire | nocentes | quando ad me venient?' I have suggested that the last passage would gain in vigour by the deletion of 101 (above, p. 28).

If 15 is deleted, *claudit* might be considered in 17: this would combine better with present *obsidet* and *venit*. On our hypothesis Juvenal is not so much recording historical events as citing type-names of general significance;[27] cf. 1. 49 'exul ab octava Marius bibit'; 14. 305 f. 'dispositis praedives amis vigilare cohortem | servorum noctu Licinus iubet'. In 16 Ruperti proposed *Longini*; but the accusative is legitimate (Courtney), and the mansion was famous (Plin. *Epist.* 7. 24; R. Syme, *Roman Papers*, 2. 662 f.).

10. 36–42   quid si vidisset praetorem curribus altis
             extantem et medii sublimem pulvere circi
             in tunica Iovis et pictae Sarrana ferentem
             ex umeris aulaea togae magnaeque coronae
             tantum orbem, quanto cervix non sufficit ulla?
             quippe tenet sudans hanc publicus et, sibi consul
             ne placeat, curru servus portatur eodem.

Democritus would have had a good laugh if he could have seen the praetor at the games wearing triumphal insignia, with a slave to hold the crown over his head. In 41 *consul* is surely impossible; at this period a praetor normally presided at the games (Courtney on 8. 194), and the scene has not changed since 36 *praetorem*. Courtney, who calls attention to the problem (on 36), tentatively suggests *praeses* instead of *consul*; but the change from *praetor* to *praeses* after five lines gives the pointless kind of variation that good Latin usually avoided. The same criticism could be directed at any similar noun.

Perhaps the lost word was a proper name; the lively particularization would not clash with *praetorem*. For instance, *Celsus* would provide a typical pun on the literal meaning of the adjective. The height of the praetor is emphasized by 36 *altis*, 37 *sublimem*, to say nothing of the big crown; note also Tert. *Apol.* 33. 4 'hominem se esse etiam triumphans in illo sublimissimo curru admonetur'. The arrogant implications of the

---

[27] Tacitus had recently reminded the world of the downfall of Cassius Longinus (*Ann.* 16. 7. 1 'opibus vetustis'), Seneca (15. 60. 4 'villam globis militum saepsit'; 15. 64. 4 'praedives'), and Lateranus (15. 60. 1); for Juvenal's use of the *Annals* see R. Syme, *Roman Papers*, 3. 1148 ff.

name would suit *sibi placeat* (as well as giving a contrast with *servus*); cf. Hor. *Epist.* 1. 8. 17 'ut tu fortunam, sic nos te, Celse, feremus'.

In making this suggestion I am influenced by another debatable passage. At 8. 193 f. Juvenal describes noblemen who 'sell their degradation' by appearing on the stage, even when they have not been coerced by the emperor: 'vendunt nullo cogente Nerone, I nec dubitant celsi praetoris vendere ludis'. It is generally supposed that *celsi* describes the elevated position of the presiding praetor, but an interlinear gloss in P adds *proprium*, i.e. treats *Celsi* as a proper name.[28] This would give a sharper contrast with *Nerone*, and would justify the emphatic position of the word in front of *praetoris*: Juvenal is underlining the relative unimportance of the man, and the contrasted Emperor would himself be *celsus* in the imperial box. Of course there is also a pun on the literal meaning of the word: when it is said that *celsus* must mean 'high' in a context referring to a presiding praetor, one must remember that the proper name would itself have the requisite associations. For the combination of type-name and description (*Celsi praetoris*) cf. 10. 202 'ut captatori moveat fastidia Cosso'. |

10. 81–6   'perituros audio multos.'
          'nil dubium, magna est fornacula.' 'pallidulus mi
          Bruttidius meus ad Martis fuit obvius aram;
          quam timeo, victus ne poenas exigat Aiax
          ut male defensus. curramus praecipites et,
          dum iacet in ripa, calcemus Caesaris hostem.'

The downfall of Sejanus causes alarm among his associates, notably Bruttidius Niger. *victus Aiax* is often said to stand for Tiberius, but Madvig regarded both *victus* and *male defensus* as incompatible with that view (*Opuscula Academica*[2] (1887), 35 f., followed by Housman, *Classical Papers*, 615); the latter point is uncertain, as Tiberius could claim that he had been badly supported in the past, but *victus* is decisive. In this contest between brawn and brains Ajax, a hero strong in defence, must be the tough prefect of the praetorian guard, just as the wily Ulysses of the *armorum iudicium* corresponds to Tiberius. It may now be added that the sculptures in the grotto of Tiberius at Sperlonga represent crises in the career of Ulysses.[29]

[28] Thus J. M. Stahl, *RhM* 48 (1893), 159; J. G. Griffith, *Mnem.* 15 (1962), 260 f. But there is no need to identify the man as P. Juventius Celsus, praetor 106.

[29] For the representation of Ulysses in the Sperlonga sculptures, and their association with Tiberius, see A. F. Stewart, *JRS* 67 (1977), 76 ff. It has been suggested (I cannot trace by whom) that the retrieval of the body of Achilles was chosen to recall the famous episode when Tiberius brought his brother's body back from Germany (*Epiced. Drus.* 171

But the passage is difficult to understand. Madvig supposed that the pallor of Bruttidius[30] is humorously ascribed to a bad declamation about Ajax, but it is much more direct to connect Ajax with Sejanus himself. As Sejanus is dead, he would have to be taking his revenge as a ghost (Hertzberg cited by Courtney); but the Ajax of mythology was still alive when he killed the cattle in mistake for his false friends (14.286 'hic bove percusso mugire Agamemnona credit'). Nor is it easy to argue that the speaker pretends to be afraid of Ajax (Sejanus) when he is really afraid of Ulysses (Tiberius); the irony would only have point if Sejanus were still alive and in a position to take revenge. The remark does not lead naturally to the thought that the corpse of Sejanus should be kicked (86); even if we assign the sentences to different speakers, the change from irony to realism would be too abrupt.

Perhaps one should cut the knot and read *non timeo*[31] (admittedly *quam timeo* is a combination found at Plaut. *Most.* 543); following some editors I assign a separate speaker for 84-6. I spell out what this speaker leaves discreetly allusive: 'I'm not afraid that as in the myth defeated "Ajax" will run amok and attempt revenge on those who have failed him (but rather that victorious "Ulysses" will, and for the same reason); so now that the former is safely down, let us put the boot in.' The corruption would have been caused by somebody who saw that it was Tiberius who was running amok, and assumed that he must be 'Ajax'. |

10. 191-5   deformem et taetrum ante omnia vultum
                            dissimilemque sui, deformem pro cute pellem

'abstulit invitis corpus venerabile fratris'; Val. Max. 5. 5. 3; Sen. *Dial.* 11. 15. 5 'corpus Drusi sui sibi vindicantem'). This is a very interesting idea, as Tiberius must have prided himself on his exploit: it would explain the prominence given to a relatively unimportant legend (for which see Bömer on Ov. *Met.* 13. 280). But if one sculpture had so personal a reference, the same should be true of the other three.

Scylla suggests Tiberius's ex-wife Julia, who was banished to Rhegium, where the unfilial monster had her cave; for the interpretation of her dogs as lovers cf. *Ciris* 77 ff. with Lyne's note. Polyphemus (the uncouth son of Neptune) would be a good nickname for Agrippa Postumus (the uncouth son of the admiral), who lived on an island and was outwitted by Tiberius. When Ulysses fails to snatch the Palladium from Diomedes, one remembers that Horace associates the latter with Agrippa (*Carm.* 1. 6. 13 ff.), who was to oust Tiberius for a time. The reason for the association in Horace is not clear: could Agrippa have connected his name with Argyrippa, the hero's city? For such fantasies cf. T. P. Wiseman, *G & R* 21 (1974), 153 ff. = *Roman Studies* (1987), 207 ff.

[30] J. Ferguson in his entertaining commentary (1979) sees a play on Bruttidius Niger's name and *pallidulus*; cf. 8. 187 'velox . . . Lentulus' with Courtney's note.

[31] I have a feeling that I heard this idea floated many years ago in discussion, but if so, I cannot remember its author.

> pendentisque genas et talis aspice rugas
> quales, umbriferos ubi pandit Thabraca saltus,
> in vetula scalpit iam mater simia bucca.

In this description of old age the repetition of *deformem* is scarcely credible, as Housman points out (on 6. 504). *deformem ... vultum* is supported by Virg. *Georg.* 4. 254f. 'horrida vultum I deformat macies'. The adjective may be less precise with *pellem* (even at the best of times the body has less defined features than the face); one looks for something more specifically meaning 'loose', to balance *pendentis* and *rugas*.

I propose *follentem*, 'baggy': the word is attested at Jerome *Epist.* 22. 28. 3 'omnis his cura de vestibus, si bene oleant, si pes laxa pelle non folleat'. Add Apul. *Met.* 9. 13. 2 'cervices cariosa vulnerum putredine follicantes'; Jerome *Epist.* 22. 34. 3 'laxae manicae, caligae follicantes, vestis grossior'; Isid. *Orig.* 23. 2. 30 'simiae Graecum nomen est, id est pressis naribus; unde et simias dicimus quod suppressis naribus sint et facie foeda, rugis turpiter follicantibus' (note Juvenal's description of monkeys below); *CGL* 5. 361. 2 'follescit tumescit'. The picture goes back to Lucilius 622 M, 'ego si, qui sum, et quo folliculo nunc sum indutus, non queo' (where the context suggests an ageing body). Jerome is imitating Roman satire, including Hor. *Serm.* 1. 3. 30ff. 'rideri possit eo quod I rusticius tonso toga diffluit' (Shackleton Bailey for *defluit*) 'et male laxus I in pede calceus haeret'; elsewhere he has a few borrowings from Juvenal.[32]

At 195 *iam*, Courtney comments 'I do not know how to explain this word; it would most naturally go with *mater* and imply that apes do not bear young until late in life, but ... this is zoologically false.' J. Ferguson has proposed *Garamantis simia*, which has been accepted by Courtney in his text of 1984; this would give an amusing parody of Virg. *Aen.* 4. 198, *Garamantide nympha.* My own tentative solution is *iam marcens simia* (*LCM* 8. 5 (1983), 80); I compare Lucr. 3. 946 'si tibi non annis corpus iam marcet'; Ov. *Met.* 7. 314 'marcentia guttura' (of an elderly ram); Plin. *Nat.* 15. 52 'celerrime in rugas marcescunt pannucea' (of shrivelled apples). This would sustain the emphasis on loose skin begun by *follentem*.

11. 56–7   experiere hodie numquid pulcherrima dictu,
              Persice, non praestem vita et moribus et re.

> vita *Φ*: vitae *P* et moribus *cod. det. et fortasse P*: nec moribus *Φ*.

[32] D. Wiesen, *St Jerome as a Satirist* (1964), 9f., 153ff.

The hiatus of *vita et* is intolerable, and not to be supported by other instances in Juvenal. Buecheler proposed *vitae tibi moribus*, but Courtney rightly regards *vitae moribus* and *re* as unbalanced. Housman (p. liv) well cited Cic. *Fin.* 1. 65 'hoc ... vita et factis et moribus comprobavit'; in fact Cicero quite often combines *vita* and *moribus*.

Courtney cites my own proposal (made by letter), *tibi vita et moribus et re*; he points to the possibility of *tibi* (spelt *tivi*) falling out before *vita* (I might add, after *-tē*). I also suggest that if the unemphatic pronoun is inserted at all, it goes best at the second place in the clause, i.e. after *non praestem*.

11. 100–2   tunc rudis et Graias mirari nescius artes
              urbibus eversis praedarum in parte reperta |
              magnorum artificum frangebat pocula miles.

In the old days Roman soldiers were so uninterested in Greek art that they smashed precious cups. *in parte* shows that Juvenal is talking not of general booty but of a Roman's soldier's particular allocation. *reperta* implies that he did not know without investigation what he had got, but the hyperbole blurs the main issue; his indifference sprang not from the superfluity of his booty but from his own lack of sophistication. The point may be too slight to press, but *recepta* would be an easy change; *parte* might have contributed to a corruption.

11. 142–4   nec frustrum capreae subducere nec latus Afrae
              novit avis noster, tirunculus ac rudis omni
              tempore et exiguae furtis inbutus ofellae.

Juvenal's slave-boy is so unsophisticated that he is guilty of only the most trifling thefts. Duff, followed by Courtney, translated *omni tempore* 'all his days', but it is hard to see what this adds: if he is now an unskilled novice, he never was anything else. F. R. D. Goodyear, in his interesting review of Courtney, suggests 'on every occasion' (*Proceedings of the African Classical Associations*, 16 (1982), 59); that is still perhaps not specific enough. I suggest *omni crimine*, 'inexpert in every offence'; for the ablative cf. Ov. *Trist.* 2. 424, *Ennius ... arte rudis*; Vell. 2. 73. 1, *studiis*; Stat. *Theb.* 6. 437, *arte*. Each of the three clauses now refers not just to inexperience (*nec novit, tirunculus ac rudis, inbutus*) but to theft (*subducere, omni crimine, furtis*).

The substitution of one dactylic ablative for another is a well-attested phenomenon.[33] At 1. 156 'qua stantes ardent qui fixo gutture fumant', P and other MSS read *pectore*; the latter would wrongly

---

[33] Housman on Manil. 1. 416; Skutsch on Enn. *Ann.* 244.

suggest 'transfixed' (Virg. *Aen.* 1.44 'illum exspirantem transfixo pectore flammas'; *TLL* 6.1.716.7ff.). 6.95f. 'pavidoque gelantur | pectore nec tremulis possunt insistere plantis', is good in itself, but a little unexpected after 93, 'pertulit Ionium constanti pectore'; at 96, *corpore* (cod. det. ap. Ruperti) should at least be recorded. 15.21 'tenui percussum verbere Circes', surely refers to an instrument rather than a blow (which would suit *leni*), but 'a thin lash' remains unconvincing even as an oxymoron; I have considered *vimine*, 'wand' (cf. Stat. *Theb.* 2.30 'Lethaeo vimine mulcens'; *CGL* 2.427.5 ῥάβδος *virga vimen*). At 15.154 'tutos vicino limine somnos', editors reject P's *limite*; but cf. Virg. *Ecl.* 1.53ff. 'hinc tibi quae semper vicino ab limite saepes | Hyblaeis apibus florem depasta salicti | saepe levi somnum suadebit inire susurro'. With *crimine, vimine, limite* the accumulation of vertical strokes would encourage corruption.

12.75-9   tandem intrat positas inclusa per aequora moles
           Tyrrhenamque pharon porrectaque bracchia rursum
           quae pelago occurrunt medio longeque relincunt
           Italiam; non sic igitur mirabere portus
           quos natura dedit.

Catullus enters the portus Augusti constructed by Claudius at Ostia. 78 *igitur* seems indefensible, though it has been defended (U. Knoche, *Gnomon*, 9 (1933), 252). Housman proposed *similis*, which could have been lost between *sic* and *mi-*; but there is no need to limit the comparison to similar harbours. *ullos*, his other suggestion, would give adequate sense, but | is heavy and colourless. Not many words would have much point; one that suggests itself is *veteres*. Cf. Virg. *Ecl.* 9.46 'Daphni, quid antiquos signorum suspicis ortus?'

12.86-92   iam sequar et sacro, quod praestat, rite peracto
            inde domum repetam, graciles ubi parva coronas
            accipiunt fragili simulacra nitentia cera.
            hic nostrum placabo Iovem Laribusque paternis
            tura dabo atque omnis violae iactabo colores.
            cuncta nitent, longos erexit ianua ramos
            et matutinis operatur festa lucernis.

Juvenal celebrates the home-coming of Catullus by decorating his house inside and out. In 91, *cuncta nitent* seems repetitive after the more specific *simulacra nitentia*, and inert compared with the other details. But it is not easy to think of an appropriate verb; *virent* would suit *ramos* but not *lucernis*, and we have already had *virentem* at 85.

As a long shot I suggest *certatim*: the front door views with the decorations inside. *certare* is sometimes used of rivalry in celebration; cf. Stat. *Silv.* 1. 4. 13 '(urbes) certent laetitia'. For competition between one adornment and another see especially Calp. *Ecl.* 7. 47 f. 'balteus en gemmis, en illita porticus auro | certatim radiant'; Stat. *Ach.* 1. 15 f. 'cui geminae florent vatumque ducumque | certatim laurus'.

13. 46–50   prandebat sibi quisque deus nec turba deorum
                talis ut est hodie, contentaque sidera paucis
                numinibus miserum urguebant Atlanta minori
                pondere; nondum †aliquis sortitus triste profundi
                imperium Sicula torvus cum coniuge Pluton.

        49 aliquis *Φ*: *om. P*   50 imperium *HLOZ*: imperium aut *PSΦΣ*.

People did not steal in the days of Saturn, before there were as many gods as today. Housman saw that 49 referred to Hades, and proposed *nondum imi* (*Classical Papers*, 966, 1016 f., 1258); *aliquis* is then an interpolation to fill a lacuna. The conjecture may well be right, but one would have expected something livelier and more specific than *profundi* to define *imperium* and balance *Atlanta*; it is only *triste* that shows that the underworld is meant rather than the sea. Conceivably *Φ*'s *aliquis* should be replaced by *Erebi*; cf. Sen. *Oed.* 160 'Erebi claustra profundi'; Lucan 1. 455 f. 'non tacitas Erebi sedes Ditisque profundi | pallida regna petunt'; Stat. *Theb.* 1. 297 f. 'profundi | lege Erebi'. The proposal is palaeographically less attractive than *imi*, but *nondũere-* might have caused a muddle after *pondere.*

13. 213–16   sed vina misellus
                expuit, Albani veteris pretiosa senectus
                displicet; ostendas melius, densissima ruga
                cogitur in frontem velut acri ducta Falerno.

The man with a guilty conscience cannot enjoy the finest wines. At 213, *Setina* (Herel and Withof) is needed to balance the other wines, but there is a further difficulty. Following Duff, Courtney says that 216 *Falerno* must be identified with the *melius* of the previous line: 'the very sight of it makes him screw up his face as if it were bitter and he were drinking it'. Yet one would naturally assume a contrast between the fine wines (*Setina, Albani*, with *melius* as a | hyperbole) and something notoriously inferior; even if some sorts of Falernian were less highly regarded than before (Plin. *Nat.* 14. 62), its great name (4. 138) could not be used to typify inferior wine.

I suggest *Falisco*, wine from the *ager Faliscus* round Falerii; though the wine is not named elsewhere, Gellius speaks of viticulture in the area (20. 8. 1 'Annianus poeta in fundo suo quem in agro Falisco possidebat agitare erat solitus vindemiam hilare atque amoeniter'). Wines from Etruria were regarded in antiquity as inferior,[34] notably that from Veii south of Falerii; cf. Hor. *Serm.* 2. 3. 143 'Veientanum festis potare diebus'; Pers. 5. 147 f. 'Veientanumque rubellum | exhalet vapida laesum pice sessilis obba?'; Mart. 1. 103. 9, 2. 53. 4, 3. 49. 1. Wine from Falerii would be included in Juvenal's own damning description, 'vinum Tiberi devectum' (7. 121).

I append a few notes on my previous conjectures (above, 19 ff.), omitting those that are mentioned above. 2. 105 f. (deletion of *summi constantia. . . campis*): the passage is discussed by R. Syme, *Roman Papers*, 3. 1145 f., but Housman's difficulty remains. 6. 65: Guyet anticipated the deletion, which I regard as certain. 6. 138, 359, 395: my tentative deletions were anticipated by A. Scholte in his interesting *Observationes Criticae* of 1873 (pointed out by M. D. Reeve, *CR* 21 (1971), 328). 6. 159 *observant ubi festa mero pede sabbata reges* (*mero* Φ: *nudo* PRO Arov.): nobody accepts my *udo* (for ritual foot-washing see *RAC* 9. 743 ff.), and the very odd *mero* may be a calque for φιλῷ. 8. 170 f.: I am still tempted to believe in the deletion of *praestare Neronem . . . aetas*, which gets rid of an obscurity about the identity of Lateranus. The deletion of 9. 126 f. *velox. . . brevissima*, can be avoided if *velox flosculus* is put within commas (Courtney, following Wakefield). I still regard as highly desirable the deletion of 10. 150 and 160, and as possible the deletion of 10. 349 and 11. 48 f. *et pallet. . . solum*. 11. 112 *tacitamque* for *mediamque*, has been accepted by some, but I have never been sure about my authorship of this conjecture. 13. 23 *furtum*, 13. 108 *vectare*, 14. 269 *perditus articulis*, 15. 143 *adeo*, have found varying degrees of support. 16. 17 ff. 'iustissima centurionum | cognitio est igitur de milite, nec mihi derit | ultio, si iustae defertur causa querellae'. Courtney punctuates with Weidner *cognitio est, igitur de milite nec mihi derit | ultio*; J. P. Sullivan proposes *cognitio, etsi agitur de milite, nec . . .* (*CPh.* 79 (1984), 229). I still believe that my deletion of 18 is the simplest way to deal with *igitur* and to put *iustissima* and *iustae* in a pointed relationship.

I add a few other readings and conjectures that deserve more support than they have received: the list makes no attempt to be comprehensive. 1. 2 *rauci Theseide Cordi* (P and most editors): *Codri* Φ rightly, alluding to Virg. *Ecl.* 7. 22, and like *Theseide* to a king of Athens

[34] For the production of cheaper wines near Rome cf. N. Purcell, *JRS* 75 (1985), 16 ff.

(cf. R. Reggiani, *QUCC* 21 (1976), 125 ff.). 1. 14 *expectes eadem a summo minimoque poeta* del. Dobree. 1. 80 *quales ego vel Cluvienus: Cluvianus* is mooted but rejected by L. A. Mackay, *CPh.* 53 (1958), 236 ff., and accepted by R. A. Lafleur, *RPh.* 50 (1976), 79 ff. (both see an allusion to Helvidius *filius* from Cluviae). 1. 104 f. *molles quod in aure fenestrae* | *arguerint: molli* T. Marshall (1723), referring to the soft bit of the ear (more vivid than *molles*). 1. 125 *profer Galla caput*, is rightly assigned to the cashier by the scholiast. 1. 127–31 were transposed by Hirschfeld and rightly deleted by Jahn (as reported by Knoche); in 120–6 the clients are collecting their dole, in 132, *vestibulis abeunt*. 3. 29 *qui nigrum in candida vertunt: nigra* Wessner. 3. 242 *namque facit somnum clausa lectica fenestra*, del. Pinzger; the rich man sleeps because he is comfortable and carefree, not because the litter is stuffy. 3. 260 *obtritum volgi perit omne cadaver: vulgo* Eremita *ap.* Jahn (the adverb combines well with *omne*, and is used of promiscuous slaughter at Cic. *Sex. Rosc.* 80, Virg. *Georg.* 3. 246). 3. 295–6: Pinzger's | transposition puts *dic* in the right relationship to 297 *dicere*. 3. 298 f. *vadimonia deinde* | *irati faciunt: iurati* Scholte (the mugger is cynical rather than aggressive when he takes his victim to court). 6. 28 f. *uxorem, Postume, ducis?* | *dic qua Tisiphone, quibus exagitare colubris*: editors accept *exagitere* from some MSS, but *exagitate* (Hadr. Valesius) is more stylish (for the vocative cf. 6. 277). 6. 50 *paucae adeo Cereris vittas contingere dignae: victus* G. Giangrande, *Eranos*, 63 (1965), 26 ff. 6. 250 f. *nisi si quid in illo* | *pectore plus agitat: imo* Scholte. 6. 514 *mollia qui rapta secuit genitalia testa: rupta* cod. det. 10. 90 f. *visne salutari sicut Seianus, habere* | *tantundem: havere* Lachmann (cf. Mart. 9. 6. 4 *non vis, Afer, avere; vale* where *habere* is a variant). 10. 132 *a luteo Volcano ad rhetora misit: rutilo* Scholte. 10. 356 *orandum est ut sit mens sana in corpore sano* del. Reeve, *CR* 20 (1970), 135 f. 11. 97 *vile coronati caput ostendebat aselli: vite* Henninius, citing Hygin. *Fab.* 274, p. 149 Schmidt, *antiqui autem nostri in lectis tricliniaribus in fulcris capita asellorum vite alligata habuerunt.* 12. 13 f. *laeta sed ostendens Clitumni pascua sanguis* | *iret et a grandi cervix ferienda ministro* (*a* om. PΣ): *pascua grandis* Castiglioni ap. Vianello (the bull's origin is shown not by its blood but by its white colour).³⁵ 12. 54 f. *ac se* | *explicat angustum: angusto* Häberlin. 13. 44 f. *iam siccato nectare tergens* | *bracchia Volcanus: saccato* Schurtzfleisch. 15. 43 f. *pervigilique toro quem nocte ac luce iacentem* | *septimus interdum sol invenit: calentem* Plathner.

---

³⁵ For the white cattle of Clitumnus cf. Virg. *Georg.* 2. 146; Prop. 2. 19. 6 with Enk. For the belief that the colour came from the water see Juv. 12. 41 f. on the sheep of Baetis; Plin. *Nat.* 2. 230; M. Ninck, *Die Bedeutung des Wassers im Kult und Leben der Alten* (*Philol.* suppl. 14; 1921), 45 f.

16

Footnotes on Horace

SOME of the notes in this paper develop suggestions made summarily in my reviews of the two recent Teubner editions;[1] others are new.[2] They are written in the belief that Horace's text is less secure than is usually supposed, and that it may legitimately be questioned even when corruption cannot be decisively proved. It is a pleasure to dedicate these remarks to Charles Brink, who has done so much in so many respects for the interpretation of Horace. He has always been ready to point out that editors of Horace are too conservative; this paper may give him cause to revise his opinion.

> narrat paene datum Pelea Tartaro
> Magnessam Hippolyten dum fugit abstinens.
> (*Carm.* 3. 7. 17-18)

My first point has nothing to do with the text. The Hippolyte of this legend belonged to Iolcos in the Thessalian Magnesia; ps.-Acro adds the thought that *Magnessam* distinguishes her from the Amazon. But it is also relevant that Magnesia was associated with magnets; cf. Lucr. 6. 908-9 'quem Magneta vocant patrio de nomine Grai | Magnetum quia sit patriis in finibus ortus'. Plin. *Nat.* 36. 128 (explicitly referring to the Thessalian rather than the Lydian Magnesia), *RE* 14. 1. 474-86.

Magnetism became a regular analogy for erotic attraction; cf. Ach. Tat. 1. 17. 2 ἐρᾶι γοῦν ἡ μαγνησία λίθος τοῦ σιδήρου κἂν μόνον ἴδηι καὶ θίγηι, πρὸς αὐτὴν εἵλκυσεν, ὥσπερ ἐρωτικόν τι ἔνδον ἔχουσα, anon. *Anth. Pal.* 12. 152 Μάγνης Ἡράκλειτος, ἐμοὶ πόθος, οὔτι

---

[1] *Gnomon*, 58 (1986), 611-15, reviewing Borzsák's edition (Leipzig, 1984); *CR* 36 (1986), 227-34, reviewing Shackleton Bailey's edition (Stuttgart, 1985) (see above, pp. 192-201).

[2] In the paper as delivered I also suggested *Epist.* 1. 11. 29 *ruimus*, 2. 2. 199 *damus*; but though emendation on similar lines may be desirable, I have little faith in these particular proposals. I still hold to my interpretation of *Epist.* 1. 19. 28 (combine *pede mascula*); but it was anticipated by J. H. Waszink, *Mnemosyne*, 4. 21 (1968), 394-9.

From *Studies in Latin Literature and its Tradition in Honour of C. O. Brink*, ed. J. Diggle, J. B. Hall, H. D. Jocelyn (*Proceedings of the Cambridge Philological Society*, suppl. 15; 1989), 87-96.

σίδηρον | πέτρωι, πνεῦμα δ' ἐμὸν κάλλει ἐφελκόμενος Claud. *Carm. Min.* 29. 328–9 'ferrumque maritat|aura tenax', *RE* 14. 1. 482. So when Horace's Peleus is repelled and keeps his distance, it is paradoxical that a Magnesian lady should be so unattractive.

> 'quid si prisca redit Venus
> diductosque iugo cogit aeneo,
>   si flava excutitur Chloe
>   reiectaeque patet ianua Lydiae?'
> 'quamquam sidere pulchrior
> ille est, tu levior cortice et improbo
>   iracundior Hadria,
>   tecum vivere amem, tecum obeam libens.'   (3. 9. 17–24) |

In line 20 some commentators regard *Lydiae* as genitive, but that spoils the contrast between *reiectae* and *patet*: the person who was once excluded is now admitted. Others explain 'if my door lies open to rejected Lydia', but that is too patronizing for a suppliant; the door naturally belongs to the once sympathetic but now disdainful woman[3] (cf. 1 'donec gratus eram tibi'). On either assumption it is tactless for the man to emphasize that he previously rejected Lydia; that is no way for him to achieve a reconciliation.

These difficulties are met by Peerlkamp's *reiectoque*, which has been independently proposed by Shackleton Bailey.[4] But it perhaps puts the blame for the parting too firmly on Lydia (contrast the neutral *diductos* above); and in this elegantly balanced poem one would prefer a word that agrees with *Lydiae*. I suggest *praelataeque*, 'preferred' (for the use of the verb 'in re amatoria' see *TLL* 10. 2. 615. 76–616. 5); the word would echo the opening of the poem (2–3 'nec quisquam potior bracchia candidae | cervici iuvenis dabat', 5–6 'donec non alia magis | arsisti neque erat Lydia post Chloen'). Lydia will open her door again if Chloe is shaken off and she herself is preferred (the two verbs make a contrast); this doubly emphasizes that the man is the petitioner.

23 *iracundior* is also a little puzzling (in spite of 1. 33. 15 'libertina fretis acrior Hadriae'). Lydia surely broke off the relationship because the man was fickle (by her way of it), not because he was bad-tempered; the only reason within the poem for his bad temper would be her own fickleness, and she is not likely to concede that she was the first to offend. Nor can *iracundior* mean that the man nourished griev-ances, for that would rather be *iratior*; anyway Chloe is not the

---

[3] See W. Wimmel, *Glotta*, 40 (1962), 124–7.
[4] *Profile of Horace* (1982), 94.

suppliant, so she should not suggest that the man has kept up the quarrel too long. The humour of the poem lies in the discrepancy between lovers' professions of constancy and their behaviour in practice; that theme is disrupted by *iracundior*, coming as it does between *levior cortice* and *tecum vivere amem.*

I have considered *inconstantior*; for the combination with *levis* cf. Cic. *Sull.* 10 'si ego sum inconstans ac levis', Boeth. *Cons.* 4. 3. 23. Just as *levior* is precisely suited to cork, so *inconstantior* is precisely suited to the sea; cf. Dem. 19. 136 (on the fickleness of the populace) ὥσπερ ἐν θαλάττηι κῦμ' ἀκατάστατον, ὡς ἂν τύχηι κινούμενον. Lydia, who has the prerogative of the last word, contrasts her partner's inconstancy with her own fidelity.

Two doubts persist. It is generally assumed that the man, the only person among the four who is not named, is Horace himself; and though the sentiment of the poem would be untypical, this view suits the normal convention that the *Odes* are written *in propria persona*. If that is right, *iracundior* is supported by *Epist.* 1. 20. 25 'irasci celerem, tamen ut placabilis essem'. Yet that does not absolve us from the need to find some relevance within the poem itself. Secondly, in a comparison like 'improbo iracundior Hadria' the two adjectives ought to point in the same direction; and it might be argued that *improbo* (with its suggestion of | unreasonable excess) is closer to *iracundior* than to *inconstantior*. But the distinction is perhaps too slight to be decisive.

> eques ipso melior Bellerophonte, neque pugno
> neque segni pede victus . . .   (3. 12. 8–9)

The ablatives *pugno* and *pede* deserve more scrutiny than they have received. A man might be surpassed 'in foot', but not so easily 'in slow foot' (unless with the undesirable implication of Plaut. *Poen.* 532 'vicistis cochleam tarditudine'). Orelli–Hirschfelder see a brachylogy for 'propter pugnos minus robustos pedesve tardiores'; but *pugno* naturally means 'in respect of fisticuffs'. L. Müller takes *segni* with *pugno* as well as *pede*, but even this artificial solution produces an unexpected use of the ablative.

Perhaps *segni* has replaced the genitive of a proper name, to be combined with *pugno* as well as with *pede*; for the word-order see F. Leo, *Ausgewählte kleine Schriften* (1960), 1. 80–4. Hyginus mentions Cycnus together with Bellerophon as a participant in the games for Pelias (*Fab.* 273 'Cycnus Martis filius armis occidit †Pilum Diodoti filium, Bellerophontes vicit equo'); but nothing is said there about boxing or running. Alternatively one might look for a Roman name to balance the Greek; unfortunately the indomitable M. Sergius is described as 'neutra manu neutro pede satis utilis' (Plin. *Nat.* 7. 104). Alternatively *victus* may point to a contemporary athlete, perhaps eminent in the pentathlon; Cycnus is recorded as a gladiator's name (*CIL* 4. 2508. 21, 12. 1382).

> purae rivus aquae silvaque iugerum
> paucorum et segetis certa fides meae
> fulgente imperio fertilis Africae
> fallit sorte beatior.   (3. 16. 29–32)

Land has 'certa fides' when it can be relied on to pay the proper interest;[5] cf. Cic. *Fam.* 16. 17. 1 'et ager fidelis dici potest', Virg. *Georg.* 1. 647 'segetes tellus infida negabit?' *certa* is applicable to few estates (3. 1. 30 'fundusque mendax'), and surely not to Horace's; note especially *Epist.* 1. 7. 87 'spem mentita seges', where there is an evident analogy between Mena's Sabine farm and the poet's. The difficulty has been felt rather than answered: Lehrs met the problem by deleting the stanza and its two successors, Dillenburger implausibly comments 'inest hypothetica sententia', L. Müller 'condicional: wenn sie sicher est'. Nor is it easy to argue that Horace asks for little and receives all that he needs; that is not what is meant by reliability. Any reference to spiritual benefits would anticipate in the subject what should be reserved for the predicate (32 'fallit sorte beatior'). |

I suggest that Horace wrote 'curta fides' (i.e. his estate yielded short weight); for the collocation cf. Juv. 14. 164–6 'merces haec sanguinis atque laboris | nullis visa umquam meritis minor aut ingratae | curta fides patriae'. This balances 'silvaque iugerum paucorum' and for that matter 'purae rivus aquae' (a symbol of simplicity); for similar modesty cf. *Serm.* 2. 6. 1–3 'modus agri non ita magnus, | hortus ubi et tecti vicinus iugis aquae fons, | et paulum silvae super his foret'. Of course *curta fides* would be more disparaging than any of the other expressions, but the wry humour seems quite Horatian. There is no point in pretending that Sabine soil is uniquely reliable; it is really more tactful to admit its material disadvantages and yet to insist that it offers more than *latifundia* in fertile Africa. See 25–6 in this poem 'contemptae dominus splendidior rei | quam si . . .'.

At 31 I have accepted Bentley's *fulgente* for *fulgentem* of the MSS; he

---

[5] See Philemon, fr. 88. 10–11 (ἡ γῆ) τοὺς τόκους δ᾽ ἀνευρίσκουσ᾽ ἀεὶ | πρόφασίν τιν᾽ αὐχμὸν ἢ πάχνην ἀποστερεῖ; Bömer on Ov. *Met.* 5. 480; *RE* 9A. 2. 1847 (on Xenophon).

comments on the latter 'non places, Flacce. unde enim tua seges aut curtus ille agellus [*note the adjective*] Proconsuli Africae notus sit, nedum regulo Afro (ut volunt interpretes) ultra Garamantas senescenti?' But Bentley is surely wrong to see a reference to a Roman proconsul; as Heinze points out, *fertilis* shows that the country is treated as a private possession (for the hyperbole he compares 1. 1. 9–10 'si proprio condidit horreo | quidquid de Libycis verritur areis'). *sorte* means simply 'in lot', and could have nothing to do with the official allotment of provinces.

> intactis opulentior
> thesauris Arabum et divitis Indiae
> caementis licet occupes
> Tyrrhenum omne tuis et mare †Apulicum,
> si figit adamantinos
> summis verticibus dira Necessitas
> clavos, non animum metu,
> non mortis laqueis expedies caput. (3. 24. 1–8)

In line 4 the MSS offer *Apulicum* or *publicum* or *Ponticum*. The first vowel of *Apulia* is long; the scansion here is no more credible than at 3. 4. 10 'extra limen Apuliae'.[6] *publicum* would emphasize that the sea is common to all; cf. Ov. *Met.* 6. 349–51 'usus communis aquarum est. | nec solem proprium natura nec aera fecit | nec tenues undas: ad publica munera veni'. That would necessitate changing *Tyrrhenum* to Lachmann's *terrenum*; he cites Porphyrio's note 'non terram tantum verum etiam mare occupantem', but this is a conceivable comment even if Horace made no mention of the land. *terrenum* as a noun is rare and unconvincing in poetry; Heinze refers it to soil usable for agriculture (Liv. 23. 19. 14 'quidquid herbidi terreni extra murum erat', Colum. 3. 11. 8 'silex cui superimpositum est modicum terrenum'), but this seems too restrictive to balance the comprehensive *mare*. There is something in J. Gow's comment 'it is absurd | here to alter *Tyrrhenum*, which is good and well attested, in order to retain *publicum*, which is ill attested and not good'; he does not analyse his objection to *publicum*, but it seems to impair the balance of the line.

Palmer proposed *Tyrrhenum omne tuis et mare sublicis*, which has been

---

[6] When a child strays beyond a *limen*, the threshold of the house must be meant; cf. Hom. *Od.* 15. 450–1 παῖδα γὰρ ἀνδρὸς ἑῆος ἐνὶ μεγάροις ἀτιτάλλω | κερδαλέον δὴ τοῖον, ἅμα τροχόωντα θύραζε. The variant *Polliae* is not much better than *Apuliae* (Horace does not name unimportant people in his *Odes*), and there is something to be said for Baehrens's *pergulae*; I can cite in favour ps.-Quint. *Decl. Mai.* 13. 4 'nutriculam casam'.

accepted by Shackleton Bailey; but the word-order is faulty (see A. Y. Campbell, 2nd edn. (1953), 116–17). The tolerably attested *Ponticum* is absurd, as a reference to the Black Sea is irrelevant. On the other hand, the minor variant *Punicum* is worth considering as an old equivalent for *mare Libycum* (cf. Flor. *Epit.* 1. 1. 17 'nec defuerant qui ipso Punici maris nomine ac terrore deficerent'); by way of hyperbole Horace might contemplate a palace stretching across the Mediterranean to Africa (cf. 2. 2. 10–12 'si Libyam remotis I Gadibus iungas et uterque Poenus I serviat uni'). After *Arabum* and *Indiae* there are attractions in two other proper names; such a distribution is typically Horatian.

5 *si* is interpreted by commentators as *siquidem*, 'seeing that', which of course is a common usage. But in the present context one expects *si* to introduce a genuine hypothesis ('although you do A, if B occurs you will not escape'), and that does not give a convincing sense: as Bentley says, 'quid si non figat clavos necessitas, nonne morietur nihilo minus?' He himself proposed *sic*; he explains 'sic rerum fato contributum, ita natura comparatum, sic clavos figit necessitas ... ut nulla vi evelli possint'. Apart from A. Y. Campbell, commentators have not admitted a difficulty; but Bentley's solution ought at least to be kept on the record.

6 *summis verticibus* is explained by some as the plutocrats' own heads, but this is hopelessly confusing before 8 *caput*; again Bentley comments forcefully 'ego spondere ausim, cui clavus per cerebrum adactus sit, omni metu liberum et expeditum futurum'. He himself suggested that the heads of the nails are meant, but the construction is unclear; and we need to be told where the nails are fixed. More plausibly others refer the word to the tops of the villas whose foundations are described in the first stanza; *vertex* in the right context can mean this (Mart. 8. 36. 11–12 'haec, Auguste, tamen quae vertice sidera pulsat, I par domus est caelo sed minor est domino'), but in our passage we look for a more specific reference to buildings than is supplied by 3 *caementis*. L. Müller compares 3. 1, where 35 'caementa demittit redemptor' is followed by 37–8 'sed Timor et Minae I scandunt eodem quo dominus'; but there is nothing there so cryptic as *verticibus* without a genitive.

Campbell's *porticibus* is too particular, and though colonnades are a symbol of luxury, they are not conspicuous for height. *culminibus* would give adequate sense, but is too remote from *verticibus*. I suggest rather *imbricibus*, rain-tiles laid on top of the ordinary *tegulae*.[7] Cato says 'imbrices medias clavulis figito' (*Agr.* 21. 3), and though he is

[7] See Marquardt–Mau, *Das Privatleben der Römer* (1886), 637–8.

talking of iron plates on a mill, the use of bolts may be significant. *imbrex* may seem an unpoetical word, but it is attested at Virg. *Georg.* 4. 296 'angustique imbrice tecti'; and Horace himself has just used the even more prosaic *caementis.* |

> sis licet felix ubicumque mavis,
> et memor nostri, Galatea, vivas,
> teque nec laevus vetet ire picus
>   nec vaga cornix.
> sed vides quanto trepidet tumultu
> pronus Orion. ego quid sit ater
> Hadriae novi sinus et quid albus
>   peccet Iapyx.   (3. 27. 13–20)

In accordance with the conventions of the propempticon[8] Horace assents reluctantly to Galatea's departure, and ruefully expresses a hope that she will remember him. We should naturally suppose that *sis licet felix* means 'it is permissible for you to be happy', but when we reach *vivas* we can only translate 'may you live'; in spite of Heinze, the different subjunctives can hardly subsist together. T. E. Page suggested in his commentary that *licet* is parenthetical, and this has been accepted by Shackleton Bailey in his text; but it is difficult to dissociate *sis* from *licet* when a parenthesis produces so jerky a result. Cunningham read without comment *at memor* (which was independently conjectured by A. Y. Campbell), but *et* suits the natural movement of the propempticon; cf. Sappho 94. 7–8 L–P χαίροισ᾽ ἔρχεο κἄμεθεν | μέμναισ᾽, οἶσθα γὰρ ὥς σε πεδήπομεν.

With great hesitation I have tried *ilicet felix*: 'without more ado may you live happy and mindful of me'. In early Latin *ilicet* is a formula of dismissal ('you may go'); it thus contains the element of consent that is part of Horace's purpose. The injunction to depart also suits the propempticon (Ov. *Am.* 2. 11. 37 'vade memor nostri', Paul. Nol. 17. 9 'i memor nostri'); but a straightforward *i* is impossible here, as it would necessitate *quocumque*. In the dactylic poets *ilicet* is used in narratives to mean 'forthwith', and that also suits our context; cf. Hom. *Od.* 5. 204–5 οὕτω δὴ οἴκόνδε φίλην ἐς πατρίδα γαῖαν | αὐτίκα νῦν ἐθέλεις ἰέναι; σὺ δὲ χαῖρε καὶ ἔμπης. A subjunctive expressing a wish is harder to parallel with *ilicet*; yet for a jussive subjunctive cf. Sil. 9. 28–9

---

[8] Cf. Prop. 1. 8. 18–19 'sed quocumque modo de me, periura, mereris, | sit Galatea tamen non aliena viae'; Menander Rhetor 397. 15–16 οὐκοῦν ἐπειδὴ δέδοκται καὶ νενίκημαι, φέρε δὴ καὶ τῆι βουλήσει συνδράμωμεν; F. Cairns, *Generic Composition in Greek and Roman Poetry* (1972), 120f.

'tradant immo hosti revocatos ilicet enses, | tradant arma iube'. For the combination of *felix* and *memor* with *vivas* cf. [Tib.] 3. 5. 31 'vivite felices, memores et vivite nostri'.

In line 18 *quid sit* is all right in isolation ('I know the significance of a black Adriatic sea'), but *sit* seems too weak to balance *peccet*. I suggest *quo sit*, 'I know to what purpose the Adriatic is black'; cf. 2. 3. 9–11 'quo pinus ingens albaque populus | umbram hospitalem consociare amant | ramis?' It does not matter that *ater* is now the predicate, for the balancing *albus* is also emphatic.

In 20 *Iapyx* is the Iapygian wind that blows from the heel of Italy. The area was famous for its horses; cf. Virg. *Aen.* 11. 678 'et equo venator Iapyge fertur' (note also 3. 537–8 of the white horses at Castrum Minervae). *peccare* is used of a horse's stumble (Hor. *Epist.* 1. 1. 8–9 'ne | peccet ad extremum'), and indeed this | may be the verb's primary meaning. So when Horace says 'quid albus peccet Iapyx', he is seeing the wind as a white horse.

> tutus bos etenim rura perambulat,
> nutrit rura Ceres almaque Faustitas,
> pacatum volitant per mare navitae,
>   culpari metuit fides.   (4. 5. 17–20)

The repetition of *rura* in 17–18 is quite unconvincing, especially as *mare* follows in the third balancing clause. Fraenkel sees an imitation of old Italian *carmina*; he comments 'the exceptional harshness of the repetition of this word is in keeping with the exceptionally harsh structure of the two stanzas' (*Horace* (1957), 443 n. 5). On the contrary the awkwardness is particularly out of place in a poem of such regularity and classical perfection. Bentley comments more judiciously 'mihi quidem *rura rura* rus merum et librariorum stuporem sapere videtur', and Housman shows equal disapproval (Manil. 5. 463).

Faber's *prata perambulat* gives an agreeable alliteration, and might be right; the leisurely tone of the verb suggests that the ox is grazing rather than ploughing.[9] But the offence may lie rather in *nutrit rura* (where the variant *nutritura* has probably no significance); *rura* ('the countryside' as opposed to the town) seems too comprehensive to suit *nutrit* precisely. Bentley comments 'nihil *nutriri* dicitur, ne per metaphoram quidem, nisi quod augeri et incrementum capere potest, ut *arbores, segetes, fructus.* qui malum igitur Ceres *rura nutrire* poterit? an illa rus exiguum aut modicum reddet ingens, quale miluus pervolare

---

[9] H. P. Syndikus, *Die Lyrik des Horaz*, 2. 337 n. 44.

nequeat?' Admittedly there might be an imitation at Sil. 12. 375 (of Sardinia) 'cetera propensae Cereris nutrita favore'; but even the neutral *cetera* combines with *nutrire* better than *rura* does. *nutrit arva* would be better in sense (as that would suggest fertile ploughing-land), but the metrical anomaly is intolerable in a poem of this type and date. Cunningham's *culta* is at least worth recording.

Bentley proposed *farra*, but a reference to spelt is too particular and prosaic to balance *rura* and *mare*. On the same lines I have considered *grana*; *nutrit* would suit the swelling of the milky grain (and *alma* also has hints of nourishment). For *nutrire* of plants cf. Catull. 61. 24–5 'roscido I nutriunt umore', and especially Ov. *Fast.* 1. 704 'Pax Cererem nutrit'. As *rura* has jumped from the previous line, the missing word need not be particularly close.

> nunc et qui color est puniceae flore prior rosae
> mutatus Ligurinum in faciem verterit hispidam ... (4. 10. 4–5)

'When the complexion that is now preferable to the bloom of the purple rose has changed and turned Ligurinus into a hairy face.' Bentley comments admirably 'ergo miser ille Ligurinus iam totus facies erat, totus barba'. Accordingly he accepts *Ligurine* (Torrentius), which also gives the poem a desirable vocative; *verterit* is now intransitive. |

A. Y. Campbell pointed to a more neglected difficulty (*Horati Carmina Viginti* (1934), 51): he does not see how a rosy *complexion* can turn into a hairy *face*. As he expresses it, 'facies tum quoque exstabat dum color eius rosam superabat'. Accordingly he proposed *maciem*, which of course is intolerable with *hispidam*. Later he suppressed the conjecture and explained *faciem* as *formam* (1st edn., 1945), but that too is unconvincing.

For *faciem* I propose *filicem*, literally 'bracken'; the word is used of body-hair at Persius 4. 39–41 'quinque palaestritae licet haec plantaria vellant, I elixasque nates labefactent forcipe adunca, I non tamen ista filix ullo mansuescit aratro'. A contrast between two different plants is suggested by similar Greek poems on adolescent boys.[10] See *Anth. Pal.* 5. 28. 6 (Rufinus) ἀντὶ ῥόδου γὰρ ἐγὼ τὴν βάτον οὐ δέχομαι, 11. 53 (anon.) τὸ ῥόδον ἀκμάζει βαιὸν χρόνον· ἢν δὲ παρέλθηι I ζητῶν εὑρήσεις οὐ ῥόδον ἀλλὰ βάτον, 12. 36. 3 f. (Asclepiades?) καὶ τίς ἂν εἴποι I κρείσσονας αὐχμηρὰς ἀσταχύων καλάμας; In our passage the unfamiliar *filicem* would be corrupted almost inevitably to *faciem*, especially as a face is being talked about.

[10] See esp. S. L. Tarán, *JHS* 105 (1985), 90–107.

> forte quid expediat communiter aut melior pars
> malis carere quaeritis laboribus.
>
> (*Epod.* 16. 15-16)

Horace is advising the Romans to abandon their city, like the Phocaeans in Herodotus. In such a consultation *forte* must mean 'perhaps'; there is no merit in the view that it is the neuter of *fortis*.[11] The conventional translation runs 'Perhaps you ask collectively or the better part of you what is expedient so as to get free from bad troubles'; but the infinitive is odd even by Horatian standards. Borzsák and Shackleton Bailey accept W. Schmid's interpretation[12] 'perhaps you ask what produces freedom from troubles'; that is to say, *expediat* means something like *efficiat*, and *carere* is its direct object. But the infinitive is then even stranger; and in such a crisis one expects *quid expediat* to mean 'what gets us out of this'. Nor is the problem solved by the old explanation 'forte communiter quaeritis quid expediat, aut melior pars quaeritis carere laboribus'; it is artificial to separate *communiter* from *melior pars* and there is no clear distinction between 'what is expedient' and 'escaping from troubles'.

As the difficulty centres on *carere*, it may be significant that the verb has occurred three lines above (13 'quaeque carent ventis et solibus ossa Quirini'). As an experiment let us try *cavere*, translating 'perhaps you ask what gets us out of troubles that are hard to guard against'. It need hardly be said that *malis cavere* in this sense is not Latin; it could only be justified as a sort of calque for δυσφυλάκτοις (cf. Eur. *Phoen.* 924 δυσφύλακτα . . . κακά). For similar infinitives cf. Virg. *Ecl.* 5. 1-2 'boni quoniam convenimus ambo, | tu calamos inflare levis, ego dicere versus', Hdt. 1. 193. 2 ἀρίστη . . . Δήμητρος καρπὸν ἐκφέρειν, *Trag. Adesp.* 393 N.² ἄκαρπον καὶ φυτεύεσθαι κακήν. By Greek standards the active | infinitive is as legitimate as the passive; cf. Thuc. 7. 51. 1 χαλεπωτέρους . . . προσπολεμεῖν, Xen. *Oec.* 6. 9 αὕτη γὰρ ἡ ἐργασία μαθεῖν τε ῥᾴστη ἐδόκει εἶναι καὶ ἡδίστη ἐργάζεσθαι.[13] It is a further oddity in our passage that *expediat* lacks an object; yet at Plaut. *Pers.* 626 *expedivit* (without *se*) means 'she got clear'.

If this all seems too far-fetched, one can only repeat Horace's challenge (line 26) 'an melius quis habet suadere?'

---

[11] Thus among others B. Axelson, *Ut Pictura Poesis* (*Studia Latina P.I. Enk . . . oblata*, 1955), 50-2; he is refuted by Fraenkel, *Horace* (1957), 53-5.

[12] *Philol.* 102 (1958), 93-102; *Glotta*, 41 (1963), 143-7.

[13] See further Kühner-Gerth, *Ausführliche Grammatik der griechischen Sprache*, 2. 15-16; E. Schwyzer, *Griechische Grammatik*, 2. 364.

> ergo negatum vincor ut credam miser
> Sabella pectus increpare carmina
> caputque Marsa dissilire nenia.   (*Epod.* 17. 27–9)

Horace is suffering torments from Canidia's witchcraft. *increpare* would mean that spells make his breast resound; cf. Enn. *Scen.* 341 V² 'sed sonitus auris meas pedum pulsu increpat'. Ov. *Met.* 12. 51–2 'cum Iuppiter atras | increpuit nubes', *Trist.* 1. 4. 24 'increpuit quantis viribus unda latus'. But the *pectus* is an inappropriate sounding-board and the verb a feeble counterpart to *dissilire*. Palmer, who first pointed to the difficulty (*CR* 7 (1893), 100–1), proposed *incremare*, but there is no good authority for this word; Shackleton Bailey tried *et cremare*, but *et* is unconvincing. A. Y. Campbell proposed *ingravare* (cf. Ov. *Trist.* 3. 4. 60 'illa meos casus ingravat, illa levat'), but that too is weak compared with *dissilire*.

I propose *macerare* in the sense of 'boil', 'reduce to pulp'. This word is originally a term of cookery, but is used freely in early Latin of physical and mental distress; cf. Plaut. *Mil.* 616–17 'at hoc me facinus miserum macerat | meumque cor corpusque cruciat', *TLL* 8. 9. 35–10. 35. It is still found in the Augustan poets, though not in more serious contexts; cf. Hor. *Epod.* 14. 15–16 'me libertina neque uno | contenta Phryne macerat', *Carm.* 1. 13. 8 'quam lentis penitus macerer ignibus',[14] *Ciris* 244 'si concessus amor noto te macerat igni' (with Lyne's note). As *macerare* describes physical distress in a forceful way, it provides the requisite balance for *dissilire*.

[14] See D. West, *Reading Horace* (1967), 66–71.

17

On Housman's *Juvenal*

THE assessment of famous editions is more difficult than is sometimes supposed. Snap judgements can be made about other works of scholarship in a library or bookshop, but to criticize a textual critic it is desirable to have wrestled with the problems oneself, as well as to know the state of opinion before he came on the scene. That is a tall order with Housman's *Manilius*, so that with a few distinguished exceptions eulogies derive from Housman himself, but Juvenal at least is relatively familiar and intelligible. The present sketch is the sequel to my article in the Skutsch *Festschrift*, *BICS* supplement 51 (1988), 86 ff. (above, pp. 227 ff.), where a number of proposals are made on the text of Juvenal. Apart from Housman himself, I have used particularly the texts of Jahn, Knoche, Clausen, and now J. R. C. Martyn (Amsterdam, 1987), as well as the commentary by Courtney (note also his text of 1984).

Housman's first text of Juvenal appeared in 1905 in the second volume of Postgate's *Corpus Poetarum Latinorum*; it had a greatly abbreviated apparatus but was otherwise virtually identical with the separate edition. This was published in the same year 'editorum in usum' by Housman's friend Grant Richards; the second edition (Cambridge, 1931) has some twenty additional pages of introduction but only minimal changes elsewhere. For Housman's articles and reviews on Juvenal, I refer to the index of his *Classical Papers* (edited by J. Diggle and F. R. D. Goodyear, Cambridge, 1972). One may note especially his expositions of the Oxford fragment (pp. 481 ff., 539 ff., 621 f.), which presumably led to the invitation from Postgate, and his mauling of S. G. Owen (pp. 602 ff., 617 f., 964 ff.), whose rival Oxford text of 1903 he ignores in his own editions.

Housman's first service to Juvenal was his clear-headed and clearly expressed account of the manuscript position. On the one hand there was *P*, the ninth-century Pithoeanus, with a few congeners, on the other hand the vulgate tradition, from which with uncanny flair he singled out seven witnesses (his Ψ, roughly equivalent to Clausen's Φ). Jahn and Buecheler, against whom he was reacting, had followed P except where it offered manifest nonsense, and sometimes even then. In a typically forceful passage (p. xi) Housman points out that if Ψ were derived from P it should never be used, but seeing that it is independent, its readings must be | considered on their merits; and he listed 26 places where P had been wrongly preferred (p. xviii). Some of his expressions might seem to undervalue manuscript authority, as when he recommends an open mind about the relative merits of P and Ψ (p. xiv); after all, when an editor is about to issue his edition, he has gone beyond that preliminary agnosticism. But in practice he recognized the superiority of P, and was ready to prefer it when there was little to choose (p. xv).

When Housman mocked *Ueberlieferungsgeschichte* (p. xxviii) as 'a longer and nobler name than fudge' (Lucan, p. xiii), he was thinking of attempts to conjure up ancient editors ('Nicaeus and his merry men') from the bald assertions of *subscriptiones*; and here at least his scepticism was justified.[1] But though he could analyse acutely the relationships of manuscripts from given data, he was not much interested in looking at them within their historical context: hence some of the deficiencies of his stemma of Propertius, where it is now realized that he was wrong against Postgate.[2] On the other hand, the tradition of Juvenal suited him well: he understood the essential set-up, which was quite straightforward, and what was needed was not stemmatological refinement but the discrimination of the critic. Yet even with Juvenal a little more might have been said about the history of the tradition.[3] W. M. Lindsay in his cool review asserts that only one ancient MS survived the dark ages (*CR* 19 (1905), 463); when Housman talks of two ancient editions, he was surely right against the manuscript expert, but he does not really argue the matter. Something more is needed about the character and date of the interpolations, which are already imitated in poets like Dracontius. And when the reader is invited to consider corruption, it is never made clear enough what letter-forms and abbreviations are envisaged.

[1] J. E. G. Zetzel, *Latin Textual Criticism in Antiquity* (Salem, NH, 1981), 211 ff.

[2] J. L. Butrica, *The Manuscript Tradition of Propertius* (*Phoenix* suppl. 17; Toronto, 1984) 6 ff.; G. P. Goold, *BICS* suppl. 51 (1988), 28 ff. (who cites Housman's offensive criticisms of Postgate).

[3] See now E. Courtney, *BICS* 13 (1966), 38 ff.; R. J. Tarrant in *Texts and Transmission*, ed. L. D. Reynolds (Oxford, 1983), 200 ff.

'No amount ... of palaeography will teach a man one scrap of textual criticism';[4] and a textual critic need not be and seldom is an expert palaeographer. Housman used palaeographic arguments, sometimes to excess, to support solutions that he had reached by reason, but he never believed in altering a letter or two to see what happens.[5] Like Porson, he seems to have derived little enjoyment from collating; his gastronomic tours of France did not lead him to the Pithoeanus at Montpellier, and he did not | himself exhaust even the famous Oxoniensis, in which E. O. Winstedt as an undergraduate had discovered 36 unique lines. He relied for his reports of readings on printed sources or inspection by acquaintances; he acknowledges particular indebtedness to the collations of Mr Hosius, though he is ready enough to insult him elsewhere. When his Ψ group speaks with divided voices, one is left without a clear view of the preponderance of the tradition, but too much information may be more misleading than too little. As Housman retorted to an early work by Knoche: 'He complains that Leo and I use too few MSS and despise most of those which Mr Hosius collated and which Jahn professed to collate. We despise them because we find them despicable' (*Classical Papers*, 1106).

However superficial Housman's recension may seem, later industry has made remarkably little difference. In 1909 C. E. Stuart called attention to Parisinus 8072 (*R* in later editions), a further congener of *P*, and Housman in his second preface records interesting readings in three places (1. 70, 2. 34, 2. 45); the most striking of these is the first, where he had printed 'quae molle Calenum | porrectura viro miscet sitiente rubetam'. Here Plathner's *rubeta*, which he had not recorded, is now supported not only by *R* but by the first hand of *P* itself; it is certainly right (Housman in his second edition simply says 'perhaps'), for *viro* must be dative after *porrectura*. In the same year A. Ratti, the future Pope Pius XI, discovered in the Ambrosian Library a palimpsest containing scraps of the fourteenth satire;[6] Housman in his second preface mentions a few notable readings (p. lv), none of which was

---

[4] A. E. Housman, 'The Application of Thought to Textual Criticism', *Proceedings of the Classical Association*, 18 (1922), 68 = *Selected Prose*, ed. J. Carter (Cambridge, 1961), 131 = *Collected Poems and Selected Prose*, ed. C. Ricks (London, 1988), 325.

[5] Ibid., 142 (Carter) = p. 333 (Ricks). See also Manilius 5, pp. xxivf.; E. J. Kenney, *The Classical Text* (Berkeley, 1974), 122f.

[6] *Classical Papers*, 815 'It was a fine August morning which placed in Monsignore Ratti's hand the envelope containing this fragment, and he gives us leave to imagine the trepidation with which he opened it and the joy with which he discovered that the parchment was in two pieces instead of one. When a scholar is so literary as all this, it would be strange if he were quite accurae he ..'.

both new and true. In 1935 C. H. Roberts published a papyrus from Antinoopolis, which showed errors going back to antiquity (*JEA* 21 (1935), 199 ff.). Its most interesting novelty was a mark indicating doubt at 7. 192 'adpositam nigrae lunam subtexit alutae', which had been deleted by Prinz and Jahn (1868) without a word from Housman; in fact the best solution is that of M. D. Reeve, 'felix et [sapiens et nobilis et generosus I adpositam] nigrae lunam subtexit alutae' (*CR*, NS 21 (1971), 328).

The scrutiny of minor manuscripts since Housman has produced still less of consequence, and even the better new readings are so thinly supported that they are likely to be conjectures or accidents (for details see Knoche and Martyn). 2. 38 'ad quem subridens' (against 'atque ita subridens') may simply be derived from Virg. *Aen.* 10. 742. 5. 105 'pinguis torpente cloaca' (of a fish in the sewers) had been proposed by Rutgers, and is worth considering against *torrente*; yet the elder Pliny talks of torrents in the *cloacae* (36. 105). At 8. 38 *sic* had been proposed by Junius and endorsed by Housman; | at 8. 229 *seu personam* is questionable (see Courtney). A more interesting case is 8. 240 ff., a passage that has been plagued by bad conjectures:

> tantum igitur muros intra toga contulit illi
> nominis ac tituli quantum †in Leucade, quantum
> Thessaliae campis Octavius abstulit udo
> caedibus adsiduis gladio.

Here a stray manuscript plausibly reads *sub Leucade*, a phrase that already appears in the scholiast's note; see also Walter of Châtillon, *Alexandreis* 5. 493 f. 'cum fuso sub Leucade Caesar I Antonio' (cited by P. G. McC. Brown, *Hermes*, 114 (1986), 498 ff.).

In his apparatus criticus Housman helpfully signalled his own conjectures with an asterisk; there are some 30 such asterisks. We may begin with 6. 157 f. (on a precious ring):

> hunc dedit olim
> barbarus incestae, dedit hunc Agrippa sorori.

For the inanely repeated *dedit hunc*, which dissociates *incestae* from *sorori*, Housman printed *gestare* (lost after *-cestae*), citing Virg. *Aen.* 12. 211 'patribusque dedit gestare Latinis'. This was the kind of proposal that makes 'the hair stand up on many uninstructed heads' (Manilius 5, p. xxxiv), but it was characteristic of its author (posit the loss of an easily lost word followed by interpolation to restore the metre); Housman rightly insists that the plausibility of a conjecture does not depend on the number of letters changed. I have described *gestare* as the best emendation that has ever been made in Juvenal (*JRS* 52 (1962), 233 (above, p. 19)), and this view has been endorsed by Professor Courtney in his commentary.

Others of Housman's conjectures are almost as brilliant; like Bentley, he was at his best when things were difficult. See 3. 216 ff. on the presents given to a rich man who has lost his possessions in a fire:

> hic nuda et candida signa
> hic aliquid praeclarum Euphranoris et Polycliti,
> haec Asianorum vetera ornamenta deorum,
> hic libros dabit et forulos mediamque Minervam,
> hic modium argenti.

Here *haec* disrupts the series of *hic . . . hic*, and the demonstratives seem one too many for the flow of the passage. Theoretically one might consider a long word in place of *haec Asianorum*, such as *phaecasiatorum* (derived by C. Valesius from the widely attested *phaecasianorum*); but 'slippered gods' has no obvious meaning, and plural *ornamenta* is unattractive in opposition to *aliquid praeclarum*. Housman proposed *hic aliquid praedarum,* | *Euphranoris et Polycliti* | *aera, Asianorum vetera ornamenta deorum*.[7] The enjambment produced by *aera* is persuasive, and *ornamenta* now fits well. If this is accepted, *praedarum* must follow (since cited by Knoche from a minor manuscript without authority); Courtney reads *hic aliquid praeclarum Euphranoris et Polycliti* | *aera*; but that compromise impairs the balance.

Juvenal tells us that the young, unlike the old, do not all look the same (10. 196 f.):

> plurima sunt iuvenum discrimina, pulchrior ille
> hoc atque ille alio, multum hic robustior illo.

The second *ille* is omitted by *P* and a few other MSS; it clearly gets in the way. Housman proposed *ore alio*, 'with another face' (see his second edition, p. liii = *Classical Papers*, 878 f.); but he comments in his apparatus 'alia conici possunt velut *voltuque alio*; minus bonum videtur *aliusque alio*'. The decisive argument is provided by the scholiast's comment 'quidam pulcher est, alter eloquens' (cited not by Housman but by Courtney); this looks like a misguided explanation of *ore alio*, and is hard to explain any other way. Martyn's *eloquio*, 'stronger in eloquence than him', produces an impossible confusion of ablatives.

---

[7] Housman's proposal is commended by J. Willis, *Latin Textual Criticism* (Illinois Studies in Language and Literature, 61; Urbana, Ill., 1972), 66.

At 10. 311ff. we are told of the fate that awaits a good-looking young man:

> fiet adulter
> publicus et poenas metuet quascumque mariti
> exigere irati debent, nec erit felicior astro
> Martis . . .

Line 313 appears thus in Ψ (with a variant *exire*), which is a foot too long; *P* reads the metrical but meaningless *mariti | irati debet*. Housman proposed *lex irae debet*, pointing to 314ff. 'exigit autem | interdum ille dolor plus quam lex ulla dolori | concessit'. Nothing else that has been suggested fits in so well with the following context.

Other of Housman's conjectures are plausible even if less striking. At 4. 128 'erectas in terga sudes', the turbot's fins are described as an omen of war; Housman comments '*in terga* erigi non possunt, cum sint in tergo', and proposes *per terga*. E. W. Bower, followed by Courtney, interprets 'spines running up the back', comparing 'erigere aciem in collem' (*CR*, NS 8 (1958), 9); but when *erectas* is applied to stakes, it ought to have a more literal meaning. At 9. 60 'meliusne hic' Housman's difficulty about *hic* has not been met, nor his *melius nunc* clearly bettered (though note Castiglioni's *dic*). At 15. 89ff. Juvenal describes how everybody in an Egyptian village took part in a cannibal feast:

> nam, scelere in tanto ne quaeras et dubites an |
> prima voluptatem gula senserit, ultimus autem
> qui stetit, absumpto iam toto corpore ductis
> per terram digitis aliquid de sanguine gustat.

In 90 Housman's *ante* may seem dull, but it is difficult to refute; the word was later recorded by Knoche from a London MS without authority.

It is not the purpose of this paper to analyse the Oxford fragment of the sixth satire, where Housman hoisted his asterisk five times. At 2 'obscenum, et tremula promittit omnia dextra' he restored the metre by transposing *et* to precede *omnia*; but von Winterfeld's *promittens* gives a more natural word-order. At 8f. 'longe migrare iubetur | psillus ab eupholio' he ingeniously conjectures *psellus* and *euphono*. At 11 'munimenta umeri pulsatamque arma tridentem' he proposed in the apparatus *pulsata hastamque tridentem*, but one might prefer a long word agreeing with *tridentem*. At 12f. 'pars ultima ludi | accipit as animas aliosque in carcere nervos', his *has* and *aliusque* are obviously right. He sorted out the punctuation of 27 'quem rides? aliis hunc mimum!

sponsio fiat'. Beyond this he elucidated indecencies that were unintelligible to everybody else.

Housman had no hesitations about the authenticity of the passage: he notes at the end with the braggadocio of an earlier age 'Buechelero ... et Friedlaendero ... Iuvenalis editoribus huius aetatis celeberrimis eisdemque interpolationum patientissimis, hi XXXIV versus, quia ipsi eos non expediebant, subditivi visi sunt; quod ne ex hominum memoria excidat, quantum potero, perficiam.' One may agree that once allowance is made for the obscurity of the subject and the uncertainty of the transmission, some of the passage sounds splendidly Juvenalian: note especially 15 f. 'cum quibus Albanum Surrentinumque recuset I flava ruinosi lupa degustare sepulchri', 21 f. 'oculos fuligine pascit I distinctus croceis et reticulatus adulter' (a passage imitated by Tertullian, *Cult. Fem.* 2. 5. 2 'oculos fuligine porrigunt', like other lines that are certainly by Juvenal). But Housman has not satisfied everybody that the situation described makes sense and is relevant to the context. In particular Axelson[8] has pointed to the difficulty of the closing lines: 'novi I consilia et veteres quaecumque monetis amici' (O. 29 f.) is clumsy compared with the alternative 'audio quid veteres olim moneatis amici' (346).

Housman improved the text of Manilius and Lucan by many repunctuations, and it is well known how by moving a comma he made sense of Catullus 64. 324 'Emathiae tutamen opis, carissime nato'. Similarly at Juv. 2. 37 everybody accepts his 'ubi nunc, lex Iulia, dormis?', where previous editors had swallowed 'ubi nunc lex Iulia? dormis?' At 5. 32 he joins 'cardiaco numquam cyathum missurus amico' to the following sentence ('cras bibet Albanis aliquid de montibus'), thus sustaining the I contrast between the menu of the host and the guests. At 6. 454 ff. he points to the absurdity of 'ignotosque mihi tenet antiquaria versus, I nec curanda viris opicae castigat amicae I verba: soloecismum liceat fecisse marito'; here he punctuates after *viris* and reads *castiget* with a stray manuscript, but admits merit in the minor variant 'haec curanda viris?' In the fourteenth satire he rightly placed 23–4 between 14 and 15 (I say nothing of his rearrangement of 6. 116–21, where no proposal seems entirely satisfactory).

Some of Housman's repunctuations were less plausible: the involuted hyperbata that he delighted to detect in other Roman poets do not suit Juvenal. At 4. 11 f. he punctuates 'caecus adulator dirusque, a

---

[8] B. Axelson, *ΔΡΑΓΜΑ Martino P. Nilsson ... Dedicatum* (Lund, 1939), 41 ff. = *Kleine Schriften* (Stockholm, 1987), 173 ff.

ponte, satelles, | dignus Aricinos qui mendicaret ad axes' (that is to say, he takes *a ponte* with *mendicaret*); but he puts forward this fantastic notion with unaccustomed diffidence. Perhaps Juvenal means that Catullus has come from a beggar's mat by the Tiber, and is sinister enough to ply his trade even at Aricia (where the virtuoso performers may have congregated). At 8. 142 f. Housman punctuates 'quo mihi te, solitum falsas signare tabellas, | in templis quae fecit avus', but his comma after *tabellas* is undesirable (see Courtney); legal documents could be signed in temples, and this provides a better parallel to what follows ('quo si nocturnus adulter | tempora Santonico velas adoperta cucullo?'). At 13. 150 ff. Housman reads:

> haec ibi si non sunt, minor exstat sacrilegus qui
> radat inaurati femur Herculis et faciem ipsam
> Neptuni, qui bratteolam de Castore ducat;
> an dubitet, solitus, totum conflare Tonantem?

But he rightly doubts his own commas round *solitus*, and considers deleting the line as an interpolation (without noticing that J. D. Lewis had said that the line would be better away); other proposals are *solitum est* (Munro), *solus* (codd. dett., Leo), and *solidum* (D. R. Shackleton Bailey, *CR*, NS 9 (1959), 201). There is a further difficulty at 15. 131 ff.:

> mollissima corda
> humano generi dare se natura fatetur,
> quae lacrimas dedit; haec nostri pars optima sensus.
> plorare ergo iubet causam dicentis amici
> squaloremque rei.

Housman pointed out the unnaturalness of taking *squalorem* with *amici* as well as with *rei*; he therefore joined *sensus* to the following sentence as the first object of *plorare* (interpreting 'emotions'). A strong pause occurs in this place elsewhere in the satire (72, 147, 159), and *ergo* can come third word in the sentence (Housman cites 15. 171); but this may be less natural when it is second word in the line. As an alternative, Housman suggested genitive *census* ('endowment'); for other proposals see Courtney. |

Housman made some suggestions for lacunae that he did not signal with his asterisk. At 1. 155 ff. his insertion must be on the right lines:

> pone Tigellinum, taeda lucebis in illa
> qua stantes ardent qui fixo gutture fumant,
> ⟨quorum informe unco trahitur post fata cadaver⟩
> et latum media sulcum deducit harena.

Here it is often said that the subject of *deducit* is *taeda*, derived as Latin allows from the ablative of 155; but the burning of a single individual would not produce a trail of light, and a furrow in the sand must be more literal. Housman is less convincing when he proposes a lacuna after 1. 131. From 95 to 126 Juvenal has dealt with the *sportula*; then from 127 to 131 he gives a meagre and irrelevant summary of the client's day; then at 132 we are told 'vestibulis abeunt veteres lassique clientes'. Rather than assume a lacuna, it seems best to delete the five irrelevant lines with Jahn (as reported by Knoche); as they are lively in themselves, they presumably originate from a genuine satiric source. Housman's suggestion of a lost line after 2. 169 is much more plausible. A less convincing case is 8. 159 ff.:

> obvius adsiduo Syrophoenix udus amomo
> currit, Idymaeae Syrophoenix incola portae
> hospitis adfectu dominum regemque salutat.

Housman admits that after the subject has been repeated by epanalepsis, the verb *salutat* is not wanted; he suggests that a line may have fallen out after 160. Leo's *salutans* had independently occurred to him (second edition, p. li), but this plausible idea is not recorded in the apparatus.

Something has fallen out at 3. 109, where *P* reads 'praeterea sanctum nihil ab inguine tutum', and various stop-gaps have been tried by manuscripts and editors. Housman himself printed *nihil aut tibi ab inguine*, but Juvenal does not elide at the trochaic caesura of the fourth foot. He made a more interesting supplement at 3. 203 ff. (describing the poor man's modest furniture):

> lectus erat Codro Procula minor, urceoli sex
> ornamentum abaci, nec non et parvulus infra
> cantharus et recubans sub eodem marmore Chiron.

Here the scholiast refers to marble statuettes; on the other hand, marble is too grand for the sideboard, and in any case now irrelevant. C. Valesius proposed *sub eo de marmore* (which gives a weak demonstrative), Housman much more convincingly *sub eodem e marmore*. As an alternative I have toyed with *rupto de marmore*, to underline the tawdry appearance of the man's ornaments.

Housman's text brackets 17 lines as interpolations, but he was responsible for none of these deletions himself: see 3. 113, 3. 281, 5. 66, 6. 188, 8. 124, 8. 258, 9. 119, 11. 99, 11. 161, 11. 165–6, 12. 50–1, | 13. 90, 13. 166, 14. 208–9 (as well as 6. 126, which is poorly attested, and 6. 346–8, which have to go if the Oxford fragment is accepted). At 7. 50ff. he considers:

> nam si discedas, [laqueo tenet ambitiosi
> consuetudo mali], tenet insanabile multos
> scribendi cacoethes et aegro in corde senescit;

but to say no more, after the general *discedas* there is an anticlimax at *multos* (at *BICS* suppl. 51 (1988), 99f. (above, pp. 246f.) I argue that something has been displaced by line 51). He rightly suspects 8. 134 'de quocumque voles proavum tibi sumito libro', but does not notice that Ribbeck had questioned the line. He plausibly casts doubt on 8. 223 ('facetiarum lepori officere mihi videtur'), 13. 153 (see above), and 14. 119 (which had already been questioned by Duff).

Housman often makes conjectures where it would be better to posit an interpolation. There is a striking instance at 6. 63ff. (on the reactions of women to the dancer Bathyllus):

> chironomon Ledam molli saltante Bathyllo
> Tuccia vesicae non imperat, Apula gannit,
> sicut in amplexu, subito et miserabile longum;
> attendit Thymele: Thymele tunc rustica discit.

Here Housman transposed *gannit* and *longum*, awarding himself two asterisks, but Guyet's deletion of 65 seems certain; the conjecture was not known to me when I made it independently in *JRS* 52 (1962), 235 (above, p. 22). The impossible *miserabile longum* is removed more economically than by Housman; the proper names are put in a pointed relationship (add this to the instances collected at *BICS* suppl. 51 (1988), 95 (above, p. 240)); and *sicut in amplexu* gives the plodding explanation of *gannit* that is characteristic of a gloss.

Juvenal says that famous ancestors are of no avail if you behave disgracefully in front of their statues (8. 1ff.):

> stemmata quid faciunt, quid prodest, Pontice, longo
> sanguine censeri, pictos ostendere vultus
> maiorum et stantis in curribus Aemilianos
> et Curios iam dimidios umerosque minorem
> Corvinum et Galbam auriculis nasoque carentem,
> quis fructus generis tabula iactare capaci
> Corvinum, posthac multa contingere virga
> fumosos equitum cum dictatore magistros
> si coram Lepidis male vivitur?

7

In 7 Housman proposed *pontifices* for *Corvinum* (ineptly repeated from 5) and accepted Withof's *posse ac* for the meaningless *posthac*; but it is simpler to omit 7 with Ψ, and better still to delete 6–8 with Guyet and Jachmann (for the arguments see Courtney). It may seem inconsequential to say 'what avails it to boast of the Curii when you live badly in front of the Aemilii?' | (cf. Courtney, p. 384); but for such a distribution of examples see Nisbet and Hubbard on Horace, *Odes* 1. 7. 10.

At 8. 108 ff. Juvenal describes how extortionate governors loot even the most trifling possessions:

> nunc sociis iuga pauca boum, grex parvus equarum,
> et pater armenti capto eripietur agello,
> ipsi deinde Lares, si quod spectabile signum,
> si quis in aedicula deus unicus; haec etenim sunt
> pro summis, nam sunt haec maxima. despicias tu
> forsitan imbellis Rhodios unctamque Corinthon:
> despicias merito.

Housman rightly objected to the *inanis strepitus verborum* at *haec etenim sunt | pro summis, nam sunt haec maxima*; he proposed *quis sunt haec maxima, despicias tu | forsitan. imbellis Rhodios unctamque Corinthon | despicias merito*. That disrupts the natural sequence *despicias . . . Corinthon: despicias merito* (as does Manso's deletion of 111 *si quis . . .* 112 *despicias tu*). It seems best to delete *haec etenim . . . haec maxima* and to restore the metre by something like *deus unus* (thus Heinecke and Heinrich).

At 8. 199 ff. the degenerate nobleman becomes a *retiarius*, who is worse than other kinds of gladiator:

>   et illic
> dedecus urbis habes, nec murmillonis in armis
> nec clipeo Gracchum pugnantem aut falce supina;
> damnat enim tales habitus, sed damnat et odit,
> nec galea faciem abscondit: movet ecce tridentem.

Line 202 is absurdly repetitive (while *sed* is meaningless); if it is deleted (thus Ruperti), the pieces of equipment are set against each other in Juvenal's usual manner. But Housman incredibly transposes *sed damnat et odit* and *movet ecce tridentem*, thereby destroying the climax.

At 11. 167 f. Housman proposed *nervi* in the apparatus for *Veneris*, and *ramitis* in the text for *divitis* (p. xxx 'the conjecture of which I expect to hear most evil'); but it may be enough to delete with Jachmann the irrelevant 168 f. 'maior tamen ista voluptas I alterius sexus' (*NGG* (1943), 216 ff.). At 15. 97 f. 'huius enim quod nunc agitur miserabile debet I exemplum esse cibi sicut modo dicta mihi gens' Housman proposed *si cui* for *sicut* (accepting the poorly attested *tibi* for *cibi*); but the lines are nonsense (see Courtney), and should be deleted with Guyet. Consider again 16. 17 f. (on the alleged advantages of military justice) 'iustissima centurionum I cognitio est igitur de milite, nec mihi derit I ultio, si iustae defertur causa querellae'. Here Housman proposed *inquit* for the meaningless *igitur*; I believe that the simplest solution is to delete 18, assigning the thought to a centurion (*BICS* suppl. 51 (1988), 109 (above, p. 259)). |

Sometimes where a difficulty had been solved by deletion, Housman turns a blind eye to the problem. There is an interesting case at 1. 81 ff. where Juvenal is saying that wickedness is now worse than ever before:

> ex quo Deucalion nimbis tollentibus aequor
> navigio montem ascendit sortesque poposcit
> paulatimque anima caluerunt mollia saxa
> et maribus nudas ostendit Pyrrha puellas,
> quidquid agunt homines, votum timor ira voluptas   85
> gaudia discursus nostri farrago libelli est.
> et quando uberior vitiorum copia?

Lines 85-6 are untrue, disruptive, and produce a top-heavy sentence; they were rightly deleted by the neglected Scholte (with the familiar change to *ecquando* at 87). E. Harrison independently made the same proposal at the Cambridge Philological Society in 1920, but though his colleague Housman was present he did not express dissent either then or later (*CR* 51 (1937), 55).

Housman disregarded many other proposals for deletion, or mentioned them in the apparatus when he might have marked them in the text. I select some notable cases in a list that in no way aims at completeness:[9] 1. 14 (Dobree), 1. 137-8 (Ribbeck), 3. 104 (Jahn), 3. 242 (Pinzger), 4. 17 (Ribbeck), 4. 78 (Heinrich), 5. 63 (Ribbeck), 6. 138, 359, 395 (Scholte), 6. 530 (Paldamus), 7. 15 (Pinzger), 7. 93 (Markland), 7. 135 (cod. U), 9. 5 (Guyet), 10. 146 (Pinzger), 10. 323 (Heinrich), 10. 365-6 (Guyet), 13. 236 (Jahn), 15. 107 *nec enim*... 108 *putant* (Francke). Since Housman's edition deletions have been made by G. Jachmann (*NGG* (1943), 187 ff.), U. Knoche (who usually expelled

---

[9] See also E. Courtney's interesting study, *BICS* 22 (1975), 147 ff. He considers 40 lines 'pretty certainly spurious' (p. 160), but does not include a fair number of interpolations that I should regard as likely or at least possible.

the wrong lines), and M. D. Reeve (note especially *CR*, NS 20 (1970),
135 f. for the excision of 10. 356 'orandum est ut sit mens sana in
corpore sano'). I have made some further suggestions at *JRS* 52 (1962),
233 ff. (above, pp. 19 ff.); here I revive two points about Hannibal that
have not attracted much attention. 10. 148 ff. 'hic est quem non capit
Africa Mauro | percussa Oceano Niloque admota tepenti, | rursus ad
Aethiopum populos aliosque elephantos'. Line 150 gives an unconvincing asyndeton (not solved by Astbury's *rursum et ad*), a false suggestion that Hannibal's empire extended far south, and a cryptic
reference to 'other elephants'; a concurrence of oddities should always
arouse suspicion. 10. 159 ff. 'vincitur idem | nempe et in exilium prae-
ceps fugit atque ibi magnus | mirandusque cliens sedet ad praetoria
regis, | donec Bithyno libeat vigilare tyranno'. Line 160 prosaically fills
up a gap in the story, *nempe* is used elsewhere by the interpolator
(3. 95, 13. 166), and *magnus* shows a misunderstanding of | *mirandus*:
Hannibal was an object of astonishment not because he was a great
man but because he was a client.

Housman argues forcibly in his introduction for the recognition of
interpolations (pp. xxxi ff.), and he may have thought himself radical
compared with Buecheler, who deleted one line, and Friedlaender,
who deleted none at all (whereas Jahn had expelled 70). In practice he
was untypically conservative, largely because of the prevailing state of
opinion; and perhaps he preferred to show his ingenuity by verbal
conjecture. In fact in an author like Juvenal, where there is a significant
number of interpolations, nothing should be taken for granted; unsatisfactory lines can be deleted with much more confidence than in a
text that has not been tampered with. Many of the interpolations tend
to follow recurring patterns;[10] usually they are metrical explanations
rather than glosses turned into verse. There are a fair number of
marginal cases that may legitimately be questioned even where proof
is impossible; it is absurd to think that doubts cannot be raised unless
guilt can be proved. Textual critics are not simply concerned with
grammatical absurdities, and in the great classical authors they look for
something more felicitous than what satisfied a fourth-century schoolmaster. 'Improving the author' it is called by a curious *petitio principii*, but
Housman at least should have been free from that misconception.

Housman did well to use the scholia as a guide to the ancient text

---

[10] I give some instances at *JRS* 52 (1962), 233 f. (above, pp. 19 f.); see also E. Courtney,
BICS 22 (1975), 161. For a more general treatment of the typology of interpolations see
R. J. Tarrant, *TAPA* 117 (1987), 281 ff.

(p. xxviii 'our purest source of knowledge'), but sometimes he may attach too much significance to imprecise or ambiguous comments.[11] At 4. 5 ff. Juvenal says that Crispinus's riches do not matter:

> quid refert igitur quantis iumenta fatiget
> porticibus, quanta nemorum vectetur in umbra,
> iugera quot vicina foro, quas emerit aedes?
> nemo malus felix, minime corruptor et idem   8
> incestus, cum quo nuper vittata iacebat
> sanguine adhuc vivo terram subitura sacerdos.

For 8 *minime* Housman read *qum sit* on the basis of the scholia (joining the two sentences together); but there is no need to pursue his reasoning, as he virtually recanted in the second edition (p. xv). The simplest solution is to delete 8 with Jahn; the point is not the unhappiness of the wicked but the general contempt in which they are held. The interpolator failed to appreciate that *incestus* was the postponed subject of *fatiget*, *vectetur*, *emerit*, and so introduced a new line; for similar misunderstandings on his part see *BICS* Suppl. 51 (1988), 97 (above, p. 243). |

At 9. 133 f., after mentioning the homosexuals who flock to Rome, Juvenal proceeds:

>   altera maior
> spes superest: tu tantum erucis inprime dentem.
> gratus eris, tu tantum erucis inprime dentem.

Thus the Pithoeanus, but the repetition is intolerable; the vulgate tradition omitted the last line. In 1889 (*Classical Papers*, 107 f.) Housman confidently proposed *derit amator* for *altera maior* (omitting the last line and making metrical adjustments before *derit*); he supplied one of his unconvincing palaeographical justifications (*derit* turns into *diter*, and 'the difference between *diteramator* and *alteramaior* is not worth considering'). In his edition he takes seriously the scholiast's comment 'multos inberbes habes tibi crescentes' (which previously he had waved aside); he now supplies *spes superest: turbae properat quae crescere molli* | *gratus eris*. But great obscurities will remain (see Courtney), notably the need to provide a transition to 135 *haec exempla para felicibus*.

Juvenal's slave, unlike the rich man's, will be home-born, so that you can order your drink in Latin (11. 147 f.):

> non Phryx aut Lycius, non a mangone petitus
> quisquam erit et magno; cum posces, posce Latine.

[11] E. Courtney, *BICS* 13 (1966), 41 ff.

For *et magno* (Ψ) *P* reads *in magno* (which would have to mean 'when you ask for a pint'); neither reading is convincing. Housman proposed and printed *qui steterit magno*, a conjecture that goes back at least to 1891 (cf. Manilius 1, p. xxxvii); he cites the scholium 'quales vendunt care manciparii', but that may simply be an attempt to interpret the vulgate reading ('sought at a great price'). In fact the emphasis should not be on the price of the rich man's slaves but on their alien origin. G. Giangrande proposed *Inachio* (*Eranos*, 63 (1965), 3 ff.); that does not seem a natural word for 'Greek' in so prosaic a context (E. Courtney, *BICS* 13 (1966), 41), but there are attractions in some epithet that balances *Phryx, Lycius, Latine.*

Violent revenge on the trickster will bring you odium (13. 178f.):

> sed corpore trunco
> invidiosa dabit minimus solacia sanguis.

Naturally Housman saw that *minimus* is meaningless (cf. Manilius 1, p. lxvi); he proposed and printed *solum*, positing the loss of the word before *solacia*. He cited the scholiast 'nihil inde lucri habebis nisi invidiosam defensionem'; but this may simply be a loose paraphrase. His alternative proposals *nimium* (with *invidiosa*) or *damni* seem more forceful, but one really expects an adjective or participle to balance *trunco*. Wakefield proposed *missus*, Martyn *nimius* (with a cod. det.), but I might have expected something livelier on the lines of *saliens*, 'spurting'. It is a case for the obelus. |

At 14. 267ff. Juvenal addresses the merchant who suffers at sea while conveying saffron from Cilicia:

> Corycia semper qui puppe moraris
> atque habitas, coro semper tollendus et austro,
> perditus †ac vilis† sacci mercator olentis.

Housman saw that *P*'s *ac vilis* does not go well with *perditus* (while Ψ's *a siculis* is obvious nonsense). He conjectured and printed *ac similis*, i.e. the merchant turns as yellow as his cargo; he cited the scholiast's *tu foetide*, but that may simply be a muddled gloss on *sacci olentis*. In fact seasickness seems too temporary an affliction to characterize the man (especially in view of the repeated *semper*); Housman says that he is called *perditus* because he cries *perii* in a storm (Manilius 1, p. xxxvi), but again one looks for a more permanent attribute. At *JRS* 52 (1962), 237 (above, p. 27) I proposed *perditus articulis* (he is arthritic from living in a damp ancient ship); cf. Persius 1. 23 'articulis quibus et dicas

cute perditus "ohe"' (where *articulis* is Madvig's necessary conjecture
for *auriculis*).

Some other asterisked proposals fail to convince, though they
usually contribute to the argument. 6. 50f. 'paucae adeo Cereris vittas
contingere dignae I quarum non timeat pater oscula'. Here Housman's
teretis vittas is too mild to balance the following clause, and Giangrande's *Cereris victus* seems to give the required point (*Eranos*, 13
(1965), 26ff.); Housman himself had suggested something like *Cereris
contingere munera dignae* (second edition, p. xlvi). 6. 194ff. 'quotiens
lascivum intervenit illud I ζωὴ καὶ ψυχή, modo sub lodice relictis I uteris
in turba': Housman saw that the endearments of octogenarian women
cannot be described as 'recently left under the blanket'. He regarded as
certain (p. xxx) his own *ferendis*, 'only to be endured', and it is undoubtedly on the right lines (see Courtney); but I prefer my own
loquendis, which may combine better with *uteris* (*BICS* suppl. 51
(1988), 96f. (above, pp. 242f.)). At 9. 118 Housman rejects *cum... tunc*
as a solecism, only to produce the questionable elision *tum est his*.
12. 12ff. '(taurus) nec finitima nutritus in herba, I laeta sed ostendens
Clitumni pascua sanguis I iret et a grandi cervix ferienda ministro' (*iret
et grandi P*). Housman pointed to the ambiguity of *sanguis iret* of the
walking bull, and proposed *et grandi cervix iret ferienda ministro*; but the
origin of the bull was shown by his colour rather than his blood.
Castiglioni proposed *grandis* for *sanguis*, and I have considered *tergus*;
that leaves Housman's problem about *a* with the gerundive (not elsewhere in Juvenal), especially as the scholiast glosses by dative *sacerdoti*.
13. 47ff. (on the small number of gods in Saturn's day) 'contentaque
sidera paucis I numinibus miserum urguebant Atlanta minori I pondere;
nondum †aliquis sortitus triste profundi I imperium Sicula torvus cum
coniuge Pluton'. Here the meaningless *aliquis* is omitted by *P* and is
presumably an interpolation. Housman supplied *imi*, but a proper
name would be more forceful; I have suggested *Erebi* (*BICS* suppl. 51
(1988), 108 (above, p. 258)). I refrain from discussing 14. 71, where |
Housman ingeniously proposed 'si facit ut civis sit idoneus'; I once
doubted this (*JRS* 52 (1962), 237 (above, p. 26)), as Courtney does for
different reasons, but am now unable to make up my mind.

I turn now to those of Housman's conjectures that are confined to
the apparatus. He points to the faulty tense at 2. 167f. 'nam si mora
longior urbem I †indulsit pueris, non umquam derit amator' (the problem is not solved by Clausen's *indulget*, as the verb has jumped from
165 *indulsisse*); he suggests *praebuerit*, and I have tried *induerit* (*BICS*

suppl. 51 (1988), 91 (above, p. 234)). 8. 47ff. 'tamen ima plebe Quiritem I facundum invenies, solet hic defendere causas I nobilis indocti; veniet de plebe togata I qui iuris nodos et legum aenigmata solvat'; here Housman suggests *pube togata* (to avoid a pointless contrast with *ima plebe*), but he does not mention *togatus* (Scriverius), which elegantly balances *Quiritem*.[12] At 10. 184 'huic quisquam vellet servire deorum?' he reasonably suggested *nollet* to sustain the irony. A more intractable place is 10. 326f. '†erubuit nempe haec ceu fastidita repulso (*repulsa* Ψ) I nec Stheneboea minus quam Cressa excanduit'; here Housman proposed *coepto* for *nempe haec*, but a line has probably fallen out (Markland, Courtney). At 12. 78f. 'non sic †igitur mirabere portus I quos natura dedit' (on the harbour at Ostia), Housman saw unlike some editors that *igitur* is meaningless in the context; his *similes* is too restrictive and his *ullos* too dull, and I have tentatively considered *veteres* (above, p. 257).

Housman does not cite nearly enough conjectures by others; here I record a few cases of particular interest. Jahn placed 3. 12-16 (on Egeria's grove) to follow 3. 20; this is a necessary transposition, but either something has been lost after 11 (Ribbeck), or 11 should be marked as a parenthesis (my own solution, *BICS* suppl. 51 (1988), 92f. (above, pp. 236f.)). At 3. 260f. 'obtritum volgi perit omne cadaver I more animae' Eremita proposed the adverb *vulgo*, 'indiscriminately'; *vulgus* would refer to the common people in general, not like *turba* to a particular crowd. 6. 44 'quem totiens texit perituri cista Latini'. In this bedroom farce Latinus, who owns the chest, should be the injured husband rather than the concealed lover; Palmer's *redituri* (cited by Owen) is worth reviving (cf. Hor. *Serm.* 1. 2. 127 *vir rure recurrat*, etc.). 8. 219ff. (the matricide Orestes is favourably contrasted with Nero) 'nullis aconita propinquis I miscuit, in scaena numquam cantavit Orestes, I Troica non scripsit'. Weidner's witty *Oresten* was ignored by Housman, and the conjecture had to be made again by C. P. Jones, *CR*, NS 22 (1972), 313. At 10. 90f. 'visne salutari sicut Seianus, habere I tantundem' Lachmann proposed *avere* (cited by Jahn), which balances *salutari* much better. The verb is normally confined to the imperative, but for the infinitive cf. Mart. 9. 6. 4 'non vis, Afer, havere: vale'. 11. 96f. 'sed nudo latere et parvis frons aerea lectis I vile coronati caput ostendebat aselli'. Henninius proposed *vite*, a certain emendation that I has been ignored; he cited the paraphrase at Hyginus, *Fab.* 274

[12] In the same passage P. G. McC. Brown plausibly deletes 'solet hic defendere causas I nobilis indocti' (*CQ*, NS 22 (1972), 374).

'antiqui autem nostri in lectis tricliniaribus in fulcris capita asellorum vite alligata habuerunt'. 13. 43 ff. (the simple life of the gods in Saturn's time) 'nec puer Iliacus formonsa nec Herculis uxor l ad cyathos, et iam siccato nectare tergens l bracchia Vulcanus Liparaea nigra taberna'. Housman records and ought to have accepted Schurtzfleisch's *saccato* (the nectar's sediment is strained as with wine); he mentions the scholiast's note 'exsiccato faeculento aut liquefacto', where the second word gives the clue.[13] I have recorded some other neglected conjectures, and put forward some new ones, at *JRS* 52 (1962), 233 ff. and *BICS* suppl. 51 (1988), 86 ff. (above, pp. 18 ff. and 227 ff.).

Where it is a question of weighing one reading against another, Housman's decisions are usually difficult to refute. But at 1. 2 he reads 'rauci Theseide Cordi' (thus *P*), where *Ψ* offers *Codri*; *Codrus* is not only a type-name for a bad poet (from Virg. *Ecl.* 7. 22), but combines pointedly with *Theseide* to suggest the kings of early Athens. At 1. 125 f. a client receives the *sportula* on behalf of his wife, who is alleged to be resting in a closed litter: '"Galla mea est", inquit, "citius dimitte. moraris? l profer, Galla, caput. noli vexare, quiescet."' The scholiast assigns *profer, Galla, caput* to the cashier (cf. p. xliv), and this leads better to *noli vexare*; it also seems best to accept *Ψ*'s *quiescit* rather than to derive an idiomatic future from *P*'s *quiescaet* ('don't disturb her because she is resting now' is more to the point than 'if you disturb her, you'll find that she is resting'). At 7. 114 Housman follows *P* in calling the charioteer 'russati . . . Lacernae', but the cloak used in country drives (1. 62) was perhaps too cumbrous for a race; *Ψ*'s *Lacertae* ('Lizard'), is an excellent name for a quick mover (Courtney cites *ILS* 5293), and as lizards are usually green there is a pointed combination with *russati*. At 8. 4 f. (on a nobleman's battered statues) Housman reads 'et Curios iam dimidios umeroque minorem l Corvinum'. Here 'impaired as to the shoulders' (*umeros P*) is better than 'diminished by a shoulder' (*umero* cod. det.): a statue does not lose a shoulder without losing an arm as well.

Even when he does not debate the text, Housman sometimes gives explanations that are open to challenge. I do not believe that 1. 28 *aestivum . . . aurum* refers to light-weight rings for summer wear (for the use of the adjective cf. 4. 108, also on Crispinus); or that 1. 144 *intestata senectus* means that old age among patrons is unattested (I delete 144 *subitae . . .* 145 *et*); or that 3. 4 f. *gratum litus amoeni* l *secessus* illustrates a

---

[13] Martyn attributes *exsaccato* to Schurtzfleisch and *saccato* to myself, an honour I never claimed; the proposal was already known to J. Jessen, *Philologus*, 47. 1 (1888), 320, to whom it is assigned in Housman's edition of 1905.

genitive of quality[14] (I propose *limen*): for all these points I refer to the discussion at *BICS* suppl. 51 (1988), 86ff. (above, pp. 227ff.). At 1. 149 *omne in praecipiti* | *vitium stetit* Housman interprets 'vice has come to its extreme limit' (*Classical Papers*, 613f.); that does not convey the precarious position of vice, a thought that leads to the following *utere velis*, 'use all your energies to attack it'.[15] 7. 61f. *aeris inops, quo nocte dieque* | *corpus eget*. Housman comments that the body needs food night and day rather than money, and mentions sympathetically Ribbeck's *quom*; but this spoils the paradox that we are using up resources even while we sleep.

No critique of Housman's *Juvenal* can ignore his extraordinary style of debate. His admirers sometimes imply that his opponents deserved all they got, but his gibes are scattered too widely for that defence to be tenable. He could be generous to the schoolmaster S. T. Collins, who at 16. 25 *quis tam procul absit ab urbe?* (of a defending pleader), irrefutably proposed *adsit* (p. lvii 'we ought all to be ashamed that the correction was not made before'). He was indulgent to J. D. Duff's 'unpretending school-edition' (p. xxix) and to the commentary of H. L. Wilson, who quoted his own work respectfully and made no claims of his own (*Classical Papers*, 611ff.). But to professional rivals he was persistently offensive, and not just to Owen but to Buecheler and Leo (even Jahn among the dead); and the effect on rising scholars was inhibiting. He rebukes non-critics who at Propertius 3. 15. 14 read *molliaque immittens* (v. l. *immites*) *fixit in ora manus* (p. xii); that must be a reprisal against Phillimore, who in his 1901 edition had criticized Housman's boldness in conjecture. He denounces the author of the *Thesaurus* article who by relying on Buecheler's text had failed to pick up *aeluros* at Juv. 15. 7 (pp. lvf., repeating his Cambridge inaugural of twenty years before); his solemn rodomontade was absurdly disproportionate to its object[16] ('this is the felicity of the house of bondage' etc.), and caused lasting offence. This reversion to the manners of previous centuries was due not just to a love of truth, 'the faintest of the passions', as he called it, though error grated on him more than on most; the explanation must surely lie in an underlying unhappiness[17] that found a more creditable outlet in his poetry. All this makes one

---

[14] Housman cannot have found the passage straightforward: in 1900 he had actually considered taking *amoeni secessus* as a nominative plural (*Classical Papers*, 518).

[15] F. O. Copley, *AJP* 62 (1941), 219ff.; D. A. Kidd, *CQ* 14 (1964), 103ff.

[16] See esp. Edmund Wilson, *The Triple Thinkers* (London, 1938), 83ff. = C. Ricks (ed.), *A. E. Housman: A Collection of Critical Essays* (Englewood Cliffs, NJ, 1968), 14ff.

[17] For a realistic view see R. P. Graves, *A. E. Housman, The Scholar-Poet* (Oxford, 1981).

sceptical of the claim that Housman was uniquely objective; less
original scholars may find it easier 'to suppress self-will', to use his own
phrase (Manilius 5, p. xxxv).

None of this dislodges Housman from his position: he continues to
impress alike by his subtle and original poetry, now more justly
valued,[18] the energy of his prose style (especially by academic standards), and his formidable intellectual and rhetorical powers. The
Juvenal remains the most stimulating introduction to textual criticism
that there is, and a classic | demonstration of a particularly English
mode of scholarship, impatient of theory, sparing of words, displaying
no more learning than necessary, going for the vital spot, empirical,
commonsensical, concrete, sardonic. Housman himself said that 'a
textual critic engaged upon his business is not at all like Newton investigating the motion of the planets: he is much more like a dog hunting for fleas';[19] but the irony should not mislead. Though he himself
had felicity of instinct (as every good editor must), he probably showed
it less persistently than some other great critics.[20] It is his lucidity of
mind and argumentative power that place him next to Bentley, and
one can never disagree without being conscious that something may
have been missed.

Housman's dominance is so great[21] that it is difficult to avoid the
cult of personality, but eulogies concentrate on the most brilliant feats
without looking at an edition as a whole. In textual criticism there are
horses for courses, and Housman found Juvenal well-suited to his
talents: the style was vigorous and incisive, but it did not strain normal
Latin usage. Even so, his solutions were often unconvincing, and not
just because the edition was undertaken in haste, 'for the relief of a
people sitting in darkness' (p. xxxvi); he had twenty-five years to
change his mind before the second edition, though his manner of
argument may not have made retraction easy. It is not that he was too
acute for his author, the criticism that used to be orthodox; as he
emphasized himself in his London 'Introductory Lecture',[22] the great
classical writers had a standard of finish that is lacking in more recent

[18] See C. Ricks (above, n. 16), 1 ff. (with other contributions to this collection), and
(above, n. 4), 7 ff.

[19] Carter (above, n. 4), 132 = Ricks (above, n. 4), 326.

[20] This point is made by G. P. Goold, *BICS* suppl. 51 (1988), 28.

[21] For two notable recent assessments of Housman as a scholar see C. O. Brink,
English Classical Scholarship (Cambridge, 1986), 168 ff.; H. D. Jocelyn, *Philology and Education* (Liverpool Classical Papers, 1; Liverpool, 1988), 22 ff.

[22] Carter (above, n. 4), 9 ff. = Ricks (above, n. 4), 265 f.

literature. The truth of the matter is that in textual criticism, as in other scholarly activities, you win some and you lose some: new evidence is noticed, fresh arguments are devised, and no edition is sacrosanct. We should not surrender to Housman's authority, and assume that nothing remains to be done: there is no greater incentive for finding corruptions in a text than the fact that corruptions have already been found.

18

The Dating of Seneca's Tragedies, with Special Reference to *Thyestes*[1]

SENECA's tragedies are notoriously difficult to date.[2] They are sometimes included in special subjects on Neronian literature, but according to the preface of Tarrant's *Agamemnon* (p. 7), they might equally
well be regarded as Claudian, Gaian, or even Tiberian. I have not
myself been able to attain a level of scepticism that Tarrant in his
Thyestes has now abandoned (p. 10), but one must remain conscious at
every turn that there are few certainties in this debate. In the first
section of this paper much of the material is tralatician, but I have tried
to identify the more important arguments and to put the emphasis my
own way. In the later sections some of the observations on *Thyestes*
may be less familiar.

I. THE CHRONOLOGICAL FRAMEWORK

It will be convenient to divide the reign of Claudius into two parts:
first, 41–8, when Messalina was empress and Seneca was in his long
exile in Corsica; second, 49–54, when Agrippina was empress and
Seneca was tutor to her son Nero. The reign of Nero may be divided in
the same way: first, 54–62, when Seneca held a dominant though latterly
declining position; second, the period from his retirement in 62 till his
forced suicide in 65 in the aftermath of the Pisonian conspiracy. The
plays in the corpus (excluding the clearly spurious *Octavia*) are *Hercules
Furens, Troades, Phoenissae, Medea, Phaedra, Oedipus, Agamemnon*,

---

[1] This article is based on a paper read to Seminar Boreas on 27 Nov. 1987 in the
University of Leeds. I am grateful to all who contributed to the discussion.

[2] See esp. Th. Birt, *NJA* 27 (1911), 352 ff.; K. Münscher, *Philologus* suppl. 16. 1 (1922),
84 ff.; O. Herzog, *RhM* 77 (1928), 51 ff. (with bibliography of earlier work); O. Zwierlein,
Prolegomena zu einer kritischen Ausgabe der Tragödien Senecas (*AAWM*, 1983, 3), 233 ff. For
summaries see the introductions to Fantham's *Troades* (9 ff.) and Tarrant's *Thyestes*
(10 ff.).

Proceedings of the Leeds International Latin Seminar, 6 (1990), 95–114.

Thyestes, *Hercules Oetaeus* (the order in the *codex Etruscus*). Our aim is to slot these plays into a chronological framework.

The most generally accepted piece of evidence comes from the | mock-dirge in the *Apocolocyntosis* that sardonically bewails the death of Claudius: 'fundite fletus, edite planctus, | resonet tristi clamore forum ...' (12. 3. 1 f.). In these two lines alone there are imitations of *Troades* 131 'fundite fletus, satis Hector habet' and *Hercules Furens* 1108 'resonet maesto clamore chaos'; and the resemblances do not stop there.[3] Therefore both *Troades* and *Hercules Furens* were composed by 54; for the skit must have been written soon after the death of Claudius. Some confirmation is provided by the reference to the *lusus Troiae* at *Troades* 777 ff. 'nec stato lustri die | sollemne referens Troici lusus sacrum, | puer citatas nobilis turmas ages'. Nero participated in the *lusus Troiae* when he was 9 at the memorable secular games of 47 (Tacitus, *Annals* 11. 11. 2), and Seneca is likely to have made his tactful allusion after he became the boy's mentor in 49. A few years later Nero would no longer be flattered by references to the accomplishments of his childhood,[4] and that would certainly be true after he became emperor in 54.

I turn now to *Medea*. In her opening monologue the embittered heroine prays for world-wide upheaval, including the joining of the two seas at the Isthmus of Corinth (35 f.). A reference has been seen to Nero's abortive attempt at a canal (Suetonius, *Nero* 19. 2),[5] but that belonged to the very end of his reign; in fact such an allusion would be tactless, and the project had already been mooted by Julius Caesar and Gaius (Pliny, *Natural History* 4. 10). Much more significant evidence is provided by the chorus on navigation, which looks forward to the conquest of Ocean (375 ff.):

> venient annis saecula seris,
> quibus Oceanus vincula rerum
> laxet et ingens pateat tellus,
> Tethysque novos detegat orbes,
> nec sit terris ultima Thule.

As has often been pointed out, this looks like a compliment to Claudius's invasion of Britain in AD 43. It need not be an immediately contemporary compliment, but at least one thing may be affirmed with confidence: after the death of Claudius in 54 Seneca would not go out

---

[3] O. Weinreich, *Senecas Apocolocyntosis* (Berlin, 1923), 112 ff.; Münscher (n. 2), 98 ff.

[4] Herzog (n. 2), 93 suggests AD 53 for *Troades*, the date of Nero's speech *pro Iliensibus*; but by that date the *lusus Troiae* might seem less topical.

[5] Thus for instance W. M. Calder III, *CJ* 72 (1976–7), 3.

of his way to write an inorganic passage that could only have been taken as a tribute to the dead emperor. I attach particular importance to this kind of argument: we should look not only for allusions to recent happenings but for remarks that would be implausibly tactless after a particular date.

We may next ask: is it more likely that *Medea* was written in Corsica between 43 and 48 or in Rome between 49 and 54? The lines | on the conquest of Ocean are at variance with most of the ode,[6] which is a conventional denunciation of navigation, and one might be tempted to argue that they are a later addition, tacked on in gratitude after Seneca was restored. But that is quite uncertain: even when in exile Seneca was anxious to please Claudius (as is shown by his obsequious *Consolatio ad Polybium*), and even after his restoration he might have written a conventional ode with a flattering afterthought. Though Corsica gave Seneca ample leisure for composition, the writing of plays was perhaps a metropolitan activity that needed the stimulus of public applause; it is not natural to argue with Herzog[7] that recitations could have been organized by family and friends. It also makes sense if the plays were written when Seneca was Nero's tutor, and interested in the role of poetry in moral education; after 54 he might be too busy and too distinguished (for drama was a frivolity compared with philosophy). I add for what it is worth that in 51-2[8] Seneca's brother Gallio was proconsul in Corinth, where he showed a wise indifference to the activities of certain trouble-makers.[9] That would be quite a good moment for Seneca's Corinthian play.

At this point the sceptic will say: 'Some of the plays seem to have been written before the death of Claudius, but why should they not belong as early as Tiberius?' That leads us to a passage of Quintilian cited by Cichorius:[10] 'memini iuvenis admodum inter Pomponium ac Senecam etiam praefationibus esse tractatum an "gradus eliminat" in tragoedia dici oportuisset' (8. 3. 31); these *praefationes* seem to have been part of the preliminaries of a recitation (cf. Pliny, *Epistulae* 1. 13. 2 'an iam recitator intraverit, an dixerit praefationem'). Quintilian heard this debate when he was *iuvenis admodum*; as he was born about 33, this might point to a time about 51-3. Seneca returned from exile in 49,

---

[6] D. Henry and B. Walker, *CPh.* 62 (1967), 180.

[7] Herzog (n. 2), 60.

[8] *PIR*² I. 757; A. Plassart, *REG* 80 (1967), 372ff.

[9] Acts 18: 17 καὶ οὐδὲν τούτων τῷ Γαλλίωνι ἔμελεν.

[10] C. Cichorius, *Römische Studien* (Leipzig and Berlin, 1922), 426ff.; Zwierlein (n. 2), 244f.

Pomponius from governing Germany in 50–1. The recitations in question were presumably those of new plays; therefore Seneca was writing at least some of his plays in the early 50s. The argument is cumulative: one must be struck by the number of leads that converge on the later years of Claudius.

Here I mention briefly a false clue.[11] Seneca's enemies alleged that he wrote more poetry after Nero developed an enthusiasm, that is to say after his accession: Tacitus, *Annals* 14. 53. 3 'obiciebant etiam eloquentiae laudem uni sibi adsciscere et carmina crebrius factitare postquam Neroni amor eorum venisset'. We need not believe an allegation of this kind, which might be very imprecise. More important, *carmina* is unlikely to refer to tragedies. There is no | evidence that Nero ever wrote in this genre, and a parallel passage clearly refers to lighter forms of verse: Tacitus, *Annals* 14. 16. 1 'ne tamen ludicrae tantum imperatoris artes notescerent, carminum quoque studium adfectavit, contractis quibus aliqua pangendi facultas necdum insignis erat'.

I come next to *Phaedra*. Here Hippolytus makes some trenchant remarks, modelled on Ovid (*Metamorphoses* 1. 144 ff.), on the degeneration of family relationships (555 ff.):

> a fratre frater, dextera gnati parens
> cecidit, maritus coniugis ferro iacet,
> perimuntque fetus impiae matres suos;
> taceo novercas: mitius nil est feris.

Of course some will see snide allusions to the Julio-Claudian court,[12] in particular the murder of Claudius by Agrippina in 54 and of Britannicus by Nero in 55; but as Roman audiences were quick to sense contemporary references, it is inconceivable that Seneca should have risked a *frisson* in the recitation-hall. Rather one must turn the argument on its head and say that the play antedates the deaths of Claudius and Britannicus. Similarly when Seneca says *vitioque potens regnat adulter* (987), that would surely be impossible in the early years of Nero, when there were rumours about his own relationship with Agrippina (Dio 61. 10. 3);[13] the probable falsity of such allegations does not rule out this argument.

That seems to put *Phaedra* back to the reign of Claudius; then the

---

[11] Birt (n. 2), 352 f.; Münscher (n. 2), 101 ff.; they are rebutted by Herzog (n. 2), 52 ff.

[12] This common approach is carried to extremes by J. D. Bishop, *Seneca's Daggered Stylus* (Beiträge zur klassischen Philologie, 168; 1985).

[13] Herzog (n. 2), 91.

adulter might suggest Silius, Messalina's lover, with whom she perished in 48. In the aftermath of her death, when it was now safe to talk, Seneca could have brooded on wicked women who framed innocent men, which is what Phaedra did to Hippolytus and Messalina (anyway by his way of it) to Seneca himself. One doubt remains over the reference to the malignity of stepmothers, *taceo novercas* (558, cited above). A commonplace, it is true, and central to the theme of the play, but difficult for a courtier to say at the exact moment when Agrippina was displacing Britannicus with her own son Nero. That might encourage us to put *Phaedra* as early as 49, the year before Claudius adopted Nero; but nothing is certain.

That brings us to *Agamemnon* and *Oedipus*, which share a notable feature: in the choruses Seneca devises new metres by modifying the standard Horatian lines.[14] It is difficult to dissociate these innovations from the theories of Caesius Bassus, who used the words *adiectio* and *detractio* to explain formations of this kind.[15] Bassus dedicated his treatise to Nero,[16] so it is sometimes argued that these | two plays should be put after the change of emperor in 54.[17] These metrical experiments were surely not Seneca's first attempt at tragic choruses, but we must not aim at too great precision: Bassus's ideas may have been current in the later years of Claudius, or he might have dedicated his treatise to Nero when he was still only a talented boy. I attach much more importance to the subject-matter of *Agamemnon*: the early years of Nero were not the time to write about a forceful wife who killed a triumphant king. Tiberius had executed a poet, perhaps Mamercus Scaurus, because he had reproached Agamemnon in a play:[18] that would be a small offence compared with hints of murder by the new Clytemnestra.

Similar considerations apply to *Oedipus*. When rumours began about the incest of Nero and Agrippina (Tacitus, *Annals* 14. 2), some time before her death in 59, that was not the best moment for a time-serving poet to write on such a theme. There is also the passage where Jocasta first invites Oedipus to kill her (1032ff.), and then speaks of

[14] See Tarrant's commentary, 372ff.
[15] F. Leo, *De Senecae Tragoediis Observationes Criticae* (Berlin, 1878),132f. attributed the theory to Varro. R. Heinze, *Die lyrischen Verse des Horaz* (*Verhandlungen der Sächsischen Akademie der Wissenschaften*, 70. 4; 1918), 21ff., and Münscher (n. 2), 86ff., point to new elaborations by Bassus.
[16] Rufinus, *GL* 6. 555. 22 'Bassus ad Neronem de iambico sic dicit. . . .'
[17] Münscher (n. 2), 88.
[18] Tac. *Ann.* 6. 29. 3; Suet. *Tib.* 61. 3.

striking her own womb (1038 f. 'hunc, dextra, hunc pete | uterum capacem, qui virum et gnatos tulit'); comparisons have been drawn with Agrippina's alleged last words to the centurion, 'ventrem feri' (Tacitus, *Annals* 14. 8. 5; cf. also *Octavia* 368 ff. 'caedis moriens illa ministrum | rogat infelix utero dirum | condat ut ensem; | "hic est hic est fodiendus" ait | "ferro, monstrum qui tale tulit"'). One interpreter[19] thinks that the lines in *Oedipus* were written not to rebuke but to amuse Nero, another talks of political codes, a third considers the possibility that the play was kept secret. Of course sinister hints must have been intended if the passage was written in the aftermath of Agrippina's murder, but there is no need for such an assumption; the scene is modelled on Sophocles,[20] and *ventrem feri* is a commonplace of declamation.[21] Once again the more credulous theories should be reversed: not only are the lines not politically motivated, but their appearance is evidence that the play was written before the death of Agrippina in 59.

II. INDISCRETIONS IN *THYESTES*?

We come now to *Thyestes*, which presents the most intriguing chronological problems of all. Here the corruption of courts is portrayed as nowhere outside Tacitus, and already in the second speech the Fury predicts the coming horrors (40 ff.):

> fratrem expavescat frater et natum parens
> natusque patrem, liberi pereant male, |
> peius tamen nascantur; immineat viro
> infesta coniunx, bella trans pontum vehant . . .

These lines are highly relevant to the development of the play, but in the first part of Nero's reign a more contemporary reference would inevitably be suspected. The brother that fears brother would be seen as Britannicus, who was murdered by Nero; the parent who fears the son would be Agrippina; the wife who threatens the husband would be Agrippina again. In the same way when Thyestes says later in the play 'venenum in auro bibitur—expertus loquor' (453), he would have

[19] W. M. Calder III, *CJ* 72 (1976–7), 5; J. D. Bishop, *CJ* 73 (1977–8), 292; J. H. W. G. Liebeschuetz, *Continuity and Change in Roman Religion* (Oxford, 1979), 164 f. For a summary see E. Lefèvre, *ANRW* 2. 32. 2. 1250 ff.

[20] O. Zwierlein, *Phaedra und ihre Vorbilder* (*AAWM* 1987, 5), 44 f., citing Soph. *OT* 1256 f.

[21] N. T. Pratt, *Seneca's Drama* (Chapel Hill, NC, and London, 1983), 191, citing Sen. *Contr.* 2. 5. 7 'caede ventrem ne tyrannicidas pariat'.

seemed to refer to Nero's poisoning of Britannicus in 55, so graphically described by Tacitus (*Annals* 13. 15. 3–16). It is impossible to believe that Seneca wrote such indiscreet passages when he was Nero's first minister.[22]

Even if we put the play back to the reign of Claudius, some difficulties still remain. Atreus is made to say 'ut nemo doceat fraudis et sceleris vias, | regnum docebit' (312 f.); if this was intended as a cautionary tale for the boy Nero, it seems a tactless thing to say when Seneca had just been brought back from exile. Perhaps the play should be assigned to the Corsican period, when Seneca could be brooding about *regnum* as he had known it under Tiberius, Gaius, and now Claudius. When the chorus praises the simple life uncorrupted by power (391 ff., 446 ff.), some have sensed the attitudes of the poet's own exile;[23] when Thyestes expresses hope and fear on his return (404 ff.), the mixture of moods could have something autobiographical about it. Yet if Seneca wrote the play in this early period, it is strange that the Fury should say 'ob scelera pulsi cum dabit patriam deus | in scelera redeant' (37 f.): we know from Cicero how sensitive exiles were about their experience. Messalina might not have liked the line about wives threatening husbands, and Claudius would certainly not have liked the line about transporting wars across the sea: 'bella trans pontum vehant' (43). Though one is reluctant to believe that Seneca's plays were written for secret circulation and private enjoyment, we have not yet found a time when *Thyestes* could have been recited without embarrassment.

III. FITCH'S BREAKTHROUGH

At this juncture I turn to the article by John G. Fitch on 'Sense-Pauses and Relative Dating in Seneca, Sophocles and Shakespeare' in *AJP* 102 (1981), 289 ff. He argues on stylistic and metrical grounds that *Thyestes* and *Phoenissae* were written later than the other plays. I | begin with a point that he makes relatively late in his paper but which seems the most decisive part of it.

It is well known that in Silver Age poetry the *o* at the end of a word is often shortened;[24] this happens with third-declension nouns like

---

[22] The point is taken by Herzog (n. 2), 71; but he sees a criticism of the regime written after or preferably before Seneca's period of power.

[23] Herzog (n. 2), 72 ff.

[24] Some material is collected by R. Hartenberger, *De o finali apud poetas Latinos ab Ennio usque ad Iuvenalem* (Diss. Bonn, 1911); but he does not draw enough distinctions about

imago, pronouns like *nemo*, first-person verbs like *cerno* or *videbo*, particles like *immo*, but not of course with ablatives like *servo*, except curiously with gerunds like *vincendo* (*Troades* 264) and *vigilando* (Juvenal 3. 232). For dating purposes I attach less importance to nouns or particles; here the final *o* is normally shortened in Seneca, and in the case of trisyllabic nominatives like *regio* it is always shortened; therefore the statistics will be distorted by the desirability of using particular words. Much more important evidence is provided by short final *o* in the first person singular of verbs, whether present or future. Here Fitch's figures for the licence do seem statistically significant: *Agamemnon* 1, *Oedipus* 1, *Troades* 2, *Phaedra* 4, *Medea* 5, *Hercules Furens* 5, *Thyestes* 18, *Phoenissae* 27. This observation must count as a notable breakthrough (Tarrant, *Thyestes* 11), especially in view of the difficulty of establishing other metrical variations as a criterion of date.[25]

Fitch also points out that changes of speaker in the middle of a line, if looked at as a proportion of all changes of speaker, are considerably more frequent in *Thyestes* than in the other plays; but he recognizes himself that the picture may be affected by the incidence of *antilabe* (cross-talk in half-lines), which is partly determined by the dramatic possibilities of the play.[26] He next turns to the incidence of all sense-pauses of a semicolon or more in the middle of a line; here the figures for internal pauses as a percentage of all pauses are *Agamemnon* 32.4, *Phaedra* 34.4, *Oedipus* 36.8, *Medea* 47.2, *Troades* 47.6, *Hercules Furens* 49, *Thyestes* 54.5, *Phoenissae* 57.2. These variations are less arresting than the discrepancy with final *o*, but they seem to be a sign of increasing flexibility of verse technique; Fitch points to comparable developments in Sophocles and Shakespeare. That tends to confirm one's instinct that the short *o*s are a sign of lateness rather than earliness; the Latin poets in general were moving towards greater laxity in this respect.

IV. THE CORONATION OF THYESTES

It is time to look at another historical allusion that may not have been correctly interpreted. After Atreus has bound the diadem round the

---

parts of speech and position in the line. See also D. Armstrong, *Philologus,* 130 (1986), 113f., 129ff.

[25] O. Zwierlein (n. 2), 233ff.

[26] Fitch himself cites H. D. F. Kitto, *AJP* 60 (1939), 178ff., who points to the limitations of such stylostatistics in determining the dates of Sophoclean plays.

head of his brother Thyestes (544 'imposita capiti vincla venerando |
gere'), the chorus remarks that even a king who bestows kingdoms on
others may himself be uneasy (599 ff.):

> ille qui donat diadema fronti,
> quem genu nixae tremuere gentes,
> cuius ad nutum posuere bella
> Medus et Phoebi propioris Indus
> et Dahae Parthis equitem minati,
> anxius sceptrum tenet et moventes
> cuncta divinat metuitque casus
> mobiles rerum dubiumque tempus.

The Dahae who have abandoned their wars lived east of the Caspian,
on the northern frontier of the Parthian empire; here they are said to
have threatened the Parthians with their cavalry, the very weapon in
which the Parthians excelled. The *exemplum* is so specific and so
irrelevant to anything in the play that it must allude to events in
Seneca's own time.

Otto Herzog[27] thought that the king who bestowed kingdoms was
Claudius, who in 41 restored Mithridates to the Armenian throne
(Tacitus, *Annals* 11. 8. 1 'monente Claudio in regnum remeavit').
Claudius was able to do this because of civil war in Parthia[28] between
the king Vardanes and his brother Gotarzes; and Tacitus mentions in
the same context that Gotarzes was supported by the very Dahae that
we meet in Seneca (*Annals* 11. 8. 4 'interim Gotarzes Daharum
Hyrcanorumque opibus auctus bellum renovat'). But the historical
situation does not in fact fit Seneca: so far from imposing a general
peace in the East, Claudius only succeeded in Armenia because of the
lack of such a peace in Parthia. When Seneca goes on to say that his
king wields the sceptre anxiously, Herzog sees an allusion to the rebellion of Scribonianus against Claudius in 42. But these would be
dangerous words for Seneca to utter even in the privacy of a Corsican
exile; after all, he wanted to return.

Tarrant ad loc. sees a resemblance to Nero; he compares the

---

[27] Herzog (n. 2), 77 ff.
[28] For the confusing Parthian history of the period see J. G. C. Anderson, *Cambridge
Ancient History*, 10 (1934), 747 ff.; K.-H. Ziegler, *Die Beziehungen zwischen Rom und dem
Partherreich* (Wiesbaden, 1964), 64 ff.; N. C. Debevoise, *A Political History of Parthia* (1968),
166 ff. For numismatic evidence see W. Wroth, *Catalogue of the Greek Coins in the British
Museum, Parthia* (London, 1903); D. Sellwood, *An Introduction to the Coinage of Parthia*
(London, 1971).

opening of Seneca's *De Clementia* (AD 56), where Nero claims to impose peace on the world (1. 1. 2):

ego vitae necisque gentibus arbiter; qualem quisque sortem statumque habeat, in mea manu positum est; quid cuique mortalium fortuna datum velit, meo ore pronuntiat; ex nostro responso laetitiae causas populi urbesque concipiunt; nulla pars usquam nisi volente propitioque me floret; haec tot milia gladiorum, quae pax mea comprimit, ad nutum meum stringentur; quas nationes funditus excidi, quas transportari, quibus libertatem dari, quibus eripi, quos reges mancipia fieri quorumque capiti regium circumdari decus oporteat, quae ruant | urbes, quae oriantur, mea iuris dictio est.

But no allusion to Parthian affairs, such as is suggested by *Dahae*, seems to fit this interpretation precisely. In AD 60 Nero put Tigranes on the Armenian throne (Tacitus, *Annals* 14. 26. 1), but Seneca would not wish to denigrate Corbulo's victories that had made this possible; and it was premature to talk of a general conciliation, for Tigranes was expelled in the following year. Nero's later coronation of Tiridates did not take place till 66 (Dio 63. 4–5), the year after Seneca's death, but the scheme was already being mooted in 63, when Tiridates placed his diadem at the foot of Nero's statue (Tacitus, *Annals* 15. 29. 1 'tum placuit Tiridaten ponere apud effigiem Caesaris insigne regium nec nisi manu Neronis resumere'). But the historical facts tell even more strongly against this particular reference: Tiridates was the brother of the Parthian king and imposed by him on Armenia, and the moves for a coronation by Nero were an attempt to save Roman face after the disastrous defeat of Paetus in 62. In such circumstances Seneca could not imply that Nero's success was an illusion: nobody thought that he had succeeded.

Surely any reference to a Roman emperor makes the anachronism too glaring in the context of Thyestes and Atreus. The man who bestows diadems on the brow and receives veneration on the knee must be an eastern King of Kings, such a ruler as there had always been in that part of the world. Once that has been granted, we may look for hints of more contemporary events such as would suggest themselves to people living in Seneca's time. We have seen that the Parthians were in disarray for most of Claudius's reign (above, p. 301), but the situation changed in 51 when Vologaeses became king. He put his brother Tiridates on the throne of Armenia (Tacitus, *Annals* 12. 50. 1) and his brother Pacorus on the throne of Media Atropatene (Josephus, *Antiquitates Judaeorum* 20. 74); but the Parthians had nothing like the universal success suggested by the lines in *Thyestes*. They had setbacks in Armenia in 53 and again in 55.[29] They were harassed by the revolt of the king's son Vardanes (Tacitus, *Annals* 13. 7. 2)[30] and by a prolonged rebellion in Hyrcania. Then there were the brilliant campaigns of Corbulo in 58 and 59 when he captured the key cities of Armenia.[31] This all seems to confirm the view that we had formed on other grounds (p. 299): the earlier years of Nero were not a suitable time for this play.

Another and later date may be put forward. When Atreus crowns his brother Thyestes, Seneca seems to be alluding to the dramatic scene in 61, when the Parthian king Vologaeses, in the presence of an | assembly of noblemen, bound the diadem[32] of Armenia round the head of his brother Tiridates (Tacitus, *Annals* 15. 2. 4 'diademate caput Tiridatis evinxit'); the solemn rite had a significance that was not simply formal.[33] The new Parthian assertiveness was explained by the fact that the long Hyrcanian rebellion was now over (Tacitus, ibid. 'mandavitque (Monaesi) Tigranem Armenia exturbare, dum ipse positis adversus Hyrcanos discordiis vires intimas molemque belli ciet, provinciis Romanis minitans'); all this corresponds to the omnipotence of the king in *Thyestes*, and in particular to the pacification of the Dahae, who lived immediately north-east of Hyrcania. But Seneca suggests that in spite of the defeat of Paetus in 62 the Parthian success is insecure; just as the reconciliation between Atreus and Thyestes is not genuine, so the Parthian king will soon resume his traditional national habit of feuding with his brother. In the same way Horace had emphasized that proud Eastern kings are subject to external pressures (*Odes* 1. 26. 5 'quid Tiridaten terreat') and the vicissitudes of fortune (1. 35. 11 f., 3. 1. 5 f.); in particular when Prahates regained the Parthian throne in 26 BC, the poet consoled himself with the reflection that true kingship lies in virtue (2. 2. 17 ff.):

> redditum Cyri solio Prahaten
> dissidens plebi numero beatorum
> eximit Virtus populumque falsis
>   dedocet uti
> vocibus, regnum et diadema tutum
> deferens uni propriamque laurum

[29] Anderson (n. 28), 757 ff.
[30] Ibid. 759 f., 879.   [31] Ibid. 760 ff.
[32] H.-W. Ritter, *Diadem und Königsherrschaft* (Vestigia, 7; 1965).
[33] D. Cannadine and S. Price, *Rituals of Royalty: Power and Ceremonial in Traditional Societies* (Cambridge, 1987).

> quisquis ingentis oculo inretorto
> spectat acervos.

Horace only became as philosophical as that when his own side was losing,[34] and Seneca would be no different.

V. THE MAILED HORSEMEN OF THE DANUBE

There is another historical allusion at *Thyestes* 629f.: 'feris Hister fugam | praebens Alanis'. A confusion has been suspected with the Alani north of the Caucasus (below, Section VI),[35] but, although Seneca's geography can be indifferent to fact, it is inconceivable that in a matter of strategic significance he made a mistake of this kind; one remembers his practical approach to the Parthian problem at the beginning of Nero's reign (Tacitus, *Annals* 13. 6. 3). Tarrant and others are surely right to refer to the kindred Rhoxolani,[36] whose name has been thought to mean 'Red Alans'; these were a nomadic Sarmatian | people who under continuing pressure from the east had now reached the north bank of the lower Danube. Tacitus vividly describes their heavy cavalry (*cataphracti*) with their encasing coats of mail (*Histories* 1. 79. 3); as in other periods in the history of war, such formations were difficult to resist if they could keep moving (*Histories* 1. 79. 2 'ubi per turmas advenere vix ulla acies obstiterit'). Their novel and distinctive armament and tactics, so different from those of the lightly armed and mobile Scythians, are already described in Valerius Flaccus (6. 231 ff.): 'cum saevior ecce iuventus | Sarmaticae coiere manus fremitusque virorum | semiferi. riget his molli lorica catena, | id quoque tegmen equis'.[37] Such coats of mail are worn by horsemen on Trajan's column;[38] these have been identified

---

[34] So Cicero pretends to find consolation in philosophy for Piso's escape: *Pis.* 43 'quae est igitur poena, quod supplicium? id mea sententia quod accidere nemini potest nisi nocenti'; 95 'equidem, ut paulo ante dixi, non eadem supplicia esse in hominibus existimo quae fortasse plerique'; 98 'mihi cui semper ita persuasum fuerit non eventis sed factis cuiusque fortunam ponderari'.

[35] A. B. Bosworth, *HSCP* 81 (1977), 222 n. 21.

[36] *RE* Suppl. 7. 1195 ff.; T. Sulimirski, *The Sarmatians* (London, 1970), 134 ff.; J. J. Wilkes in *Rome and her Northern Frontiers*, ed. B. Hartley and J. Wacher (London, 1983), 255 ff.; S. F. Ryle, *Hermathena*, 143 (1987), 93 ff.

[37] R. Syme, *CQ* 23 (1929), 129 ff. For later accounts of these armoured brigades see R. M. Rattenbury, *CR* 56 (1942), 113 ff.

[38] L. Rossi, *Trajan's Column and the Dacian Wars*, revised J. M. C. Toynbee (London, 1971), 125 (with plates 27 and 33); Wilkes (n. 36), 272 pls. II and III (see also 257 for a relief from South Russia).

with the Rhoxolani, but the resemblance does not extend to all details of their equipment.[39]

The Rhoxolani were in diplomatic and perhaps military contact with the eminent Ti. Plautius Silvanus Aelianus,[40] who was legate of Moesia (to the south of the lower Danube), probably from 60 to 67,[41] though some go a few years earlier. Plautius mentions the transaction in a self-assertive inscription[42] by the well-known Mausoleum of the Plautii, which still stands where the via Tiburtina crosses the Anio: 'regibus Bastarnarum et Rhoxolanorum filios, Dacorum fratr⟨es⟩ captos aut hostibus ereptos remisit'. At the time of these events he had relinquished a large part of his army for the Armenian campaign: 'motum orientem Sarmatar. compressit, quamvis parte⟨m⟩ magna⟨m⟩ exercitus ad expeditionem in Armeniam misisset'. Tacitus records that to meet the Armenian crisis of 61–2 a legion had been pulled out of Moesia and assigned to Paetus (*Annals* 15. 6. 3 'addita quinta (legione) quae recens e Moesis excita erat'). Surely the hurried troop-movement implied by *excita* is the very one mentioned in the inscription.[43]

Of course the Rhoxolani could have been causing trouble for some years previously: we do not know when they reached the Danube. According to Strabo or rather his earlier source, they were still east of the Borysthenes (Dnieper) at a time when the Sarmatian Iazyges lived to the west (7. 3. 17), but by the reign of Tiberius the Iazyges are found in the Hungarian plain.[44] All we can say is that about 62, the date we are considering for *Thyestes*, the Rhoxolani were highly topical: Plautius settled over 100,000 barbarians to the south of the Danube, perhaps Dacians who had experienced the *motum orientem Sarmatarum* of which the inscription speaks. Plautius's activities at the time were

---

[39] F. B. Florescu, *Das Siegesdenkmal von Adamklissi: Tropaeum Traiani* (Bucharest and Bonn, 1965), 660 ff. and *Die Trajanssäule* (Bucharest and Bonn, 1969), 116 f. (with plates 58d and XXVIII).

[40] *PIR* P 363; *RE* 21. 35 ff.; L. Halkin, *AC* 3 (1934), 121 ff.; L. R. Taylor, *MAAR* 24 (1951), 29 n. 42.

[41] A. Stein, *Die Legaten von Moesien* (Budapest, 1940), 29 ff.; his dating is endorsed by R. Syme, *Antichthon*, 11 (1977), 85 = *Roman Papers*, 3 (Oxford, 1984), 1005; M. T. Griffin, *Seneca* (Oxford, 1976), 245, 456.

[42] *CIL* 14. 3608 = *ILS* 986; M. McCrum and A. G. Woodhead, *Select Documents of the Principates of the Flavian Emperors... A.D. 68–96* (Cambridge, 1961), No. 261.

[43] Otherwise M. Hofmann, *RE* 21. 37.

[44] Plin. *Nat.* 4. 80–1; Tac. *Ann.* 12. 29–30; R. Syme, *Cambridge Ancient History*, 10 (1934), 305; A. Mócsy, *Pannonia and Upper Moesia* (London, 1974), 39. For a general view of the Sarmatian migrations see M. Rostovtzeff, *Iranians and Greeks in South Russia* (Oxford, 1922), 115 ff.; F. G. B. Millar, *The Roman Empire and its Neighbours*[2] (London, 1981), 281 ff.; Wilkes (n. 36), 255 ff.

significant and memorable: he intervened against the | Scythians as far away as Chersonesus,[45] near Sebastopol in the Crimea, a sign of the new strategic concern about migrations in the area.

VI. THE GATE THROUGH THE CAUCASUS

There seems to be a neglected historical allusion[45a] at *Thyestes* 369 ff., where the chorus catalogues kings of the East who lack the true *regnum* of the virtuous man:

> reges conveniant licet
> qui sparsos agitant Dahas,
> qui rubri vada litoris
> et gemmis mare lucidis
> late sanguineum tenent,
> aut qui Caspia fortibus
> recludunt iuga Sarmatis,
> certet Danuvii vadum
> audet qui pedes ingredi
> et (quocumque loco iacent)
> Seres vellere nobiles:
> mens regnum bona possidet.

The king who walks across the frozen Danube is presumably one of the Sarmatians (whether Rhoxolani or another tribe) that Plautius had to deal with; but more might be made of the preceding clause (374 f.) *aut qui Caspia fortibus* | *recludunt iuga Sarmatis.* The verb *recludunt* suggests a reference to the so-called Caspian Gates,[46] the pass of Darial ('the gate of the Alans'), a hundred miles north of the modern Tbilisi, where the Georgian Military Highway runs through the formidable barrier of the central Caucasus.[47] The pass should properly be called the Caucasian Gates, as Pliny complains on two occasions;[48]

[45] *ILS* 986 'Scytharum quoque rege[m] a Cherronensi, quae est ultra Borustenem, opsidione summoto'.

[45a] The reference to the Caspian Gates at *Thy.* 374 ff., which I thought had been missed, has now been noticed by R. Syme, *Acta Classica*, 30 (1987), 59 ff. Some of his other material overlaps with my own (particularly in Section VI), and he is ready to accept Fitch's late date for *Thyestes*. [46] A. R. Anderson, *TAPA* 55 (1928), 135 ff.

[47] For some local colour see Fitzroy Maclean, *To Caucasus, the End of all the Earth* (London, 1976), 154 (with illustrations in preceding pages and facing p. 81).

[48] Plin. *Nat.* 6. 30 (quoted in text); 6. 40 'corrigendus est in hoc loco error multorum, etiam qui in Armenia res proxime cum Corbulone gessere. namque ii Caspias appellavere portas Hiberiae quas Caucasias diximus vocari, situsque depicti et inde missi hoc nomen inscriptum habent.' If the misnomer gained particular currency when Corbulo held the Eastern command, that might be a further argument for giving *Thyestes* a Neronian date.

it must be clearly distinguished from Alexander's Caspian Gates to the south of the Caspian, south-east of Tehran. In one of these passages Pliny states that the gates included a physical obstacle (*Natural History* 6. 30):[49]

ab iis sunt Portae Caucasiae magno errore multis Caspiae dictae, ingens naturae opus montibus interruptis repente, ubi fores additae ferratis trabibus, subter medias amne diri odoris fluente citraque in rupe castello quod vocatur Cumania communito ad arcendas transitu gentes innumeras, ibi loci terrarum orbe portis discluso.

A more recent writer has described 'a gorge (8m. long) of singular beauty, shut in by precipitous mountain walls nearly 600ft. high, and so narrow that there is only just room for the carriage-road and the | brawling river Terek side by side'.[50]

In AD 35 the Iberians, who lived south of the central Caucasus in the modern Georgia, let the Sarmatians through the pass to attack the Parthians in Armenia: Tacitus, *Annals* 6. 33. 3 'sed Hiberi locorum potentes Caspia via Sarmatam in Armenios raptim effundunt'.[51] Josephus says of the same episode Ἀλανοὺς (Ἀλανοὶ codd.) δὲ δίοδον αὐτοῖς διδόντες διὰ τῆς αὐτῶν καὶ τὰς θύρας τὰς Κασπίας ἀνοίξαντες ἐπάγουσι τῷ Ἀρταβάνῳ (*Antiquitates Judaeorum* 18. 97); 'having opened the Caspian Gates' corresponds closely to Seneca's *recludunt*, though it may be anachronistic to use the expression 'Caspian Gates' of events quite so early. These passages should not tempt us to put *Thyestes* back to the last years of Tiberius; Parthia was in poor shape at that time,[52] and it was not the moment to talk of their imposing a general peace (*Thyestes* 601 ff., above p. 301). Tacitus makes it clear in the same context that the incursion of 35 was not an isolated intervention: *Annals* 6. 33. 2 'Pharasmanes (king of Iberia) . . . accire Sarmatas, quorum sceptuchi utrimque donis acceptis more gentico diversa induere'. Even a hundred years later Pharasmanes II of Iberia let the Alans through the Caspian Gates to attack his neighbours the Albani.[53]

---

[49] Procopius, *Bell.* 1. 10. 4 attributes the gate to Alexander, who was never in fact there: δίοδος γὰρ οὐδεμία τὸ λοιπὸν φαίνεται, πλήν γε δὴ ὅτι ὥσπερ τινὰ χειροποίητον πυλίδα ἐνταῦθα ἡ φύσις ἐξεῦρεν, ἢ Κασπία ἐκ παλαιοῦ ἐκλήθη . . . 9 ὅπερ ἐπειδὴ ὁ Φιλίππου Ἀλέξανδρος κατενόησε, πύλας τε ἐν χώρῳ ἐτεκτήνατο τῷ εἰρημένῳ καὶ φυλακτήριον κατεστήσατο.

[50] *Encyclopaedia Britannica*[11], 5 (Cambridge, 1910), 552.

[51] J. G. C. Anderson (n. 28), 777; A. B. Bosworth, *HSCP* 81 (1977), 221 ff.

[52] Anderson (n. 28), 747 ff.; Debevoise (n. 28), 158 ff.

[53] Dio 69. 15. 1; Bosworth (n. 51), 228 ff.

In particular the Caucasus had a topical strategic significance towards the end of Nero's reign. In 66, the year after Seneca's death, when Nero went on his last visit to Greece, he was planning an expedition to the Caspian Gates: see especially Tacitus, *Histories* 1. 6. 2 'quos idem Nero electos praemissosque ad claustra Caspiarum et bellum quod in Albanos parabat opprimendis Vindicis coeptis revocaverat'.[54] Here *in Albanos* is a puzzling anticlimax: the preposition implies hostile action, but the Albani lived not in the modern Georgia south of the Gates but in the modern Azerbaijan, south of the Caucasus on the eastern (Caspian) side. Mommsen plausibly emended to *Alanos*,[55] the barbarians to the north of the range. It has been argued that the consolidation of Hiberia and Albania made more strategic sense,[56] but perhaps this was not a grandiose enough project for an expedition led by the emperor himself with a specially formed 'phalanx Alexandri Magni' (Suetonius, *Nero* 19. 2). We have seen from the intervention of Plautius in the Crimea (above, p. 306) a new awareness of the menace from the north-east, and there may have been some thoughts of turning the Black Sea into a Roman lake;[57] perhaps there were now visions of a simultaneous thrust through the Caucasus to strike at the heartland of the Sarmatian tribes.[58] Where Alexander was believed to have gone (because of the | confusion about the Caspian Gates) Nero might be eager to follow; as with Julius Caesar's Parthian expedition of 44 BC, the megalomaniac enterprise may have played a part in turning informed opinion against its author.

Mommsen's conjecture derives a little support from Lucan 8. 222 ff. (Pompey claims to have spared the Parthians in 66–65 BC):

> si vos, o Parthi, peterem cum Caspia claustra
> et sequerer duros aeterni Martis Alanos

[54] So also Pliny, *Nat.* 6. 40 'et Neronis principis comminatio ad Caspias portas tendere dicebatur cum peteret illas quae per Hiberiam in Sarmatas tendunt'; Suet. *Ner.* 19. 2 'parabat etiam ad Caspias portas expeditionem'; Dio 63. 8. 1.

[55] See also Anderson (n. 28), 777; D. Magie, *Roman Rule in Asia Minor* (Princeton, NJ, 1950), 2. 1418 n. 63; Chilver on Tac. *Hist.* 1. 6; R. K. Sherk, *ANRW* 2. 7. 2 (1980), 992; M. T. Griffin, *Nero: The End of a Dynasty* (London, 1984), 228 f., 299 n. 36.

[56] A. B. Bosworth, *Antichthon*, 10 (1976), 74 and *HSCP* 81 (1977), 225 f.

[57] Anderson (n. 28), 774. He cites Josephus *BJ* 2. 366–7 (Agrippa advises the Jews against revolt by emphasizing the power of the Roman empire): τί χρὴ λέγειν Ἡνιόχους τε καὶ Κόλχους καὶ τὸ τῶν Ταύρων φῦλον, Βοσπορανούς τε καὶ τὰ περίοικα τοῦ Πόντου καὶ τῆς Μαιώτιδος ἔθνη; παρ' οἷς πρὶν μὲν οὐδ' οἰκεῖος ἐγιγνώσκετο δεσπότης, νῦν δὲ τρισχιλίοις ὁπλίταις ὑποτάσσεται, καὶ τεσσαράκοντα νῆες μακραὶ τὴν πρὶν ἄπλωτον καὶ ἀγρίαν εἰρηνεύουσι θάλασσαν. This speech is assigned by Josephus to AD 66, but may more accurately reflect conditions under Vespasian (Anderson loc. cit.).

[58] Anderson loc. cit.; the emphasis is put on the Crimea by Millar (n. 44), 290.

> passus Achaemeniis late decurrere campis
> in tutam trepidos numquam Babylona coegi.

Pompey never reached the Gates,[59] and the name Alani is anachronistic for his time; but the lines (perhaps written as late as AD 64) may glance at Nero's projected campaign. Similarly, if Seneca wrote *Thyestes* in 62, his reference to 'Caspian ridges' might have been influenced by recent Sarmatian incursions, the sort of thing that is likely to have happened to provoke Nero's violent reaction.

VII. CONSEQUENCES

We have now reached a conclusion similar to Tarrant's (*Thyestes* 12 f.), though in part by a different route: stylistic and historical arguments converge to date *Thyestes* in the latter part of Nero's reign, in 62 to be precise. *Phoenissae* must go together with *Thyestes*, in view of Fitch's evidence about the high incidence of short final *o*; but for this the order in the *codex Etruscus* could be chronological (above, p. 293). A late date is acceptable[60] for a play that lacks choruses and shows other evidence of incompleteness. The theme of the aged Oedipus would suit an ageing Seneca, just as *Oedipus Coloneus* was thought to suit the venerable Sophocles. The clash of brother against brother might have been a tactless subject when Nero was the rival of Britannicus, or soon after he had disposed of him. It should be noted that Zwierlein[61] followed Leo in putting *Phoenissae* after *Oedipus* because of the likely priority of a parallel. It may seem less satisfactory that Conte[62] saw imitation of *Phoenissae* in Lucan's proem (where one naturally thinks of the younger man as imitator); but even if the resemblances are significant, Lucan may only have begun his poem in 62 or 63.[63]

Our chronology has further consequences. Münscher[64] used the metrical simplicity of the choruses of *Thyestes* as an argument for a very

---

[59] For Pompey's Caucasian campaign see Magie (n. 55), 358 f., 1225 f.; A. N. Sherwin-White, *Roman Foreign Policy in the East 168 BC–AD 1* (London, 1984), 195 ff.

[60] Münscher (n. 2), 119 ff.

[61] Zwierlein (n. 2), 238 f., citing *Phoen.* 173 ff. (Oedipus to Antigone) 'ades atque inertem dexteram introrsus preme I magisque merge; timida tunc parvo caput I libavit haustu vixque cupientes sequi I eduxit oculos'. This seems an unusually specific reference to *Oed.* 961 ff. 'gemuit et dirum fremens I manus in ora torsit. at contra truces I oculi steterunt et suam intenti manum I ultro insecuntur, vulneri occurrunt suo'.

[62] *Maia*, 18 (1966), 49 f., citing *Phoen.* 298, 300, 414 f.; Zwierlein (n. 2), 246 ff. (with bibliography of Lucan's imitations of Seneca).

[63] F. M. Ahl, *Lucan* (Ithaca, NY, and London, 1976), 352 f.

[64] Münscher (n. 2), 62 ff.; he is rebutted by Herzog (n. 2), 95 f.

early date; but though one may concede that the most complicated metrical systems were not the first to be attempted, that | does not mean that all the plays can be neatly arranged in a sequence of increasing complexity. W. M. Calder III[65] put *Thyestes* before *Agamemnon*: the prologues both deal with the crimes and punishments of Tantalus, but the one in *Thyestes* is more closely integrated with the rest of the play.[66] Similarly Zwierlein[67] put *Thyestes* before *Medea*; the opening speeches in both plays mention the turning back of the sun, but in *Thyestes* the description is more obviously related to the subsequent action. If we are right that *Thyestes* is late, that tends to confirm the difficulty, too often underestimated, of establishing arguments about priority. Everybody was familiar with the eating of the children and the turning back of the sun, and it was not inevitable that the more integrated treatment should have been written first.

There are also inconvenient consequences for my own view of *Hercules Oetaeus*. It is widely believed that this play is not by Seneca, and there are some abnormalities of metre and diction that in my opinion have been considerably exaggerated.[68] I have argued elsewhere[69] that the work is Senecan and very late; I see a hint of Nero in the concluding prayer 'et si qua novo belua voltu I quatiet populos terrore gravi I tu fulminibus frange trisulcis' (1992 ff.). But it must be acknowledged that *Hercules Oetaeus* has at most four instances of verbs with short final *o*.[70]

I add a few footnotes from the Flavian period to show the continuing importance of Seneca's concerns in *Thyestes*. In 69 the trans-Danubian Rhoxolani crossed the river in force, but their armour-plated horsemen were overwhelmed in the mud and slush (Tacitus, *Histories* 1. 79). In 70 Sarmatians, perhaps Rhoxolani, killed in battle the governor of Moesia, Fonteius Agrippa,[71] but were defeated by his

[65] *CPh.* 71 (1976), 29 f.

[66] For thematic links in *Thyestes* see H. M. Hine, *Papers of the Liverpool Latin Seminar*, 3 (1981), 259 ff.   [67] Zwierlein (n. 2), 241 f.

[68] R. Jakobi, *Der Einfluss Ovids auf den Tragiker Seneca* (Untersuchungen zur antiken Literatur und Geschichte, 28; 1988) collects many interesting parallels between Ovid and Seneca. The pattern seems similar in *HO* and the other plays, but he persists in finding fault with the author of *HO*; in questions of authenticity it is natural τὸν πεσόντα λακτίσαι πλέον, but in fact decisive criteria are rare.

[69] *Homo Viator: Classical Essays for John Bramble*, ed. M. Whitby, P. Hardie, M. Whitby (Bristol, 1987), 249 ff. (above, pp. 209 ff.); see also M. Rozelaar, *ANRW* 2. 32. 2 (1985), 1348 ff.

[70] *HO* 282 *ibo*, 740 *cerno* (both in elision), 1435 *video*, 1837 *sedabo*. Note also at 1862 the gerund *lugendo* with short final *o*.

[71] Jos. *BJ* 7. 90–4; R. Syme, *Antichthon*, 9 (1977), 85 f. = *Roman Papers*, 3 (Oxford, 1984), 1006 f.

successor. In 72 the trans-Caucasian Alani made a devastating raid on Parthia;[72] the Romans fortified a strong-point near Tbilisi, as recorded in an inscription (*ILS* 8795). When Valerius wrote the *Argonautica*, he must have been aware of the strategic topicality of Colchis (south of the Caucasus on the Black Sea side); in a description of a barbarian warrior he suggests operations at the Caspian Gates (5. 603f. 'iam pervigil illum I Medus et oppositis exspectat Hiberia claustris'). A little later Statius imagines a command for Vitorius Marcellus in the same area (*Silvae* 4. 4. 63f. 'aut Histrum servare datur metuendaque portae I limina Caspiacae'); here *metuenda* implies not just rugged topography but a threat from the Alans to the north. But in spite of such references the Flavians, unlike Nero, were aiming at consolidation rather than expansion. |

I append a final postscript from the *Dialogus* of Tacitus. In the year 75,[73] shortly before he died,[74] Curiatius Maternus was contemplating a seditious swan-song, a tragedy called *Thyestes*. We should resist any temptation to assign the extant play to Maternus; in spite of the surprising incidence of short final *o*, the style and metrics are too Senecan in other respects, the matter is not dangerous enough for comment by Tacitus, and far from dominating the East, Vologaeses was now asking Vespasian for help (Suetonius, *Domitian* 2. 2). But the *Dialogus* reminds us of one thing: Seneca was writing in a society where the family feuds of Greek myth seemed potentially relevant to Roman dynastic struggles, at a time when a calculating statesman might hesitate to say too much. In his tragedies Seneca could not help drawing on his experience of the world, and he understood at first hand the temptations of power that ruined Thyestes, but he had not yet utterly despaired of Rome or his own position. When he speaks of the crimes of kings, one cannot answer for his underlying motivation, which may not have been fully apparent even to himself, but at least at the most obvious level he is hinting less at the Julio-Claudians than the Arsacidae.

[72] Jos. *BJ* 7. 244–51; E. Täubler, *Klio*, 9 (1909), 18ff.; Magie (n. 55), 575, 1438 n. 24; A. B. Bosworth, *Antichthon*, 10 (1976), 67ff.

[73] R. Syme, *Tacitus* (Oxford, 1958), 104ff., 670ff.

[74] Alan Cameron, *CR* 17 (1967), 258ff.

19

Cola and Clausulae in Cicero's Speeches

IN a volume dedicated to Kenneth Dover an article on prose colometry should not come amiss. Questions of word-order are relevant, as
are rhythmical patterns, so much more complicated than in the poets;
progress will ultimately depend on a combination of linguistic instinct
and clear-headedness about statistics. It may seem more anomalous
that the following remarks are based on Cicero's speeches, but here as
elsewhere a Latin author may have something to offer even to Hellen-
ists. Cicero's *Kunstprosa* is derived from Greek oratory, and his clausulae can be paralleled in the contemporary inscription of Antiochus of
Commagene;[1] but because of the sheer bulk of his writings as well as
the nature of his sentences (persistently rhythmical but still very
varied), he provides a better testing-ground for colometry than
perhaps any Greek.

I shall begin with Eduard Fraenkel, whose contributions to the study
of Greek and Latin colometry were as innovating and as interesting as
anything he ever wrote. He used passages in the Roman poets where
the sentence overruns the couplet to identify the colon-boundaries:[2]
thus he cites Catull. 113. 2 f. 'facto consule nunc iterum | manserunt duo
. . .' (the ablative absolute forms a colon that ends with the penta-
meter), Mart. 11. 11. 2 f. 'et mihi secura pocula trade manu | trita
patrum labris et tonso pura magistro' (*participia coniuncta* similarly
produce independent cola). He used Wackernagel's law (on the
tendency of unstressed pronouns and the like to occupy second place)

Some aspects of this article were discussed in a paper read in the University of St
Andrews in Nov. 1988. Prof. M. L. West clarified my mind on colometry in the London
train, and Dr M. Winterbottom made helpful comments on the penultimate draft; I am
grateful to both.

[1] *OGIS* 383; E. Norden, *Die antike Kunstprosa*, 2nd edn. (Leipzig and Berlin, 1909),
i. 140 ff.
[2] 'Kolon und Satz', *NGG* (1932), 197 ff. = *Kleine Beiträge zur klassischen Philologie*
(Rome, 1964), i. 73 ff.

From *Owls to Athens: Essays on Classical Subjects presented to Sir Kenneth Dover*, ed. E. M.
Craik (Oxford, 1990), 349–59.

to show where cola begin;[3] cf. Cic. *Cat.* 2. 7 'uno me hercule Catilina exhausto I levata mihi et recreata res publica videtur' (where the position of *mihi* confirms the break after the ablative absolute). He pointed out that vocatives often mark the end of a colon[4] (as does 'Mr Speaker'); cf. *Verr.* 2. 1. 63 'oppidum est in Hellesponto Lampsacum iudices I in primis Asiae provinciae clarum et nobile' (where the modern habit of printing a comma before as well as after the vocative is usually misleading).

But these are all special cases that happen only from time to time. Much | more important are the recurring cadences at the ends of internal cola; these are far more regular in Cicero[5] than many people realize, and fully deserve the name of 'clausulae'. In his pioneering work Zieliński[6] confined himself to the ends of sentences, where the divisions are most clear-cut and the preferred clausulae can be established most objectively. When he turned to internal rhythms in his second study,[7] he relied too much on preconceptions and mechanical rules rather than on his ear and his sense of what was being said; thus at *Pis.* 50 he was prepared to articulate 'quae cum plurimae leges veteres I tum lex Cornelia maiestatis I Iulia de pecuniis I repetundis planissime vetat' (where the separation of *repetundis* from *pecuniis* is patently absurd).[8] Such arbitrariness has led many to be too sceptical about the possibility of establishing internal rhythms.

Fraenkel, on the other hand, in his last word on the subject made use of clausulae without forgetting his natural feeling for how ancient prose breaks up.[9] His treatment has also the great advantage of concentrating on particular passages where the reader can see the system in action; more theoretical accounts soon get lost in a tangle of figures[10] without making the main lines clear or presenting enough specific examples for the reader to react against. Fraenkel's book has

---

[3] 'Kolon und Satz II', *NGG* (1933), 319 ff. = *Kl. Beitr.* i. 93 ff.

[4] 'Noch einmal Kolon und Satz', *SBAW* (1965), 2.

[5] *De Or.* 3. 173 'neque librariorum notis sed verborum et sententiarum modo interpositas clausulas in orationibus esse voluerunt'.

[6] *Das Clauselgesetz in Ciceros Reden* (*Philol.* suppl. 9. 4; 1904).

[7] *Der constructive Rhythmus in Ciceros Reden* (*Philol.* suppl. 13. 1; 1914). W. Schmid is no clearer (*Hermes* Einzelschr. 12; 1959).

[8] Criticized by H. D. Broadhead, *Latin Prose Rhythm* (Cambridge, 1922), 27.

[9] *Leseproben aus Reden Ciceros und Catos* (Rome, 1968). See the review by E. Laughton, *JRS* 60 (1970), 188 ff.; he also gives a useful summary of Fraenkel's earlier writings on colometry.

[10] Thus even H. Aili, *The Prose Rhythm of Sallust and Livy* (Studia Latina Stockholmiensia, 24; 1979); K. Müller comments in his review 'aurem tuam interroga' (*Gnomon*, 58 (1986), 12 ff.).

been undervalued by some[11] because of his disregard for statistical data, and colleagues remember the days when he would claim to have discovered a new clausula in Cato on the strength of two instances. But he makes an important caveat when he says that he is primarily concerned with colometry rather than with rhythm (p. 14). The student of the subject must both follow the sense and listen to the rhythm; when a natural sense-break, even a fairly slight one, coincides with a familiar clausula, that is prima-facie evidence that there is an objective incision. But the rhythms at the ends of minor internal cola are less regular than those at the ends of sentences, and it must be emphasized very strongly that we cannot always expect one of the most familiar patterns.

Before turning to actual specimens of Ciceronian prose, I shall remind the reader of the most common types of Ciceronian clausulae, as they appear from the ends of sentences. It should be noted that the last syllable of the clausula | (here marked 'x') may take any form (just as in a hexameter); that is to say, *radunt, radit, rado,* and *rasa* (nominative) give interchangeable endings.[12]

1.	$-\cup-\ -\times$	Cretic + spondee or trochee
	$\cup\cup-\ -\times$	(with resolution of first long syllable)[13]
	$-\cup\cup\ -\times$	(the familiar *esse videatur*)
	$-\cup-\ \cup\times$	
2.	$-\cup-\ -\cup\times$	Double cretic
	$-\cup\cup\ -\cup\times$	(with resolution)
	$\cup\cup-\ -\cup\times$	”　　　　”
	$---\ -\cup\times$	(molossus + cretic)
	$-\cup-\ -\cup\times$	(choriambus + cretic)
3.	$-\cup-\times$	Trochaic metron (two trochees or trochee + spondee), often preceded by $-\cup-$ or $---$
4.	$-\cup-\cup\times$	Hypodochmiac (cretic + iambus)

For a demonstration I have chosen *Phil.* 10. 1, a passage discussed by Habinek, *Colometry*, 140 ff. Though he provides much interesting

---

[11] T. N. Habinek, *The Colometry of Latin Prose* (Univ. of California Publ. Class. Stud. 25; 1985), 8 ff.

[12] One commonly thinks of *radit* as a trochee (as the second vowel is short), but strictly speaking at the end of a colon it is a spondee (as the second syllable is closed by a consonant); see M. L. West, *Greek Metre* (Oxford, 1982), 8 f.

[13] For such resolutions see K. Müller's edition of Curtius Rufus (Munich, 1954), 758 ff. (the best treatment of prose-rhythm in any classical Latin author).

material on ancient punctuation and the evidence from citations, he deliberately underplays prose-rhythm, by far the most valuable criterion, on the mistaken ground that it prejudices the discussion; in fact in any treatment of colometry all factors must be looked at together. For present purposes I have followed Habinek's divisions, which he distinguishes by one or two vertical strokes according to their importance; the index figures refer to the type of clausula (see above), which is recorded by him only on lines 4 and 10.

1   maximas tibi Pānsă grātiăs ⁴ |
2   omnes et habere et ăgēre dēbēmŭs ¹ ‖
3   quī cum hŏdīernō dĭĕ ² |
4   senatum te habiturum non ārbĭtrārēmŭr ¹ ‖
5   ut Marci Bruti |
6   praestantĭssĭmī cīvĭs ¹ |
7   litteras accepisti ‖
8   ne minimam quidem moram interposuisti |
9   quin quam primum |
10 maximo gaudio et gratulatiōne fruĕrēmŭr ¹ ‖

1. I think that the first colon ends at *gratias*; otherwise it has 22 syllables, which is too long. The clausula is satisfactory, and the following *omnes* is emphasized. In placing vocatives, the shape of the components is a significant | factor; *Laterensis* or *Antoni*, when preceded by a trochee, often ends a colon, while a name like *Pansa* more naturally occupies the penultimate position. 3. There is a clear incision after *die*; adverbial phrases often make cola in Greek and Latin, and the matter is clinched by unemphatic *te* in the second position in the next clause. Possibly the monosyllable *cum* is not elided but followed by a hiatus.[14] 5. Appositions sometimes occupy separate cola, but not necessarily so. As the components here are short and *Marci Bruti* gives an unsatisfactory clausula (much more so than the single word *accepisti* below), I take lines 5 and 6 together. 6. Those who articulate according to the major syntactical units will not admit an incision after *civis*; but the clausula is good, an extended genitive can make a single colon, and the clause is rather long if there is no break between *ut* and *accepisti*. 8. The *clausula heroica* ('hexameter-ending') is less disagreeable in Cicero (particularly in internal clausulae) when it does not end with a disyllable or trisyllable, i.e. when it does not

---

[14] Cf. J. Soubiran, *L'Élision dans la poésie latine* (Études et Commentaires, 63; 1966), 374. So the Gallus papyrus has *tum erunt* as an anapaest; cf. above, p. 118.

suggest the regular rhythms of a Latin hexameter verse.[15] 9–10. If taken together these lines give a colon of 20 syllables, which seems too long. Habinek marks a minor incision after *primum*, but I should rather risk putting a colon-ending after *gaudio*; again we must get rid of modern ideas about punctuation. This splits up 9–10 more evenly, and gives a double-cretic clausula (type 2) at *maximo gaudio*, provided that hiatus is posited before *et*. As this raises issues of some consequence, an extended discussion follows.

Though we expect elision to operate in prose the same way as in verse, an expectation abundantly confirmed in the clausulae, it is a priori plausible that hiatus should occur at the end of a colon (just as at the end of a hexameter); and Fraenkel, for instance, suggests in a couple of places that hiatus is present (*Leseproben*, 29, 146). H. D. Broadhead had gone some way further in his interesting and still significant book on *Latin Prose Rhythm*; observing that 'the end of a kolon can sometimes be determined by the presence of hiatus or *syllaba anceps*' (p. 32), he cites *Lig.* 1 'sed quoniam diligentia ĭnĭmīcī | investigatum est quod latebat'. He then adds 'this is a highly subjective technique, and to be applied only when other resources fail'; but this is much too pessimistic. In fact the recognition of hiatus seems to be a significant and disregarded method for determining the boundaries of cola in Latin.[16]

Let us begin with a simple case like *Marc.* 30 'nunc certe pertinet [2] | esse te talem [1H] | ut tuas laudes obscuratura | nulla umquam sit oblivio [2]'. Here there is an obvious sense-break after *talem*, and we naturally assume that *esse te talem* | is a type-1 clausula ($-\cup--\times$) followed by hiatus (here symbolized by '[H]'); but if the case were taken in isolation, some might elide the *-em* of *talem* and assume a type-3 clausula ($-\cup-\times$). Things are clearer when a hiatus produces a markedly better clausula than an elision does. See *Sex. Rosc.* 54 'finge aliquid saltem commode [2H] | ut ne plane videaris id facere [1] | quod aperte facis'; the rhythm would be much less convincing if the final vowel of *commode* were elided. *Sest.* 68 'res erat et causa nostra eo iam loci [2H] | ut erigere oculos et vivere videremur'; nobody with ears could believe that the last syllable of *loci* is elided. *Lig.* 11 'non habet eam vim ista accusatio [2H] |

---

[15] F. W. Shipley, *CP* 6 (1911), 410 ff.

[16] Conditions are different in Greek, where long vowels are not normally elided, and some authors are reluctant to use hiatus at all; for bibliography see M. D. Reeve, *CQ*, NS 21 (1971), 514 with n. 2. Where the ban is not total, the presence of hiatus may be a guide to the colometry; cf. Dem. 18. 169 τῆι δ' ὑστεραίαι | ἅμα τῆι ἡμέραι | οἱ μὲν πρυτάνεις ..., cited by L. Pearson, *AJP* 96 (1975), 138 ff.

ut Q. Ligarius condemnetur'. In many such cases it is noteworthy that the final word in the colon takes the shape of a cretic (*commode*) or iambus (*locī*); just as in verse, one may see a reluctance to elide the final long vowel of such a word before a following short vowel.[17]

There is no doubt in the above passages about where the colon ends, and the recognition of hiatus adds no extra information. The case is more interesting where smaller units are concerned, and there might be reasonable doubt about whether to subdivide and how (as at *Phil.* 10. 1 *maximo gaudio* discussed above). See for instance *Sex. Rosc.* 12 'eo prorumpere hominŭm cupĭdĭtātem ¹ᴴ | et scĕlŭs ĕt audacĭăm ²ᴴ | ut non modo clam vērum ĕtiam hĭc ĭn fŏrŏ ²ᴴ | antĕ trĭbūnāl tŭŭm ² | Marcĕ Fānnĭ ³ᴴ | ante pedēs vēstrŏs iūdĭcēs ² | inter ĭpsă sūbsēllĭă ² | caedēs fŭtūrae sĭnt ¹'. Here it is obvious that a colon ends after *audaciam* (before the *ut* clause), and the hiatus tells us nothing extra. It will be less generally agreed that a colon ends after *cupiditatem* (this raises the same questions as the separation of *gaudio* and *et gratulatione* cited above); but the fact that hiatus produces a much better rhythm than elision tends to confirm that there is an objective incision. The same is true after *foro* and *Fanni* (for the evidence is cumulative); and when we see how much the sentence is subdivided, that encourages us to make further subdivisions, for instance after *subsellia*.

I select a few other instances out of many possibilities. *Sest.* 103 'sed tamen haēc vĭa āc rātĭŏ ¹ | rei publicae cāpĕssēndae ¹ᴴ | olim erat magis pērtĭmēscēndā ¹ | cum multis in rebus | multĭtūdĭnĭs stŭdĭŭm ¹ᴴ | aut pŏpŭlī cŏmmŏdŭm ²ᴴ | ab utilitate rei pūblĭcae dĭscrĕpābat. ³' I have marked hiatus after *capessendae*, *studium*, *commodum*, and in the last two cases the rhythm would be impaired without it; once again this encourages us to break up the sentence into small units. *Cael.* 1 'sed adulescentem inlustri ingenio indūstrĭa grātĭa ²ᴴ | accusari ab eius filio | quem ipse in iudicium ᴴ | et vocet ĕt vŏcārĭt ³.' The double cretic at *industria gratia* (if hiatus is posited) suggests that *adulescentem* with its attributes makes a colon (the unit is long enough); the incision after *iudicium* is natural though the clausula is not one of the commonest (−−−⌣⌣×), as a break is often found before the first *et* of a pair. *Har. Resp.* 2 | 'cepi equidēm frŭctŭm māxĭmŭm ²ᴴ | et ex consurrectione ōmnĭŭm vēstrŭm ¹ᴴ | et ex comitatu pūblĭcānōrŭm. ¹' Once again there is an incision before 'both' and 'and'. *Har. Resp.* 11 'potestne referre dē mĕā dŏmŏ ⁴ | quae ut dixi | sōla ĭn hāc ŭrbĕ ¹ᴴ | omnī rĕlĭgĭŏnĕ ¹ᴴ | omnibus iudiciis lībĕrāta ĕst? ³' It might be debated whether *omni*

---

[17] Soubiran, *L'Élision*, 437 ff.

religione is an independent colon; the emphasis on *sola, omni, omnibus* encourages such a view, and this is supported by the clausula if hiatus is posited. *Pis.* 21 'itaque dĭscēssŭ tŭm mĕō ²ᴴ | omnes illi nefārĭī glădĭī ¹ | de manibus crudēlīssĭmĭs ēxcĭdērŭnt. ³' The clausula after the iambic *meo* (provided that hiatus is posited) confirms that as often the adverbial phrase makes an independent colon;[18] once this is granted, one is encouraged to subdivide further after *gladii*, as extended subjects also make independent cola.[19] *Phil.* 3. 15 'primum in Caesarem ut malĕdīctă cŏngēssĭt ¹ | deprompta ex recordatione īmpŭdīcĭtĭae ¹ᴴ | ēt stŭprōrŭm sŭōrŭm ³'. Fraenkel marks the colon-ending at *congessit*, noting that the following participial clause makes an independent colon (*Leseproben*, 115); he might have added an incision at *impudicitiae*, where the possible break suggested by the sense is supported by the rhythm if hiatus is accepted.

It must be admitted that there are some clear breaks where the clausula would be better if there were no hiatus, but such places are by comparison infrequent. See for instance *Sex. Rosc.* 43 'nonne optatissimum sibi putant esse | filios suos rei familiari māxĭmē sērvīrĕ | et in praediis colendis | operae plurimum studique consumere?', *Cael.* 34 'ideō vĭām mūnīvĭ | ut eam tu alienis viris comitata celebrares?' In such cases we should probably admit hiatus and accept the less favoured clausula; 'cretic + molossus' is not uncommon at the ends of internal cola. But even if we see elision in such circumstances and think of something like the hypermetric syllables occasionally found in verse, that would not affect our main point: hiatus is the norm at the end of a colon, and in doubtful cases the improvement of the rhythm by the assumption of a hiatus is itself evidence for the colometry.

These thoughts about hiatus suggest another line of inquiry which may be left to others to follow up. Ancient theorists suggest that when a word ends with a certain consonant, it is 'rough' for certain other consonants to begin the next word. Cf. Cic. *De Or.* 3. 172 (of a style that is 'aequabiliter fluentem') 'id adsequemini si verba extrema cum consequentibus primis ita iungentur ut neve aspere concurrant neque vastius diducantur' (the latter clause refers to unwanted hiatus), *Orat.* 150 'ne extremorum verborum cum insequentibus primis concursus aut hiulcas voces efficiat aut asperas', Quint. 9. 4. 37 'ceterum consonantes quoque, earumque praecipue quae sunt asperiores, in commissura verborum rixantur, ut s ultima cum x proxima, quarum tristior

---

[18] Cf. Fraenkel, *Leseproben*, 218, 'praepositionaler Ausdruck kolonbildend'.
[19] Ibid. 201 ff.

etiam si binae colliduntur stridor est, ut *ars studiorum'*. I am not aware
that it has ever been properly worked out which *coniunctiones verborum*
are avoided; the | question cannot be settled at a glance, as we are talk-
ing of tendencies rather than of absolute rules, but with computer
technology it should be possible to establish whether in fact Cicero has
a different distribution from a less mellifluous author (such as Sallust)
or a non-literary text. The collection of statistics is complicated by a
further consideration, but if this is once recognized it might be turned
to advantage: if there are clear conventions about undesirable col-
locations of letters, they presumably cease to operate at the ends of
cola. So if we found that a particular collocation (of consonants or
vowels) that tended normally to be avoided by Cicero appeared at a
place where sense or rhythm led us to suspect the end of a colon, that
would give some corroboration that our suspicion was justified.

I turn now to another possible technique for determining the
boundaries of cola in Cicero. It is well known that the Roman elegists
have few instances of *atque* before a consonant, and that most of these
are likely to be corrupt.[20] Hexameter poets are less strict, but even they
show considerable inhibitions.[21] In the same way Cicero[22] usually
avoids *atque* before a consonant except where it produces a desirable
clausula (as at *Verr.* 3. 208 *atque disceditis*, 3. 212 *atque recreasti*, 3. 215
atque contemptum, Sull. 15 *atque vultu*). For his normal practice cf. *Verr.*
5. 92 'o tempus miserum *atque* acerbum provinciae Siciliae. o casum
illum multis innocentibus calamitosum *atque* funestum. o istius nequitiam *ac* turpitudinem singularem'; here the first *atque* comes before a
vowel, the second *atque* before a consonant to assist the clausula, and
ac before a consonant when not in the clausula. Other prose authors
show the same tendency.[23]

Fraenkel notes that rhythmical factors may have played a part in
Cato's predilection for *atque* before consonants,[24] and he comments on
the clausula *atque curare* in the rhetorical letter that is optimistically
ascribed to the mother of the Gracchi.[25] But it may not have been

[20] M. Platnauer, *Latin Elegiac Verse* (Cambridge, 1951), 78 ff.
[21] B. Axelson, *Unpoetische Wörter* (Lund, 1945), 83 ff.; J. A. Richmond, *Glotta*, 43 (1965),
78 ff.; O. Skutsch, *The* Annals *of Ennius* (Oxford, 1985), 63.
[22] J. Wolff, *Jahrb.* suppl. 26 (1901), 637 ff. (but he is only interested in clausulae at the
ends of sentences).
[23] H. Hagendahl, *La Prose métrique d'Arnobe* (Göteborg, 1937), 198 ff.; Axelson, *Unpoetische Wörter*, 83 f. n. 72; J. B. Hofmann and A. Szantyr, *Lateinische Syntax und Stilistik*
(Munich, 1965), 720.
[24] *Leseproben*, 130.
[25] Ibid. 162 n. 3.

appreciated that ante-consonantal *atque* provides a prima-facie criterion for determining the boundaries of internal cola. See for instance *Sull.* 34 'harum omnium rerum ¹ | quas ego in consulatu ³ | pro salute rei publicae ² | suscepi ātquĕ gēssĭ ³ | L. ille Torquatus ¹ | cum esset meus contubernalis in consulatu ³ᴴ | atque etiam in praetura fuisset ³ | auctor adiutor particeps exstitit ²', *Har. Resp.* 10 'reperietis enim | ex hoc toto prodigio ātquĕ rēspōnsŏ ¹ | nos de istius scelere ac furore ³ᴴ | ac de impendentibus periculis maximis ² | prope iam voce Iovis Optimi Maximi praemoneri ³'.

As with hiatus, the technique is most useful when we consider the less | obvious cases; I give only a selection of many possible instances, some exhibiting hiatus as well. *Verr.* 1. 1. 16 'ea mansit in condicione ātquĕ pāctŏ ³ᴴ | usque ad eum finem | dum iudices reiecti sunt'. *Imp. Pomp.* 71 'vestram voluntatem ¹ᴴ | et rei publicae dignitatem ³ᴴ | et salutem provinciarum ātquĕ sŏcĭōrŭm ¹ | meis omnibus commodis ² | et rationibus | praeferre oportere ¹' (the extended object makes a series of cola). *Clu.* 194 'cuius ego furorem ātquĕ crūdēlĭtātĕm ³ | deos immortalis | a suis aris ātquĕ tēmplĭs ³ | aspernatos esse confido ¹' (the prepositional phrase makes a colon). *Leg. Agr.* 2. 5 'cum ad animi mei fructum ¹ᴴ | ātquĕ lāĕtĭtĭăm ¹ | duco esse permagnum ¹'. 2. 15 'sic confirmo Quirites ³ | hac lege agraria pulchra ātquĕ pŏpŭlārĭ ¹ | dari vobis nihil . . .'. *Cat.* 3. 18 'quamquam haec omnia Quirites ¹ | ita sunt a me administrata ¹ᴴ | ut deorum nutu ātquĕ cōnsĭlĭŏ ¹ᴴ | et gesta et provisa esse videantur ¹'. 4. 12 'tum fugam virginum ātquĕ pŭĕrōrŭm ¹ᴴ | ac vexationem virginum²⁶ Vestalium perhorresco ¹'. 4. 21 'sit Scipio clarus ille ³ | cuius consilio ātquĕ vīrtūtĕ ¹ᴴ | Hannibal in Africam redire ³ᴴ | atque Italia decedere coactus est ²'. *Mur.* 29 'deinde vestra responsa ātquĕ dēcrētā ¹ᴴ | et evertuntur saepe dicendo ¹ᴴ | et . . .' (the extended subject makes a colon, and there are incisions before 'both' and 'and'). *Arch.* 26 'ut etiam Cordubae natis poetis ³ | pingue quiddam sonantibus ātquĕ pĕrēgrīnŭm ¹ | tamen auris suas dederet ²'. *Dom.* 145 'si in illo paene fato rei publicae ²ᴴ | obieci meum caput ⁴ | pro vestris caerimoniis ātquĕ tēmplĭs ³ | perditissimorum civium furori ātquĕ fērrŏ ³'. *Balb.* 31 'o iura praeclara ¹ᴴ | ātquĕ dīvīnĭtŭs ² | iam inde a principio Romani nominis ² | a maioribus nostris comparata ³'. *Planc.* 1 'si huius salus ob eam ipsam causam esset infestior ² | quod is meam sălūtĕm ātquĕ vītăm ³ | sua benivolentia praesidio custodiaque texisset ¹' (*sua* is emphatic). *Rab. Post.* 25 'suas fortunas ātquĕ fāmăm ³ | libidini regiae

---

²⁶ The repetition of *virginum* is unattractive, and if the word were deleted the colon would be a better length.

commisisse'. *Phil.* 6. 2 'cum vos universi ³ᴴ | ūnā mēnte ātquĕ vŏcē ³ᴴ | iterum a me conservatam esse rem publicam ² | conclamastis'. *Phil.* 10. 20 'nos ita a maioribus instituti ³ᴴ | atque imbuti sumus ² | ut omnia consilia ātquĕ fāctā ³ᴴ | ad dignitatem et ad virtutem referremus ¹'.

Sometimes *atque* appears before a consonant without helping the rhythm, but some of these cases may be caused by a faulty text. See *Verr.* 3. 48 'atque perinde loquor'; better the variant 'atque haec perinde loquor' (as at *Quinct.* 83). *Verr.* 5. 127 'in urbe nostra pulcherrima atque ornatissima ² | quod signum quae tabula picta est ¹ | quae non ab hostibus victis ¹ | capta atque deportata sit?' The manuscripts vary between *deportata* (where *atque* gives no help to the rhythm) and *adportata* (which makes no sense); perhaps *asportata* (as at 4. 80, 88, 110, 5. 185; *deportare* should give a destination). *Cat.* 3. 11 'sceleris manifesti atque deprehensi'; read *deprensi*, as is always legitimate. *Arch.* 19 'saxa atque solitudines voci respondent, | bestiae saepe immanes cantu flectuntur ātquĕ cōnsīstŭnt ¹'; Clark accepts the first *atque* from Quintilian (five citations), | where Cicero's manuscripts have *et*, but the rhythm tells against him. *Arch.* 21 'urbem amicissimam Cyzicenorum ¹ᴴ | eiusdem consilio ᴴ | ex omni impetu regio ²ᴴ | atque totius belli ore ac faucibus ² | ereptam esse ātquĕ sērvātăm ¹'; the variant *ac totius* seems preferable. At *Sest.* 81 Peterson's Oxford text reads 'cum rem publicam a facinerosissimis sicariis et a servis ¹ | esse oppressam atque conculcatam videretis ¹'; here *conculcatam* is a conjecture by Gulielmius for the meaningless *occultam*, and the variant *occupatam* gives a more satisfactory rhythm.

Cicero uses *atque* before consonants more freely in his earlier speeches, notably the *Rosciana* of 80 BC and even the *Verrines* of 70; cf. *Verr.* 4. 107 'quam circa lacus lucique sunt plurimi ²ᴴ | atque laetissimi flores ¹ | omni tempore anni ³' (here *atque* produces an extra cretic, perhaps a sign of early exuberance). In stereotyped phrases in particular the archaic *atque* seems to be retained; cf. *Sex. Rosc.* 32 'cum ferro atque telis venistis', *Leg. Agr.* 2. 74 'in capite atque cervicibus nostris conlocare ³', *Mur.* 1 'bene atque feliciter eveniret ³'. I have also noticed some instances where two superlatives are combined: *Rab. Perd.* 13 'superbissimi atque crudelissimi regis ¹', *Mur.* 59 'fortissimo atque florentissimo viro ⁴', 83 'honestissimi atque sapientissimi viri iudicabunt ³'. There are other exceptions to our rule, but considering the quantity of the material, unambiguous cases are rather few. We are entitled to say that at least in speeches later than 70 BC *atque* before a consonant will normally begin the clausula, and should be assumed to do so unless considerations of sense point clearly the other way.

The evidence from hiatus, *atque*, and unemphatic pronouns[27] all points the same way: fairly short units are being produced, often of no more than ten syllables. What is more important, the evidence is abundant enough for us to extrapolate to the much larger number of places where there is no hiatus, no *atque*, and no unemphatic pronoun. This supports the thoroughgoing subdivision of sentences adopted by Fraenkel (with prepositional phrases and the rest counting as separate cola); and indeed it is entirely natural that set-piece speeches to large audiences should be delivered in short bursts (like 'government of the people | by the people | for the people').[28] Now of course breaks must vary in length and significance (with no sharp distinction between the major and the minor, but rather a continuous gradation), and of course the clausulae before the minor pauses tend to have a less stereotyped rhythm; but if we argue from the clear cases to the less clear even the minor pauses can often | be identified. Fraenkel is also justified in his use of the word 'colon' even for the lesser subdivisions of a sentence (the ancient practice seems to have varied). Broadhead reserves the term for significant syntactical units, and calls the shorter subdivisions 'articuli'; but this involves arbitrary decisions about nomenclature in many places where no practical consequences are involved. If the shorter units often show the favoured clausulae (much more than Broadhead admitted), and if they are sometimes followed by hiatus, then they need not be differentiated in kind from the larger units. If a unit admits, or is capable of admitting, hiatus at the end, let us call it a colon.

If a colon is identified in this way, let us next consider what normally is its maximum length; here again we can extrapolate from the small sense-units that are confirmed as cola by Wackernagel's law, pen-ultimate *atque*, and clausula (especially when it is supported by hiatus). I have gone through the Ciceronian passages analysed by Fraenkel in his *Leseproben* (admittedly often chosen for their eloquence and

---

[27] Fraenkel's observation about Wackernagel's law is most illuminating when it produces short cola that might not otherwise be recognized; see e.g. *Quir.* 16 'deinde ipse ad extremum ¹ | pro mea vos salute ³ | non rogavit solum | verum etiam obsecravit ³'. *Sest.* 134 'homo flagrans cupiditate gloriae ⁴ | tenere se non potuit'.

[28] For the limitations of conventional punctuation in English see R. Quirk *et al.*, *A Comprehensive Grammar of the English Language* (London, 1985), 1606 ff. Thus in the sentence 'The newspaper article on the recent conflict was utterly misleading' there is a break in the spoken language at 'conflict' (after the extended subject).

marked prose-rhythm). I begin to feel some disquiet when he gives a
colon of more than 16 syllables, and note that the same size was given
by du Mesnil a century ago as a normal maximum.[29]

Quinct. 83 (*Leseproben*, 54) 'debueris aut potueris Publium Quinctium de possessione deturbare' (25 syllables); probably divide after
potueris (clausula type 3 with resolution) and *Quinctium* (type 2). *Imp.
Pomp.* 30 (p. 60) 'per quam legionibus nostris iter in Hispaniam Gal-
lorum internicione patefactum est' (28 syllables); certainly divide after
nostris (clausula 1) and *Hispaniam* (clausula 2). Ibid. 'quae saepissime
plurimos hostis ab hoc superatos prostratosque conspexit' (23 syllables); divide after *hostis* (clausula 1). *Cat.* 2. 17 (p. 35) 'ex quibus
generibus hominum istae copiae comparentur' (18 syllables); divide
after *hominum* (with hiatus), before the emphatic *istae. Sull.* 4 (p. 69)
'quem cum videas hoc honore auctoritate virtute consilio praeditum'
(23 syllables); divide after *auctoritate* (clausula 3). *Sull.* 5 'an vero | in
quibus subselliis haec ornamenta ac lumina reipublicae viderem | in his
me apparere nollem' (23 syllables in the middle colon); divide after
subselliis rather than *vero.* Ibid. 'cum ego illum in locum atque in hanc
excelsissimam sedem dignitatis atque honoris' (22 syllables), 'multis
meis ac magnis laboribus et periculis ascendissem' (20 syllables); divide
after *locum* (with hiatus), *sedem* (clausula 1), *laboribus* (clausula 4). *Arch.*
29 (p. 72) 'non cum vitae tempore esse dimittendam commemora-
tionem nominis nostri' (24 syllables); divide after *tempore* (clausula 2
with hiatus), and perhaps *dimittendam. Dom.* 91 (p. 81) 'tuo praecipiti
furori atque impio sceleri restitissem' (19 syllables); divide after *furori*
(clausula 3 with hiatus).

This leads us to a further question: how many long syllables in
sequence are tolerable? According to Blass's law, Demosthenes avoids
a sequence of three or more short syllables;[30] Latin was a much heavier
language, and here too many | long syllables may have seemed objec-
tionable. *Imp. Pomp.* 30 'testes nunc vero iam omnes orae atque omnes
terrae gentes nationes'; from *testes* to *nat-* gives a sequence of 16 long
syllables, but there is surely a colon-ending after *orae* (with hiatus), and
below the reading *exterae gentes ac* should be preferred. *Sest.* 5 'quibus
initiis ac fundamentis hae tantae summis in rebus laudes excitatae
sunt'; 17 long syllables in a row is too many, and a colon ends at *fundamentis. Sest.* 58 'Antiochum Magnum illum maiores nostri magna belli

---

[29] Cited by L. Laurand, *Études sur le style des discours de Cicéron*, 2, 4th edn. (Paris, 1938),
138 n. 1.
[30] K. J. Dover, *OCD*, 2nd edn., 888.

contentione terra marique superatum ᴵᴴ | intra montem Taurum
regnare iusserunt'; 15 long syllables on end is too many, and the first
clause too long (30 syllables); divide after *illum, nostri, contentione*
(clausula 3), noting that *Magnum, maiores*, and *magna* balance one
another. *Sest.* 73 'magna rerum permutatione impendente | declinasse
me paulum ᴵᴴ | et spe reliquae tranquillitatis praesentes fluctus tem-
pestatemque fugisse'; there is surely a colon-end at *tranquillitatis*
(clausula 3) reducing the sequence of long syllables from 11 to 9. *Sest.*
87 'qui si homines despecti et contempti tantam rem publicam sustinere non potuissent'; the sequence of 11 long syllables from *homines*
to *pub-* as well as the length of the clause as a whole (25 syllables)
encourages us to make an incision after *contempti*.

Prose-rhythm is still an underdeveloped subject in both Greek and
Latin. The basic prosodic rules are not established beyond doubt;
Zieliński[31] says that *sc* at the beginning of a word lengthens the previous syllable, but when I read 'ipse sceleratus' before a pause (*Pis.* 28),
I hear *esse videatur*. Even the behaviour of mute and liquid may vary
from author to author; Konrad Müller has shown that in Curtius Rufus
patris may in certain circumstances count as a trochee,[32] but for
Fraenkel the first syllable in Cicero is invariably short. The textual
critic of a rhythmical author must repeatedly use clausulae to dis-
criminate between variants; most now know this when considering
sentence-endings, but few are sufficiently sensitive to internal rhythms.
It is sometimes said that a conjecture should never be made simply for
the clausula; the dogma is refuted by Cic. *Phil.* 13. 27 *munera rosit* (a
sentence-ending describing the bribes taken by one Mus), where Clark
was certainly right when he proposed *munera arrosit* (a type-1 clausula
instead of a 'hexameter-ending'). It seems possible that even works not
regarded as notably clausulated might have a characteristic thumb-
print, that with modern technology might provide a criterion for
authenticity: are the rhythms of *Ephesians* distributed differently from
those of *Corinthians?* But here I imitate the *recusatio* of the Augustan
poets who in declining to undertake a difficult enterprise were content
to hint at a more appropriate author.

---

[31] *Clauselgesetz*, 174 f.   [32] Edn., p. 770.

20

The Style of Virgil's *Eclogues*

THE style of a poet is the most important thing about him, the element that cannot be translated, without which nobody but a scholar could endure to read him. But it is also the hardest part to characterize, which is why we all prefer to talk about other matters. Lists of vocabulary and metrical statistics provide useful raw material, but they may communicate very little; a count of dactyls does not tell us what the *Eclogues* are actually like. I believe that here as elsewhere the best approach is to concentrate on particular passages where the idiosyncrasy of the poet appears in its most undiluted form. Such passages give a flavour to the whole, but this quality is easily dissipated in a statistical treatment; after all, in most works of literature, including even the *Eclogues*, there are many lines that could have belonged somewhere else.

Virgil in the *Eclogues* set out to do a Theocritus in Latin, that is to say to transfer the charm and precision of a very individual poet to his own slow-footed language. Partly of course he does the trick by specific imitations, and commentators have collected a store of more or less parallel passages, which for the most part will be omitted here. Such parallels are most evocative when they preserve the movement of the original; thus at 8. 41 *ut vidi, ut perii*, 'when I saw, then I was lost' the use of the second *ut* as a correlative[1] strains the possibilities of Latin, but it recalls the Theocritean prototype χὼς ἴδον ὡς ἐμάνην (2. 82). Then there is the notorious case of 8. 58 *omnia vel medium fiat mare*, 'let everything become mid-ocean'; Theocritus had said πάντα δ᾽ ἔναλλα γένοιτο, 'let everything become contrary' (1. 134), and by a process of free association more characteristic of modern than classical poetry Virgil represents ἔναλλα 'contrary', as if it were ἐνάλια, 'in the sea'. But quite apart from parallel passages there is a more indirect

---

[1] S. Timpanaro, *Contributi di Filologia e di storia della lingua latina* (Rome, 1978), 219 ff., citing (p. 274) Cat. 62. 45 'sic virgo, dum intacta manet, dum cara suis est', 62. 56.

Proceedings of the Virgil Society, 20 (1991), 1–14.

imitation of style that cannot be associated with any single model. This type of imitation is really the more subtle, though it is harder to pin down; in the same way | the best parodies are not the sort most common in antiquity, where a well-known line is modified by some ridiculous adaptation. The really clever parodies suggest the idiom of the original in an absurd way without referring to any particular passage; such is Calverley's skit on Browning, 'The Cock and the Bull', or the hexameter of Persius that catches the quintessence of the old Roman tragedians, *Antiopa aerumnis cor luctificabile fulta* (1. 78).

The *Eclogues* deal with what Milton called 'the homely slighted shepherd's trade', and so they affect a simplicity that is an accomplishment of art. That is why Tityrus at the beginning of the book plays on a thin oat, *tenui avena*, with reference to the style of the poems as well as the shape of the instrument; in the same way Virgil at the end of the last eclogue says that he has been weaving a basket from slender hibiscus, 'dum sedet et gracili fiscellam texit hibisco'. Words for rustic objects like *avena*, 'oat', and *fiscella*, 'basket' give a suggestion of simplicity; however natural oats and baskets may have been in the context, the ancient sensitivity to levels of diction was such that they must have seemed to lower the style. Just as Theocritus talks of onions and snails, and the more realistic Greek epigrammatists describe cottage utensils and artisans' implements, so Virgil flavours his bucolics with thyme and garlic, chestnuts and cheese. Theocritus had one great advantage: by writing in a kind of Doric, however bogus it often was, he produced a whiff of the countryside, and because of the dialect's poetic status he could do this without seeming prosaic or banal. In view of the very different literary traditions of Latin, Virgil could not go to the backwoods for poetic expressions. His efforts in this direction were very limited: we may note the archaic 'nec vertat bene' for 'ne vertat bene' (9. 6), perhaps *his* for *hi* in a passage whose interpretation is disputed (3. 102 'his certe—neque amor causa est—vix ossibus haerent'), most notoriously *cuium pecus* for 'whose flock?' (3. 1). That provoked the well-known retort 'dic mihi, Damoeta: cuium pecus anne Latinum?' (Vita Donati 43), and Virgil did not venture again on what Catullus would have called the language of goat-milkers (*caprimulgi*).

Apart from words for rustic objects, the most striking thing about the vocabulary of the *Eclogues* is the number of diminutives. There are only three proper diminutives in the whole of the *Aeneid*, *palmula* (5. 163), *sagulum* (8. 660), and most memorably *parvulus Aeneas*

(4. 328). In the *Eclogues*, on the other hand, there are a dozen diminutives, words like *agellus, gemellus, luteolus, munusculum, novellus*, with no fewer than | thirteen instances of *capella*, 'a nanny-goat'; this is out of line with other serious poetry apart from Catullus and elegy. Other instances of unpoetical words are not very common; *suavis*[2] occurs 4 times and *formosus* 16 times, though they were avoided in the *Aeneid* and most other epic. In spite of the sprinkling of rusticity, there is plenty of stylistic heightening; the Latin poetic vocabulary is freely used, words like *amnis* (5. 25), *pontus* (6. 35), *ratis* (6. 76), poetic plurals like *otia* (1. 6, 5. 61) or the notorious *hordea* for barley (5. 36), forms like *arbos* (3. 56) or *risere* (4. 62), infinitives like *suadebit inire* (1. 55), retained accusatives like *suras evincta* (7. 32), Grecisms like *suave rubenti* (4. 43). It is true that Tityrus mentions *caseus* or cheese (1. 34), not a word that could be found in epic, but when he invites Meliboeus to supper he turns to a more dignified periphrasis, *pressi copia lactis* (1. 81). It is this blend of the commonplace and the exquisite that gives the *Eclogues* some of their characteristic quality.

'The most prominent single characteristic of Theokritos' style is his repetition or partial repetition of words': I quote Dover's commentary (p. xlv), and I base my analysis partly on his. The repetition of a single word is too common to need much illustration, but one may note in particular the *geminatio* of a proper name (2. 69 *a Corydon, Corydon*, Theoc. 11. 72 ὦ Κύκλωψ Κύκλωψ). More typical[3] are lines like 1. 74 'ite meae, felix quondam pecus, ite capellae', where a word in the first foot is repeated in the fifth; by a rather mannered distribution *meae* is attached to the first *ite* and *capellae* to the second. The same pattern can be seen in Theocritus: cf. 1. 64 ἄρχετε βουκολικᾶς, Μοῖσαι φίλαι, ἄρχετ' ἀοιδᾶς. Another type can be seen at 6. 20f. 'addit se sociam timidisque supervenit Aegle, | Aegle Naiadum pulcherrima'; here the subject is repeated with some expansion, though the figure does not permit a second verb. Such epanalepsis is in no way particularly bucolic, but significantly is found at Theocritus 1. 29f. μαρύεται ὑψόθι κισσός, | κισσὸς ἑλιχρύσῳ κεκονιμένος. A more characteristically bucolic idiom occurs when a whole clause is repeated with slight modifications: 'Daphninque tuum tollemus ad astra: | Daphnin ad astra feremus; amavit nos quoque Daphnis' (5. 51 f.). So in Theocritus βουκολιάζεο Δάφνι· τὺ δ' ᾠδᾶς ἄρχεο πρᾶτος, | ᾠδᾶς ἄρχεο, Δάφνι, ἐφεψάσθω δὲ Μενάλκας (9. 1 f.).

---

[2] B. Axelson, *Unpoetische Wörter* (Lund, 1945), 35 ff.
[3] R. Gimm, *De Vergilii stilo bucolico quaestiones selectae* (Diss. Leipzig, 1910), 80 ff.

That leads us to more complex repetitions where we shall take as prototype Theocritus 1. 4 ff., which must have derived particular prominence from its place in the early editions: |

> αἴ κα τῆνος ἕλῃ κεραὸν τράγον, αἶγα τὺ λαψῇ.
> αἴ κα δ' αἶγα λάβῃ τῆνος γέρας, ἐς τὲ καταρρεῖ
> ἁ χίμαρος· χιμάρῳ δὲ καλὸν κρέας, ἔστε κ' ἀμέλξῃς.

'If he chooses the horned goat you will take the she-goat, and if he takes the she-goat for his prize, the kid falls to you; a kid's flesh is fine until you milk her.' Here words for 'take', 'she-goat', and 'kid' reappear at different places in the line, sometimes in a different tense or case; the lines derive their charm from the ringing of the changes. The pattern is not confined to bucolic poetry, and is found also in Callimachus's *Hymn to Apollo* (2. 9 ff.):

> ὡπόλλων οὐ παντὶ φαείνεται, ἀλλ' ὅτις ἐσθλός·
> ὅς μιν ἴδῃ, μέγας οὗτος, ὃς οὐκ ἴδε, λιτὸς ἐκεῖνος·
> ὀψόμεθ', ὦ Ἑκάεργε, καὶ ἐσσόμεθ' οὔποτε λιτοί.

'Apollo does not appear to everybody but to him that is good. Who sees him, he is great; who has not seen him, he is lowly. We shall see you, Apollo, and we shall never be lowly.' Virgil must have felt the movement as typically bucolic, and so we find similar juggling with words in the eighth eclogue when he assesses the relative guilt of Medea and Cupid (8. 48 ff.):

> crudelis tu quoque, mater.
> crudelis mater magis, an puer improbus[4] ille?
> improbus ille puer; crudelis tu quoque, mater.

Commentators are offended by the pointlessness of it all: Heyne wished to delete the last two lines, and Coleman finds the triple repetition of *crudelis* and *mater* very jejune. In fact Virgil is using a pattern that he regarded as particularly Theocritean; no doubt this pattern has its origin in the jingles of shepherds, but in the hands of a poet the artlessness is contrived.

The same movement is found in the bucolics of Calpurnius, and it has been observed also by modern imitators. Tennyson's 'Come down o maid from yonder mountain height' is a beautiful pastoral poem, and everybody knows 'the moan of doves in immemorial elms', reflecting Virgil's onomatopoeic 'nec gemere aeria cessabit turtur ab ulmo' (1. 58). Less attention | is paid to what goes before: 'and sweet is every

---

[4] In view of the following line I take *improbus* to be predicative, not attributive.

sound, Sweeter thy voice, but every sound is sweet'; here in a line
and a half Tennyson shows that he has caught one of the most
characteristic features of the bucolic idiom. The point has not been
lost on so gifted a verse-composer as J. B. Poynton; see his rendering
of Shakespeare's 'In such a night as this':[5]

> advenit, ecce, leo, Thisbe nec viderat ipsum.
> umbra est, quam vidit; visa tamen aufugit umbra.

Another form of balance is found in the poetic competitions where
one shepherd caps the song of another, naturally in the same
number of lines; the movement is familiar not only from Theocritus
but from the rival choruses of Catullus's epithalamium. The pattern
must have its antecedents in popular poetry: Dover quotes the
Greek children's song where one speaker says: 'Where are my roses,
where are my violets, where is my beautiful parsley?' and the other
replies: 'Here are the roses, here are the violets, here is the beautiful
parsley.'[6] The possible complexities of the pattern may be seen from
the end of Virgil's seventh eclogue (61 ff.):

Corydon: Populus Alcidae gratissima, vitis Iaccho,
             formosae myrtus Veneri, sua laurea Phoebo;
             Phyllis amat corylos: illas dum Phyllis amabit,
             nec myrtus vincet corylos nec laurea Phoebi.
Thyrsis: Fraxinus in silvis pulcherrima, pinus in hortis,
             populus in fluviis, abies in montibus altis:
             saepius at si me, Lycida formose, revisas,
             fraxinus in silvis cedat tibi, pinus in hortis.

Here we should observe the degrees of correspondence not only
between one speaker and another but within each separate quatrain
and often within single lines. We may notice in particular the paratactic comparison, most simply illustrated from the opening of
Theocritus 1; instead of saying 'your piping is as sweet as the
whisper of the pine' we find instead 'sweet is the whisper of the
pine-tree and sweet too is your piping'. Another bucolic pattern may
be seen very clearly in the second of these two stanzas: the statement of the first two lines 65–6 is followed by the hypothesis, *saepius
at si me, Lycida formose, revisas*, which leads to the | conclusion in the

---

[5] J. B. Poynton, *Versions* (Oxford, 1936), 100, translating Shakespeare, *Merchant of Venice*.

[6] PMG 852 ποῦ μοι τὰ ῥόδα, ποῦ μοι τὰ ἴα, ποῦ μοι τὰ καλὰ σέλινα; | ταδὶ τὰ ῥόδα, ταδὶ τὰ ἴα, ταδὶ τὰ καλὰ σέλινα.

last line. For the same movement we may compare Theocritus(?)
8. 41 ff.:

> πάντᾳ ἔαρ, πάντᾳ δὲ νομοί, πάντᾳ δὲ γάλακτος
> οὔθατα πιδῶσιν καὶ τὰ νέα τράφεται,
> ἔνθα καλὰ Ναῒς ἐπινίσσεται· αἱ δ᾽ ἂν ἀφέρπῃ
> χὠ τὰς βῶς βόσκων χαἰ βόες αὐότεραι.

Everywhere is spring, and everywhere pastures, and everywhere udders gush
with milk and younglings are fattened where fair Nais comes; but if she goes
away, the cowherd and the cows dry up.

The shepherds' monologues, as well as their dialogues, seem to be
influenced by popular poetry. This is seen most clearly with the
repeated refrains, which tend to break speeches into snatches; but
even when there is no refrain, there may be a lack of orderly progres-
sion. Stories are not told in any systematic way; the narrative about the
capture of Silenus (6. 14 ff.) is quite exceptional. In Damon's love-song
(8. 17 ff.) the reader has to piece together what is going on,[7] a natural
consequence of the broken-up character of the bucolic style; the same
is true to some extent with Corydon in 2 and Gallus in 10, though in
the latter case the fluctuating movement of Gallus's own elegies seems
to play a part. Tityrus in the first eclogue cannot give a coherent
account of himself; though this is meant to suggest the rustic wise-
acre's garrulity and love of mystification, Virgil may have been
influenced in his strategy by the inherent bittiness of shepherds' songs.
As T. E. Page pronounces on *modulans alterna notavi* (5. 14), 'You
cannot sing and play a pipe at the same time.'

Another kind of disjointedness in bucolic arises from the frequency
of parenthesis. Sometimes this involves quite a long hyperbaton; for a
possible instance see 9. 37 f. 'id quidem ago et tacitus, Lycida, mecum
ipse voluto | si valeam meminisse neque est ignobile carmen'. Here
editors usually regard *id* as the object of *voluto*, but this does not
combine satisfactorily with the idiomatic *id ago*, 'I am busy with that'; it
might be more elegant to take *voluto* with *carmen* and to mark off the
intervening phrases with dashes. Sometimes a parenthesis gives an
impression of spontaneity, which is of course achieved by art; cf. 3. 93
'frigidus. o pueri—|fugite hinc—latet anguis in herba', where the dis-
ruptive *fugite hinc* indicates the speaker's sudden alarm. See also 8. 109
'parcite—ab urbe venit—iam parcite, carmina—Daphnis'; here the
separation of *venit* from *Daphnis* is highly mannered, but at the same

---

[7] B. Otis, *Virgil, A Study in Civilized Poetry* (Oxford, 1964), 105 ff.

time it indicates the excitement of the speaker and produces a climax with the lover's name. For an even longer hyperbaton see 9. 2 ff.:

> o Lycida, vivi pervenimus, advena nostri
> (quod numquem veriti sumus) ut possessor agelli
> diceret 'haec mea sunt; veteres migrate coloni'.

Here the long separation of *nostri* from *agelli* puts great emphasis on the possessive, and the parenthesis helps to suggest the breathless indignation of Moeris.

Ellipse is another feature that is colloquial at least in origin. It is found in the clipped civilities of Theocritus (14. 1 f.):

> χαίρειν πολλὰ τὸν ἄνδρα Θυώνιχον—ἄλλα τοιαῦτα
> Αἰσχίνᾳ. ὡς χρόνιος—χρόνιος—τί δέ τοι τὸ μέλημα;

'A very good day to friend Thyonichus.—The same to Aeschinas. It's a long time.—A long time.—What's the trouble?' So too the beginning of the third eclogue (a passage directly imitated from Theocritus (4. 1 ff.):

> Dic mihi, Damoeta, cuium pecus? an Meliboei?
> Non, verum Aegonis.

Sometimes the ellipse is more mannered than genuinely colloquial. 'quo te, Moeri, pedes?' (9. 1) may look idiomatic, but it is not what anybody would actually say; it is as artificial as 'whither away?' So too when Menalcas forgets an astronomer's name, the interrupted construction gives an illusion of spontaneity: 'in medio duo signa Conon—et quis fuit alter | descripsit radio totum qui gentibus orbem . . .?' (3. 40). Ellipse may also be used for euphemistic reasons; Virgil would not dream of imitating the rustic obscenities of Theocritus, still less the unimaginable bad language of real *pastores*, a rough body of men, so he contents himself with the discreet impropriety of 'novimus et qui te' (3. 8).

A marked feature of the Theocritean style is the number of appositions, | which suggest the disjointed afterthoughts of colloquial discourse; cf. 15. 19 f. ἑπταδράχμως κυνάδας, γραιᾶν ἀποτίλματα πηρᾶν, | πέντε πόκως ἔλαβ' ἐχθές, ἄπαν ῥύπον, ἔργον ἐπ' ἔργῳ ('yesterday he bought five fleeces, seven-drachma dog-skins, pluckings of antiquated haversacks, nothing but filth, one job after another'). Appositions in the *Eclogues* are much less conspicuous, but there is one notable type that is mannered rather than colloquial; this is the appositional sandwich as in 1. 57 'raucae, tua cura, palumbes'. This pattern is not paralleled in Theocritus, but is attested in Archilochus and Greek epigram.[8] Otto Skutsch has commented on the resemblance between 'raucae, tua cura, palumbes' and a line in Propertius 'et Veneris dominae volucres, mea turba, columbae' (3. 3. 31); he plausibly suggests a common source in Gallus,[9] and has named the construction the 'schema Cornelianum'. The word-order appears intermittently in later Latin poetry, and Juvenal still uses it for sardonic effect (7. 120 'veteres, Maurorum epimenia, bulbi', 'old onions, the rations of Moors'); no extant work favours it so much as the *Eclogues*, but it must be regarded as a neoteric rather than a bucolic feature.

Some of the elements that I have been mentioning are brought together in a concentrated form in a passage in the ninth eclogue (23 ff.):

> Tityre, dum redeo—brevis est via—pasce capellas,
> et potum pastas age, Tityre, et inter agendum
> occursare capro—cornu ferit ille—caveto.

This is an isolated snatch of song, typical of the bittiness to which I have referred. The passage is broken up by two parentheses (*brevis est via* and *cornu ferit ille*) that hint at the disorganized character of colloquial speech, though once again Virgil's disorganization is deliberately organized. We may also note the repeated reiteration of key words to produce the traditional bucolic jingle: *Tityre Tityre, pasce pastas, age agendum.* And there is a distinctive metrical point that I have not yet dealt with, the so-called bucolic diaeresis.

A diaeresis occurs when a word ends at the end of a foot, and the bucolic diaeresis is sometimes defined as any word-break at the end of the fourth foot; thus on this definition there would be a bucolic diaeresis after *cornu ferit*. Such word-breaks are notably common in Theocritus, and more common in the *Eclogues* than in Virgil's other hexameters; but a more restrictive definition brings out more clearly a distinguishing | characteristic of bucolic poetry. According to this a bucolic diaeresis occurs when there is not only a word-break but a pause in sense at the end of the fourth foot, as after *brevis est via* in the passage under discussion; by the normal rules of the Latin hexameter this pause is preceded by a dactyl, often produced by a pyrrhic word of two short syllables (as here *via*). The bucolic diaeresis in this strict sense is much more common in the *Eclogues* than in Virgil's other works: I have counted 62 cases in the *Ecologues* compared with 4 in

[8] An authoritative treatment of the figure is provided by J. Solodow, *HSCPh.* 90 (1986), 129 ff.

[9] O. Skutsch, *RhM* 99 (1956), 198 f.; he also cites *Ecl.* 10. 22 'tua cura Lycoris'.

Aeneid 2 (including one incomplete line). If we look at the distribution of these 62 cases the effect is even more striking: the early third eclogue has 10, the early seventh eclogue has 12, and though the first eclogue has only 4, 3 of these occur in the first eleven lines, where the characteristic tone is being established. It is also worth noting that the grander manner of the fourth eclogue allows no place for a bucolic diaeresis in the strict sense (i.e. followed by a pause).

Other metrical points may be mentioned more summarily. One feature with a higher incidence than in the *Aeneid* is a line like 'Daphnin ad astra feremus: amavit nos quoque Daphnis' (5. 52); here after *feremus*, that is to say after the trochee in the third foot, there is not only a word-break but a pause. This so-called feminine caesura is often found with Greek words, as at 2. 6 *o crudelis Alexi*; significantly there are three of these caesuras in the first seven lines of the early second eclogue. Then again the runs without strong punctuation at the end of the line are shorter than in the *Aeneid*, even if the statistics are exaggerated by the short snatches of dialogue between the shepherds. The relatively frequent elision of long vowels that is so characteristic of the *Aeneid* is much less common in the *Eclogues*; but such a feature is too negative to give us much sense of the tone of the poems.

I shall mention briefly a few metrical abnormalities. Quadrisyllabic endings may be noted at 2. 24 *Actaeo Aracyntho*, 6. 53 *fultus hyacintho*, 10. 12 *Aonie Aganippe*; in all these cases the last word is Greek, and the Greek effect is underlined by a preceding hiatus or in one instance by an irrational lengthening; metrical licences often come two by two. Sometimes there is a shortening of a long final vowel before another vowel, again in the Greek manner; the abnormality is encouraged by the Greek name at 2. 65 *o Alexi*, though not at 8. 108 *an qui amant, ipsi sibi somnia fingunt?* The effect is more typically bucolic when the licence is combined with a bucolic diaeresis, as at 6. 44 *ut litus 'Hyla Hyla' omne sonaret.* | Here the first final *a* is long by Greek accidence, and the second is shortened by Greek correption before the vowel; the scansion of the same word in two different ways, a favourite Hellenistic trick,[10] here gives hints of an echo. So again at 3. 78 f.:

> Phyllida amo ante alias: nam me discedere flevit
> et longum 'formose, vale vale' inquit 'Iolla'.

The final *e* of the second *vale* is shortened before *inquit*, suggesting that the speaker is moving into the distance. Perhaps in passing I may

---

[10] Nisbet–Hubbard on Horace, *Odes* 1. 32. 11; N. Hopkinson, *Glotta*, 60 (1982), 162 ff.

give my version of the situation, which is different from the usual
account. Phyllis wept that Menalcas was going, and said 'goodbye,
goodbye my beautiful'. One naturally assumes that she is going to say
'my beautiful Menalcas', but then by a surprise she adds 'Iolla'; it
transpires that she is going off with Menalcas, and that the farewells
are being addressed to the other man.

Some of the features that I have been discussing are not specifically
bucolic, and we must look for further antecedents. Horace described
the style of the poems as *molle*, soft;[11] of course that is one side of
Theocritus, but as a Hellenistic poet he could also be crisper and
spikier than the *Eclogues* ever are. Virgil must have owed much to
Catullus and no doubt Gallus for his emotional sentimentality, har-
monious resonances, bright colouring, and elaborate word-patterns. If
this paper deals only incidentally with these aspects it is because I wish
to isolate the more purely bucolic elements, but a full analysis of the
style would recognize an element of neoteric *mollitia* that is not really
Theocritean. When Horace characterized the *Eclogues* he combined
molle with *facetum*; as Quintilian saw (6. 3. 20), *facetum* refers not to
humour, though there is humour in the *Eclogues*, but to a neatness and
elegance that may be distinguished from the lush sensuousness of the
neoterics proper.

Here it must be emphasized that in spite of a dominant tone,
ancient poetry-books are not necessarily written in a uniform style.
Theocritus himself shows a considerable variation between the purely
bucolic idylls and the mime-like *Adoniazusae* (15), and Virgil introduces elements that properly belong to different types of poem; in
such cases Kroll talked of the crossing of the genres,[12] but where the
abnormality is incidental Francis Cairns's term 'inclusion'[13] seems
more appropriate. For a simple instance see the beginning of the song
of Silenus (6. 31f.): |

> namque canebat uti magnum per inane coacta
> semina terrarumque animaeque marisque fuissent.

Here *uti* is clearly Lucretian, particularly at that place in the line, and
so is some of the vocabulary, though not the use of *que*. I have already
referred to the subsequent lines on Hylas (6. 43f.)

[11] Hor. *Serm.* 1. 10. 44f. 'molle atque facetum | Vergilio annuerunt gaudentes rure
Camenae'.
[12] W. Kroll, *Studien zum Verständnis der römischen Literatur* (Stuttgart, 1924), 202ff.
[13] F. Cairns, *Generic Composition in Greek and Roman Poetry* (Edinburgh, 1972), 158ff.

> his adiungit Hylan nautae quo fonte relictum
> clamassent, ut litus 'Hyla Hyla' omne sonaret.

Here a neoteric effect is produced not only by the scansion of *Hyla Hyla* but by the learned allusiveness of *quo fonte*. Another style is found in a snatch of song by Corydon at 7. 29 f.:

> saetosi caput hoc apri tibi Delia parvus
> et ramosa Micon vivacis cornua cervi.

That is the manner of dedicatory epigram, even if it is written in two hexameters rather than an elegiac couplet. Then again, at 8. 80 'limus ut hic durescit et haec ut cera liquescit' the rhyming jingle suggests a magic spell. For a more thoroughgoing conflation of styles one may turn to the tenth eclogue, where the bucolic themes give way to a pastiche in hexameters of the love-elegies of Gallus:

> a te ne frigora laedant!
> a tibi ne teneras glacies secet aspera plantas!
> ibo et Chalcidico quae sunt mihi condita versu
> carmina pastoris Siculi modulabor avena.   (10. 48–51)

Here one may note the sentimental *a*, the sentimental theme of the ice taken from Gallus by Propertius,[14] followed by the resolute *ibo*, suggesting (as Gallus himself must have done) the fluctuating moods of the lover.

The most persistent change of style is in the fourth eclogue, where Virgil himself describes his matter as *paulo maiora*, 'somewhat grander': |

> ultima Cumaei venit iam carminis aetas;
> magnus ab integro saeclorum nascitur ordo;
> iam redit et Virgo, redeunt Saturnia regna,
> iam nova progenies caelo demittitur alto.
> tu modo nascenti puero, quo ferrea primum
> desinet ac toto surget gens aurea mundo,
> casta fave Lucina,[15] tuus iam regnat Apollo.   (4–10)

This resonant passage is intended to suggest a sacred chant, though it is more resonant than the Jewish Sibylline oracles to which Virgil owes so much of his content. We may note the almost entirely end-stopped lines and the formal patterning in groups of 2 + 2 + 3; groups of 7 are

---

[14] Prop. 1. 8. 7 f. 'tu pedibus teneris positas fulcire pruinas, | tu potes insolitas, Cynthia, ferre nives'.

[15] Against the general opinion I put a comma after *Lucina* and interpret 'provided that Lucina favours the birth, Apollo is already as good as reigning' (*BICS* 25 (1978), 62 (see above, p. 56)).

in fact attested in the Jewish prototypes. But the most striking feature is the incantatory rhyming of *o*: *integro, ordo, virgo, caelo, alto, puero, quo, toto, mundo, Apollo*.[16]

The fourth eclogue has a manner of its own in other respects. One may note *saeclorum*, a molossus without elision in the centre of the line; there are 10 instances of this neoteric pattern in 63 lines, a greater incidence than in the other *Eclogues* and considerably greater than in the *Aeneid*. The artistic distribution of adjective and noun, again in imitation of Catullus 64, is also more marked than usual, even if there is only one 'golden' line in the strict sense: 28 'incultisque rubens pendebit sentibus uva'. Then there is the grandiloquent address to the baby himself (48 ff.)

> adgredere o magnos (aderit iam tempus) honores,
> cara deum suboles, magnum Iovis incrementum.

Here *incrementum* at the end of the line produces a spondeiazon almost unique in the *Eclogues*, though found occasionally in Theocritus; the rustic word is given dignity by its position, producing an ambiguity characteristic of this oracular poem. In the following lines we meet some more resonant rhymes (50 ff.), again quite unlike the normal style of the *Eclogues*:

> aspice convexo nutantem pondere mundum,
> terrasque tractusque maris caelumque profundum;
> aspice, venturo laetentur ut omnia saeclo. |

As the poem nears its end the tone suddenly changes (55 ff.):

> non me carminibus vincet nec Thracius Orpheus
> nec Linus, huic mater quamvis atque huic pater adsit,
> Orphei Calliopea, Lino formosus Apollo.
> Pan etiam, Arcadia mecum si iudice certet,
> Pan etiam Arcadia dicat se iudice victum.

Coleman calls attention to the apparently pointless repetitions, which he regards as a possible indication of textual corruption. I believe that his observation could be explained in a different way: Virgil is changing gear and reverting in a rather exaggerated way to his normal bucolic idiom. In much the same way Catullus in his eleventh poem, after using the Sapphic metre inappropriately for cynical gibes at his friends and tasteless invective against his lady, reverts in his last stanza to a genuinely Sapphic image, the flower broken by the ploughshare.

---

[16] This was pointed out in an early article by R. G. Austin, *CQ* 21 (1927), 100 ff.

I conclude with the last lines of the tenth eclogue: evening appropriately closes the poem and the book:

> surgamus: solet esse gravis cantantibus umbra,
> iuniperi gravis umbra; nocent et frugibus umbrae.
> ite domum saturae—venit Hesperus—ite capellae.

Here we have the same jingling repetition that we found at the beginning of Theocritus 1: *gravis, gravis, umbra, umbra, umbrae*. At *iuniperi gravis umbra* there is the enanalepsis that has already been mentioned, for it is surely wrong to understand *est*; that would disrupt the correspondence with the next clause, where *et frugibus* balances *cantantibus*. It may also be suggested that *gravis umbra* is a delicate oxymoron of the sort familiar in sophisticated Roman poetry: a shade in all its senses is naturally *levis*. In the penultimate line we have the soft feminine caesura after the trochee in the third foot, and in the last line the even more typical bucolic diaeresis, the break after *Hesperus*. Also characteristic are the parenthesis *venit Hesperus*, the repetition of *ite* in the first and fifth feet, the artificial distribution by which *saturae* is combined with the first *ite* and *capellae* with the second; there seems also to be a whimsical implication that the audience like the animals now have had their fill. The poem closes with a Grecism for the Evening Star (*Hesperus*), and a | diminutive for the humble nanny-goats (*capellae*), the word that is found in the *Eclogues* thirteen times; the blend of the poetic and the familiar that is so typical of these poems is here given special emphasis. Virgil has ended the book with his bucolic signature-tune, and if I am asked to define the bucolic style I can only point to these lines and say 'That is what it is like.'

21

How Textual Conjectures are Made

In his introduction to Manilius 5, Housman gives a formidable list of the qualities needed for emending a classical text. 'To read attentively, think correctly, omit no relevant consideration, and repress self-will, are not ordinary accomplishments; yet an emendator needs much besides: just literary perception, congenial intimacy with the author, experience which must have been won by study, and mother wit which he must have brought from his mother's womb'.[1] It is not difficult to see that there is something autobiographical about this passage, and Housman goes on to say that he would not have edited Manilius if he had not thought he was fit for the task. To emend so technical and corrupt a text undoubtedly needs a combination of intuition and reasoning power, and in Housman's case the latter may even have predominated. As G. P. Goold has recently emphasized,[2] 'Housman's genius as a textual critic rested upon his power of logical analysis: far beyond the abilities of most scholars he could spot the difficulties in a flawed manuscript text; the record of his successes in solving them, however, shows him to merit, though still a distinguished place, yet one on a lower level.'

Yet Housman understood as well as anybody the part of instinct in textual conjecture. In the same preface he describes how in a quotation from de la Mare's 'Fare Well' he came | across 'the rustling harvest hedgerow', and saw in a flash what the poet had really written (i.e.

An earlier version of this paper was read in Nov. 1989 to the Corpus Classical Seminar in Oxford. It draws in part on my discussion of the text of Juvenal at *JRS* 52 (1962), 233-8 (above, pp. 18-28); *BICS* suppl. 51 (1988) (= *Vir Bonus Discendi Peritus, Studies in Celebration of Otto Skutsch's Eightieth Birthday*, ed. N. Horsfall), 86-110 (above, pp. 227-60); *ICS* 14 (1989), 285-302 (above, pp. 272-92); of Catullus at *PCPS*, NS 24 (1978), 92-115 (above, pp. 76-100); of Horace at *Gnomon*, 58 (1986), 611-15; *CR*, NS 36 (1986), 227-34 (above pp. 192-201); *PCPS* (suppl. 15; 1989) (= *Studies in Latin Literature and the Tradition in Honour of C. O. Brink*, ed. J. Diggle, J. B. Hall, and H. D. Jocelyn), 87-96 (above, pp. 261-71).

[1] *M. Manilii Astronomicon Liber Quintus* (London, 1930), p. xxxv.
[2] *BICS*, suppl. 51 (1988), 28.

'rusting').[3] Even in his paper on 'The Application of Thought to Textual Criticism' he underlines that in making conjectures (as opposed to judging them) the intuitive element plays an important part:[4] 'A textual critic engaged upon his business is not at all like Newton investigating the motion of the planets: he is much more like a dog hunting for fleas ... If a dog is to hunt for fleas successfully he must be quick and he must be sensitive. It is no good for a rhinoceros to hunt for fleas: he does not know where they are, and could not catch them if he did.' He goes on to say that because every textual problem is possibly unique, textual criticism cannot be reduced to rules.

Housman also said that 'no amount ... of palaeography will teach a man one scrap of textual criticism';[5] and it is notorious that good textual critics may be indifferent palaeographers and good palaeographers indifferent critics. Of course information about letter-forms, abbreviations, and common corruptions never comes amiss, and Housman made abundant use of such expertise when it suited his purpose. But an obsession with letter-forms can become a snare: we have all met old articles, even by Housman himself, where an elaborate sequence of misreadings is posited that becomes more speculative at every move. It must be remembered that copyists read by the word, just as we do,[6] rather than by individual letter. I once heard in a radio news-bulletin that a certain athlete was suffering from 'frost-bite, I mean fibrositis'; and I saw in a newspaper the other day a puzzling reference to Chalkidice, only to find that I had misread 'Chalkface'. Many corruptions in classical texts are of this kind, and it is the textual critic's job to clutch out of the air a word with perhaps no more than a general resemblance to the transmitted reading.

Housman claimed to have no inkling of *Ueberlieferungs\geschichte*,[7] which he regarded as a longer name for fudge. He was thinking of the attempt to conjure up ancient editions from the meagre evidence of *subscriptiones*, and here at least his scepticism was justified. The fact remains that though he knew as well as anybody the need to determine the interrelationships of manuscripts, he was not himself primarily interested in handling them. With Juvenal it did not matter: the

[3] Manilius 5 (n. 1), pp. xxxv–xxxvi.
[4] *The Classical Papers of A. E. Housman*, ed. J. Diggle and F. R. D. Goodyear (Cambridge, 1972), 3. 1059.
[5] Ibid. 1058.
[6] J. Willis, *Latin Textual Criticism* (Illinois St. in Lang. and Lit. 61; Urbana, 1972), 53–6, 74–8.
[7] *D. Iunii Iuvenalis Saturae*, 2nd edn. (Cambridge, 1931), p. xxviii.

manuscript set-up was essentially simple, and he identified and described it with wonderful clarity of mind and expression. With Propertius it was very different, and he wasted much ingenuity emending readings that should have been eliminated from the tradition.[8] In fact 'to omit no relevant consideration' is even more difficult than 'to repress self-will', and not even Housman achieved either completely.

All this suggests that in textual conjecture, as in other branches of scholarship, there is no single approach, and that we should be careful to choose our ground with a realistic regard both to the subject-matter and our own capacities. If the relevant text requires significant new work on the manuscripts, we should be wary about making conjectures till we are sure of the facts. But beyond this, the author himself (as opposed to his transmission) must be right for us. I could not myself emend the *Aetna* or the *Anthologia Latina* because I have no instinct about what the authors might have written, nor do I care. I could not emend Ovid because he is too clever, or Propertius because he is too imprecise (or anyway his transmitted text gives that impression). I could not emend Manilius because I find the astronomy too complex as well as the corruptions. It may be added that there is no point in emending authors where nothing needs to be done or nothing can be done. On the other hand, where a number of plausible conjectures have already been made there are probably more to be found.

In the following sketch I shall describe how one textual critic, some of whose conjectures have been accepted by some people other than himself, was led to make particular | proposals.[9] This procedure must seem very self-centred: textual critics are like poets on a very small scale, and so are much too indulgent to their own brain-children. Yet it may be instructive to trace the process of investigation, not after it has been organized and rationalized in a published article, but as it actually occurred; I should make it clear at the beginning that I take a less exalted view than Housman of the textual critic's qualifications and procedures. The result must seem too haphazard and untheoretical for *Materiali e discussioni*. This may be evidence of a British empiricism and

[8] J. L. Butrica, *The Manuscript Tradition of Propertius* (*Phoenix* suppl. 17; Toronto, 1984), esp. 6–7; G. P. Goold, *BICS* suppl. 51 (1988), 28–30.

[9] For general accounts of textual conjecture see L. Havet, *Manuel de critique verbale, appliquée aux textes latins* (Paris, 1911); J. Willis, op. cit. (n. 6); M. L. West, *Textual Criticism and Editorial Technique applicable to Greek and Latin Texts* (Stuttgart, 1973), 53–9; E. J. Kenney, *The Classical Text* (Berkeley, 1974), index s.v. 'conjecture'; D. R. Shackleton Bailey, *Profile of Horace* (London, 1982), 104–20 (reprinting his 1962 lecture on *Bentley and Horace*); L. D. Reynolds and N. G. Wilson, *Scribes and Scholars*, 3rd edn. (Oxford, 1991), 207–41 and 288–94.

dislike of generalization, but it perhaps says something about one aspect of textual conjecture. Other textual critics may operate otherwise, and it would be interesting to hear the experience of those who have worked with different and perhaps more difficult authors.

I shall begin with the first conjecture I ever published,[10] on Cicero, *Philippics* 2. 103: 'ab hac perturbatione religionum advolas in M. Varronis . . . fundum Casinatem. quo iure, quo ore?' Thirty years ago I set the passage in a test-paper, and one student translated 'by what right, by what authority?' Obviously *quo ore* cannot bear this meaning, but he had seen that it must be a genuine question to balance *quo iure*; as he had not prepared his work properly, his natural common-sense was not blurred by received opinion. Once it was clear that the passage was corrupt, and that a parallel to *quo iure* was required, it took only a few seconds to think of *quo more*, 'by what precedent?' Merguet's lexicon to Cicero supplied the required parallels (some of which I may have subconsciously remembered): *Sex. Rosc.* 126 'quo iure aut quo more aut qua lege venierint quaero' (*more* Ernesti: *modo* codd.); *Verr.* 3. 118 'quo id iure atque adeo quo id potius more fecisti?' (*more* cod. det.: *ore* cett.); 3. 198 'quo more, quo iure, quo exemplo?' (*more* Ruhnken: *modo* codd.); *Dom.* 43 'quo iure, quo more, quo exemplo legem nomi|natim de capite civis indemnati tulisti?'; *Vat.* 30 '(scire cupio) quo exemplo quo more feceris'. Finally, as always in Cicero one must test the clausula, which proved highly satisfactory: *quo iure quo more?*, $-\cup--\times$.

Several lessons can be drawn from this trivial episode. The most important stage in conjecture is to know that there is a corruption; if we are sure of that, and refuse to be shaken by general opinion, then the solution may be easy. The critic must understand what the classical feeling for symmetry requires: there is simply no way that *quo ore* can be a question parallel to *quo iure*, still less an exclamation. The critic should not be isolated from teaching in some magnificent research institute, for in meeting the difficulties of others one may find out something for oneself; but we must all hope for students who are sensible and lazy rather than stupid and docile. The solution may come in a flash without any conscious exercise of the mind, though it will often be influenced by a subconscious memory. For that reason we must read and re-read texts, without relying on concordances and computers; these come into play only at the later stage of testing and verification, which is much harder work than making the conjecture itself.

[10] *CR*, NS 10 (1960), 103–4.

I turn to another passage that cries out for the restoration of symmetry. Catullus is describing the pretentious format of Suffenus's new book (22. 6-8):

> cartae regiae, novi libri,
> novi umbilici, lora rubra, membranae,
> derecta plumbo et pumice omnia aequata.

I was greatly puzzled because *novi libri*, which refers to the work as a whole, is not parallel to the other items, which refer to particular features; it is particularly unfortunate that the phrase comes second in the list, and one can have no confidence in Kroll's excuse 'ohne den Verszwang hätte C. sie vor den *chartae regiae* genannt'. I began to think of particular components of a book, papyrus for instance; that immediately suggested *bybli*[11] (probably genitive), which was gratifyingly close to the much commoner *libri*; then I found from the dictionary that *bibli* was the Latin form. At this point an embarrassing | thought struck me, that was soon confirmed: *biblus* is feminine, like βύβλος in Greek. Then I looked at the *apparatus criticus*, as a more methodical reader would have done in the first place, and found that the reading of the transmission was not *novi* but *nove*, the medieval spelling of *novae*. It gives one confidence in a conclusion when an important item of evidence that had not been taken into account is seen to point in the same direction.

For a different kind of faulty balance see Catullus 63. 64: when Attis recalls his past popularity he laments 'ego gymnasi fui flos, ego eram decus olei' (*fui* **O**: *sui* **GR**). Either perfect *fui* or imperfect *eram* could be defended in isolation, but if they appear together, there must be significance in the variation, which is not the case here: editors have not been resolute enough to insist on this. At first sight the alliteration of *fui flos* is so satisfying that I turned my attention to *eram*; I considered *heri* (for the *h* is optional), but the quantity of the second syllable is so uncertain that the word is avoided in classical poetry. Perhaps then *fui* is corrupt. I tried *prius*, which is fairly innocuous, but does not explain the corruption. Then I noticed that Baehrens (one of the few editors who were aware of the difficulty) had tentatively suggested *mei*; this encouraged me to work on the meaningless variant *sui* rather than the superficially meaningful *fui* (always a good principle, though I do not claim that I deliberately adopted it here). This led me to think of *ego gymnasi suus flos*[12] which is good Latin and suits

---

[11] *PCPS*, NS 24 (1978), 96-7 (above, pp. 81-2).   [12] Ibid. 100 (above, p. 86).

the context; this could easily have produced *sui*, which in view of the
similarity of *s* and *f* would have been quickly changed to *fui*. A conjecture that was designed to cure the discrepancy of *fui* and *eram* has
also dealt with the variant *sui*. It may be noted that though I rejected
Baehrens's *mei*, it helped me to a proposal of my own; because of
situations like this editors should be much readier than they are to
record conjectures even when they do not accept them.

At *Carmina* 3. 1. 41–4 Horace observes that luxuries do not soothe
distress:

> quodsi dolentem nec Phrygius lapis
> nec purpurarum sidere clarior
> delenit usus nec Falerna
> vitis Achaemeniumque costum ... |

Here I was mildly surprised by *sidere clarior* and wrote in my margin
sindone; I may have half-remembered what I later turned up, Martial
4. 19. 12 'nec sic in Tyrio sindone tutus eris'. I saw at once that this was
a silly idea, for muslin unless qualified by an adjective is distinguished
by *tenuitas* rather than brightness; but the textual critic must try
ranging shots, and my margins contain a lot of absurdities that I hope
will never be revealed. So I allowed my doubts to be stilled.

A long time afterwards in an idle moment another thought struck
me: the three other luxuries in the stanza are characterized by a
geographical epithet (*Phrygius*, *Falerna*, *Achaemenium*), but the purple
fabrics have no such adornment. Now it is true that *Carm.* 2. 9. 1
begins 'non semper imbres nubibus hispidos manant in agros', though
in the parallel clauses that follow there are mentioned the Caspian Sea,
the lands of Armenia, and the oak-groves of Gargano; in that passage
there is much to be said for the conjecture *Istricos* (recorded by Orelli);
but even if such a solution is rejected, it is easier to have the first clause
out of line (referring to a scene that is imagined as present) than the
second item in a series of four. As soon as it is recognized that the
latter is impossible, the solution presents no problem. What place is
associated with purple? Tyre, obviously, but by no device can Tyre be
made to fit the metre. Anywhere else? I was on holiday at the time, and
working without reference-books (which tend to slow down a textual
critic), but though puzzled by the scansion of *Sidone* as a dactyl,[13] I felt
that it must be permissible. This indeed turned out to be the case: see

---

[13] *LCM* 5 (1980), 151–2 (above, pp. 144–6).

Mart. 2. 16. 3 'quid torus a Nilo, quid Sidone tinctus olenti?'; 11. 1. 2 'cultus Sidone non cotidiana'.

I turn now to a less obvious sort of symmetry that seems to have been impaired by corruption. Juvenal says that those who write on conventional epic themes avoid the risk of offending powerful contemporaries (1. 162–4):

> securus licet Aenean Rutulumque ferocem
> committas, nulli gravis est percussus Achilles
> aut multum quaesitus Hylas urnamque secutus.

All seems straightforward, and the text has never been doubted, but I began to be worried by one point. The first clause is sar|castic, as it suggests that Virgil was a *lanista* promoting a fight of gladiators. So also is the third clause: *urnamque secutus*, 'following the jug', is a comic way of describing Hylas's fall down the well. But there is nothing remotely humorous about *percussus Achilles*, which might have occurred in any serious epic poet. It is a recurring principle of textual criticism that when two clauses out of three show a certain tendency, the third ought to correspond.

The first thing to do was to localize the corruption: it obviously lay in *percussus*. By coincidence I had been collecting a number of words in Juvenal where the prefix had been altered. This led me to think of *excussus Achilles*,[14] which would refer to the hero's exposure when he was disguised as a girl on Scyros: the reference to the *Achilleid* of Statius, not Juvenal's favourite poet, would balance those to the *Aeneid* and to the *Argonautica* of Valerius. I then noticed that *ex-* might have fallen out after *est*, but that was an afterthought, as palaeographic explanations often are in my experience.

This leads to a passage in the same poet where the balance has been impaired in another way. At 3. 106–8 Juvenal describes how a Greek flatters his patron on the most unseemly occasions:

> laudare paratus
> si bene ructavit, si rectum minxit amicus,
> si trulla inverso crepitum dedit aurea fundo.

In the last line commentators have seen references to drinking to the last drop, or alternatively the game of cottabus, all in vain. If an anticlimax is not to be produced, there must be a vulgarity more vulgar than its two predecessors, and the sense can only be *si bene cacavit*;

---

[14] *BICS*, suppl. 51 (1988), 88–9 (above, p. 231).

what is more, this is the only thing that gives point to *aurea*. But now *inverso* is inexplicable, though some have tried to explain it.

I first fiddled with the letters and produced things like *insperso* (too weak) and *immerso* (bad grammar); we have seen already how such false starts may be part of the critical process. Then once again I considered changing the prepositional prefix: this led me quickly to *adverso*.[15] I had an idea that I had met | this word in a context referring to an echo, but I could not find it anywhere, and a search in *TLL* proved fruitless. Finally, a year later I remembered that my own note on Hor. *Carm.* 1. 20. 8 dealt with echoes, and there I discovered what I had vaguely remembered: *Consolatio ad Liviam* 220 'at vox adversis collibus icta redit'.

Another case of imbalance, even if a less obvious one, may be suspected at Lucan 9. 157–9, where Pompey's son is cursing the gods of Egypt:

> omnia dent poenas nudo tibi, Magne, sepulchra:
> evolvam busto iam numen gentibus Isim
> et tectum lino spargam per volgus Osirim . . .

My difficulty was that while *spargam per volgus* is particularly suited to Osiris, whose body was torn limb from limb by Seth and scattered around Egypt, *evolvam busto* seems to have no special application to Isis. This led me to suspect *busto*; I thought of *bysso*,[16] the fine linen associated with Isis in which her mummified body was wrapped. Then I noticed a sequence about dress that I had previously missed: Pompey's body was left naked on the shore, Isis was to be unwrapped from her winding sheet, Osiris though clothed in linen was to suffer the even worse indignity of dismemberment.

My change of *busto* to *bysso* was made not by a conscious examination of every letter; it was a single process, like the original corruption. To suspect a corruption sometimes involves use of the rational faculties, but to cure it need be no more intellectual than solving a clue in a crossword-puzzle: the only difference is that it requires knowledge of a language that is not one's own. I give as another instance a couplet in Catullus, where he hopes that his friend 'Allius' will not be forgotten (68. 49–50):

> nec tenuem texens sublimis aranea telam
> in deserto Alli nomine opus faciat.

---

[15] Ibid. 90.

[16] *Acta Antiqua Academiae Scientiarum Hungaricae*, 30 (1982–4), 314–15 (above, pp. 187–8).

I was puzzled by *sublimis*, even though commentators cited Hes. *Op.* 777 ἀερσιπότητος ἀράχνης: it is not clear how a high roof helps the image, and *sublimis* seems too grand an adjective for the context. What word that looks like *sublimis* is more | appropriate to spiders? If the question is posed in this form, *subtilis* must present itself instantane-ously;[17] it combines well with *tenuem*, *texens*, *telam*, and suits the thought that decay is caused by slight but persistent agencies.

I have been baffled since I was a student about how to translate Lucretius 3. 1042 'ipse Epicurus obit decurso lumine vitae': the mixed metaphor of *decurso lumine* might be tolerated in Propertius, who sometimes writes in a loose and impressionistic way (anyway if we believe his manuscripts and most of his editors), but not in a poet as precise as Lucretius. First I fiddled with *decurso*, in vain; then I noticed that *lumine* was full of the downward strokes that are so often confused (especially before men learned not before time to dot their *i*s). We want a word with similar letters that means not 'light' but 'course'. When the problem is put in this form, it can be solved in one move, *limite*;[18] this word is often misunderstood when the meaning is not 'boundary' but 'path'. It is argued in favour of *lumine* that it suits the solar imagery implied by *obit* ('set') and sustained in the following lines: 'qui genus humanum ingenio superavit et omnis | restinxit, stellas exortus ut aetherius sol'. But *limes* also suits the imagery as it can be used of celestial bodies.[19]

At *Carmina* 4. 10. 4–5 Horace predicts what the boy Ligurinus will say when he grows a beard,

> nunc et qui color est puniceae flore prior rosae
> mutatus Ligurinum in faciem verterit hispidam.

Ligurine (cod. det.) is rightly accepted by most editors: this removes the suggestion that the boy will be 'totus barba' (Bentley's phrase). But in searching the commentators I saw that A. Y. Campbell had noticed another difficulty that had escaped everybody else:[20] what is the point of saying that a rosy *complexion* will turn into a hairy *face*? As Campbell himself expressed it, 'facies tum quoque exstabat dum color eius rosam superabat'. He proposed *maciem*, which does not suit *hispidam*. I tried various things like *cariem*, which is much worse; but at | this prelimin-

---

[17] *PCPS*, NS 24 (1978), 107–8 (above, pp. 94–5).

[18] For this conjecture see R. G. M. Nisbet and M. Hubbard, *A Commentary on Horace, Odes I* (Oxford, 1970), 325 (on 1, 28, 7).

[19] *TLL* 7. 2. 1411. 22 ff.

[20] *Horati Carmina Viginti* (Liverpool, 1934), 51.

ary stage one is content with words of the right shape but the wrong meaning, or the right meaning but the wrong shape (a better approach, as it may lead to a synonym).

Then I remembered that in the many poems on the same theme in the *Greek Anthology*, two types of plant are sometimes contrasted: see 5. 28. 6 (Rufinus) ἀντὶ ῥόδου γὰρ ἐγὼ τὴν βάτον οὐ δέχομαι, 11. 53; 12. 36. 3–4. (I had noted the point in commenting on *Carm.* 1. 25. 17, and so read more carefully than usual the discussion of such poems by S. L. Tarán;[21] it is a good idea to write commentaries as one's own notes are easier to remember than other people's.) So what prickly plant looks like *faciem*? This question led me in a single move to *filicem*. I knew I had met something similar elsewhere, I thought in a satirist; I first tried Horace (for one's memories do not need to be accurate), then Persius, where the index produced 4. 41 'non tamen ista filix ullo mansuescit aratro'. I am fairly sure that this conjecture is right, but most of the credit should go to A. Y. Campbell, who spotted the corruption (much more difficult than solving it). The textual critic should pay particular attention to wild editors like Campbell and Peerlkamp; though their proposals are usually nonsense, they are good at noticing difficulties, and do not try to lull us to sleep with bland assurances.

The corruption of *filicem* to *faciem* seems to me a very typical one: a rare word is displaced by something much commoner that begins with the same letter and otherwise has a general resemblance. As a possible instance of the same process I cite an idea about Statius, *Silvae* 4. 3. 50–3, which was sparked off by a paper read by Dr Kathleen Coleman (for though textual criticism is not exactly a co-operative activity, it may be stimulated by a general discussion):

> hi caedunt nemus exuuntque montis,
> hi ferro scopulos trabesque levant;
> illi saxa ligant opusque texunt
> cocto pulvere sordidoque tofo.

The first two lines refer to timber, but *scopulos* seems intrusive: to smooth rocks and beams one needs different implements. I cannot now remember whether Dr N. M. Horsfall's *corylos* came before or after my contribution; this is ingenious, but too | particular to balance *trabes*. Rather than fiddle with individual letters, I tried to reverse the dyslexia of the copyist, and so produced *scolopas*, 'stakes';[22] the Greek

[21] *JHS* 105 (1985), 90–107.
[22] Published in K. M. Coleman's edition of Statius, *Silvae* 4 (Oxford, 1988), 116–17.

word is acceptable in a technical context, and Dr Coleman's commentary supplies data on the engineering process.

A somewhat different category of corruption seems to arise at Juvenal 3. 4–5. The poet is saying that though Cumae is a lonely place, it has compensations:

> ianua Baiarum est et gratum litus amoeni
> secessus.

Housman took *amoeni secessus* as a genitive of quality; for the unusual combination with the adjective *gratum* he cited Hor. *Serm.* 1. 1. 33 'parvola ... magni formica laboris'. But the phrase remains worrying (perhaps because *secessus* has to mean something like 'secludedness'); earlier he had been ready to take *amoeni secessus* as a nominative plural, which he would not have done if there had been an obvious interpretation.

If there is a corruption it must be in *litus*, which does not seem to balance *ianua* satisfactorily. In looking for something more suitable that began the same way (as most corrupted words do), I hit on *limen*:[23] Cumae is the gateway to the Bay of Baiae, which could certainly be described as *amoeni secessus*. Only then did I notice that *-men* could have been swallowed by *ameni*, with the consequential expansion to *litus*; I have found this quite a common process. Years after I had jotted this idea in my margin I saw the relevance of Stat. *Silv.* 4. 3. 97–8 'huius ianua prosperumque limen | arcus' (elsewhere on the *via Domitiana*); and Dr Coleman's note on the passage called my attention to the Arco Felice, which still stands at Cumae itself. Here again it is gratifying when evidence in support of a conjecture is noticed only after the conjecture has been made.

For a possibly similar corruption see Juvenal 6. 194–6, describing octogenarian women who use Greek terms of endearment:

> quotiens lascivum intervenit illud
> ζωὴ καὶ ψυχή, modo sub lodice relictis
> uteris in turba. |

relictis is clearly indefensible (see Housman and Courtney): elderly women who use these endearments in a crowd have not 'recently left them under the blanket'. Housman saw that a gerundive would give the right contrast and proposed *ferendis* ('only to be endured'); at the same time he suggested a not particularly plausible explanation of the

[23] *BICS*, suppl. 51 (1988), 91–2 (above, pp. 234–5).

corruption. Apart from this I felt unhappy about *uti ferendis*; I thought a verb of speaking would be better (for *uti verbis* is a natural locution), and this naturally suggested *loquendis* ('only to be spoken').[24] I only considered the cause of the corruption after I had made the correction: *locēdis* could have been swallowed by *lodice* and *relictis* supplied to fill the gap.

In making a conjecture it is necessary to know what part of speech it ought to be. Consider Catullus 84. 5–6, where the poet is deriding Arrius's use of aspirates:

> credo sic mater, sic liber avunculus eius,
> sic maternus avus dixerat atque avia.

Editors tell us that by calling the man's uncle 'free', the poet is imputing servile status to the rest of the family; but this is much too complicated, quite implausible (for why should the uncle be any different?), and totally irrelevant to the point at issue. The same line of argument can be used against *Cimber* (Heinsius) and *Umber* (Riese), and indeed any adjective we care to think of. So what part of speech was the missing word? The answer can only be 'an adverb', one that would be generally applicable to all the relatives. I might then have reasoned that the adverb should be of trochaic shape, and that *-er* should therefore be retained; I could then have tried Gradenwitz's reverse lexicon, as I have done on many other occasions (though it has not so far led me to a conjecture). In fact, as far as I can remember, *semper* presented itself as what the sense required,[25] and I only thought up palaeographic explanations afterwards.

It is indeed a merit in a conjecture if it gets rid of an over-complicated interpretation; in some of the passages that I marked as a student because I found it difficult to remember the translation, I now regard the text as corrupt. For one unwel‖come involution see Juvenal 13. 213–16, where we are told that a man with a guilty conscience cannot enjoy the finest of wines:

> sed vina misellus
> expuit, Albani veteris pretiosa senectus
> displicet; ostendas melius, densissima ruga
> cogitur in frontem velut acri ducta Falerno.

The first thing needed is to change *sed vina* to *Setina* (Herel and Withof), a conjecture curiously not accepted by Housman; the three

---

[24] Ibid. 96–7 (above, pp. 241–2).
[25] *PCPS*, NS 24 (1978), 110 (above, p. 98).

wines now balance in a way highly characteristic of Juvenal.[26] But we
are not out of the wood yet: instead of *Falerno* we surely expect an
inferior wine. Courtney comments: 'The better wine is identified with
the Falernian, the only vintage that could rival Alban and Setine: the
very sight of it makes the man screw up his face as if it were bitter and
he were to drink it.' This is ingenious but much too difficult for me.

It is not easy to think of a substitute for *Falerno*. First I tried the
mechanical change of letters that Housman criticized, and arrived at
Salerno. Could *Salerno* be an adjective? No. Could the place-name be
used as a substitute for the product? Not where it is balancing *Albanum*
and *Setinum*. Was there any evidence that Salerno was notorious for
bad wine? No. Finally I turned in desperation to the dictionary and
went systematically through it looking for place-names beginning with
F and preferably *Fa*. That soon brought *Falerii* with its adjective
Falisco,[27] which would suit Juvenal's view that wine brought down the
Tiber was bad (7. 14 *vinum Tiberi devectum*). I could find no parallel for
Faliscum as the name of a wine, but tried Nissen;[28] he referred me to
Gell. 20. 8. 1 for viticulture in the *ager Faliscus*.

Juvenal's fondness for three balancing words may also be invoked at
6. 107-9 (describing the disfigurements of a gladiator):

> praeterea multa in facie deformia, sicut
> attritus galea mediisque in naribus ingens
> gibbus et acre malum semper stillantis ocelli.

I understood some of the difficulties from Housman's note: it | is
difficult to see how a lump in the middle of the nostrils could be caused
by the chafing of the helmet; equally unconvincing is the use of *que* to
join *attritus galea* and *mediis in naribus* (which is not co-ordinate).
Housman accepted *galeae* (Hadrianus Valesius), taking *attritus* as a
noun: instead of a top-heavy sentence we now have three parallel disfigurements, each described in a longer clause than its predecessor.
But it seemed to me that the corruption should rather be looked for in
sicut, which is awkwardly otiose for so conspicuous a place in the line.
So we are looking for a trochaic word with a resemblance to *sicut* and
probably beginning with an *s* to describe a disfigurement produced by
the rubbing of a helmet. I juggled with the letters, trying obvious
substitutes like *l* for *i*, and the answer came from nowhere: *sulcus*.[29]

---

[26] *BICS*, suppl. 51 (1988), 95 (above p. 240).
[27] Ibid. 108-9 (above, pp. 258-9).
[28] H. Nissen, *Italische Landeskunde*, 2.1 (Berlin, 1902), 366 n. 2.
[29] *JRS* 52 (1962), 235 (above, p. 22).

Afterwards I noticed that Buecheler had proposed *ficus*, but in its medical sense this word is not used of sores on the face.

I proceed to other places where I have relied on a hunch about the distribution of words. Horace says that however much a rich man extends his domain, his only sure destiny is the palace of Hades (*Carm.* 2. 18. 29–32):

> nulla certior tamen
> rapacis Orci fine destinata
> aula divitem manet
> erum. quid ultra tendis? . . .

I say nothing here about *fine destinata*, which has distracted people's attention from the much more puzzling *manet erum*. My ear tells me that the sentence ends at *divitem manet*; *erum* at the beginning of the next line is a nasty surprise, and a break after the initial iambus sounds all wrong (an intuition confirmed by a scrutiny of similar lines in Horace). There is no point in thinking up a word to replace *erum*, as the difficulty will not go away. The only escape is to take together *erum quid ultra tendis?*, which must mean 'why do you strain proprietorship further?'[30] I had already collected instances of accusatives like *agere civem*,[31] but this was quite secondary: the | important stage was to trust one's instinct that *manet* ends the sentence.

At 4. 48–9 Juvenal mentions the informers who would prosecute the fisherman if he failed to present his turbot to the emperor:

> dispersi protinus algae
> inquisitores agerent cum remige nudo.

For a long time I felt unhappy about the position of *algae*; it depends on *inquisitores*, but its place at the end of the line would sooner suggest a relationship with *dispersi*. I considered *alga* (but *in* would be expected); I asked myself whether *protinus algae* or something similar could mean 'all along the seaweed' (nonsense); I looked for another nominative participle to which *algae* could be hooked (hopeless). In any case the sense of the passage rquired that the *inquisitores* should be hunting out the worthless seaweed. Many years after I first saw a problem, I thought of *dispersae* (genitive):[32] the seaweed is scattered by wind and waves, but the *inquisitores* track it down. Though this

---

[30] R. G. M. Nisbet and M. Hubbard, *A Commentary on Horace, Odes II* (Oxford, 1978), 309–10.

[31] Op. cit. (n. 18), 396 with op. cit. (n. 30), 309.

[32] *BICS*, suppl. 51 (1988), 93–4 (above, p. 238).

proposal was prompted by a feeling about the distribution of words, it seemed to improve the sense: the *inquisitores* were not going to remonstrate with the fisherman on the shore but prosecute him in the courts (the natural meaning of *agere cum*).

I add a more speculative case that begins with a feeling about punctuation. In accordance with the conventions of the propempticon Horace assents reluctantly to Galatea's departure (*Carm.* 3. 27. 13–14):

> sis licet felix ubicumque mavis
> et memor nostri, Galatea, vivas.

One would naturally suppose that *sis licet felix* means 'it is permissible for you to be happy', but *vivas* can only be a wish, 'may you live': the two subjunctives are incompatible. T. E. Page suggested that *licet* is parenthetical; but it is difficult to dissociate the word from *sis*, especially when the result is so disjointed. I became convinced that the passage must be corrupt, but could not think of a substitute for *licet*: anything like *precor* was too remote to be convincing. Then I considered the | possibility that *sis licet* was corrupted from *scilicet*; but though the change was an easy one I could not persuade even myself that *scilicet* gave a satisfactory sense. But that wrong track led me to consider *ilicet*, 'without more ado may you live happily'.[33] The archaic word is found in epic narratives, and for a closer parallel I have noted Sil. 9. 28–9 'tradant immo hosti revocatos ilicet enses, | tradant arma iube'; as usual the work has to be done at the stage of verification rather than when one is actually making the proposal.

For another kind of problem see Juvenal 1. 142–6; the rich man, having gorged himself on peacock in solitary state, dies in the bath, to the delight of the clients whom he has starved in life:

> poena tamen praesens, cum tu deponis amictus
> turgidus et crudum pavonem in balnea portas.
> hinc subitae mortes atque intestata senectus,
> et [it **AL**²] nova nec tristis per cunctas fabula cenas:
> ducitur iratis plaudendum funus amicis.

As Madvig and Housman saw, old men do not fail to make wills because of a heavy meal; it may be added that *intestatus*, unlike English 'intestate', need not imply that the subject is dead (cf. Juv. 3. 273–4 'ad cenam si | intestatus eas'). Housman himself interpreted 'old age is unattested', but that is far too vague a generalization; at the very least the satirist would have to say 'old age is unattested among greedy

[33] *PCPS*, suppl. 15 (1989), 92 (above, p. 267).

patrons'. Conjectures are unconvincing: I find Corelli's *intemptata* as unintelligible as Madvig's *infestata*.

Knoche deleted 144–5. 145 is too good to lose, but his conjecture led me to suggest that 144 alone should be deleted;[34] in a text like Juvenal's that is known to be seriously interpolated, interpolation must always be considered as a possible solution to problems. I then noticed that we had excised not only the intractable *intestata senectus* but the generalizing plural *subitae mortes*, which interrupts a series of vivid singulars; I collected similar cases of disruptive plurals[35] in other interpolations in Juvenal. As we have seen before, a solution that kills two birds | with one stone has much to commend it. *et* remains intolerable, but as Housman pointed out, the poorly attested *it* gives good sense.

The sudden transition from the heavy meal to the funeral, without an explicit mention of the death, finds a striking parallel at Persius 3. 102–3 'uncta cadunt laxis tunc pulmentaria labris. | hinc tuba, candelae' (a parallel that I noticed only after I had recognized a similar sequence in Juvenal). But an oddity remained that I had failed to account for: if Juv. 1. 144 is deleted, then *hinc* is the work of the interpolator; but if he had been aware of the parallel in Persius, he might not have thought interpolation necessary. This led me many years after my original suggestion to propose 'hinc [subitae mortes atque intestata senectus | et] nova nec tristis per cunctas fabula cenas';[36] this also gets rids of the impossibly weak *et* without the need to accept the thinly supported *it*. There are several lessons to be learned from this problem: we should not hesitate to delete in a text known to be interpolated; we should be ready to build on suggestions made by our predecessors (in this case Housman and Knoche) without necessarily accepting them; and one's own first thoughts are not always one's last ones.

Most of the above conjectures are relatively simple ones, and I include in that category the deletion of a line. A few critics such as Housman could heal more complex corruptions, but they are easier to admire than to imitate; one of my few attempts in that direction is the passage in Catullus when the girl asks the poet for the loan of his litter-bearers (10. 24–7):

> hic illa, ut decuit cinaediorem,
> 'quaeso' inquit 'mihi, mi Catulle, paulum
> istos commoda; nam volo ad Serapim
> deferri ...'

---

[34] *JRS* 52 (1962), 234 (above, p. 21).　　　[35] Loc. cit. (n. 34).
[36] *BICS*, suppl. 51 (1988), 87–8 (above, pp. 229–30).

My starting-place was the conviction that *commoda* cannot be imperative: such a shortening of the final vowel is unparalleled in classical Latin poetry (except with a few common words like *puta*), but if it were permissible it would surely occur again. *commode enim* (Munro) is very clumsy, and gives a unique elision at this place in the line; *da modo* (again Munro) is quite unconvincing at the end of the sentence. In searching the com|mentators for guidance, I noticed that Ellis took *commoda* as neuter plural in the sense of 'loans'; it seemed more satisfactory to understand 'perquisites' (I remembered such passages as Juvenal 16. 7), for Catullus claimed that he had acquired eight litter-bearers serving with Memmius in Bithynia. Ellis was ready to take *commoda* in apposition to *istos*, but I cannot believe that that is Latin. Yet a part of *iste* is highly appropriate in the context: that imposes *ista* or better *istaec* (for in this part of the book Catullus does not give his hendecasyllables a trochaic base).[37] If that is so, *commoda* needs a verb to govern it; *quaeso* is not so used in classical Latin, but *quaero* is an easy change. That in turn suggests the punctuation *'quaero' inquit 'mihi, mi Catulle, paulum | istaec commoda'*;[38] but though one can persuade oneself that each move is necessary, it is obvious that a sequence of such conjectures can only be speculative.

For another instance of deep-seated corruption see Catullus 68. 37-40, where the poet is apologizing for not sending poems to his friend:

> quod cum ita sit, nolim statuas nos mente maligna
> id facere aut animo non satis ingenuo
> quod tibi non utriusque petenti copia posta est:
> ultro ego deferrem copia siqua foret.

As I could not translate *utriusque*, I started with the conviction that it was corrupt: it is alleged to refer to line 10 'muneraque et Musarum hinc petis et Veneris', but that is too far back, and in any case 'the gifts of Venus and the Muses' are one and the same (a *carmen venustum*, not a poem and a girl). I am not now sure of the process that led me to *hucusque*,[39] but I think it was by playing with the letters (as inexpert critics do, according to Housman) rather than by considering the thought. I then turned to 39 *copia*, which seems to spoil the contrast between particular specimens and the store on which Catullus might have drawn. Here I certainly played with the letters, trying *e* for *o* (a

---

[37] M. Zicàri, *SIFC* 29 (1957), 252-3; O. Skutsch, *BICS* 16 (1969), 38.
[38] *PCPS*, NS 24 (1978), 93-4 (above, pp. 78-9).
[39] Ibid. 105-6 (above, p. 92).

common corruption in Catullus) and *l* for *i*. That led to *exempla*, which was highly satisfactory in sense, though | reached by a palaeographic path. That necessitated in turn an active verb such as *posivi* or better *paravi*, and I also should have preferred *nulla* to *non*; but when changes are made on this scale, the chance of getting everything right becomes remote.

It is possible to make a conjecture without understanding it. When he was editing Virgil, Sir Roger Mynors called my attention to the difficulties at *Aen.* 3. 684–6, which I had never examined sufficiently:

> contra iussa monent Heleni, Scyllam atque Charybdim
> (inter utramque viam leti discrimine parvo),
> ni teneant cursus.

He tolds me that he accepted *Scyllamque Charybdimque inter* (Heinsius) and *teneam* (an ancient variant), but he was still puzzled by *utramque viam leti discrimine parvo* (for it was not sensible to talk of two separate ways through the straits). I immediately suggested *utrimque* from no more than a feeling that 'on either side' suited a context about Scylla and Charybdis; but I had to admit that I could not follow the construction. Mynors accepted the conjecture,[40] and suggested that *viam* was an instance of 'the accusative in apposition to the sentence'. I have since been told that my proposal may have been anticipated, but my informant could not tell me where.

Most of the above conjectures, even *exempla*, still convince me, though judgement in this area is notoriously subjective. I come now to several more speculative ideas (some would say 'even more speculative'). At 68. 59–60 Catullus compares the relief provided by his friend 'Allius' to that given to a weary traveller by a mountain stream,

> qui cum de prona praeceps est valle volutus
> per medium densi transit iter populi.

I was puzzled by *densi*: in the condition of traffic in the ancient world the adjective seems exaggerated for a road near a mountain area. I first tried juggling with the letters, but this produced nothing. Then I asked myself (as I should have done in the first place) what kind of adjective would be expected to go with *populi*. A word for 'hurrying' seemed possible, but *rapidi* is not actually used of people, and *celeris* detroys the rhyme with | *populi*. Then I thought of *properi*[41] (the archaic tone is acceptable in Catullus); if this rare word was once corrupted to *populi*,

---

[40] *P. Vergili Maronis Opera*, ed. R. A. B. Mynors (Oxford, 1969), ad loc.
[41] *PCPS*, NS 24 (1978), 108 n. 49 (above, p. 95 n. 49).

then anything might have been supplied to restore some approximation to sense. As has often been pointed out, the plausibility of a conjecture does not depend on its closeness to the transmitted reading.

For a still bolder speculation see Juvenal 10. 191–5, where the satirist is describing the hideousness of the old:

> deformem et taetrum ante omnia vultum
> dissimilemque sui, deformem pro cute pellem
> pendentisque genas et talis aspice[42] rugas
> quales, umbriferos ubi pandit Thabraca saltus,
> in vetula scalpit iam mater simia bucca.

I felt a vague disquiet at the repetition of *deformem*: anaphora is all very well, but not where *vultum* is given three epithets and *pellem* only one. My doubts were greatly strengthened when I noticed that in a comment on another passage (6. 504) Housman called the repetition *vix credibile*. Once again we have to decide which place is corrupt. *deformem* goes very well with *vultum* (I picked up from the dictionary Virg. *Georg.* 4. 254–5 *horrida vultum | deformat macies*). But the body at the best of times has less defined features than the face: to agree with *pellem* one looks for an adjective meaning 'loose' to balance *pendentis* and *tales rugas*.

Such a word is hard to find: as *deformem* must have been influenced by the previous occurrence of the word, the missing epithet need not be particularly close. I looked through the dictionary for words beginning with *de-*, but found nothing suitable. Then I tried a trick I had found to work before: remove the *de* and expand *formem* into a trisyllable. As inspiration was still lacking, I had recourse again to the dictionary, and worked mechanically through words beginning with *fo*; fortunately I had at hand Lewis and Short rather than the *Oxford Latin Dictionary*, which ends about AD 200. As a result I came up with | *follentem*, 'baggy',[43] a word I did not know; cf. Jerome, *Epist.* 22. 28. 3 *si pes laxa pelle non folleat*; 22. 34. 3 *caligae follicantes*; Isid. *Orig.* 12. 2. 30 *rugis turpiter follicantibus* (he is talking of monkeys like Juvenal below). This again is one of the conjectures that pleases its author more than the world at large. The moral is that one should not be afraid of using the dictionary, but the labour is tedious unless we are sure that the text is corrupt.

---

[42] In preparing the present paper I transcribed *aspice* as the nonsensical *aspera*, which may have been influenced by *rugas*; many corruptions are as irrational as this.

[43] *BICS*, suppl. 51 (1988), 106 (above, p. 255).

At 195 Courtney in his commentary pointed to the difficulty of *iam mater*. J. Ferguson proposed *Garamantis simia*, which is not close enough, particularly at the vital beginning of the word; I have myself suggested *iam marcens simia*,[44] which would provide another reference to loose and wrinkled skin. Here I mention the point only to emphasize that in making conjectures one will often depend on the diagnosis of others.

I now record a conjecture even more reckless than *follentem*; I should willingly suppress it if I could think of a better way. In a famous simile Horace compares the emergence and disappearance of words with that of leaves (*Ars Poetica* 60-2).

> ut silvae foliis pronos mutantur in annos,
> prima cadunt, ita verborum vetus interit aetas,
> et iuvenum ritu florent modo nata vigentque.

The passage is incoherent as it stands, even after *pronos* has been emended to Bentley's *privos*. Some scholars suggest a supplement after *prima cadunt*, on the lines of *porroque cadentibus altera primis succrescunt* but this seriously disrupts the balance of the *ut* and *ita* clauses. Housman took *prima cadunt ita verborum* together (followed by a full-stop); but to say nothing of the word-order, *prima cadunt* does not correspond adequately to the more general *mutantur* (see Brink's commentary).

prima cadunt simply gets in the way, and desperate measures are needed. The first question in such circumstances should always be: what part of speech would be desirable here? The answer is an adverb, to be taken with *mutantur*. The number of adverbs that fit the metre cannot be many: words ending in *-ter* will not scan, words ending in *ē* will scan only with difficulty. | That suggested a long word ending in *-tim* and preferably beginning with *p*. I have proposed *particulatim*[45] but have not yet found anybody to believe me. It is recorded of Ovid that when he was asked to name his three best lines and some of his friends his three worst, they produced the same answers.[46] Textual critics sometimes have a similar experience.

Most of the above conjectures have already been published, sometimes long after I first thought of them (for one's partiality is so great that it is best not to hurry); but I add here a couple of recent attempts.

[44] *LCM* 8 (1983), 80.
[45] *Gnomon*, 58 (1986), 615.
[46] Seneca, *Controversiae* 2. 2. 12.

Virgil has been describing the division of labour among the bees, comparing it with that of the Cyclopes (*Georgics* 4. 176-8):

> non aliter, si parva licet componere magnis,
> Cecropias innatus apes amor urget habendi
> munere quamque suo.

I found myself perplexed by the relation of the last three words to the rest of the sentence, and my doubts were increased by Conington's evident embarrassment: '*munere suo* seems a modal ablative, belonging not to anything expressed in the sentence, but to the notion of working implied in *non aliter urget*'. Having started with this purely verbal point I then considered the wider context: though *amor habendi* is an attested phrase, it is not directly relevant to the bees' working habits that are under discussion. As always, one's suspicions are greatly increased when two different scruples reinforce one another.

This led naturally to the thought that *habendi* is corrupt. When a suspected word begins with *h*, I automatically remove the first letter to see what happens (the sort of thing that Housman tells us not to do): thus at Juvenal 10. 90-1 'visne salutari sicut Seianus, habere | tantundem', I replaced the weak *habere* with *avere*,[47] only to find that Lachmann had done the same (knowledge concealed from us by most editors). The same procedure in the Virgilian passage leads almost as easily to *agendi*: the bees' love of work is not only notorious but highly relevant to the context, and *munere quamque suo* now fits in excellent|ly. Having reached this point I consulted Geymonat's edition (as I ought to have done earlier), and there I found from the apparatus that Peerlkamp had already considered *agendi*. Such anticipations are a disappointment to all but the most generous temperaments, but they increase the chances that an idea might be right.

Here is another recent conjecture that has not yet been published (though Professor James Willis has given it encouragement by letter). Juvenal is describing how the rich patron will devour the best game and fish as he dines alone (1. 135-6):

> optima silvarum interea pelagique vorabit
> rex horum vacuisque toris tantum ipse iacebit.

But is *optima silvarum* really a natural way of describing the best venison and boar-meat? Would the phrase not sooner suggest that the patron is munching high-quality timber? I look for a noun on the lines

---

[47] *BICS*, suppl. 51 (1988), 110 (above, p. 260).

of *munera* (cf. Hor. *Epist.* 1. 6. 5 *quid censes munera terrae?*), for one aims in the first instance at a pattern rather than the actual word; but *munera* is remote from *optima*, and it does not provide the necessary idea of excellence. Better *praemia*, which could have been abbreviated to *pmia*; the dictionary yields Hor. *Epod.* 2. 35–6 (which I may have half-remembered) 'pavidumque leporem et advenam laqueo gruem I iucunda captat praemia'; Nem. *Ecl.* 2. 67–8 'praeterea tenerum leporem geminasque palumbes I nuper, quae potui, silvarum praemia misi'; *TLL* 10. 2. 715. 25 ff.

This whole paper will be regarded by conservative critics as an instance of what some of them would call *cacoethes coniciendi*. Before we accept this criticism, let us look at the passage in Juvenal from which this slogan is derived (7. 50–2):

> nam si discedas, laqueo tenet ambitiosi
> consuetudo mali, tenet insanabile multos
> scribendi cacoethes et aegro in corde senescit.

Some of the difficulties in these lines are familiar: *ambitiosi mali* is a strange phrase, *multos* is too limiting after *nam si discedas* (which has a general application), *consuetudo mali* appears to originate from a gloss on *cacoethes* (*consuetudo mala* says the scholiast), in any case a *cacoethes* is not an itch but a growth or ulcer (see Courtney). Hence Jahn deleted 51, reading *ambitiosum* in 50, and this has been accepted by Clausen. I

In trying to translate the sentence into English (an exercise that should be recommended to conservative critics), I became aware of a further difficulty; if a *cacoethes* is an ulcer then the genitive *scribendi* is unintelligible. I first thought of *scribenti*, which necessitated a new line in place of the trebly impossible 51. Then I had a better idea, *scribendo*: I remembered Lucretius 4. 1068 *ulcus enim vivescit et inveterascit alendo* (or to be more accurate, I half-remembered the line and then looked it up). The only thing left was to provide a mechanical explanation for the loss of the line, which is always worth trying, though it must be highly speculative (particularly in the present context, where the insertion of a gloss is being posited as well as the loss of a line). That suggested something with the following pattern:

> nam si discedas, laqueo tenet ambitiosum
> scribendi ⟨studium, gliscitque atque usque gravescit
> scribendo⟩ cacoethes et aegro in corde senescit.[48]

[48] Ibid. 99–100 (above, pp. 245–6).

To be sure, *scribendi cacoethes* is a well-known phrase, but that is no reason for retaining it. Scholte deleted 1. 85-6 'quidquid agunt homines, votum timor ira voluptas | gaudia discursus nostri farrago libelli' (reading *ecquando* for *et quando* at the beginning of the next line); in any case *gaudia* and *discursus* do not make a good pair. What is more, M. D. Reeve[49] deleted 10. 356 'orandum est ut sit mens sans in corpore sano', a line that used to be admired by headmasters. Let the reader who is sorry to lose these familiar quotations look at the contexts and listen to the arguments.

Such then are the random recommendations of one very sceptical textual critic: as Horace says to Numicius, 'si quid novisti rectius istis, | candidus imperti, si non his utere mecum' (*Epist.* 1. 6. 67-8). But wait a minute: can that really be right? How can he describe his own precepts in the same sentence both as *his* and *istis*, particularly in a context where a contrast is being drawn between two possible approaches? Otto Skutsch tried to meet the difficulty by taking *istis candidus imperti* together;[50] but though *impertire* with an accusative and ablative | is a legitimate construction in early Latin, here there is no *me*. The fault surely lies in *istis*, and yet some part of *iste* would suit the contrast with Horace's own views. Many years ago I thought of *istic*, 'if you over there know anything better'; I must have vaguely remembered such passages as Cic. *Att.* 3. 8. 2 'nunc istic quid agatur magno opere timeo'. But then Skutsch told me to my chagrin that the proposal is attributed to G. Wagner in H. Schütz's commentary (1883), where it has languished ever since.

It is clear from the above discussion that though no two instances are exactly the same, certain situations recur. The most important common factor is the overwhelming conviction that the transmitted text cannot be right. Housman said that those who know Latin can tell that a passage is corrupt when they cannot understand it;[51] he added with his usual offensive candour that some editors find even sound texts hard to understand. But sometimes one senses that a passage is corrupt even when it can be literally translated. It is not enough for the great classical authors to produce an occasional felicity: the structure must cohere, and the words must be the right words. Things may be particularly treacherous when the transmitted reading is derived from an edition of late antiquity. But even if it scans and makes a vague sort

---

[49] *CR*, NS 20 (1970), 135-6.
[50] *Hermes*, 88 (1960), 504-5.
[51] *M. Manilii Astronomicon Liber Primus* (London, 1903), p. 1.

of sense, we must have a higher conception of classical perfection than what satisfied a fourth-century *grammaticus*.

When we have decided that a passage will not do, there are certain stock moves we can make. We must decide where the corruption is, and what part of speech it ought to be; but even that decision may depend on instinct as much as reason. We should start from the thought, as the best critics advise; yet in real life we usually find ourselves playing with the letters as well. We should be aware of the common palaeographic confusions, particularly in the text we are studying; yet in the end there is an irrational element in most corruptions, and manuals like Havet's are of less use than one's own experience. Ideally we should have an accurate recall of most that we read; but a vague impression that can be verified, or even a subconscious memory, may serve us just as well. We should clear the ground | as much as we can by rigorous logical analysis; but not all cases call for an intellectual treatment, and even when they do, logic alone will not give us the answer. We must try to repress self-will, as Housman tells us, but the only people who succeed completely are those who never think of anything for themselves.

It is only seldom that one makes a conjecture, and as with all academic activity we should observe the circumstances and try to renew them. I have mentioned the need to justify a position in teaching or discussion; one hears oneself saying things that one did not know one knew. Conjectures are not made in the Bodleian Library: the spectacle of so much earnest activity is inhibiting; so also the abundance of learned works to explain away difficulties. Conjectures can be made on uncrowded trains, if one is operating from a plain text without any aids of scholarship. They can be made on holiday, when one feels no obligation to be busy, and the relaxed mind summons up and integrates things long forgotten. The period after Christmas is particularly productive, when everything is shut and one is slouched in an armchair half-asleep. The Muse of Textual Conjecture (let us call her Eustochia) only visits those who have worked, but she does not visit us when we are actually working. Even in the natural sciences, scientific method is sometimes less deductive than people once liked to suppose. At the beginning you collect the evidence, and at the end you test your hypothesis; but at the moment of discovery you may simply be snatching at fleas.

22

The Orator and the Reader
Manipulation and Response in Cicero's *Fifth Verrine*

THE title of this book must not be taken too literally but needs interpretation by the reader. Though much Latin literature suggests the presence of an audience, it was recorded not on tape but papyrus. Speeches have a notably ambiguous status: they reconstruct the style and techniques of living oratory, but once they were issued to the world they were no longer spoken. Not even the content need be the same,[1] for in his published versions Cicero added political manifestos (as in the *Pro Sestio*), omitted procedural technicalities (everywhere), or shifted his stance to suit a developing situation (as in the *Catilinarians*). He expanded some remarks against Piso into a comprehensive invective, he never spoke the famous *Second Philippic*, and the *Pro Milone* that failed is not the one that we have. The present essay deals with the *Fifth Verrine*, which purports to have been delivered in 70 BC at the trial of Verres for extortion as governor of Sicily, but as the defendant withdrew into exile after the first preliminaries, not a word was actually uttered. Even if Cicero had a draft of the speech ready for delivery, he would rewrite it in a triumphal spirit when he knew that he had won. He was now not so much persuading a jury as justifying a successful prosecution.[2]

A problem of presentation arises with any discussion of Cicero's speeches: the text goes on for so long that comment soon becomes

---

This paper is based on a talk given in London in March 1989 at a refresher course organized by the Association for the Reform of Latin Teaching.

[1] J. Humbert, *Les Plaidoyers écrits et les plaidoiries réelles de Cicéron* (Paris, 1925) emphasizes the unreality of Cicero's published speeches; W. Stroh, *Taxis und Taktik: Die advokatische Dispositionskunst in Ciceros Gerichtsreden* (Stuttgart, 1975), the reality.

[2] Shortly after the case against Verres, juries in extortion trials became predominantly equestrian (by the *lex Aurelia*) rather than exclusively senatorial. This may in some respects have influenced Cicero's written version.

From *Author and Audience in Latin Literature*, ed. T. Woodman and J. Powell (Cambridge, 1992), 1–17, 216–18 (a volume dedicated to David West).

diffuse. To meet this difficulty I shall concentrate on a fiftieth part of the *Fifth Verrine*, a page deploring the destruction of a Roman fleet by the pirates near Syracuse (5. 92-5). Such a procedure may be acceptable to David West, who in his treatment of Lucretian imagery, Virgilian similes, and Horatian word-play has shown how to select significant examples with a general application.[3] What is more, I shall discuss each sentence immediately after it has been quoted, even though this disrupts the continuity of the whole. Talk about literature too often loses sight of the words on the page, and the arrangement here adopted may persuade some readers to respond to the Latin as well as the comment. There will | be few technical terms and no abstract theory,[4] only concrete instances of the symbiotic relationship of orator and reader; but some general conclusions will be suggested at the end.

O tempus miserum atque acerbum provinciae Siciliae! o casum illum multis innocentibus calamitosum atque funestum! o istius nequitiam ac turpitudinem singularem! (5. 92)

What a wretched and bitter moment for the province of Sicily! What a calamitous and deadly catastrophe it was for many innocent people! How unprecedented that man's profligacy and iniquity!

Cicero's reader would not skip and skim in the modern manner, aiming at no more than the general drift. He would declaim the passage aloud[5] (or get a trained *anagnostes* to do so), mouthing the repeated *o* (an emotional word in Latin), and emphasizing the parallelism of the three resonant clauses. This is the grand style of oratory (*grande genus orationis*), designed to rush an audience into enthusiasm and action: the best reader would have been something of an orator himself, a person with *gravitas* and *auctoritas* as well as an understanding of style, who could at least hint at the orotundity of a great

[3] D. West, *The Imagery and Poetry of Lucretius* (Edinburgh, 1969), 'Multiple-Correspondence Similes in the Aeneid', *JRS* 59 (1969), 40-9, 'Horace's Poetic Technique in the Odes', in C. D. N. Costa (ed.), *Horace* (London, 1973), 29-58.

[4] For some of the theoretical problems raised by 'response' and 'reception' see W. Iser, *The Implied Reader* (London and Baltimore, 1974); S. Fish, *Is there a Text in this Class?* (Cambridge, Mass., 1980); J. P. Tompkins, *Reader-Response Criticism: From Formalism to Post-Structuralism* (London and Baltimore, 1980); R. C. Holub, *Reception Theory: A Critical Introduction* (London and New York, 1984).

[5] For reading aloud cf. J. Balogh, 'Voces paginarum', *Philologus*, 82 (1927), 84-109 and 202-40; G. L. Hendrickson, 'Ancient Reading', *CJ* 25 (1929), 182-96; W. V. Harris, *Ancient Literacy* (Cambridge, Mass., 1989), 226. B. M. W. Knox, 'Silent Reading in Antiquity', *GRBS* 9 (1968), 421-35, makes some qualifications, but a speech more than anything needs to be declaimed.

performer. In practice this was beyond most people: a Greek secretary, however literate, could not provide the *timbre* of a Roman senator;[6] schoolboys might try out their voices, but Cicero's aims were not primarily educational; even a statesman would not imitate the delivery of a real oration[7] when he was receiving no stimulus from an audience.[8] Every reading of a speech, as of other works of literature, was to some extent a fresh occasion, like the staging of a play or the performance of a piece of music, and, quite apart from the degree of professionalism, different readers must have produced different effects.

The rhythmical quality of Cicero's speeches must have been particularly difficult to recapture. At the end of most sentences he adopts a favoured metrical pattern, the so-called 'clausula',[9] whether $-\cup--\times$[10] (*atque funestum*), or $-\cup-\times$ (*singularem*), or $-\cup--\cup\times$ (*-inciae Siciliae* belongs to this type, with the first two short syllables of *Siciliae* substituted for a long). We cannot suppose that many Romans consciously thought in terms of long and short syllables (crotchets and quavers, as we might describe them), yet we hear of an audience applauding at a *dichoreus* or double-trochee in the clausula ($-\cup-\times$): 'hoc dichoreo tantus clamor excitatus est ut admirabile esset' (Cicero, *Orator* 214). Clearly the more receptive listeners found aesthetic pleasure in the rhythm; as Cicero rightly says, 'what music can be found sweeter than | balanced speech, what poetry more harmonious than an artistically rounded period?' (*De Oratore* 2. 34 'qui enim cantus moderata oratione dulcior inveniri potest? quod carmen artificiosa verborum conclusione aptius?'). The movement of formal prose was an integral part of the meaning, the untranslatable quality that gave it its distinction and appeal, but the reader also had a contribution to make. If he proved inadequate, he could destroy a work as surely as a bad actor or musician.

[6] Cicero laments the death of his *anagnostes* Sositheus, whom he describes as *festivus puer* (*Att.* 1. 12. 4); but would he have trusted him to read aloud one of his own speeches?
[7] For the importance of *actio* or delivery (gesture as well as voice) see *Rhet. Her.* 3. 19–27; Cic. *Or.* 56 'not without reason Demosthenes assigned the first and second and third places to delivery'; Quint. 11. 3. Add R. Volkmann, *Die Rhetorik der Griechen und Römer* (Leipzig, 1885), 573–80; J. Martin, *Antike Rhetorik* (Munich, 1974), 353–5.
[8] Tacitus connects the decline of oratory under the Empire with the lack of great occasions and the stimulus they provided (*Dial.* 38–40).
[9] For a summary see R. G. M. Nisbet, *Cicero: In Pisonem* (Oxford, 1961), xvii–xx; for the cadences at pauses within the sentence cf. E. Fraenkel, *Leseproben aus Reden Ciceros und Catos* (Rome, 1968); R. G. M. Nisbet, 'Cola and Clausulae in Cicero's speeches' in E. M. Craik (ed.), *Owls to Athens* (Oxford, 1990), 349–59 (= above, pp. 312–24).
[10] A cross is used to indicate the so-called 'syllaba anceps' found at the end of a clause (as of a hexameter line).

The following sentence also demands a reader with different expectations from our own:

una atque eadem nox erat qua praetor amoris turpissimi flamma, classis populi Romani praedonum incendio conflagrabat.

On one and the same night the governor was on fire with the flame of an iniquitous passion, and the fleet of the Roman people with a conflagration kindled by pirates.

Reactions to literature can change very quickly, and twenty years later Cicero might seem to have crossed the line between the grand and the inflated;[11] but some at least of the original readership must have appreciated hyperbole,[12] and far-fetched analogy, and a metaphor that was not yet dead. In a world where houses were more combustible than our own and fire brigades less efficient, they could understand the horror of conflagration; Cicero himself was to play on such fears when he described the incendiarism of Catiline.[13] The formal phrase *classis populi Romani* is designed to activate patriotic reflexes, as 'Royal Navy' once did. Words for 'pirate' like *praedo* suggested not the picturesque ruffians of our childhood, Long John Silver or Captain Hook, but vicious terrorists who threatened the lives and the livelihood of some of Cicero's own readership. As for Verres's iniquitous passion, we should not forget that many Romans had a strong sense of decorum,[14] which is not the same as puritanism. Young men might be indulged within limits (*Pro Caelio* 39–50), but responsible persons, such as the reader is encouraged to think himself, would deplore anything that impaired the authority and efficiency of a provincial governor.

adfertur nocte intempesta gravis huiusce mali nuntius Syracusas.

At dead of night there is brought to Syracuse the heavy news of this disaster.

After his grandiose exclamations Cicero varies his tone: narratives were written in a simple style[15] to produce credibility, though in the | *Verrines* alleged fact and tendentious comment cannot easily be separated. Here the restrained solemnity is designed to affect the

[11] For the 'inflated' style see *Rhet. Her.* 4. 15; Longinus 3. 3 with D. A. Russell, *'Longinus' on the Sublime* (Oxford, 1964), 72.

[12] For hyperbole see *Rhet. Her.* 4. 44 (citing 'aspectu igneum ardorem adsequebatur'); P. R. Hardie, *Cosmos and Imperium in Virgil's Aeneid* (Oxford, 1986), 241–92.

[13] Cicero *Att.* 1. 14. 3 'totum hunc locum quem ego varie meis orationibus soleo pingere, de flamma, de ferro ... valde graviter pertexuit'.

[14] P. Brown, *The Body and Society* (London, 1989), 19–29.

[15] For *narratio* cf. Volkmann, op. cit. (n. 7), 148–64; H. Lausberg, *Handbuch der literarischen Rhetorik* (Munich, 1960), 163–90; Martin, op. cit. (n. 7), 75–89.

reader beyond the literal meaning of the words. The postponement of
the subject adds to his suspense. He is encouraged to sense a contrast
between the stillness of the night[16] (more noticeable in ancient towns
than in our own) and the ensuing hubbub, and to draw on his experience, or perhaps rather his reading, to produce a feeling of sympathetic involvement. Compare Xenophon on the destruction of the
Athenian fleet at Aegospotami (*Hellenica* 2. 2. 3): 'It was night when
the ship arrived with news of the disaster. A wailing ran from the
Peiraeus to the city ... During that night no one slept.' Or Demosthenes in the *De Corona* on the fatal loss of Elatea (18. 169), a much
quoted passage[17] that must have been familiar to educated readers: 'It
was evening when a messenger arrived with the news that Elatea had
been captured ... The generals were summoned, the trumpeter was
ordered to attend. The city was full of commotion. The next day at
dawn ... the citizens went to the ecclesia.' So Macaulay on the relief of
Londonderry (*History of England*, ch. 12): 'It was the twenty-eighth of
July. The sun had just set: the evening sermon in the cathedral was
over; and the heart-broken congregation had separated; when the
sentinels on the tower saw the sails of three vessels coming up the
Foyle.' A carefully worded narrative may give an impression of
objectivity even while it is eliciting a subjective response.

curritur ad praetorium quo istum ex illo praeclaro convivio reduxerant paulo
ante mulieres cum cantu atque symphonia.

There is a rush to the governor's residence, where Verres had been escorted
from his fine dinner-party a short time before—by women, with singing, and a
chorus of Greeks.

Any competent reader would see that *praeclaro* was ironic, but his
expression might vary from the deadpan to the heavily sarcastic. He
could be relied on to remember that Verres had pitched his marquees
at the entrance to the Grand Harbour of Syracuse, south of the
Arethusa fountain;[18] here in his summer camp, as Cicero calls it (5. 96
aestiva), he had entertained married women at lavish picnics. The
ordinary Roman might have enjoyed aristocratic magnificence from

---

[16] For *nox erat* to set the scene in poetry cf. A. S. Pease, *P. Vergili Maronis liber quartus*
(Cambridge, Mass., 1935) on Virg. *Aen.* 4. 522.

[17] See the commentary by H. Wankel, *Demosthenes Rede für Ktesiphon über den Kranz*
(Heidelberg, 1976), ad loc.

[18] *Verr.* 5. 30, 5. 80 *post Arethusae fontem.* R. G. C. Levens, *Cicero: The Fifth Verrine
Oration* (London, 1946), 118 interprets *post* as 'farther inland'; rather 'farther south', away
from the central parts of the Insula.

afar,[19] but Cicero has his eye on the more energetic members of the governing class, who would feel varying degrees of indignation or envy at the luxury of a superior whom in some cases they might hope to supplant. As Antonius is made to say in the *De Oratore*, the orator should urge his audience towards love or hate, envy or goodwill, preferably by working on | existing emotions, but if nothing is obvious, 'by sniffing out their feelings and expectations'.[20]

In this delightful spot, when his fleet sailed past to do battle with the pirates, Verres had taken the salute[21] in sandals, wearing a purple cloak and ankle-length tunic, and propped up by one of his girl-friends: 5. 86 'stetit soleatus praetor populi Romani cum pallio purpureo tunicaque talari, muliercula nixus in litore'. Quintilian cites this vivid scene as an instance of the realism ($\dot{\epsilon}\nu\acute{\alpha}\rho\gamma\epsilon\iota\alpha$, *sub oculos subiectio*)[22] that encourages the reader to visualize; though such pictures are evidence of literary power rather than actual knowledge, they were regarded as an effective method of persuasion. Quintilian adds that the reader could fill in details that have not been described: 'I for my part seem to see the face and eyes and unseemly blandishments of both of them, and the silent turning away and apprehensive modesty of the bystanders' (8. 3. 65 'ego certe mihi cernere videor et vultum et oculos et deformes utriusque blanditias et eorum qui aderant tacitam aversationem ac timidam verecundiam').[23] He advises the speaker not to imitate the inclination of Verres's body as he leans against the woman (11. 3. 90 'non enim ... inclinatio incumbentis in mulierculam Verris imitanda

---

[19] J. Griffin, 'Propertius and Antony', *JRS* 67 (1977), 21–2 = id., *Latin Poets and Roman Life* (London, 1985), 39–41.

[20] *De Or.* 2. 185–6 'in ea cogitatione curaque versor ut odorer quam sagacissime possum quid sentiant quid existiment, quid exspectent quid velint, quo deduci oratione facillime posse videantur'.

[21] For a memorable instance of 'taking the salute' see Virg. *Aen.* 6. 754–5 'et tumulum capit unde omnis longo ordine posset | adversos legere et venientum discere vultus'.

[22] For realism cf. H. Caplan, [*Cicero*] *ad C. Herennium* (London and Cambridge, Mass., 1954), 404–7; Lausberg, op. cit. (n. 15), 399–401; G. Zanker, *Realism in Alexandrian Poetry* (London, 1987), 39–54.

[23] See Sterne, *Tristram Shandy*, 2. 11 'The truest respect which you can pay to the reader's understanding is to halve this matter amicably, and leave him something to imagine, in his turn, as well as yourself. For my own part, I am eternally paying him compliments of this kind, and do all that lies in my power to keep his imagination as busy as my own.' I owe this passage to Iser, op. cit. (n. 4), 31, 275; he also (79) cites Dugald Stewart, *Elements of the Philosophy of the Human Mind*, 1 (London, 1792), 483: 'In reading history and poetry, I believe it seldom happens, that we do not annex imaginary appearances to the names of our favourite characters. It is, at the same time, almost certain, that the imaginations of no two men coincide upon such occasions' (see the whole context for other 18th-cent. views).

est'); he is discouraging exaggerated gestures, but his warning shows his readiness to think of the episode in visual terms. All this suggests that the writer's imagination was understood more literally than sometimes nowadays, and that readers were expected to picture things that were not explicitly in the text.[24] If that is so, every reader could provide a particular colouring of his own.

In fact the details of this scene seem to be instances of the fibs (*mendaciuncula*) that Cicero regards as permissible in invective (*De Oratore* 2. 241); in the same spirit he will later describe how Verres's eyes were splashed by the victorious pirates' oars (5. 100). It is entirely credible that the governor wore a purple cloak in a Greek city (5. 31, 5. 137 'tu praetor in provincia cum tunica pallioque purpureo visus es'); but it is not likely that Cicero had precise information about the particular occasion in so secluded a place. Informality of dress was a profitable theme in invective[25] because it showed a disregard for social position and the dignity of office.[26] The ordinary person might wear sandals without criticism, but Cicero's readers would expect better things of a *praetor populi Romani* (again the formal phrase) when they themselves had to endure a Roman summer in a clammy toga and tight boots.[27]

After his party Verres returned to his *praetorium*; a right-thinking Roman would understand what is not explicitly stated, that Government House required higher standards of behaviour. He would pick up the gibe in the apparently factual *paulo ante*: if it was nearly *intempesta nox*, | 'the unseasonable time of night', then Verres stayed up too late for a man with duties in the morning. *reduxerant* at first sight suggests a magistrate's escort of attendants and hangers-on, but by the time we reach the end of the sentence we see that this impression was misleading: the governor's procession has become more like a band of *comissatores*, young men who roamed the streets after a party in search of further pleasure. The postponed subject *mulieres* is meant to shock or amuse: respectable women would not be present on such occasions, so the reader on Cicero's wavelength (a man) could speak the word with

[24] One may compare the mnemonic techniques that depended on visualizing imaginary scenes: *Rhet. Her.* 3. 30–9; Cic. *De Or.* 2. 350–60; Quint. 11. 2. 17–22; F. A. Yates, *The Art of Memory* (London, 1966); H. Blum, *Die antike Mnemotechnik* (Spudasmata, 15; Hildesheim and New York, 1969).

[25] Cf. W. Süss, *Ethos* (Leipzig and Berlin, 1910), 253; Nisbet, op. cit. (n. 9), 194.

[26] For dress 'expressing the man' see Sen. *Epist.* 114. 6 (on Maecenas). British royalty has shared the Roman view, with the significant exception of Edward VIII.

[27] Mart. 12. 18. 5 'sudatrix toga'; Tert. *De Pallio* 5. 2 'calceos nihil dicimus, proprium togae tormentum'.

scorn and astonishment. Singing was an expected part of the *comissatio*, but it had no place in a governor's escort; so *cantu* as well as *mulieres* might be emphasized with distaste. The Greek word *symphonia* refers to a group of musicians such as Verres had recently appropriated from a captured pirate-ship (5. 64); a skilled speaker (perhaps not a Greek *anagnostes*) could pronounce the word in a knowing way to suggest the decadence of foreign culture. Cicero's readers are invited to construct a picture of the governor rolling home; to share some fun with them about the follies of the great, especially when they were great no more, was an easy way of engaging their sympathy.

Cleomenes, quamquam nox erat, tamen in publico esse non audet; includit se domi.

Although it was night, Cleomenes does not venture to appear in public, but shuts himself indoors.

Cleomenes was the Syracusan commodore who in the flight from the pirates had led his squadron from the front (5. 88–9); the point would amuse the more chauvinist Roman reader, just as Gilbert's Duke of Plaza Toro encouraged the least warlike Victorians in their contempt for south European armies. Such a reader might not reflect that because of their inexperience in seamanship, Roman navies had to rely heavily on the despised Greeks. In the ancient world leaders— even emperors—were expected to be visible, and it was easy to stir up comment on their disappearance; yet a dozen years later even Pompey barricaded himself in his house to escape the gangs of Clodius (Asconius 41 Kiessling–Schoell). In fact no sensible person would face a hostile demonstration in the middle of the night, but though Cicero's *quamquam* is misleading, he could rely on most readers not to notice.

neque aderat uxor quae consolari hominem in malis posset.

Nor was the wife at hand who could comfort the fellow in his troubles. |

The implications of this sentence are more damaging than the surface meaning. The wife of Cleomenes was called Nike or 'Victory', an irony that cannot have escaped competent readers, though it is not brought out explicitly. Neither could they forget that she was the object of Verres's 'iniquitous passion'; they might not be too shocked by the relationship in itself (any more than Nelson's admirers by Lady Hamilton), but the promotion of Cleomenes to secure his absence could not be condoned.[28] Here it is implied that Nike could not

---

[28] There is no suggestion that Cleomenes is being sent to his death, as in the similar triangle of King David, Bathsheba, and Uriah the Hittite (2 Sam. 11).

comfort her husband because she was comforting Verres instead.[29]
When Cicero is in a malicious mood, we must look not only at what he
says but at what he stops short of saying: innuendo is recognized by
the rhetorical theorists (they called it *emphasis* or *significatio*),[30] and
anybody who had followed the context could easily supply the unspoken thought. For such collaboration with the reader compare
Demetrius (probably Cicero's contemporary): 'As Theophrastus says,
one should not speak out everything in precise detail, but leave some
things for the hearer to work out and understand for himself. When he
grasps what you have not expressed, he will be more than your hearer,
he will be a witness on your behalf, and more kindly disposed towards
you, for you have given him the opportunity to exert his intelligence
and he feels he has done so. To express everything as to a fool is to
accuse your hearer of being one.'[31]

huius autem praeclari imperatoris ita erat severa domi disciplina ut in re tanta
et tam gravi nuntio nemo admitteretur, nemo esset qui auderet aut dormien-
tem excitare aut interpellare vigilantem. (5. 93)

But our remarkable commander-in-chief kept such strict control over his
household that in so great a crisis, with such heavy tidings to be reported,
nobody was admitted, there was nobody who ventured either to rouse him
while he slept or to interrupt him when he was awake.

huius imperatoris refers to Verres not Cleomenes, though the latter is
described as *imperator* below. Moderns who exaggerate the admitted
ambiguity of language might find confusion here, but words must not
be taken in isolation: a competent reader would follow the context and
see the function of *huius* and *autem*. He would understand the irony of
imperatoris, a word repeatedly attached to Verres (as well as of *praeclari*
and *disciplina*): commanders were only acclaimed by this title when
they had won an important victory. He would interpret Verres's som-
nolence as a lack of *vigilantia* (watchfulness, a prized Roman virtue);
yet even in modern times, when communications are far better,
persons in authority | should not be wakened up if nothing can be done
till day. When Cicero goes on to say *interpellare vigilantem*, the more

---

[29] So in June 1940, when France was on the verge of defeat, Churchill commented on
the Comtesse de Portes, the mistress of Paul Reynaud, the French Premier, 'She had
comfort to give him that was not mine to offer' (M. Gilbert, *Winston S. Churchill*, 6
(London, 1983), 536). Once again the suggestion of sexual licence, directed principally at
the woman, conveys an impression of political irresponsibility.

[30] Volkmann, op. cit. (n. 7), 445–6; Lausberg, op. cit. (n. 15), 450–3.

[31] Demetrius, *On style* 222, trans. G. M. A. Grube, *A Greek Critic: Demetrius on Style*
(Toronto, 1961), 111.

alert reader would spot another innuendo: he is being tempted to
suspect what is not in fact said, and may be quite untrue (for how could
anybody know?), that Verres was up to no good with the commodore's
wife.

iam vero re ab omnibus cognita, concursabat urbe tota maxima multitudo.

When in due course the matter was known to everybody, a huge crowd milled
about over the whole city.

An ancient reader would understand the urban environment, and
sympathize with the concern of the crowd. When public life is
conducted in the open air, 'a chill rumour' in Horace's phrase 'seeps
from street-corner to street-corner' (*Satires* 2. 6. 50 'frigidus a rostris
manat per compita rumor'). If trouble came in the middle of the night,
a public-spirited or curious citizen went outside to see what was
happening, as when Propertius had a row with Cynthia (4. 8. 2). In the
alleys of an old city a crowd soon built up, and Cicero needs only a few
words to communicate a sense of crisis. It is unlikely that he had
precise evidence for the details, but most readers would be content
with an account that seemed plausible in the situation. Much ancient
oratory, and history, is neither obviously true nor obviously false, but a
reasonable guess at the sort of thing that might well have happened.[32]

non enim sicut antea erat semper consuetudo, praedonum adventum significa-
bat ignis e specula sublatus aut tumulo, sed flamma ex ipso incendio navium et
calamitatem acceptam et periculum reliquum nuntiabat.

Contrary to the invariable previous practice the approach of the pirates was
signalled not by the raising of fire on a watch-tower or hill, but flame from the
actual burning of the ships announced both the disaster that had been suffered
and the danger that remained.

Signalling by fire is attested in the historians (even if Aeschylus's
beacon-speech was a fantasy), and flames in the night encourage the
reader to visualize; compare Macaulay's line on the Armada 'And the
red glare on Skiddaw roused the burghers of Carlisle' (just as with our
passage, 'burghers' appeals to the solid virtues of the expected readership). Here Cicero presents a more piquant drama: the disaster was
signalled by the actual burning of the ships. This had taken place as

[32] For amplification beyond the evidence in history and biography cf. T. P. Wiseman,
Clio's Cosmetics (Leicester, 1979); A. J. Woodman, *Rhetoric in Classical Historiography*
(London, 1988); M. J. Wheeldon, '"True Stories": The Reception of Historiography in
Antiquity', in A. Cameron (ed.), *History as Text* (London, 1989), 36–63; C. B. R. Pelling,
'Truth and Fiction in Plutarch's Lives', in D. A. Russell (ed.), *Antonine Literature* (Oxford,
1990), 19–52.

evening fell (5. 91) at Helorus, fifteen miles south of Syracuse: at the |
time the cause of the fire would not be clear (the pirate-ships could
themselves have been destroyed), and by the middle of the night,
when the 'grave news' arrived, the flames might no longer be visible.
One suspects a picturesque variation of stereotyped phrases like 'messenger of his own disaster'. But a sympathetic reader would be persuaded by the particularity of the detail, which suggests truthfulness to
the uncritical: compare the *Historia Augusta* and *Robinson Crusoe*, to
name only secular texts.

cum praetor quaereretur, et constaret neminem ei nuntiasse, fit ad domum eius
cum clamore concursus atque impetus.

When the governor was looked for, and it was established that nobody had
informed him, there is a mass rush to his residence accompanied by shouts.

In this whole passage Cicero does not simply narrate alleged facts:
by the repetition of key words he encourages the reader to form an
impression of turmoil. Thus *concursus* echoes *curritur* and *concursabat*
above, and *clamore* is echoed by *clamore* below (for shouting was one of
the more democratic elements in the Roman political process); note
also the recurring reference to night and fire. At first sight we might
assume that the protesting crowd consisted of Syracusan Greeks: in
fact they were Roman citizens, the only people allowed to live on the
Insula (5. 84) where the governor's residence was situated (4. 118),
merchants at serious risk from the pirates and natural allies of Cicero.
This all becomes clear at the end of the paragraph, but the better-
informed Roman would understand the situation from the start. The
original readership of any ancient work might contribute to its interpretation facts that are less obvious to us.[33]

tum iste excitatus, audit rem omnem a Timarchide, sagum sumit—lucebat iam
fere . . . (5. 94).

Then wakened at last, he learns the whole business from Timarchides, puts his
uniform on (it was now more or less light) . . .

Timarchides was a freedman of Verres, an agent (we are told) in
some of his shadier transactions, who had been privileged to join him
and Nike at his parties on the sea-front. Many readers would accept

---

[33] E. Fraenkel, *Horace* (Oxford, 1957), 26–7 maintains that poems do not require
knowledge of anything outside the poem. In fact quite a lot is presupposed, though some
readers could contribute more than others: everybody had to know who Maecenas was,
but only the inner circle would be aware that Trebatius was a swimmer (Cic. *Fam.*
7. 10. 2; Hor. *Sat.* 2. 1. 8).

the suggestion (probably not a sincere one) that familiarity with Greeks should be discouraged; they would certainly feel it improper that a Roman governor should be briefed by such a person, though in many provinces this must have been inevitable. The more literate would appreciate the | irony of the formal *sagum sumit*,[34] when it is the unwarlike Verres who is dressing for battle (a significant type of scene since the *Iliad*). The mention of daybreak (like *tum . . . excitatus* above) is not simply factual but underlines Verres's procrastination (*fere* perhaps betrays exaggeration). A civilian reader would not stop to ask what could be done about the pirates in the middle of the night.

procedit in medium, vini somni stupri plenus.

He steps forth, heavy with drink, sleep, and debauchery.

Cicero's ideal reader could convey by his voice the mock grandiloquence of *procedit in medium*: when a Roman governor appeared, you knew he was there. The ancient world gave only erratic help with punctuation, and modern editions are often misleading; but an experienced reader would see that the clause ended at *medium*, before the deflating climax. A modern scholar will suspect a literary commonplace when a surprised army or general is said to be the worse for drink,[35] but a Roman would think that a Roman defeat needed a particular explanation. As for Verres's 'debauchery', the reader is being encouraged to construct a story out of isolated scenes that give the impression of corroborating one another: we are shown in turn the mixed parties on the shore (the only reliable detail), the girl-friend at the review of the fleet, women trooping to the *praetorium* after the symposium, Verres's reluctance to be disturbed at night, his exhaustion the morning after. Cicero was so pleased with his phrase *vini somni stupri plenus* that he applied it later both to Gabinius (*Post reditum in senatu* 13) and Clodius (*De haruspicum responso* 55); though this tells against the truth of the remark, most Romans would see nothing wrong with elaborating the case against a discredited enemy.

excipitur ab omnibus eiusmodi clamore, ut ei Lampsaceni periculi similitudo versaretur ante oculos; hoc etiam maius hoc videbatur, quod in odio simili multitudo hominum haec erat maxima.

He is received by everybody with shouting of such a kind that his similar danger at Lampsacus floated before his eyes; the present danger seemed all the

---

[34] Th. Mommsen, *Römisches Staatsrecht* (Leipzig, 1887–8), 3. 2. 1247 n. 2.
[35] Ennius, *Ann.* 288 Skutsch; Virg. *Aen.* 2. 265, 9. 236; Livy 8. 16. 9, 25. 24. 2, etc.

greater because amid similar animosity the crowd of people on this occasion was greatest.

Nobody could have known what was floating before Verres's eyes, but most Roman readers would be happy to go along with speculations of this kind; similarly at 5. 161 'toto ex ore crudelitas eminebat',[36] they would | see only psychological probability[37] and convincing realism. Cicero expects people to recall that in his early career Verres was nearly burned alive by a mob at Lampsacus when on his way East to serve as a *legatus* (2. 1. 63–9). Such an episode from the defendant's past life[38] could be thought to corroborate what happened at Syracuse; in fact Cicero's account of the latter may have been overdrawn to make it correspond with the former.

tum istius actae commemorabantur, tum flagitiosa illa convivia.

Then his beach-parties were recounted, then those scandalous banquets.

Again Cicero is expecting the kind of reader who would resent Verres's ostentatious luxury. *actae* refers to sophisticated beach-parties;[39] the word was a humorous substitution for the more normal *acta*, 'achievements'.[40] The attitude to Cicero's puns must have varied from person to person, and generation to generation: thus 2. 121 *ius Verrinum* ('Verrine justice' and 'hog-broth') was criticized in Tacitus (*Dialogus* 23. 1) among other writers. But quite apart from questions of taste, other people's jokes present problems when they are read aloud. One has to see them coming,[41] and this may not be easy if the work is unfamiliar; even then the reader has to be a master of timing. This is particularly the case with Cicero's jokes, which usually depend not on a comic situation but a felicitously unexpected phrase (as can be seen

---

[36] Aulus Gellius comments on Cicero's words in this passage: 'tanti motus horrorisque sunt ut non narrari quae gesta sunt sed rem geri prorsus videas' (10. 3. 10).

[37] For physical appearance as an indication of character (*effictio, characterismus*) see *Rhet. Her.* 4. 63; E. C. Evans, 'Physiognomics in the Ancient World', *TAPhS* 59. 5 (1969). In oratory characters are presented as unambiguously good or bad; cf. D. A. Russell, 'Ethos in Oratory and Rhetoric', in C. B. R. Pelling (ed.), *Characterization and Individuality in Greek Literature* (Oxford, 1990), 197–211.

[38] For arguments *ex ante acta vita* see Volkmann, op. cit. (n. 7), 369–75; Stroh, op. cit. (n. 1), 251 n. 48.

[39] J. Griffin, *Latin Poets and Roman Life* (London, 1985), 91.

[40] *actae* is in fact Philippson's conjecture for *acta* of the manuscripts (cf. 5. 63 'in acta cum mulierculis iacebat ebrius' and 5. 82); it is needed to balance *convivia* (cf. Cic. *Cael.* 35 'accusatores . . . Baias actas convivia . . . iactant'). The person who miscopied the word must have been an incompetent reader who could not see a joke.

[41] Quint. 1. 1. 34 'sequentia intuenti priora dicenda sunt, et quod difficillimum est dividenda intentio animi, ut aliud voce aliud oculis agatur'; Lucian, *Adv. Ind.* 2.

from the fact that they are much more successful in Latin than in English). All this shows once again how much Cicero relied on the contribution of the reader.

tum appellabantur a multitudine mulieres nominatim.

Then the crowd called out at the women by name.

The ideal reader, and the ideal reader's wife, would think that ladies should not be talked about (Thucydides 2. 45. 2); still less should they attract the barracking (*convicium*) that characterized Roman 'popular justice'.[42] He would recall that Cicero had named these people in his earlier descriptions of the picnics on the shore. There was Tertia (5. 31, 40), the daughter of the mime-actor Isidorus and mistress of a musician from Rhodes: the particulars, which could be recited with disgust, would suggest that Cicero knows all. When he said that Verres valued his women less for their lineage than their merits (5. 31), he relied on the reader to interpret the compliment nastily: the sardonic twist to a conventional motif was a kind of humour that appealed to the Romans.[43] Apart from Nike, whom we have met already, there was also Pipa, the | wife of Aeschrio (the name sounds disgraceful in Greek), whose affair with Verres was recounted in verses[44] that circulated throughout Sicily (5. 81). Readers with predictable attitudes would feel a blend of disapproval and glee; with luck some might be able to supply the lines, which were clearly unsuitable for quotation in a speech.

tum quaerebant ex isto palam tot dies continuos per quos numquam visus esset ubi fuisset quid egisset; tum imperator ab eo praepositus Cleomenes flagitabatur.

Then they asked Verres to his face where he had been and what he had done for all those days on end through which he had never been seen. Then they shouted for the commander-in-chief he had appointed, Cleomenes.

The crowd's insolence to Verres is unexpected and may be fictitious: when a Roman magistrate appeared in public, he was supported by a

---

[42] H. Usener, 'Italische Volksjustiz', *RhM* 56 (1900), 1–28 = id., *Kleine Schriften* (Leipzig and Berlin, 1912–13), 4. 356–82; E. Fraenkel, 'Two Poems of Catullus', *JRS* 51 (1961), 46–53 = id., *Kleine Beiträge zur klassichen Philologie* (Rome, 1964), 2. 115–29; A. W. Lintott, *Violence in Republican Rome* (Oxford, 1968), 6–10.

[43] P. Plass, *Wit and the Writing of History* (Madison, Wis., 1988), 30–1.

[44] For such pasquinades see Cic. *QF* 2. 3. 2 'cum omnium maledicta, versus denique obscenissimi in Clodium et Clodiam dicerentur'; P. Veyne, 'Le folklore à Rome', *Latomus*, 42 (1983), 13–15; A. Richlin, *The Garden of Priapus* (New Haven, Conn. and London, 1983), 94–6.

fearsome display of *imperium*, in this case six stalwart lictors with canes and axes. If Cicero had actually delivered his speech, his disrespect for office might have disturbed a senatorial jury; but now that Verres was disgraced and in exile, readers from a wider milieu could enjoy an account of his discomfiture. They would appreciate the merciless scene where the crowd shouts 'We want Cleomenes'; failure met with little sympathy in the Roman political world (or the Greek for that matter). The less subtle would find it hilarious to give a defeated Greek the majestic title of *imperator*, just as when years later Cicero called Clodia *imperatrix* (*Pro Caelio* 67).

neque quicquam propius est factum quam ut illud Uticense exemplum [de Hadriano] transferretur Syracusas, ut duo sepulchra duorum praetorum improborum duabus in provinciis constituerentur.

As near as no matter the precedent of Utica was transferred to Syracuse, so as for two burial-places for two wicked governors to be instituted in two provinces.

The reader is assumed to recall the episode of Utica in 83 BC when the crowd burned the governor Hadrianus in his own residence.[45] I have deleted *de Hadriano* as an intrusive gloss that impairs the balance of Utica and Syracuse; contemporaries with political awareness could supply the name, and if anybody had forgotten it no harm would be done. It seems strange that Cicero condones this outrage against the governor of a province, but again the crowd consisted of Roman merchants, a class that | he was trying to cultivate. At the end of the sentence there is a reminiscence of the tragedian Accius, *video sepulcra duo duorum corporum*, 'I see two sepulchres of two bodies';[46] the line was certainly familiar to Cicero, as he quotes it at *Orator* 156. The well-read reader would enjoy the pleasure of recognition, and feel well-disposed to an orator who took his culture for granted; the less learned would not feel slighted as there would be no reason for puzzlement. Much reminiscence in Latin literature works, or fails to work, in the same sort of way.

verum habita est a multitudine ratio temporis, habita tumultus, habita etiam dignitatis existimationisque communis, quod is est conventus Syracusis civium Romanorum, ut non modo illa provincia verum etiam hac re publica dignissimus existimetur.

But the throng paid regard to the crisis, to the civil commotion, to the dignity and reputation of the community; for such is the Roman citizen body at

---

[45] *Verr.* 2. 1. 70; Livy, *Per.* 86; Lintott, op. cit. (n. 42), 8–9.
[46] Accius fr. 655 Ribbeck (*TRF*³) = *inc.* 33 Warmington (*Remains of Old Latin* 2. 574).

Syracuse that it is regarded as a credit not only to the province of Sicily but to the Roman Republic as well.

Having appealed to his less scrupulous readers' baser emotions, Cicero is skilfully backtracking. He had seemed to advocate the incineration of a governor in his own *praetorium*, but now he hastily explains that the Roman citizens at Syracuse were too responsible to do any such thing. His flattering of this community would win the sympathy, if not of the senatorial jury that he is purporting to address, at least of much of his original readership.

confirmant ipsi se, cum hic etiam tum semisomnus stuperet arma capiunt, totum forum atque Insulam quae est urbis magna pars complent. (5. 95)

They draw courage from one another; when Verres was even then in a semisomnolent stupor, they take up arms; they man the whole forum and Island, which comprises a large part of the city.

Again Cicero loads his narrative to win the co-operation of his readers. Many would identify with the Roman citizens who rallied to the defence of their interests; correspondingly they would deplore the irresponsibility of the governor, who was the right person to organize resistance. In other circumstances a leader can be praised for insouciance in the face of danger: Drake had time to finish the game, Wellington attended the Duchess of Richmond's ball, and the Romans could admire men of action who knew how to enjoy their *otium*. But as Verres lost his battle with the pirates, patriots would readily believe that he was half-|asleep. In fact though he may well have been negligent in his preparation of the fleet, it is difficult to see that his conduct at the time of the battle made any practical difference.

We can better understand Cicero's conspiracy with his reader if we compare a later piece of invective, the surviving fragment of Caelius's speech against C. Antonius, the uncle of Mark Antony; it is a commonplace that the original reader used earlier literature to interpret a text, but for us it is also legitimate to use a later parallel to illuminate a manner of writing.

namque ipsum offendunt temulento sopore profligatum, totis praecordiis stertentem, ructuosos spiritus geminare, praeclarasque contubernales ab omnibus spondis transversas incubare, et reliquas circumiacere passim. quae tamen exanimatae terrore hostium adventu percepto, excitare Antonium conabantur, nomen inclamabant, frustra a cervicibus tollebant; blandius alia ad aurem invocabat, vehementius etiam nonnulla feriebat; quarum cum omnium vocem tactumque noscitaret, proximae cuiusque collum amplexu petebat; neque

dormire excitatus neque vigilare ebrius poterat, sed semisomno sopore inter
manus centurionum concubinarumque iactabatur. (Quintilian 4. 2. 123–4 =
Malcovati, *Oratorum Romanorum fragmenta*, 2nd edn., fr. 17, p. 483)

They find the governor prostrate in a drunken slumber, snoring with all his
vitals, redoubling flatulent eructations, with his fine female tent-mates from all
the camp-beds lying crosswise over him, and the rest of the women sprawling
higgledy-piggledy around. Even so they were startled out of their wits when
they perceived the onset of the enemy; they tried to rouse Antonius, they
shouted out his name; they made to lift him by the shoulders, in vain. One
called coaxingly in his ear, others hit him quite vigorously, and as he recognized
every one of them by voice and touch, he tried to put his arms round the neck
of whoever was nearest; but he could neither sleep on being wakened nor stay
awake as he was drunk, but in a semi-somnolent slumber was bundled from
hand to hand by his centurions and concubines.

This fragment has a number of things in common with our passage
from the *Fifth Verrine*. In both a provincial governor on trial for extortion is accused of negligence at the approach of an enemy. In both he is
somnolent, drunk, and distracted by discreditable women. In Cicero
the crowd tries to rouse the slumbering Verres, in Caelius the women
try to | rouse the slumbering Antonius: both passages emphasize words
like *dormire, vigilare, excitare*. Caelius calls the camp-followers *contubernales* or tent-mates; so Cicero had referred in his speech to *illud contubernium muliebris militiae* (5. 104). In particular we may note *cum
semisomnus stuperet* at the end of the Ciceronian passage and *semisomno
sopore* at the end of Caelius's fragment. Alan Cameron has pointed out
that the latter phrase is oddly tautologous (especially as *sopore* was
used above), and he has conjectured *semisomno stupore*;[47] his proposal is
supported by the parallel in Cicero, which he does not record. All this
tends to show that Caelius was imitating Cicero and going one better
than his master, but his very exaggerations make clearer the conventions of invective. The more sensible readers of both speeches would
see that some elements were overdrawn, but that would not seem to
matter. A speech by Cicero was not just a manifesto but an entertainment.

Rhetoric is the art of persuasion, and Cicero uses all its techniques
on his original readers. He senses their views on incompetent governors, defeated commodores, and luxurious mistresses, and he works on
their patriotic instincts, factional interest, moral convictions, envy, and
sense of humour. Sometimes he will invoke prejudices that he does not

[47] A. Cameron, 'Caelius on C. Antonius (*ORF*² fr. 17)', *CR*, NS 16 (1966), 17.

himself hold (as notoriously in the *Verrines* in his disdain for Greek art), but he is not utterly cynical: an orator will write and speak best when he is swept along by his own eloquence (*De Oratore* 2. 189–90), and shares the emotions that he helps to generate. He does not work by consulting the textbooks, though he has read them all, but by applying general principles imaginatively to particular situations: sometimes a circumstantial narrative will carry conviction, sometimes a self-evident fabrication will make his adversary ridiculous; more often he is content to exaggerate, selecting and slanting, making the more plausible points carry the less. There is no reason to believe that Verres was an innocent victim: parts of the *Verrines* are supported by details that could not have been invented without being refuted. But in other circumstances Cicero could have tilted the argument the other way: thus in the *Pro Fonteio* and *Pro Flacco* he stresses the unreliability of provincial witnesses, and in the *Pro Murena* and *Pro Caelio* he shows an indulgent attitude to the life of pleasure. He has no feeling that a prosecution should not be pressed too vehemently, or that Verres should be spared once he had admitted defeat. He is now playing not just to win a good case but to confirm his own position in the courts and public life.

Beyond this immediate object Cicero has a larger aim, the creation of a prose classic comparable with anything in Greek oratory. His expected audience cannot be defined (expressions like 'the ideal reader' are vague | at the best of times), but it would include a cultivated minority in future generations. The literary and political purposes of the work overlap: in the ancient world the literary public admired rhetorically effective arguments, while politically minded persons expected an orator to delight (*delectare*) as well as to inform (*docere*) and to excite (*movere*). But the *Verrines* are too long for purely practical needs, and though eloquence was appreciated in Roman courts, the degree of polish and elaboration would have been impossible for a speaker facing unexpected situations in the real world. If we consider the written works that we have and not the orations that might have been, Cicero's aims in the *Verrines* begin to seem more literary than political, and this is as true of the small-scale effects as of the larger design.

It may be objected against the tenor of this chapter that an author's intentions cannot be gauged: we have only the text to go on, which we can interpret as we choose, and have no other access to the orator's mind. Certainly slips of the pen are possible, and unforeseen felicities, or ambiguities that have not been consciously designed. Yet oratory is so practical an art that even in its literary form the uncalculated elements are more marginal than in poetry: it is easier to talk of Cicero's purpose in the *Verrines* than of Virgil's in the *Aeneid*, let alone that of twentieth-century writers, who have had an undue influence on contemporary discussion (modern critics read more Joyce than Johnson). We can bring to bear not only what we find in the text itself but our knowledge of the genre, the needs of the case, and human nature in general. Above all, we have enough of Cicero's writings to know what he was like: he had an astute mind and a lucid style, and it is not difficult to identify his overall aims and the means he adopted to achieve them. The notion of 'intention' always raises problems of definition, as we do many things deliberately but without conscious reflection;[48] but though on any particular occasion we may be mistaken, Cicero's purposes are in principle no more opaque than those of any living politician or colleague.

Written words are symbols in ink that need a receiver to activate them; this is true of all literature, but oratory depends to an unusual extent on the living voice. What then could the reader contribute to the speech that was never spoken? At the most obvious level, a familiarity with literary Latin that Romans possessed in very different degrees; also, if possible, some acquaintance with the political and practical issues. Misunderstandings had to be avoided (easier for those who knew the language), non-existent punctuation supplied (some variation was possible), innuendo and irony expressed, allusions and parodies spotted, jokes seen and communicated. Blanks in the narrative might be filled in, | for just as in interpreting a painting, we sometimes have to supply what is suggested rather than stated. If the reader had imagination, he could visualize select scenes in his own way, an aspect of reading that is too often neglected. Above all, the reader had to have some feeling for the sound and rhythm of formal prose, and be able to reproduce it out loud. But though the speech could not happen without him, he remained subordinate to the author. It is of the essence of oratory that the speaker should know what he is doing, and though we may fail to notice his sleight-of-hand, we can follow in its main lines what he is willing us to see.

---

[48] A. Sheppard, *Aesthetics: An Introduction to the Philosophy of Art* (Oxford, 1987), 94–113.

23

Adolescens Puer (Virgil, *Eclogues* 4. 28-30)

I N the *Liverpool Classical Monthly* Dr John Pinsent has enabled scholars to air their theories before others could think of them or they themselves repent of them. Among many other services he has found space for notes on the sexual language of antiquity, when they might have impaired the stylistic unity of primmer journals. As a modest contribution to these studies I voice some suspicions about what must seem an unlikely source in Virgil's *Fourth Eclogue*.

After mentioning the conception and babyhood of his *Wunderkind*, Virgil proceeds to a later stage of growth (26-8):

> at simul heroum laudes et facta parentum
> iam legere et quae sit poteris cognoscere virtus,
> molli paulatim flavescet campus arista.

That is to say, even the untilled plain will grow yellow with corn-ears (a continuation of the idyllic features of the previous lines). *molli* makes something of an oxymoron with *arista*, which is usually thought of as spiky, but the corn-ears are soft because they are new.

It is generally accepted that in this poem the development of the boy is paralleled by changes in the state of the world; the pattern recalls myths about the divine child who grows with the vegetation that in some sense he personifies (M. P. Nilsson, *Geschichte der griechischen Religion* 1³ (Munich, 1967), 315-19, 579-81). In these circumstances it is natural to see in line 28 a hint of the first down of adolescence; boys in antiquity were in no hurry to shave, as the ἴουλος or *lanugo* was thought attractive, and in some circles at least the *depositio barbae* was a significant ceremony (see Dio 48. 34. 3 on Octavian, Crinagoras, *Anth. Pal.* 6. 161 on Marcellus, J. Marquardt and A. Mau, *Das Privatleben der Römer* (Leipzig, 1886), 599-600). Cf. Hom. *Il.* 24. 348 πρῶτον ὑπηνήτῃ, τοῦ περ χαριεστάτη ἥβη, Theoc. 15. 85 πρᾶτον ἴουλον ἀπὸ κροτάφων καταβάλλων, Herodas 1. 52 with Headlam's parallels, Pacuv. *Trag.* 362

From *Tria Lustra: Essays and Notes presented to John Pinsent*, ed. H. D. Jocelyn with the assistance of Helena Hurt (Liverpool Classical Papers, 3; Liverpool, 1993), 265-7.

nunc primum opacat flore lanugo genas, Virg. *Aen.* 8. 160 *tum mihi prima genas vestibat flore iuventas* (which tells against Scaliger's *flora* in Pacuv. loc. cit.), 10. 324 *flaventem prima lanugine malas*, Ov. *Met.* 6. 718 *flavescere malae*, 9. 398 *paene puer dubiaque tegens lanugine malas* with Bömer, Mart. 1. 31. 5 with Citroni, E. Eyben, *Latomus*, 31 (1972), 692–3. For analogies between adolescent hair and corn cf. Call. *H.* 4. 298 f. παῖδες δὲ θέρος τὸ πρῶτον ἰούλων | ἄρσενες ἠιθέοισιν ἀπαρχόμενοι φορέουσιν (ἴουλος can mean 'a corn-sheaf' as well as 'down'), Asclepiades of Adramyttium, *Anth. Pal.* 12. 36. 3 f. καὶ τίς ἂν εἴποι | κρείσσονας αὐχμηρὰς ἀσταχύων καλάμας; Strato, ibid. 12. 215. 2 καὶ καλάμη γὰρ ἔσῃ, S. L. Tarán, *JHS* 105 (1985), 90–2. For the particular comparison of *arista* with bristles cf. Varr. *Ling.* 6. 45 *etiam in corpore pili ut arista in spica hordei horrent*, Pers. 3. 115 *excussit membris timor albus aristas*. For *molli* as an epithet of the first hair of adolescence cf. Lucr. 5. 672 f. *nec minus in certo dentes cadere imperat aetas | tempore, et impubem molli pubescere veste, | et pariter mollem malis demittere barbam*, 5. 888 f. *tum demum puerili aevo florente iuventas | occipit et molli vestit lanugine malas*, Mart. 10. 42. 1. For *paulatim* cf. Asclepiades of Adramyttium, *Anth. Pal.* 12. 36. 1 f. ὅτε λεπτὸς ὑπὸ κροτάφοισιν ἴουλος | ἕρπει.

Virgil continues in the following line (29) 'incultisque rubens pendebit sentibus uva'; again he is describing the spontaneous profusion of the new Golden Age. But if there is a suggestion of the boy in 28 *molli*... *flavescet*... *arista*, then the ambiguity must be sustained in line 29; there is no escape from this conclusion, as anything else would give an intolerable anticlimax. Before we consider other manifestations of male puberty, it must be emphasized that we are talking not of the primary meaning (which obviously concerns vegetation) but of oblique hints, such as are familiar in the *Eclogues*, and | particularly in this oracular poem. Even the god of Delphi posed riddles with a sexual significance; cf. Apollodorus 3. 15. 6 (to Aegeus) ἀσκοῦ τὸν προύχοντα ποδάονα, φέρτατε λαῶν, | μὴ λύσῃς, πρὶν ἐς ἄκρον Ἀθηναίων ἀφίκηαι, Eur. *Med.* 679 ff., J. Fontenrose, *The Delphic Oracle* (Berkeley and Los Angeles, 1978), 356.

In these circumstances I shall list a few parallels that spell out bluntly what in our passage is left decently inexplicit. For *rubens*... *uva* cf. Strato, *Anth. Pal.* 12. 222. 3 τῇ χερὶ τοὺς κόκκους ἐπαφώμενος (of an assault on a boy by a wrestling-master); a κόκκος was a red excrescence on the kermes-oak, similar to cochineal, and an important source of ancient dye (R. J. Forbes, *Studies in Ancient Technology*, 4 (Leiden, 1956), 100–4). Note also Auson. *Cento Nuptialis* 105 f. (p. 216

Peiper = p. 138 Green) *aperit ramum qui veste latebat | sanguineis ebuli bacis minioque rubentem* (from Virg. *Ecl.* 10. 27). For *sentibus* of pubic hair cf. anon. *Anth. Pal.* 12. 40. 3 f. γυμνὴν Ἀντιφίλου ζητῶν χάριν, ὡς ἐπ᾽ ἀκάνθαις | εὑρήσεις ῥοδέαν φυομένην κάλυκα (*sentes ἄκανθαι CGL* 7. 256), Asclepiades of Adramyttium 12. 36. 2 μηροῖς ὀξὺς ἔπεστι χνόος (note also βάτος of facial hair at Rufinus, *Anth. Pal.* 5. 28. 6, anon. 11. 53. 2). For *incultis* cf. Pers. 4. 41 *non illa filix ullo mansuescit aratro*; the boy is not *pumice mundus* (Hor. *Epist.* 1. 20. 2; cf. H. Blümner, *Die römischen Privataltertümer* (Munich, 1911), 438-9). For *pendebit* cf. Lucil. 534 ff. M. *ibat forte aries, inquit, iam quod genus! quantis | testibus! vix uno filo hosce haerere putares, | pellicula extrema exaptum pendere onus ingens, Priapea* 52. 7 *pulcre pensilibus peculiati* (I owe these passages to J. N. Adams, *The Latin Sexual Vocabulary* (London, 1982), 57); note also Cels. 7. 18. 1 *dependent vero ab inguinibus per singulos nervos quos cremasteras Graeci vocant* (Galen 4. 635 K).

The next line (30) runs *et durae quercus sudabunt roscida mella* (again referring to the new Golden Age); now that we have got so far, there can be no turning back. For *durae quercus* cf. Novius, *Atell.* 21 (*puerum*) *cuius iam ramus roborascit*, Hor. *Epod.* 12. 19 f. *cuius in indomito constantior inguine nervus | quam nova collibus arbor inhaeret* (perhaps *indomito* means *inculto*, cf. Pers. 4. 41 cited above, Tac. *Dial.* 40. 4 *indomitus ager habet quasdam herbas laetiores*), H. Akbar Khan, *CPh* 64 (1969), 91-2 (on the hamstrung alder at Catull. 17. 18), my own comment on Sen. *HO* 1099 *stipite* in *Homo Viator*, ed. M. Whitby, P. Hardie, M. Whitby (Bristol, 1987), 247 (above, p. 207), J. N. Adams, op. cit. 23-4. For *sudabunt* cf. Mar. Victorin. *Defin.* p. 39. 2 ff. *turpis translatio . . . ut si quis patrationem definiens lacrimas dicat Veneris fatigatae* (cf. Lucil. 307 M), *quem sudorem melius nominaret.* For *roscida* cf. *Priapea* 48. 3 *non ros est, mihi crede, nec pruina . . .*, Pfeiffer on Call. *Hecala* fr. 260. 19 δρόσον (*intellegi potest de semine Hephaesti*), Dover on Ar. *Clouds* 977, though his particular interpretation of that passage remains controversial (cf. Jeffrey Henderson, *The Maculate Muse* (New Haven, Conn. and London, 1975), 145). It is harder to parallel *mella* directly, though Porphyry has a mystical passage associating honey with the pleasure of generation (*De Antro Nympharum* 16 ταὐτὸν δὲ τῇ ἐκ συνουσίας ἡδονῇ παρίστησιν αὐτοῖς ἡ τοῦ μέλιτος); yet for modern usage cf. *Grande Dizionario della lingua italiana*, 10 (Turin, 1978), s.v. *miele* 5 *fluido seminale*, E. Partridge, *Dictionary of Slang and Unconventional English*, 8th edn. (London, 1984), s.v. 'honey' ('C. 19-20 low slang').

Some of the above passages cross the boundary of the obscene, but not everybody was like Strato or Martial; there were more serious ways of writing about sexuality, a fact that is obscured by an exclusively lexicographical approach. The coming of puberty was the occasion of an important *rite de passage*, the assumption of the *toga virilis* (Marquardt-Mau, *Privatleben*, 123–34). A medical examination could be required that was to seem indecent to Christian sensibilities: cf. Justinian, *Inst.* 1. 22

nostra autem maiestas dignum esse castitate nostrorum temporum bene putavit, quod in feminis et antiquis impudicum est visum esse, id est inspectionem habitudinis corporis, hoc etiam in masculos extendere, |

Codex 5. 60. 3 indecoram observationem in examinanda marium pubertate resecantes iubemus: quemadmodum feminae post impletos duodecim annos omnimodo pubescere iudicantur, ita et mares post excessum quattuordecim annorum pubescere existimentur, indagatione corporis inhonesta cessante

(cf. Ar. *Wasps* 578), Rossbach, *Die römische Ehe* (Stuttgart, 1853), 404–6, P. E. Corbett, *The Roman Law of Marriage* (Oxford, 1930), 51–2. Yet in Virgil's day respectable and responsible Romans would rather have shared the attitude of St Augustine's father: *ubi me ille pater in balneis vidit pubescentem et inquieta indutum adulescentia, quasi iam ex hoc in nepotes gestiret, gaudens matri indicavit* (*Conf.* 2. 3. 6). Such considerations would apply particularly to the child of the *Fourth Eclogue*, who is meant to suggest the hoped-for offspring of the dynastic marriage of Antony and Octavia (cf. *BICS* 25 (1978), 63–4 (above, pp. 58–60)).

It may be further observed that the analogy between human and vegetable fecundity was developed even in poetry of the highest style, notably in descriptions of the union of heaven and earth: cf. Aesch. *Danaides* fr. 125. 22 f. Mette ὄμβρος δ' ἀπ' εὐνάεντος Οὐρανοῦ πεσὼν | ἔκυσε Γαῖαν ..., Lucr. 1. 250 ff., 2. 991 ff., Virg. *Georg.* 2. 325 ff. *tum pater omnipotens fecundis imbribus Aether* | *coniugis in gremium laetae descendit.* Our passage is less grand than that, as suits the difference of genre, and the sensuous imagery has a closer analogy at *Pervigilium Veneris* 9 ff. (on the birth of Aphrodite): *tunc cruore de superno spumeo pontus globo* | ... *fecit undantem Dionem de marinis imbribus.* For this myth cf. Hes. *Theog.* 190 f. ἀμφὶ δὲ λευκὸς | ἀφρὸς ἀπ' ἀθανάτου χροὸς ὤρνυτο, where West comments 'there may be an allusion to τὸ ἀφρῶδες τοῦ σπέρματος' (p. 213); he cites among other parallels Nonn. *Dion.* 13. 439 ff. ὁππότε γὰρ γονόεσσα κατάρρυτος ἄρσενι λύθρῳ | Οὐρανίη μόρφωσε λεχώιον ἀφρὸν ἐέρση | καὶ Παφίην ὤδινε.

The *Fourth Eclogue* encourages a search for ambiguities, and in the

speech *Ad Sanctum Coetum* that Eusebius attributed to the Emperor
Constantine a religious significance was suggested for the oaks and the
honey (ch. 20, vol. 1, p. 285 Heikel): ἴσως δὲ καὶ τοὺς τὸν θεοῦ πόνον
ἀσκοῦντας τῆς ἑαυτῶν καρτερίας γλυκύν τινα καρπὸν λήψεσθαι
διδάσκων. In fact the poem was less other-worldly than has sometimes been thought, and Virgil less virginal. Already in the first century
AD Valerius Probus was embarrassed by *Aen.* 8. 405 f. *placidumque
petivit | coniugis infusus gremio per membra soporem*; he absurdly bowdler-
ized the passage by reading *infusum* (Serv. ad loc., cf. H. D. Jocelyn,
LCM 9 (1984), 20–1). Ausonius knew better (*Cento Nuptialis* p. 219
Peiper = p. 139 Green, with some plagiarism from Gellius 9. 10. 1, cf.
L. Holford-Strevens, *Aulus Gellius* (London, 1988), p. 107 n. 24):

quid etiam Maronem Parthenien dictum causa pudoris, qui in octavo Aeneidos,
cum describeret coitum Veneris atque Volcani, αἰσχροσεμνίαν decenter
immiscuit? quid? in tertio Georgicorum de summissis in gregem maritis
[3. 123 ff.], nonne obscenam significationem honesta verborum translatione
velavit?

24

Four Conjectures on Catullus 64

non flavo retinens subtilem vertice mitram,
non contecta levi velatum pectus amictu,
non tereti strophio lactentis vincta papillas.   (63–5)

AT the wedding of Peleus and Thetis the coverlet on the bed portrayed the deserted Ariadne on the sea-shore. Each of the above three lines contains six words that correspond to similar words in the other lines: *non, non, non*; *retinens, contecta, vincta*; *mitram, amictu, strophio*; *subtilem, levi, tereti*; *vertice, pectus, papillas*; *flavo, velatum, lactentis*. It is clear from this analysis that in the second line *velatum* is anomalous, and not simply because it is awkwardly combined with *non contecta*; we look for a picturesque adjective, especially one describing colour. Unsatisfactory attempts have been made to emend the text: Baehrens records *bullatum* (Fea), *vesanum* (Riese), *nudatum* (Schwabe), *niveum per* (Mähly), *niveum tum* (Baehrens himself at one time, but *tum* is otiose); Ellis in his Oxford text added *laniatum* (Owen), *violatum* (Haverfield); T. Kakridis proposed *decoratum* (*PhW* 44 (1924), 501).

I suggest *variatum*, 'mottled'. At Hor. *Carm.* 2. 5. 10 ff. 'iam tibi lividos l distinguet Autumnus racemos l purpureo varius colore' (a passage with erotic imagery) A. Y. Campbell comments 'designat poeta virginis adultae mammas venis errantibus variegatas' (1945 edition, London); but he cites no parallel. The verb is used below at 350 f. 'cum incultum cano solvent a vertice crinem l putriaque[1] infirmis variabunt pectora palmis' (of mourning mothers beating their breasts); these lines come from the Fates' grisly epithalamium, with its annunciation of the birth and bloodthirsty deeds of Achilles. If Catullus wrote *variatum* in line 64, *variabunt* in 351 could be a sinister reminiscence; compare also *flavo retinens . . . vertice* with *cano solvent a vertice*, and *vincta papillas* with *putria . . . pectora*. In ancient literature descriptions of works of art sometimes foreshadow the future action whether by resemblance or contrast.[2]

---

[1] *putriaque* is plausible for *putridaque* of the transmission (cf. Hor. *Epod.* 8. 7 'mammae putres'); the conjecture is assigned to Heinsius by M. L. Earle, *RPh.* 27 (1903), 271.

[2] P. Friedländer, *Johannes von Gaza und Paulus Silentiarius* (Leipzig and Berlin, 1912), 1 ff.; S. Bartsch, *Decoding the Ancient Novel* (Princeton, NJ, 1989); see also above, p. 208.

huc huc adventate, meas audite querellas
quas ego vae misera extremis[3] proferre medullis
cogor inops ardens, amenti caeca furore.   (195–7)

In her address to the Eumenides Ariadne is describing her own help-
lessness. For a similar accumulation of adjectives see Ov. *Met.* 14. 217
'solus inops exspes, leto poenaeque relictus'. Bömer supplies further
parallels: Acc. *Trag.* 415 'exspes expers desertus vagus', Ov. *Her.* 6. 162
'erret inops exspes', 12. 1 'exul inops contempta' (apparently interpolated), *Ibis* 113 'exul inops erres', *Met.* 13. 510 'nunc trahor exul
inops'. But in our passage *ardens* refers to Ariadne's blazing anger, and
so interrupts the sequence of words suggesting desperation.

I propose 'cogor inops amens ardenti caeca furore'. *amens*, 'dis-
traught', makes a satisfactory pair with *inops*, 'helpless', and is made
easier by the fact that *mentis inops* (like *inops animi*) is an attested locution (Ov. *Ars* 1. 465, *TLL* 7. 1. 1756. 30ff.). *amens* combines well with
caeca; cf. Cic. *Sest.* 17 'caecus atque amens', Lucan 7. 747 'amentes
aurique cupidine caecos'. On the other hand, *amenti* with *furore* adds
nothing; distinguish Lucan 10. 147f. 'caecus et amens I ambitione
furor', where *amens* is qualified by *ambitione* (the combination with
caecus is in fact more significant for our passage). For the collocation of
ardens and *furor* cf. 64. 124 'ardenti corde furentem', Virg. *Aen.* 9. 760f.
'sed furor ardentem . . . I egit in adversos', Apul. *Met.* 9. 2. 2 (of a mad
dog) 'ardentique prorsus furore venaticos canes invasisse', Lact. *Phoen.*
18 'ardens caedis amore Furor'.

hic, qualis flatu placidum mare matutino
horrificans Zephyrus proclivas incitat undas,   270
Aurora exoriente, vagi sub limina Solis,
quae tarde primum clementi flamine pulsae
procedunt, leviterque sonant plangore cachinni;
post vento crescente magis magis increbescunt,
purpureaque procul nantes ab luce refulgent: 275
sic tum vestibuli linquentes regia tecta
ad se quisque vago passim pede discedebant.   (269–77)

The departure of the wedding-guests is compared to the waves that
come thicker and faster with the dawn breeze. Doubt has been caused
by 276 *vestibuli*. The *vestibulum* was a forecourt in front of the palace

---

[3] *ex imis* is an early conjecture for *extremis* (see also D. F. S. Thomson, *RhM* 113
(1970), 89ff.); yet cf. Ov. *Her.* 4. 70 'acer in extremis ossibus haesit amor', *TLL* 5. 2. 1998.
62ff.

(also mentioned at 293 'vestibulum ut molli velatum fronde vireret'); in that case the *regia tecta* must be the buildings round the court, though the phrase would refer more naturally to the palace as a whole. Schrader proposed *vestibulo* (accepted by G. P. Goold) or *vestibulis*, but the degree of emphasis imposed by the word's position is still a little strange: how else would the guests be expected to leave? One might try to see a contrast with 271, where the waves in the simile are driven towards the portals of the sun; unlike most editors, I take *sub limina solis* with *incitat*, not *exoriente*. See Fraenkel's note on Aesch. *Ag.* 1180 ff. λαμπρὸς δ' ἔοικεν ἡλίου πρὸς ἀντολὰς | πνέων ἐσᾴξειν, ὥστε κύματος δίκην | κλύζειν πρὸς αὐγὰς τοῦδε πήματος πολὺ | μεῖζον (where he cites our passage). If this interpretation is correct, the balance of *limina* and *vestibulo* would be purely formal, as sometimes happens in multiple-correspondence similes; as the portals of the sun are metaphorical, they do nothing to make the analogy more vivid.

J. Mähly suggested in place of *vestibuli* a nominative plural on the lines of *Thessalii* (*NJPhP* 103 (1871), 352); Baehrens considered *festini*, to underline the analogy between the guests and the waves. I propose rather *vestiflui*, 'with flowing robes', to be combined with *sic* (taking *linquentes regia tecta* as a separate clause). *vestifluus* is attested at Auson. *Technopaignia* 11. 6 'vestifluus Ser' (of a Chinese in silk robes).[4] It was conjectured by Turnebus, but not accepted by recent editors, at Petr. 133. 3 vers. 3 f. 'quem Lydus adorat | †septifluus' (where the other side of the tradition offers *semper flavius* or *semperfluus*); for flowing Lydian robes Courtney cites Xenophanes fr. 3, Sappho fr. 39 L–P, Aesch. fr. 59 Nauck–Radt ὅστις χιτῶνας βασσάρας τε Λυδίας | ἔχει ποδήρεις, Aristaenetus 1. 15 Λύδιός τε καὶ ποδήρης χιτών (*The Poems of Petronius* (Atlanta, 1991), 36). The adjective is likely to be archaic and suits Catullus's poem; cf. 64. 52 *fluentisono*.

vestiflui would make the relevance of the simile much more explicit. The waves are like the wedding-guests not just because of their babble (273 *cachinni*) or because they come thicker and faster (274 *increbescunt*). The point of 275 *purpurea ... ab luce refulgent* is surely to emphasize the colour of the guests' finery, while *nantes* draws a comparison with their gliding motion. In the same way *vestiflui* would point back to the flowing water of the simile.[5] For the image it is enough to compare Herrick:

---

[4] For imitations of Catullus in Ausonius see the index to Green's commentary; note also above, pp. 83–4.

[5] Cf. M. S. Silk, *Interaction in Poetic Imagery* (Cambridge, 1974), *passim*.

When as in silk my *Julia* goes
Then, then (me thinks) how sweetly flowes
That liquefaction of her clothes.

> quare agite optatos animi coniungite amores.
> accipiat coniunx felici foedere divam,
> dedatur cupido iam dudum nupta marito.   (372–4)

The Fates now directly address Peleus and Thetis. *nupta* balances *marito* precisely, but *coniunx* does not balance *divam* so well. One difficulty is that *coniunx* can be applied either to the husband or the wife, and in an epithalamium more naturally refers to the wife. It is more serious that the word is not used exclusively of mortals, an implication highly desirable in this passage (cf. 20 'tum Thetis humanos non despexit hymenaeos'), but can describe either a god (68. 139) or a goddess (Virg. *Aen.* 1. 47 etc.); note especially 329 'adveniet fausto cum sidere coniunx' (of Thetis), [Sen.] *Octavia* 706 f. 'talis emersam freto | spumante Peleus coniugem accepit Thetin'.

I suggest *iuvenis*; Peleus was one of the *lecti iuvenes* of line 4. The word suits the bridegroom in an epithalamium; cf. 61. 56 ff. 'tu fero iuveni in manus | floridam ipse puellulam | dedis', 62. 23 'et iuveni ardenti castam donare puellam', Stat. *Silv.* 1. 2. 81, Claud. 14. 5 'ne cessa, iuvenis, comminus adgredi'. It may be argued that *coniunx* picks up *coniungite* in the previous line; but equally the verb might have influenced the corruption of *iuvenis* to a word with only a superficial resemblance.

25

The Survivors: Old-Style Literary Men in the Triumviral Period

THE triumvirate marks a convenient break in literature as well as in history. Cicero died in 43 with the revived Republic, a calamity not just for oratory but for Rome's whole intellectual life. Cinna, the earliest of the neoteric poets on some definitions of that vague term, had been lynched on the day of Julius Caesar's funeral.[1] Cornificius, another friend of Catullus, was killed in Africa in 42; he belonged to a vanishing generation when poetry could still be a part-time activity, and a man of affairs could write an 'epyllion' on Glaucus the fish-tailed god. The triumvirate also saw the emergence of three great literary innovators, Virgil, Horace, and Sallust (for the *Epistles* to Caesar, which purport to be earlier, are not authentic).[2] Soon afterwards Maecenas began to give literature more systematic 'guidance', if that is the word, than could have been contemplated in the Republic or even the Dictatorship.

But everybody does not disappear at once: people straddle the generations who represent a former way of looking at things. Tacitus has an alert eye for such survivors, whose death is a reminder of historical change; thus in AD 22 he records the funeral of Junia, sister of Brutus and widow of Cassius, sixty-three years after the battle of Philippi (*Ann.* 3. 76. 1). With such people our first intimation that they were still alive may be the news that they are dead, and modern instances sometimes surprise us in the obituaries. When a poet dies young, his associates may long outlive him: Joseph Severn, who nursed Keats by the Spanish Steps, survived him for fifty-eight years, and Edward Trelawny, who cremated Shelley on the shore, survived him for fifty-nine years.

A shorter version of this paper was read on 16 June 1992 at an Oxford seminar on the triumvirate chaired by Professor Fergus Millar and myself.

[1] Ovid, *Ibis* 539–40; Plut. *Brut.* 20. 6; E. Courtney, *FLP = The Fragmentary Latin Poets* (Oxford, 1993), 212.

[2] R. Syme, *Sallust* (Berkeley, 1964), 318–51. For imitation of Sallust in Horace's *Epodes* see above, pp. 166, 169.

On the other hand, some survivors continue to be significant, for periodization in literature is even more misleading than it is in history. Decisive shifts of political power do sometimes occur, for instance at the battle of Philippi, but revolutions of taste are not so complete at the time as they are made to appear in retrospect. In the first two decades of the nineteenth century we think of the major British poets as Blake, Wordsworth, Coleridge, Keats, perhaps Shelley; but at the time they were Scott, Southey, Campbell, and Rogers, together with Byron, who after too long an eclipse may now have been restored to his rightful position. When we come to the 1920s, we find that students of English concern themselves with Eliot and Joyce, possibly to excess; but if we wish to know what writers were prominent at the time, we have only to look at the eight pall-bearers at Thomas Hardy's funeral. Apart from Baldwin, the Prime Minister, and MacDonald, the Leader of the Opposition, they were Barrie, Galsworthy, Gosse, Housman, Kipling, and Shaw, while conspicuous in the congregation were such people as Arnold Bennett and John Masefield, soon to become Poet Laureate in succession to Robert Bridges.

When we turn to the triumviral period we find that some of the survivors can be identified from Horace, *Sat.* 1. 10, written perhaps about 35 BC. In the first place, there were the archaizing *grammatici* whose proper respect for the roots of Roman poetry made them too resistant to new standards of classicism; the literary triumphs of the triumvirate and later owed much to the rich and cultivated patrons who were displacing the scholars as arbiters of taste.[3] The *grammatici* made pedantic criticisms of the *Eclogues* as later of the *Aeneid*;[4] they disparaged Horace for his candour about Lucilius's verbosity and imprecision (*Sat.* 1. 4. 6–13, 1. 10); in the *Epistles* he attributes the disappointing reception of the *Odes* to his failure to canvass influential critics (1. 19. 35–40); both in the *Satires* and *Epistles* he treats it as a degradation of poetry to be used for educational purposes (*Sat.* 1. 10. 74f. 'an tua demens | vilibus in ludis dictari carmina malis?', *Epist.* 1. 20. 17–18). Two of these *grammatici* are mentioned in the cryptic passage prefixed to *Satires* 1. 10 on one side of the manuscript tradition:

> Lucili, quam sis mendosus, teste Catone
> defensore tuo pervincam, qui male factos
> emendare parat versus, hoc lenior ille

---

[3] For some of them see R. Syme, *CQ*, NS 31 (1981), 424–5 = *Roman Papers*, 3 (Oxford, 1984), 1419–20.
[4] Schanz–Hosius, *Geschichte der römischen Literatur*, 2 (Munich, 1935), 96–8.

> quo melior vir ⟨et⟩ est longe subtilior illo
> qui multum †puer et loris et funibus udis
> †exoratus, ut esset opem qui ferre poetis
> antiquis posset contra fastidia nostra
> grammaticorum equitum doctissimus.

These lines are disfigured by textual corruption[5] and cannot belong to the poem as it stands;[6] but whether they are the work of another satirist or an early version by Horace himself, they are surely not a late forgery but reveal something authentic about the literary controversies of the period.

First comes Valerius Cato,[7] who was more interesting than most of his fellow-scholars. He had once himself been one of the new poets from Cisalpine Gaul, the author of a *Dictynna* and a *Lydia*, and an important influence on the whole movement; hence the well-known epigram plausibly attributed to Furius Bibaculus (17 M):

> Cato grammaticus, Latina Siren,
> qui solus legit et facit poetas.

legit seems to be generally misunderstood: the word means not 'reads' (which does not suit *solus*) but 'chooses', ἐγκρίνει,[8] for Cato had exercised his main influence not as a schoolmaster but as a critic, who could be said to have formed a new canon single-handed. That is why Gallus says in the papyrus poem that he does not fear the judgement of Cato provided that Lycoris approves (above, p. 111), and Bibaculus himself jokingly compares him with the great Hellenistic critics (2. 7, cited below). Cato lived well beyond the triumviral period to an impoverished old age, and Bibaculus describes how his villa at Tusculum was repossessed by his creditors (2 M):

> Catonis modo, Galle, Tusculanum
> tota creditor urbe venditabat.

---

[5] Reisig proposed *multum puerum est ... exhortatus* (see Heinze's note); Nipperdey preferred *multum pueros*. Passages with an eccentric transmission are particularly exposed to corruption; cf. Virg. *Aen.* 2. 567–88; Juv. 6. O. 1–34.

[6] C. Nipperdey, *Opuscula* (Berlin, 1877), 490–4; E. Fraenkel, *Hermes*, 68 (1933), 392–9 = *Kleine Beiträge zur klassischen Philologie* (Rome, 1964), 200–8, contradicting G. L. Hendrickson, *CPh.* 11 (1916), 249–69 and M. Rothstein, *Hermes*, 68 (1933), 70–83.

[7] Schanz–Hosius, 1 (Munich, 1927), 287–8; Courtney, *FLP* 189–91. His influence is played down, perhaps excessively, by R. P. Robinson, *TAPA* 54 (1923), 98–116; N. B. Crowther, *TAPA* 66 (1971), 108–9.

[8] For literary canons see R. Pfeiffer, *History of Classical Scholarship* (Oxford, 1968), 206; Nisbet–Hubbard on Horace, *Odes* 1. 1. 35, above, pp. 115–16. *facit* may refer to Cato's encouraging criticism of younger poets; this formulation avoids a tautology after *legit* (as Mr P. G. McC. Brown suggests to me).

> mirati sumus unicum magistrum,
> summum grammaticum, optimum poetam,
> omnes solvere posse quaestiones,
> unum deficere expedire nomen.
> en cor Zenodoti, en iecur Cratetis.

This sad story shows the progressive decline[9] of literary men when they live too long. The Latin Siren who had imposed new standards of mellifluousness on Roman poetry and lured the more adventurous young poets to his way of thinking seemed to some people even in the triumvirate a voice from the past, to be criticized himself for his indulgence to old-fashioned satirists.

The second critic mentioned in the problematical lines is not named but characterized, so we shall have to guess who he is. We are told that he was less subtle than Valerius Cato, that he relied on corporal punishment to inculcate an appreciation of early Roman poetry, and that he was the most learned of equestrian schoolmasters, *grammaticorum equitum doctissimus*. This is surely Horace's old teacher, Orbilius of Beneventum,[10] who was already 50 in 63 BC and lived to be 100 (Suet. *De Gramm.* 9). He seems to have obtained equestrian status in the army (Suet. loc. cit. 'in Macedonia corniculo mox equo meruit, functusque militia studia repetit'); the parallel with *corniculo* suggests that *equo* marks a rank rather than simply service in the cavalry (unless Suetonius has misunderstood a joke). Suetonius also quotes the line of Bibaculus (3 M) 'Orbilius ubinam est, litterarum oblivio?' He himself thought that Orbilius had lost his memory, others that his style of teaching was the death of literature.[11] In fact after *ubinam est?* the phrase may mean that he is literature's forgotten man.[12]

Another survivor was Furius Bibaculus himself. He was born at Cremona, according to Jerome (though his date of 103 is too early for a man clearly junior to Valerius Cato), and it is tempting to identify him with the Furius who is addressed in several poems by the Cisalpine Catullus.[13] Like Catullus he wrote lampoons in hendecasyllables, and Furius Bibaculus's epigram on the repossession of Cato's villa bears

---

[9] If Cato was 70 at the time of this epigram, the date is unlikely to have been earlier than 20 BC (Courtney, *FLP* 193).

[10] Schanz–Hosius, 1. 580; for his discipline see Hor. *Epist.* 2. 1. 70; Domitius Marsus 4 M.

[11] J. J. Hartman, *Mnem.* 29 (1901), 145–7; Courtney, *FLP* 194.

[12] Cf. Schanz–Hosius, 1. 580.

[13] Catullus 11, 16, 23, 26; W. A. Heidel, *CR* 15 (1901), 215–17; E. H. Green, *CJ* 35 (1939–40), 348–59; Courtney, *FLP* 119–200 (hesitant about the identification).

some resemblance to Catullus's epigram to Furius on a similar problem (26): 'Furi, villula vestra (nostra *v.l.*) non ad Austri | flatus opposita est neque ad Favoni | ... verum ad milia quindecim et ducentos' (the pun in *opposita est*, both 'exposed' and 'mortgaged', is capped by Bibaculus's *expedire nomen*, with its suggestion of both grammatical and financial problems). Macrobius ascribes to a Furius a hexameter poem called *Annales* in at least eleven books, and other authorities refer to *Annales Belli Gallici* or *Pragmatia Belli Gallici*,[14] which looks like an epic on Caesar's Gallic War. That would suit the Furius who is sent by Catullus on a mission of renunciation to Lesbia (probably as a hated rival), and whose readiness to go anywhere with the poet is described with ironic exaggeration (11. 13 ff.):

> sive trans altas gradietur Alpes
> Caesaris visens monimenta Magni,
> Gallicum Rhenum, †horribilesque ulti-
> mosque Britannos.

It may be objected that Bibaculus was hostile to Julius Caesar: see Tac. *Ann.* 4. 34. 5 'carmina Bibaculi et Catulli referta contumeliis Caesarum leguntur, sed ipse divus Iulius, ipse divus Augustus et tulere ista et reliquere' (if his lampoons had been aimed only at Augustus one would expect Tacitus to have written *Catulli et Bibaculi*). But that does not rule out his authorship of a poem on the Gallic War,[15] for though the enmities of the late Republic were intense, they could be resolved very quickly. Nor can one argue that military epic does not suit a supposedly 'new poet' like Bibaculus; for though his epigrams had close affinities with Catullus, poets do not divide into parties as neatly as is sometimes supposed, and there is nothing to suggest that he wrote anything in the Alexandrian manner.

At *Sat.* 2. 5. 40 f. Horace refers derisively to a poet called Furius in connection with the Alps: 'seu pingui tentus omaso | Furius hibernas cana nive conspuet Alpes'. Porphyrio explains that Furius Bibaculus had written an unlucky line about Jupiter spluttering snow over the Alps: 'Iuppiter hibernas cana nive conspuit Alpes' (fr. 15 M). Horace's *tentus* suggests an inflated style, and *omasum*, a Gallic word for tripe (*CGL* 2. 138. 29), suits the Cisalpine origin of Bibaculus. Bentley

---

[14] Schol. Ver. *Aen.* 9. 379 'in annalibus Belli Gallici', ps.-Acro on Hor. *Sat.* 2. 5. 41 'Furius Vivaculus in pragmatia belli Gallici' (*pragmatia* is also found at Porph. *Epist.* 1. 19 praef., and is the scholiast's word rather than the poet's).

[15] Courtney, *FLP* 199–200, against Nipperdey, op. cit. (n. 6), 499–500 and E. Fraenkel, *Horace* (Oxford, 1957), 130.

further speculates that the bibulous Furius (Plin. *NH* praef. 24 'Bibaculus erat et vocabatur') was 'non minus cibi appetens quam vini' (on *Sat.* 1. 10. 37). It is an intriguing thought that the bloated hexameter poet derided by Horace is the long-surviving epigrammatist from Cremona, and that both may be Furius the acquaintance and apparent rival of Catullus.

In view of his unlucky line about the Alps, Furius must be the 'Alpinus' whom Horace had already mocked at *Sat.* 1. 10. 36 ff.:

> turgidus Alpinus iugulat dum Memnona dumque
> diffingit Rheni luteum caput, haec ego fingo.

I refer *luteum caput* to the silt-bearing waters of the Rhine before it enters Lake Constance[16] (not the literal source, which would not be muddy). It is less plausible to apply the phrase to the mouth of the river,[17] as that does not combine well with the Alps. *diffingit* (supported by Porphyrio as well as the preponderance of the tradition) means 'remoulds' (*Odes* 1. 35. 39, 3. 29. 47), and I suggest that it might refer to the transformation of water into ice (perhaps with the support of an ablative like *albisque pruinis*); in Bibaculus's turgid line the subject could have been Jupiter, as with *conspuit* in the parallel passage. The variant *diffindit* (*defindit* E) is thought to refer to the Rhine delta, but even Bibaculus should have seen that with *caput* it could only suggest the splitting of a head. *diffindit* would exemplify the idiom by which a poet is said to do what he describes,[18] and so would convincingly balance *iugulat*, but this is also true of *diffingit* as explained above. Horace's *dum* confirms that a contemporary poet is in question and not some earlier Furius, but it is strange to find the Alps and the Rhine still a theme in the triumvirate; a possible explanation will be suggested towards the end of this paper (p. 412).

In *Satires* 1. 10 Horace is fighting current trends in literature on two fronts: as well as archaizing *grammatici* and bad epic poets there were the survivors of the neoteric movement, who were as distasteful to him

---

[16] Strabo 4. 3. 3, 7. 1. 5, *RE* 1A. 734; Kristine Müller (ed.), *The Rhine* (Insight Guides, 1991), 87: 'Lake Constance is also the destination for the immense mass of debris and silt carried along by the Alpenrhein. 200 years ago the estuary was an extensive area of marsh and bogland'; ibid. 133: 'heavy sedimentary deposits have made it necessary for most of the river to be diverted into Lake Constance via a man-made canal'. Alternatively the *luteum caput* of the Rhine might be at the western end of the lake, where there is also mud.

[17] For *caput* in this sense see Caes. *BG* 4. 10. 5 (interpolated); Lucan 2. 52 'indomitum Rheni caput'; Courtney, *FLP* 197–8.

[18] C. O. Brink, *PCPS*, NS 33 (1987), 32; G. Lieberg, *Poeta Creator* (Amsterdam, 1982).

as he no doubt was to them. They are presented as over-exquisite poseurs who were unfamiliar with the manly writers of Old Comedy:

> quos neque pulcher
> Hermogenes umquam legit neque simius iste
> nil praeter Calvum et doctus cantare Catullum.   (17–19)

Porphyrio identifies the ape with Demetrius, who is paired with Hermogenes at the end of the satire; he thinks that *simius* describes the man's physical appearance,[19] but it is more likely to refer to the unoriginality of his tastes (cf. *nil praeter*). He calls Demetrius a *modulator* or musician, a word used by Horace of Hermogenes at *Sat.* 1. 3. 130. *cantare* seems to suggest that these people recite[20] Calvus and Catullus in the affected way characteristic of their profession, perhaps also that they keep on at it (cf. *cantilena*).

Horace seems to regard music as an undesirably aesthetic activity, as well as socially disreputable, and he thinks that its practitioners have no business to meddle with real literature. Later in the same satire he shows his resentment when this popular clique ventures on literary criticism (1. 10. 78–80):

> men moveat cimex Pantilius aut cruciet quod
> vellicet absentem Demetrius aut quod ineptus
> Fannius Hermogenis laedat conviva Tigelli?

Elsewhere he complains that Fannius had been presented with a bookcase and his bust whereas nobody reads his own poetry (*Sat.* 1. 4. 21 ff.). In the last lines of the book Demetrius and Hermogenes are told to go and wail among the easy chairs of their female pupils, whom they may have taught both music and poetry (1. 10. 90–1):

> Demetri, teque Tigelli,
> discipularum inter iubeo plorare cathedras.

As well as the idiomatic sense of 'go to the devil' (κλάειν, οἰμώζειν), *plorare* seems to suggest over-emotional singing and maudlin elocution. Horace was always to admire so-called masculine poets like Archilochus, Alcaeus, and Aristophanes who were more distinguished

---

[19] 'propter maciem et parvitatem corporis'. I suggest *pravitatem*, 'misshapenness'; cf. Cic. *Leg.* 1. 15 'corporis pravitates'; *Tusc.* 4. 29.

[20] For performances of poetry see K. Quinn, *ANRW* 2. 30. 1. 155–8. Cf. the 'late-neoteric' recital at Pers. 1. 33 ff. 'rancidulum quiddam balba de nare locutus I Phyllidas Hypsipylas, vanum [*P*: vatum *cett., edd.*] et plorabile siquid I eliquat ac tenero subplantat verba palato'. For the overlapping problems raised by Cicero's *cantores Euphorionis* (*Tusc.* 3. 45) see W. Allen, *TAPA* 103 (1972), 1–14; C. J. Tuplin, *CQ*, NS 29 (1979), 358–60.

for energy than beauty; here with characteristic sexism he seems to imply that 'neoteric' poetry was a girls' subject, like music.[21]

Tigellius Hermogenes appears elsewhere in the *Satires* as a singer (1. 3. 129, 1. 9. 25) and minor literary man (1. 4. 70 f. 'libellos | quis manus insudet vulgi Hermogenisque Tigelli'). He is identified by Porphyrio and some modern authorities[22] with Tigellius Sardus, also described as a *cantor* (1. 3. 3 f.). Then indeed he would be a link with the past; the Sardinian was the victim of a lampoon by Calvus (fr. 3 M 'Sardi Tigelli putidum caput venit'), a protégé of Caesar, and as such mentioned several times by Cicero in 45 BC (*Fam.* 7. 24. 1 'hominem pestilentiorem patria sua', 2 'bellum tibicinem et sat bonum cantorem', *Att.* 13. 49. 1, 50. 3, 51. 2). But though the two musical Tigellii were presumably connected by blood, adoption, or manumission, they can hardly be the same man:[23] the Sardinian is recently dead at *Sat.* 1. 2. 1 ff., mourned by a motley company of *mimae* and *balatrones*, while Hermogenes is very much alive at 1. 10. 90 (cited above).[24] The Sardinian survived long enough to enjoy the patronage of Octavian (1. 3. 4 ff. 'Caesar qui cogere posset, | si peteret per amicitiam patris atque suam, non | quidquam proficeret'); but Horace's particular hate is Hermogenes, who continues the affectations of a past generation.

Demetrius and Hermogenes were at most hangers-on of the neoterics, but the movement had a few more significant survivors. One of these may have been Ticida, who had praised Cato's *Lydia* (fr. 2 'Lydia doctorum maxima cura liber') and is mentioned by Ovid in conjunction with Cinna and Cornificius as well as Cato (*Trist.* 2. 433–8). He is usually identified with the person of that name put to death by Metellus Scipio in Africa in 46;[25] but Messalla combines him with Bibaculus and Valerius Cato as people he has nothing to do with,[26] and this tends to suggest that he was still alive in the triumviral period. The recipient of Ticida's love-poetry, whom he called Perilla,[27] was really a

---

[21] S. F. Bonner, *Education in Ancient Rome* (London, 1977), 27–8; E. Rawson, *Intellectual Life in the Late Roman Republic* (London, 1985), 46–7.

[22] Porph. on *Sat.* 1. 2. 1, 1. 3. 1; B. L. Ullman, *CPh.* 10 (1915), 270–9; F. Münzer, *RE* 6A. 943–6; R. Syme, *CQ*, NS 36 (1986), 274 = *Roman Papers*, 5 (1988), 627.

[23] Fraenkel, *Horace* 86 n. 2; N. Rudd, *The Satires of Horace* (Cambridge, 1966), 292–3.

[24] Ullman, op. cit. 274–5, fails to get round this difficulty.

[25] *Bell. Afr.* 46. 3; Münzer, *RE* 6A. 845–6; T. P. Wiseman, *Cinna the Poet* (Leicester, 1974), 189; Courtney, *FLP* 228–9.

[26] Suet. *De Gramm.* 4. 3 'eosdem litteratores vocitatos Messalla Corvinus in quadam epistula ostendit, non esse sibi dicens rem cum Furio Bibaculo, ne cum Ticida quidem aut litteratore Catone'.

[27] It may be suggested that she was given her pseudonym because she scorched her victims, like Perillus who devised the brazen bull for Phalaris. Cf. Prop. 3. 24. 13

Metella according to Ovid (*Trist.* 2. 438) and Apuleius (*Apol.* 10), and Münzer[28] proposed an identification with the notorious wife of Lentulus Spinther, son of the consul of 57. Elsewhere[29] he suggested that she was the daughter of Clodia and Metellus Celer, that is to say Ticida's Perilla was the daughter of Catullus's Lesbia, an intriguing link with the past. She is probably also to be identified with the Metella of Hor. *Sat.* 2. 3. 239 ff. 'filius Aesopi detractam ex aure Metellae I scilicet ut decies solidum absorberet, aceto I diluit insignem bacam'; the son of the famous actor Aesopus was M. Clodius Aesopus, presumably a client of the Clodii, so this is another connection with Clodia Metelli. We know from Cicero that Clodius and Clodia were interested in the stage,[30] so here as with Demetrius and the two Tigellii we glimpse the raffish world of actors, singers, and minor poets that had continued from the late Republic and was despised by the grandees who made up the literary establishment.

A more certain survivor was Aemilius Macer[31] of Verona, who lasted till 16 BC according to Jerome. Ovid (born 43) thought him worth cultivating in his old age and heard him recite his didactic poetry (*Trist.* 4. 10. 43 f.):

> saepe suas volucres legit mihi grandior aevo,
> quaeque nocet serpens, quae iuvat herba, Macer.

This couplet alludes to the *Ornithogonia*, a work on metamorphosis modelled on Boeo, and the *Theriaca* (probably also an *Alexipharmaca*),[32] modelled on Nicander. These works were probably written long before: Quintilian twice pairs Macer with Lucretius, describing him as *humilis* (10. 1. 87), and treating him as a good poet who was surpassed by Virgil (12. 11. 27). The fragments confirm that he represented the drier side of the Alexandrian movement at Rome, but this still had its devotees, and his material on snakes was used by Lucan and Pliny.

'correptus saevo Veneris torrebar aeno', where the image is connected with Phalaris by W. R. Smyth, *CQ* 43 (1949), 122–5; he also cites 2. 25. 11 f. Add now M. B. Skinner in *Tria Lustra*, ed. H. D. Jocelyn (Liverpool, 1993), 303–4.

[28] *RE* 3. 1235 with suppl. 3. 223.

[29] *Römische Adelsparteien und Adelsfamilien* (Stuttgart, 1920), 341. For the argument see D. R. Shackleton Bailey, *Cicero's Letters to Atticus*, vol. 5, p. 412, and for a summary Wiseman, op. cit. (n. 25), 112.

[30] Wiseman, loc. cit. Cicero uses imagery from the theatre against both Clodius and Clodia (*Sest.* 116, *Cael.* 65).

[31] H. Dahlmann, *AAM* (1981), 6; J. P. Néraudeau, *ANRW* 2. 30. 3. 1708–31; Courtney, *FLP* 292–9.

[32] A. S. Hollis, *CQ*, NS 23 (1973), 11.

A more significant survivor was Parthenius.[33] He had been brought from Bithynia at the end of the Mithridatic War by Cinna, perhaps the poet himself[34] rather than his father, and must have had a fundamental influence on the new trends in Roman poetry. His propempticon (*Suppl. Hell.* 639) and apparently a poem about Zmyrna (641) had been imitated by Cinna; his epicedeion on Arete (608–14) by Calvus in his elegy on Quintilia;[35] his *Leucadia* perhaps by Varro Atacinus;[36] his use of Euphorion by Gallus (compare 620 Γρύνειος Ἀπόλλων with Virg. *Ecl.* 6. 72 f.); his languid line Γλαύκῳ καὶ Νηρῆι καὶ εἰναλίῳ Μελικέρτῃ (647, perhaps from the propempticon) by Virgil himself (*Georg.* 1. 437), whom he is said to have tutored in Greek (Macr. *Sat.* 5. 17. 18).[37] His prose synopsis of obscure romantic myths, the ἐρωτικὰ παθήματα, had been dedicated to Cornelius Gallus, presumably in the 40s BC when Gallus was poetically active (see below). He is said by the Suda to have survived till the reign of Tiberius; that is impossible, as by AD 14 he would have been over 100, but he probably lived long enough to influence the young prince's poetical tastes (for which cf. Hor. *Epist.* 1. 3). Hence Suet. *Tib.* 70. 2 'fecit et Graeca poemata imitatus Euphorionem et Rhianum et Parthenium, quibus poetis admodum delectatus, scripta omnium et imagines publicis bibliothecis inter veteres et praecipuos auctores dedicavit, et ob hoc plerique eruditorum certatim ad eum multa de his ediderunt'; for amateurs in literature retain the preferences of their youth long after they have ceased to be dominant, as we see also from the *Ciris.*[38] But in the Augustan period Parthenius's rejection of traditional epic was beginning to seem out of date, and after his death Erucius pictured him being choked in the underworld because he had called the *Iliad* a dung-hill (*Anth. Pal.* 7. 377):[39]

---

[33] W. Clausen, *GRBS* 5 (1964), 187; N. B. Crowther, *Mnem.* 29 (1976), 66–71 (too sceptical about his influence).

[34] Wiseman, op. cit. (n. 25), 47–8; Courtney, *FLP* 212–13.

[35] R. Pfeiffer, *CQ* 37 (1943), 23–32 = *Ausgewählte Schriften* (Munich, 1960), 133–47.

[36] The transitional poet Varro Atacinus was born in Narbonensis in 82 (Jerome), wrote a *Bellum Sequanicum* in the 50s BC, and turned in the 40s to Greek imitations (notably the *Argonautae* and *Leucadia*). At *Sat.* 1. 10. 46 Horace mentions his satires, probably from his earlier period; apart from his age there is nothing to suggest that he survived to the triumvirate. See further E. Hofmann, *WS* 46 (1928), 159–76; Courtney, *FLP* 235–53.

[37] There might be a hint of Parthenius at *Ecl.* 10. 57 (Gallus is speaking) 'Parthenios canibus circumdare saltus' (primarily referring to the Arcadian mountain).

[38] The work is Augustan, dedicated to Messalla, and written by a retired politician in the 'neoteric' manner that had appealed to him in his youth.

[39] The epigram is attributed by the MSS to Parthenius of Phocaea (4th cent. AD), but that cannot be right (Gow-Page, *Garland of Philip*, 2. 287). The slave's collar may allude to Parthenius's enslavement in war (G. Giangrande, *CR*, NS 16 (1966), 147–8).

ἤλασε καὶ μανίης ἐπὶ δὴ τόσον ὥστ' ἀγορεῦσαι
πηλὸν Ὀδυσσείην καὶ πάτον Ἰλιάδα·
τοιγὰρ ὑπὸ ζοφίαισιν Ἐρινύσιν ἀμμέσον ἧπται
Κωκυτοῦ κλοιῷ λαιμὸν ἀπαγχόμενος.

Classical norms were now reasserting themselves.

Mention of Parthenius brings us to his friend and patron Cornelius Gallus; he was still a dominating influence, as is shown by the admiring imitations of Virgil and Propertius, but in the 30s BC he seems to have turned from poetry to a public career. His mistress Lycoris was a celebrity of the 40s, Virgil's eulogies in the *Eclogues* should be placed about 39 (for Maecenas is nowhere mentioned in the whole work), and the fragment from Qaṣr Ibrîm was most probably written at the end of Caesar's dictatorship (above, p. 125). The fragment disappointed many scholars, and one of them was unwise enough to pronounce it a forgery (p. 432), but the intermittent roughness of style may be paralleled in the epigrams of Catullus. Even if his grander elegies had survived, they might seem to look back rather than forwards (and not simply because of neoteric preciosity): Virgil's *Eclogues* had suddenly made earlier poetry look a little heavy.

Some of the other poets mentioned in the *Eclogues* may deserve the name of survivor. When the modest shepherd says that he is inferior to Varius[40] and Cinna but cackles like a goose among swans (9. 36 'inter strepere anser olores', echoed by Prop. 2. 34. 84), Servius comments 'alludit ad Anserem quendam, Antonii poetam,[41] qui eius laudes scribebat' (he cites Cic. *Phil.* 13. 11 for Antonians of this name). Anser appears as an erotic poet at Ov. *Trist.* 2. 435 'Cinna quoque his comes est Cinnaque procacior Anser | et leve Cornifici parque Catonis opus'; though a precise chronological sequence need not be expected in this passage, it at least suggests that the man belonged to the older generation. Bavius and Mevius, who are damned in a single line (*Ecl.* 3. 90 'qui Bavium non odit, amet tua carmina, Mevi') may also have written old-style poetry (contrasted with the *nova carmina* of Pollio); this guess is helped a little by Jerome's notice that Bavius died in Cappadocia in

---

[40] Varius seems to have been senior to Virgil, and some of his poems may be earlier than the Epicurean *De Morte* (about 43 BC), but as his famous *Thyestes* is dated to 29, it is difficult to treat him as a survivor.

[41] Another Antonian poet was Cassius of Parma, who must have written elegy; cf. Hor. *Epist.* 1. 4. 3 (to Tibullus) 'scribere quod Cassi Parmensis opuscula vincat' (humorously derisive). He did not long survive the triumvirate, as Octavian had him executed after Actium (Val. Max. 1. 7. 7).

35 BC.[42] Mevius had satirized the incident of Aesopus and the pearl (Porph. on Hor. *Sat.* 2. 3. 239, above, p. 398), perhaps in the 40s BC; when Horace prays for his shipwreck in a mock-propempticon (*Epod.* 10), he must be thinking of his pretentious verses, so the man may have written a serious propempticon that Virgil and Horace thought old-fashioned.

Codrus at first sight looks like a survivor (*Ecl.* 5. 11, 7. 22, 26): the Greek name evokes the king of Athens who was proverbial for antiquity (*Corp. Paroem. Graec.* 1. 296 πρεσβύτερος Κόδρου· ἐπὶ τῶν παλαιῶν καὶ πολυχρονίων). A fragment of Valgius (2 M) shows that 'Codrus' stood for somebody definite, unlike most of the shepherds' names in the *Eclogues*, and that his old-world quality was found attractive by some:

> Codrusque ille canit quali tu voce canebas
> atque solet numeros dicere, Cinna, tuos,
> dulcior ut numquam Pylio profluxerit ore
> Nestoris aut docto pectore Demodoci.

The most plausible explanation is Rostagni's neglected theory:[43] he identifies Codrus with Messalla, who had the eloquence of a more gracious age (note also *Corp. Paroem. Graec.* 1. 84 εὐγενέστερος Κόδρου). Valgius seems to have belonged to the circle of Messalla, and is suggested by the *Panegyricus Messallae* as a more suitable eulogist: 179 f. 'est tibi qui possit magnis se accingere rebus I Valgius: aeterno propior non alter Homero'. Messalla is praised at *Catalepton* 9 for the grace of his Greek poetry (13 ff.):

> pauca tua in nostras venerunt carmina chartas
> carmina cum lingua, tum sale Cecropio,
> carmina quae Phrygium, saeclis accepta futuris,
> carmina quae Pylium vincere digna senem.

The poem goes on to say that these Greek poems were pastoral (17 f. 'molliter hic viridi patulae sub tegmine quercus I Moeris pastores et Meliboeus erant'); that would suit Corydon's compliment at *Ecl.* 7. 21 ff. 'nymphae noster amor Libethrides, aut mihi carmen I quale meo Codro concedite (proxima Phoebi I versibus ille facit)', for it is only the less agreeable Thyrsis who is critical (7. 26 'invidia rumpantur

[42] Domitius Marsus mocked Bavius in his *Cicuta*, but the date is uncertain (Courtney, *FLP* 300-1).

[43] 'Virgilio, Valgio e ... Codro. Chi era costui?', *Studi in onore di Luigi Castiglioni* (Florence, 1960), 2. 809-33 = *Virgilio minore*, ed. 2 (Rome, 1961), 405-27.

ut ilia Codro').[44] Messalla was born in 59 according to Jerome, clearly too late to suit his role at Philippi,[45] in 64 according to moderns, who posit a confusion with the consuls of 59; one is tempted to suggest 65, for Horace's address to his coeval wine-jar (3. 21. 1 'o nata mecum consule Manlio') is really addressed to Messalla. So if Rostagni's identification is correct, Codrus is not a survivor after all but a very distinguished man of the new generation who wrote in a traditional way.

We cannot dismiss Pollio[46] as simply a voice from the past: as a tragedian (Virg. *Ecl.* 8. 10, Hor. *Sat.* 1. 10. 42), historian (N.-H. on *Odes* 2. 1), friend of poets (Virg. *Ecl.* 4. 10, Hor. *Sat.* 1. 10. 85), and founder of Rome's first national library, he was one of the dominating literary personages of the triumvirate. Yet unlike Messalla he straddled the generations, having first appeared as the young brother of the Asinius who made off with Catullus's table-napkin; when the poet says 'est enim leporum | differtus[47] puer ac facetiarum' (12. 7 f.), the compliment shows that he already belonged to the same smart set. He was the recipient of Cinna's *Propempticon* in 56 BC, a poem learned and obscure enough to need a commentary by the Augustan Hyginus (Charisius 171 B = 134 K). Though in his histories he showed a certain anti-Ciceronianism in both substance and style (cf. Sen. *Suas.* 6. 24), he retained an essentially Republican independence. But in spite of his distinction in so many fields he was beginning to be marginalized, and it is a sign of the times that the less talented Maecenas, who is not mentioned in the *Eclogues*, was able to poach his poets. The *Georgics* are dedicated to Virgil's new patron, and Horace's compliments in his great ode to Pollio (2. 1) are nothing to what he did for Maecenas.

Pollio brings us to the prose writers, who as always dominated the literary scene more than our modern syllabuses suggest. Timagenes[48] had been brought to Rome from Alexandria by Gabinius in 55; his

---

[44] It was later too readily assumed that Codrus was a bad poet; cf. Juv. 1. 2 'rauci Theseide Codri' (*Cordi* editors with *P*), where Codrus balances Theseus as an early king of Athens (R. Reggiani, *QUCC* 21 (1976), 125 ff.).

[45] For Messalla's date of birth see A. Valvo, *ANRW* 2. 30. 3. 1666–9.

[46] J. André, *La Vie et l'œuvre d'Asinius Pollion* (Paris, 1949); J.-P. Néraudeau, *ANRW* 2. 30. 3. 1732–50; G. Zecchini, ibid. 31. 2, 1265–96.

[47] I feel some hesitation about Passerat's *differtus* (for the transmitted *dis(s)ertus*); the point is not that Pollio was full of humour but that he knew a good joke from a bad one. Though no exact parallel presents itself, one wonders whether *disertus* could convey the idea of discrimination; cf. Varr. *LL* 6. 64 'ut holitor disserit in areas sui cuiusque generis res, sic in oratione qui facit disertus'.

[48] P. M. Fraser, *Ptolemaic Alexandria* (Oxford, 1972), 1. 518–19, 2. 746–7; M. Sordi, *ANRW* 2. 30. 1. 775–97.

sardonic wit and anti-Roman stance[49] would have been less easy for a later arrival, and when he went too far for Augustus, Pollio protected him. The Epicurean centre in the villa of the Pisones at Herculaneum survived till about the beginning of our period, with papyri recording the names of Virgil, Varius, Quintilius (Varus), and Plotius (Tucca),[50] but Philodemus and Siro soon disappear from the record; Servius tries to see Siro in the *Eclogues* under the mask of Silenus (6. 13), but an epigram attributed to Virgil speaks as if he were now dead (*Catalepton* 8. 1 'villula quae Sironis eras'). Epicureanism was to become less fashionable, and the great library mouldered undisturbed till it was smothered by Vesuvius. Horace derides several minor Stoic moralists,[51] whose reputation for having written a lot suggests that they were survivors from the previous generation: 'loquacious' Fabius, who is described as a Pompeian (Porph. on *Sat.* 1. 1. 13), Plotius Crispinus, who wrote long-winded sermons in verse (*Sat.* 1. 4. 15 etc.), Stertinius, author of 220 books (ps.-Acro on *Epist.* 1. 12. 20) and teacher of the art-dealer Damasippus (*Sat.* 2. 3. 33, 296), himself a survivor.[52] At a more serious level Octavian himself was to take over a new wave of Greek philosophers, of whom the first was Athenodorus[53] (Calvus), son of Sandon; he was in Rome at least from 44, when Cicero consulted him when writing *De Officiis* (*Att.* 16. 11. 4, 16. 14. 4), and lived to be 82 (Lucian, *Macrobioi* 21).

It is beyond the scope of this sketch to deal with the greatest survivor of them all, the one who had lived the longest and written the most. Varro[54] was born in 116, and in spite of his wealth came through the proscriptions to write the *De Gente Populi Romani*, the *De Imaginibus* (his collection of portraits also called *Hebdomades*), and finally the *De Re Rustica* in 37. Though he said then in his eightieth year that the time had come to pack his bags (1. 1), he was good for another decade, and in Pollio's library he was the only living writer to be commemorated by a bust (Plin. *Nat.* 7. 115), presumably because he was too old to envy.

---

[49] Hor. *Epist.* 1. 19. 15; Sen. *Cont.* 10. 5. 22; Sen. *De Ira* 3. 23. 4; *Epist.* 91. 13 'felicitati urbis inimicus'.

[50] But not of Horace (as once was proposed); see M. Gigante and M. Capasso, *SIFC* 7 (1989), 3–6; M. Gigante, *Virgilio e gli Augustei* (Naples, 1990), 9–22.

[51] Rawson, op. cit. (n. 21), 49, 53.

[52] Cic. *Att.* 7. 23. 2; Macr. *Sat.* 2. 3. 2; Rawson, op. cit. 88–9.

[53] C. Cichorius, *Römische Studien* (Berlin, 1922), 279–82; G. W. Bowersock, *Augustus and the Greek World* (Oxford, 1965), 32; M. J. McGann, *Studies in Horace's First Book of Epistles* (Brussels, 1969), 26–32; E. Rawson in M. Griffin and J. Barnes (eds.), *Philosophia Togata* (Oxford, 1989), 243–5.

[54] Rawson, op. cit. (n. 21), esp. 136–9, 198–9, 235–47.

For he was not just a survivor but a pre-Ciceronian man; in spite of all his efforts he never learned to impose a construction and a message on his undigested particulars.[55] Like the Rip Van Winkle figure of his own Menippean satire[56] he was now living in an unfamiliar world; but it could be said on the other side, as Cicero pointed out, that the Romans were strangers in their own city till he taught them to think about their roots: 'nam nos in nostra urbe peregrinantis errantisque tamquam hospites tui libri quasi domum deduxerunt, ut possemus aliquando qui et ubi essemus agnoscere' (*Acad.* 1. 9). His old-fashioned antiquarian researches were to provide the raw material for the Augustan vision of Rome, whether in the *ab urbe condita* or the *Aeneid*, not to mention his more superficial influence on the greatest poem of the triumvirate, the *Georgics*.

Cornelius Nepos[57] was almost as old as Varro: when he says that Fortune willed that he should survive Atticus (*Att.* 19. 1) that implies that he was the older man and pushes his birth back to about 110 BC. He was a member of the Republican literary establishment, received two lost books of letters from Cicero, and was the author of a work on chronology in three volumes that had the merit of setting Roman history against a Greek background (Catull. 1. 6 'omne aevum tribus explicare cartis'). In these he may have mentioned his fellow-Cisalpine Catullus (cf. 1. 3 f. 'namque tu solebas | meas esse aliquid putare nugas'), as his model Apollodorus had done with Greek poets in his *Chronica*, and in the dedication to his book Catullus responds gracefully (1. 8–10):

> quare habe tibi quidquid hoc libelli
> qualecumque quidem patroni ut ergo
> plus uno maneat perenne saeclo.

Bergk's *patroni ut ergo*, 'in consequence of the patron' (for the transmitted *patrona virgo*), seems necessary to give the poem coherence;[58]

---

[55] R. Syme, *The Roman Revolution* (Oxford, 1939), 247 'The old scholar lacked style, intensity, a guiding idea'. For an element of logical organization in Varro see E. Rawson, *Roman Culture and Society* (Oxford, 1991), 327–31.

[56] 491 Buecheler 'Romam regressus ibi nihil offendi quod ante annos quinquaginta, cum primum dormire coepi, reliqui'.

[57] See T. P. Wiseman, *Clio's Cosmetics* (Leicester, 1979), 157–66; J. Geiger, *Cornelius Nepos and Ancient Political Biography* (Historia Einzelschriften, 47; 1985); F. Millar, *Greece and Rome*, 35 (1988), 40–55; N. Horsfall, *Cornelius Nepos: A Selection, including the Lives of Cato and Atticus* (Oxford, 1989).

[58] See esp. G. P. Goold in J. A. S. Evans (ed.), *Polis and Imperium* (Toronto, 1974), 253–64 and *LCM* 6 (1981), 235–8; in the latter article he cites Germain Audebert of Orleans (16th cent.) 'donabo tamen atque consecrabo | qualiscumque sit ut tuo favore | plus uno

and *saeclo* is an allusion to the long vistas shown in Nepos's own *Chronica*. But it is important to observe that in the conditions of Republican literature Nepos was the book's patron, not the poet's;[59] he may have helped with the promotion of the poems and a little condescending flattery, but Catullus did not owe him his estate at Sirmio or expect guidance from him on what to say about Julius Caesar. In the changed political circumstances of the triumvirate Nepos worked away at his biographies, mainly of people too remote to raise presentational problems; but when he admits with a show of candour that Atticus had links with Antony (*Att.* 12. 2 'non est enim celandum'), he betrays an awareness that the world had changed.

Our next survivor is one of the most influential and least read of the Augustan writers, Vitruvius.[60] He seems to have finished his *De Architectura* in the early 20s BC, but he presumably began it much earlier, as he was professionally known to Julius Caesar (1 praef. 2; 2. 9. 15–16); the dedication of the second book makes him sound quite decrepit, even allowing for the pretence of modesty conventional in a preface ('mihi autem, imperator, staturam non tribuit natura, faciem deformavit aetas, valetudo detraxit vires'). His inelegant style[61] is hard to characterize fully because of the lack of contemporary technical writing, but with its anacolutha and oddities of vocabulary it certainly gives an old-fashioned impression. P. Thielscher tried to make him a survivor in a more pointed sense by identifying him with the notorious Mamurra (*RE* 9A. 1. 427 ff.): it would indeed be an edifying cautionary tale if the broken-down old architect is none other than Julius Caesar's ostentatious chief-of-staff, who had fiddled contracts in Gaul to build an immense personal fortune, and is familiar in Catullus under the sobriquet of Mentula (115 etc.). Unfortunately this pleasing fantasy has nothing particularly in its favour,[62] though the two men may have been related.

maneat perenne saeclo' (what text of Catullus did he read?). For another humanist rewriting of the passage see J. H. Gaisser, *Catullus and his Renaissance Readers* (Oxford, 1993), 127–9, 173–4.

[59] Wiseman, op. cit. 173, points out correctly that Nepos was not Catullus's patron, but is wrong to use this as a knock-down argument against Bergk's conjecture.

[60] P. Gros, *ANRW* 2. 30. 1. 659–95 (with bibliography); Rawson, *Intellectual Life* (n. 21), 86–8, 184–200. For links with the circle round Octavia see 1 praef. 2 'per sororis commendationem'; Cichorius, op. cit. (n. 53), 261–9; Nisbet–Hubbard on Horace, *Odes* II, pp. 153–4.

[61] E. Wistrand, 'De Vitruvii Sermone' in *Apophoreta . . . V. Lundström oblata* (Göteborg, 1936), 16–52 = *Opera Selecta* (Stockholm, 1972), 22–58; L. Callebat, *ANRW* 2. 30. 1. 696–721 (perhaps too sympathetic).

[62] P. Ruffel and J. Soubiran, *Pallas*, 11 (1962), 123–79; R. E. A. Palmer, *Athenaeum*, NS 61 (1983), 343–61.

I turn now to the jurists, who tend not to be regarded as literary men, though they are much more significant than minor poets; like antiquarians, they improved with age, and even in times of political upheaval still found plenty to do. A notable instance was Trebatius Testa,[63] who apart from his legal works wrote nine books *de religionibus*, and was the recipient of Cicero's *Topica*. He was also the recipient of the programmatic satire in Horace's second book, written about 30 BC, where the poet professes to seek counsel's opinion about the advisability of continuing with satire. Twenty-five years earlier, when Trebatius was on Caesar's staff in Gaul, Cicero had written letters to him which were also full of legal jokes. In the satire he is represented as advising Horace to swim three times across the Tiber as an alternative to writing poetry (2. 1. 8); in the correspondence Cicero had joked with him about swimming in the English Channel (*Fam.* 7. 10. 2 'sed tu in re militari multo es cautior quam in advocationibus, qui neque in Oceano natare volueris studiosissimus homo natandi'). In the satire he advises Horace to soak himself with drink in the evening (2. 1. 9), and indeed he may owe his cognomen Testa to this propensity; in a letter of 44 BC Cicero describes how after an evening with Trebatius he came home *bene potus*, but was still able to verify a point of law in his library (*Fam.* 7. 22). In both the former letter and the satire it is interesting to note the easy relationship between the ambitious young man and the eminent senior; but in the letter Trebatius is the ambitious young man, in the satire he has survived to be an eminence himself. He lived to pronounce on the divorce of Maecenas and Terentia (*Dig.* 24. 1. 64), who were still married in 16 (Dio 54. 19, *RE* 6A. 2259).

Another eminent jurist was Alfenus Varus,[64] who does not receive as much attention from literary scholars as he deserves. He was a survivor from the cultured circle round Servius Sulpicius Rufus,[65] whose *responsa* he collected, and his own rulings are often cited in the *Digest* from the epitomes by Paullus and an anonymous hand. A flavour of the man's breadth of approach emerges from his treatment of the nature of identity (*Dig.* 5. 1. 76); a panel of *iudices*, he says, remains the same even when all the individual *iudices* have been replaced, just as with a

---

[63] O. Lenel, *Palingenesia Iuris Civilis* (Leipzig, 1888–9), 2. 343–52; *RE* 6A. 2251–61.

[64] Lenel, op. cit. 1. 38–54; Schanz–Hosius, 1. 596; L. De Sarlo, *Alfeno Varo e suoi Digesta* (Rome, 1940); A. Watson, *Law Making in the Later Roman Republic* (Oxford, 1974), 162–7.

[65] R. Syme, *CQ*, NS 31 (1981), 421–7 = *Roman Papers*, 3 (1984), 1412–22; Rawson, op. cit. (n. 21), 209–12.

legion or a *populus* or a ship when all its planks have been replaced, and just as we ourselves remain the same people, even though the philosophers say that the particles of which we are constructed leave our bodies every day and have their place taken by others.[66] His rulings are still of interest to lawyers, as appears from the article by Alan Rodger on 'Mrs Donoghue and Alfenus Varus'.[67] A asked B to show him his ring, and while B made to do so it fell from his grasp into the Tiber; here Alfenus seems to have thought that A's request constituted something similar to a *mandatum* so that he was liable for the loss.

Alfenus is most familiar to most people from his appearance in Virgil's ninth eclogue, where the dispossessed Moeris describes an unfinished poem in his honour by the Virgil-like Menalcas (26–9):

> immo haec, quae Varo necdum perfecta canebat:
> 'Vare, tuum nomen, superet modo Mantua nobis,
> Mantua vae miserae nimium vicina Cremonae,
> cantantes sublime ferent ad sidera cycni.'

As an eminent jurist Varus was charged with the confiscation of land in Cisalpina in 41;[68] in fact he himself came from Cremona, according to Porphyrio's commentary on Horace (*Sat.* 1. 3. 130). This assertion has been doubted by some,[69] but Porphyrio often shows knowledge about prosopography, and the note in question contains other reliable information; local antecedents would give Varus particular expertise and authority, and would explain why Virgil sought his intervention. The swans of Mantua can only be the poets, that is to say Virgil himself; when we read in the *Georgics* 'et qualem infelix amisit Mantua campum | pascentem niveos herboso flumine cycnos' (2. 198 f.), that seems to be evidence, usually disregarded, that the poet has lost his land.[70] But Varus did not succumb to flattery, and in his adjudication he left the Mantuans only the marshier ground (Serv. auct. *Ecl.* 9. 10 'quod per iniquitatem Alfeni Vari qui agros divisit praeter palustria

---

[66] Watson, op. cit. 189–91. However when Servius says that he studied Epicureanism under Siro (*Ecl.* 6. 13), this looks like confusion with Quintilius Varus, the Epicurean friend of Virgil and Horace (above, n. 50, *RE* 24. 899–902).

[67] *Current Legal Problems*, 41 (1988), 1–22 (citing *Dig.* 19. 5. 23).

[68] T. R. S. Broughton, *The Magistrates of the Roman Republic*, 2. 377–8.

[69] R. Syme, *Roman Papers*, 7 (Oxford, 1991), 474–5; Porphyrio's information is accepted by G. Alföldy, *Epigrafia e ordine senatorio* (Rome, 1982), 350. Of course confusion is possible again with Quintilius Varus, who is described as *Cremonensis* by Porphyrio on Hor. *Ars P.* 438, Hieron. *Chron. olymp.* 189.

[70] F. Vollmer, *Sitzungsb. der Münch. Akad.* 1909. 9, 6–7; C. G. Hardie in B. Levick (ed.), *The Ancient Historian and his Materials* (Farnborough, 1975), 109–12.

nihil relictum sit'); the commentator cites a speech against Alfenus which he attributes to 'Cornelius' (identified on insufficient grounds with the poet Gallus), complaining that he had left the Mantuans nothing but water.[71] That explains Virgil's *nec perfecta* (*Ecl.* 9. 26, cited above); it is not surprising in the circumstances that he did not complete his panegyric.

Alfenus Varus was consul suffect in 39 BC, and as he was a *novus homo*, that puts his birth back to the 80s. We may already have met him as a young man in the reproaches of Catullus, 'Alfene, immemor atque unanimis false sodalibus' (30. 1); if in fact he came from Cisalpina, that would give a point of contact. The poem is written in the rare and difficult 'greater Asclepiads', a metre used by Catullus only here and by Horace only in three odes. In one of these odes Horace urges a certain Varus, who owns an estate at Tibur, to grow no tree in preference to the vine: 'nullam, Vare, sacra vite prius severis arborem' (1. 18. 1). This Varus is usually said to be Horace's friend Quintilius Varus (*Odes*, 1. 24), but the *fundus Quintiliolus* at Tivoli, already attested in the tenth century, is not decisive evidence for the identification (*RE* 24. 901–2). Horace models his line on a poem by Alcaeus also in greater Asclepiads (342 L–P μηδ᾽ ἓν ἄλλο φυτεύσῃς πρότερον δένδριον ἀμπέλω), but he could have chosen this particular motif because Varus had been addressed in the same metre by Catullus a generation before. The last line of the ode warns that Bacchic revels may have undesirable concomitants (1. 18. 14 ff. 'quae subsequitur caecus amor sui | et tollens vacuum plus nimio gloria verticem | arcanique fides prodiga perlucidior vitro'); though there is humorous exaggeration, the admonition has more point when addressed to a successful lawyer like Alfenus Varus than to an Epicurean and literary man like Quintilius Varus. It is true that political activity by Alfenus Varus is not recorded after his consulship, but he could have continued with his much more important legal work. Porphyrio says that he was honoured with a public funeral (Hor. *Sat.* 1. 3. 130), but as this must have been a mark of his legal rather than his political distinction, it could have happened well after his consulship.

As the identification is controversial, one is tempted to seek support in a further hypothesis. The opening line of Horace's ode suggests that he regarded the vine as a kind of tree; as he is closely following Alcaeus (342 cited above), there is no need for a special explanation, yet the formulation has particular point when it is remembered that jurists

---

[71] L. P. Wilkinson, *The Georgics of Virgil* (Cambridge, 1969), 31.

were interested in such questions of definition.[72] Gaius tells us that a man lost his case about cutting down vines because he called them *vites* rather than *arbores*, the only term sanctioned by the Twelve Tables (*Inst.* 4. 11. 3–4). Ulpian comments 'vitem arboris appellatione contineri plerique veterum existimaverunt' (*Dig.* 47. 7. 3, cf. 43. 27. 3); Alfenus must be included among the *veteres*, and the *Digest* quotes his ruling that *pomum* includes nuts, figs, and dessert grapes.[73] See further Hor. *Epist.* 1. 18. 15 'alter rixatur de lana saepe caprina', where Porphyrio gives two explanations: either goats' wool is something of no importance, or the issue is whether goats' hair is properly included in the term 'lana'; the second explanation is correct, as is shown by the opinion of Ulpian: 'lana legata etiam leporinam lanam et anserinam et caprinam credo contineri' (*Dig.* 32. 70. 9). So in the first line of his ode Horace may be mocking the pedantry of the lawyers as well as alluding to Alcaeus and Catullus; such ingenuity was not beyond him.

Alfenus poses a further problem at Horace, *Sat.* 1. 3. 129 ff., where the poet mocks the Stoic view that the *sapiens* is potentially a good shoemaker:

> 'ut quamvis tacet, Hermogenes cantor tamen atque
> optimus est modulator; ut Alfenus vafer, omni
> abiecto instrumento artis clausaque taberna
> tonsor[74] [sutor *v.l.*] erat, sapiens operis sic optimus omnis
> est opifex solus, sic rex.'

Here Porphyrio comments 'urbane autem Alfenum Varum Cremonensem deridet qui abiecta sutrina quam in municipio suo exercuerat Romam petit magistroque usus Sulpicio iuris consulto ad tantum pervenit ut et consulatum gereret et publico funere efferretur'. The latter part of the note is circumstantial and reliable, and as we have seen, the statement that Alfenus came from Cremona should not be too readily dismissed; the story about his early life in trade is presumably derived from Horace himself, and belongs to a familiar

---

[72] See A. Watson, *The Law of Succession in the Later Roman Republic* (Oxford, 1971), 134–54.

[73] *Dig.* 50. 16. 205 'idem [Paulus] libro quarto epitomarum Alfeni: qui fundum vendidit, "pomum" recepit [excepted]: nuces et ficos et uvas dumtaxat duracinas et purpureas et quae eius generis essent, quas non vini causa haberemus, quas Graeci τρωξίμους appellarent, recepta videri'.

[74] *tonsor* (Bland. vet.) should be preferred to *sutor*, the generally transmitted reading (C. O. Brink, *PCPS* 33 (1987), 22–5); when Horace provides two analogies to the Stoic aphorism about the *sutor*, it is appropriate that he should mention two different skills.

category of invention about the antecedents of eminent persons.[75] It is usually denied that Horace was referring to the jurist, as the impertinence to an important consular would have been too great.[76] But if Alfenus was an unimportant tradesman, nobody would be interested in his change of occupation; and there was no need for Horace to call him *vafer*, a word too easily associated with lawyers (note *Sat.* 2. 2. 131 'vafri inscitia iuris', an important parallel). It may be argued that if this Alfenus really is the jurist, that is inconsistent with the suggestion that a friendly ode is addressed to him; but in Roman political life invective could give way to eulogy very quickly (see above on Bibaculus and Caesar). The imperfect *tonsor erat* (as opposed to *est modulator* of Hermogenes) may also be thought to tell against the view that Alfenus was alive at the time of *Odes* 1. 18, but the point may simply be that he remained a barber even when he shut up shop.

Virgil returns to Varus with the dedication of the sixth eclogue; the date could be apprioprately 39, the year of Varus's consulship, for if any of the eclogues were written significantly later, one would expect Maecenas to be mentioned somewhere.

> nunc ego (namque super tibi erunt qui dicere laudes,
> Vare, tuas cupiant et tristia condere bella)
> agrestem tenui meditabor harundine Musam.
> non iniussa cano. si quis tamen haec quoque, si quis
> captus amore leget, te nostrae, Vare, myricae,
> te nemus omne canet; nec Phoebo gratior ulla est
> quam sibi quae Vari praescripsit pagina nomen.   (6-12)

This passage shows that Varus was still looking for panegyrics, just as in the ninth eclogue, but Virgil brushes him off with a graceful *recusatio*. The reference to Phoebus suggests that Varus had himself a role in literature, as opposed to simply patronage. Servius *auctus* (i.e. Donatus) comments on 9. 35 *Vario* 'nonnulli sane Alfenum Varum volunt, qui licet iuris consultus et successor Servii Sulpicii esset, etiam carmina aliqua composuisse dicitur; sed hoc teste Horatio falsum est qui Varium poetam laudat'. It is not clear whether *aliqua carmina* is based on actual knowledge, but even if it is not, the reference to Phoebus cited above does seem significant.

[75] W. Süss, *Ethos* (Leipzig and Berlin, 1910), 248; R. G. M. Nisbet, *Cicero, In Pisonem* (Oxford, 1961), 194.

[76] Fraenkel, *Horace* 89-90; C. O. Brink, *PCPS* 33 (1987), 35 n. 15; Syme, loc. cit. (n. 69).

Tenney Frank[77] associated Donatus's comment with Catullus 22:

> Suffenus iste, Vare, quem probe nosti,
> homo est venustus et dicax et urbanus,
> idemque longe plurimos facit versus ...   (1 ff.)

He suggested that 'Suffenus' (not an attested name) is a pseudonym for Alfenus (for as we have seen, the Alfenus of Catullus 30 may well be the rising jurist); he added the thought that just as Alfenus suggests ἀλφή or profit (which suits *Epod.* 2. 67 *fenerator Alfius*), so Suffenus suggests *sub fenus*, 'under debt' (the ablative would have been more natural). By Frank's account the Varus to whom the poem is addressed (so also Catull. 10. 1) must then be somebody other than Alfenus (perhaps Quintilius Varus, also described as *Cremonensis*); but with all the vocatives in the world to choose from, why pick on the real cognomen of Suffenus? If Frank is right in his identification, it seems better to suppose that the pretentious Suffenus that Varus knows so well is none other than himself (that would explain *iste*). If this construction has anything to be said for it, we should have a coherent picture of a real survivor. Young 'Suffenus' is a polished man about town (Catull. 22. 12 f. 'qui modo scurra | aut si quid hac re tritius[78] videbatur'), anxious for his own indifferent poetry to be taken seriously (22. 6 f. 'cartae regiae novae bibli,[79] | novi umbilici, lora rubra, membranae'); and as a very distinguished jurist Alfenus is still seeking commemoration from the rising star of the new age, his fellow-countryman Virgil.

However that may be, the dedication of the sixth eclogue presents another problem. Virgil says that other poets will wish to celebrate Varus's campaigns, *tristia condere bella* (6. 7), but he does not tell us what campaigns these are. Servius refers to wars in Germany, and this may be right in general terms, though Servius *auctus* mixes up the later Varus who lost the legions. Virgil's tenth eclogue provides a pastiche of Gallus describing operations in the north (47 f. 'Alpinas, a dura, nives et frigora Rheni | me sine sola vides'); but the date is far from clear.[80] However we do know that in 43 Plancus triumphed *ex Raetis*,[81] and

---

[77] *CQ* 14 (1920), 160–2.

[78] I accept *tritius* (Pontanus) for *tristius* (codd.); see M. C. J. Putnam, *Hermes*, 96 (1968), 552–8 = *Essays on Latin Lyric, Elegy, and Epic* (Princeton, NJ, 1982), 30–6. *scurra* is used in its older complimentary sense.

[79] See above, p. 81.

[80] See above, p. 127.

[81] For his colony at Augusta Rauricorum (Augst) see C. M. Wells, *The German Policy of Augustus* (Oxford, 1972), 36. The Raeti are further east.

Varus could have continued operations near Lake Constance. This leads to yet another question: when Virgil said that others would write military panegyric on Varus, had he anybody in mind? The clever young poets seemed to have lost the taste for commemorating battles, so Varus would need to try a survivor like himself; and nobody was more suitable than Furius Bibaculus, also from Cremona, who could supply a continuation of his *Annales* on the Gallic War. Anyway that would explain why Furius is still describing the Alps and the Rhine at the same time that Horace is writing his first book of *Satires* (1. 10. 36 f.), twenty years after Caesar's campaigns.

In the spring of 32 the death took place of the antiquarian Atticus, a conspicuous survivor in every sense of the term. His ashes were interred at the fifth milestone on the Appian Way, and everybody who mattered showed up (Nep. *Att.* 22. 4 'comitantibus omnibus bonis'). Agrippa, his son-in-law, would have been there, and Balbus of Gades, who was summoned to the death-bed (*Att.* 21. 4). Cicero's son ought to have come, for the old man had arranged the bills of exchange when he was purporting to study at Athens (*Att.* 12. 24. 1, 12. 27. 2); Terentia is less certain, though she lived to be 103 (Val. Max. 8. 13. 6). Among literary men there was no reason for Virgil or Horace to appear, perhaps not even survivors like Valerius Cato and Furius Bibaculus, for they might not have moved in such distinguished society even in their palmier days. But I should have expected to see Varro, if his health had permitted and he was not marooned on his estates, certainly Nepos, the dead man's biographer, and Pollio of course, with his research assistant Ateius Philologus,[82] who had once taught Clodius's brothers, not to mention Messalla Rufus,[83] consul of 53 and an augur for fifty-five years, who had written both *de auspiciis* and *de familiis*. Then there was Trebatius the jurist, who was still going strong, with Alfenus Varus if he was still alive, and Q. Aelius Tubero,[84] the prosecutor of Ligarius in 46, who turned with more success to law, where his style was too archaic even for the lawyers (*Dig.* 1. 2. 2. 46), and to history, where he imitated Thucydides. At a respectful distance one might have seen Tiro, Cicero's freedman and editor of his literary remains, provided that he could have forgiven Atticus for his accommodation with Antony (for some freedmen took *fides* very seriously). Then there were the people that Atticus had helped from good nature

[82] Schanz–Hosius, 1. 580 f.; Rawson, op. cit. (n. 21), 73 f.
[83] Schanz–Hosius, 1. 600; Rawson, 302.
[84] Schanz–Hosius, 1. 322 f.; Wiseman, op. cit. (n. 57), 135–9.

or calculation, Volumnius (if he was still around) who had appeared memorably in Cicero's letters as patron and lover of Gallus's Cytheris and perhaps was a minor versifier himself,[85] and Julius Calidus whom Nepos considered the most elegant poet that his age had produced after the deaths of Lucretius and Catullus (*Att.* 12. 4). This is so astonishing a judgement even for Nepos that the name has been thought a corruption in the text, but a corruption of what? If the truth must be told, we know very little about the survivors, for the very good reason that they have failed to survive.

---

[85] Cic. *Fam.* 9. 26. 2 'infra Eutrapelum Cytheris accubuit'; Courtney, *FLP* 234.

26

Tying down Proteus: The Limits of Ambiguity and Cross-Reference in Horace's *Odes*

I T is one of the penalties of growing older that people invite me to draw contrasts between then and now. 'How', they ask, 'do the students compare with those of the 1950s, and how has the study of Latin changed?' My answer to the first question is easy: students nowadays have more interest in literature as such, they write about it in a more sophisticated way, they are better than their predecessors in many other respects, except that they don't know Latin as well. It is more difficult to identify the most important changes in the subject, but I think I should say this. We used to suppose that a passage had one meaning, and now we like to look for a spread of meanings. We used to comment that the first part of this line of Horace has been taken in two different ways, and the second part has been taken in three different ways, making six interpretations in all, and then by rigorous analysis we blocked off five of these interpretations until one survivor was left, and it was declared the winner. Nowadays everything is different. We recognize that the meaning of poetry may be an elusive thing, and that Horace like other poets of his period is not always easy to pin down. In old-fashioned language he might be called Protean, like the Old Man of the Sea who assumed many shapes. In the more modern idiom he is called 'polysemous'.

It is always easier to follow particular illustrations than abstract generalizations, so let me turn to a very familiar poem, Horace's so-called Soracte Ode:

> vides, ut alta stet nive candidum
> Soracte, nec iam sustineant onus
> silvae laborantes, geluque
> flumina constiterint acuto?   (1. 9. 1–4)

It is now held by many critics that the white mountain in some sense symbolizes old age,[1] and foreshadows the contrast later in the poem

This unpublished paper was the opening lecture at the conference of the Classical Association at Durham on 5 Apr. 1993. The tone is informal but the issues are serious.

[1] L. P. Wilkinson, *Horace and his Lyric Poetry* (Cambridge, 1945), 130–1; M. G. Shields, *Phoenix*, 12 (1958), 166–73.

between white hair and the green sap of youth (17 'donec virenti canities abest'). But the editors of the *Odes* have neglected this polysemous interpretation, and here I have a confession to make. Twenty-five years ago, when I was even more cautious than I am today, I was far from clear that the mountain conveyed hints of old age. I wished to concentrate on the literal scene, I could not find a satisfactory parallel for this particular instance of symbolism, and I saw no necessity to look for hidden meanings any more than in the ode's prototype in Alcaeus. Now I have changed my mind, but not simply because the polysemous interpretation is an interesting idea. I believe that there are objective reasons for this approach, and it is part of the thesis of this paper that in so subjective an area we should look as much as we can for objective reasons.

The argument depends on detail, so I ask you first to turn to Horace's ode to Valgius (2. 9). Valgius has been writing mournful elegiac poetry, and Horace is urging him to desist; he points out that in the natural world ice and storms do not last for ever. 'nec Armeniis in oris, | amice Valgi, stat glacies iners | menses per omnis' (4 ff.): *glacies* clearly corresponds to a chilling of the human heart. 'aut Aquilonibus | querqueta Gargani laborant' (6 f.): *laborant* suggests an analogy with human suffering. 'et foliis viduantur orni' (8): *viduantur*, 'are bereft', makes us think of human bereavement.

Now let us turn back to the Soracte Ode: the imagery is partly the same as in the other poem, but the analogy with human misery is no longer explicit. If we look at the second clause, the suffering woods, the *silvae laborantes*, correspond exactly to the suffering woods of the Valgius Ode, and so an analogy with human tribulations may be recognized here as well. In the same way the sharp frost (*gelu acuto*) in the third clause of the Soracte Ode corresponds to the rigid ice of the Valgius Ode; we are encouraged to think again of the grief that chills and pierces the heart. And now comes the crux of the argument: if the second and third clauses of the Soracte Ode have a metaphorical as well as a literal implication, the same should be true of the first clause about the snow-white mountain-peak. So Mount Soracte suggests something other than itself, and that is presumably old age.[2] Indeed there is nothing ultra-modern about this kind of interpretation. Housman recognized it when he wrote 'On Wenlock Edge the wood's in trouble'—that is to say *laborant*, with its hint of human troubles. And

---

[2] For the grimness of mountains see above, p. 209 n. 34.

already in 1715, when Congreve published his rather free translation of the Soracte Ode, he saw an analogy with human life:

> Trembling the Groves sustain the weight and bow
> Like aged Limbs which feebly go
> Beneath a venerable Head of Snow.

So that is one instance of multiple meanings: Soracte is both a mountain and a symbol of old age. I turn now to Horace's ode to the battered ship:

> o navis, referent in mare te novi
> fluctus. o quid agis? fortiter occupa
>   portum. nonne vides ut
>   nudum remigio latus,
> et malus celeri saucius Africo
> antemnaeque gemant . . .?   (1. 14. 1-6)

Some scholars have thought that the ship that the poet addresses is a real ship, but this view is hard to sustain: in the first stanza it is told to be bold and run to harbour (2f.), in the following lines we learn that its oars, mast, and rigging are all in bad shape, in the last stanza it is urged to avoid the Cyclades (19f. 'interfusa nitentis | vites aequora Cycladas'), superfluous advice if it is too battered even to start the voyage. In the last stanza we are also told that the ship was once a cause of worry and weariness to Horace (17 'nuper sollicitum quae mihi taedium'), but that now it is his heart's desire, his *desiderium*; this seems too emotional a way of talking about a real ship. So some scholars have held that the ship is not a real ship but a woman,[3] and indeed there are epigrams in the Greek Anthology where such comparisons are made; but in these epigrams remarks about battered rigging refer to decrepit courtesans,[4] and this does not seem to suit Horace's *desiderium* in the last stanza. Alternatively it has been argued that the ship represents Horace's poetry-book;[5] but the references to a broken mast and groaning yard-arms seem rather an extreme way of describing the agonies of authorship. I think that the least difficult explanation is still the one that fits best with ancient conventions: the ship is a political ship, which accounts for Horace's past anxieties and present hopes. I shall not call it the Ship of State, as Horace doesn't seem to be on

---

[3] See esp. A. J. Woodman, *CPh.* 75 (1980), 60-7.

[4] Rufinus, *Anth. Pal.* 5. 44; H. D. Jocelyn, *CPh.* 77 (1982), 330-5.

[5] W. S. Anderson, *CPh.* 61 (1966), 91 (who considers but rejects the hypothesis); N. K. Zumwalt, *CW* 71 (1977), 249-54.

board; rather the ship represents the institutions of government with which he is now in sympathy.

I didn't think that this explanation would satisfy everybody, so I tackled one of the clever young critics on Horace's ship; I shall name no names as he may have changed his mind by this time, though on the other hand he may not. I said to him: 'Some people think that Horace's ship is a real ship, some think it's a political ship, some think it's a woman, some think it's a poetry-book, some think it's Horace's life and various other things I've now forgotten; now what do you think?' I guessed what he would say, and he said it. He told me it was all these things simultaneously, a real ship, a political ship, a woman, a poetry-book, and Horace's life. I next asked him if there was anything the poem was not about—a silly question that got the answer it deserved. He conceded that it was not about a football-match.

My next question was more cunning. I said to him, 'When you say that Horace's ship is all these things, you might be taken in one of two ways. You might be saying that the meaning of any poem is no more than what different people at different times have taken it to mean. Or alternatively you might be saying that when Horace wrote the poem about the ship, he actually thought of it as open-ended in the way that you suggest. Now which of these two approaches represents your position? Here I met with a great surprise. I thought he would adopt the first interpretation: we all know that up-to-date critics don't talk any more about poets' intentions, and some of them are even prepared to say that no interpretation is more valid than any other. This is a deplorable attitude, and I say this not simply because it makes scholarship pointless; but it must be conceded that if you choose to define meaning in so unsubtle a way, the position has a certain perverse consistency.

In fact the critic's reply shocked me even more: he said that Horace meant the poem to be open-ended. Now I agree that Horace might have written a poem that was polysemous to a limited extent: the ship might have been a real ship and at the same time a political ship, just as Soracte is a real mountain and at the same time suggests old age. I don't think that this is consistent with the poem that we actually have, but it could have been written otherwise. But it is inconceivable to me that any ancient poet could have written anything as open-ended as my interlocutor suggested. We don't want to go as far as Fraenkel, who took the romantic view that the odes must all spring from personal experience, but Horace was not just composing intellectual cryptograms for critics to be clever about. I find it inconceivable that he did not know or care whether he was talking about politics or poetry or a woman.

I turn now to another ode addressed to a ship, in this case the one that is about to convey Virgil to Greece (1. 3). A growing number of scholars now see in it a secondary meaning: by their way of it the voyage suggests Virgil's heroic endeavours to sail on the vast sea of epic poetry.[6] It is well known that in the Augustan poets, including Horace himself, sailing the seas is sometimes a metaphor for writing epic,[7] but circumstances alter cases; as Horace himself points out, just because a nut is hard outside you mustn't assume the same of the olive.[8] If a reference to the *Aeneid* could be found in the ode, such an interpretation would enliven and enrich a rather boring poem, but as always we need to look at the words and the arguments.

> sic te diva potens Cypri,
>   sic fratres Helenae, lucida sidera
> ventorumque regat pater
>   obstrictis aliis praeter Iapyga,
> navis, quae tibi creditum
>   debes Vergilium, finibus Atticis
> reddas incolumem precor
>   et serves animae dimidium meae.
> illi robur et aes triplex
>   circa pectus erat, qui fragilem truci
> commisit pelago ratem
>   primus . . .   (1. 3. 1–12)

The ode opens with a prayer to the maritime Venus and to Castor and Pollux, the brothers of Helen: it is said for some reason to be a significant clue that Venus was mother of Aeneas and that Helen plays a part in book 2 of the *Aeneid*. Next Aeolus, the father of the winds, is urged to constrain them; that is thought to be a pointer to the beginning of *Aeneid* I. In line 9 of the ode the first navigator is said to have had triple bronze, *aes triplex*, round his heart; this is alleged to be an allusion to *Aeneid* 10. 784, where the phrase is also found, and the considerable difficulties about chronology are simply brushed aside. When Horace describes the first ship as breakable, *fragilem* (10), we are

---

[6] W. S. Anderson, loc. cit.; C. W. Lockyer, *CW* 61 (1967–8), 42–5; J. V. Cody, *Horace and Callimachean Aesthetics* (Brussels, 1976), 87–9; D. A. Kidd, *Prudentia*, 9 (1977), 97–103; R. Basto, *Vergilius*, 28 (1982), 30–43.

[7] *Odes* 4. 15. 3 f.; Cody, op. cit. 82–7; G. Davis, *RhM* 132 (1989), 331–45.

[8] *Epist.* 2. 1. 31 'nil intra est olea, nil extra est in nuce duri'. This ironic line should be taken to heart by many modern critics.

told that this represents *tenue*, subtle,[9] and so has something to do with Callimachus's theories about poetry; in fact 'breakable' is not the same as 'subtle', and there is no reason why the first epic should be described in terms appropriate to small-scale poetry. The critics have failed to prove that Virgil's ship has any allegorical element; such resemblances as there are to the *Aeneid* can be explained by the fact that both the epic and the ode describe the sea in traditional poetic ways.

We can go further: some features of the ode point against any reference to the *Aeneid*. In line 6 Horace asks the ship to deliver Virgil safely to Attica; if he had been thinking of Aeneas, it would have made more sense to refer to Troy. He goes on to criticize the first navigator in a way conventional in a propempticon or sending-off poem;[10] though his words seem exaggerated, they have some sort of point if he is talking about the separation of friends. But surely he cannot be thinking here of epic poetry: it is fair enough to say that the epic poet is undertaking a heroic and hazardous enterprise, but Horace would not wish to suggest that the first epic poet, that is to say Homer, showed unnatural hardihood. When he goes on to describe ships as *impiae* (23), that suits the criticisms of navigation traditional in the propempticon, but is too extreme to describe the boldness of the epic poet. Yet even here the critics are not at a loss, and an allusion has been seen to the *pietas* that pervades the *Aeneid*.[11] Such irrelevant associations are now very common in literary studies, but they illuminate nothing except the confusion of those who find them.

I turn now to another ode where hidden references have been seen to poetry: see 1. 20, where Horace is inviting Maecenas to have a drink with him.

> vile potabis modicis Sabinum
> cantharis, Graeca quod ego ipse testa
> conditum levi, datus in theatro
> cum tibi plausus . . .

On the face of it this is the usual sort of invitation-poem where the poor poet apologizes to a richer friend for his simple entertainment;[12]

---

[9] Cody, op. cit. 88–9.

[10] F. Jäger, *Das antike Propemptikon und das 17. Gedicht des Paulinus von Nola* (Rosenheim, 1913); K. Quinn, *Latin Explorations* (London, 1963), 239–73; Nisbet and Hubbard on *Odes* 1. 3.

[11] Kidd, op. cit. (n. 6), 100.

[12] Philodemus, *Anth. Pal.* 11. 44; Catull. 13; Hor. *Epist.* 1. 5; *Odes* 4. 12.

as happens elsewhere (*Epist.* 1. 5. 4 ff., above, pp. 1–3), the drink has a sentimental association for the recipient, in this case the applause in the theatre that followed Maecenas's recovery from illness. But Steele Commager argued over thirty years ago that the modest wine that Horace offers stands for the ode itself:[13] in that case drinking the wine is a metaphor for reading the poem. The verb *condere* is used of constructing a poem as well as storing wine; *levi*, 'I smeared', would suit the oil that was used to preserve papyrus rolls (*Ars Poet.* 332); Sabine wine in a Greek jar suits Latin poetry in Greek metres. This interpretation is now accepted by a growing number of scholars, but I believe that in spite of its ingenuity it fails to explain the poem as a whole.

Commager thought that the emphatic *ego ipse* tells in his favour, but there is no need for this to be so: if the sentence is understood in its literal sense, Horace is emphasizing that he laid down the wine with his own hands, instead of leaving the job to a servant. And there is a parallel passage that tells against him, where Horace speaks in similar terms of a wine that he laid down to celebrate his own escape from the falling tree:

> hic dies anno redeunte festus
> corticem adstrictum pice dimovebit
> amphorae fumum bibere institutae
>   consule Tullo.   (3. 8. 9–12)

Now it is implied in yet another poem that Maecenas's recovery from illness and Horace's escape from the tree were astrologically linked, presumably because they happened at the same time:

> utrumque nostrum incredibili modo
> consentit astrum. te Iovis impio
>   tutela Saturno refulgens
>   eripuit volucrisque Fati
> tardavit alas, cum populus frequens
> laetum theatris ter crepuit sonum:
>   me truncus illapsus cerebro
>   sustulerat, nisi Faunus ictum
> dextra levasset . . .   (2. 17. 21–9)

We certainly don't need to assume that when Horace talks of drinking a commemorative wine he is describing something that actually

---

[13] S. Commager, *The Odes of Horace* (New Haven, Conn., 1962), 326; M. C. J. Putnam, *CJ* 64 (1969), 153–7 = *Essays on Latin Lyric, Elegy, and Epic* (Princeton, NJ, 1982), 102–6; E. Gowers, *The Loaded Table* (Oxford, 1993), 220.

happened. But there is some awkwardness in supposing that in one of these parallel poems (3. 8) the wine is to be understood literally as wine, and that in the other (1. 20) it is to be understood metaphorically as the poem itself.

Let us now look at the last stanza of 1. 20 and see how it suits the idea that Horace's wine stands for the poem:

> Caecubum et prelo domitam Caleno
> tu bibas uvam; mea nec Falernae
> temperant vites neque Formiani
> pocula colles.   (1. 20. 17 ff.)

If cheap Sabine wine represents Horace's ode, then the metaphor must be sustained if the poem is not to be broken-backed, but it is hard then to see the significance of the Caecuban and the other fine wines. You might try to argue that they represent the grander poetry written for instance by Virgil, who lived in Campania, but what then is the point of saying to Maecenas 'It's all very well for you to drink Caecuban'? That would imply that while Maecenas read and enjoyed Virgil's poetry, Horace did not. My friend Professor Putnam thinks that Caecuban suggests the applause of the crowd that was so agreeable to Maecenas in the first stanza;[14] Horace then modestly remarks that his own eulogies have less to offer. This is too complicated for me; when I read interpretations of this kind I can only repeat the lines 'Oh what a tangled web we weave | When first we practise to deceive.' A contemporary who was familiar with other invitation-poems would take the ode in the sense usual in such poems: Horace's life-style cannot match that of the luxurious Maecenas, but his modest wine will show the seriousness of his friendship. The case is parallel to that of the propempticon to Virgil (1. 3) and the allegorical ship (1. 14): if we are familiar with the literary conventions that apply to a particular type of poem, we shall be less tempted to look for extraneous interpretations.

I turn now to yet another poem where critics have seen a reference to Horace's own poetry, the last poem of Book 1.

> Persicos odi, puer, apparatus.
> displicent nexae philyra coronae;
> mitte sectari, rosa quo locorum
> sera moretur.
> simplici myrto nihil adlabores

---

[14] Putnam, op. cit. 156–7 (= *Essays* 105–6). See also C. Macleod, *Greece and Rome*, 26 (1979), 25 = *Collected Essays* (Oxford, 1983), 229.

> sedulus curo: neque te ministrum
> dedecet myrtus, neque me sub arta
> vite bibentem. (1. 38)

In my simple way I took this to be a recommendation of simplicity of life;[15] Persian luxury was proverbial, and *apparatus* is often used in similar contexts. I added the thought that the poem's simplicity (which is highly appropriate to the theme) makes an effective contrast with the grand manner of the preceding Cleopatra Ode, and gives an agreeable and characteristic end to the book. But Don Fowler in his excellent article on poetic closure didn't like my comment;[16] he called it 'uncharacteristic waffle'. I am grateful to him for calling my waffle 'uncharacteristic'.

Dr Fowler thinks that the poem's position at the end of the book shows that it is largely a literary manifesto in favour of unpretentious poetry. I am not at all sure. Of course the beginnings and ends of books are often the occasion for a literary manifesto, but they do not always have to be so; sometimes they are significant poems in other ways. It is true that Horace sometimes represents his odes about love and wine as slight,[17] but I wonder if immediately after the Cleopatra Ode he would carry false modesty so far as to characterize his poetry in general as *simplex*. If the poem is praising simplicity of life, everything is clear: when he tells the boy not to go looking for late roses, one thinks of the Greek epigrams where a slave is sent shopping for the symposium;[18] there is also a very important allusion to the Epicurean doctrine that we should be content with what lies ready to hand.[19] When Horace describes the slave as wearing myrtle as well as his master, that follows another traditional motif: at unpretentious parties the attendants are also unpretentious, as we find for instance in the eleventh satire of Juvenal (136–60). But if we think that the simplicity recommended is simplicity in literature, we cannot say what is represented by the slave-boy and his myrtle-garland. Far from enriching the poem, a reference to poetry seems to me to blur the effect.

But the champions of the polysemous interpretation have other arguments to adduce. When Horace rejects Persian elaboration, with its clear reference to proverbial Persian luxury, J. V. Cody sees also a

---

[15] Nisbet–Hubbard, *Odes* I, p. 423; S. Borzsák, *Živa Antika*, 25 (1975), 76–87.

[16] *Materiali e Discussioni*, 22 (1989), 97.

[17] *Odes* 1. 6. 20, 2. 1. 39 f., 3. 3. 69 ff.

[18] Nisbet–Hubbard, *Odes* I, pp. 421–2.

[19] Ibid. on 1. 31. 17.

reference to the line of Callimachus: 'assess poetry by its skill, not by the Persian land-measure' (*Aetia* 1. 1. 17–18).[20] Worse follows. The next poem in the collection (*Odes* 2. 1) compares the writing of recent history with walking on hot ash (7 f.): Cody compares the epigram of Callimachus (44. 2 Pf.) where he says 'fire lies under the ash', though there Callimachus is talking of smouldering passions. The preceding ode (1. 37 on Cleopatra) contains an epic simile about the hunter pursuing the hare (19 ff.): here Cody compares the epigram of Callimachus about a hunter's unwillingness to pursue a wounded hare (31 Pf.), though that epigram refers to the lover's preference for the unattainable. Having found these irrelevant parallels to Callimachus in 1. 37 and 2. 1, Cody thinks that they support his view that there is a reference to Callimachean poetics in the intermediate ode, 1. 38. Again and again we find that the people who write most fluently about literature are quite unrealistic about how a poem might actually come to be written.

This leads me to make some general remarks about the contemporary taste for hunting cross-references between one poem and another. It has always been accepted that there are some significant arrangements in Horace's *Odes*. The first and last poems in the different books are carefully placed, so also the middle poem. The six consecutive 'Roman Odes' (3. 1–6) have the same metre and a general similarity of theme. There are other significant juxtapositions, for instance the two odes on Fortune (1. 34 and 1. 35). But a credulous age has taken things much further, so that almost every poem is seen to have cross-references to its predecessor and successor, sometimes also to the ode that is the same distance from the end of the book as it is from the beginning. Two whole volumes have recently been devoted to this kind of inventiveness,[21] and it will be enough to amuse you with a few of many instances.

1. 14 is the poem on the political ship that we have already mentioned; it is thought significant that the next poem begins with Paris's voyage from Sparta. 1. 20 describes the applause when Maecenas recovered from illness, an illness not actually mentioned in the ode; the following poem asks Apollo and Diana to avert war, famine, and pestilence. 1. 27 compares an overpowering girl-friend with Charybdis;

[20] Cody, op. cit. (n. 6), 31–44. He observes that Cicero mentions *verborum apparatum* (*De Or.* 2. 355). Even so, *Persicos apparatus* could not possibly refer to an elaboration of literary style rather than of life-style.

[21] M. S. Santirocco, *Unity and Design in Horace's Odes* (Chapel Hill, NC, 1986); D. H. Porter, *Horace's Poetic Journey* (Princeton, NJ, 1987).

the following poem deals with the death by drowning of the mathema-
tician Archytas. 1. 29 describes Iccius's departure on an expedition to
Arabia; the following poem is a kletic hymn to Venus inviting her to
come from Cyprus. And while we are on the theme of travel, the third
poem of the first book deals with Virgil's voyage to Greece, the third
poem of the second half of the book (1. 22) says that the *integer vitae*
has nothing to fear when marching through the desert. These
imaginary relationships can be extended almost indefinitely.

Those who believe in these interconnections, and they include some
excellent scholars, should be confronted with a simple dilemma. On the
one hand, they might argue that the odes were written as an integrated
sequence: yet it can easily be shown that they do not appear in chronological order, and if they were composed as a unity it is strange that
Horace should not have made the connections more significant and
recognizable. Alternatively, it could be maintained that Horace wrote
the individual odes independently, but when he came to arrange his
book he paid attention to resemblances of the kind now suggested. This
is certainly true of a limited number of cases, and there are others where
some difference of opinion is possible; but interrelationships of the com-
plexity that is being posited would be quite impossible to organize,
especially when we consider that the order is affected by mechanical
metrical principles, such as the alternation of Alcaics and Sapphics at the
beginning of Book 2. When I put my difficulty to one advocate of complex relationships he suggested that when the books were finished
Horace changed words here and there to bring about the desired effects.
This is to underestimate the difficulty of changing words in a complex
and carefully integrated ode, and also the pointlessness of doing it to
achieve such trivial results. It may be asked why so many resemblances
can be detected between one ode and another. To this end I reply that
some of the resemblances are imaginary, and some unimportant, while
those that remain can be explained by the fact that the odes were written
on recurring themes in a more or less unified style.

I turn now to two problems in the last poem of Book 3, which for a
change really is about Horace's poetry:

> exegi monumentum aere perennius
> regalique situ pyramidum altius.

Scholars debate about the meaning of *situs* here. In one sense the word
means 'positioning', 'establishment', Greek θέσις,[22] just as *aram Druso*

---

[22] Thus D. Korzeniewski, *Mnem.* s. iv, 21 (1968), 29–34.

sitam (Tac. *Ann.* 2. 7. 2) is an altar set up for Drusus. In its other sense *situs* means 'mould' or 'decay', and so some have interpreted it here.[23] The sense of 'establishment' must be primary: when Horace says that his monument is loftier than the pyramids, he is emphasizing their fixity rather than their weakness, and the phrase must balance *aere perennius*. But Professor Woodman ingeniously argues that there is a conscious ambiguity:[24] at first sight *situs* suggests fixity, but when Horace goes on to say that wind and rain will not destroy his monument we realize that *situs* can also refer to the crumbling of buildings.[25] In some moods I should like this explanation to be true, as *situs* undoubtedly bears the two meanings suggested. On the other hand I find a particular difficulty where the two suggested implications are as incompatible as they are here; for if *situs* can suggest 'decay', that diminishes the impressiveness of Horace's own monument. It may be agreed that cases occur in Latin poetry where the full implication of a passage cannot be grasped without reading back. But this is easier when an extra dimension is being added than when the new element conspicuously contradicts the necessary meaning of the words in their immediate context. One would like to see other instances of this alleged phenomenon, for these questions can only be decided by the accumulation of relevant detail.

I turn now to a problem about the implications of *deduxisse* later in the same poem.[26]

> dicar qua violens obstrepit Aufidus
> et qua pauper aquae Daunus agrestium
> regnavit populorum, ex humili potens
> princeps Aeolium carmen ad Italos
> deduxisse modos.   (3. 30. 10–14)

I suspect that in its most literal sense of 'derive' the verb may have been a technical term of metrics or music to describe transposition from one system to another, but so far I haven't noticed any instance of such a usage in Latin or anything similar in Greek. Most modern critics, whenever they see the verb *deducere*, assume a reference to the *deductum carmen* (Virg. *Ecl.* 6. 5), the fine-spun song of the imitators of Callimachus,[27] but if *deduxisse* suggests 'to have spun finely' that does

---

[23] V. Pöschl, *Horazische Lyrik* (Heidelberg, 1970), 251–5.

[24] *Quality and Pleasure in Latin Poetry*, ed. T. Woodman and D. West (Cambridge, 1974), 117–22.

[25] Mart. 8. 3. 5 'et cum rupta situ Messalae saxa iacebunt'.

[26] Pöschl, op. cit. (n. 23), 257–9, Woodman, op. cit. (n. 24), 124–5.

[27] Pöschl, 258, Woodman, loc. cit.

not cohere with *ad Italos modos*; in any case there is considerable oddity in connecting Horace's monumental structure with fine spinning. Some scholars see a reference to bringing home prisoners for a triumph,[28] but again there is some awkwardness with *ad Italos modos*, and there is no clue in the poem so far to encourage so particular an interpretation. The image of colonizing has been tried,[29] and is prima facie more plausible. Horace says he will be spoken about in his native Apulia, where Daunus ruled rustic tribes; just as the legendary Daunus colonized Apulia, so Horace could say that he settled Greek poetry in Italy; the word *princeps*, which means 'first' when applied to Horace, would also remind us that Daunus was a prince. Professor Woodman has ingeniously suggested that when Daunus is described as poor in water, *pauper aquae*,[30] that hints at the poverty of indigenous Italic verse; if that is so, we might then try to see *deduxisse* as a metaphor from irrigation.[31] That would allow three possible implications for the verb: deriving in the literal sense, colonizing, and irrigation. These three implications can perhaps be felt together, as they are all similar usages of the same word and do not contradict one another, but for me it simply blurs the point to see further allusions to spinning and bringing home prisoners.

For a change I now turn to a passage where I see a double implication that most people would deny: I refer to the end of the Pyrrha Ode.

> miseri quibus
> intemptata nites. me tabula sacer
> votiva paries indicat uvida
> suspendisse potenti
> vestimenta maris deo.   (I. 5. 12–16)

It is generally recognized that in this poem an analogy is suggested between Pyrrha and the sea: both have changing moods and a deceptive glitter. What then are we to make of the last stanza where the shipwrecked poet, who will sail (i.e. love) no more, dedicates his wet clothes to the god that rules the sea, *potenti maris deo*? If the poem is not to dissolve in anticlimax the double meanings should be sustained to the end, and I used to think that this necessitated Zielinski's conjecture *deae* for *deo*: Venus is a maritime goddess as well

---

[28] I. Borzsák, *Act. Ant. Hung.* 12 (1964), 144–6; A. Hardie, *Stud. Class.* 21 (1983), 49–57.
[29] E. Maróti, *Act. Ant. Hung.* 13 (1965), 97–109.
[30] Op. cit. (n. 24), 123–4.
[31] Virg. *Georg.* 1. 169 *rivos deducere*, with Mynors's note.

as the goddess of love. I now accept Kinsey's theory that the pun can be sustained if we keep *deo* as the ambiguous 'deity';[32] thus Virgil says of Venus *ducente deo*, not *dea* (*Aen.* 2. 632). I am tempted to go further and accept an idea of Professor Quinn's, put forward very tentatively and immediately withdrawn:[33] *maris* is the genitive both of *mare*, 'the sea', and of *mas*, 'the male'. It is left ambiguous whether the poet is dedicating his clothes to Neptune who rules the sea (the normal situation) or to Venus who rules males (Horace's particular situation). This theory may seem fanciful, but it is supported by a similar pun in the *Satires* not noticed by Quinn (2. 8. 14f.): 'procedit fuscus Hydaspes I Caecuba vina ferens, Alcon Chium maris expers'. That means at first sight that the Chian wine has no share of the sea, has no brine in it, as Galen says is true of some Chian wine.[34] But Housman instead applied *maris expers* to Alcon,[35] just as *fuscus* is applied to Hydaspes: the slave had nothing male about him. Housman talks as if these two interpretations were alternatives, but they should both be felt together. In fact clear-cut puns are more typical of Horace than an evocative spread of meaning such as we find so often in Virgil.

Before I try to sum up my position, I shall give you a final illustration, this time not from a Horatian ode but from an English sonnet. Milton's invitation-poem to Mr Lawrence ends with a dry Horatian sentence:

> He who of those delights can judge, and spare
> To interpose them oft, is not unwise.

If you look up the commentators on Milton you will find two interpretations of the verb 'spare'. Some say that the meaning is 'he who refrains from interposing them oft'; that is to say, you shouldn't take too many days off. Others say that the meaning is 'spares the time to interpose them oft'; that is to say, you should take a lot of days off. Then along comes the influential critic Stanley Fish,[36] who makes sensible remarks elsewhere about how the interpretation of a passage is determined by the situation and the reader's expectations in that situation. That ought to have led him to the correct conclusion:

---

[32] T. E. Kinsey, *Latomus*, 23 (1964), 502–5.

[33] K. Quinn, *Latin Explorations* (London, 1968), 194, n. 2. See also Nisbet–Hubbard on *Odes* 2. 5. 20.

[34] Galen, 10. 833 K οὐ μὴν οὐδ᾽ εἰώθασι τοῖς εὐγένεσιν οἴνοις ... μιγνύναι τῆς θαλάσσης ἐν Λέσβῳ, καθάπερ οὐδ᾽ ἐν Χίῳ Ἀριουσίῳ.

[35] *Classical Papers* (Cambridge, 1972), 861–2.

[36] S. Fish, *Is there a Text in this Class?* (Harvard, 1980), 148–52.

Milton is using 'spare' in the Horatian sense of *parcere*, 'to refrain',[37]
and he is taking the Epicurean view that it is a good thing to relax
occasionally.[38] But that is not the conclusion that Professor Fish
reaches. He sees instead a calculated ambiguity between the two interpretations: by his way of it, Milton is leaving it open whether he is
recommending a lot of holidays or only a few. To quote Fish, 'the lines
first generate a pressure for judgment—"he who of those delights can
judge"—and then declines to deliver that judgment'; but who except a
professional critic would ever imagine that Milton's expression 'can
judge' was meant to lead to a suspension of judgement? Now of course
Milton knew all about multiple implications: the first words of *Paradise
Lost*, 'Of man's first disobedience', play on the name Adam, the
Hebrew for mankind or a man, and at the same time allude to 'the
man' in the first lines of the *Odyssey* and the *Aeneid*. But it is quite a
different matter to take the last lines of the sonnet in two completely
incompatible ways. Only the Delphic oracle talked like this, and the
Delphic oracle had particular reasons for being polysemous.

But it is out of fashion to accept simple and obvious interpretations.
Such readings are nowadays called 'reductive', which is a smart put-
down word, much as 'simplistic' was twenty years ago, and 'analytic' was
forty years ago. I hope I have made it clear that I am far from rejecting all
polysemous interpretations; indeed I have sometimes come under fire
for seeing too many meanings in Latin rather than too few. The poetry of
the Augustan period is rich in subtle associations that will be slightly different for different readers, so that it is not always possible to define
them exhaustively. But there is a curious idea now going round that no
speculation that flits across the over-active mind need ever be rejected.
On the contrary, it diminishes a poem to see irrelevant complications,
and it is a part of intelligent comprehension to exclude notions that
simply blur the point. We have to block out extraneous associations as if
they were background noises that must not be allowed to interfere with
our conversation with the author.

A number of reasons may be suggested for the over-interpretation
that is now so prevalent. It has come from the study of English and
other modern languages, and these studies have been largely based on
twentieth-century literature; but Eliot and Joyce may be open-ended

[37] Hor. *Odes* 1. 28. 23, 3. 8. 26, 3. 28. 7 f. 'parcis deripere horreo|cessantem Bibuli con-
sulis amphoram'; *Sat.* 2. 2. 58 'ac nisi mutatum parcit defundere vinum'; *TLL* 10. 1. 332.
19 ff.
[38] Nisbet–Hubbard on Hor. *Odes* 2. 3. 6, citing Epicurus, *Epist.* 3. 131, Lucr. 2. 23
'interdum'.

to a degree that does not suit the more public and accessible state-
ments of Latin literature. In modern English criticism more attention
is sometimes paid to originality and imagination than the obligation to
get things right; indeed the very concept of 'getting things right' seems
to some critics (not the best ones) meaningless in this context. It is a
further problem with dead languages that none of us knows them
quite well enough to exclude all misunderstandings; an inexperienced
student faced with a difficult unseen may be excused for finding it quite
exceptionally polysemous. I may also mention the belief of modern
critics that the poets of antiquity shared their own concerns to the
same degree, which is why those critics prefer to comment on verbal
ambiguities or theories about poetry rather than imperialistic politics
and self-centred ethics. They themselves rightly point out that we all
let our own preconceptions distort our reading of an author; but they
do not seem to see how easily this argument can be turned against
their own interpretations.

Some literary critics no longer even try to look at writings within
the context of the time when they were written. One of them has
told me that people like myself who aim to look at literature historically will be swept away by the tides of history. Well, the tides of
history flow in different directions, and classical scholars who try too
hard to keep up sometimes miss the tide by a decade or two and are
left gasping on the shore. The zeal for over-complicated interpretations is thought very up-to-date, but in fact it was common in
antiquity, especially in the period of the decline. We find in that
period self-absorbed coteries, without the stabilizing influence of a
broadly educated literary public, and so imposing their own schematic theories on an earlier age that they had not the historical insight
to understand. The ancient interpreters of Homer found an enthral-
ling adventure-story too banal, and so looked for more sophisticated
interpretations; thus when Odysseus protects himself with moly
against the wiles of Circe they tell us that moly stands for reason.[39]
The commentators on Virgil correctly recognized political allegory in
some places, and so thought they had to see it all over the place.
Neoplatonists understood nothing straightforwardly if they could
devise some anachronistic allegory, and their undeniable intellectual
subtlety made their influence on human thought all the more
pernicious. But it would be a pity if Latin poetry of all subjects is to

[39] F. Buffière, *Les Mythes d'Homère et la pensée grecque* (Paris, 1956), 150, 292, H. Rahner,
Greek Myths and Christian Mystery (Eng. trans., London, 1963), 179–222.

be asphyxiated by the desiccated scholasticism that has deservedly
given metaphysics such a bad name.

I am now coming to the end of my paper, and I wish to offer you
three quotations to take away with you. The first is a famous dictum of
Epicharmus, indeed it is the only famous dictum of Epicharmus, and it
may be commended to all who read or hear discussions of poetry: I am
referring of course to his injunction 'Keep sober, and remember to disbelieve.'[40] My second quotation is from Horace's own ode to Licinius
(2. 10): 'you will fare best if you don't press out to sea the whole time or
hug the shore too timidly'; his metaphor refers to political discretion,
but the middle course that he recommends is also applicable to the
search for multiple meanings. My third quotation is the advice given
by Eidothea to Menelaus in the fourth book of the *Odyssey* (414 ff.): 'As
soon as you see Proteus settled down, then remember your power and
your strength, and hold him there though he is eager to elude you. He
will try you out by assuming the shape of every creature under the sun,
but hold him tight and press him all the more; and when he resumes
his proper shape ask him how you can return home safely.' Ladies and
gentlemen, may you steer a steady course between the Scylla of reduc-
tionism and the Charybdis of the polysemous; stop your ears against
the sophistries of over-subtle theorists, for they will wreck you on a
rocky shore; let no literary critic's wand induce you to renounce intelligible human speech, but protect yourselves with the antidote of
rationality. I wish you all a happy conference and a safe home-coming.

---

[40] Kaibel, *Com. Graec. Frag.*, p. 137 νᾶφε καὶ μέμνασ' ἀπιστεῖν· ἄρθρα ταῦτα τᾶν
φρενῶν.

ADDENDA

Old articles always include some things that one would now express differently; there is no point in trying to rewrite them, but I record a few supplements and corrections. I also note some later bibliography in a list that in no way aims at completeness.   R.G.M.N.

1. For Vinnius add M. J. McGann, *CQ*, NS 13 (1963), 258–9. For Fuscus add S. J. Harrison, *CQ*, NS 42 (1992), 543–7. P. 4, Martial 5. 6. 9 ff. refers to Parthenius, Domitian's chamberlain rather than his doorkeeper.

2. Konrad Müller produced revised editions of his text of Petronius in the Tusculum series (3rd edn., Munich, 1983); for his later more conservative view on interpolations see pp. 471–5 of that edition. Of my own conjectures III. 9 *ingrata* was anticipated by E. Rohde, *Jahrbücher f. Philologie*, 119 (1879), 847; 60. 5 *commissio* and 108. 9 [*sine morte*] were proposed simultaneously by J. Delz in his review of Müller in *Gnomon*, 34 (1962), 676–84. Other conjectures I no longer wish even to consider, for instance 74. 13 *ambubaiam non meminisse*, 117. 6 *serviliter vestiti*, 128. 1 *neglegens odor*.

In 1992 W. V. Clausen published a 'revised edition' of his Oxford text of Persius and Juvenal; he made only a few changes, and the work must now be considered out of date (see M. D. Reeve, *CR*, NS 43 (1993), 173–4). My review should be read in conjunction with my article of 1988 (Ch. 15 in the present volume, occasionally supplemented in Chs. 17 and 21); note especially the notes on 1. 29 (p. 228), 1. 144 f. (p. 229), 3. 298 (p. 260), 6. 588 (p. 244), 7. 50 ff. (p. 245). My deletion of 6. 65 was anticipated by Guyet (reported by Courtney in his commentary); my tentative deletions of 6. 138, 359, 395 by A. Scholte, *Observationes Criticae*, 1973 (pointed out by M. D. Reeve, *CR*, NS 21 (1971), 328); my conjecture of *et* for *aut* at 8. 201 by Lubinus (in his text but not his commentary).

3. See now also H.-J. van Dam's commentary on Statius, *Silvae* II (Leiden, 1984), 187 ff. and 450 ff.; at 276 ff. and 454 f. he argues inadequately against my conflation of the two Pollae; at 502–4 he gives more parallels for 'images of the dead'. For the *univira* see further S. Treggiari, *Roman Marriage* (Oxford, 1991), 233–6.

4. For the Sibylline Oracles see also E. Schürer, *The History of the Jewish People in the Age of Jesus Christ* 3², ed. G. Vermes, F. Millar, and M. Goodman (Edinburgh, 1986), 618–54; J. J. Collins in J. H. Charlesworth (ed.), *Old Testament Pseudepigrapha* (London, 1983), 317–472 (including translation) and *ANRW* 2. 20. 1 (1987), 421–59; H. W. Parke, *Sibyls and Sibylline Prophecy in Classical Antiquity* (London, 1988), especially 145–51; D. S. Potter, *Prophecy and History in the Crisis of the Roman Empire* (Oxford, 1990), 95–140.

5. See also Chs. 21 and 24. On Cat. 61. 109–13 add R. Mayer, *PCPS*, NS 25 (1979), 69–70, S. J. Harrison, *PCPS*, NS 31 (1985), 11–12 (proposing *cava* for *vaga*). At 66. 74 W. S. Watt, *CPh.* 85 (1990), 129–30 proposes *nostri* (*nr̄i*) for *vere*.

6. The Gallus papyrus has generated a considerable bibliography, from which I list a selection: G. Giangrande, *QUCC*, NS 5 (1980), 141–53 (rejecting authorship by Gallus); A. S. Hollis, *CQ*, NS 30 (1980), 541–2; S. Mazzarino, *Quaderni Catanesi*, 2. 3 (1980), 7–50 (dating to 32 BC) and *Helikon*, 20–1 (1980–1), 3–26 (on Lycoris); J. K. Newman, *Latinitas*, 28 (1980), 83–94; M. C. J. Putnam, *ZPE* 39 (1980), 49–56; G. Zecchini, *Aegyptus*, 60 (1980), 138–48 (dating to 30–27); A. Barchiesi, *Atene e Roma*, NS 26 (1981), 153–66; G. O. Hutchinson, *ZPE* 41 (1981), 37–42 (dating to the Illyrian campaign of 35–33 BC); R. Whitaker, *Acta Classica*, 24 (1981), 87–96 (note p. 89 on *templa legam*); F. Graf, *Gymnasium*, 89 (1982), 21–36 (who points out (n. 18) that the *praetexta* mentioned in n. 42 was by the younger Balbus, not Pollio); D. E. Keefe, *CQ* 32 (1982), 237–8; G. Petersmann, *ANRW* 2. 30. 3 (1983), 1649–55; H. Schoonhoven, *ZPE* 53 (1983), 73–8; J. Fairweather, *CQ* 34 (1984), 167–74; G. Danesi Marioni, *Disiecti Membra Poetae*, 1 (1984), 88–98; A. M. Morelli and V. Tandoi, ibid. 101–16; A. M. Morelli, ibid. 2 (1985), 140–83 (with bibliography).

I call particular attention to the article by F. Brunhölzl, *Codices Manuscripti*, 10 (1984), 33–40; he alleges that the papyrus is an incompetent forgery, it is not clear by whom. His arguments are quite inadequate, as is recognized by more recent writers: see G. Ballaira, *Paideia*, 42 (1987), 47–54 (with bibliography on palaeographic aspects); J. Blänsdorf, *ZPE* 67 (1987), 43–50; G. Lieberg, *Latomus*, 46 (1987), 527–44; A. M. Morelli, *Disiecti Membra Poetae*, 3 (1988), 104–19; C. U. Merriam, *Latomus*, 49 (1990), 443–52. Note also the authoritative pronouncement in favour of authenticity by G. Cavallo in *Lo spazio letterario di Roma antica*, 2 (Rome, 1989), 324 n. 67.

There is a short commentary on the papyrus by E. Courtney, *The*

Fragmentary Latin Poets (Oxford, 1993), 263–8. Note especially his discussion of *Cons. Liv.* 267 ff. (cited previously by several scholars) 'pars erit historiae totoque legetur in orbe' l . . . 288 'nec sua prae templi nomina fronte leget'.

8. See also Ch. 21, pp. 343–4. For *sidere clarior* some editors cite Hom. *Il.* 6. 295 ἀστὴρ δ᾽ ὣς ἀπέλαμπεν (of a robe). The absence of a geographical place still seems to me decisive against *sidere*.

9. For a view of Ovid's exile similar to my own (rejecting theories about political plots) see G. P. Goold, *ICS* 8 (1983), 94–107.

10. For a view of the ninth epode in some respects similar to my own see E. Kraggerud, *Horaz und Actium* (*Symbolae Osloenses* suppl. 26, 1984), 66–128. For *puppes sinistrorsum citae* see C. B. R. Pelling, *CQ*, NS 36 (1986), 177–81, who argues that the phrase refers to Antony's right wing that Agrippa had drawn north. For the battle see further J. M. Carter, *The Battle of Actium* (London, 1970), 215–27, Pelling's commentary on Plutarch's *Antony* (Oxford, 1988), 272 ff.

12. See also the review by J. Delz, *Gnomon*, 60 (1989), 495–501 (with textual discussions and a further list of *errata*); both reviews should be read in conjunction with Professor Shackleton Bailey's courteous reply, *Philologus*, 134 (1990), 213–28. For my own conjectures see also Ch. 16 in this volume (with occasional references in Ch. 21); add to my list *Ars* 120 *inornatum* (cf. Hom. *Il.* 1. 119 ἀγέραστος) . . . *Achillem* (*Gnomon*, 58 (1986), 614), which Professor W. S. Watt has persuaded me not to withdraw. At *Carm.* 3. 2. 13, where I tentatively proposed *dulci decorum est* (cf. *Omnibus*, 15 (1988), 16–17), S. J. Harrison cites against me Ach. Tat. 3. 22.1 ἀλλ᾽ ὑπὲρ φίλου, κἂν ἀποθανεῖν δεήσῃ, καλὸς ὁ κίνδυνος, γλυκὺς ὁ θάνατός (*RhM* 136 (1993), 91–3).

13. See further V. Tietze Larson, 'The *Hercules Oetaeus* and the Picture of the *sapiens* in Senecan Prose', *Phoenix*, 45 (1991), 39–49. For injury of the offending part (p. 207) see for instance H. P. Syndikus on Catull. 108, p. 123 n. 10, Ov. *Am.* 2. 10. 34, Dewar on Stat. *Theb.* 9. 133, R. MacMullen, *Chiron*, 10 (1986), 159, *RE* 4A. 2069 ff. (*talio*). For a scruple about the late date of *HO* (p. 210) see above, p. 310. D. R. Shackleton Bailey suggests that the play's incidence of homoeoteleuton is abnormal for Seneca (*RFIC* 120 (1992), 68).

15. p. 236 n. 9. A reputable *haruspex* would not inspect the entrails of frogs (pointed out by S. Braund, *CQ*, NS 40 (1990), 502–6); therefore Juv. 3. 44 f. 'ranarum viscera numquam | inspexi' is not inconsistent with the eminent *haruspex* Umbricius. At 6. 195 I have no authority for such spellings as *locendis* for *loquendis*, though *locuntur* for *loquuntur* is

common. The tentative deletion of 10. 16 was suggested by M. D. Reeve though never published; it should be restored to him. At 10. 17 *claudit* was suggested as a variant by Guyet (Professor James Willis informs me).

16. At Hor. *Carm.* 3. 12. 9 in support of my *Cycni* for *segni* N. Horsfall points out that after the fifth century AD the *c* could be softened in pronunciation (*CR*, NS 40 (1990), 447). At *Epist.* 1. 11. 28 ff. 'navibus atque | quadrigis petimus bene vivere. quod petis hic est, | est Ulubris' (cited in n. 2), I still doubt *petimus*, which should be differentiated from *petis*; for my tentative *ruimus* with the infinitive cf. Lucan 7. 751 'scire ruunt' (*v.l. volunt*), Stat. *Theb.* 7. 177 (with Hill's note), Claud. *Rapt. Pros.* 3. 386–7.

17. p. 273. For Housman's view of the history of Juvenal's tradition see not just his *obiter dicta* at pp. xxv and xli of his text but his *Classical Papers*, 1106–7; for more recent accounts see E. Courtney, *BICS* 14 (1967), 38–50, R. J. Tarrant in *Texts and Transmission*, ed. L. D. Reynolds (Oxford, 1983), 200–3.

18. The article by R. Syme that in places overlaps my own (my note 45a) has been reprinted in his *Roman Papers*, 6 (1991), 269–86 (see especially 282–6).

19. See now A. M. Riggsby, 'Elision and Hiatus in Latin Prose', *Class. Ant.* 10 (1991), 328–43.

21. p. 346. My conjecture *limite* for *lumine* at Lucr. 3. 1042 was suggested by Pius in 1511 and also noted by Lambinus in 1570 (Professor M. F. Smith informs me). For *loquendis* (p. 349) see above on Ch. 15.

23. p. 383. Pfeiffer's note on Call. *Hec.* 260. 19 is relevant, but the passage itself is not; see A. S. Hollis's commentary, fr. 70. 4.

BIBLIOGRAPHY OF R. G. M. NISBET

(Books, chapters of books, and articles are included together with a selection of reviews. Items to be found in the present collection are marked with an asterisk.)

Review of G. Highet, *Juvenal the Satirist*, in *JRS* 45 (1955), 234–5.

'The *Invectiva in Ciceronem* and *Epistula Secunda* of Pseudo-Sallust', *JRS* 48 (1958), 30–2.

*'Notes on Horace, *Epistles* I', *CQ*, NS 9 (1959), 73–6.

'Cicero, *Philippics* ii. 103', *CR*, NS 10 (1960), 103–4.

Cicero, *In Pisonem*, edited with text, introduction, and commentary (Oxford, 1961).

Review of A. Boulanger and P. Wuilleumier (eds.), *Cicéron, Philippiques* i–iv, in *CR*, NS 11 (1961), 135–6.

'Cicero, *De Provinciis Consularibus* 6', *CR*, NS 11 (1961), 201.

Review of P. Wuilleumier (ed.), *Cicéron, Philippiques* v–xiv, in *CR*, NS 11 (1961), 235–6.

'The *Commentariolum Petitionis*: Some Arguments against Authenticity', *JRS* 51 (1961), 84–7.

Review of R. G. Austin (ed.), *Cicero, Pro Caelio*, 3rd edn., in *JRS* 51 (1961), 266–8.

'*Romanae Fidicen Lyrae*: The Odes of Horace', in J. P. Sullivan (ed.), *Critical Essays on Roman Literature: Elegy and Lyric* (London, 1962), 181–218.

*Review and discussion of K. Müller (ed.), *Petronii Arbitri Satyricon* and W. V. Clausen (ed.), *A. Persi Flacci et D. Juni Juvenalis Saturae*, in *JRS* 52 (1962), 227–38.

Review of H. Kasten (ed.), *Cicero, pro Murena*, in *CR*, NS 12 (1962), 311–12.

'Persius', in J. P. Sullivan (ed.), *Critical Essays on Roman Literature: Satire* (London, 1963), 39–71.

Review of J. Cousin (ed.), *Cicéron, Pour Caelius, Sur les provinces consulaires, Pour Balbus*, in *CR*, NS 13 (1963), 300–2.

'The Speeches', in T. A. Dorey (ed.), *Cicero* (London, 1965), 47–79.

Review of J. Cousin (ed.), *Cicéron, Pro Sestio, Contre Vatinius*, in *CR*, NS 16 (1966), 335–7.

Review of M. Ruch (ed.), *Cicéron, Pro Marcello oratio*, in *Gnomon*, 38 (1966), 775–7.

Review of I. Opelt, *Die lateinische Schimpfwörter und verwandte sprachliche Erscheinungen*, in *Gnomon*, 39 (1967), 67–72.

Review of V. Grassmann, *Die erotische Epoden des Horaz*, in *CR*, NS 17 (1967), 163–4.

Review of W. Wili, *Horaz und die augusteische Kultur*, in *CR*, NS 18 (1968), 55-7.

Review of C. Ricks (ed.), *A. E. Housman: A Collection of Critical Essays*, in *Essays in Criticism*, 19 (1969), 232-9.

Review of E. Doblhofer, *Die Augustuspanegyrik des Horaz in formalhistorischer Sicht*, in *CR*, NS 19 (1969), 173-5.

A Commentary on Horace: *Odes*, Book I (with M. Hubbard) (Oxford, 1970).

Review of P. Grimal (ed.), *Cicéron, Contre L. Pison*, in *CR*, NS 21 (1971), 61-3.

Review of H. P. Syndikus, *Die Lyrik des Horaz: eine Interpretation der Oden. Erstes und zweites Buch*, in *CR*, NS 25 (1975), 212-14.

A Commentary on Horace: *Odes*, Book II (with M. Hubbard) (Oxford, 1978).

'Felicitas at Surrentum (Statius, *Silvae* 2. 2)', *JRS* 68 (1978), 1-11.

*'Virgil's Fourth *Eclogue*: Easterners and Westerners', *BICS* 25 (1978), 59-78.

*'Notes on the Text of Catullus', *PCPS*, NS 24 (1978), 92-115.

*'Elegiacs by Gallus from Qaṣr Ibrîm' (sections IV-VIII, section IV in collaboration with P. J. Parsons), *JRS* 69 (1979), 140-55.

*'*Aeneas Imperator*: Roman Generalship in an Epic Context', *PVS* 18 (1978-80), 50-61.

*'*Sidere Clarior* (Horace, *Carm.* 3. 1. 42)', *LCM* 5 (1980), 151-2.

Review of K. Quinn (ed.), *Horace: The Odes*, in *Phoenix*, 36 (1982), 181-3.

*'Great and Lesser Bear (Ovid, *Tristia* 4. 3)', *JRS* 72 (1982), 49-56.

'Alcestis in Barcelona', *ZPE* 52 (1983), 31-6 (with P. J. Parsons and G. O. Hutchinson).

'Iam mater simia (Juvenal 10. 195)', *LCM* 8 (1983), 80.

'Some Problems of Text and Interpretation in Horace *Odes* 3. 14 (*Herculis ritu*)', *PLLS* 4 (1983), 105-19.

Review of D. R. Shackleton Bailey, *Profile of Horace*, in *CR*, NS 33 (1983), 23-7.

'Varia Historia' (review article on *Cambridge History of Classical Literature*, II), *JRS* 73 (1983), 175-9.

*'Horace's *Epodes* and History', in T. Woodman and D. West (eds.), *Poetry and Politics in the Age of Augustus* (Cambridge, 1984), 1-18, 197-200.

*'Sacrilege in Egypt (Lucan 9. 150-161)', *Acta Antiqua Academiae Scientiarum Hungaricae*, 30 (1982-4), 309-17.

'The Poets of the Late Republic', in J. Boardman, J. Griffin, O. Murray (eds.), *The Oxford History of the Classical World* (Oxford, 1986), 479-94 = *The Roman World* (Oxford, 1988), 101-16.

Introduction to C. Macleod, *Horace: The Epistles* (Rome, 1986), vii-x.

Review of S. Borzsák (ed.), *Q. Horati Flacci Opera*, in *Gnomon*, 58 (1986), 611-15.

*Review of D. R. Shackleton Bailey (ed.), *Q. Horati Flacci Opera* in *CR*, NS 36 (1986), 227-34.

*'The Oak and the Axe: Symbolism in Seneca, *Hercules Oetaeus* 1618 ff.', in M. Whitby, P. Hardie, M. Whitby (eds.), *Homo Viator: Classical Essays for John Bramble* (Bristol Classical Press, 1987), 243-51.

*'Pyrrha among Roses: Real Life and Poetic Imagination in Augustan Rome', review article on J. Griffin, *Latin Poets and Roman Life*, in *JRS* 77 (1987), 184-90.

*'Notes on the Text and Interpretation of Juvenal', in N. Horsfall (ed.), *Vir Bonus Discendi Peritus: Studies in Celebration of Otto Skutsch's Eightieth Birthday* (*BICS* suppl. 51; 1988), 86–110.

Review of T. P. Wiseman, *Roman Studies*, in *CR*, NS 38 (1988), 380–3.

Review of H. P. Syndikus, *Catull: Eine Interpretation*, I. *Die Kleinen Gedichte*; III. *Die Epigramme*, in *JRS* 78 (1988), 218.

*'Footnotes on Horace', in J. Diggle, J. B. Hall, H. D. Jocelyn (eds.), *Studies in Latin Literature and its Tradition in Honour of C. O. Brink* (*PCPS* suppl. 15; 1989), 87–96.

*'On Housman's *Juvenal*', *ICS* 14 (1989), 285–302.

*'The Dating of Seneca's Tragedies, with Special Reference to *Thyestes*', *PLLS* 6 (1990), 95–114.

*'Cola and Clausulae in Cicero's Speeches', in E. M. Craik (ed.), *Owls to Athens: Essays on Classical Subjects presented to Sir Kenneth Dover* (Oxford, 1990), 349–59.

Review of R. F. Thomas (ed.), *Virgil, Georgics*, in *CR*, NS 40 (1990), 260–3.

*'The Style of Virgil's *Eclogues*', *PVS* 20 (1991), 1–14.

*'How Textual Conjectures are Made', *Materiali e Discussioni*, 26 (1991), 65–91.

*'The Orator and the Reader: Manipulation and Response in Cicero's *Fifth Verrine*, in T. Woodman and J. Powell (eds.), *Author and Audience in Latin Literature* (Cambridge, 1992), 1–17, 216–18.

'La Vita', in *Enciclopedia Oraziana* (Rome, 1992), 1–8.

Review of D. R. Shackleton Bailey (ed.), *M. Valerii Martialis Epigrammata*, in *CR*, NS 42 (1992), 50–1.

Review of E. Courtney, *The Poems of Petronius*, in *CR*, NS 42 (1992), 444–5.

*'*Adolescens Puer* (Virgil, *Eclogues* 4. 28–30)', in H. D. Jocelyn (ed.), *Tria Lustra: Essays and Notes presented to John Pinsent* (Liverpool Classical Papers, 3; Liverpool, 1993), 265–7.

*'Four Conjectures on Catullus 64' (unpublished).

*'The Survivors: Old-Style Literary Men in the Triumviral Period' (unpublished).

*'Tying down Proteus: The Limitations of Ambiguity and Cross-Reference in Horace's *Odes*' (unpublished).

INDEX NOMINUM ET RERUM

INDEX VERBORUM

INDEX LOCORUM